Psychology
at Work

Psychology at Work

An Introduction
to Industrial and
Organizational
Psychology

second edition

Lilly M. Berry

San Francisco State University

£38.99 s/c
D/B

Boston, Massachusetts   Burr Ridge, Illinois   Dubuque, Iowa
Madison, Wisconsin   New York, New York   San Francisco, California   St. Louis, Missouri

McGraw-Hill

A Division of The McGraw·Hill Companies

PSYCHOLOGY AT WORK: AN INTRODUCTION TO ORGANIZATIONAL PSYCHOLOGY
International Editions 1998

Exclusive rights by McGraw-Hill Book Co – Singapore, for manufacture and export. This book cannot be re-exported from the country to which it is consigned by McGraw-Hill.

10 09 08 07 06 05
20 09 08 07 06 05 04 03 02 01
PMP   BJE

Library of Congress Cataloging-in-Publication Data

Berry, Lilly M.
    Psychology at work: an introduction to industrial and
    organizational psychology / Lilly M. Berry. – 2nd ed.
        p.   cm.
    Includes bibliographical references and index.
    ISBN 0-697-20173-2
    1. Psychology, Industrial.   I. Title.
    HF5548.8.B395   1997
    158.7–dc21   97-13527
                                                     CIP

hhtp:/www.mhhe.com

When ordering this title, use ISBN 0-07-115963-0

Printed in Singapore

Contents

Preface   xiii

*P*reface

My friend and coauthor of the original *Psychology at Work,* John P. Houston, has retired. In this second edition, however, I continue many features we included in the first edition. Foremost among these is the text's student orientation. This will continue to be a book especially for students.

As before, the text provides a thorough coverage of the field of I/O psychology. I intend for the text to be a complete course of study, as well as a useful reference after students have gone on to careers or graduate school. I attempt to give them a sense of where the field has been, what is happening now, and what the future might hold for the myriad issues that are I/O psychology. A focus on the connections between the scientific aspects of the field and real-life work situations treats both science and practice seriously. Thus, this is a book on *psychology* that is relevant to people in real-world organizations.

The text and chapter organization continue to follow a problem-solving approach, although I have made some changes in the sequence of chapters. The overall aim of the book is to provide an understanding of the individual and to solve the problems of human behavior at work. In the first section, I describe in general terms how psychology can be used to accomplish these two purposes. The second section shows the first reorganization. At the request of users, I have moved the material on motivation and job satisfaction to a later section. Now, the section II chapters focus on personnel issues. Beginning with job study and selection chapters, and ending with chapters on training and performance appraisal, I attempt to define ways of establishing an effective work force. Following this is a new third section that focuses on creating an effective social organization of work. Chapters on motivation, satisfaction, leadership, organizational design, and interactions, show ways to enhance the quality of life at work. The last section addresses the need to solve human problems at work. A variety of problems affect employees, which in turn affect their job performance. These problems and their prevention are discussed in the chapters on stress, employee health, and work design.

I hope I have succeeded in writing a student-friendly textbook. I have tried to write clearly, so as to make the meaning apparent to those who are not *already* familiar with the subject matter. Also, because I know students themselves have a heavy workload, I have tried to make the material interesting. In writing, I have envisioned readers at the junior or senior level in college. To benefit most from this text, students should have had a basic introductory course in psychology. Other courses would be helpful, such as research methods, however, I do not assume they have had this background. My own teaching experience suggests that many students want their I/O course early in their educational programs before they have done much preparation.

The text contains several learning aids. Each chapter begins with a preview. At the end of major divisions within a chapter, I have developed a brief review of the "main points" to help students remember the material. At the end of each chapter, there is a review summary and a list of study questions. The primary purpose of the questions is to aid students who want to know "what to study." By asking these particular questions, I am suggesting that this material is important, and in fact, the questions might be used to guide classroom discussions. Also at the end of each chapter is a "Consider This" assignment. Most of these are case studies. Others are general issues for thought and discussion. Finally, an extensive glossary of terms is included at the end of the book. Words and phrases printed in bold throughout the text are listed in the glossary.

A number of people have been helpful to me in preparing this second edition. First, I acknowledge those instructors who used the book in their classes and thank them for their comments and suggestions. I received student reactions also, including a number from students at San Francisco State University. I thank them and their professors for making their comments available. Finally, I recognize and thank those who reviewed the revision. I found their suggestions helpful. The reviewers follow:

Allan Jones,
University of Houston

Susan Murphy,
University of Houston

David Day,
Pennsylvania
State University

Karen Duffy,
State University of
New York at Geneseo

John Binning,
Illinois State University

Lilly M. Berry

Section I

Using Psychology at Work

In this introductory course of study, I begin the analysis of human work by looking at the background of Industrial/Organizational (I/O) Psychology. In section I, there are two chapters. The first reviews the past and identifies some important directions for I/O psychology. The chapter ends with a note on the future of the field. Chapter 2 provides a general discussion of the methods I/O psychologists use in their research and work in organizations. In this chapter, I attempt to recognize the many different approaches used in understanding work behavior and in solving work problems.

Welcome to the field of industrial/organizational (I/O) psychology! In this chapter, you will discover that I/O psychology has a rich history. It started with the work of some turn-of-the-century scientists. These were the first psychologists, and they were among the first to recognize that psychology could be used in business. You will learn what kind of work modern I/O psychologists do and how they develop their careers. You will see into the future of the field and even may get some ideas as to how you could develop a career in I/O psychology.

Women have a long history of doing wage-earning work. These factory workers are stitching the center seam of silk ties by hand.

$\mathcal{C}$ h a p t e r 1

Contents

I/O Psychology: Then and Now

A long time before New York and Chicago were discovered, there lived an alchemist who sold an unfailing prescription for making gold from eggs. He sold it at a high price, on a contract that he was to refund the whole sum in case the prescription was carried through and did not yield the promised result. It is said that he never broke the contract and yet became a very rich man. His prescription was that the gold-seeker should hold a pan over the fire with the yolks of a dozen eggs in it and stir them for half an hour without ever thinking of the word hippopotamus. Many thousands tried, and yet no one succeeded. The fatal word, which perhaps they never had thought of before, now always unfortunately rushed into their minds, and the more they tried to suppress it, the more it was present.

H. Münsterberg

Hugo Münsterberg, a professor of psychology at Harvard University at the turn of the century, told this story to a group of businessmen to interest them in applying psychology in marketing. He pointed out that the alchemist may not have known how to turn eggs into gold, but he certainly knew how to turn *psychology* into gold. Münsterberg himself was not unlike the alchemist. During his life, he popularized psychology. He spent much of his time talking to business managers, advertisers, lawyers, and politicians. He showed them how to use the information about behavior that research labs were amassing. In the process of selling psychology, he also amassed a fortune by knowing how to turn psychology into gold for himself.

APPLYING PSYCHOLOGY

Prescientific Applications

Münsterberg and the alchemist were not the first to apply psychology. We have a long history of using our understanding of human behavior to get what we want from the world. Ordinary, commonsense psychology has been used for many purposes—to get money and power, to control our own lives, and to change other people. For example, decision making is an age-old problem. Decisions may be based on inferences about the relationship between behavior in a test situation and in a later performance. Such an inference is apparent in a famous decision made by King Solomon. Two women appeared before him, each claiming to be the mother of one child. After hearing the case, Solomon offers to divide the child in half and give each a portion. The king believes that this will expose the true mother because she, unlike the false mother, would rather give up her child than win at such a cost. He is correct, of course, and the two women show the expected behavior: One agrees to the splitting, the other begs him to give the "whole" child to her rival. In applying his understanding of behavior, King Solomon gained respect as a judge (1 Kings 2).

We have long used knowledge of human behavior at work. Consider occupational training, for example. Apprenticing is the traditional method of training.

It is based on the necessity for active practice and feedback for effective learning. Records of apprenticing exist as far back as the Babylonian laws of Hammurabi in 2100 B.C. (Douglas, 1921). Ability testing, too, has a long history. Ancient Greeks employed this method of sampling a person's abilities to predict satisfactory job performance (Doyle, 1974).

Applications of Scientific Psychology

Scientific psychology did not actually appear until the latter part of the last century. Prior to this time, human behavior was considered by philosophers. In the 1870s, however, philosophers, physiologists, and medical researchers began to study behavior with the experimental method. Informal labs were established first, mainly for demonstrations. Then, in 1879 at the University of Leipzig in Germany, Wilhelm Wundt created a laboratory specifically for the experimental study of human behavior. This marked the beginning of psychology as a science. Scientific study of behavior increased rapidly from that time. By 1900, most European and American universities had developed "psychology departments." Experimental laboratories were established in those departments. Undergraduate majors in psychology were accepted and the first Ph.D.s were awarded. The American Psychological Association (APA) grew from 31 members in 1892 to 127 in 1902. The *American Journal of Psychology* was founded for publishing psychological research.

In this setting of rapid growth, **industrial/organizational (I/O) psychology**[1] was born. It had a dual parentage. On the one hand, it grew out of research in which the new scientific method was used to solve behavioral problems in industry. For example, new ways to increase efficiency were scientifically developed. On the other hand, some of the new scientists cultivated **applied psychology** as a necessary adjunct to basic psychology. This view, that applied psychology should grow in conjunction with the basic laboratory science, was unacceptable to many scientists of the time. They believed that research results should not be used until the science was older. Psychology is still too young, they said, and too little is known about the laws of behavior. Others thought psychology would be contaminated if it recognized applied psychology as a legitimate subfield. For many years, Edward Titchener held this view. As director of the experimental lab at Cornell University, Titchener was influential in American psychology. He hoped to maintain the field as a solid science. If it was to retain its newly acquired scientific status, he believed it should stay pure like mathematics or physics. A physicist would not do engineering, so, he reasoned, a psychologist should not be involved in applications.

The opposing view, that application was an important adjunct to basic science, was promoted by some experimental psychologists and contemporaries of Titchener. These scientists believed that just as applications of physics, mathematics, and chemistry give meaning and usefulness to those sciences, so too do applications of psychology give reason and purpose to our basic science. The most notable early champion of this view was Münsterberg. He thought that psychological science was useful in the business world but that it had not been marketed. In his public speeches, he noted that industry had made extensive use of the knowledge derived from physical science, but only education and medicine were using psychology's discoveries. He hoped this would change, and we will see that it has changed.

[1]Terms printed in bold type are listed in the glossary at the end of the book.

Branches of Applied Psychology

From the early discussion of applications came a division between basic and applied psychology with distinct branches in the different applied areas. Undoubtedly, you are familiar with some. Clinical psychology, for example, is a widely recognized branch. This dualistic aspect of psychology has continued to the present day (Schonpflug, 1993). The branches of applied psychology have retained much of their independence from basic psychology, as some applied psychologists believe they should (Levy-Leboyer, 1992). Applied psychologists must solve practical problems, and they often cannot wait for solutions to come from the basic psychology laboratory. Instead, they rely on their own research and theory development, as well as relevant work from other disciplines.

The branch of applied psychology currently known as industrial/organizational or I/O psychology has had several names. Early in the century, it was called economic psychology, business psychology, and vocational psychology. To some great extent, even the term *applied psychology* referred more to this branch of applications than to any other. For most of its existence, however, the field has been known as industrial psychology. About 25 years ago, I/O psychology became its official name.

The Subject Matter of I/O Psychology

From the beginning, the aim of many of those who wanted to apply psychology was to promote the use of basic psychological science in solving work problems. In his introduction to *Business Psychology* (1915), Münsterberg wrote:

> **The understanding of psychology is one of the most important roads to success for the modern business man. Industrial and commercial work are in thousand-fold contact with the mental life. Salesmanship and advertising, learning and training for technical labor, choosing the right position and selecting the right employe[e], greatest efficiency at work and avoidance of fatigue, treatment of customers and of partners, securing the most favorable conditions for work and adapting the work to one's liking, and ever so many other problems stand today before the business world and cannot be answered but by psychology. (p. v)**

Today's industrial/organizational psychology is as broad as the business psychology Münsterberg described. It is defined now, as then, as the study of behavior at work. This means that I/O psychology is almost as big as the entire field of psychology because the work situation is almost as big as life. People spend at least a third of their time working. All kinds of life activities go on at work, just as they do at home and at school.

The subject matter of I/O psychology includes a wide variety of behaviors that occur in the work setting: We study the "composition" of the work itself, from assembly line production to executive management. We look for ways to improve the process of selecting people for jobs. We design and evaluate programs for training, career development, and employee counseling. We are concerned also with work motivation, rewards for quality work, turnover, and job satisfaction. Work problems involving alcohol abuse, occupational stress, and sexual harassment need our solutions. We try to understand and improve leadership and supervision. We study the organization's structure and the effects it has on people, and we develop working conditions to accommodate the individual worker. As you can see, whatever affects work or occurs in the workplace is within the domain of this broad field. It encompasses almost all of applied psychology at one level or another.

*M*ain
*P*oints

Historically, ordinary commonsense psychology has been used by people to meet their own needs. Similarly, knowledge of human behavior has been used since ancient times to deal with problems in the workplace. When psychology became a science at the end of the nineteenth century, the idea that it should be an applied as well as a basic science was debated. The result was a division of the field that remains today. In addition to the basic research side of psychology, there are applied branches of psychology.

Industrial/organizational (I/O) psychology is the modern version of one of the original applied psychologies. Over the years it has been called by various names, including business psychology. Now, as in the early days, I/O psychology is the study of behavior at work and the application of behavioral knowledge to solve problems and meet the needs of the workplace.

I/O PSYCHOLOGY IN THE PAST

A description of the activities of those who study and practice in a field defines that field in terms of its boundaries and content. In this section, I describe the beginnings of I/O psychology by looking into the lives of its earliest proponents. Then, I review some trends in the research done over the years, and point out some external factors that influenced the field's growth.

The Pioneers

Sometimes science historians try to identify and crown one person as the "father of our science." This is not a good idea because it ignores what others said and did before and during that person's work. I agree with Roback (1952) who dedicated his *History of American Psychology* to "the obscure and forgotten who were either prematurely cut off by a cruel fate or whose feeble voice could not be heard above the din of their more dynamic colleagues." Usually, the very early originators of a movement are not heard. Sometimes their ideas are not published broadly, or their ideas may be so radical they cannot be accepted.

In addition to giving the forerunners their due, another reason for looking at history is that we periodically need to rethink how our science has developed. Psychology's noted historian, Edwin G. Boring (1950), proposed that modern history cannot be written simply by adding a new chapter to the old. "Strange as it may seem," he said, "the present changes the past; and, as the focus and range of psychology shift in the present, new parts of the past enter into its history and other parts drop out (p. ix)." What seemed nonsense at one time, later might be seen as prophetic insight. What seemed unrelated, might later be recognized as a developing branch of the field. I/O psychology has evolved in this way, growing out of several different lines of work.

Hugo Münsterberg

The story of Münsterberg began in Germany where he studied at the University of Leipzig under Wundt. As a student, Münsterberg showed signs of the creative thinker he was to become. For example, in his student research, he developed a theoretical position in direct opposition to Wundt's, something that did not happen between Wundt and his students. (Wundt's students accepted *his* view of human behavior.) As a result of their disagreement, Münsterberg was dismissed from the project.

After Münsterberg received his Ph.D., he taught at the University of Freiburg. There, he continued the controversial study he had begun in Wundt's laboratory and published an article describing his theoretical position. Wundt and his supporters were very critical of the article, but the American professor William James called it a masterpiece. At the time, James was working on a theory and found Münsterberg's ideas complementary to his own. James was so interested in the young scholar's work that he invited him to come to Harvard University. At Harvard, Münsterberg took over the small experimental laboratory that James had set up and turned it into an expansive, well-equipped facility (Landy, 1992). As a result, students flocked to the University to study under him.

Münsterberg's interests in psychological applications came out of some later work in which he attempted to define and organize the systems of knowledge. In a paper published in 1903, he observed that although knowledge does come from the development of scientific theory, knowledge also comes from practical experience. The usual view was that everything known in the practical sciences was already known in the basic sciences. Münsterberg, however, proposed that the human sciences did not operate in this manner and that applied psychology could actually contribute new knowledge to basic science.

One of the strongest of Münsterberg's research interests was in the application of psychology to various vocational testing problems. For example, in 1912, he did the groundwork for one of the earliest personnel selection tests. While talking with an executive at a railway company, Münsterberg described how it was possible to do studies on the causes of streetcar accidents and to use the results to identify and hire safe operators. Impressed with the idea, the executive hired him to do such a study. In the study, which was one of the first field experiments to be done, Münsterberg used his knowledge of the experimental method to design a simulation of the streetcar in traffic in order to observe the operator's behavior. He used skilled streetcar operators in the study and recorded the effects of varying the direction and progress of pedestrians, horses, and cars relative to the streetcar.

Although Münsterberg published relatively few articles reporting research done in his lab, he wrote theoretical papers and a number of books on a range of subjects—ethics, psychotherapy, education, and economic psychology. His book, *Psychology: General and Applied,* was his most influential work. It functioned as a vehicle for displaying his broad scope and ability to synthesize ideas from many sources (Roback, 1952).

During the last few years of his life, Münsterberg devoted himself almost entirely to promoting economic psychology. He wrote articles for popular magazines, conducted lecture tours, and talked with people about the value of applying psychology. Typically, in these promotions, he began by observing that other sciences—physiology, chemistry, physics, and mathematics—had been used for profit making. Psychology could be too, he said. He described business problems in which knowledge of human behavior could be helpful. For example, in employment selection, psychological research could be used to develop tests matched specifically to the needs of a particular business. Münsterberg had high hopes for the use of psychology in this way. He believed the business psychologist would become the middle person between scientific psychology and the industrial world.

Münsterberg's promotion of applied psychology did pay off, of course. The year after he died in 1916, the journal that has become the primary professional publication for I/O psychology, the *Journal of Applied Psychology,* made its debut. In this first volume, the editors noted:

> **The psychologist finds that the old distinction between pure and applied science is already obscured in his domain; and he is beginning to realize that applied psychology can no longer be relegated to a distinctly inferior plane. (** *Journal of Applied Psychology,* **1917, foreword)**

Münsterberg had a flashy but short career. Not only was he prominent within psychology but also, because of his involvement in business and governmental affairs, he was a well-known public figure in the United States and Europe. However, within three or four years after his death, he appeared to have been forgotten. References to his books and scientific articles had all but disappeared from the psychological literature (Landy, 1992). In fact, his contributions remained undervalued and his importance to applied psychology went unrecognized until recent years when his name began to appear in I/O psychology textbooks as the historical "father" of the field. Landy's (1992) study of Münsterberg's life indicated a complex explanation for the professional scorn. One important factor was that the field was undergoing some wrenching transitions. Münsterberg was involved in several of these, such as the proper role of applied psychology. Another factor was his personal style. Münsterberg's work showed that he was a visionary, however, he also was a headline seeker. He was critical—even condescending, with his American colleagues, yet he was easily offended by any outright or even implied criticism from them. Undoubtedly, this behavior must have irritated his associates. Still, many admired him, and his students were devoted to him. Knight Dunlap, one of those students, expressed how they felt about him.

> **There was at least one giant in those days, although his publications do not show it. Münsterberg made no converts . . . but I think the modern trends in American psychology . . . are easily traceable to Münsterberg as their father. . . . He radiated scientific impulses and profoundly altered the course of American psychology. (Boring & Lindzey, 1932, p. 42)**

James McKeen Cattell

The star performer in early applied psychology was Münsterberg. However, he was not the only one who thought of using psychology in business. James McKeen Cattell was another contributor to the field's development. Cattell initiated and directed much of the mental testing movement that began in the late 1800s and monopolized the attention of applied psychologists for decades.

Cattell was Wundt's student also, although he was American born. He received his doctorate at Leipzig in 1886. Shortly thereafter, he went to Cambridge University in England to study with Francis Galton, who had been researching **individual differences** in intelligence. Cattell had always been interested in this view of behavior. Even in Wundt's laboratory, where such studies had not been done, Cattell's research concerned individual differences. He preferred to learn how people differ, rather than how they are similar. At Cambridge, Galton was using a new method to study individual differences that involved the statistical evaluation of large numbers of subjects. Although this method is commonplace today, it was not at that time. In the late 1800s, scientific research was done by means of an **introspective method** carried out by two or three "observers," usually the researcher and assistants. Galton's statistical method was a radical departure from this procedure but appropriate for Cattell's needs.

The study of individual differences is linked to some practical applications. For example, suppose we have two job applicants. The way we behave toward each will depend on how much of some characteristic X we believe they each have. (X might be a job skill, for example.) Often, we do not know an applicant's level of X, but we guess and act accordingly. Of course, we are likely to be somewhat inaccurate and our actions somewhat off base. If, however, we could discover how the applicants *differ* in X, we could act more correctly. (We might offer one a job.) What we need is a measure of X. Cattell meant to provide such measures. First, he used the **statistical method** to study many people and discover ways people differ. From this discovery, he developed a measure–the mental test. Cattell's mental test was meant to assess a variety of intellectual capacities and to provide information on the range of differences in a tested group.

Cattell believed in the value of applied psychology. In 1893, he wrote about the future of testing. He predicted that public testing programs for everyone would be created. For example, people could be tested to find out if they were overworked and needed a vacation. A test could tell them whether a particular occupation would be right for them. Psychological methods could be used for diagnosing ailments and providing cures–not just physical ailments but also social disorders. Cattell believed that psychological measurement would become important in social progress. It is interesting to note that while he was making these predictions, testing was being promoted at the World's Fair that year. Psychology had an exhibit that included a display of experimental equipment and a testing lab for people interested in learning about their mental abilities (Roback, 1952).

Cattell promoted applications of psychology in industry, not from the soapbox but from behind the executive's desk. He founded and edited journals that published scientific research; thus, to a great extent, Cattell channeled psychological research by his control over the journals. More than this, he was successful in softening the reactions of experimental psychologists to applied psychology. In the early days, the attitude of many psychologists was that no self-respecting scientist would engage in this activity. Within a decade or so, however, attitudes changed. I believe this was largely a result of Cattell's work. Granted, his success was helped by Münsterberg's stage-setting; but, as we see in many history-making actions, his timing was right. In 1921, Cattell established the first successful business devoted to psychological consulting. It was, and is today, called **The Psychological Corporation.** He hired psychologists on a contract basis to work with businesses in solving work problems. Payment for consultation was divided between the consultant and the consulting firm, with much of the profit channeled into research and education in applied psychology. Cattell financed The Psychological Corporation by selling $10 shares to his friends and associates. He was open with them about its purpose: The firm would sell expert knowledge to industry. The board of directors of the corporation consisted of 20 leading psychologists. Edward Titchener, the most prominent experimental psychologist of the day and previous vocal opponent of applied psychology, was a member of the board.

Cattell never lost his belief in the future of applied psychology. On the 25th anniversary of the American Psychological Association (APA) in 1917, he predicted that in another 25 years those working in applied psychology would outnumber those teaching psychology. Twenty years later in 1937, he noted that the applied divisions of APA had increased to three—clinical, industrial, and educational psychology. However, their numbers had not increased as much as he had predicted. Was he right in the long run? In some ways he was. In 1996, almost 80 years later, there were many new applied divisions, as table 1.1 shows. In terms of members, applied psychology has become well established in APA. At least, the clinical branch has. There are now large numbers of clinical members. This change has shifted the focus of APA from general scientific issues to clinical interests. This shift in APA has resulted in stronger allegiance to APA divisions, and the establishment of a new professional association, the American Psychological Society (APS). APS is meant to emphasize the scientific side of psychology, particularly in basic academic research in which APA is now weak. I/O psychologists belong to both APA and APS.

Walter Dill Scott

Another who has been called the "father" of I/O psychology is Walter Dill Scott. Like most originators, however, he did not work alone. Harlow Gale, who went before Scott, should be recognized for his work in the psychology of advertising. In 1896, Gale, a psychology instructor at the University of Minnesota, began a series of experimental studies of advertising. He wanted to find out what made people pay attention to advertisements (Kuna, 1976). Publication of these studies in a scholarly journal, however, did not attract much attention. Psychologists who read the journal probably were not interested in the subject, and advertisers were not likely readers of such a publication.

Advertising at the turn of the century was evolving. There were two views concerning the information that should go into an ad. These two viewpoints differed primarily in what was assumed about the consumer. In one view, people were

Table 1.1   Divisions of the American Psychological Association

Division	Title
1	General Psychology
2	The Society for the Teaching of Psychology
3	Experimental Psychology
5	Evaluation, Measurement, and Statistics
6	Behavioral Neuroscience and Comparative Psychology
7	Developmental Psychology
8	Society for Personality and Social Psychology
9	Society for the Psychological Study of Social Issues
10	Psychology and the Arts
12	Clinical Psychology
13	Consulting Psychology
14	Society for Industrial and Organizational Psychology
15	Educational Psychology
16	School Psychology
17	Counseling Psychology
18	Psychologists in Public Service
19	Military Psychology
20	Adult Development and Aging
21	Applied Experimental and Engineering Psychologists
22	Rehabilitation Psychology
23	Society for Consumer Psychology
24	Theoretical and Philosophical Psychology
25	Experimental Analysis of Behavior
26	History of Psychology
27	Society for Community Research and Action: Community Psychology
28	Psychopharmacology and Substance Abuse
29	Psychotherapy
30	Psychological Hypnosis
31	State Psychological Association Affairs
32	Humanistic Psychology
33	Mental Retardation and Developmental Disabilities
34	Population and Environmental Psychology
35	Psychology of Women
36	Psychology of Religion
37	Child, Youth, and Family Services
38	Health Psychology
39	Psychoanalysis
40	Clinical Neuropsychology
41	American Psychology–Law Society
42	Psychologists in Independent Practice
43	Family Psychology
44	Society for the Psychological Study of Lesbian and Gay Issues
45	Society for the Psychological Study of Ethnic Minority Issues
46	Media Psychology
47	Exercise and Sports Psychology
49	Group Psychology and Group Psychotherapy
50	Addictions
51	Society for the Psychological Study of Men and Masculinity

From APA Division Interest Form. Copyright © 1997 American Psychological Association. Reprinted by permission.

rational buyers who would evaluate a product objectively; therefore, an ad should be a straightforward presentation of the facts. In the other view, buyers based their decisions on subjective impressions of the product; thus, advertising should appeal to the person's emotions and make a positive impression (Kuna, 1976).

Thomas Balmer was one of the advertising people interested in discovering which view was correct. Balmer thought the scientific method of psychology might settle the issue, and he hired Scott to do some advertising studies. Although Scott did bring the scientific method to Balmer's project, his use of it was not as objective as some might have hoped. Primarily, he followed the principles of psychology as they were known at the time. He used two well-known psychological constructs in advising advertisers. One was the concept of suggestibility in which the normal person was seen as suggestible and easily persuaded. The other concept was that of ideomotor action. In this, it was believed that a thought contained a tendency to act, and the act would occur unless a conflicting thought prevented it (Kuna, 1976).

As a result of Scott's use of these concepts in his studies, many advertisers came to view the consumer as impressionable. If they wished to persuade the consumer, Scott advised, their ads must present the product information in a manner that would fill the consumer's awareness completely. Mention of any information that might suggest *not* buying the product was taboo. How would an advertiser develop an ad then? Scott had two suggestions: the direct command and the return (or "cents off") coupon. The direct command features an active verb, such as "drink," followed by the brand name, "Super Cola." The direct command, Scott said, is obeyed impulsively. That is, if no choice is offered, we tend to do as we are told. The return coupon gives us an immediate way to comply with the command. We clip the coupon and plan to take it to the store (Scott, 1914).

Scott was successful in promoting applied psychology because he took his ideas directly to the people who would be interested. For instance, he spoke to people in advertising and wrote articles for their magazines. A report of his work with Balmer was published in an advertising journal, and his book, *The Theory of Advertising,* was marketed in the advertising community. Later, in 1915, when he left his position at Northwestern University and became the first professor of applied psychology at the Carnegie Institute of Technology, he made similar contacts. During his first year at Carnegie, Scott met Edward Woods, a prominent Pittsburgh businessman. Woods was interested in what qualities were needed for good salesmanship and in how to recognize people with sales potential. This contact led to a deal between Scott and Woods. Woods would finance a research center at Carnegie, at which Scott would study the issue of salesmanship and answer Woods's questions. Scott's studies did uncover some answers. One study led to the development of the application blank for use as a selection device. Scott also published another book of advice, *Aids in the Selection of Salesmen.*

Scott had a knack for consulting and worked easily with advertisers and business executives. In 1919, he organized the Scott Company, which was the first consulting firm specifically aimed at solving personnel selection problems. Although it survived only a few years, it provided an example for later personnel consultants.

Frederick W. Taylor and the Gilbreths

Simultaneously with the mainstream developments in applied psychology, Frederick W. Taylor, an engineer, and Frank and Lillian Gilbreth, an engineer and a psychologist, were progressing along another avenue in industry. Although Taylor and the Gilbreths did not collaborate in their research, their work came to be known collectively as the **time and motion studies.** Mainly, what they had in common was their use of the scientific method to solve performance problems in field settings.

After apprenticeship training, Taylor went to work in 1878 in the steel industry. Over the next 10 years, he moved up in the organization to foreman and then to chief engineer. As foreman, Taylor was faced constantly with having to decide what was the best way to do a job; what was an adequate workload; and what was an equitable pay rate. Being a methodical person, he found that the rule-of-thumb procedure typically used to answer such questions was not to his liking. Consequently, he developed a method, which he called **scientific management,** for making these decisions. Scientific management was an application of the experimental method being used in research. His studies began with observation and timing of work methods, equipment uses, or work/rest periods. These observations then were compared with measures of production, allowing conclusions to be drawn.

The much publicized shoveling study at Bethlehem Steel Works illustrates the method. Taylor began the study by making detailed observations of how shoveling work was being done. He also collected information about the workers, their tools, and the materials they shoveled, which consisted mostly of iron ore and coal. He noted that each worker brought his own shovel to work and used it for both materials. He weighed the load a shovel could carry and found that it varied from about 3.5 pounds for coal to about 38 pounds for iron ore. In the second phase of the study, Taylor set out to establish the optimal shovel load that would allow a worker to move the most material in a working day. For this, he set up an experiment with two shovelers using different shovels over a period of days. They started with a large shovel, which would permit heavy loads, and gradually changed to smaller shovels. The results of the study showed that the best shovel for all materials was one that carried 21 pounds. This meant that two different shovels would be needed for the different materials.

Taylor used the results of the shoveling study to redesign the work at Bethlehem Steel. Specifically, he convinced his superiors to buy shovels of the proper size. Similar studies had shown other ways to improve efficiency, and the changes Taylor was able to institute included not only new shovels but a new way of managing. He started a planning department to schedule and assign work. He had each worker's performance level recorded and gave bonuses to those with high production. Trainers were provided for those who fell behind. Finally, he documented the impact of these interventions and showed that the costs of shoveling had been cut in half.

Taylor's critics said that he was merely trying to squeeze more work out of the workers (e.g., Ryan & Smith, 1954). This criticism is likely due to Taylor's expressed aim of increasing work efficiency. However, he did not believe that this necessarily meant exploitation. In fact, he denounced both industrial exploitation of workers and worker exploitation of industry. He saw scientific management as a way to improve the organization. It would provide higher wages for labor, lower prices for consumers, and more business for the company (Taylor, 1916).

Frank Gilbreth's early experience was similar to Taylor's. His career began in 1885 as a bricklayer's apprentice, and he rose rapidly in the construction industry. By 1900, he had his own business. Also like Taylor, Gilbreth was a keen observer of the work process. For example, he noticed the various actions workers used to perform the same job. Although they might be equally proficient, he found that no two worked in exactly the same way. Fast work was done in one way and slow work in another. Workers used still other methods when showing someone how to perform the job. After years of observing these differences, Gilbreth decided to find the best way to perform a given task. He devoted himself entirely to studying work methods. In addition to his personal observations, he began photographing the work process. This was the beginning of motion study.

Motion study became a highly refined technique in the hands of Frank and Lillian Gilbreth. This husband and wife team adapted the motion picture camera for photographing a worker's movements. For example, they added a device for marking time intervals on the film. With this equipment, they were able to record both a movement and the time it required. As a result of such innovations, the Gilbreths developed **micromotion study,** a method used in equipment design research in which the fundamental elements of an operation are analyzed (Barnes, 1940).

Frank Gilbreth did extensive study of bricklaying and developed some improvements. One was a scaffold that incorporated a workbench and reduced the number of motions involved in picking up bricks. He also developed a streamlined method of bricklaying in which the number of motions required to lay one brick was reduced from 18 to less than a quarter of that number. The innovations that resulted from his motion study escalated production from 120 bricks placed per hour to 350 per hour, three times the average of the old work method.

The bricklaying studies used able-bodied workers. However, some of the Gilbreths' later studies were aimed at determining the most efficient design of jobs for disabled employees. Their interest in this need resulted from the observation that World War I veterans who were disabled found it almost impossible to get jobs when they returned home. Believing that this was a critical need and that society was obligated to provide work for these veterans, the Gilbreth team conducted motion studies and developed strategies whereby the nation's disabled labor force could be helped. Their motion studies explored the workers' limitations and demonstrated that by designing jobs to fit the worker, veterans could be proficient on civilian jobs if they had the opportunity (Gotcher, 1992).

Development of the Field

The work of individuals shows the origins of a developing field. A history of the personalities involved in I/O psychology is difficult to continue, however, because so many more people were involved as the field became better established. Another way to view the development of I/O psychology is to look at what issues have evolved. In this section, let us consider the development of the subject matter that concerns I/O psychologists.

Although there were relatively few applied psychologists in the early 1920s, some were finding work in private industry. They worked for department stores, insurance companies, and manufacturers. They selected, trained, and evaluated employees, particularly sales personnel (Katzell & Austin, 1992). Similarly, in the university laboratories, the primary interest of the applied psychologists was employment testing. Although they talked about how psychology could be applied to a range of work situations, most seemed too busy with testing to get started on other applications. In 1926, Viteles reviewed the literature appearing in technical journals and found that 65 percent of the articles reported studies of tests and other methods of vocational selection.

Much of the work in testing had actually begun prior to World War I, and military involvement of psychologists during the war contributed to this focus. At the time, applied psychologists were reputed to be testing experts, and many of those who went into military service worked on constructing tests for evaluating inductees. In 1917, the Secretary of War established the Committee on Classification of Personnel to address this need for military testing. The Committee was headed by psychologists Walter Dill Scott, Edward L. Thorndike, and W. V. Bingham. Later that year, 2 million soldiers participated in the first large-scale group administration of an intelligence test. This written test, the **Army Alpha,** was one developed by psychologists specifically to classify inductees into appropriate work. A few months later, a second intelligence test came out, the **Army Beta,** a nonlanguage test that was administered to 100,000 illiterate or non-English-speaking soldiers. Of course, this focus on testing was not easily lost, and after the war, the psychologists went on to develop selection tests for civilian work.

The field in the early 1930s looked much the same as in the 1920s. The 1935 *Psychological Abstracts*[2] showed continuing emphasis on testing and selection. There was some study of industrial efficiency. For example, a series of field experiments, which became known as the **Hawthorne studies,** took place during this decade. Although these studies were aimed at improving the company's operations, it was the somewhat accidental discovery of the importance of social relationships at work that captured attention (Katzell & Austin, 1992). By the end of the 1930s, however, researchers had broadened their focus. The *Journal of Applied Psychology* contained comparatively fewer testing studies. Interest in applying psychology to other vocational activities and in exploring its uses in solving traffic problems was on the increase (Darley, 1968).

Then, the country was caught up in another war. World War II had a significant impact on the field. Many psychologists went into the armed services, and others were hired into adjunct civilian positions. The 1945 *Psychological Abstracts* showed that a large amount of military research being done during the time dealt with testing. Two other major activities of the military psychologist were (1) mental health assessment and counseling of service personnel, and (2) participation with engineers on teams designing military equipment. Emerging from this latter experience was a line of research that ultimately came to be known as **engineering psychology**. The reasoning of military project leaders in teaming psychologists with engineers to design military machinery was that psychologists knew what to expect from a human operating this equipment. After the war, these psychologists continued working on design research in their civilian labs, and in 1947, the first article on human engineering appeared in the *Journal of Applied Psychology*.

In the civilian sphere at this time, much of the research related to personnel selection or industrial efficiency. In addition, there was some study of social

---

[2]A reader's guide to publications on psychological issues.

conditions in the workplace, including motivation, job satisfaction, and supervision. The **human relations movement** eventually emerged from this social emphasis. In a similar vein, the coming movement in industrial employee relations was being forecasted by the study of job training, supervision, and industrial working conditions (Yoder, 1945).

In the 1950s, there were more changes. Human engineering studies increased, and the issue of automation surfaced. Although industrial efficiency was still of interest, this research now centered on monotony and motivation. The previous wartime emphasis on vocational counseling had almost disappeared. Studies of personnel had less to do with testing than they had before. Industrial psychologists had broadened their interests to include social aspects of work, such as communication, supervision, and morale (Darley, 1968). The human relations movement had burgeoned everywhere. Books were being written on this subject, mainly addressing communication problems and instructing readers on how to set up programs to help workers communicate better (e.g., Maier, 1952).

Both the human relations and the human engineering movements were signs of a new attitude. Earlier, industrial psychology had been concerned mainly with increasing profits. The new "human" approach was more altruistic and focused on the mutual adjustment of the worker and the organization. This could be seen in books on the psychology of personnel. These books combined information on selection, training, and evaluation with new knowledge of employee attitudes, communication, and social conditions to produce two major divisions—the management of workers and the satisfaction of workers (e.g., Bellows, 1954).

Organizational psychology rose in the 1960s from the multidisciplinary study of the social conditions of work, which already had spawned the popular human relations trend. Although organizational psychology was broader and more concerned with the organization itself, it had much in common with human relations. Texts on organizational psychology coming out in the 1960s included discussions of motivation, satisfaction, interpersonal relations, and organizational design (e.g., Katz & Kahn, 1966). Leadership was an exciting topic in this new work. The texts also presented material on social processes, such as communication, conflict, and decision making (e.g., Bass, 1965). This focus on the organization was so important that by the end of the decade we were considering an official name change. Early in the 1970s, APA Division 14 became the "Division of Industrial and Organizational Psychology."

In the 1960s and 1970s, personnel selection changed as a result of legal developments. The 1964 **Civil Rights Act,** as well as a number of court cases involving employment discrimination, encouraged test developers to rethink some of their basic assumptions. Questions of what a job applicant legitimately could be asked on a test were considered. Applicants and employees, and lawmakers and courts demanded that employers using a selection test be able to show the test's relevance to the job. Many employers changed their approach to selection. There was less of the previous wholesale, indiscriminate use of commercial tests. Psychologists working in industry began to conduct large-scale test validation studies to evaluate their companies' tests. Other companies stopped using tests altogether and sought alternatives. Consequently, such selection devices as the assessment center began to draw attention (Ash & Kroeker, 1975; Dunnette & Borman, 1979). These developments resulted in improved methods for analyzing jobs and validating tests, and the foundation was laid for a sophisticated new selection research technology to appear in the 1980s.

On the organizational side of the field, individual and group behavior within the social setting of work continued to interest researchers in the 1970s. One issue in the forefront at this time was work motivation. By the early 1970s, several theories had been advanced, and research literature was accumulating around these theories. By the middle of the decade, however, this work was almost at a standstill. Most well-known theories seemed to be quite limited, and researchers began asking different questions about the motivational issue. Some directed their research at the effects of societal changes, such as the entry of more women and minorities into the work force and the apparent dissatisfaction of young workers (Korman, Greenhaus, & Badin, 1977). Other psychologists attempted to alter motivation with interventions meant to increase employee participation at work. Organization development (OD) was presented as a way to humanize an organization. OD practice caught on rapidly, and I/O psychologists explored its effectiveness in many different work settings (Alderfer, 1977).

*M*ain *P*oints

You should remember six people who are important in the history of I/O psychology: Münsterberg, Cattell, Scott, Taylor, and the Gilbreth team. Münsterberg played an important part in beginning the field by introducing and legitimizing the idea that science and practice could progress simultaneously. He became a well-known public lecturer, writer, and consultant to business on the uses of psychology. Cattell did research on individual differences in mental ability. He founded research journals and established one of the earliest consulting firms. Scott also started a consulting firm. He is known for his work in advertising, salesmanship, and selection. Taylor, who devised time studies of work processes, was among the first to use the experimental method to solve industrial problems. The Gilbreths similarly used the research method in motion studies to design efficient work procedures.

From the beginning, research in I/O psychology has featured personnel selection. To some extent, this resulted from psychologists' involvement in World War I, during which important tests were developed. Selection and other personnel issues dominated the field during the early years. This emphasis changed later. Research following World War II increasingly dealt with the social conditions of work, and the human relations movement was initiated. This, in turn, led to the emergence of organizational psychology.

I/O PSYCHOLOGY NOW

Where has our history led us? There are two ways to answer this question. We can look at the current subject matter of the field and at the people in the field. In this section, let us consider the people in I/O psychology. The remaining chapters of this book focus on the subject matter.

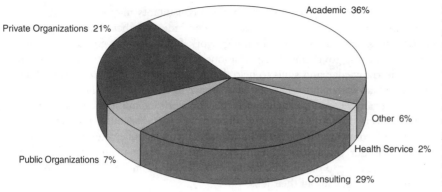

Academic 36%

Private Organizations 21%

Other 6%

Health Service 2%

Public Organizations 7%

Consulting 29%

Figure 1.1. *Where I/O psychologists work. Private organizations include high-tech industry, financial and nonfinancial services, consumer products, and telecommunications. Public organizations include federal, local, and state governments and agencies, and the military. (Total is 101 percent because of rounding error.)*

From Ann Howard, The Multiple Facets of Industrial-Organizational Psychology. *Arlington Heights, Illinois: Society for Industrial and Organizational Psychology, 1990, pp. 9, 11. Reprinted by permission.*

Professional Work in I/O Psychology

Where do I/O psychologists work and what do they do? For those with a Ph.D., there are four major work settings: academic institutions, business and industrial organizations, public or governmental agencies, and external consulting firms (see figure 1.1). I/O psychologists in colleges and universities work in both psychology departments and business schools. They teach, conduct research, and participate in university administration. The particular mix of these activities depends on the academic institution. Those who work in research-oriented universities are involved in research more than in any other facet. Those in teaching-oriented institutions focus on education. In addition to their primary work, many academics do independent consulting. Howard (1990) found that more than one-third of the academic psychologists had second jobs, usually as consultants.

Other I/O psychologists are hired by business or governmental organizations as employees. Typically, they do not have the job title of "I/O psychologist." Instead, they are personnel administrators, directors of training, organizational research supervisors, and human resource directors. These I/O psychologists generally do three types of work: research, management, and internal consulting. Their research is practical, done mainly for the benefit of the employer and not necessarily for publication. For example, the psychologist may conduct an employee attitude survey or develop an employment test. Most I/O psychologists in industry do a certain amount of supervision and managerial work. Howard (1984) pointed out that for the I/O psychologist in industry, promotions tend to move the person from specialty work to general management. As an **in-house consultant,** the I/O psychologist provides expert advice on human resource problems, including development and implementation of special intervention programs. Although there are some similarities between in-house and **external consulting,** there are some important differences. In-house consultants are employees, not contractors. An advantage for internal consultants is that they can develop and follow projects over a longer period of time. When something goes wrong, the internal consultant is there to put it right (Kissler, 1985). In contrast, the external consultant must get in, get results, and get out.

I/O psychologists who are external consultants may work for a consulting firm or be self-employed. A recent survey indicated that about three-fifths of those whose primary job is consulting, work for consulting firms that contract with business or government organizations (Howard, 1990). External consultants use their knowledge and skills to help the organization solve its human problems. The external consultant offers services similar to those of the in-house psychologist. For example, one consultant said that his work includes job analysis and employee selection, design of training and performance evaluation programs, development of compensation systems, and health and safety evaluations (Robinson, 1987). Another consultant added career and succession planning and organizational downsizing to this list (Lupton, 1988). Table 1.2 indicates what some external consultants say about their jobs.

Professionalization of I/O Psychologists

Whatever their work, I/O psychologists must keep abreast of developments in the field. Becoming a professional means making a commitment to lifelong learning. One way to do this is to participate in the activities of professional groups, such as APA, APS, APA Division 14—the **Society for Industrial and Organizational Psychology (SIOP)**, and the Academy of Management. Professional associations help members stay current in several ways. They offer research journals and other publications. They sponsor conventions at which new research and issues of general importance are discussed. They also contribute to our identity as psychologists, represent the profession in public affairs, and provide us with ethical standards. I/O psychologists are committed to certain values. All ethical psychologists respect human dignity and worth. We are devoted to increasing our knowledge of behavior and to using this knowledge to protect human rights and promote human welfare. The American Psychological Association (1992) has published a list of specific ethical principles derived from these values that are used to govern the behavior of psychologists. In general, these principles specify that a psychologist must be responsible and competent; personally moral and sensitive; respectful of the integrity and rights to privacy of others; interested in promoting public understanding of psychology; and concerned with the welfare of clients and research subjects.

Licensing

Any psychologist who offers services for a fee to the public is required by law to be licensed by the state. For I/O psychologists, this law applies to most who do business as external consultants. They need to be licensed just as a clinical psychologist who has a private practice must be. Almost all 50 states have licensing laws that cover I/O consultants. The purpose, from the state's point of view, is to protect the public from individuals who are not qualified to offer psychological services. The process of licensing is meant to ensure that the practitioner is competent and ethical. To get a license, applicants typically must have a Ph.D. and a year or two of supervised postdoctoral experience. They also must pass a written examination and be approved by an ethically oriented review panel.

Table 1.2   What I/O Consultants Say about Their Work

I believe one of the attractions offered by consulting firms is the variety of work. For example, a review of assignments that have been accomplished or that are being carried by consultants with our firm during the last six months would encompass all of the section headings of any major textbook written about the field of I/O psychology.

> P. R. Jeanneret, A comment on making career decisions in I/O Psychology—Is there variety in a consulting career? _TIP_[a], Nov. 1989, 27(1), p. 63.

Like most people, I suspect, my career progression has been a combination of interest and serendipity. . . . I found I enjoyed the variety of working in a number of different organizations because, while the basic issue of risk may be the same, it will always be different given a specific organizational setting and cast of characters.

> D. E. Lupton, A consultant's view of being a consultant: Part III: The national consulting firm. _TIP_, Feb. 1988, 25(2), p. 40.

There are very few "clients" out there who can "use" what we want to give them. There are, however, nearly unlimited clients with specific problems that, if we really listened, we might be able to respond to in a way that would make the client see the benefit in our approach. Clients have problems and needs, not a desire to do "research."

> P. M. Connolly, Marketing professional services: A plan for finding receptive clients. _TIP_, May 1987, 24(3), p. 36.

If the services that one offers are not being utilized, then either they are not in demand, or the services are not perceived as worth the cost. The challenge is to create services in response to market needs in order to add value to organizational quests for increased competitive advantage. If we are effective consultants, we will help clients achieve their goals, and they will see value in what we do.

> M. R. Cooper, A consultant's view of being a consultant: Part IV: A worldwide strategy & human resource consulting firm. _TIP_, May 1988, 25(3), pp. 36–37.

What's required to be a good consultant? Aside from technical and professional competence, from my perspective there are a number of important factors. In our business, the kind of work we do has a very practical applied problem-solving character. We've got to deliver something that is useful and present it to clients in a way that they can understand how they can use it.

> J R. Hinrichs, I/O careers in consulting. _TIP_, Aug. 1984, 21(4), p. 21.

Persistence is a key to success in consulting: persistence in marketing, in providing consistently superior service, in getting financing, search for the best staff, and so forth. . . . Persistence means working very long hours to meet a commitment; it means attending to the details that separate the best in any field from everyone else; and it means continuing to make contacts and develop new clients in the face of disinterest and even outright rejection.

> D. S. Cohen, A consultant's view of being a consultant. _TIP_, May 1987, 24(3), p. 61.

An individual proprietor must have a strong sense of independence, willingness to accept risk, and a high tolerance of ambiguity. One of the most difficult aspects of independent consulting is unpredictable cash flow. Tolerance, persistence, and patience are necessary because it is difficult to sell I/O services to people who are unaware of the benefits.

> D. D. Robinson, A consultant's view of being a consultant: Part II: The small established consulting firm. _TIP_, Aug. 1988, 24(4), p. 45.

Of all the things I/O psychologists do, probably the most difficult involves getting specific recommendations implemented once a project is "complete." In essence this skill is needed to ensure effectiveness of an intervention as our involvement diminishes. This is a problem and a frustration for both internal and external consultants whose work tends to be of a "project" versus "process" consulting nature. How do you convince a client to keep you involved after you've made a recommendation or a project appears complete?

> P. M. Connolly, Implementing solutions as a consultant. _TIP_, Aug. 1986, 23(4), p. 35.

[a] _TIP_ is an acronym for _The Industrial Organizational Psychologist._

To the extent that I/O psychologists do individual assessment and one-on-one counseling, licensing is meant to provide the necessary assurance of ethical practice in this field. Most I/O psychologists approve of this (Howard, 1990). However, some do not believe licensing is needed when the practice does not involve work with individuals. When the I/O psychologist's client is an organization, rather than an individual, there seems to be less need for protection. We do not think of "sick" organizations as being vulnerable to unscrupulous "healers" and in need of protection by the state, but we do think of individuals in this fashion. Thus, the issue of licensing for I/O psychologists is a controversial one, and we will hear more about it in the future (Howard & Lowman, 1985; Schmitt, 1991).

Education of I/O Psychologists

There are several routes to education in I/O psychology. Each will determine to some extent the type of work for which the person is prepared. Ph.D. programs in I/O psychology require at least four years of study beyond the bachelor's degree in addition to a dissertation based on a candidate's original research. Some programs also require an internship in which the student gains hands-on experience in the practice of I/O psychology in a work setting. In general, a Ph.D. is required for most academic positions, for licensed private practice as an external consultant, and for many positions in business and government in which a person does research and/or internal consulting.

Another way to get an education in I/O psychology is through a program that offers a master's degree in the field. Master's degree programs usually take no more than two years to complete. They require coursework and a thesis. Many require an internship or field experience. Individuals with a master's degree in I/O psychology are most likely to work in business and government organizations (Howard, 1990). They often have job titles similar to Ph.D. psychologists in these organizations, such as training specialist, personnel systems analyst, executive recruiter, and compensation consultant (Berry, 1990). A listing of master's and doctoral programs in I/O psychology can be found in the appendix.

A third way to get an education in I/O psychology is through an undergraduate program that offers a bachelor's degree in psychology with a concentration in I/O. So far, not many of these programs are available (Peters, 1985). They tend to be fairly general and are meant to prepare the student for graduate study or work in entry-level jobs in human resources. In addition to general requirements for psychology majors, such a program can include I/O specialty courses, business courses, labs in which students learn I/O-related work skills, and field placements in which students get work experience (Downey, Knight, & Saal, 1987). By itself, this level of education does not lead to professional work, but it does appear to make the person competitive for jobs in industry. One survey showed that those who graduated with an I/O emphasis went into various lines of work, including general business administration, sales, and specific human resources fields. For example, I/O-related job titles included employee representative, human resource assistant, and personnel specialist (Taylor, 1990).

I/O psychologists work in various settings. In universities, they teach and do research on work-related issues. In businesses and in government agencies, they do human resource administration, organizational research, and internal consulting. As external consultants, they perform the same kind of work but on a contract basis, and in this they must be licensed because they are providing services to the public.

Work as an I/O psychologist requires an education in the field. Numerous programs are available to students interested in a Ph.D. or master's degree. I/O psychologists who work as university faculty members need to have a Ph.D. in I/O psychology, as do external consultants. Some work being done in business and in government agencies, such as organizational research, can also require a Ph.D. Other work in business and government can be done with a master's degree.

THE FUTURE OF I/O PSYCHOLOGY

When a historical analysis approaches the period in which the analyst lives, identifying the developing trends becomes an especially difficult process. Edwin G. Boring (1950) noted his own caution in interpreting events of the previous 20 years in the history of psychology. Other historians agree that the patterns in the recent past are hard to see (Darley, 1968). Forecasters have a different problem. They must observe and interpret the present. The trick is to understand today and use it to predict tomorrow. The forecaster identifies present trends and then dashes forward in time, carrying these potential influences to their very limits. Of course, if the field developed in a vacuum without outside influences to affect the path of progress, then forecasters probably could make accurate predictions by employing this strategy. However, unexpected societal changes have modified the direction and growth of I/O psychology in the past, and these effects are likely to continue. My task at this point is to identify some ways in which the field may be redirected in the future. The historical review has suggested two categories of influence: internal and external conditions. In this final section of chapter 1, I identify some factors in each category and describe some ways the field may be influenced.

Internal Conditions

The New Generation of I/O Psychologists

Some changes in the field will occur because of the impact of the unique people who pursue I/O psychology as a career. The personal influences of the originators of the field were certainly important. At any point in our history, we can evaluate the field according to who is doing what and for what personal reason. We should not ignore this in anticipating our future. You and I, because of who we are and what we value, will change the course of the field. In order to predict this effect, we need to know the characteristics of people who will choose I/O psychology as a profession.

Curtis By Ray Billingsley

What can be said about us as a whole? Already, there are many more of us than there were, and this growth is likely to continue. According to APA's directories, membership in Division 14 in 1960 was 734. Twenty-five years later in 1985, membership had increased to 2,500. These numbers are adequate to show the rate of increased interest in the field, but they do not reflect the actual numbers of us, because some people who have a career based on I/O psychology are not Division 14 members. This is likely to be true of those whose highest degree is a master's. Recently, the field has become more popular among students because it seems to offer more employment opportunity than other areas of psychology. To students who like psychology but who do not want an academic or clinical career, getting a master's degree and a job in business is an appealing option.

One thing that sheer numbers do is increase the public's awareness of the field. At present, the average person is not very knowledgeable about I/O psychologists. We are usually mistaken for clinicians. The business world, however, has developed an increased appreciation of what we can offer. The increased numbers of people with I/O backgrounds who work in industry as employees or consultants have exposed the field to a wider audience. There also appears to be an increasing tendency for people with I/O degrees, both at the master's and doctoral levels, to work in industry, which is likely to improve the public awareness of the field (Cederbloom, Pence, & Johnson, 1984).

Another aspect of the new I/O psychologists' influence has to do with their individual interests and values. For quite awhile, the focus of I/O psychologists has been on human rights. This can be seen, for example, in the human relations work of the 1960s and in the current study of organizational climate. I believe this humanistic stance will continue to reflect the makeup of I/O people, and because of their increased numbers, humanism will eventually have a pronounced effect on the field. Another issue likely to be important to these new I/O psychologists is the meaningfulness of work. It may be that society's values are changing with respect to work, and if so, the new I/O psychologist probably will carry them to fulfillment. Work has always been an important part of our lives, but attitudes toward it have varied. Perhaps we are nearing a time when it is common to expect that basic rights include both having work and having meaningful work.

In addition, like the work force in general, I predict that I/O psychologists of the future will be of different ethnic, gender, and age proportions than in the past. The entire work force is aging (Tolliver, 1983), and it has more women and members of ethnic minority groups. We can expect this change in I/O psychology as well. I see some signs of it already, particularly in terms of the numbers of women entering the field. Howard (1990) found that among those receiving their doctorates during the 1980s, 39 percent were female. This contrasts sharply with the 8 percent of I/O psychology doctorates awarded to women in the 1960s. The interests of a more diverse group of I/O psychologists are likely to differ from those of previous generations, not only because they will be working in a different world but because of their own personal values.

Finally, I/O psychology appears to be developing beyond its American boundaries. Increasingly, the field is mentioned as a growing area of emphasis in universities around the world (Bazar, 1994). The International Association of Applied Psychology, which is a professional affiliation for many I/O psychologists, has published several articles over the past few years describing I/O activity in various countries. For example, the development and growth of I/O research in Spain over the past few years has been reported. The authors indicated that the same type of progress is expected throughout the European Community, and they predicted more cross-national collaboration in research and practice (Peiró & Munduate, 1994).

Threads of the Past

Several issues currently under study are likely to continue to occupy us in the future. Research on the personnel function is one of these issues. Employers will need methods to make selection decisions as long as there are more applicants than jobs. New selection research is likely to run the gamut of today's issues but will provide more emphasis on the relationship between tests and job performance criteria. For a number of reasons, I believe that a particular focus will be on ways to evaluate work performance. We still need valid selection devices, and these depend on accurate assessment of performance.

Training is likely to be the focus of some significant new research as well. There has been a concern for a long time that we know too little about executive behavior. Perhaps within the next decade or so, there will be more study of the executive, particularly because there seems to be an increasing interest in the development of managers. In a related vein, current interest in organizing will continue, because I/O psychologists and executives alike are interested in better organizations. Research on organizational climate and culture looks like an area of growth. This will lead to a more serious concern about the interaction of an organization and its intercultural work force.

External Conditions

In this section, I consider three broad societal changes that are likely to affect the field as a whole. These changes include the continuing development of information technology, an evolving work force, and increasing movement toward international business.

Information Technology

The ability to handle the vast amounts of information that computers make possible will certainly influence I/O psychology research. The changes have begun already. For example, computer techniques are available for analyzing jobs and training employees. Methods for evaluating large amounts of research data also have appeared, such as meta-analysis. We are likely to see this type of work in every area of I/O psychology.

Information technology undoubtedly will have an impact on jobs and organizations. However, predictions in the late 1970s and 1980s of a technology catastrophe have not been realized. Blackler (1988) reviewed some of these early forecasts, noting the prediction of (1) widespread unemployment due to replacement by automated machinery; (2) extreme simplification of jobs and elimination of many supervisors; and (3) resistance of employees to information technology. Although some signs of these changes have appeared, the effect has not been severe.

Some unanticipated problems relating to information technology are occurring, however. Most notable is the impact on the organization as a social entity. In one business firm, the goals and structure of the organization were altered in the process of integrating new technology (Shani & Sena, 1994). Often, social interaction among employees is reduced by such measures, as are the benefits that can result from interaction. Work groups are replaced by individual employees working independently but with the same computerized information sources. Such changes are likely to have rippling effects on the performance and supervision of employees. Security is another problem that can result, especially when telecommuting employees have remote access to an company's computerized data banks (Halachmi, 1992). Although the effects of information technology are not likely to be as extreme as the early forecasters thought, these latest developments do indicate that we need to pay attention to the day-to-day users of this equipment.

The New Work Force

The social conditions of the latter half of the twentieth century are changing the fabric of the work force. Birth rate, life expectancy, standard of living, and new politics surrounding immigration and fair employment practices are altering society. The work force of the twenty-first century is expected to be older and more balanced with regard to gender and ethnicity. These changes will affect the research and practice of the I/O psychologist. In response to the older work force, we are likely to see an increase in research on the effects of aging on cognitive, physical, and interpersonal work abilities. Problems of testing and evaluating older applicants and retraining older workers for new jobs will require more attention. We also will see some research on retirement and leisure activities.

The increase of female and minority employees has already begun to have an effect. For example, there is interest in evaluating these employees for managerial work. Especially as more women and ethnic minorities enter I/O psychology, this research is likely to continue. We will probably see more interest in alternate work schedules and settings as well. Job sharing, flexible work hours, and work at home are innovations likely to become common topics. Child care and other family issues, such as marital stress, will not be unusual issues for the I/O researcher.

The International Workplace

Another external condition that will redirect the field is the increasing amount of business done across national boundaries. Many large corporations headquartered in the United States now have branches in other countries. American workers increasingly are finding that foreign firms are employing them. The Japanese automobile industry in this country is a case in point.

American companies can establish their labor forces in other countries in either of two ways. They can take American workers with them or hire citizens of the host country. In either case, there is potential for problems. If Americans go to work in the other country, they need to be selected and trained to perform their jobs and adapt to living in the new country. If the company hires host country nationals, alternative selection and training issues are relevant. In addition, interpersonal issues, such as communication and supervision, pose challenges (Tung, 1981). Clearly, if the move toward international business continues, as I believe it will, all these human issues will become relevant to the I/O psychologist. We can expect to see the field respond by developing special selection and training procedures and by improving cross-cultural communication. Already we are getting involved. Howard's (1990) survey of I/O consultants revealed that 27 percent have done contract work outside the United States.

*M*ain *P*oints

I/O psychology is likely to change in the future because of the people who are attracted to the field. A new generation of I/O psychologists will bring their unique interests and values to the field. These new psychologists will be men and women of varying cultural backgrounds, and the values they bring are likely to be more humanistic than in the past. However, because some needs of industry persist, the future I/O psychology also will retain threads of its past. I/O psychologists will continue to contribute to the personnel function and to organizational improvement.

External conditions will affect the future. Information technology undoubtedly will influence the way I/O research and practice are done. In some ways but not all, the effect will be positive. Also likely to affect the future is the changing national work force. A diverse work force, including older, ethnic minority, and female members, will change the research I/O psychologists do and the problems they solve. A third condition is the increasingly international workplace. U.S. companies are operating in other countries, and foreign firms are here. I/O psychologists already are interested in the international company because of the organizational and personnel problems it presents.

CHAPTER SUMMARY

Industrial/organizational (I/O) psychology is an applied psychology in which principles and methods of psychology are used to address real-world issues of human behavior at work. The field has a comparatively long history, with roots in the late nineteenth century when scientific psychology began. Several turn-of-the-century notables were important in introducing and promoting the application of psychology in the business world. These include Münsterberg, Cattell, and Scott, all of whom were influential in bringing the academic world to accept the legitimacy of applied psychology. Taylor and the Gilbreths promoted the field by putting psychology to work in industry. Some social and economic developments in the twentieth century have been significant in the evolution of I/O psychology. World Wars I and II, in particular, were critical in determining the direction of the field. Personnel selection became a major focus as a result of World War I. From World War II, an emphasis on using psychology in machine design emerged. The 1960s Civil Rights movement further changed the course of the field, particularly because of its impact on personnel selection issues.

I/O psychologists currently are involved in several types of work. Some are professors who conduct research and teach. Others, employed in business, industry, and government, perform a variety of research, administrative, and consultative work. Still others provide external consultation in these settings. Individuals who are professionals in I/O psychology need to have at least a master's degree in the field; those who do external consulting as psychologists need a Ph.D. and a license to practice.

A number of factors are expected to influence the direction of I/O psychology in the future. The changing work force, more diverse now than it was in the past, is an example. The group choosing I/O psychology as a career reflects this change as well. Information technology is a second condition likely to affect the field. Increase in international business is a third. New issues and new techniques for research and practice in I/O psychology will no doubt result from these developments.

STUDY QUESTIONS

1) What is applied psychology, and how does I/O psychology fit into this broader category?

2) Who were the "parents" of I/O psychology, and what did they do to earn such a distinction?

3) In what ways were World Wars I and II important in the development of I/O psychology?

4) What does the modern I/O psychologist do in his or her job?

5) Do I/O psychologists need to be licensed? If so, under what conditions? If not, why not?

6) What level of education is required for an I/O psychologist?

7) What kinds of social conditions can be expected to influence the development of I/O psychology in the future?

CONSIDER THIS

ISSUE

Can the present change the past? Strangely enough, it can. At least, it can change what we remember about the past and how we interpret it. The psychology historian, Edwin G. Boring (1950) thought so. He observed that because the focus of the field changes from time to time, its connection to the past changes also. When I/O psychology branches into new research areas, as a growing field does, the background of those areas becomes relevant to its history.

This effect can be seen in a recent report of the now-relevant study of disabled workers that was done by Frank and Lillian Gilbreth to provide employment for the disabled worker. The Gilbreths' motion studies have long been cited as being important in the history of I/O psychol-ogy. However, in the past, only their studies addressing the design of jobs for the ablebodied were described. With our more recent interest in employing disabled workers, we are now interested in discovering another part of the past. Following World War I, a vast number of disabled American soldiers returned home to a life in which they had absolutely no opportunity to go back to work. Seeing this situation, the Gilbreths began to use their motion study method to redesign jobs so that they could be performed by these disabled workers (Gotcher, 1992).

This previously ignored bit of history is now a part of I/O psychology's past. What else is going on now that will appear in our past? Do the new directions I forecast in this chapter suggest that we may discover other pioneering work or even other "pioneers" we have ignored?

what's in this chapter?

I/O psychologists use many of the same methods to do their research as other psychologists use. They emphasize particular techniques, however, because of what they study and the nature of the workplace. In this chapter, you will learn about the variety of research methods and analytical techniques used for studying work behavior. You will discover how I/O psychologists approach the questions they want to answer. You will see how experiments and observational studies are done. You will learn how to carry out a survey, including what to think about when writing survey questions. You also will find out how I/O psychologists make sense of the data they collect by using statistics.

Direct observation is a research procedure used for conducting studies in the workplace. The researcher uses a checklist to record information about a worker's activities during short periods of the work day.

Chapter 2

Methods of Study and Research

Contents

In 1942 the U.S. Treasury was considering the imposition of a special 'victory tax' which was to be deducted directly from wages. A complication arose because a campaign had been conducted to persuade wage-earners to buy war loan on a deduction-from-wages plan. The question was what would happen to this system if direct taxation on wages were instituted. Would wage-earners now decide they were paying enough directly out of wages and no longer wish to continue their purchase of war loan? . . . A psychological research survey was conducted which involved careful interviewing of a selected sample of the population. The conclusion was that there would be no interference provided the tax was introduced to the workers in a suitable way. The tax was instituted.

C. J. Adcock

Now it is difficult to imagine working without having taxes withheld from one's paycheck! This is an example of how psychological research has been used to answer practical work-related questions. As we will learn in later chapters, there are many occasions when we need to find out how employees will react to changes in work policies and procedures, and the survey is one means of finding out. In this how-to chapter, I discuss how I/O psychologists conduct a survey and other research. The material included emphasizes general methods that can be applied in a variety of situations. More specific tools and techniques are discussed in other chapters along with the particular issue to which they apply. For instance, research methods for evaluating employment tests are discussed with other testing issues in chapter 5. In this chapter, my intention is to interpret research methodology in a broad and general sense. When an I/O psychologist goes to work, whether in an academic institution or in industry, he or she must do both research and fact-finding on the route to solving behavioral problems. Further, the I/O psychologist is expected to know how to accomplish all the tasks: The individual must evaluate the problem or need, plan and budget a study, analyze data, and present the findings coherently to people who are not psychologists.

Introducing Behavioral Research

Research on people at work can be conducted with the experimental method. In the last chapter, we saw that the basic experiment not only marked the birth of scientific psychology, but it also appeared in the work of the originators of I/O psychology. Recall, for instance, that Hugo Münsterberg did a field experiment in an effort to learn about streetcar accidents. He used a simulated street scene and tested the abilities of accident-free and accident-repeating operators to anticipate a simulated collision. Today's I/O psychologists also conduct experiments in the field or in their laboratories. Other I/O research is done through observational study. A trained observer can directly observe and record work behavior, or workers can be asked about their behavior or opinions. The latter, in which we are asking for a self-observation, is the survey method. These experimental and observational research methods are standard ones used by psychologists to study all kinds of behavior.

Both methods have distinct purposes that provide us with different types of information. Observational studies give information about the extent to which two or more behavioral variables are associated. Because it is a well-controlled simulation of real life, the experiment gives information about the extent to which one variable acts as a cause of another. Each method is appropriate for different research objectives, and each has different constraints that must be considered. The experiment is the most powerful tool for evaluating the impact of individual causal variables on behavior; however, it is an expensive method in terms of researcher and participant time. Sometimes it cannot be used at all. For example, you would not conduct an experiment in which you systematically subjected employees to a dangerous working condition. This would be unethical. If you had to research the dangerous condition, you would use an observational method to study employees who had already had such exposures, even though this approach might not provide the exact information you need. Observational methods can be used for studying ethically sensitive problems because they do not involve manipulation of variables.

There are alternatives to the experimental and observational methods for solving problems in work organizations. These other methods usually are not included in discussions of research methodology because they are more accurately **fact-finding** or study methods. In a broad approach to the research process, however, these methods are worth consideration. One such method can be referred to as "resource accounting." It includes efforts the researcher makes to find out what information is already available. Library searches for published studies and community searches for informal data often are necessary. For instance, community census data are sometimes helpful when social problems affect what goes on in the organization. Resource accounting also includes organizational searches. Company files typically contain a wealth of information on employees, on policies and procedures, and on the history of organizational activities. In addition, research may have been done in the organization, if not on the very problem being considered, then on something closely related. Someone may have written a report that is now waiting on a dusty shelf. In any research endeavor, some amount of resource accounting should be done. Making use of such available resources frequently results in money saved.

Behavioral Causes and Effects

Each of the standard research methods have particular strengths and weaknesses. Some are helpful when the researcher knows very little about the behavior in question. Observational methods are good for this type of exploratory research. If you want to know what causes a particular behavior, however, observational methods are not enough. They cannot tell you whether a particular variable causes the behavior in question, although they can suggest possible causal relationships. To test a hypothesis about a causal relationship, you must do a controlled experiment, and here is why.

In general, behavior is conceptualized as having a network of causes, such as depicted in figure 2.1. Suppose we want to uncover the causes of behavior A. The particular nature of behavior A is understood as being the outcome of several sources of influence. These sources vary in strength; therefore, some have stronger effects on behavior A than others. Nonetheless, it is the entire network of causes that determines the character of the behavior.

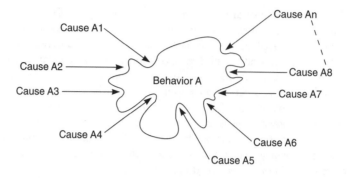

Figure 2.1. *Behavior shaped by a causal network. Note that the combined causes determine the total character of behavior A.*

If we knew the identity of the variables that make up the **causal network** of a particular behavior, then we could evaluate the importance of each variable in shaping the behavior. We could do this by conducting a series of experiments. In each experiment, we would control all the variables except one, which would be manipulated by varying its strength in different experimental conditions. The comparative impact of the variable at its different strengths would then be measured by evaluating any changes in behavior A in these experimental conditions. We would repeat this process, manipulating one causal variable at a time while stabilizing the others, until we had evaluated all variables in the causal network. In doing so, we would learn the extent to which the variables cause the specific behavioral pattern.

Of course, we typically do not know the identity of the variables in a causal network. The best we can do, usually, is to form hypotheses about their identity and then test those hypotheses in experiments. In such cases, we can try to control some variables that we think might be operating and do our best to neutralize those we cannot identify. In this way, we can use the experimental method to build knowledge about the sources of the behavior.

For this kind of investigation, we need a method that enables us to control the effects of some variables while we manipulate and evaluate others. The experiment is the only technique that allows us to do this. Observational methods do not provide any way to control or manipulate variables. With observational techniques, we can take a sample or a slice of behavior and analyze it, but the behavior sampled is allowed to occur freely without researcher intervention.

Observational methods are helpful in that they give us ideas about what "causes" to examine in an experiment. Consider an example. Suppose we conduct an observational study of leadership in an interacting group. First, we observe the group's interaction and record instances in which "leading" behavior was shown. Then, we have each member of the group complete a questionnaire in order to collect additional information, such as their gender and age, job satisfaction, and attitudes toward conformity. Upon analyzing the data, we find that some of the questionnaire responses are related to our measure of leadership behavior. Suppose we find that job satisfaction and leadership behavior are related, in that those with high job satisfaction scores also show a high incidence of leading activity, whereas those with low job satisfaction scores do not. To understand this, we consider three alternative explanations. First, it may be that high job satisfaction causes the person to engage in leading, and low satisfaction causes the person to withdraw. Second, it may be that the reverse is true: Engaging in leadership may cause the person to become more satisfied, but when the person cannot lead, satisfaction is lowered. Third, some other behavioral characteristic X (e.g., self-confidence) may be causing the person to be both satisfied and leaderlike.

Which is it? All three hypotheses sound reasonable, but our observational data cannot go any farther in answering this question. A series of experiments can, however. Initially, we need some new subjects for the control and the experimental groups. To test the possibility that satisfaction brings about leadership, we need to perform some operation so that subjects in the experimental group have a different level of satisfaction than those in the control group. To test the possibility that leadership causes satisfaction, we need to do something that would change the level of leadership in the experimental condition. In either experiment, if the predicted effect occurred, there would be a notable difference in the way the subjects in the experimental and control groups behaved. Only then would we conclude that the manipulated variable is a cause of the resulting behavior. If neither manipulation affected the subjects' actions, then we might decide to design other studies to investigate the possibility of a larger structure, of which both satisfaction and leadership are a part.

PROGRAMS FOR SOLVING BEHAVIORAL PROBLEMS

Assessing the Need

The first step in solving behavioral problems is becoming aware that there is one. Many problems in the workplace, which I/O psychologists are called on to solve, involve discrepancies between what people are doing and what other people think they ought to be doing (Mager & Pipe, 1970). Sometimes, instead of doing what they are supposed to be doing, workers are doing something else, and at other times, they are not doing anything. In either case, a problem is perceived, usually by management. The next step, as shown in figure 2.2, is to assess the nature of the problem.

Techniques for Needs Assessments

To study a problem, it is helpful to approach it as if some need existed that was not being met and to use a systematic procedure for assessing the nature of this need. Any of several systematic methods for **needs assessment** can be employed. For example, the problem can be explored by means of "resource accounting" in which company records and resources are accessed. At this point, the researcher looks for information previously gathered by the organization. Information from outside sources, such as research journals, should be reviewed as well.

A needs assessment can involve some observational study also. If direct observation of work activities is possible, information can be obtained from observing the work process, the setting, and the interactions of the people doing the work. An important task for the researcher in this type of study is to record observations carefully. Survey techniques also can be used to analyze the problem. A short questionnaire can be developed and used as a written survey or as a protocol for interviewing people who may have knowledge of the problem.

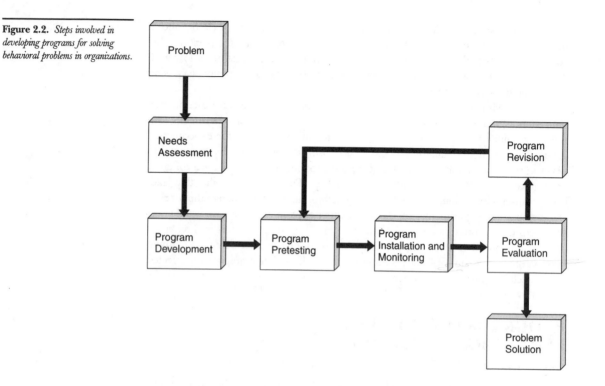

Figure 2.2. *Steps involved in developing programs for solving behavioral problems in organizations.*

Mager and Pipe (1970) have devised an analytical procedure for needs assessment in which the basic principles of reinforced behavior are used to guide the assessment and plan interventions. Mager and Pipe pointed out that the underlying basis of a performance discrepancy must be identified before appropriate solutions can be devised. They suggested two questions that will help reveal the general nature of a problem. One question is whether the problem has occurred primarily because employees lack necessary knowledge and skill. Sometimes people do not do what is expected of them because they do not know how. They might never have learned how, or they might have learned and then forgotten. If such knowledge and skill deficiencies are behind a problem, then the best solution would involve some kind of training. A formal skills training program might be required if workers just never knew, or practice and feedback might be needed if they have forgotten. The second question is whether the performance problem is due to low motivation. That is, are there any incentives for performing as desired? Sometimes there are social costs to doing what the boss wants. Nonperformance might actually be rewarded. For example, people sometimes ignore safety measures because coworkers provide social rewards for those who dare to risk danger. It also may be that the performance simply does not matter or that there are obstacles to performance. For example, employees sometimes neglect certain of their responsibilities because they are too busy with other work. If such motivational factors are causing the performance discrepancy, then the best solution would involve adding incentives or making some change so the desired performance is rewarded.

Program Development and Evaluation

Once the needs assessment is done and we have a clear idea of the problem, the next step is to develop a program of interventions for solving it. In developing the program, as in assessing the need, research methodology is helpful. Research and study techniques can be used to pretest the program. In addition, we should build into the program's design some way of evaluating the outcome. **Program evaluation** is a sensitive issue. People who develop intervention programs want them to be effective. Generally, we have no desire to discover that our programs do not work, and the fear of finding out is part of the reason why program evaluation often is done halfheartedly or not at all. However, if we have designed a really good program, then surely we want to be able to demonstrate that fact.

Evaluation research is conducted by means of an experimental procedure, and it allows us to show the effectiveness of the program. In an evaluation study, we design the program, run it, and evaluate it as if we are doing an experiment. That is, we hypothesize that the intervention program will take care of the problem, and then we evaluate this hypothesis experimentally. The data we collect, following administration of the program, are measures of the problem-involved behavior, and they will show whether this hypothesis can be supported. An example of an evaluation study appears later in this chapter.

Conclusions Concerning Problem-Solving Techniques

If you get the idea that the research process is cyclical, you are right (see figure 2.3). We begin with an observational study to gather ideas that can be tested in experiments. Following this, we design and pretest an experimental study or program. The pretest can indicate changes that should be made before running the program. The program then is conducted and its outcome evaluated. Program evaluation determines the effectiveness of the interventions and indicates whether there is a need for revisions before the program is accepted for routine use. If the results are as expected, the program can be accepted. If not, further observational and/or experimental study is needed for modifying the program.

To solve a problem at work, first identify the problem. Needs assessment techniques are good for this. You can assess a need in several ways: by observing employees, by surveying employees and managers, and by checking records to see if the problem has been noticed before. One helpful approach is to assume the problem results from people not doing what their jobs require, and then ask whether this is because they do not know how or because they are not motivated.

Once you know what kind of problem you have, the next steps are (1) to develop a program of interventions that might solve it, and (2) to evaluate whether or not the program actually solved the problem. In both steps, but particularly in program evaluation, you will use a cycle of research, including an experimental procedure.

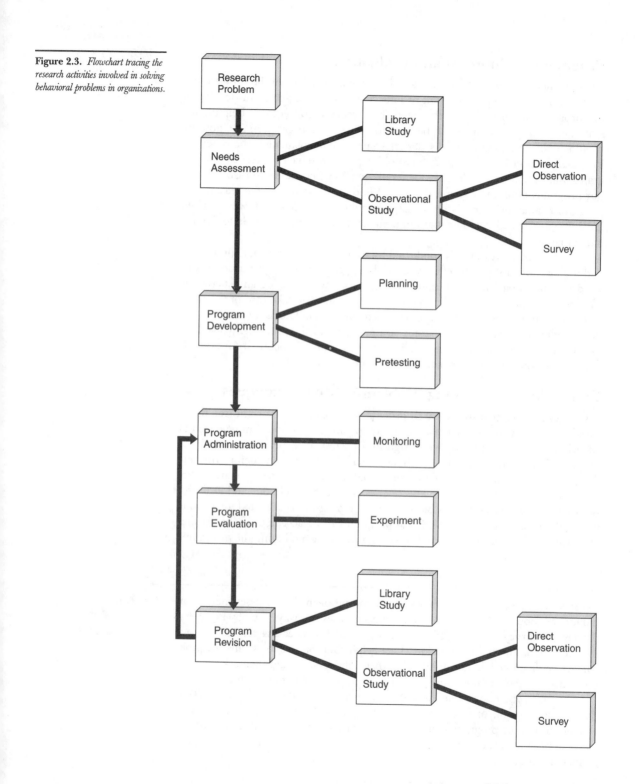

Figure 2.3. *Flowchart tracing the research activities involved in solving behavioral problems in organizations.*

Research Problem

Needs Assessment

Library Study

Observational Study

Direct Observation

Survey

Program Development

Planning

Pretesting

Program Administration

Monitoring

Program Evaluation

Experiment

Program Revision

Library Study

Observational Study

Direct Observation

Survey

THE EXPERIMENTAL METHOD
History and Definitions

A now-classic set of **field experiments,** known as the Hawthorne studies, were begun about 1925 and continued for several years at the Western Electric Company's Hawthorne plant (Roethlisberger, 1941). In one series, the relationship between the amount of factory illumination and the worker's productivity was studied. This particular series of experiments became well known, not because of what was discovered about the relationship of light to production but because it demonstrated the complex causes of human behavior. Briefly, the first experiment involved increasing the level of illumination for an experimental group and comparing the group's work output to that of a control group in which no change in illumination was made. Surprisingly, members of both groups increased their output. In another experiment, illumination was decreased for the experimental group and left unchanged in the control group. Exactly the same effect on output occurred. Members of both the control group and the experimental group increased their production. In search of an answer to this puzzle, the researchers undertook other similar experiments. Finally, they concluded that they had been neglecting to consider a very effective social cause of behavior: Their own presence and attention to the workers were acting as motivators of productivity!

The **experiment** is a simulation of real life, but it is not a duplicate because not all conditions in the life situation are represented. The intent, however, is to create a situation as close as possible and especially to incorporate the conditions most important to the behavior under study. Because the experiment is a simulation, control of behavioral variables is possible. Since the experimenter has recreated a slice of life in the simulation, it becomes possible to stabilize or control variables that are suspected antecedents of the behavior and to vary others.

Bailey and Ford (1994) argue that a good way to understand the nature of the experiment is to recognize that it is like theater. The playwright is actually a theorist who proposes that certain effects will occur in the audience when the plot is played out on stage by the actor. In like manner, the experimenter, in the role of research designer, proposes that certain changes will occur when the conditions of the experiment are presented to the subject. Like the actor, the experimenter delivers a script in introducing and guiding the subject through the experiment. However, unlike the actor, the experimenter has little freedom in conveying this information to subjects. To maintain control over the experiment, he or she must keep strictly to the script.

The Experiment Dissected

Probably the most important phase in an experiment is the initial planning. A good plan means better control, fewer unforeseen procedural problems, clearer understanding of results, and increased savings of time. Table 2.1 provides a checklist to help guide the planning phase.

Experiments are meant to test hypotheses about the nature of some cause-effect relationship. Typically, the experimenter hypothesizes that one behavioral variable operates so as to produce another. Changes in the one variable can be expected to cause changes in the other, and the experimental hypothesis is stated in these terms. The null hypothesis, which the experiment is designed to reject, is a statement that negates the meaning in the experimental hypothesis, generally by specifying that there is no relationship between the variables.

Independent and Dependent Variables

The variable that the experimenter believes acts as a causal agent is the one manipulated in the experiment. The experimenter produces changes in this variable, called the **independent variable,** in order to see whether resulting changes will occur in another variable. This manipulated variable is considered independent because of its hypothesized relationship to the other variable. It is not influenced by the measured or dependent variable, that is, it operates *independently*.

The aspect of behavior, which is measured and thought to be affected or influenced by the independent variable, is called the **dependent variable.** The state of this variable is *dependent* on or determined by the independent variable. For example, in a recent experiment, two independent variables—the need for and use of a program for employee drug testing—were evaluated for their effects on job applicants' attitudes toward the company—the dependent variable (Crant & Bateman, 1990). One hypothesis was that applicants would have less positive attitudes toward companies that tested applicants and employees for drug use. A second hypothesis was that applicants would be more positive toward drug testing if the company appeared to have a need for it because of problems with employee drug use.

To conduct an experiment, the experimenter must define both variables operationally. Although cause-effect relationships can be discussed in general terms, experimental tests of hypotheses can be made only with specific behaviors. The hypotheses to be tested must be phrased in terms of "specific condition A results in specific behavior X." It is by means of defining the independent and dependent variables operationally that we make this transition from the general to the specific. For example, in the experiment mentioned in the previous paragraph, the need for drug testing was operationalized by a description of the extent to which the company had high rates of accidents, absenteeism, and employee theft. The dependent variable—job applicant's attitude toward the company—was operationalized as the applicant's reaction to a series of statements about the company (Crant & Bateman, 1990).

Operational definitions have two important characteristics. They are specific behavioral statements that define the variables, as well as operations that the experimenter can perform. These operations allow the experimenter to maintain control over the experiment and measure the behavior that occurs. The operational definition of the independent variable is something that the experimenter can do to produce the desired variations in this variable. In the case of the dependent variable, the operational definition is something that the experimenter can observe and measure, something that will show the effects of the independent variable if there are any.

Table 2.1	**Checklist Used in Planning the Design of an Experiment**

_____ Determine need/appropriateness of experimental method.
_____ Define and operationalize independent variables(s).
_____ Develop procedures for manipulating independent variable(s).
_____ Define experimental and control groups.
_____ Decide how nuisance variables will be controlled.
_____ Develop experimental and null hypotheses.
_____ Define and operationalize dependent variable(s).
_____ Develop dependent variable measures and instruments.
_____ Specify comparisons between groups.
_____ Develop plans for data analysis.
_____ Decide sampling questions: Who? How many? Assigned to groups on what basis?
_____ Decide operational procedures for conducting experiment.
_____ Enumerate materials and equipment needed.
_____ Develop budget for financing the experiment.
_____ Write report outline.

Experimental Controls

Earlier, I suggested that there are many causes for any one behavior. The purpose of experimentation is to take the proposed causal factors one at a time and study their individual impact on the behavior in question. While we are investigating the effects of one variable, all the others become **nuisance variables** (also called confounds). These variables interfere with or contaminate our study of the relationship between one independent variable and a dependent variable.

There are two ways to deal with nuisance variables. We can control them by standardizing them, that is, by making sure they do not vary between the experimental and control groups. We also can control them by making sure that whatever influence they do have is thoroughly scattered so as to have no consistent effect on either group. In the first case, to control by standardization, we must know the identity of these variables. We must know what they are so that we can set up experimental conditions to maintain them in some constant state. In this way, their influence will be the same on the experimental and control groups. Then, when we measure the dependent variable, the contribution from these nuisance variables will be like adding a constant number to all scores. As a result, when we look at the difference between people in the experimental and control groups, we see the impact of the independent variable beyond any influence from the nuisance variables. For example, in the experiment relating to drug testing (Crant & Bateman, 1990); certain variables that could influence a job applicant's attitude toward a company, such as salary, benefits, and job location, were controlled by standardization. All subjects were given the same information about these variables.

The second way of controlling nuisance variables can be used even if we do not know their identity. Because we typically do not know all the variables that affect behavior, this procedure is employed routinely. Again, the idea is to spread the effects of the variables over the experimental and control groups so that they will have no differential impact. The strategy is to assign subjects randomly to the experimental and control groups. How does random assignment ensure this control? Consider some personal characteristic X that can be operating as a nuisance variable. We assume that people will vary in terms of how much X they have. Some have high levels and some have low levels. If we assign the subjects to groups by flipping a coin, which is one method of randomizing, the different groups that result will have a similar mix of high and low X subjects. When we look at group behavior after we have scattered a variable this way, any effect from this variable will be equalized across the different experimental conditions.

Experimental and Control Groups

The groups of subjects in an experiment are designed around the independent variable. There are two types of groups: **experimental** and **control groups**. There may be just one of each, or there may be more than one experimental group, depending on the number of variations in the independent variable. Often, the control group experiences the "naturally occurring" condition in which the independent variable is not changed, and the experimental groups experience conditions in which the independent variable is manipulated to reach particular levels. In other studies, control groups are those in which the independent variable is established at a certain level. In any case, the control group is used as a comparison or standard for the experimental group(s).

To conduct an experiment, subjects are exposed to the conditions either of the experimental group or of the control group, and their resulting behavior is measured. The valuable information drawn from the experiment is the difference between the behavior of subjects in these different groups. This comparison between the groups informs us about the effect of the independent variable. If the behavior of members of one group differs greatly from that of the other group, given the experiment has been done well, the experimenter can conclude that there is support for the experimental hypothesis (Kirk, 1968).

Experiments in I/O Psychology

The experimental procedure has been used in I/O psychology in three ways. First, laboratory experiments with work-related content are conducted in universities and other research laboratories. For example, in a study of performance evaluation (Farh & Dobbins, 1989), two groups of undergraduates were given job tasks to perform and then asked to complete an evaluation of their work. In the experimental group, the students were allowed some time to review their coworkers' tasks before they did their self-evaluations. Students in the control group were not allowed to see their coworkers' work. Following their self-ratings, students in both groups were evaluated by a "supervisor." (This was another student whose task was to review and evaluate the work of several "subordinates.") The experimental hypotheses being tested were that students from the experimental group, having comparative information from reviewing their coworkers' work, would produce (1) more accurate self-ratings when compared to objective measures and (2) self-ratings that were in closer agreement with the supervisor's rating than students in the control group who did not have comparative information available.

A second way the experiment is used in I/O psychology is when the procedure is carried out in the field setting. A study investigating some causes of job stress among shopfloor workers provides an example (Martin & Wall, 1989). Two independent variables were evaluated for their effects on subjects' responses to a measure of psychological strain. Work demands on attention, and responsibility for costly equipment were the two independent variables. The study was conducted in an electronics manufacturing plant, and the subjects were shopfloor employees who were making circuit boards for computers. The company's practice in designing jobs was such that existing jobs were markedly different in terms of attentional demands and cost responsibility, which actually made the experiment possible, that is, various levels of these two independent variables already existed. Further, the company's practice of rotating employees through these different jobs meant that any individual differences in propensity for stress were held constant.

The third use of the experiment in I/O psychology is different from the first two in that it has a slightly different purpose, that of evaluation. Both laboratory and field experiments are done to discover new knowledge about work behavior. However, some field experiments are carried out to evaluate the effects of a program of interventions. Although any type of program can be evaluated in this way, training program evaluation provides us with numerous examples. In one such experiment (Latham & Frayne, 1989), a group of employees were trained in self-regulatory skills to improve job attendance. Several months after training was complete, behavioral measures of job attendance and sick leave use were taken and compared with measures obtained from a control group of employees who had not yet received the experimental training. In this study, the evaluation was aimed at determining whether the immediate positive effects of the training would last as long as six to nine months.

Example: An Evaluation Study

A good way to learn how to do an experiment is to perform one. In this section, let us go step-by-step through an evaluation experiment. Suppose you have recently been placed in charge of training employees in an insurance company. The employees you will be training are a group who check claims forms for accuracy. If the claims are inaccurately or incompletely filled out, they are returned for correction. Accurate claims are passed on to analysts who evaluate the claim. Analyst time is saved if the claims checkers are efficient, and because analysts are higher paid employees, this also means that money is saved. It stands to reason that the company wants its claims checkers to learn their jobs well and quickly.

Planning the Experiment

Part of your job is to determine whether special training would help produce efficiency, and if so, what type of training would be best. You decide to use an experimental research design to evaluate the effects of different training activities that your company might use. (The experimental study will disrupt work to an extent; however, you believe the disruption to be minor and ultimately worth it in order to find out which training program leads to quick learning.)

Suppose you decide to consider two aspects of training at this time: (1) pretraining given to trainees prior to the usual job instruction and (2) method

Table 2.2	Example: Experimental Design for Evaluating Pretraining of Insurance Claims Checkers		
Independent Variables	**Groups**		
	Control *(n = 20)*[a]	*Experimental 1* *(n = 10)*	*Experimental 2* *(n = 10)*
Amount of pretraining	none	4 hours	4 hours
Method of pretraining	none	classroom	individual study

[a]In psychological research, *n* refers to the number of subjects.

of pretraining. These are your independent variables. You decide to use the present method of on-the-job training (OJT) in the control condition. Employees in the control group will be instructed as usual and receive no pretraining. Employees in the experimental groups will be pretrained before they receive the usual OJT. You will manipulate the method so that you have two different pretraining "levels" and two experimental groups. Pretraining will be given by the classroom method to one experimental group and by an individual study method to the other. In sum, these operational definitions result in three groups of subjects: (1) control group with no pretraining; (2) experimental group 1 with pretraining by classroom method; and (3) experimental group 2 with pretraining by individual study method. Table 2.2 summarizes this design.

Next, the procedure for pretraining must be planned. Training material will include laws pertaining to claims, nature of the claims forms, and description of common checker errors. In the classroom training, this material will be covered by lecture, discussion, and coaching. In the individual study training, the material will be presented in a workbook for trainees to study privately.

You will want to control some variables. For example, through your library study, you became aware that the length of training may affect learning; therefore, you decide to control this by standardizing training time. You design your program so that both the classroom group and the individual study group receive four hours of pretraining. You are also concerned about some individual differences that can affect the training evaluation. You recognize that people differ in intelligence and ability to read and absorb material. This difference will be controlled by random assignment of trainees to the three groups in the experiment, a strategy that will prevent one group from being filled with high-ability trainees and another with low-ability trainees. It also occurs to you that those in the individual study group may not cover all the material in the workbook during the allotted time. To ensure exposure to all topics in the workbook, you decide to introduce a pacing mechanism that will move the trainees along. The material in the workbook will be divided into small sections, and trainees will study these for specified periods of time.

You also must operationalize the dependent variable and develop dependent measures. Skill acquisition of the claims checkers is your dependent variable, and you decide to operationally define skill acquisition as job proficiency. You reason that if a trainee has acquired the skill, then he or she will be proficient on the

Table 2.3   Example: Null and Experimental Hypotheses in Claims Checkers' Pretraining Experiment

Hypotheses Relating to Independent Variable 1: Pretraining

Null Hypothesis:	There is no difference in skill acquisition between the pretraining method and the standard OJT method.
Experimental Hypothesis:	There is quicker skill acquisition in the pretraining method than in the standard OJT method.[a]

Hypothesis Relating to Independent Variable 2: Method of Pretraining

Null Hypothesis	There is no difference in skill acquisition between the classroom and the individual method of pretraining.
Experimental Hypothesis:	There is a difference in skill acquisition between the classroom and the individual study method of pretraining.[b]

[a]This experimental hypothesis is directional because improvement is expected to occur in the pretraining condition.
[b]This experimental hypothesis is nondirectional. Whether the classroom or the individual study method is more effective is not specified.

job. You decide to measure proficiency in two ways; therefore, you will have two dependent measures of skill acquisition. For one, you will count the number of forms accurately checked during the trainee's first three days on the job after being trained. The total number will consist of forms checked by the employee minus the number returned by the quality control officer. Your second measure will be a rating of the trainee's potential, completed by a supervisor at the end of the first three days. You believe this will measure something beyond productivity, such as interpersonal skills necessary in being a good employee.

As shown in table 2.3, you have two experimental hypotheses: One is that pretraining will result in improved trainee skill. The other is that the method of pretraining will affect skill acquisition, although you are unsure which method will be superior. The comparisons you will make in analyzing your data emerge from these hypotheses. To test the first hypothesis, you decide to combine the data from the two experimental groups and compare it to the data from the control group. Your comparison will tell you whether there is an overall improvement due to pretraining. To test the second hypothesis, you compare the data from experimental group 1 with that from experimental group 2, which will say whether there is any effect due to the particular training method. These planned comparisons are listed in table 2.4.

Other details of the experiment must be decided. You must answer some sampling questions. Who will the subjects be, and how will they be assigned to groups? In field research, the identity of the subjects may be decided for you, as they are in this example. Your subjects are newly hired employees. At other times, as when we conduct basic research in a university laboratory, we select subjects who represent the population to which we are going to generalize the research.

How many trainees will you have in the experiment? The answer depends on how strong you want the test to be. If you have too few subjects, your

Table 2.4

Example: Planned Comparisons for Testing Hypotheses in Claims Checkers' Pretraining Experiment

1. To test the first experimental hypothesis concerning the effect of pretraining, compare the mean of the control group with the mean of the combined experimental groups.

2. To test the second experimental hypothesis concerning the effect of pretraining method, compare the mean of the experimental group 1 with the mean of the experimental group 2.

results are unlikely to show an effect even if there is one. On the other hand, you can have too many subjects. Then, you risk making "mountains out of mole-hills." Even if the real effect is very weak, it is likely to show up and mislead you into thinking it is substantial. What you need in most cases is a medium-sized sample. Generally, about nine or ten subjects in each group you are going to compare will be adequate.

The final aspect of planning is to complete the procedures for running the experiment and to get the materials and equipment that will be needed. In this example, you will need to map out exactly when and where you will conduct pretraining sessions. You will need to develop training materials and the instruments for measuring skill acquisition.

Analyzing Experimental Data

Once the experiment has been conducted and the data collected, you must summarize and present the results in a brief form. Rather than list the raw scores of each trainee, you must reduce the detail and summarize the groups' behavior. The meaning of the data can be grasped more easily in this fashion. Data are summarized with **descriptive statistics**. These are ways of describing the group of people included in the study. One way to summarize the behavior of subjects is to calculate the percentage who behaved in one way as opposed to another, or who fell into a particular behavioral category. Other descriptive statistics include measures of central tendency and variability.

A data summary generally includes a measure of central tendency for each of the groups studied. **Central tendency measures** indicate the average behavior of the group. A typical measure of central tendency used in experimental data summaries is the arithmetic *mean*. The mean is calculated by adding all the scores in a group and dividing this sum by the total number of scores. Another measure of central tendency is the *median*. The median is the middlemost score, or the score with half the subjects scoring above and half scoring below it. By arranging the scores in order and then counting off half, you calculate the median. When should you use the median instead of the mean as your measure of central tendency? Generally, you use the mean if scores are distributed in a roughly symmetrical fashion, with most falling in a middle range and declining gradually to the

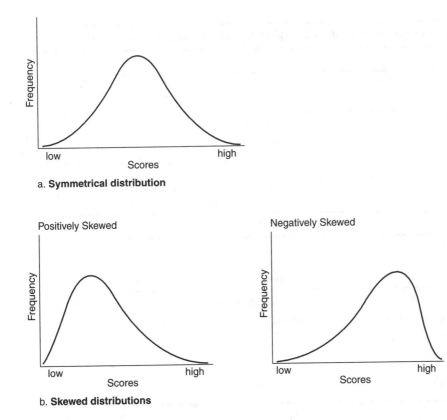

a. **Symmetrical distribution**

Positively Skewed

Negatively Skewed

b. **Skewed distributions**

Figure 2.4. *Symmetrical and skewed distributions of scores. (a) In symmetrical (normal) distributions, most scores cluster in the middle of the range. (b) In skewed distributions, they accumulate at one end of the range. When the distribution is positively skewed, scores cluster at the low end; when it is negatively skewed, scores are at the high end of the range.*

extremes so that only a few scores are very high or very low. If the distribution of scores is very skewed, then you should use the median. The median is less influenced by extreme scores. It gives a more accurate description of the average score in distributions in which most scores are either very high (negative skew) or very low (positive skew); see figure 2.4. If you need to use the median, then you also must have a different set of inferential techniques that use the median rather than the mean as the basic unit of comparison (Denenberg, 1976).

Variability measures are also needed in a data summary as an indication of the variability or dispersion of the scores; that is, you should show how different or similar the scores are. Two commonly used indicators of dispersion are the *range* and the *standard deviation*. Which one is required depends on which measure of central tendency you use to describe the data. If the data call for the median, the appropriate measure of variability is the range. The standard deviation is appropriate when the mean is required. The standard deviation is a measure of how much the scores deviate from the mean score; thus, the mean is used to calculate and interpret it. If a group has a very small standard deviation, then we understand that the scores are very similar and clumped around the mean score. If the group has a very large standard deviation, then the scores are widely different and spread out around the mean. Formulae for these measures of central tendency and dispersion are listed in table 2.5 for quick reference.

*T*able 2.5   Descriptive Statistics Frequently Used for Summarizing Data

Measures of Central Tendency

Mean: $\overline{X} = \dfrac{\Sigma X}{n}$ | Median

To calculate the mean score:	*To calculate the median score:*
1. Total all raw scores (ΣX).	1. Arrange scores in order.
2. Divide by the number of scores (*n*).	2. For odd number of subjects, find the middle score, which is the median.
	3. For even number of subjects, find the two middle scores; halfway in between these scores is the median.

Measures of Variability

Standard Deviation: $s = \sqrt{\dfrac{\Sigma(X - \overline{X})^2}{n-1}}$ | Range

To calculate the standard deviation of scores:	*To calculate the range of scores:*
1. Subtract the mean score ($\overline{X}$) from each raw score (X) to compute *n* difference scores.	Subtract the lowest score from the highest.
2. Square each difference score.	
3. Sum the squared difference scores and divide by $n-1$.	
4. Find the square root of the amount in step 3.	

*T*able 2.6   Example: Data Summary Table for Claims Checkers' Pretraining Experiment

Group	n	Mean Score	Standard Deviation (s)
Control	20	15.4	3.02
Pretraining[a]	20	28.55	2.96
Experimental Group 1	10	30.6	2.32
Experimental Group 2	10	26.5	1.96

[a]Note: Score refers to the number of claims forms accurately processed by trainees three days following employment. Experimental groups 1 and 2 combined.

It is often helpful to present research data in tables and graphs in order to depict the behavior of groups. In our example, you need to calculate the mean and standard deviation of the proficiency scores for each of the three groups and present summary statements in a simple table for easy reference. You probably will want to construct a bar graph using this same summary information to dramatize the differences among the groups. Table 2.6 and figure 2.5 depict data that you

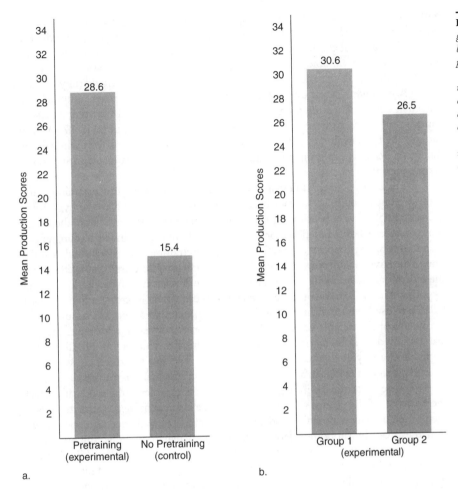

Figure 2.5. *Example: Bar graphs demonstrating differences between groups in claims checkers' pretraining experiment. Variations in the independent variable are conventionally placed on the horizontal axis of a graph, and the dependent measure is displayed on the vertical axis. (a) The graph on the left shows mean scores of subjects in the experimental and control groups. (b) The graph on the right shows mean scores of subjects in the two experimental groups.*

might have collected in the training study. Table 2.6 contains mean proficiency scores and standard deviations for each group. (Remember, the proficiency score is a three-day production measure.) In figure 2.5, these mean scores are displayed in two bar graphs. Figure 2.5a shows the performance of the experimental subjects compared to the control group, and figure 2.5b illustrates the performance of the two experimental groups.

In addition to summarizing the data, you will want to test your hypotheses. Hypothesis-testing is, after all, the purpose and primary advantage of the experimental method. In this experiment, therefore, you will compare the behavior of the control subjects with that of the experimental subjects. If, as you hypothesized, pretraining is effective in improving proficiency, the measures taken from these groups will be significantly different. How do you know if they are? **Inferential statistics** help answer this question. Inferential statistics are mathematical procedures that help you decide or infer the relationship between variables. Here we return to the original point: Does a supposed cause of behavior really function as such? Inferential statistics used in experiments are tools for determining whether the manipulation of the independent variable was effective in substantially changing the dependent variable.

Inferential statistics techniques have been devised for a variety of purposes. A commonly used one is the **t-test.** It is useful to researchers routinely involved in experimental research (Denenberg, 1976). Steps for conducting a t-test to compare mean scores from two independent groups are listed in table 2.7. As you can see, the t-test evaluates the mean scores of the groups and tells you whether the difference between the groups is significant or simply due to a chance variation in people's behavior.

In using the t-test to evaluate the difference between your pretraining and control groups, you need to refer back to the hypotheses. The way the hypotheses are stated will have a bearing on how you evaluate the t-statistic. Hypotheses are phrased in terms of a directional or nondirectional prediction. In the training experiment, you have proposed a directional effect: Pretraining will *improve* skill acquisition. You have also proposed a nondirectional effect: The classroom method and the individual method will *differ* in their effects on trainee improvement. Directional hypotheses allow you to compute a one-tailed t-test, which is stronger than the two-tailed test used with nondirectional hypotheses. Sometimes you are unsure about the nature of the independent variable's effect on the dependent variable, but you are interested in knowing if any effect occurs. In this, you have a nondirectional hypothesis, and you should use a two-tailed test. The two-tailed test allows you to take advantage of evidence in either direction to support your hypothesis.

The t-test results in a single number that represents the extent to which the behavior of the groups differed. If the t-value is small, it means that the experimental manipulation probably did not affect behavior. Whether an experimental hypothesis can be supported depends on the particular hypothesis, the amount of risk the experimenter is willing to take for an incorrect conclusion, and the size and direction of the t-value. How large does the t-value need to be? This is really a question of how willing you are to risk being incorrect in inferring support for your hypothesis. There are some conventions that psychologists use in making this decision. Typically, when doing basic scientific research, we do not want to risk being wrong with a greater than 5 percent chance. This is why you see experimental results reported at the .05 significance level (also called alpha level). In such studies, there is a 5 percent probability that the observed result was actually a chance occurrence. This alpha level is a cautious stance, however. In daily life, we make many riskier decisions. In fact, some decisions in life are based on 50-50 odds or a 50 percent chance of being wrong. In your evaluation research, if you decide to accept an alpha level greater than .05, bear in mind that you are just that much more likely to be wrong.

With these cautions in mind, you are ready to evaluate the performance of your training program. Looking at the mean scores of your groups, you notice that there is not much difference between the two pretraining groups, but there is improvement in the scores of those getting pretraining compared to the controls. You predicted this type of effect; therefore, you will want to see if the difference is

Table 2.7   Procedures for Calculating a T-Test Comparing the Means of Two Independent Groups

Testing the Difference Between Two Independent Means

$$t = \frac{\bar{X}_1 - \bar{X}_2}{S_{\bar{X}_1 - \bar{X}_2}}$$

Steps in Calculating t:

1. Calculate the difference between the means: $\bar{X}_1 - \bar{X}_2$: Subtract the mean of the experimental group from the mean of the control group.

2. Compute the sum of the squares (SS) for each of the groups being compared:

    $$SS = \frac{\Sigma X^2 - (\Sigma X)^2}{n}. \text{ For the first group:}$$

    a. Square each of the raw scores: X^2. Sum the squared scores for the group: ΣX^2.

    b. Sum the raw scores for the group: ΣX. Square this sum: $(\Sigma X)^2$.

    c. Subtract the squared sum $(\Sigma X)^2$ from the sum of the squared scores ΣX^2. Divide the remainder by the number of subjects in the group: n.

3. Repeat the process in step 2 to calculate the sum of the squares (SS) for the second group.

4. Calculate the estimated within-group variance: $S_w^2 = \frac{SS_1 + SS_2}{n_1 + n_2 - 2}$

    a. Add the sum of the squares for the first group to the sum of the squares for the second group.

    b. Add the number of subjects in each group, and subtract 2 from the sum.

    c. Divide the total obtained in step 4a by the number obtained in step 4b.

5. Calculate the standard error of the difference between means: $S_{\bar{X}_1 - \bar{X}_2} = \sqrt{S_w^2 \left(\frac{1}{n_1} + \frac{1}{n_2} \right)}$

    a. Divide the number of subjects in each group into 1, and add the results.

    b. Multiply this sum by the within-group variance (S_w^2), obtained in step 4.

    c. Find the square root of the result.

6. Calculate the value of $t = \frac{\bar{X}_1 - \bar{X}_2}{S_{\bar{X}_1 - \bar{X}_2}}$

    Divide the standard error of the difference obtained in step 5 into the difference between the group means obtained in step 1.

7. Evaluate the value of t:

    a. Calculate the degrees of freedom: $df = n_1 + n_2 - 2$.

    b. Determine if the test is one tailed (directional hypothesis) or two tailed (nondirectional hypothesis).

    c. Determine the acceptable level of risk of wrong inference; alpha level convention is .05 or less.

    d. Consult a table of the t-distribution found in appendices of most statistics textbooks (e.g., see J. L. Bruning and B. L. Kintz, *Computational handbook of statistics*, 2d ed. Glenview IL: Scott, Foresman, 1977).

large enough to support your hypothesis. You calculate a t-test to evaluate the size of this difference. Following the procedure specified in table 2.7, I have calculated a t-test for your study, as shown in table 2.8. I have assumed that you wanted to take a cautious stance and have set the significance level at .05. At this level, with the one-tailed test appropriate for your directional hypothesis, the value of t is significant. It indicates that your pretraining successfully improved skill acquisition as hypothesized. There was no significant difference, however, between the methods of training. Consequently, you recommend that the insurance company should pretrain new employees, but it might just as well use the less expensive individual study method.

*M*ain
   *P*oints

Three kinds of I/O experiments are done: lab experiments on work-related issues; field experiments involving employees in work-site studies; and evaluation experiments on intervention programs. The classic Hawthorne studies were among the first field experiments.

The experimental procedure allows the researcher to control what goes on in a study and to test hypotheses about the nature of work behavior and events. The experimenter hypothesizes that one factor (the independent variable) causes changes in another factor (the dependent variable). By operationally defining and manipulating the independent variable, the researcher controls what the subject experiences in the experiment. By defining and measuring the dependent variable, the researcher discovers whether changes in the subject's behavior resulted from that experience. To prevent undesirable factors from entering the study, the researcher controls the experiment, typically by randomly assigning subjects to experimental and control groups.

Data collected on the dependent variable are first summarized with descriptive statistics. Descriptive statistics, such as mean scores, show how the experimental and control groups behaved. Then, these statistics are used to calculate inferential statistics, such as t-test values, which allow conclusions to be drawn about the hypothesis.

THE OBSERVATIONAL METHOD

Unlike the experiment, **observational methods** do not allow control and manipulation of variables. As a result, these methods are used for exploring rather than for testing hypotheses about causes. They are appropriate when beginning research programs or when behavior is little understood. If experiments cannot be done, as in dangerous situations, they are useful as well. Sometimes they are employed because an experiment is too costly.

Observational methods produce information about the **covariance** of behavioral variables. They allow the researcher to say that two variables are connected in such a way that when one changes, the other changes. However, these methods do not provide evidence about causal relationships between variables. For example, breathing coal dust covaries with the development of black

Section I: Using Psychology at Work

*T*able 2.8

Example: Testing Hypotheses in the Claims Checkers' Pretraining Experiment

Testing Hypothesis 1 on the Effect of Pretraining

	Group 1: Combined Experimental Groups		Group 2: Control Group	
	Classroom	*Individual Study*		
Raw Scores	27	25	14	15
	29	27	16	12
	28	28	10	22
	32	26	16	20
	32	24	18	15
	32	31	11	16
	32	27	18	17
	33	26	17	11
	28	25	16	15
	33	26	13	16
Mean Scores	$X_1 = 28.55$		$\bar{X}_2 = 15.4$	
Sum of Squares	$SS_1 = 15{,}478.6$		$SS_2 = 4{,}497.4$	
Estimated Within-Group Variance	$S_w^2 = 525.68$			
Standard Error of the Difference	$S_{\bar{x}_1 - \bar{x}_2} = 7.25$			
T-Test	$t = 1.81$			

Degrees of freedom: $df = 38$

One-tailed test with alpha at .05

Difference is significant.

Testing Hypothesis 2 on the Effect of Pretraining Method

	Experimental Groups	
	Group 1: Classroom	*Group 2: Individual Study*
Mean Scores	$\bar{X}_1 = 30.6$	$\bar{X}_2 = 26.5$
Sum of Squares	$SS_1 = 8{,}422.4$	$SS_2 = 6{,}316.8$
Estimated Within-Group Variance	$S_w^2 = 818.84$	
Standard Error of the Difference	$S_{\bar{x}_1 - \bar{x}_2} = 12.8$	
T-Test	$t = 0.32$	

Degrees of freedom: $df = 18$

Two-tailed test with alpha at .05

Difference is not significant.

lung disease in miners. Although we may believe that there is a causal relationship between the two, unless we do experimental studies in which coal dust exposure is manipulated and other variables are controlled (as in animal research), we cannot conclusively show that the coal dust inhaled by miners causes black lung disease. It is always possible that some other variable associated with being a coal miner is responsible for the disease.

Observational study can be done through direct observation or through surveys. In **direct observation,** the researcher observes and records what people are doing; thus, he or she has a somewhat direct contact with the behavior under study. In the **survey,** however, people are asked to say what they are doing, feeling, or thinking, and the researcher records what they report. The research relationship is more indirect in this case because the data are filtered through the individual as well as through the researcher. In a sense, the survey participant is acting both as the observer and the observed; therefore, the accuracy of these observations depends largely on the person's ability to self-analyze.

The two forms of observational study, then, differ in their risks of a wrong inference. In direct observation, the researcher may infer an internal state from the observed behavior. For example, you can observe someone engaged in problem solving and infer that the person is highly motivated to achieve. In the survey, informants report on their own internal states. For example, you might ask participants to estimate their level of achievement motivation, and you assume they can do this. Both inferences may be inaccurate, of course. In direct observation, the researcher may be wrong about the meaning of the behavior observed. In surveys, the informant may have little self-insight.

The Method of Direct Observation

Direct observation is used to study particular kinds of behavior. For example, whenever a behavioral pattern is highly complex or relatively unknown, direct observation is the best way to begin. When the behavior involves interaction, as in group activities, this method again is appropriate. Direct observation is useful also when other methods are constrained by conditions of the study. For example, if a behavior might be distorted by self-report, or if individuals are not motivated to participate in a survey, direct observation is an option.

How do you do direct observation? Do you just watch, or is there more to it than this? Primarily, it is watching, but there are ways to make the watching process systematic and to produce written records of the observation. These techniques include procedures for group process analysis and activity process analysis.

Observational Techniques

Group process analysis is useful when the behavior under study is the action taking place within a group or between two groups. In any group or team activity, there is a task or work to be done. This is the purpose of a group. In addition to the task, there also exists the group's process. Group process is the way the task is accomplished, and it includes the group's interpersonal activities. A researcher may want to study the group's process in order to understand why one group functions better than another or why some forms of group interaction are effective. For example, the researcher may be interested in learning how a group manages conflict.

In planning a group process study, the researcher must decide a number of issues. What behaviors will be studied? When and for how long will the group be observed? What instruments will be used for data collection? Typically, the researcher will take a time sample of the group's interaction. The time sample consists of a single period of time, or several periods of a few minutes each, in which

Observer's Report: Leadership Activities

Group: *Affirmative Action Committee*
Time: From *10:00A.M.* To *10:30A.M.*
Date: *10/16/81*   Observer: *Williams*
Major Task Activity: *Planning report development and writing*

Group Members (identified by initials)

	BR	SR	JD	MN	ED	BW	—
Task oriented							
Information seeking	✔✔	✔	✔	✔		✔	
Information giving	✔	✔✔	✔✔✔	✔		✔	
Summarizing	✔✔			✔✔✔	✔		
Interpreting	✔	✔✔		✔	✔		
Testing for decision readiness	✔✔✔		✔	✔✔	✔		
Calling for decision	✔✔		✔		✔		
Maintenance oriented							
Encouraging participation	✔	✔		✔	✔✔	✔	
Harmonizing conflict		✔			✔		
Testing for process satisfaction			✔		✔	✔✔	

Comments: *Group under time pressure. BR previously elected responsible to superiors*

Figure 2.6. *Sample instrument used in group process analysis. This checklist is an observer's report of leadership behavior occurring in an active group.*

the researcher observes and records the group's activities. To conduct the observation, the researcher needs to develop instruments for recording the behavior under study. The recording instrument can be a checklist that the observer can use to document the observation, noting the specific behaviors that occurred and when they occurred in the time sample. Figure 2.6 shows a checklist for recording leadership behavior.

Another issue that requires attention has to do with how to minimize disruption of the group when an observer is present. The observed behavior should be as natural as possible, yet people often behave differently when they are being watched. The researcher can deal with this **observer effect** by having the observer sit in an unobtrusive location. Another strategy is to simply allow the group to settle down and become accustomed to the observer before any data are collected.

The researcher needs to consider the possibility of problems resulting from observer unreliability or error in the study due to inaccurate observation. Observers can overlook behavior or "see" behavior that did not occur. It is best to use observers who are consistent with themselves over time and consistent with other observers taking the same time sample. How do we get such observers? Training them certainly helps. If they know exactly what behavior is to be recorded and how to recognize it, mistakes are likely to be fewer and reliability higher.

Activity process analysis is like group process analysis in the way it is conducted. A time sample is taken, and observers use prepared recording instruments. Similarly, the same problems occur. The difference between the two methods is primarily in the content of the study. In activity process analysis, focus is on the task or work activity, and emphasis is on the individual worker rather than on a group. The technique generally is used to analyze activities of an individual operator on a job. It is useful when the researcher wants to know: "What is the operator doing?" Process charts and flow diagrams that map the course of the work are common outcomes. Activity process analysis is sometimes used to design the spatial arrangement of interactive work units.

The Survey Method

The survey is appropriate when the study involves internal states and when it is not appropriate to infer these states from behavior. Study of certain behavioral content, such as attitudes and opinions, traditionally has used this method. Some behavior, such as past behavior, may not be accessible by any other means (Schuman & Kalton, 1985). The survey is a commonly used method for research in industry. It is particularly helpful when the people to be studied are in different locations or when everyone in a large organization must be consulted. It is convenient when direct observation is too expensive or too disruptive of the work, or when individuals simply are not available for observation.

In addition to the limitations of observational methods in general, the survey has unique constraints. The desired information must be available to the informant, and the informant must be motivated to respond. To the extent that either condition does not hold, the data gathered will be inaccurate and/or incomplete. The researcher considering a survey needs to confront these constraints early in the research planning phase.

Survey Techniques

Surveys are administered in three ways: by mail, by telephone, and by face-to-face interview. Each has advantages and disadvantages. The researcher must weigh these and decide what is best for the particular project. The mail survey is comparatively inexpensive and allows the informant to remain anonymous. Anonymity may encourage some to respond who might not otherwise. Unfortunately, mail surveys typically show a low response rate. Having only about one-third of the surveys returned is not unusual. To boost the return rate, some researchers have sacrificed the anonymity feature in order to prompt the reluctant informant. If a record is kept showing who has returned the survey and who has not, follow-up is possible. The researcher can mail out another request or call and ask the person to complete the survey.

In a personal interview, either over the phone or face-to-face, the informant is directly asked the questions included in a survey. This method results in a higher response rate with more complete information. Explanations also can be provided for questions that the informant does not understand. Personal interviews are more expensive than mail surveys, however. Interviewers have to be hired, trained, and paid. The telephone survey is less expensive than the face-to-face interview because it does not involve paid travel time to conduct the interviews, although it does involve the cost of telephone service.

Questionnaire Construction

Regardless of the type of survey, a questionnaire is required. Unless one can be borrowed from another research project in which the same sphere of behavior was investigated, a questionnaire must be constructed for the study. Whether the researcher borrows or constructs a survey instrument, the prime consideration is **content adequacy,** or the extent to which the questionnaire adequately samples the issue. Schriesheim et al. (1993) developed a procedure for assessing content adequacy. The procedure used a panel of evaluators to examine the questions and determine the extent to which important aspects of the issue are addressed. Other considerations that need to be taken into account in developing a questionnaire are summarized in table 2.9. Briefly, decisions must be made about the nature of the questions, the response format, and the organization of the questionnaire.

Writing Questions

In writing questions, the researcher needs to be aware of several constraints of question construction. First, consider the language of the question. The researcher must make every effort to use vocabulary that is well understood by the survey participants. Informants must understand the meaning of the terms in exactly the same way that the researcher does. This is extremely important. If questions are not clear, there will be error in the survey because informants will interpret a question in various ways. Schuman and Kalton (1985) demonstrated the potential for this type of problem and recommended the pretesting of all questions, even ones that seem clear to the researcher. They described a survey that included an item asking whether "the lot of the average man" was getting better or worse. They discovered that the phrase was confusing to many participants. It was interpreted as referring "to a lot of average men," "to the size of housing lots," and in one case "to cemetery lots!" (p. 643).

A second constraint in developing questions concerns the accessibility of information. The researcher must consider whether informants are likely to know the answers to questions. If this is not clear, open-ended questions can help. In open-ended questions, informants respond in their own words. Such questions can reveal the extent to which an informant has information about the question. An alternative strategy, for cases in which information is likely to have been forgotten, is to incorporate memory prods into the question. For example, a question might begin with "when the Civil Rights Act was passed in 1964" in order to trigger memories about discrimination.

A third constraint refers to the motivation of participants. Questions can be constructed to increase motivation to respond. If the research is about sensitive issues, questions should be phrased to illustrate their relevance. A survey that appears important and necessary is more likely to get responses than one that seems prying. Response bias can be a problem as well. For example, some behaviors are more or less socially desirable, and responses to questions about these behaviors can reflect our motivation to describe ourselves positively. As a case in point, it is desirable to be an independent thinker; therefore, many of us describe ourselves in this way although we actually follow opinion leaders. Including a phrase in the questionnaire item to caution respondents about such tendencies can help encourage unbiased responses.

Table 2.9   Considerations in Planning a Questionnaire for Survey Use

Considerations in Evaluating a Survey

1. Content adequacy: Do the items provide a representative sample of the behavior under study?
2. Content contamination: Do the items ask for irrelevant information?

Considerations in Writing Questions

1. Respondent's language ability: Are some words too difficult?
2. Common vocabulary and frame of reference: Does the question have the same meaning for researcher and respondent?
3. Clarity: Is the question worded clearly?
4. Single meaning: Can the question be interpreted in some way other than what is intended?
5. Accessibility of information: Is the respondent likely to have access to the information? Did the respondent ever know the answer to the question?
6. Respondent's motivation: Is the respondent likely to be motivated to answer the question and to answer truthfully?
7. Respondent's right to privacy: Does the question concern a sensitive issue?
8. Socially desirable responding: Does the question suggest a socially desirable answer?

Considerations in Arranging for Responses

1. Open or closed questions: Is the question's issue reasonably well understood? Can specific answers be devised?
2. Combination of open and closed questions: Does the answer need to be explained?

Considerations in Structuring the Questionnaire

1. Number of questions: How many questions are necessary to obtain the required information?
2. Sequence: How might the questions be arranged to encourage the respondent's participation?
3. Anonymity: Will the respondent wish to remain anonymous?

Questionnaire Structure

To determine the kinds of responses needed, the researcher must consider the objectives of the survey. If the purpose is to classify the informant on a clear, well-understood dimension of behavior, then the closed response format is best. Closed questions ask you to respond by choosing from a list of alternative responses. (The familiar multiple-choice examination uses closed questions.) If the researcher also needs the reason for an answer or must gauge the level of the informant's information or opinion, then open questions are appropriate. Open questions are like essay

Table 2.10 — Time Planning for a Survey

Development Stages	Time Phases								
	1	2	3	4	5	6	7	8	9
Prepare, pretest, and revise questionnaire.	x	x	x	x					
Plan, pretest, and revise operational procedures.	x	x	x						
Hire and train interviewers.		x	x	x					
Plan sample design and select sample.		x	x	x					
Plan, outline, and write preliminary and final reports.		x	x					x	x
Collect data.					x	x	x		
Analyze data.						x	x	x	

questions; they ask you to devise your answer in your own words. A questionnaire can contain either open or closed questions, or some combination.

How many questions will the survey contain, and how will they be arranged? A battery of questions gives more complete information than a single question on an issue. However, the researcher must consider the amount of time it takes to complete the survey. If the survey is long and cumbersome, many people will not want to fill it out. Shorter questionnaires are usually more acceptable. Typically, questions are arranged in logical order. This allows informants to follow a train of thought. Some researchers place interest-arousing questions at the beginning of a questionnaire for motivational purposes. Roberson and Sundstrom (1990) found an effective way to do this. They arranged their survey items in an order that matched participants' priorities, and they obtained a high rate of return as a result.

The Survey Process

As with other research, surveys require planning. In fact, there are comparable phases in conducting a survey as in an experiment. These stages include (1) developing and pretesting the research plan, (2) collecting data, (3) analyzing data, and (4) preparing a report. Some phases can overlap with others. For example, data processing and analysis often begin before all the data are collected. Table 2.10 demonstrates a survey time plan.

Planning and Development
To get a survey started, the first steps are to develop a preliminary plan of operation and to find or construct and pretest the questionnaire. The plan of operation should identify all aspects of the study, including the sample, methods for quality control,

and financing. Financing the survey is considered at this time because many projects fail due to inadequate budgeting. In developing the budget for a survey, the researcher must plan for a variety of expenses. All phases of planning and conducting the survey will have labor and materials costs. A portion of the researcher's salary and wages for interviewers and data analysts may need to be budgeted.

The researcher needs to plan for certain problems that will arise. For example, what should be done about unanswered questions? Does the whole questionnaire get thrown out if some questions are not answered? Because most researchers want to salvage as much of the information as possible, they are inclined to accept incomplete questionnaires. The problem of incomplete questionnaires is similar to the problem of low survey response rates in general. Whether people decline to respond altogether or merely decline to answer some questions, the researcher must be concerned about the validity of drawing conclusions from the data and generalizing to others who were not surveyed. Pretesting the questionnaire on a small sample of subjects before running the study can help identify problematic questions and suggest ways to make the order of the questions more appealing. An additional strategy, which can be used after data are collected, has been devised by Viswesvaren et al. (1993). They suggest a way to calculate an estimate of what the average nonrespondent might say. Comparing this estimate with the data from respondents, it is then possible to assess the extent to which conclusions from the study are generalizable.

Data Collection and Analysis

To conduct a survey, the questionnaire is administered; the data are collected; and quality control procedures are applied. Spot-checking and supervision of interviewers may be needed, depending on the survey. If answers are not self-coding, someone will have to do this; coding can include translating of open-ended responses into numerical categories. Data then are tabulated and evaluated as planned. Descriptive and inferential statistics are calculated and results interpreted. At this point, the research report should be completed. Table 2.11 shows what goes into the report.

Analyzing Survey Data

Survey data can be described and analyzed with a variety of statistical methods, depending on the nature of the data and the purpose of the research. As with an experimental study, the survey researcher first will summarize data in an organized form. Typically, descriptive statistics, such as measures of central tendency (e.g., medians) and dispersion (e.g., range), are reported with bar graphs and tables to display data visually. Other inferential statistical procedures allow conclusions to be drawn about the nature of the behavior under study.

Correlations

One statistical method frequently used to analyze survey data is the correlational technique. A **correlation** is a measure of the degree to which one variable is related to another. Although its use is not confined to observational research, it is especially appropriate for these methods because the purpose of observational research is to discover relationships between different aspects of behavior. The researcher may want to learn about the relationship between two psychological variables, a

Table 2.11	**Outline of the Research Report: A Standard Form for Experimental and Observational Research**

Research Report

Title of Report:	
Author's Name and Affiliation:	
Abstract:	Brief summary of the entire research report.
Introduction:	Brief review of other relevant research uncovered in the library study. Discussion of related theory. Statement of the problem being studied and reasoning that led to the present study. Statements of the null and experimental hypotheses.
Method:	Description of the research methodology used. Statements of the operational procedures and instruments or apparatus. Description of subjects or participants.
Results:	Thorough description of the data collected; presented in data summaries and graphic displays. Descriptions of statistical tests and results of data analyses. Conclusions about support for hypotheses.
Discussion:	Discussion of the meaning of the research results. Statements of relevance to existing knowledge. Ideas for further research.
References:	Complete reference resources on all works specifically cited in the report.

physical and a psychological variable, or a demographic and a psychological variable. For example, we may be interested in the relationship between job satisfaction and occupational stress; physical well-being and psychological health; or the work attitudes of employees in different occupations (Koenker, 1974).

A correlation between two variables tells us the degree and manner in which they covary. The two may be strongly related, weakly related, or not related at all. The strength of a correlation ranges from .00 (no relationship) to 1.00 (perfect relationship). Very infrequently, however, do we find correlations above .90 in behavioral research. What are considered strong correlations range from .70 to .90. However, the strength of a correlation depends on the number of participants in a survey. Smaller correlations are meaningful and of significant strength when they have come from large samples. Thus, the statistical significance of correlations should be included in a report. Information on correlation significance can be obtained easily from tables included in statistics books.

Two variables may show either a **positive correlation** or a **negative correlation.** Looking at the direction as well as at the strength, we see the range of possible correlations as being –1.00 to .00 to +1.00. (The convention is to show the sign only if it is negative. Unsigned correlations are understood as positive.) When two variables are positively correlated, they operate in the same manner. As one increases, the other increases; as one decreases, the other decreases. For example, long-term exposure to coal dust is positively correlated with the development of black lung disease. When two variables are negatively correlated, they operate in opposing ways. As one increases, the other decreases. For example, the amount of a family's disposable income tends to be negatively correlated with the number of children in the home. (Disposable income is the amount of money left after the bills are paid.)

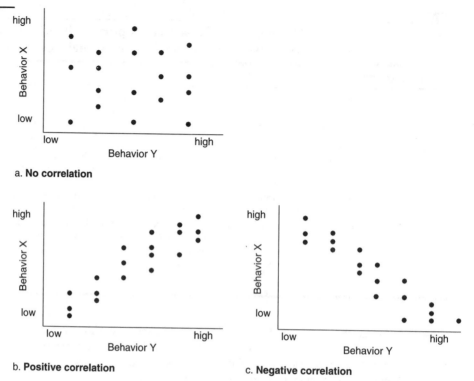

Figure 2.7. *Scattergrams showing (a) no correlation, (b) positive correlation, and negative correlation between hypothetical behaviors X and Y.*

a. **No correlation**

b. **Positive correlation**

c. **Negative correlation**

Scattergrams demonstrate the meaning of a correlation graphically (see figure 2.7). In the scattergram, a number of scores on two measures of behavior are plotted on a graph. Scores on behavior X are entered on the vertical axis, with those on behavior Y on the horizontal axis. The degree to which scores are "scattered" indicates the strength of the correlation. Scores scattered all over the graph, as in figure 2.7a, indicate little or no correlation. When scores are grouped together as in figure 2.7b and c, a stronger relationship exists. Signs of the correlation are shown also. In figure 2.7b notice that the high X scores are associated with high Y scores (and low X scores with low Y scores). This indicates a positive correlation. In figure 2.7c, a negative relationship is shown, as high X scores are associated with low Y scores (and vice versa).

There are several ways to compute a correlation. Which you choose will depend on the kind of data you have. Of particular importance in this respect is whether responses are dichotomous, such as true-false, or continuous, such as ratings. One of the most frequently used correlational statistics for continuous data is the Pearson product-moment coefficient, r. A number of available reference books specify the formulae and computational procedures for correlational techniques. They give directions on how to decide when to use one procedure rather than another, as well as exact instructions on how to calculate the statistic (cf., Bruning & Kintz, 1977). Most researchers possess at least one of these reference books.

Direct observation techniques are used in I/O research. Group process analysis is a way to observe group interactions. Activity process analysis is used to study work procedures. In all direct observation studies, the researcher needs an instrument that allows quick and accurate recording of relevant behaviors. One problem is that observers are not always accurate and reliable. Another problem is that when people are being observed, they may not behave the same as when they are not.

Surveys are used to gather various information, including knowledge and opinions. However, researchers should be reasonably sure that participants actually have and are willing to share their information. Surveys can be administered by mail or phone, or in person. They are relatively inexpensive. Anonymity is an advantage of the mail survey; however, low response rates are a problem.

You may need to construct a questionnaire for a survey. If so, make sure your questions cover the issue well. Write questions so that participants understand what is being asked. Try to avoid response biases. Decide whether to use the closed or the open response format.

Survey data can be summarized with descriptive statistics, such as the median and range of responses. Inferential statistics allow the researcher to draw conclusions about the survey results. Correlational analysis is one inferential method. A correlation shows the nature and strength of association between two variables. Correlations can be positive or negative.

CHAPTER SUMMARY

I/O psychologists use analytical research methods to study work behavior. Some studies are meant to discover basic knowledge that contributes to the science; others are aimed at solving practical problems in industry. The research process is cyclical, and this is aptly demonstrated by a field study. Such a study is often initiated because someone notices a discrepancy between expected and actual performance. The need underlying this discrepancy is assessed by means of fact-finding and research techniques, and the problem is further explored with observational studies. At this point, the I/O psychologist attempts to develop hypotheses about what can solve the problem. These hypotheses are either tested in a field experiment or used as the basis for a program of interventions that is later experimentally evaluated to determine its effectiveness in solving the problem.

Two types of research methods are used, depending on the particular purpose of the study. The experiment, which can be done in the laboratory or in a field setting, is particularly good for testing cause-effect relationships. To conduct an experiment, the researcher develops hypotheses that describe the predicted cause of the behavior being studied. The researcher simulates the hypothesized causal conditions and measures the effects on the subjects' behavior.

Behavior of the experimental and control subjects is summarized with descriptive statistics, and hypotheses are tested with inferential statistics.

Observational methods are useful for exploring issues when not enough is known about a behavior to hypothesize its causes. These methods also are useful when experiments are not feasible, as when an experiment might disrupt work or endanger workers. Observational methods provide information about associations between variables, but they cannot determine cause-effect relationships. Direct observation is a way to study behavior in a natural setting, and it is useful when the purpose is to learn about group interactions and work activity processes. The survey is an observational method useful when the purpose is to learn about internal states, such as attitudes, that cannot be observed directly. Surveys are conducted by means of a questionnaire. The questionnaire can be mailed to participants or used to interview participants by telephone or in person. As with experimental research results, the behavior of participants in observational studies and surveys must be summarized with descriptive statistics and evaluated with inferential statistics. Correlational analysis is used to evaluate the nature and extent of associations between variables.

STUDY QUESTIONS

1) How does needs assessment contribute to research done in field settings?

2) Why are experiments better for testing cause-effect relationships than observational methods?

3) In a laboratory experiment designed to test the effects of pay increases on productivity, what are the independent and dependent variables? How might these variables be operationally defined?

4) Define these terms: mean, median, range, standard deviation, inferential statistics, statistical significance.

5) What are the two main forms of observational research, and what specific techniques are involved in this research?

6) In what situation(s) is direct observation best, and how is it done?

7) What are some constraints of the survey?

8) What difficulties should the researcher be aware of in constructing survey questionnaires?

9) What meaning can be derived from a correlation coefficient? How is a negative correlation interpreted?

CONSIDER THIS

APPLICATION

The American work force is changing in terms of the number of women who are working outside their homes. More women have paid jobs now than in the past, even married women with young children. In addition, it appears that working women carry the major responsibility for the household and child care duties. Some of these women have this added responsibility because they are single parents. Others have working spouses who do not fully share the work at home.

Here is an issue to which you can apply your understanding of the research methodology described in this chapter. The following are some questions that you might answer with a well-designed study using direct observation, surveys, or experimental procedures.

1) Considering cultural backgrounds, are the women in some families more likely to have jobs than the women in other families? Are there cultural differences in the willingness of the spouses to share in work at home?

2) Are American men unprepared to perform a full share of work at home? Do the husbands of these working women simply not know how to perform housework and child care?

3) Are there ways to get housework and child care done other than (a) making it the woman's responsibility, and (b) splitting it between the woman and her spouse?

4) Do popular media, such as television and movies, portray working men and women accurately? Do they present a picture of men and women that reflects their changing roles at work and at home?

How would you design studies to answer these questions? Are some questions best studied with direct observation or with surveys? Can any of these questions be answered through experimentation? Where would you find the subjects for such studies? What information would you need to obtain from the subjects? What would your hypotheses be?

Section II

Establishing a Strong Work Force

In any organization, some of the work that must be done centers on the workers themselves; that is, the focus is on the human resources of the organization. Organizational members involved in human resources work are often found in personnel divisions, and much of what they do is related to personnel psychology. As I point out in chapter 1, personnel psychology essentially constituted I/O psychology earlier in our history. It occupies relatively fewer of us now, but it is still important in the field. Psychologists in industry often perform personnel functions, and many such practitioners still refer to themselves as being "in personnel."

Generally, human resource work endeavors to establish a strong work force in the organization. This is done in a variety of ways, as the material in this section demonstrates. First, the personnel function includes some work that needs to be done prior to accepting and evaluating job applications, such as analyzing jobs and recruiting applicants. This is covered in chapter 3. Second, skilled employees need to be hired. As described in chapters 4 and 5, the personnel psychologist has a long history of involvement in the development of methods for employee selection, particularly selection testing. Third, psychologists engage in orienting and training employees. New employees usually need training; sometimes experienced employees do, too. Fourth, the focus is on performance evaluation. We can improve the work force by giving employees feedback about their performance on the job. These subjects are discussed in chapters 6 and 7. Personnel work includes developing methods for training and evaluating performance and for fostering worker improvement.

The material covered in this section should convey the message that an understanding of how employees are selected, trained, and evaluated is important in gaining insight into their behavior in the organization. This will become apparent in the next section, in chapters that address the need to improve work performance through an understanding of what motivates and satisfies employees.

what's in this chapter?

This is the first of three chapters that focus on issues of personnel selection. In this chapter, you will learn about legally fair employment and how employers comply with the requirements of specific laws on equal employment opportunity. Second, you will learn about the need for studying jobs prior to hiring, and you will find out why job analysis is necessary before effective selection can be done. Third, you will discover that recruitment is a necessary preliminary step to employee selection, as it ideally results in a large pool of qualified applicants. Finally, through step-by-step directions, you will learn how to perform all these procedures.

A traditional and favored way to recruit new employees is current employee referrals. This is done by posting information about a company's job openings and inviting current employees to inform their acquaintances about positions available.

Chapter 3

Preparing for
Employee
Selection

In her indifferent wandering she turned into Jackson Street, not far from the river, and was keeping her way along the south side of that imposing thoroughfare, when a piece of wrapping paper, written on with marking ink and tacked up on the door, attracted her attention. It read, "Girls wanted—wrappers & stitchers." She hesitated a moment, then entered. . . .

[A] foreman in an apron and shirt sleeves, the latter rolled up to his shoulders, approached.

"Do you want to see me?" he asked.

"Do you need any help?" said Carrie, already learning the directness of address.

"Do you know how to stitch caps?" he returned.

"No, sir," she replied.

"Have you ever had any experience at this kind of work?" he inquired. She answered that she had not.

"Well," said the foreman, scratching his ear meditatively, "we do need a stitcher. We like experienced help, though. We've hardly got time to break people in." He paused and looked away out of the window. "We might, though, put you at finishing," he concluded reflectively.

Theodore Dreiser

Some features of the employment process have remained the same since this interview took place a little more than one hundred years ago in 1889. First, job advertisements today may be glossier, but the public posting of available positions is still used as a method of recruiting. Second, although other selection methods are available now, the required interview with the foreman or supervisor has persisted. Also, even though many modern employers look at other applicant qualifications, experience is considered by many to be of prime importance. Other features of the employment process have changed drastically since then. Our fair employment laws did not exist in 1889, for example. Then, it was not unlawful to recruit and hire on the basis of the worker's gender, as in "Girls Wanted."

Today's **personnel selection** function has three basic elements: (1) studying the job to be performed, (2) recruiting a pool of applicants for the job, and (3) selecting the best from the applicant pool. These aspects of personnel are interrelated, of course. To hire the right person for a job, we must know the requirements of the job. A job analysis may be needed to define the necessary qualifications a person must have to do the job. After worker qualifications are determined, the job needs to be advertised so that people with these qualifications, or with a reasonable probability of developing them, will apply. Knowing what the job requires and recruiting those with potential contributes to making the final hiring decision easier.

The overriding issue of selection is how to get the best available people for jobs. Although this depends on the particular job, there are usually many more people available than there are positions open. Thus, the primary aim of personnel specialists is to find better methods for selecting the most qualified out of the many who apply. There are several ways to accomplish this. Some personnel researchers are working on new selection devices for measuring job potential. Others are concerned with fair employment. They are interested in finding ways to select employees without placing ethnic minority and female applicants at a disadvantage. In fact, the issue of employment discrimination is a thread that runs through all elements of the personnel function. For example, affirmative action recruiting is meant to increase the number of minority and female applicants, and selection studies are routinely done to establish that selection devices do not discriminate unfairly against these applicants.

In this chapter and in chapters 4 and 5, these varied issues of personnel selection are addressed. This chapter explores some important preliminary steps. First, because employment discrimination is important in various aspects of the selection process, we will take a close look at this issue. Following this, we must consider methods of job analysis because we need to know what the job involves in order to select for it. Finally, recruitment is covered. In chapter 4, the methods of selection, including applications, interviews, and assessment centers, are the major concern. The issue of selection testing is given full consideration in chapter 5.

UNFAIR EMPLOYMENT DISCRIMINATION

It seems redundant to say *unfair* discrimination because, in terms of ordinary language, discrimination *is* unfair. In technical language, however, this qualifier is needed in order to differentiate between the acceptable discriminating function of personnel selection devices and the use of these devices to affect someone's employment status unfairly. The main legitimate purpose of tests, interviews, applications, and other such tools is to help us discriminate between applicants who are likely to be productive employees and those who are not. (The same can be said of educational tests and evaluations. The college entrance test you took discriminated between you and others who would be less successful in college.) **Unfair discrimination** does not refer to this discriminating feature of the selection tool. Rather, it is discrimination that uses applicant characteristics that are irrelevant to job success, such as an applicant's religion, race, or sex.

Legal History of Employment Discrimination

Signs of concern about unfair employment discrimination in this country began to appear in the early 1960s. The **Equal Pay Act (EPA)** of 1963 was the first of several formal measures. The EPA provided for setting pay according to the job instead of according to the person who held the job. It became unlawful to pay a female or minority employee less money than a male or majority employee for doing the same job. This provision seemed straightforward: All employees doing the same jobs were to be paid the same. However, a question surfaced, particularly with respect to male and female employees. What constituted the *same* job? Having the same job title seemed one way to gauge this, but what if men and women having the same job title did somewhat different work? What if their titles were different, but their duties were the same? These questions, coupled with our observation that we have traditionally paid different wages for "men's" work and "women's" work, led to the current issue of **comparable worth.** Proponents of comparable worth interpret the question of equal work not to mean identical work but work that is comparable in terms of its worth to the employer. They say that the idea of equality in pay needs to be expressed in terms of equal pay for work of equal value. Jobs that have equal value are those that are comparable in terms of their requirements for skill, effort, and responsibility (Taylor, 1989).

Over the next few years, a number of legislative acts were passed.[1] The Civil Rights Act of 1964 included a section, **Title VII,** referring specifically to employment. For the first time in our history, it became unlawful for an employer to refuse to hire, to fire, or to otherwise adversely affect a person's employment status because of that person's race, color, religion, sex, or national origin. In 1967, Congress passed the **Age Discrimination in Employment Act (ADEA),** recognizing age as another personal characteristic that should be protected against employment discrimination. The protected class includes persons between the ages of 40 and 70. Finally, the 1973 **Rehabilitation Act** and the 1990 **Americans with Disabilities Act** have extended protection to qualified disabled employees. Prior to the passage of these measures, employment discrimination by race, sex, age, and disability was not unlawful.

During the 1970s, a flurry of activity centered around the interpretation of Title VII of the Civil Rights Act. Much of this activity occurred within the judicial system. Throughout the decade, the Supreme Court reviewed a variety of employment discrimination cases brought under Title VII. In 1971, the Supreme Court heard what has become a classic employment discrimination case, *Griggs v. Duke Power Company.* In that case, the company was found to have violated Title VII even though the employer had not *intended* to discriminate. The Court held that the discriminatory *consequence* of the employment practice mattered, not the motivation of the employer; therefore, unintentional discrimination also was illegal. Further, the Supreme Court required that the discriminating practice be eliminated unless the employer could show proof that the practice was demanded by business necessity. That is, a selection device with a discriminating effect was acceptable only if it was a reasonable or valid[2] measure of job performance and in this way necessary for business. In the *Griggs* case, the employer had been requiring that employees have a high school diploma, and pass a general intelligence test and a mechanical comprehension test before they were hired or promoted into the job in question. The Court decided that the employer must discontinue use of the high school requirement and the general intelligence test because the evidence failed to indicate job relevance. That is, business necessity could not be shown for these requirements because neither the diploma nor the test predicted success on the job. Rather, both tended to disqualify African American applicants and employees (U.S. Office of Personnel Management, 1979).

By the end of the 1980s, further developments were in the air. A decision made by the Supreme Court concerning questions of employer responsibility for answering charges of discrimination and for proving the business necessity of selection procedures sparked a debate in Congress. Several bills were proposed during the 1990–91 congressional sessions, culminating in the passage of the Civil Rights Act of 1991. The act supported much of the meaning of the Civil Rights Act of 1964 and the interpretations by the judicial system. For example, it emphasized that the employer must demonstrate that a challenged employment practice is job

[1]These legislative documents can be found in the *Code of Federal Regulations* in your university library's government publications section.

[2]Validity is discussed at length in chapter 5. Briefly, validity of a selection device refers to its accuracy in assessing a person's potential performance on the job.

relevant. It amended the 1964 act in one respect. It ruled out the past practice of considering the applicant's race or gender in deciding passing scores on job tests (Varca & Pattison, 1993).

Uniform Guidelines of 1978

During the 1970s, the federal government began to show more interest in employment practices. In 1972, Title VII of the Civil Rights Act was amended to bring state and local government employers under its auspices and to establish the **Equal Employment Opportunity Commission (EEOC)** as the monitoring agency. Several federal agencies, including the Office of Federal Contract Compliance (OFCC) and the EEOC, began formal scrutiny of the new law. These federal agencies developed separate interpretations of Title VII. By the end of 1976, two completely separate sets of compliance guidelines existed, and these frequently disagreed on how employers were to eliminate discrimination. You can imagine what happened. Employers who held federal contracts were caught in a particular bind. They were regulated by both EEOC and OFCC guidelines. Employment practices acceptable to the EEOC frequently were not acceptable to the OFCC, and vice versa.

By 1977, it was clear that the government needed a single, unified position on employment discrimination defined in everyday terms. Methods for determining the existence of discrimination needed to be developed, and employers needed to be advised about these methods. Committees were formed of legislative and legal experts, federal agency administrators, I/O psychologists, and employers, and were given the responsibility of developing this unified governmental position. By mid-1978, the document was published, aptly entitled the *Uniform Guidelines on Employment Selection Procedures*. All four federal agencies endorsed it. Although there have since been amendments and clarifications, it is still the *Uniform Guidelines* of 1978 to which employers look for direction.

Title VII covers any practice that affects a person's employment opportunities. The *Uniform Guidelines* define this "practice" as any procedure used to make selection decisions, including tests, interviews, applications, and entry requirements. "Employment opportunities" refer to selection for initial hire, as well as for termination, transfer, promotion, entry into training programs and labor unions, and salary assignments. In other words, any device or practice used to make any of these personnel decisions is subject to EEOC regulations.

Do these regulations apply to everyone? Suppose you hire a caretaker for your child and a teenager to cut your lawn. Do you need to consult the *Uniform Guidelines*?[3] If this is the extent of your activities as an employer, the answer is no. The guidelines do cover private and public employers and other bodies, such as labor organizations and employment agencies. However, the *size* of the employer is important. Employers with fewer than 15 employees working no longer than 20 weeks a year are not subject to these regulations.

Discrimination Defined

According to the guidelines, a discriminatory practice is one that has an **adverse impact** on the employment opportunities of individuals of any race, ethnic group, or sex, unless it can be justified as a business necessity.

[3]This and similar questions are answered in a 1979 government publication referred to as the *Questions and Answers*.

Examine this definition carefully. First, notice that this is a practical definition. If a selection device shows an adverse impact and it cannot be justified, it is discriminatory. If it does not have this effect, it is not discriminatory. Second, notice that the measure is "class blind" in that *any* race or ethnic group and *both* sexes are protected by this definition. (Other regulations, such as the ADEA and the Rehabilitation Act, specify a particular protected class that does not include everyone.) This class blind aspect of the definition is relevant when we consider what has come to be known as reverse discrimination. In reverse discrimination terminology, the protected group is the majority group rather than a minority group, or males rather than females. Third, notice that an adverse impact may be justified as a business necessity. This has a very narrow meaning. Showing business necessity is showing proof that the selection device has a valid relationship to job performance. For example, if a Chinese language test is used to select waiters in a restaurant, the test may have an adverse impact on non-Chinese groups. However, the test may be justified as a business necessity if the patrons of the restaurant speak only Chinese; thus, job performance would require an employee to speak Chinese, and the language test would be a valid requirement.

Assessing Adverse Impact

The guidelines describe methods for determining whether an employment practice is discriminatory. Selection procedures used in hiring and promoting are evaluated with these methods. Three key concepts are necessary for understanding how adverse impact is assessed: the bottom-line concept, the selection ratio, and the four-fifths (80 percent) rule of thumb. The **bottom-line concept** says where to start. We begin by looking at the "bottom line" or the overall selection outcome; that is, we consider those who were actually hired by the selection process. The **selection ratio** is the proportion of individuals who pass a selection hurdle. At the bottom line, the selection ratio is the number hired divided by the number who applied. The **four-fifths rule of thumb** is a way of determining adverse impact by comparing the selection ratios of different groups. Any group should be selected at a rate equal to or greater than 80 percent of the most heavily selected group. If the selection ratio is less than this, adverse impact is shown. Two overall adverse impact assessments are made—one by sorting applicants by race or ethnicity and another by sorting applicants by sex. For each sorting, we begin with a bottom-line assessment. If this shows *no* adverse impact, then we need go no further than the bottom-line assessment. However, if the bottom line does show adverse impact, then we must do a component assessment. In this, we identify the component of the multiple-hurdle selection process responsible for the effect. The step-by-step procedures for conducting these assessments are shown in the example in figure 3.1.

Clearly, careful recordkeeping is necessary for adverse impact assessment. We must have records of the ethnicity and sex of each applicant, and we must be able to track all individuals through the selection hurdles. Two questions are relevant here. The first concerns how to get this individual information. If applicants apply in person, we might simply scrutinize their appearance and surname. However, this "eyeball" method of data collection is prone to error and is *not* recommended. A brief self-report form in which the individual can provide his or her own data is a better method. The form provides an easy way to keep ethnicity and

Figure 3.1. *Computing adverse impact: Example of sorting applicants into racial/ethnic groups. Bottom-line assessment is done initially. If it shows adverse impact, as in this example, a component assessment must be computed to identify the selection device(s) responsible for this adverse effect.*

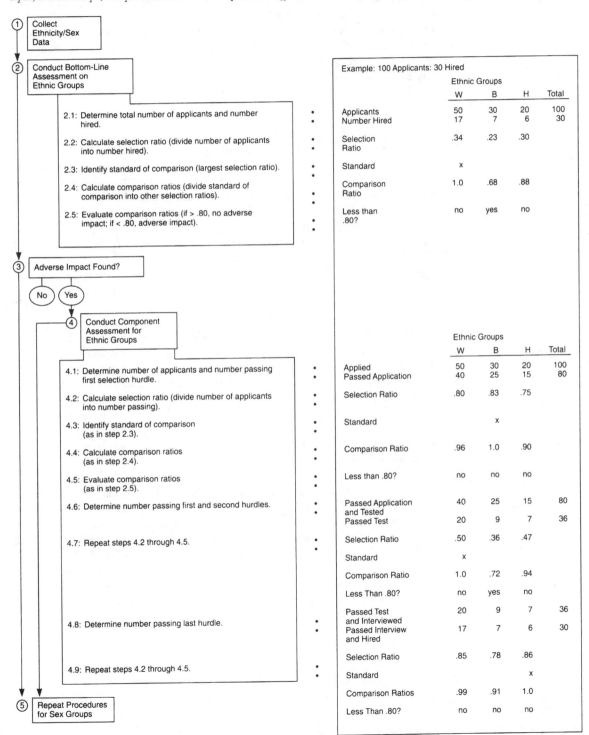

① Collect Ethnicity/Sex Data

② Conduct Bottom-Line Assessment on Ethnic Groups

2.1: Determine total number of applicants and number hired.

2.2: Calculate selection ratio (divide number of applicants into number hired).

2.3: Identify standard of comparison (largest selection ratio).

2.4: Calculate comparison ratios (divide standard of comparison into other selection ratios).

2.5: Evaluate comparison ratios (if > .80, no adverse impact; if < .80, adverse impact).

Example: 100 Applicants: 30 Hired

	Ethnic Groups			
	W	B	H	Total
Applicants	50	30	20	100
Number Hired	17	7	6	30
Selection Ratio	.34	.23	.30	
Standard	x			
Comparison Ratio	1.0	.68	.88	
Less than .80?	no	yes	no	

③ Adverse Impact Found?
No / Yes

④ Conduct Component Assessment for Ethnic Groups

4.1: Determine number of applicants and number passing first selection hurdle.

4.2: Calculate selection ratio (divide number of applicants into number passing).

4.3: Identify standard of comparison (as in step 2.3).

4.4: Calculate comparison ratios (as in step 2.4).

4.5: Evaluate comparison ratios (as in step 2.5).

4.6: Determine number passing first and second hurdles.

4.7: Repeat steps 4.2 through 4.5.

4.8: Determine number passing last hurdle.

4.9: Repeat steps 4.2 through 4.5.

	Ethnic Groups			
	W	B	H	Total
Applied	50	30	20	100
Passed Application	40	25	15	80
Selection Ratio	.80	.83	.75	
Standard		x		
Comparison Ratio	.96	1.0	.90	
Less than .80?	no	no	no	
Passed Application and Tested	40	25	15	80
Passed Test	20	9	7	36
Selection Ratio	.50	.36	.47	
Standard	x			
Comparison Ratio	1.0	.72	.94	
Less Than .80?	no	yes	no	
Passed Test and Interviewed	20	9	7	36
Passed Interview and Hired	17	7	6	30
Selection Ratio	.85	.78	.86	
Standard			x	
Comparison Ratios	.99	.91	1.0	
Less Than .80?	no	no	no	

⑤ Repeat Procedures for Sex Groups

gender data separate from the selection decision process. The second question concerns the ethnic groups that must be considered in the assessment. We do not need to assess our procedures for adverse impact against every possible ethnic group. Only those groups that make up as much as 2 percent of the total local labor force need to be identified. Employers must have current information on the labor pool from which employees are drawn in order to calculate this. Such information usually can be obtained from labor statistics collected by the county or counties from which the organization draws its applicants.

Rectifying Adverse Impact

What do we do if we find an adverse effect on one of the protected groups? The first step is to conduct the component assessments and determine the source of the adverse impact, as shown in figure 3.1. When the responsible component has been located, a number of alternatives are considered. To begin, the difference in the selection ratios can be examined by means of a statistical test to establish that the effect is significant and not simply a chance variation. The guidelines offer the four-fifths rule of thumb simply as a quick procedure for evaluating differences in selection ratios. It is not meant to supplant statistical analysis. If a statistical test does show that the selection difference is significant, however, something must be done about the selection device. One answer the guidelines offer is to eliminate the device. A similar answer is to replace the device with one that does not show adverse impact. In either case, eliminating the adverse impact takes care of the problem, at least as far as the guidelines are concerned. When these regulations were first published, this is in fact what often happened, particularly when a test showed adverse impact. Because tests tend to be sensitive to differences among applicants and are relied upon to reduce the applicant pool (by disqualifying applicants with low potential), they also more frequently tend to show adverse impact. Many employers who wanted to avoid EEOC attention, either replaced their tests with less sensitive devices or stopped using tests altogether. This may not have been in their best interests, however (Wollack, 1994). Less sensitive tests contain more error and are less valid measures. Also, when a test is simply discarded, there is naturally more reliance placed on interviews and other selection methods. As we will see, these other methods in general are not as valid as tests.

There are other ways to rectify adverse impact. The employer can revise the selection device and/or justify it as a business necessity. As I indicate in the example on page 72, when the restaurant uses a Chinese language test to screen waiters, the test is likely to show adverse impact on both white and African American applicants. The employer may provide evidence to justify its use because performance on the test is significantly related to performance on the job. This is the nature of the argument for business necessity. The evidence must show that a device is a *valid* measure of a real job requirement; that is, proof must come from a validity study, which will be discussed in chapter 5.

Affirmative Action

Although employment discrimination discussions usually center on selection issues, fair employment does extend to other aspects of the personnel function, including recruitment of job applicants. **Affirmative action** is one of those discrimination issues that often relates directly to recruitment. In the reasoning of the *Uniform Guidelines* (1978), if we eliminate those selection procedures that unfairly discriminate against applicants and employees and substitute fair selection devices, *eventually* we will have equality in employment. Theoretically, at least, representation of all racial/ethnic and sex groups in all job classes will become comparable to their numbers in the labor force. However, the process is likely to take a long time. Affirmative action recruiting is meant to hurry the change. It is an extra step taken beyond what the law requires to correct the past inequity. Affirmative action requires organizations to do a better job in recruiting applicants. A serious affirmative action program results in larger numbers of minority members and females than would ordinarily appear in the applicant pool. These increased numbers in the applicant pool increase the probability of a qualified minority or female employee being hired.

In actual practice, the term *affirmative action* is sometimes used in a casual way to convey the idea of fair employment. Using the term in job ads typically is meant to say the organization will not unfairly discriminate and will give a fair opportunity to all interested applicants. Despite this intent, affirmative action is understood by many people as preferential selection, in which women and minorities exclusively are sought for open positions. The confusion in understanding this term probably has several sources, such as (1) the profligate use of this term instead of "equal employment opportunity" to mean fair employment; (2) the fact that some organizations are legally required to do preferential or quota hiring; and (3) the practice of some organizations to voluntarily engage in preferential hiring.

When an organization is brought to court because it has failed to hire minorities or women, the court may impose a **hiring quota**. The hiring quota, which is meant to increase the diversity of the work force, legally requires this organization to do preferential hiring. However, most organizations do not have court-ordered hiring quotas. When they advertise as an affirmative action employer, it means either they are engaging in affirmative action recruiting and fair employment, or they have a self-imposed practice of preferential hiring. Such a practice sometimes is adopted when an organization finds that its work force is not as diverse as it should be.

Whether an organization actually has engaged in voluntary preferential selection or simply is believed to have done so, reactions often are negative. Research indicates that preferential treatment usually is evaluated negatively, although this depends on whether the individual has benefitted in some way by preferential treatment (Summers, 1995; Tougas & Beaton, 1993).

Currently, considerable opinion on this issue is being expressed. In 1995, following the U.S. government's review of federal employment requirements and during California's dismantling of the affirmative action programs at the University of California, a public debate was reported in newspapers nationwide. In daily discussions, some defined affirmative action as a means for hiring unqualified individuals and as a form of reverse discrimination. Others countered that affirmative action had given employment opportunities to people who had not had opportunities in the past. It is likely that we will hear more public discussion of this issue. Human resource professionals and I/O psychologists alike will need to be alert to new developments in affirmative action and fair employment practices, as changes in the law may modify recruitment and selection of employees.[4]

[4]For more information on this issue, see the "Consider This" discussion at the end of this chapter.

For more than 30 years, we have had laws explicitly addressing the rights of workers to be treated fairly in obtaining and performing work. Fair treatment includes equal opportunity for qualified applicants regardless of their race, sex, religion, age, or medical condition. Specific laws have been passed to provide protection for groups of people classified in these ways. Most important is Title VII of the Civil Rights Act. Implementation of Title VII has resulted in major changes in how employers approach and conduct the hiring process. Employers must document that their selection procedures have no adverse impact on applicants, and they must attempt to increase the diversity of their employee groups. Affirmative action programs provide a way for employers to be proactive. However, such programs have recently been spotlighted by public criticism.

DETERMINING JOB REQUIREMENTS

The first step in finding and hiring effective employees is to determine the job's requirements. We must know what the job entails before we can find the right person to do it. **Job analysis** is the way to study the job. There is more interest in job analysis now than there was in the past. Psychologists have always said there was a need for it, especially for developing selection tests. However, it can hardly be said that job analysis was really promoted. Prien (1977) observed that textbooks of the past treated job analysis as something "any fool can do." I would not like to give this impression. Job analysis is the systematic method by which job requirements are determined. As such, it is the very foundation of much of what I/O psychologists do.

It is useful to begin this discussion of job analysis by defining some basic terms used in studying jobs. A **position** is a set of tasks and duties that one person performs. A **job** is a group of related positions in which the major tasks and duties are either identical or sufficiently similar that individuals occupying the positions do basically the same work (McCormick, 1979). A **job family** is a group of related jobs. Generally, job analysis is aimed at the job level, although recent interest in transporting analyses from one organization to another sometimes has us thinking in terms of job families.

Uses of Job Information

An understanding of the job is necessary for several personnel functions. In the next two chapters, you will see that job information is used for selection purposes. To be sure that a selection program performs effectively and does not discriminate unfairly, the personnel specialist must know what the job involves. In addition, job information is needed for other purposes. It is used in setting wages, developing training programs and evaluating job performance. Wooten (1993) demonstrated that it can be used to advantage in planning for future staffing needs. His study focused on the need for developing current employees for entry level managerial positions. He found that many abilities and skills required in managerial positions are required also in secretarial positions. Because of this, secretarial positions could provide a career path to management.

Job Evaluation

Job information is necessary for compensation plans. Before we go on, let us take a close look at this important use of job analysis information. There are several methods by which wage policies can be decided. The simplest one is to find out what the market will bear. Usually, this means setting the wage at the lowest level at which someone will take the job. In more complex wage-setting methods, monetary value is assigned according to the intrinsic worth of the job. Collectively, these complex methods are called **job evaluation**.[5] They include whole-job ranking, factor comparison, and the point system (McCormick, 1979).

To some extent, all job evaluation methods rely on job analysis information. The simplest, **whole-job ranking,** is a holistic method of evaluating a job. In this, all jobs in an organization are simply judged and ranked in terms of their overall value to the organization. The factor and point methods require a thorough understanding of the job before reasonable judgments concerning job value can be made. In **factor comparison,** job characteristics (factors) valuable to the organization, such as physical demands and responsibility for others, are specified. Also, certain jobs are identified in which the pay is considered fair. These fairly paid jobs function as benchmarks or reference points in assigning value to the job factors. Other jobs then are assessed as to the extent to which they are similar to the benchmark job in having these valuable or compensable factors. The **point system** also uses compensable factors. The factors are judged in terms of their dollar value and are assigned points to represent this value. Individual jobs then are evaluated as to the extent that they contain these compensable factors. The factor points are summed to determine the level of pay for each job.

Job evaluation methods have become important in the discussion of pay discrimination and comparable worth. As mentioned earlier, the view of comparable worth is that equal pay is appropriate for jobs having equal value. The more sophisticated methods of job evaluation appear to have potential for helping us make better judgments of what are equal values. Although the holistic judgments of whole-job ranking are thought to produce compensation plans that carry existing wage inequities into perpetuity, the factor comparison and point methods are considered less likely to do so, because they make better use of job information and have ways to compare jobs. The point system provides ways to weight the different job factors according to their value. Because of this, the point system is an effective method of creating an unbiased compensation plan (Davis & Sauser, 1991; 1993).

Types of Job Information

Because job analysis information is used in a variety of ways, it is not surprising to find that job analysis methods differ in their ability to produce particular types of information. Basically, two kinds of job information are generated through job analysis: task information and worker qualifications information. Task information

[5]Job *evaluation* is not simply another term for job *analysis* although they sound similar.

Table 3.1	**Samples of Duties and Task Statements for a Psychology Department Secretarial Job**

Duty:	Receive, screen, and route incoming departmental requests and materials.
Tasks:	Receive, screen, and route phone calls and office visitors to appropriate faculty and staff.
	Receive and distribute departmental mail.
Duty:	Prepare drafts and final copy of instructional materials, departmental correspondence, and department and university forms.
Tasks:	Type examinations, class handouts, and other instructional materials.
	Type university forms for personnel actions, administrative actions, and course proposals.
	Assist department typist in typing backlog of various materials as needed.
Duty:	Implement procedures for acquisition and maintenance of departmental equipment, materials, and services.
Tasks:	Order, receive, and arrange for storage of office supplies.
	Perform minor servicing of office copiers, duplicating machines, and other equipment.
	Order major service and repair of office equipment.

includes statements about what work is done, how it is done, and for what purpose. It also can include statements about equipment and materials; special working conditions, such as hazards; and relationships with other people, such as supervisors and subordinates. (Sample task statements generated from a job analysis are shown in table 3.1.) Worker qualifications information includes statements about the knowledge, skills, and abilities (**KSAs**) that are necessary for a worker to do the job successfully.

The job analysis techniques discussed in the following section provide both types of information, although they differ in the extent to which they emphasize either task or worker information. The purpose of the job analysis will indicate the kind of information needed and suggest appropriate methods (McCormick, 1976). Most reviewers of research on this issue have concluded that there is no one best way to do a job analysis (cf. Hakel, 1986; Zedeck & Cascio, 1984). One technique may be superior for one purpose and inferior for another. Even for just one use, such as developing a selection program, more than one type of job analysis may be needed (Levine, Ash, & Bennett, 1980; Prien, 1977; Veres, Lahey, & Buckly, 1987).

Job Analysis Methods

As a method of collecting information, job analysis can be viewed as a form of observational research. Direct observation and survey research are used routinely to do job analyses. In addition, special instruments and procedures have been developed. These include task analysis, critical incidents, the job element method, and the Position Analysis Questionnaire, all of which incorporate standard research techniques. Figure 3.2 gives an overview of the process of job analysis.

A job analysis is begun as any research project is, with the study of available resources. The _Dictionary of Occupational Titles_ (DOT) (1991) provides general

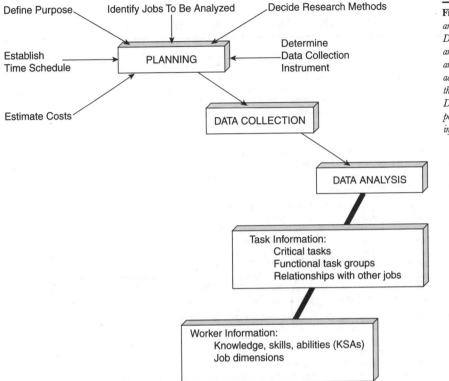

Define Purpose Identify Jobs To Be Analyzed Decide Research Methods

Establish
Time Schedule → PLANNING ← Determine
Data Collection
Instrument

Estimate Costs

DATA COLLECTION

DATA ANALYSIS

Task Information:
  Critical tasks
  Functional task groups
  Relationships with other jobs

Worker Information:
  Knowledge, skills, abilities (KSAs)
  Job dimensions

Figure 3.2. *Flowchart of job analysis. First, the study is planned. During this stage, the method of job analysis is decided and instruments are obtained. Second, data on work activities are collected. During the third stage, data are analyzed: Depending on the method used, pertinent task and/or worker information is extracted.*

descriptions of work activities in many different occupations (see table 3.2 for some examples). Descriptions of the job under study or of similar jobs also are frequently available in an organization's files, as are training and operations manuals. Performance records can provide further information about necessary skills, frequent errors, and difficulties encountered on the job.

What we do after this initial document study depends on the specific job analysis; however, a number of observational research techniques often are used. For example, the job analyst might directly observe the work being done. A worker's activities during a number of short periods during the work day can be recorded by means of a checklist. A mechanical recording, such as a videotape, can be used also, although such a record still will need to be transcribed. Another use of the observational method involves role playing in which the *analyst* performs the job and then records all the work activities. Obviously, this method has limitations, as the job analyst may not have the ability to role-play the job. For example, the method would hardly be appropriate for analyzing the jobs of firefighters and helicopter pilots. Other job analyses engage the job incumbent in self-observation. For example, activity diaries require incumbents to record all work activities they perform during a specified time period.

Survey techniques are frequently used in job analysis as well. Both questionnaires and individual and group interviews are routinely used. For example, job

Table 3.2

Samples from DOT. Tasks and Activities of Five Jobs

709.384–010
Fire-Extinguisher Repairer
(any ind.)

Repairs and tests fire extinguishers in repair shops and in establishments, such as factories, homes, garages, and office buildings, using handtools and hydrostatic test equipment: Dismantles extinguisher and examines tubings, horns, head gaskets, cutter discs, and other parts for defects. Replaces worn or damaged parts, using handtools. Cleans extinguishers and recharges them with materials, such as soda water and sulfuric acid, carbon tetrachloride, nitrogen, or patented solutions. Tests extinguishers for conformity with legal specifications, using hydrostatic test equipment. May install cabinets and brackets to hold extinguishers. May sell fire extinguishers.

709.484–010
Silk-Screen-Frame
Assembler (any ind.) frame
builder, silk-screen; setter-up,
silk-screen frame.

Builds frames for silk or metal screens used to stencil identifying or operational data on parts or products following blueprints: Bends bar stock to specified shape and dimensions to form frame, using vise and handtools. Solders joints, using soldering iron. Measures and marks location of holes on frame, using rule. Drills and threads holes, using drill press and handtap. Screws guides and stops in holes for use in positioning part in frame.

209.587–026
Mail Clerk (clerical)
mailroom clerk; mail sorter;
postal clerk.

Sorts incoming mail for distribution and dispatches outgoing mail: Open envelopes by hand or machine. Stamps date and time of receipt on incoming mail. Sorts mail according to destination and type, such as returned letters, adjustments, bills, orders, and payments. Readdresses undeliverable mail bearing incomplete or incorrect address. Examines outgoing mail for appearance and seals envelopes by hand or machine. Stamps outgoing mail by hand or with postage meter. May fold letters or circulars and insert into envelopes [FOLDING-MACHINE OPERATOR (clerical)]. May distribute and collect mail. May weigh mail to determine that postage is correct. May keep record of registered mail. May address mail, using addressing machine [ADDRESSING-MACHINE OPERATOR (clerical)]. May be designated according to type of mail handled as MAIL CLERK, BILLS (clerical).

539.367–014
Water-Quality Tester
(paper & pulp)

Reviews data from meters, recorders, and sampler, and inspects equipment in mill to insure compliance with government standards: Records readings from plant measuring devices, such as recorders and meters. Removes and replaces record charts. Computes effluent flow from chart for sampling period. Collects waste water sample, using sample bottle. Submits samples to laboratory for testing. Writes report on findings. Observes operation of mill effluent system to determine areas of abnormal pulp spills, leaks, or defects in piping. Inspects machine sampling and measuring devices to determine source of problem or if equipment is malfunctioning. Reviews sampling and operational reports to insure that results are within limits of water quality standards. Conducts tests, such as pH and dissolved oxygen, to ascertain effluent levels. Notifies supervisor of excessive fluctuation in water-flow or major breakdown in equipment. Records findings on daily logsheet.

709.682–010
Autoclave Operator
(chem.) II

Operates series of high pressure autoclaves to test fabricated uranium fuel elements for leakage and ruptures in zirconium cladding and weld: Loads fuel elements in metal baskets and places baskets into tank of autoclave, using crane. Closes tank lid, using torque wrench. Turns valve to admit specified amount of water into tank, and closes exhaust outlet of tank. Activates electric heating element, adjusts control knobs, and observes gauges to obtain specified temperature and pressure. Monitors gauges to prevent rise in temperature and listens for alarm signal that indicates leak or rupture of one or more fuel elements. Presses button to cut off heat elements, opens exhaust water valve to dump hot water, and opens valve to admit cold water to cool elements. Opens autoclave, removes basket, and replaces tested elements. Records serial number of ruptured elements. Periodically tests quality of deionized water in autoclave, using special equipment.

Source: *Dictionary of Occupational Titles,* 4th ed., 1977. U.S. Government Printing Office, Washington, D.C.

incumbents can be presented with a list of tasks or work activities in questionnaire form and asked to respond to the ones the job includes. The task statements and other items included on such questionnaires may have emerged from an observational study (as described previously), or they may have resulted from a series of interviews. Interviews with individual workers are frequently conducted to clarify or gather additional information after observation or after an activity diary has been reviewed. Actually, interviews can be used instead of observations and questionnaires to provide primary data. Incumbents and supervisors, or "subject-matter experts

(SMEs)" as these job-knowledgeable persons are often called, are regularly asked to generate statements about work objectives, duties, task activities, and worker qualifications. Depending on the size of the organization and on the purpose of a job analysis, **SME committees** also can include the company president, vice presidents, and unit managers. These individuals can be valuable because they are able to convey a broad view of the overall purpose and objectives of the job (Robinson, 1981).

Task Analysis

In job analysis, the point is to identify important aspects of the job. **Task analysis** is a method developed by the U.S. Department of Labor (1972) that accomplishes this through a multiple-step process focused on the duties and tasks of the job. (Other methods, as we will see, focus directly on worker requirements.) In task analysis, the task universe is first defined through direct observation and surveys of job-knowledgeable persons. The task universe is a listing of all the job's tasks. Next, incumbents are asked to respond to the list of tasks through a questionnaire. Typically, they are asked to indicate what tasks their job includes; how much time they spend on each task; how frequently each is performed; and how important each task is to the job as a whole. The questionnaire also may call for judgments concerning how long it takes employees to learn the tasks and how difficult and critical they are. (Task criticality refers to the extent to which poor performance on the task would negatively affect success on the job.) Specific task evaluations likely will be more useful than general overall ratings. Sanchez and Levine (1989) found that judgments of overall importance largely reflected judgments of criticality and difficulty in learning the task. Further, they found that combining the latter two judgments actually provided a more reliable estimation of task importance than the overall rating.

In subsequent steps of task analysis, the job analyst evaluates the questionnaire data, identifying important tasks, sorting them into different job functions, and extracting worker requirements that appear necessary for each function. Worker requirements are the knowledge, skills, and abilities **(KSAs)** necessary for task performance (Gavin, 1977). This process is outlined in figure 3.3.

One value of task analysis is its job relatedness. In this systematic procedure, we never lose sight of the work itself. By documenting each stage of the process, the job analyst maintains direct contact with the actual work. Job relatedness has been important in issues of fair employment, and as we will see in chapter 5, it is essential in the validation of certain job-content tests.

Critical Incidents

In the late 1940s following some research for the Air Force, Flanagan (1954) introduced the **critical incidents** technique as a way to establish requirements for several military jobs, such as those of Air Force officer, pilot, and research scientist. With this technique, incumbents and supervisors are asked to describe specific incidents of behavior that are critical to success or failure on the job. These are the behavioral incidents that make or break the job. Job behaviors characterizing poor, average, and superior workers can be described with this technique. Although questionnaires can be used for this purpose, the data collection process generally begins with a structured interview in which an individual is asked about the nature of the critical incidents, such as that described in table 3.3. Once the data have been collected, the job incidents are submitted to an evaluative process, and the job analyst

Figure 3.3. *The process of task analysis. The task universe is defined through direct observation and survey procedures. In phase 2 of the process, the data are analyzed. The analysis includes evaluating tasks, inferring required KSAs and organizing a description of necessary worker qualifications.*

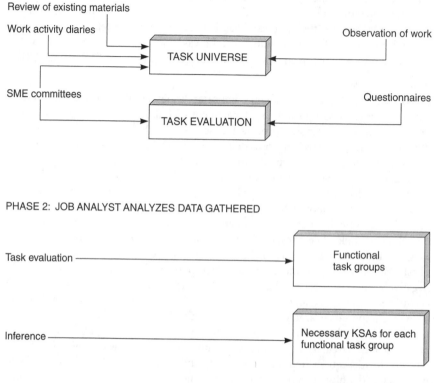

PHASE 1: JOB ANALYST WORKS WITH SUBJECT-MATTER EXPERTS (SMEs)

Review of existing materials

Work activity diaries

Observation of work

TASK UNIVERSE

SME committees

Questionnaires

TASK EVALUATION

PHASE 2: JOB ANALYST ANALYZES DATA GATHERED

Task evaluation ⟶ Functional task groups

Inference ⟶ Necessary KSAs for each functional task group

Organization ⟶ Worker qualifications: Required knowledge, skill, and ability (KSAs)

sorts and orders the incidents. The particular categorization reflects the purpose of the job analysis. When used for selection, incidents should be categorized according to worker qualifications, or KSAs.

The critical incidents method was developed specifically for identifying the important requirements of a job. Because it is based on actual descriptions of work activities, it provides a good deal of job relatedness. Another value is that minimal inference and abstract reasoning are required from individuals reporting critical incidents. Descriptions of work activities are concrete and factual. Specifying exactly what is done to make the activity successful or unsuccessful is a central feature of the technique.

Job Element Method

Use of the critical incidents technique for identifying the important aspects of a job led to further study of this approach and to the development of the **job element**

Table 3.3   Sample Form Used in Critical Incidents Interviews

"Think of the last time you saw one of your subordinates do something that was very helpful to your group in meeting their production schedule." (Pause till he indicates he has such an incident in mind.) "Did his action result in an increase in production of as much as one percent for that day?—or some similar period?"

 (If the answer is "no," say) "I wonder if you could think of the last time that someone did something that did have this much of an effect in increasing production." (When he indicates he has such a situation in mind, say) "What were the general circumstances leading up to this incident?" _____

_____

_____

"Tell me exactly what this person did that was so helpful at that time." _____

_____

"Why was this so helpful in getting your group's job done?" _____

_____

"When did this incident happen?"_____

"What was this person's job?" _____

"How long has he been on this job?" _____

From J.C. Flanagan, "The critical incident technique" in *Psychological Bulletin,* 1954, 51, 4, 327–358. Copyright © 1954 by the American Psychological Association. Reprinted with permission.

method. Developed by Primoff (1975), this method is used to identify the basic aspects of behavior or KSAs required in a job. As in the critical incidents technique, the method is used to specify the job elements that distinguish superior workers from workers who are marginally acceptable. To conduct the job analysis with this procedure, the analyst forms an SME committee that includes such people as job incumbents and supervisors. The SME committee produces a list of KSAs its members think are necessary for job performance. Once the list has been generated, each of these "job elements" is rated by the committee in terms of its relative importance to the job. From an analysis of these ratings, a list of critical job requirements is drawn up. These critical requirements are categorized into broad groups of worker qualifications, and they are used to guide the development of the selection program.

 The job element method yields a job analysis that has a less direct connection with work activities than the task analysis and critical incidents techniques; thus, job relatedness is not as easily demonstrated. In task analysis, KSAs are inferred from the job content. Although this inference represents a weak link between work activities and worker requirements, the inference and the weakness also is present in the job element method. The inference is perhaps simply less apparent. Without first making the tasks explicit, SMEs infer worker requirements from their knowledge of the job. For some purposes, such as those in which job relatedness must be shown, this omission of the job content can be a serious weakness.

 The value of the job element method is in terms of its ability to produce job analyses that can be transported from one organization to another. Because it can be used to identify common core elements of jobs, the method might be used to develop a taxonomy of job elements. Such a taxonomy could make job analyses very inexpensive because the analysis would become a process mainly of matching the elements of a job with those in the taxonomic list. Transportable job analyses based on a taxonomy are likely to become more important in the future, particularly when the analysis is used for establishing the validity of selection tests. Research indicates that job families are internally similar enough for a test that is found valid for a job family in one setting to be considered valid in another (Zedeck & Cascio, 1984). Thus, highly-detailed job analyses may be unnecessary, and broad methods such as the job element technique are acceptable because they can place the job within a job family (Schmidt, Hunter, & Pearlman, 1981).

Position Analysis Questionnaire

McCormick and his associates developed the **Position Analysis Questionnaire (PAQ)** from research in which job element techniques were used (McCormick, 1976; McCormick, Jeanneret, & Meacham, 1972). Like the job element method, the PAQ is worker oriented rather than task oriented. The questionnaire contains items referring to 194 different job elements categorized in six groups: information input, mental processing, work output, relationships with others, job context, and other job characteristics. Table 3.4 lists the types of elements included in these six categories. The PAQ makes job analysis a less time-consuming process. In doing a PAQ study, we begin by having job-knowledgeable persons check off elements listed on the PAQ that apply to the job in question. Then they rate those elements as to their degree of criticality. Analysis of the data results in grouping the identified job elements into categories of related items called job dimensions. The data also are analyzed to show the weight or the importance of each job dimension to the total job; thus, a list of critical worker requirements is produced.

The PAQ is like the job element method in having the potential for producing transportable job analyses. Identification of job dimensions makes it possible to determine the extent to which jobs in one location are like those in another. Such information, under certain conditions, may mean that a selection device used in one organization is appropriate for use in another, eliminating the cost of a full job analysis at the other location.

A criticism of the PAQ is that it requires the respondent to have a high level of verbal ability. This may be a problem if the questionnaire is completed by job incumbents who do not have the necessary verbal skills. One solution is to have job analysts complete the PAQ because they are more likely to have high verbal skills. Evidence that job analysts can produce PAQ analyses that are as accurate as those done by job incumbents has been reported (Smith & Hakel, 1979). However, other research has questioned this conclusion (Harvey & Lozada-Larsen, 1988). It probably depends on the job. Another questionnaire, the Job Element Inventory (Cornelius & Hakel, 1978), modeled after the PAQ, avoids this problem because it requires a lower reading level. Research evaluating the inventory indicates that it is otherwise comparable to the PAQ (Harvey et al., 1988).

Table 3.4 — PAQ Job Element Categories

Category	Subject Matter of Items
Information input (where and how worker gets information to use on job)	Sources of job information Sensory and perceptual processes Estimation activities
Mental processes	Decision making, reasoning, and planning/scheduling Information-processing activities Use of learned information
Work output (physical activity)	Use of tools, devices, and equipment Manual activities Entire body activities Level of physical exertion Body positions and postures Manipulation and coordination activities
Relationships with others	Communication Interpersonal relationships Amount of personal contact Types of personal contact Supervision and coordination
Job context (physical and social work environment)	Physical working conditions Physical hazards Personal and social job elements
Other job characteristics	Apparel required Licenses required Work schedule Job demands and responsibilities

Adapted from E. J. McCormick, P. R. Jeanneret, and R. C. Meacham, *Position Analysis and Questionnaire*. Copyright © Purdue Research Foundation, Purdue University, W. Lafayette, Indiana.

Main Points

Job analysis is a way to study a job. There are various reasons we need to study jobs. The information is needed for selection, training, performance evaluation, and for setting wages. Job evaluation, which is distinct from job analysis, is a way to put a dollar value on jobs. The more sophisticated job evaluation methods rely heavily on information from job analysis.

Although standard research methods are used in job analysis, special techniques also exist. These include task analysis, the critical incidents technique, the job element method, and the Position Analysis Questionnaire. These methods vary in their ability to provide two types of job information: task information and worker qualifications information. The purpose of the job analysis will indicate which type of information is needed and what is the most appropriate method for obtaining it.

RECRUITING JOB APPLICANTS

Once we have analyzed the job and understand its worker requirements, it is time to think about recruiting applicants. In the past, recruitment received little attention from I/O psychologists. We seemed to care only that there were enough applicants to make selection realistic, and typically, there are enough. Whenever unemployment is high, job ads draw large numbers of applicants, particularly in some fields. For example, an announcement of a position in law, medicine, and college teaching has been reported to draw as many as 300 to 400 letters of response (Dorfman, 1982). Recently, I/O psychologists have become interested in recruitment because the process has become more than simply finding applicants. The real objective of recruitment is to find particular people who have specific qualifications or potential and get them to apply. This points to the relationship between recruitment and selection. Recruitment can provide a large pool of high-potential job applicants.

Discrimination and Affirmative Action in Recruitment

In describing the nature of the **chilling effect**, the *Uniform Guidelines* (1978) comment on recruitment discrimination. The chilling effect is a discriminatory practice affecting an organization's applicant pool. That is, a business firm can have a reputation in the local community as being uninterested in or "chilly" toward certain groups of potential employees. Before employment discrimination became illegal, "chilliness" was blatant. Some advertisements would contain a line suggesting that women or some minority group may as well not apply for the job. Such statements are no longer lawful; however, more subtle versions of these sentiments remain. Word gets out that women or minority members will not be hired even if they apply, or that they will not be promoted, or that in some fashion they will be at a disadvantage to work for this company. Whenever this kind of discriminatory practice becomes known, members of the affected group(s) do not bother to apply. Thus, the organization produces a chilling effect.

As mentioned previously, the *Guidelines* define affirmative action as a way to speed the process of equality in employment by active recruitment of applicants. Affirmative action recruiting is a way for an employer to reverse its reputation of being chilly and to increase the diversity of its work force.

In setting up an affirmative action program, some questions arise. What minority groups should be included? What specific actions should be taken? How does the company know when it has done enough? The organization can use local labor force statistics to determine what groups to include. The local labor force is the group of individuals available for work in a local geographical area, such as a county. Counties collect data on the proportion of various ethnic groups in the area. Usually, the organization sets a goal for increasing the numbers of its minority and female employees to reflect the proportion of these groups in the local labor force. If the available workers are 35 percent female, 30 percent African American, and 10 percent Mexican American, then the organization should try to fill new openings to bring their total work force to these proportions.

Table 3.5   Targeting the Recruiting Effort

Ask	Consider
Who will be recruited?	Worker requirements from job analysis Affirmative action plans
How will the opening be announced?	Ads in major newspapers, community newspapers, and professional and trade journals Radio and television broadcasts Public and private employment agencies Bulletin boards at community service agencies College placement offices Company's own newsletter and bulletin boards
What should the announcement include?	Job requirements Compensation and benefits Description of the company Procedures for applying Special appeals for special applicants

From E. J. McCormick, P. R. Jenneret, and R. C. Mecham, *Position Analysis and Questionnaire.* Copyright © 1969 Purdue Research Foundation, Purdue University, W. Lafayette, Indiana.

Recruitment Techniques

The question of recruitment is one of effectively disseminating information about the job opening. Table 3.5 contains suggestions for accomplishing this. Three questions need to be asked. The first concerns the applicants to be recruited: Who are they? To decide, the recruiter must consider needs for special skills, as well as affirmative action goals. The next questions address recruitment techniques. Where should the announcement be placed? The answer to this depends on the particular applicant sought. Advertisements need to be placed where potential applicants are likely to see them. Ask yourself whether there are particular publications that the potential applicant reads. Finally, what information should the advertisement contain? Barber and Roehling (1993) provided an answer. They analyzed the advertisement information that job seekers use in deciding whether to apply for an advertised position. They found several aspects of the job and the ad itself to be important. Where the company was located, and how much the job paid were the two most important items of information. The subjects also were interested in benefits and were attracted to one organization that listed a three-week vacation. The researchers also found that the amount of information in the ad was important. Subjects reacted negatively to ads that contained little information.

Recruitment is routinely done by advertising in newspapers, trade journals, and other such publications. The hope is that these are read by the particular group of applicants targeted for hire. Employment agencies can also be notified of job openings. These include publicly operated state employment offices, as well as private agents called **headhunters.** For a fee, private agencies attempt to locate appropriate applicants for the organization. Although newspaper ads and employment agencies do find applicants, they may not be fully effective. Some research has shown that employees recruited through these sources are more likely to quit prematurely (Saks, 1994).

Two traditional and favored methods of recruiting are (1) accepting unsolicited applications from people who "walk in off the street," and (2) informing current employees of job openings and accepting their referrals. **Current employee referrals** have been used to fill all kinds of jobs, from those requiring no special skills to those demanding long periods of preparation. Businesses report that they find most of their production and clerical employees by accepting "walk ins" and current employee referrals (Gorlin, 1982). According to one study, these informal methods are effective in finding employees who can cope on the job. The researchers reported that informally recruited employees had received accurate information and had realized their job expectations (Saks, 1994). In contrast, newspaper ads and employment agencies are weak sources of realistic job information, as they provide few details or only positive information.

College Recruiting

If you visit your college placement office, you will probably find that several local and national companies have scheduled interviews with students who are about to graduate, particularly students in business and technical majors, such as engineering. The recruitment process has been described as "job marketing," that is, as a way to sell job seekers on the prospect of employment with a company (Maurer, Howe, & Yee, 1992).

Although it may be an appealing way to get job applicants, there is evidence that college recruiting is not entirely satisfactory. A major problem is reflected in the high turnover rate among employees who are recruited in this manner (Rendero, 1980). Although high turnover may be due to an unrealistic view of work that students hold, there is probably more to it than this. First, recruiters do not always provide realistic information about the job and the organization. Rynes and Boudreau (1986) did a survey of *Fortune* 1000 companies in an effort to explore college recruitment practices. They found that company brochures were used as the primary method of conveying information to prospective applicants, and recruiters generally received little training for doing their job. Second, recruiters do not always make valid estimations of the extent to which a student would fit into an organization. One study questioned whether recruiters are able to assess the congruence between applicants' work values and the organization's culture and values. In fact, applicants who were judged to fit the organization had work values that were more similar to the recruiter's than to the organization's (Adkins, Russell, & Werbel, 1994). Other research indicates that a recruiter's interpersonal skills and similarity in gender and education can affect a student's interest in a job. Thus, the picture seen in college recruitment is one in which the student is (1) given only general and overly positive printed information; (2) interviewed by someone who has not been trained in what to look for or even in how to conduct an interview; and (3) influenced to join the company by the recruiter's personal attributes.

Realistic Job Previews

The **realistic job preview** is an innovation that reflects the close relationship between recruitment and selection. The person being recruited is given a preview of what the job and the organization actually are like, and the selection specialist gets a preview of the applicant's response to the job. In general, the method supplies more realistic information for the applicant and results in a better applicant pool. The manner in which the preview is conducted varies considerably, however. The preview can consist simply of an interview in which the recruit is told honestly about the drawbacks of the job. For example, if long hours or stressful conditions are expected, the person is told. At the other extreme, the job preview consists of a sample of work that the recruit performs under realistic conditions.

Realistic job previews appear to have some advantages. They may help the applicant make a more reasoned decision about a position with the company, and as a result, reduce turnover. Previews also may reduce the wear and tear on an individual who otherwise would engage in trial-and-error job hopping until the right job is found. (It is not unusual for college graduates to leave their first job within a couple of years.) It has been difficult to show that job previews actually do have these effects, however. Some organizations have reported lower turnover among employees who were given a realistic job preview (Wanous, 1977), but evidence for reducing turnover has not been impressive in other companies (Reilly et al., 1981).

As a matter of fact, we are not clear as to why turnover is reduced *when* it is. Wanous (1977) proposed that previews lower expectations about the job; lowered expectations are easier satisfied; and satisfaction lowers turnover. The results of an analysis of several job preview studies supported this view (Premack & Wanous, 1985). On the other hand, Meglino et al. (1988) observed that the preview can be designed to reduce both overly positive expectations and overly negative impressions. When their recruits got both kinds of information, turnover was lower than when they received only information to reduce positive expectations. In another study, Meglino, DeNisi, and Ravlin (1993) found that recruits who were given a preview and who had been previously exposed to the job were more likely to quit the job during a probationary period than after the probation.

---

*M*ain
*P*oints

Recruiting is the process of finding particular applicants. Applicants often are needed who have unique job qualifications or who can improve the diversity of the work force. To begin recruitment, the organization must consider these needs in deciding where to announce the opening and what details to include.

Recruiting is accomplished by means of a variety of techniques, both formal (such as newspaper ads) and informal (such as current employee referrals). Informal methods appear to be more effective in finding employees who will stay on the job. College recruiting is attractive to many companies. However, the practice is problematic because it results in high turnover. The realistic job preview is a technique that possibly provides a solution to the problem of high turnover of new employees. The typical preview conveys more and more accurate job information than other recruitment techniques. The rationale is that this will prevent premature turnover by helping applicants make more reasoned decisions about accepting a job.

CHAPTER SUMMARY

The primary question of personnel selection is how to find the best employees. Over the years, employers have had many ideas about what the "best employee" is like and about how to recognize him or her as an applicant. Some of these ideas have led to practices that unfairly discriminate against some applicants. In the 1960s and 1970s, legislation was passed to protect American workers from unfair practices. These measures include Title VII of the 1964 Civil Rights Act. The *Uniform Guidelines on Employment Selection Procedures,* based on Title VII, defines procedures by which employers can evaluate their own practices for fairness.

To find the best employee, the employer must know what the job requires. A variety of job analysis techniques are available for studying jobs and determining their requirements. Depending on the method used, the job analysis will show the tasks and duties of the job and/or the worker qualifications required by the job. This type of information is useful also for personnel functions other than selection. For example, job analysis is used in evaluating the worth of jobs for compensation plans and in developing recruitment programs.

The purpose of recruitment is to find applicants who have a high probability of being well qualified. Because qualified individuals may not be aware of a job opening or of their potential to perform well, recruitment needs to be deliberate and focused. Announcements of openings and efforts to encourage applicants need to be based on realistic information about the position and the organization. Affirmative action is an effort to recruit minority and female applicants, particularly when these groups are underrepresented in an organization's work force. A variety of recruitment techniques are available, including the realistic job preview, which is both a recruitment and a selection device.

STUDY QUESTIONS

1) What federal measures protect employees from unfair discrimination? Who are the protected groups, and what personnel practices do these measures cover?

2) What are the steps in conducting an adverse impact assessment?

3) What is the difference between job evaluation and job analysis?

4) In what ways are observation and survey research used in conducting a job analysis?

5) What are the steps involved in conducting a task analysis?

6) What is the difference between a critical incidents study and a job element study?

7) What are the advantages and disadvantages of using the PAQ for job analysis?

8) Why is affirmative action considered a recruitment issue?

9) When is an affirmative action plan likely to include a hiring quota?

10) What are the best recruitment techniques?

CONSIDER THIS

CONTROVERSY

In early 1995, while the U.S. government reviewed its employment requirements and the University of California dismantled its affirmative action programs, a public debate was being reported in newspapers nationwide. In the debate, affirmative action was defined as preferential selection and described as a program for hiring unqualified employees. There were two complaints: (1) that affirmative action resulted in reverse discrimination, that is, against white men, and (2) that because it promoted preferences for unqualified people, it stigmatized the very ones it was meant to help.

The U.S. Labor Department responded but found little evidence of reverse discrimination. There were fewer than 100 reverse discrimination cases among the 3,000 discrimination cases heard by the courts during 1990–94 (Ross, 1995). A White House report agreed that when affirmative action is done correctly, it does not lead to reverse discrimination. However, because affirmative action sometimes is not implemented correctly, federal employers were asked to check their programs and eliminate any quota or preference for the unqualified (Benac, 1995).

News reporters and columnists addressed the question of whether affirmative action harms those it is supposed to help. Civil rights advocates insisted that it had helped, and had given opportunities to people who had not had opportunities before (Freedman, 1995). An African-American professor wrote about the stigma attached to affirmative action. "Admitting that you have been helped by affirmative action is usually tantamount to admitting deficiency." She argued that discarding affirmative action would not change the fact that the qualifications of female and minority students and faculty are routinely doubted. In spite of the stigma, she believed affirmative action has helped. "Without affirmative action, it would never have occurred to any large, white research university to consider me for professional employment, despite my qualifications" (Painter, 1995).

Should we continue to extend special employment opportunities to minority members and women, or is special consideration of some job applicants unfair to others? Should affirmative action revert to its original meaning, that is, a way to enhance recruitment, rather than remain a hiring quota? At one time, we needed to do something to increase the diversity of America's work force. Do we still need to do this, or is the work force diverse enough?

what's in this chapter?

In the previous chapter, you learned what must be done prior to meeting and evaluating job applicants. Now, in chapter 4 (and later in chapter 5), you will learn some selection methods you can use to make the hiring decision itself. You will get information about particular selection devices: What they do best and the kinds of problems that may occur when you use them. You will discover that there are a variety of ways to get information on an applicant's work history. These methods include various types of application blanks, biographical inventories, résumés, and reference checks. In addition, you will learn how to use assessments of a job applicant's current behavior to make a selection decision. Interviews, assessment centers, and selection tests are all useful for assessing current behavior. In chapter 4, you will learn how a job interview can be effective, and you will find out how assessment centers are used in managerial selection. You will learn about selection testing in the next chapter.

Hardly anyone is ever hired without being interviewed at least once. Most are interviewed several times before they finally see the immediate supervisor of the job.

Chapter 4

Contents

William Congreve observed: "Married in haste, we repented at leisure" (1972, *The Old Bachelor*, act 5, scene 1, line 255). The modern interviewer might profitably paraphrase this: "Hired in haste, we repented at leisure." Yet one of the earliest findings of the McGill studies on the job interview was the remarkably early point in the interview at which decisions were reached (Webster, 1964). Springbett's (1954) study showed that his eight experienced interviewers reached their decision in an average of just under 4 minutes.

D. H. Tullar, T. W. Mullins, and S. A. Caldwell

Four-minute interview decisions are to I/O psychologists as three-minute eggs are to egg salad lovers: underdone. Finding and hiring the best person for a job is a complex process of data gathering and decision making that does not occur through a flash of insight. Rather, interviewing requires prior planning, careful conduct, and more than a little time. When an interview does not meet these requirements, the employer can make a hiring decision that is regretted later.

MAKING HIRING DECISIONS

In chapter 3, you learned about the first two steps in the selection of new personnel. The job must be analyzed and a large pool of applicants need to be drawn in by recruitment efforts. Now, in chapter 4, comes the big question. How do you determine who among these applicants is best to hire? This question is the major concern of selection specialists and is crucial to the organization because selection decisions can cost or save enormous amounts of money. For example, the productivity and loyalty of those who are hired can result in costs or savings. The problem in selection is to accurately predict who in the applicant pool will become capable, productive, and loyal employees. If the right applicants are identified, there is a savings; if not, there is a cost to the organization.

The personnel selection process primarily is reductionistic. It is meant to reduce a pool of applicants with unknown potential to the one best person for the job. This reductionistic process is accomplished by putting applicants through **multiple hurdles.** That is, applicants are examined in a series of steps by means of various selection methods, and at each step decisions are made to drop some of them from consideration. The number and identity of selection hurdles varies somewhat between organizations and depends on such factors as the type of job and the abilities and attitudes of the organization's personnel staff. Typically, however, the first hurdle is an application or résumé screening. Those who pass go on to the next hurdle, which can be a test or interview. Applicants are disqualified at each point. The final hurdle is an interview with the immediate supervisor, who usually has the last word in hiring because he or she must "live with" the new employee.

A large number of tools are available to those making these selection decisions. The tools differ mainly in the amount and type of information they provide. Some, such as applications, collect information about an applicant's *past,* for example. Such tools are based on the assumption that past behavior predicts future behavior. Others, such as tests, provide behavioral information about the *present* and are based on the assumption that present behavior predicts future behavior.

The key issue with the many, varied methods used to gather applicant information and make selection decisions is **validity**. Validity is characteristic of a selection method that performs effectively in obtaining accurate information and in yielding good selection decisions. That is, a valid selection method helps the employer hire the right person. A related issue is **reliability**. A reliable selection method performs consistently, time after time, in gathering information about an applicant. The reliability of judgments, such as those obtained from references or interviewers, is known as **interrater reliability**. This indicates whether raters agree with each other in their judgments. A method that is both reliable and valid is one that an employer can depend on to provide consistently accurate information. A method that is not reliable gives inconsistent information, as when two reference letters give conflicting views of the same applicant. A method also may not be valid, as when two reference letters give inaccurate or irrelevant information about an applicant.

Which job applicant is most likely to be a successful employee? To answer this question, selection procedures are combined in a multiple hurdle process that reduces the applicant pool to one or more who can be hired. Selection tools typically used in the multiple hurdle process are application or résumé screenings, tests, and interviews.

Some selection tools provide information about past experiences. Others examine present behavior. Two concerns about all selection tools are validity and reliability. Valid and reliable tools provide consistently accurate information about applicants, which can be used to predict who will be a good employee.

*M*ain
*P*oints

PERSONAL HISTORY ASSESSMENTS

Evaluating a person's history of education and work experience by means of an application blank is one of the oldest and still commonly used methods of selection. The basis for looking into a person's past is this: If the person has done something in the past, he or she probably can and will do it in the future. This perspective that the best predictor of future behavior is past behavior, is a recurrent theme throughout psychology.

Past experience can be viewed in two ways. We can look at a *sample* of it. That is, we can ask an applicant to describe and document a specific event in his or her past experience, or we can look at what we believe is a *sign* of it and infer that the experience occurred. For example, we may decide to use the amount of education or experience on similar jobs as signs that the person has the required knowledge and skill. The problems with some personal history methods of selection are that they ask for signs rather than samples of behavior from the past, and they limit the type of past experience considered. Researchers have pointed out that most applications and résumés are based on the implicit assumption that the *amount* of education and experience are good signs of the qualities associated with superior job performance (Schmidt et al., 1979). This approach, however, ignores the fact that there are differences in the quality of applicants' previous educational and work experiences. Some people do very well in their educational programs; others just barely muddle through. The same can be said about job performance. In addition, the KSAs associated with superior job performance may have been acquired through less formal experiences, such as volunteer work and community service, but these experiences often are ignored.

Applications and Biographical Inventories

Several procedures are available for collecting information about the applicant's past. The standard job application blank traditionally has been used to evaluate education and work experience. In an effort to answer questions about the validity of the standard application blank, I/O psychologists have developed other techniques. These include weighted application blanks, biographical inventories, and the Behavioral Consistency Method of Unassembled Examining, a procedure used for collecting information on a range of experiences.

Standard Application Blanks

Although routine information is gathered with this instrument, the standard application blank otherwise tends not to be very standard. Questions of name, address, social security number, educational degrees, work experience, and military experience are usually included. Beyond this, the other questions on an application blank usually depend on what the organization has asked in the past and on what other companies are asking.

The questions on application blanks must conform to the requirements of fair employment law. Questions about the applicant's race, nationality, religion, age, marital status, and previous arrest record regularly appeared on application blanks as late as the 1950s and early 1960s. However, fair employment regulations made them

THE WIZARD OF ID   **Brant parker and Johnny hart**

By permission of Johnny Hart and Creators Syndicate, Inc.

Section II: Establishing a Strong Work Force

unlawful. Questions about arrest records tend to be discriminatory because minority members are more often arrested, although not necessarily convicted. Therefore, it is acceptable to ask about convictions, but not about arrests because the question provides the means for discrimination. The question of age is needed currently only to verify that the applicant is within the legitimate working age range–between 18 and 70. The question on age should be no more specific than this. Information about applicants' sex and ethnicity do have to be collected in order to conduct adverse impact studies. These questions, however, do not have to appear on the application blank, and they should not. Many organizations collect the sex and ethnicity data they require for adverse impact studies by means of an "affirmative action" form that is returned and maintained separately from the application blank.

You may wonder to what extent employers have actually revised their application blanks to meet the legal requirements. Burrington (1982) reviewed a sample of applications used by state governments and found a number of items that were illegal or questionable with regard to potential discrimination. Table 4.1 lists the kinds of inappropriate items that sometimes appear on applications. Because such items provide personal information that can bias the selection decision, they need to be deleted from any employer's application blank.

Standard application blanks are used to screen applicants for minimum job requirements. This screening can be economical in that applicants who clearly are not acceptable are disqualified early. The expense of a costly process of tests and interviews can be saved in this way. Of course, it must be clear that the disqualification is appropriate. Qualifications used to screen applicants must be established by job analysis as actually being the minimum necessary for successful job performance. Research has indicated that previous work experience can be used to predict job

Table 4.1　　　　　Unfair Application Questions

Some questions are inappropriate for application blanks because they provide personal information that can bias the selection decision.

Biasing Questions		Type of Personal Information
1.	Are you married?	Gender or Marital Status
2.	Do you prefer Miss or Mrs.?	"　　　　　"
3.	How old are you?	Age
4.	When were you born?	"
5.	What year did you finish school?	"
6.	What is your race?	Race or Ethnicity
7.	Where were you born?	"　　　"
8.	Are you a native English speaker?	"　　　"
9.	Have you ever been arrested?	"　　　"
10.	Do you have any handicaps?	Disability
11.	How would you rate your health?	"

Reprinted with permission of *Public Personnel Management,* published by the International Personnel Management Association, 1617 Duke St., Alexandria, VA 22314, 703-549-7100.

performance. However, we must be careful here because certain factors can affect this relationship between past job experience and future performance. McDaniel, Schmidt and Hunter (1988) found that the accuracy of the prediction of future behavior depends on the complexity of the job and on the actual number of years of past experience. The prediction was stronger when the job was less complex and required comparatively low levels of experience (such as 3 years versus 12 years).

One way to improve the quality of application screening decisions is to look for indicators of actual past behaviors rather than mere past exposures, and establish that these past behaviors are the same as or clearly similar to the behaviors necessary on the job (Schmidt et al., 1979; Wernimont & Campbell, 1968). For example, if the job requires creative problem solving, it is better to have applicants provide information about events in which they demonstrated this ability rather than to infer the ability from their past job titles or other such credentials.

Weighted Applications and Biographical Inventories

If application blanks are going to be used to make predictions about the future behavior of applicants, then we should ask whether anything can be done to assure users of their accuracy. Owens and Schoenfeldt (1979; Owens, 1968) asked this question and illustrated how the standard application blank can be changed into a device that can be scored and used like a valid test to predict the future performance of applicants. They described two modifications of the application: **weighted application blanks** and **biographical inventories.** The weighted application blank and the biographical inventory differ in length, extensiveness of questioning, and general appearance. The biographical inventory is longer and more extensive. The weighted application looks like an application blank; the biographical inventory resembles a psychological test. Like personality tests, the biographical inventory usually incorporates the closed response format in which the applicant chooses one of several answers (as in multiple-choice items). An exception is the futures autobiography, a form of the biographical inventory in which open-ended questions are used. The futures autobiography is designed to collect information about applicants' plans and hopes for their futures (Tullar & Barrett, 1976).

Development of both the weighted application and the biographical inventory require empirical research. First, personal or biographical information (**biodata**) is collected from a sample, usually the current employees of the organization. Second, a measure of job performance is obtained on each member of the sample to use as a **criterion measure.** Third, the personal data are matched with the performance data on an item-by-item basis. This requires that each item of personal data be translated into a numerical score and correlated with the score on the performance measure. The correlation indicates the extent to which the personal item characterizes those who succeed on the job. This method of developing items for application blanks and biographical inventories is actually a validity study in which the instrument is evaluated for its ability to predict job behavior. This validation strategy is discussed more fully in chapter 5.

A wide range of personal information can be included in the biodata study (see figure 4.1). Some information may be factual and verifiable, such as education, previous employment, military service, financial condition, and place of residence. Other data may be more attitudinal and correspondingly

FACTOR	TYPES OF ITEMS
Athletic involvement	Items on participation in athletic activities and events
Social extraversion and popularity	Items on participation and effectiveness in social situations
Religious activity	Items on participation in religious and charitable organizations
Warmth of parental relationships	Items about close relationships with parents
Academic achievement	Items on expected and actual success in academic tasks
Academic interest	Items on interest and enjoyment of school

Figure 4.1. *Factors and types of items used in biographical inventories. Biodata questionnaires include both factual and attitudinal questions (see sample questions) that reflect a wide range of personal information.*

Adapted from B. J. Eberhardt and P. M. Muchinsky, "An Empirical Investigation of the Factor Stability of Owens' Biographical Questionnaire" in Journal of Applied Psychology, 67:138-145, 1982; W. A. Owens *and L. F. Schoenfeldt, "Toward a Classification of Persons" in* Journal of Applied Psychology Monograph, 65:569-607, 1979.

Sample Items

How successful were your teachers in arousing your academic interests?

In high school, how much class participation and discussion were allowed?

In general, how much did you like your high school teachers?

Hou much have you liked school?

How adequate do you feel your high school education was?

less verifiable. Because the items are validated according to the degree to which they actually predict a performance criterion, we can be less concerned about the extent to which they appear on the surface to reflect the tasks of the job.

The criterion used in the biodata study may be an indicator that the employee is a good worker, such as a performance evaluation. It also may be an indicator that the person is a good organizational citizen, such as accident rate or length of employment. Job tenure and turnover frequently are used in such studies. In choosing a criterion measure for a study, the researcher should consider not simply what measures are easy to get but also what behavior each measure describes. If the aim of the study is to predict those who stay with the organization, then turnover records are appropriate. If, however, the aim is to predict productivity or safe behavior, then supervisor ratings and accident records are more appropriate.

Correlations between a criterion measure and biodata items justify the use of biodata items for applicant screening. Those items that are strongly related to the criterion measure can be expected to predict future job behavior. Those that are not strongly related are less able to do so. The strength of the relationship indicates the strength of the prediction; therefore, item correlations can be used to assign scoring weights to item responses. Although application and biographical inventory responses are not correct or incorrect as test answers are, the principle of weighting is the same. In scoring test items, a weight of 1 is assigned for a correct answer and a weight of 0 for an incorrect answer. For biodata items, values *between* 0 and 1 are assigned. Values closer to 1 (and equal to the correlation) are given for responses strongly associated with the criterion measure; values closer to 0 are given for those with a smaller correlation.

You may be wondering just how well these instruments predict job behavior. If they are carefully developed, they can perform quite well. Reilly and Chao (1982) reviewed several biodata studies done with different occupational groups. In general, these studies showed successful results. For example, biodata instruments were used successfully to predict office workers' job performance level and turnover (Cascio, 1976; Brush & Owens, 1979). Training success also has been predicted with biodata (Drakeley, Herriot, & Jones, 1988). Biodata inventories have proved useful in selecting for military occupations (Hoiberg & Pugh, 1978; Webster et al., 1978).

Biodata Items

How does one develop a biodata instrument? Items can be obtained from several sources. Items currently appearing on application blanks used by the company can be evaluated in a biodata study. Biodata research literature can provide items also. Owens and Schoenfeldt's (1979) research is one good source; Eberhardt and Muchinsky's (1982) research is another. Russell, Mattson, Devlin, and Atwater (1990) described a procedure they used for developing items from the life histories of youthful subjects. Biodata items were constructed from personal history essays in which high school experiences played a major part. This life history procedure can be useful when applicants have no previous work experience comparable to what they will be doing on the job, as when a company hires employees for entry-level jobs with the intention of moving them by means of a "fast track" into higher positions.

Two questions are relevant when we collect biographical data for use in selection. One concerns the accuracy of the responses. Do applicants answer these questions truthfully, or do they try to make themselves look good? If applicants do respond inaccurately, what can be done about it? Mael (1991) suggested that faking and socially desirable responding can be curbed by using items that refer to discrete and external events, are objective, and correspondingly are verifiable. Factual information can be verified; however, it is difficult to determine whether an applicant is truthful on attitudinal items. Earlier research on faking most often addressed factual items that were easily verified. Responses to these items were not found to be perfectly accurate, but the inaccuracy was not great. Most people answered these objective questions honestly (Owens, 1976). They were less likely to answer subjective questions accurately, but not much less so (Shaffer, Saunders, & Owens, 1987). More recently, researchers have investigated the effects of giving directions to respondents pertaining to their accuracy. Becker and Colquitt (1992) compared responses of actual job applicants to the responses of an experimental sample who were told to try to make themselves look good. They found that subjects were able to fake the instrument. They found also that some faking occurred naturally in the job applicant sample, particularly on items that were more job relevant and less historical and objective than other items. Kluger and Colella (1993) found that faking was less likely to occur in a sample of applicants for a nursing job when they were warned against faking. Perhaps, applicants have a natural tendency to make themselves look good, which they can suppress if they are told specifically to answer honestly.

The second question about biodata raises ethical and legal concerns. These items ask about personal areas of life, and it is understandable that applicants complain about some of them. For example, questions about parental disciplinary practices can be found on biodata instruments. Even if such practices do relate to job success, one might be taken aback to encounter items of this nature on a job application. In addition to the possible invasion of privacy, the use of biodata to make selection decisions may operate to perpetuate the status quo. That is, if a company uses its present employees to develop a biodata instrument, then those hired in the future will tend to be the same kind of people as those hired in the past. This process can stagnate an organization. It also can exclude some people. If the sample used in developing the instrument included few minority members, and if new minority applicants have different personal experiences than majority employees, then they may be disadvantaged. Although such disparate effects have not been shown to be systematic (e.g., Reilly & Chao, 1982), the use of a biodata instrument should be investigated for adverse impact.

OPM's Behavioral Consistency Method

A selection device developed at the U.S. Office of Personnel Management (OPM), called the **Behavioral Consistency Method**, is similar to application and biodata instruments in that it is used to collect personal history information and is based on the rationale that past experience predicts future behavior. It is different from these other methods in that it uses samples of past behavior rather than signs, and it incorporates an open response format for the questions.

To develop a selection instrument by this method, the critical dimensions of a job are identified and ranked through job analysis. Critical dimensions are those that differentiate between superior and marginal employees. Each dimension is listed on the instrument and described briefly. The applicant is instructed to give samples of past experiences he or she believes are relevant to the dimension. Past achievements in a variety of settings can be listed, not simply those relating to paid work and education. In addition, the applicant also provides information on the outcome of the experience, the credit he or she claims in the case of team projects, and the name of someone who can verify the information. Table 4.2 provides an example. In scoring, the applicant's answers are compared to a list of differentiating job behaviors for each dimension and rated. As with any questionnaire that uses open response or essay items, scoring is difficult. The method requires skill in rating answers, which means a rater must be trained (BRE Exam Preparation Manual, 1977; Schmidt et al., 1979).

Résumés

In making selection decisions for managerial and technical positions, we frequently request résumés, which function as a special form of the application blank. The major difference is that the items of personal information included on the résumé

Table 4.2

Sample Job Dimension and Question Developed by the Behavioral Consistency Method

Sample Dimension:	Ability to get things done within a business organization.
Question:	What have you actually done in the past that demonstrates your ability to get things done within an organization?

In Writing Answers, Include:

1. What the problem or objective was
2. What you actually did and when
3. What the outcome or result was
4. Estimated percentage of the credit you claim for this achievement
5. Name, address, and phone of someone who can verify the information

Sample Answer: I analyzed a budgetary control method that had been proposed and showed that the method would have resulted in inadequate control had it been adopted. I described the difficulties in a written report and discussed them in a managerial meeting. As a result, the proposed method was not adopted and my boss praised me for the work. I did this entirely on my own. My supervisor at ABC Chemical Company, Kay Mills, can verify this.

From F. L. Schmidt, J. R. Caplan, S. E. Bemis, et al. (1979), *The Behavioral Consistency Method of Unassembled Examining*. Washington, DC: U.S. Office of Personnel Management, Personnel Research and Development Center, Research Branch.

are left to the discretion of the applicant. Some information is included in both résumés and application blanks, such as work experience and education. Beyond this, résumés vary tremendously. Some résumé writers begin with a statement of their career objective. In fact, some job seekers have two or three different résumés, with the content rearranged to suit two or three different career objectives. Other information that may be listed includes memberships in career- or work-oriented organizations, volunteer work activities, hobbies and interests, publications, awards and honors, special credentials and certificates, and sometimes a list of references. (See the sample résumé in table 4.3.)

Résumés, like applications, are used by employers to screen job applicants. However, there are problems with the résumé as a selection device. The first problem is due to the potential lack of standard information in résumés. It is unlikely that comparable information will be obtained on all applicants because the particulars of the résumé are decided by the résumé writer. Unstructured interviews, as we will see later, have this same problem, and the difficulty lies in comparing applicants on the basis of different types of information. This is comparable to grading students on the basis of different information. Suppose, for example, you were graded on your exam performance, and someone else was graded on class attendance. To the extent that applicants are evaluated on varying information, the validity of selection decision is weakened.

Résumé inaccuracy presents the second problem. Probably, résumé writers try to present a positive image, and in so doing they may write a résumé that

Table 4.3	Sample Résumé

BARBARA R. MARTIN
3091 22nd Street, Apt. 14
San Francisco, CA 94110
(415) 239–1664

Objective

Position in personnel selection, with duties in development, administration, and validation of personnel tests and other selection instruments.

Education

Coursework toward M. S. in Industrial/Organizational psychology in progress, San Francisco State University.
    Courses in I/O psychology, vocational testing, and research methodology.
B.A., Psychology, University of Oregon, 1991.
    Courses in general psychology, statistics, social psychology, and personnel psychology; outside coursework in sociology and business.

Work Experience

1994 to present: Personnel clerk, Finnegan Flight Services, Inc., San Francisco.
    Duties include preparing employment notices, screening applicants, arranging and conducting interviews, and completing employment forms and reports on all personnel actions.
1991 to 1994: Cashier, part time, Associated Students, University of Oregon.

Community Service

1989 to 1991: Volunteer reader on periodic basis, Logan Street School for the Blind, Eugene, Oregon.

References

Furnished upon request.

---

is inaccurate. Omission of negative information, inclusion of positive but inaccurate relevant information, and inclusion of positive but irrelevant information are all inaccuracies that weaken the device as a selection tool. Although there is little research on the accuracy of résumé information, it is generally thought that résumé fraud is widespread, particularly with respect to job history and educational information. Employers should verify applicants' information as much as possible. Résumé fraud, whether real or not, is an apparent problem in industry, and special businesses have come into existence for the very purpose of investigating the backgrounds of potential employees. Their advertisements, in such trade publications as *Personnel Journal,* offer services in checking job histories, educational credentials, and criminal records.

Letters of Reference

Reference letters, like other personal history devices, presumably can provide information about past behavior that can be used to predict future behavior. Previous employers, for example, have access to job relevant information on applicants that they can describe. In addition, they can be used to verify information already provided by the applicant. The question is how to obtain complete and accurate information from references.

Format of the reference technique varies from unstructured to structured. The unstructured reference letter probably is used more often. The reference person simply writes a letter about the applicant to the prospective employer, giving whatever information seems relevant and desirable. Some questionnaires sent to reference persons are equally unstructured. They include open-ended questions on a few aspects of the applicant's character, or they ask for an evaluation of the applicant's ability to perform the job. At the other extreme, the structured reference request asks for specific information or answers to a list of questions. Short essays, ratings, and forced-choice items referring to a wide range of work behaviors and qualifications have been used in the structured reference form. In a forced-choice item, the reference person selects one of two descriptors that best fits the applicant. The descriptors have been paired so that they are equally positive or equally negative; therefore, the reference person can give an overall positive recommendation and still provide some useful information to the prospective employer (Carroll & Nash, 1972). This technique also is used in performance evaluations (see chapter 7).

Using reference information for selection presents some serious problems. One problem is inconsistency. References for a single applicant do not always agree, which makes it hard to know whom to believe (Reilly & Chao, 1982). Letters of recommendation for students applying for graduate school have shown a similar lack of consensus (Baxter et al., 1981). Another problem is that the information often is incomplete and inaccurate. The inconsistency and inaccuracy may not be intentional, as it could result from the format of the reference inquiry. For example, in the unstructured reference format, as in the free-form résumé, relevant information shedding bad light on the applicant can be omitted. Because it is the reference person who decides what information will be sent in a free-form letter, we can expect that the type of information collected will vary across references. Thus, the unstructured reference format will reduce standardization in the selection process, which means that applicants have to be compared on the basis of different types of information. This situation can be improved by using a structured reference format.

Other reasons for the problem of inconsistency and inaccuracy concern the reference writer's own abilities and motivations. People vary in their ability to evaluate others, to understand questionnaire items, and to express evaluations so that it is clear to the reader exactly what is being said about the applicant. Sometimes judgments are made on the basis of inadequate information. References can be requested from persons who have had little opportunity to observe the applicant's behavior, such as when the respondent is the applicant's superior but not immediate supervisor. People who write reference letters also differ in the leniency of their evaluations and in their views of what is satisfactory performance. Just as some teachers are more lenient in evaluating students than others are, so too are some reference writers more lenient.

For most of these problems, structuring the reference format can help. Including a response category of "no opportunity to observe" will be helpful to those who may not have had close contact with the applicant. Defining a standard against which to compare the applicant is beneficial also. For example, the respondent can be asked to compare the applicant to the average or to the best employee.

Validity of the reference check also is weakened when reference persons are not motivated to respond to the request. Ryan and Lasek (1991) point out that a former employer who has negative information may be fearful that sending it would result in a defamation lawsuit filed by the former employee. Such fearfulness can result in an incomplete or overly positive reference, which can mislead the new employer. However, companies considering applicants for hire must protect themselves against potential charges of negligent hiring, and one way to do this is with thorough background checks. "Negligent hiring," a legal term, is the basis for bringing an employer to court when an employee causes some harm to another person. The charge is that the employer should have known this was likely to happen and was negligent in not finding out, as through background checks.

There are three possible solutions to this problem. One, according to Ryan and Lasek (1991), former employers can protect themselves against defamation charges when they give honest information to the reference request, if they have documentation that the information is true. For example, performance evaluation procedures that are routinely done carefully, documented, and shared with the employee can provide this evidence. A second solution for the company considering the applicant is to get help from a background-checking agency, such as those who operate to counter résumé fraud. The third solution is suggested by a recent study that validated a method of analyzing the content of the standard, free-form letter. Aamodt, Bryan, and Whitcomb (1993) were intrigued by a strategy for extracting traits from letters that was proposed by Peres and Garcia in 1962. These earlier researchers attempted to make reference letters more useful by evaluating specifically *what* the reference said rather than simply checking its positiveness. Their procedure involved identifying and counting the traits used to describe an applicant and comparing these to a previously established list of traits that are relevant to the job. In their validation study, Aamodt, Bryan, and Whitcomb (1993) found that the letter analyses were able to predict performance in a sample of graduate student teachers. Although such analyses are time consuming to do, perhaps they present employers with a way to more effectively use the free-form reference letters they are likely to receive.

*M*ain *P*oints

Assessing the applicant's personal history of work and life experience is one of the most important approaches to personnel selection today. The rationale of this approach is that past experience is a good predictor of future performance. The key is to determine what is relevant about the past and to access that information.

The application blank is a traditional way to get information about training and work experience. However, because the standard application is not very effective for this purpose, I/O psychologists have developed revisions and related strategies. Weighted application blanks provide a way to evaluate and score the information applicants give. Biographical inventories also provide scores and, because they include testlike questions on various types of biodata, they can gather information about a range of past personal experiences, not simply training and job experience. The behavioral consistency method is an open response way to collect background information about work abilities, in which applicants write short essays describing what they did in the past that proves they can do the work.

Résumés and reference checks are other ways to get information about personal history. Both methods present problems to the user because they often do not provide comparable information on applicants. This is because the material included is at the discretion of the writer rather than the employer. These methods also can yield inaccurate information, a problem that is serious for employers who rely on these background checks for legal protection.

ASSESSMENTS OF CURRENT BEHAVIOR

The selection methods discussed so far are designed to get information about the applicant's past. In contrast, selection tests, interviews, and assessment centers focus on the present. These methods use samples of the applicant's current behavior to predict job performance. The past is not completely ignored, however. In achievement tests, for example, we recognize the role of past experience in learning the information and skills demonstrated in good test performance. We can also focus interviews on past work experiences. For the most part, however, emphasis on the past is secondary to emphasis on current behavior.

Many organizations use psychological tests to gather information on applicants' current abilities. Usually, tests are given as a second hurdle in the selection process after an application screening. Written tests can contain items of job-relevant information, and performance tests can demonstrate job-relevant skills. Use of psychological tests is a major issue in selection. Testing involves considerations of validity, special administrative and interpretative techniques, and a number of fair employment questions. Because of the complexity of this issue, I delay discussion of selection testing until chapter 5.

Interviews

Hardly anyone is ever hired for work without being interviewed at least once. In fact, a new employee may have been interviewed several times—by employment agency staff, company recruiters, personnel department interviewers, and the immediate supervisor of the job—before finally being hired. Interviews have been used for early screening to get preliminary information from applicants. Interviews also are conducted late in the selection process to determine whether an applicant would be a suitable employee.

The selection interview typically has two purposes: to get information from the applicant and to judge the applicant on the basis of this information. The judgment often is used immediately if the interviewer is in a position to make a hiring decision. The interview evaluation also can be combined with other assessments of the applicant and used later to make a hiring decision. Factual information, such as previous education and experience, can be obtained in interviews. More appropriately, however, interviews are used to gather interpersonal information, such as an applicant's social ease and confidence, speaking ability, and manner of interacting. The information that is sought needs to be job relevant and fair, however. In the discussion of applications, you learned that some factual questions are inappropriate, such as age, ethnicity, religion, and marital status. These are inappropriate in the interview as well because they are not relevant to work performance and can be used to discriminate. Generally, the relevance of all interview questions needs to be established through job analysis.

Interview Validity

Is the interview a good way to get valid information to use in selection decision making? Perhaps yes; perhaps no. Current research shows that it is better than we used to believe, but still its value is determined by how carefully it is planned and conducted.

Historically, I/O psychologists studied the interview and tried to establish its validity, as they studied other selection methods. Their research showed that some methods were valid; however, there was not a great deal of favorable evidence for the interview. The interview, of course, was and is still a popular method, and the failure of the researchers to show that it was a valid way to select employees did not stop people from using it. In 1955, Ghiselli and Brown observed:

> **Many organizations that have refused to accept some other carefully evaluated selective procedures because the validity of that procedure appeared to be too low have continued to use the interview without any attempt whatsoever to evaluate its effectiveness. (p. 165)**

It is not surprising, therefore, to find that much of the newer research has accepted the interview as a selection method that is here to stay. Researchers and practitioners have focused on developing new and improved versions of the popular method. In the new versions, the interview has more structure and the interviewer has more control. Relevant questions are incorporated. Often, the interview is conducted by a panel of interviewers who share the tasks of asking questions, taking notes, and evaluating applicants.

Meanwhile, reviews of research on the effectiveness of actual interviews (some of which incorporated the new structuring and some of which did not) continued to report woefully low indicators of validity (e.g., Hunter & Hunter, 1984). Better evidence was reported, however, when researchers began to evaluate the improved interview methods as compared to the unstructured, casual conversation that traditionally has constituted the job interview. Reviewers of the research began reporting that more accurate decisions could be made if the interview was structured than if it was not (Huffcutt & Arthur, 1994; McDaniel et al., 1994; Wiesner & Cronshaw, 1988).

It may look now as if we have turned the corner on this problem. Certainly, if employers adopted the controlled, structured interview format that is being evaluated in the research, they would have a valid selection method. However, there are no signs that this has occurred yet. In order for it to occur, employers need to be convinced that the unstructured interview is not an effective way to select employees.

Interview Problems and Solutions

The typical selection interview is susceptible to a variety of contaminating variables that weaken it. Some of the most common problems and suggested solutions are summarized in table 4.4 and discussed in the next sections. Some of these problems result from human difficulties in judging other people from a

Table 4.4 — Summary of Common Problems and Errors in Selection Interviews

Problem	Source of Problem	Solutions
Inconsistent, inadequate information is obtained.	Unplanned, unstructured interview format is used. Interviewer considers early and/or negative information only.	Structure interview format. Train interviewer to delay decision. Do not require clinical judgment of interviewee.
Irrelevant traits are rated.	General rating form and standard items are used for all interviews.	Do thorough job analysis, and tailor rating items to job.
Lack of agreement exists among interviewers (unreliability).	Traits are not observable in interview. Ratings are contaminated by interviewer bias and stereotype.	Structure interview. Require ratings of observable traits only. Specify appropriate standard of comparison. Train to avoid bias.
Ratings contain contrast effects.	Inadvertent up or down grading due to contrasts of interviewee with others.	Vary order of interviews. Coach interviewers on contrast error avoidance. Specify appropriate standard of comparison.

small sample of their behavior. Others stem from the nature of the interview itself, including its sometimes dual purpose. That is, the interviewer is asked to evaluate traits that may not be demonstrated in the interview process. Then, on the basis of this information, the interviewer is asked to make difficult clinical judgments about the applicant's suitability for employment. Although interviewers are able to evaluate certain characteristics accurately, such as speaking ability, other traits, such as work motivation, are not apparent in the interview. Only those traits that can be demonstrated in the short period of the interview should be evaluated. Interviewers who purposely base their decisions on applicant characteristics that are apparent in the interview, such as interpersonal and oral communication skills, actually are more accurate in their interview judgments (Graves & Karren, 1992).

Lack of Consistent Information When an interview is conducted as a casual and rambling conversation, a door is opened to several problems. One is inconsistent information. Interviews sometimes begin with a vague request, such as "Tell me something about yourself"; thus, the information obtained can vary widely among applicants. The particular information will depend on what the applicant chooses to report. But, you may object: Does this interview not provide interesting information about an applicant that otherwise would not be gained? Although this may be true, it is also true that this interesting information may not be relevant to the job and may bias the interview evaluation. The problem resulting from this lack of consistency is that applicants will be evaluated on the basis of different information. This is as unfair as evaluating applicants with different résumé information.

Structuring the interview can deal with this problem because a **structured interview** is controlled by the interviewer rather than by the applicant. Campion and his associates (Campion, Pursell, & Brown, 1988) have noted that there are many ways to structure an interview and have suggested a procedure that they found to be valid and fair. First, a list of questions are developed from job analysis information. Questions that elicit information on important job-relevant characteristics should be included. All applicants are asked all questions in the same order. A panel of interviewers is used to record and rate the applicant's responses. In this manner, all applicants are treated in the same way, and comparisons between applicants are made on the basis of the same information.

Some interviewers like to review applications or résumés before interviewing job applicants. Is this a good idea? Probably not. From the research, it appears that doing so biases the interview evaluation. Dipboye (1982; Dipboye & Macan, 1988) proposed that the interviewer's preinterview impressions of the applicant will cause the interviewer to try to confirm these impressions in the interview session. Several studies have supported this hypothesis. In a field study, Phillips and Dipboye (1989) found that managers' preinterview evaluations were positively correlated with their postinterview evaluations, indicating that impression-confirming strategies were used. Similarly, student interviewers who reviewed applications rated applicants as showing better interview performance to the extent that they looked good on paper (Macan & Dipboye, 1994). Other research indicates that the bias also is detectable from the interviewer's behavior in the interview. Dougherty, Turban, and Callender (1994) analyzed the behavioral styles of interviewers and found that they confirmed their preinterview evaluations of the applicant. For example, they expressed positive regard toward those for whom they had positive first impressions. One way that such actions can be initiated is when the interviewer uses the application review to develop questions for individual applicants. In one study, student interviewers reviewed application materials and then developed questions for each applicant. Analysis showed that the students had used an impression-confirming strategy to develop their questions, particularly for applicants who appeared to be less suitable for the job. These applicants were more likely to receive a question seeking negative information than were the apparently suitable applicants (Binning et al., 1988). Macan and Dipboye (1988) similarly found that questions prepared for applicants with poor credentials were more likely to be negative than questions prepared for applicants with moderate or good credentials.

Job Relevance of Rated Traits—A second problem that occurs in the unstructured interview is that irrelevant information is gathered. Even if an interviewer is accurate in assessing applicant characteristics, the data will not be useful unless the characteristics are relevant to the job. Jobs that require the specific traits typically displayed in interviews can be effectively filled by interview assessments. For example, retail sales clerks must have good interpersonal skills, which can be observed easily in an interview. Interview assessments of sales clerk applicants and later sales performance have been found to be associated, indicating that the interview has good predictive validity for this job (Arvey et al., 1987). Not all jobs require interpersonal skills, however. Evaluating applicants on such skills when they are unnecessary for job performance lowers the validity of the interview and leads to decisions in which more suitable applicants are overlooked. For example, some interviewers look for people with "pleasant personalities," a characteristic more often attributed to extroverts. When a job does not require an extroverted personality, then hiring decisions made on this basis can disadvantage introverts (Fletcher, 1987). Likewise, interviewers can have a preference for assertiveness and show this preference by being more likely to hire an assertive applicant (Gallois, Callan, & Palmer, 1992). When interviewers base their decisions on such traits, they should have good reasons to believe that they are required on the job.

Conducting a thorough job analysis and using the information to develop appropriate questions for the interview, as Campion et al. (1988) have suggested, should solve the problems of information relevance. Questions that result from a job study, like questions on some applications, can address the applicant's past. That is, they can require the applicant to recall and explore a past experience at work. Questions also can be more future oriented or hypothetical. In a structured procedure known as the **situational interview,** applicants are presented with hypothetical job situations and asked how they would respond. In both interviews, answers are evaluated according to the extent to which they are similar to responses obtained from successful employees on the job (Latham et al., 1980). An example of each kind of question is shown in table 4.5.

Interview structuring by incorporating job-relevant questions is an effective way to make interviews operate more effectively. In fact, some recent research suggests that carefully structured interviews can perform as well as cognitive ability tests, which have performed well in selection. Structured interviews can obtain different information than tests, which makes them valuable to use in combination with tests (Campion, Campion, & Hudson, 1994; Pulakos & Schmitt, 1995).

Table 4.5	**Sample Structured Interview Questions and Answers**

Future-Oriented Question

Suppose you had an idea for a change in work procedure to enhance quality, but there was a problem in that some members of your work team were against any type of change. What would you do in this situation?

Answers:

(5)   Excellent answer (top third of candidates)—Explain the change and try to show the benefits. Discuss it openly in a meeting.

(3)   Good answer (middle third)—Ask them why they are against change. Try to convince them.

(1)   Marginal answer (bottom third)—Tell the supervisor.

Past-Oriented Question

What is the biggest difference of opinion you ever had with a coworker? How did it get resolved?

Answers:

(5)   Excellent answer (top third of candidates)—We looked into the situation, found the problem, and resolved the difference. We had an honest conversation with the person.

(3)   Good answer (middle third)—Compromised. Resolved the problem by taking turns, or I explained the problem (my side) carefully.

(1)   Marginal answer (bottom third)—I got mad and told the coworker off, or we got the supervisor to resolve the problem, or I never have differences with anyone.

From M. A. Campion, J. E. Campion, and J. P. Hudson Jr., "Structured Interviewing: A Note on Incremental Validity and Alternative Question Types" in *Journal of Applied Psychology,* 79:999. Copyright © 1994 by the American Psychological Association. Reprinted with permission.

Note. Both questions are intended to assess conflict resolution and collaborative problem-solving knowledge, skills, and other requirements.

Reliability of Judgments   Some other interview problems are due to the difficulty humans have in making judgments. This difficulty is shown when interview panelists do not agree in their evaluations of an applicant. This is a reliability problem; that is, the judgments are not consistent across raters. If evaluations of an applicant are accurate and valid, they will not vary greatly from one interviewer to another, yet they often do vary, particularly in unstructured interviews. This suggests that some of the weakness of the interview is actually due to rater errors.

You might guess that the process of using a structured interview can improve the interview panel's ability to judge an applicant's behavior and to produce consistent ratings. Structuring provides direction for the interview panel and questions that focus the panel on job-relevant attributes that are observable in the interview. There is some evidence to support this view. For example, the situational interview was found to improve the reliability of ratings (Maurer & Fay, 1988). A later study of structuring with past-oriented questions found that interviewer ratings were not inconsistent (Pulakos et al., 1996).

Standards of Comparison   Sometimes, the reason interviewer ratings are not reliable is that they are based on different standards. Evaluations are always made in comparison to something. An applicant is compared to other applicants or employees, or to some ideal applicant. Usually, the standard is not explicit and varies from one interviewer to another. For example, when an interviewer imagines an ideal applicant, this ideal contains some characteristics with which other interviewers agree and some with which others do not agree (Mayfield & Carlson, 1966). In areas in which the standards are not the same, we can expect that the evaluations will not agree, which is part of the reason for unreliability.

Organizations usually rely on the interviewer's conception of an ideal employee. However, there is no all-around right candidate. The ideal depends on the job. To establish that interviewers are all using the same appropriate standard of comparison, they need to be trained in the use of a structured interview format that defines the ideal employee. Briefing interviewers about what attributes to look for and providing them with job-relevant information about the right kind of person for the job can improve the reliability of their evaluations by making the standard of comparison explicit. When interviewers are given specific, job-relevant dimensions to use, they are more capable of differentiating between more- and less-qualified applicants than are other evaluators who rate applicants on the basis of general job dimensions (Osburn, Timmreck, & Bigby, 1981).

Another problem with interview comparisons results from the way in which we compare one applicant to another. Certainly, we should and do compare one applicant's test performance, job history, and interview behavior with that of other applicants for the same job. However, we have trouble if the comparisons are not standardized and done carefully. For example, we may distort the difference between applicants. This is **contrast error.** It occurs whenever an evaluation of one applicant is unduly influenced by earlier applicants. To demonstrate, suppose an interviewer sees two poorly qualified applicants and then someone who is actually about average. A contrast error results if the average person is rated higher than he or she deserves because of the influence of the below average applicants. One way to deal with contrast error is to use several interviewers, change the order in which they see the applicants, and then average their ratings. Reordering can be done easily with videotaped interviews and a group of raters working independently.

Stereotypes and Interviewer Bias Race, age, sex, and physical attractiveness of an employee are usually irrelevant to job performance. As I mentioned earlier, however, stereotypes about these characteristics were used in the past to make hiring decisions. Because awareness and acceptance of fair employment is more widespread now, interviewers are increasingly sensitive to certain types of discrimination, such as racial discrimination. For example, Mullins (1982) found higher evaluations of African American applicants among equally qualified African American and white male pairs. Also, Pulakos and Schmitt (1995) found that their experience-based interview questions were equally valid for three applicant groups varying in ethnicity. However, discrimination due to stereotypes held by interviewers does still occur. For example, male applicants may be rejected unfairly when they apply for a female-dominated job (Arvey et al., 1987), just as female applicants may be unfairly rejected when they apply for jobs requiring seemingly male attributes. One study showed that interviewers preferred "baby faced" or female applicants for jobs requiring personal warmth, while male or mature-looking applicants were preferred for jobs requiring shrewdness and leadership (Zebrowitz, Tenenbaum, & Goldstein, 1991).

Personal characteristics of both the interviewer and the interviewee can influence interview judgments. For example, the interviewer's mood was found to affect the ratings of applicants, particularly those who were not obviously qualified. When in a bad mood, the interviewer gave lower ratings to these applicants than when in a good mood (Baron, 1993). Other interviewee characteristics have been reported to affect interviewer ratings. For example, an applicant's physical attractiveness can affect the hiring decision. Both students and experienced interviewers were influenced by the applicant's attractiveness (Gilmore, Beehr, & Love, 1986). Ratings given by interviewers to applicants for managerial positions showed the effect (Cash & Kilcullen, 1985).

Structuring the interview may be helpful. However, because these errors are founded in the interviewer's own thoughts or cognitive structure, the problem is likely to require a somewhat direct intervention. It is thought that errors in evaluating applicants can be reduced by giving interviewers error-avoidance training. Research on training raters for employee performance evaluation should be consulted because the rating process is similar. This research indicates that training can help produce more accurate evaluations, particularly if raters are coached on how to avoid common errors (Thornton & Zorich, 1980).

Interviewing Recommendations

I conclude that the typical unstructured interview is not a valid way to select employees. Such an interview is burdened with numerous, serious problems that compromise its effectiveness. Varying information is collected on applicants, sometimes because control over the interview is put in the hands of the interviewee, and sometimes because the questions are developed on-the-spot from an application or résumé. The job relevance of the collected information is often doubtful because there has been no job analysis and because the questions reflect the interviewer's personal preference for employee behavior. Other weaknesses are due to difficulties interviewers have in producing reliable and valid judgments of applicants when they are given no direction on what to look for. In such cases, interviewers must rely on their own, varying conceptions of the ideal applicant, and without any training on judgment errors to avoid, they are often unable to prevent bias from entering into the evaluation of applicants.

Throughout this discussion, I have recommended that employers structure their interviews in order to solve these problems and to strengthen the method as a selection tool. Research has demonstrated that the interview is valid only when it is structured. Experience-based or situational questions that have been developed from a job analysis should be used, and interviewers need to be instructed on how to use this format and to increase their awareness of judgment errors.

Assessment Centers

During World War II, the Office of Strategic Services (OSS) needed a way to select secret service agents. Men who could perform under stress needed to be distinguished from those who could not. The answer was found in Henry Murray's (1938) personality research. In Murray's study, a group of clinical specialists, each using his own diagnostic and evaluative tools, assessed the personalities of student volunteers. The OSS adopted a similar procedure for assessing their secret service applicants. In the OSS assessment center, each candidate was observed in individual and group activities and then assessed by a staff of scientists. Because stress resistance was of prime importance, assessment activities were designed to be stressful. The candidate had to meet deadlines, surmount obstacles, and respond to unpredicted events. Since that time, other centers for personality research have been developed. MacKinnon's at the University of California and Bray's at American Telephone and Telegraph are longitudinal projects in which personality structure and change were studied. MacKinnon's (1962) spanned 20 years, and Bray's (1982) continued for more than 25 years.

The **assessment center** has become a popular technique for selecting new employees and developing current employees. In 1973, Development Dimensions International (DDI, 1977) introduced a catalog of assessment center materials and noted that assessment centers were being used by more than 300 organizations. Two years later, DDI referred to the center as a well-recognized method being used by 1,000 companies. Executives and managers (Bray, Campbell, & Grant, 1974; Neidig & Martin, 1979), sales personnel (Bray & Campbell, 1968), and a variety of military personnel (Dyer & Hilligoss, 1980), including military recruiters selected for training (Borman, 1982), have been evaluated in assessment centers. Also, they are used to select people for public sector occupations, such as fire and police work (Coulton & Feild, 1995; Feltham, 1988; Fitzgerald, 1980).

Rationale and Method

Assessment centers are meant to simulate the job realistically. For example, commonly used behavioral dimensions in managerial assessment centers include such management-related abilities as organization, planning, and decision making

Table 4.6   Common Behavioral Dimensions Used in Managerial Assessment Centers

Organization and Planning:	Ability to organize work and plan ahead for self and group
Decision Making:	Ability and readiness for making decisions
Communication Skills:	Effectiveness in expressing ideas in written and oral form
Leadership:	Ability to get others to accept ideas and to move toward task accomplishment
Tolerance for Stress:	Ability to work effectively under pressure
Flexibility:	Ability to modify goals and directions
Initiative:	Willingness to start work activities
Creativity:	Ability to develop novel and imaginative solutions to problems
Risk Taking:	Willingness to take calculated risks

(see table 4.6). The rationale behind the use of an assessment center is that an applicant who can perform a sample of the job satisfactorily probably can perform the job. How true this is depends on the extent to which the job sample reflects the whole job. Good job sampling is absolutely crucial for valid assessment centers. Like other selection devices, the center depends on job analysis to sample the job. In fact, the assessment center is organized around behavioral dimensions identified through job analysis. Activities are chosen according to their capacity for creating a situation in which these dimensions can be demonstrated. Figure 4.2 outlines the procedure for developing an assessment center. Notice the amount of work required in the planning stages.

The assessment center can be located off site or on company grounds. Time required to conduct the center ranges from one day to one week. In the typical center, from six to twelve candidates participate in individual, dyadic, and group activities. The participants are observed and evaluated by a two- or three-person team of assessors for each group of six. The assessors can be outside consultants or members of the organization's own staff. Although the choice of assessors depends on the types of activities included in the assessment center as well as on the cost of outside help, there is evidence that validity is higher when psychologists rather than managers act as assessors (Gaugler et al., 1987). If company staff is used, training certainly must be given. Training should include instruction in group observation, evaluation methods, and rating errors.

Depending on the types of activities involved, assessors observe group interactions, evaluate written inputs from candidates, and conduct interviews. They usually write individual evaluative reports and confer as a group on areas of disagreement. At the end of the assessment process, the assessors as a group report on each candidate. Typically, candidates are given oral and written feedback on their performance. In addition, the organization receives a written report that contains a detailed evaluation of each candidate's potential. Identification of areas in which development is needed also is included in the report. Clearly, the assessment center can provide much information about candidates. However, because assessment

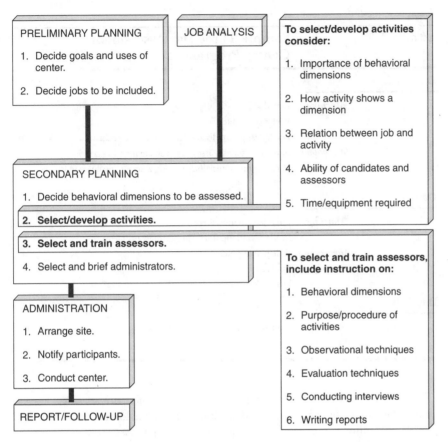

PRELIMINARY PLANNING

1. Decide goals and uses of center.

2. Decide jobs to be included.

JOB ANALYSIS

To select/develop activities consider:

1. Importance of behavioral dimensions

2. How activity shows a dimension

3. Relation between job and activity

4. Ability of candidates and assessors

5. Time/equipment required

SECONDARY PLANNING

1. Decide behavioral dimensions to be assessed.

2. **Select/develop activities.**

3. **Select and train assessors.**

4. Select and brief administrators.

To select and train assessors, include instruction on:

1. Behavioral dimensions

2. Purpose/procedure of activities

3. Observational techniques

4. Evaluation techniques

5. Conducting interviews

6. Writing reports

ADMINISTRATION

1. Arrange site.

2. Notify participants.

3. Conduct center.

REPORT/FOLLOW-UP

Figure 4.2. *Procedure for preparing an assessment center. The center depends on job analysis to determine the behavioral dimensions to be assessed. Planning the center is as important as conducting it.*

centers consume the time of employees who are taken away from their own jobs to participate or to perform as assessors, or because they require paying outside consultants, they are also quite expensive.

Assessment Center Activities

The types of activities vary considerably from one assessment center to another. Individual activities may include psychological tests and biographical inventories. Both objective and projective personality tests may be used. Candidates may be asked to perform written and oral communication exercises and the in-basket exercise. Communication exercises typically involve reading source material and preparing written and oral reports. Oral reports are delivered in meetings of the candidate group. The **in-basket exercise** requires the candidate to deal with the kind of correspondence that usually accumulates while an executive is on vacation. The in-basket contains requests, questions, directives, and various bits and pieces of information that must be handled within a specified period of time. Some requests need immediate attention, requiring the candidate to assign priorities. Solutions can involve phone calls, letters, and other personal handling, as well as delegation.

Table 4.7		Sample Three-Day Assessment Center Program
Day 1		
	Morning	Introduction
		Background interview
		Leaderless group discussion (cooperative problem)
	Afternoon	In-basket exercise; assessors evaluate morning activities
	Evening	Written communication exercise; assessors evaluate in-basket actions
Day 2		
	Morning	Interview on in-basket
		Leaderless group discussion (conflict problem)
	Afternoon	Role-playing exercise
		Oral report
		Debriefing; candidates leave
Day 3		
	Morning	Assessors' panel—discussion/evaluation
	Afternoon	Assessors write reports

Dyadic activities include role-playing exercises, such as interviews. For example, the candidate can be required to deal with a troublesome employee in a role-playing episode or to interview an applicant for a job. Assessors usually interview the candidates also, to discuss their responses to tests and their actions in the in-basket exercise.

Group exercises include the **leaderless group discussion** in which candidates work together without any assigned roles on some organizational problem. The type of problem depends on the behavioral dimension being assessed, although usually the group has a deadline and unanticipated events occur. For example, the group may work on a number of production problems and then have to deal with a drastic change in finances. Other leaderless group discussions focus on internal issues, such as competition between members over limited organizational resources. Table 4.7 lists activities that can be combined in a three-day assessment center.

Effectiveness of Assessment Centers

Do assessment centers work? To answer this question, let us consider whether they give reliable and valid predictions of performance on the job. As discussed previously, reliability and validity are important issues to address in considering any selection method. Validity of the assessment center refers to the extent to which the method can accurately predict job success. Reliability, which refers to the consistency of the assessments, is determined in two ways. Interrater reliability indicates whether the assessors agree with each other. Consistency or stability of a single assessor's ratings over time is another way to show reliability.

The accumulated research on interrater reliability shows a range of correlations, indicating that there is considerable variation in the extent to which assessors agree with each other (Schmitt, 1977). Individual differences in assessors' ability to evaluate candidates, including their tendency to commit rating errors, can account for some of this variation. Contrast errors, to which interviewers also are susceptible, have been found in assessor's ratings. For example, candidates were rated lower when they were evaluated with two high performers than when with two low performers (Gaugler & Rudolph, 1992). Secondly, the particular behavioral dimensions being evaluated can contribute to variation in assessors' ratings and to low reliability (Sackett & Wilson, 1982). As is true in interview evaluations, behavioral dimensions that can be clearly demonstrated in assessment center activities are easier to evaluate, and assessors tend to agree on them. Finally, it should be noted that the level of agreement can be affected by assessor interactions (Lowry, 1992). In the typical assessment center, assessors share their impressions of candidates. As Schmitt (1977) has pointed out, when assessors discuss candidates before evaluating them, the reliability coefficient is higher than when assessors act independently. Whether some assessors are influential in bringing the group to agree in their evaluations is not all that clear, although Klimoski, Friedman, and Weldon (1980) did find that higher-ranking assessors have an edge in this respect. However, it is possible that the interaction process itself affects the assessors. Researchers have speculated that interviewers working as a team feel more accountable to each other and as a result provide more accurate and reliable evaluations (Pulakos et al., 1996).

Evidence of reliability gives some information about validity. First, low reliability means low validity. Here's why. If assessors disagree to the extent that their ratings cannot even be used to predict each other, then it is unlikely that these ratings can predict anything else, such as job success. Second, high reliability sometimes indicates high validity, but not always. Assessors may fully agree in their evaluations of a behavioral dimension, yet the evaluation may be entirely unrelated to success on the job. How can this happen? They can be wrong in their assessment of a behavioral dimension, or the dimension itself can be unimportant to job success even if they do evaluate it accurately. This might occur because of inadequate job analysis and difficulty in determining what behavior is related to job success.

Validity of assessors' ratings is evaluated by determining how well the ratings correlate with some measure of job success. Research reviews have reported encouraging information about the ability of assessment centers to predict a variety of criterion measures of job success (Finkle, 1976; Tenopyr & Oeltjen, 1982). Bray's (1982) research at American Telephone and Telegraph provides an interesting example. Several assessments of the original sample were made over a period of 20 years on such dimensions as organizing and planning, decision making, creativity, and leadership. These assessments were then compared to a promotion criterion, specifically the organizational level reached by an individual in 10 years. Two groups were assessed. Of those persons who were predicted to reach a third level management position, 58 percent of one group reached this level, and 43 percent of the other group actually surpassed this level.

The news about assessment centers is not entirely good, however. Later reviews of research suggest that we should question the assessment center as a valid selection procedure (Zedeck & Cascio, 1984). Klimoski and Strickland (1977) questioned what assessors' ratings actually predict. First, these researchers observed that assessors' ratings usually are compared to measures of salary growth and promotion, which may not be good indicators of job performance. Second, because assessors' ratings predict raises and promotions, it may be that the assessment center is simply a way of telling managers what they already think, but at some expense. Third, they noted that assessors' ratings are better able to predict supervisors' ratings of employee *potential* than actual job performance. Other researchers have reported similar findings. A meta-analysis of 50 assessment center studies indicated that assessors' ratings were more predictive of a candidate's job potential than of his or her job performance, promotion, or career advancement (Gaugler et al., 1987). Assessors' ratings also have been found to predict supervisors' ratings better than they predict actual promotions (Feltham, 1988), and by themselves, assessment centers appeared to be no more effective in predicting supervisors' ratings of potential than were personnel record evaluations (Lowry, 1994). This research suggests that it may be as useful, and certainly cheaper, to simply use supervisors' ratings of potential in place of the assessment center.

Another issue to consider in the evaluation of assessment centers is their utility or cost-effectiveness. Cascio and Silbey (1979) did a unique study on monetary utility. By comparing the costs of using assessment centers, traditional selection procedures, and simple random assignment of employees, they hoped to discover the point at which an assessment center would become worth its cost. They found that when there are large differences in the performance of persons on the job, the payoff of the assessment center is greatest. That is, when a company's costs of having marginal (as opposed to superior) employees are high, then the cost of an assessment center, even one that shows only modest validity, is a small price to pay for improving the selection of employees.

Finally, assessment centers may operate to maintain the status quo in managerial jobs. This can be a problem also with other selection devices, such as biographical inventories, that are developed from information about present employees. Individuals who might be successful on the job, yet do not resemble the present employees, can be neglected. Organizational policies and traditions in hiring and promotion may influence who is successful in the organization. If so, then basing assessment centers on current employees will amplify these effects. Whether there is actual need for concern is not yet clear. One study reported sex bias in assessment center ratings, but the effect was not in the direction expected. Female candidates were favored over male candidates (Walsh, Weinberg, & Fairfield, 1987).

Some selection methods use the applicant's current behavior to predict future performance on the job. To be effective, such methods must say what is relevant to look for in the applicant's behavior, and give ways to assess the behavior.

The interview takes this approach, although the unstructured and casual procedure that many interviewers use is not a good example. The unstructured interview fails to identify what is relevant to discuss with an applicant, and it gives no guidance on how to judge the applicant's attributes. However, because employers like the interview for making selection decisions, I/O psychologists have investigated ways to make it do what it should do. The result is the structured interview. Structured interviews provide questions developed from job analysis that define what is relevant to observe and evaluate. They provide direction on how to judge whether an attribute has been demonstrated. The structured interview is reliable, and employers can depend on it to get accurate information.

Assessment centers are meant to simulate the job, and good ones are organized around dimensions drawn from job analysis. Candidates for a variety of jobs, such as managerial, technical, and military jobs, are examined this way. Assessment center participants do written assignments, are tested and interviewed, and participate in group activities. Multiple assessors observe and evaluate the participants' performance and report on their potential for success on the job. The level of reliability and validity varies. In some, interrater reliability is low, which means that validity is low. Also, there is a question about what assessment centers predict. Some are clearly valid for predicting salary growth and promotion. Whether this means they give a valid prediction of job performance is not so clear.

*C*HAPTER *S*UMMARY

The selection process is the third step, after job analysis and recruitment, in identifying the best person for a job. Typically, a variety of selection procedures and instruments are used in a multiple hurdle process in which the potential of each person in the applicant pool is evaluated. For this process to be effective, the employer must be confident that any selection method used is both reliable and valid. Only valid and reliable methods can provide the kind of consistent and accurate information that an employer needs to predict who will be a good employee.

Applications, biographical inventories, résumés, and reference letters are used to gather information about the applicant's past that is relevant to the job. In general, the effectiveness of these selection devices vary, with the more structured instruments being more reliable and valid. Weighted application blanks are an example. They are structured so as to obtain particular information relevant to

job performance and to provide a score. The behavioral consistency method is a similarly scorable open-response application procedure. Biographical inventories are structured to provide measures of various past personal experiences, not simply training and experience. In contrast, standard application blanks, résumés, and reference letters usually do not yield information that is job relevant, scorable, or comparable across applicants.

Interviews and assessment centers sample the job applicant's present behavior and use this to predict future job performance. To provide an accurate prediction, these methods must define the relevant behavior to observe and evaluate. Interviews are used by most organizations. However, many use an unstructured procedure that generally fails to provide accurate information about applicants. Research indicates that structured interviews designed to be job relevant are effective. They can validly predict future job performance, and they make a better choice for employers. Assessment centers, used mostly for managerial selection, are meant to provide a simulation of the job; thus, they include activities that normally are done on the job. Performance in the assessment center is observed and evaluated by trained assessors. Research has shown that assessment centers can provide reliable and valid prediction of some measures of success. They appear best for predicting salary growth and promotion. They are expensive but may be worth the expense if employee selection is improved.

STUDY QUESTIONS

1) What is the rationale for using personal history assessments in making selection decisions, and what other approach might be taken instead?

2) How do weighted application blanks differ from standard application blanks? Which is better?

3) How effective are biographical inventories in predicting job performance? What ethical issues should be considered in using these inventories?

4) What can be done to improve reference letters as a selection device?

5) What is a structured interview? How effective is it compared to an unstructured interview?

6) What are the advantages of a situational interview, and how is one developed?

7) Why are interviewer judgments often inaccurate? What might be done to improve them?

8) Who are chosen as assessors in assessment centers, and what are their functions?

9) What kinds of activities are used in assessment centers?

10) Do assessment centers work?

CONSIDER THIS

CASE

Vocational Rehabilitation Services (VRS) is a community service organization that operates a sheltered workshop for people with disabilities. In the workshop, VRS clients learn to perform a variety of light manufacturing and assembly operations mainly through on-the-job training. The agency contracts with local manufacturing companies for this work. The clients get job training and work experience and are paid a modest piece rate.

VRS is now planning to hire an executive assistant to help with the overall administration of the agency. This is a new position in this small organization, and the tasks have been carved out of the work now being done by the executive director. The intent is to give the overworked director help in two areas: (1) assistance in overall planning for the organization, and (2) specific development and monitoring of contracts.

The executive director has developed the following job description:

The executive assistant will assist the director of VRS in the agency's overall planning and evaluation. Specifically, the assistant will (1) develop grant proposals, including planning, research, and writing; (2) obtain all permits required for operating the workshop; (3) assist the director in representing the agency in contacts with community groups, businesses, and governmental agencies; and (4) coordinate and report all contract compliance efforts.

VRS needs a new procedure for hiring a qualified person for this position. The agency also wants a selection procedure that will be useful for future hiring needs throughout the organization. In the past, hiring decisions were made on the basis of a simple process: an interview with the executive director and reference checks. This process has not been satisfactory particularly because the agency has experienced very high turnover. The agency is interested in improving its selection procedures. What would you recommend?

Probably, most of your life, you have been on the receiving end of testing. You have had tests in school and maybe even have taken a job test. This is a valuable perspective, but it's not the only one.

In this chapter, you get to see the other side of it. You find out what tests are good for or whether they are good for anything, and you learn what goes into demonstrating this. Tests themselves get tested. They are evaluated in reliability and validity studies, and they have their monetary value examined in utility analyses.

Included are examples of tests, some of which are well-known. You will find out how they can be used to assess someone's job ability. Sometimes such tests are administered by computer. In fact, some tests are developed so that the computer actually works with the test taker. It does not simply present item after item; it also analyzes the answers and responds.

Taking a test may be difficult for older job applicants because of age-related losses of sensory and motor abilities. To guard against the unfair rejection of older applicants, employers need to use tests that require only the abilities used on the job.

$\mathcal{C}$ hapter 5

Contents

Using

Psychological

Tests in Selection

I said to the widow: "If in one day, between sunrise and sunset, with your own hands you can mow this field, and it be well done, I will let the case drop and you shall keep your son. But if you cannot do it, he must go.". . . For the mowing of that field is a day's work to three men, or three days' work to one man. Today, as the sun rose, she set to her task. And down there, by the end of the field, you will see her now, in a blue headcloth, with the man I have set to follow her and to ascertain that she does the work unassisted.

Isak Dinesen

Mowing a field? Is that a test? In this story, it is. Notice that the required performance is defined, standards are established, and a "passing score" is identified. That is, the widow must mow the field; she must personally mow all of it; it must be mowed in one day's time; and it must be mowed well. In addition, a test administrator is included—a man is sent to follow her and see that the testing conditions are maintained. Performance tests used at work are like this. The work required of the testee is specified; quality standards are included; and the test is monitored to control testing conditions.

Tests sometimes are relevant and valid for the purpose they are supposed to accomplish, and sometimes they are not. We might guess, for example, that the mowing test is meant to show whether the widow has enough physical stamina to do the work necessary to support a family. If so, then the test likely would give relevant information to help decide whether she should keep her son. In fact, however, the mowing test was used as a measure of motivation—to find out how desperate the widow was to have her son back home. Usually, job tests are not designed to determine a test taker's motivational level, because ability to perform the work is considered more important. Nonetheless, most tests do tap into motivation to some extent. How well you do on a performance test depends not only on your abilities but also on how motivated you are to do well. The point is, the relevance and validity of a test depend on the actual use of the test.

In chapter 4, I describe a variety of devices used to make selection decisions. Psychological tests are among them. Along with applications, interviews, and letters of reference, tests are used to predict the future behavior of a job applicant. Decisions about whether to hire an applicant, promote an employee, or send someone to training are aided by the information these selection devices provide.

REQUIREMENTS OF A GOOD SELECTION TEST

What makes a good selection test? Certainly, a test should measure relevant job behavior. This is necessary for accurate prediction of future job performance. Further, a good test must be valid and reliable. It must be administered under standard conditions and scored by means of standard procedures. Scores on the test must be evaluated against an appropriate standard (Anastasi, 1982). Some believe that the

Table 5.1	Requirements of a Selection Testing Program

1. The test must be *standardized:*

    Administration procedures must be controlled.
    Scoring procedures and answer keys must be defined.
    Appropriate norms for interpretation of scores must be established.

2. The test must be *reliable:* it must measure consistently.

3. The test must be *valid:* it must measure what it is intended to measure and be used appropriately.

4. The test must be *fair:* it must not be discriminatory.

5. The test must have *utility:* it must be economical.

"goodness" of a test should be evaluated also in terms of the utility or dollar value of the selection decision it helps to make. Table 5.1 briefly summarizes these requirements, and I discuss them in the following sections.

Standardization of Tests

In one respect, **test standardization** refers to the conditions under which a test is administered. If a test is to measure a behavior or trait accurately, then it must be administered carefully so that extraneous variables do not affect the measurement. Standardizing test conditions means keeping the conditions exactly the same each time the test is administered. Test conditions include test materials, instructions, time allowances, and even equipment and rooms. The importance of standardizing test conditions is apparent if we consider something as simple as differences in the room in which the test is given. Compare one group seated in a well-lighted room with comfortable chairs to another group in a room with a flickering light bulb and wobbly chairs. The groups are likely to differ in their performance because of the differences in the rooms.

In test standardization, we attempt to control any condition that has potential for influencing test performance. Because selection testing may be ongoing, with applicants being tested continually, test standards need to be written down. Test administrators must be trained to observe these standards to the letter. This is why they often *read* written instructions to a group of applicants. This is also why test materials, such as practice questions, test booklets, and response sheets, are so strictly controlled.

Controlling Test Scoring

Test standardization also involves scoring. Obviously, we do not want test information or scores to be contaminated by the personal biases of those grading the test. For this reason, we usually do not leave it to the discretion of the scorer as to whether a test answer is correct. Rather, we specify the right answers or the conditions under which an answer can be considered correct. Then, regardless of who does the scoring, test results will depend only on testee performance. In objective tests, such as multiple-choice and true-false tests, scoring is standardized. Correct answers are identified before the test is administered. However, in projective tests and essay examinations, scoring is not standardized in most cases. The scorer must decide on the accuracy of a response. How well a person does on these tests depends partly on the test scorer's ability to distinguish between good and poor answers, which depends in turn on the scorer's knowledge of the test material. When a standardized scoring procedure is used, however, the impact of the scorer is minimal. Even changing scorers within a single test administration has no impact on objective test scores. In fact, scoring of objective tests is often done by machine.

In another sense, test standardization refers to the sample on whose behavior test norms are established. This group, called the **standardization sample,** originally was given the test, and their scores are used to evaluate the scores of those currently being tested.

What people are included in a standardization sample? Typically, they are a large group of people who are similar in several respects to those who will be taking the test. Thus, different tests will have different standardization samples because they will be used with different applicants. For example, one test used to assess the aptitudes of applicants for a clerical job and another to evaluate technical knowledge for a government job will have different standardization samples.

Test norms are distributions of the scores of the standardization sample. Although these distributions can be expressed in a variety of ways, they usually are presented in terms of **percentiles.** A percentile indicates the number of people in the standardization sample who scored at or below a particular score. For distributions of test scores that approximate a normal bell-shaped curve, as most do, the 50th percentile corresponds to the mean score of the standardization sample. The 15th percentile is about one standard deviation below the mean, and the 85th percentile is about one standard deviation above the mean. Comparison of an individual's score with test norms makes the score meaningful. Suppose you are told that your score on a test is 102 and that this score is at the 75th percentile. This does not mean that 75 percent of your answers were correct. Rather, it tells you that 75 percent of the standardization sample scored 102 or lower; therefore, your performance was as good or better than theirs. Twenty-five percent of the standardization sample did better than you did.

Reputable commercial test developers provide standardization information for their test users. This information describes the standardization sample and specifies test norms, scoring procedures, and conditions that need to be controlled. Obviously, if a test can be purchased, much of the user's work has been done. However, if an organization must develop its own test or purchase one without standardization information, then in-house standardization research must be done.

Testing Disabled Applicants

In the past, employers often assumed that disabled and older people could not perform many jobs for which they actually were well qualified. Physical "standards" for jobs were established without the benefit of a job analysis, and therefore, qualified disabled applicants often were ruled out. Advocate groups have worked to dispel the myths about the abilities of disabled and older employees, and laws have been passed to protect employment opportunities of these individuals (see chapter 3). It is not clear whether attitudes and hiring practices have changed, however. Attitudes toward disabled and older applicants probably depend on various aspects of the selection process. One study looked at the effects of having wheelchair users disclose their disability over the phone prior to a job interview. Those who did not disclose their disability before the interview were rated more positively by the interviewer, but they were less likely to be selected for the job (Tagalakis, Amsel, & Fichten, 1988).

To guard against unfair rejection of disabled applicants, the personnel specialist needs to establish standards for the perceptual and physical requirements of the job, and a thorough job analysis is the first step. Physical ability standards are established routinely for some jobs. These are usually jobs that require superior abilities, such as the job of fire fighter. For example, a fire fighter may need to carry heavy weights, climb great heights, and run up several flights of stairs. Few jobs require such superior physical skills. Nonetheless, physical and sensory specifications do need to be established because higher standards than are warranted may be assumed without them.

Because tests must be standardized, disabled applicants should be tested under the same conditions as other applicants if possible. However, some adjustments may be necessary. A testing site may have to be moved in order to accommodate wheelchair users. Dyslexic applicants should be accommodated by a tape recording of the items, if they are applying for a job that does not require reading. Contents of written tests must be scrutinized for questions that are irrelevant to the job but discriminate against disabled applicants. For example, a test for a job that is open to blind applicants should not contain questions about colors.

To test older applicants, similar adjustments may be needed. Examination materials should be inspected. Multiple-choice answer sheets that have tiny circles to be filled in are difficult for older people to see and for persons with impaired hand and finger dexterity to use. Dexterity is important in some jobs but not in others. If it is required for a test but not for a job, older applicants can be disadvantaged. The testing experience itself may be difficult for an older applicant. Today's younger generation has grown up with tests, but older adults may have had little testing experience. Practice materials can be helpful for these applicants (Johnson & White, 1980).

Reliability of Tests

As I discuss in chapter 4, reliability of the interview reflects the consistency of judgments made by interviewers. Similarly, **test reliability** refers to a test's ability to get consistent responses. Response consistency in testing is necessary because behavior itself is consistent. Although people do change, change is gradual, and behavior tends to be stable. For example, intelligence is thought to be fairly constant, and intelligence tests need to reflect this. An IQ test given twice to the same person should show about the same score. If you took an IQ test one week and scored 105 and the next week when you took it again you scored 84, you probably would not think you became less intelligent. You would conclude that the test was inconsistent or unreliable.

Reliability indicates the extent to which a test can predict itself. If it is reliable, it will predict itself quite well. Pairs of scores earned by the same persons will be highly similar. If they are not, the test is not dependable. Also, ask yourself whether a measuring device that cannot predict itself can predict anything else. The primary purpose of testing is to forecast an applicant's future job performance. If a test is so unreliable that it produces two different estimates of a person's *present* behavior, how can we believe that it gives a good estimate of future behavior? For this reason, a valid test is a reliable test. If it is not reliable, it also is not valid.

Test-Retest Reliability

Test reliability can be estimated in four ways (see table 5.2). With the **test-retest** method, a test is administered and then readministered after a period of time. The test score and the retest score are compared to determine their similarity. If the test is reliable, the two scores will be highly similar. An assessment of test-retest reliability involves comparing the two scores of a sample of subjects in a correlational study. The overall correlation coefficient is the reliability estimate, and it shows the test's degree of **stability** over time. Although this estimate of reliability may be intuitively appealing, it is not always appropriate. For example, if test performance is improved by practice, the retest score will be contaminated by memory or practice effects, and the reliability estimate will be inaccurate.

Alternate Forms Reliability

The **alternate forms** method of assessing test reliability can be used when test-retest is inappropriate. Subjects are tested twice, as in the test-retest method; however, two different versions of the test are used. The procedure requires the construction of two equivalent test forms, one to be administered first, the other to be given later. The two test scores are correlated to determine the extent of their similarity. This method shows the temporal stability of the test. It also provides a measure of **equivalence** as the reliability estimate. That is, the correlation coefficient indicates the extent to which the two test forms measure the same behavior. There is no problem of practice effects because a different test is used in the second administration. However, the alternative forms method can be costlier than the test-retest method because constructing two tests is more time-consuming. In addition, a serious problem can result from the difficulty of developing two forms that actually are two versions of the same test. Both versions must sample the same content and ask questions about the same material. Items must be expressed in the same manner and be about the same level of difficulty.

Split-Halves Reliability

The **split-halves** method of evaluating test reliability requires only one administration and is the least costly. Following administration, the test is split in half by some systematic procedure. The two halves are scored separately, as if they were two separate tests, and the scores on these halves are correlated. The correlation coefficient indicates the degree of **internal consistency** in the test, or how consistently the same behavior is measured throughout the test.

One problem with using this method is in deciding how to split the test. Dividing it into first and second halves may not be appropriate because items may

Table 5.2 — Techniques for Determining Test Reliability

Technique	Procedure	Estimate of Reliability	Constraints
Test-retest	Same test administered twice	Stability	Practice effects; may overestimate reliability
Alternate forms	Different version of test administered the second time	Equivalence	Cost of developing two forms; difficult to develop comparable forms
Split-halves	One test administered and split in half; score halves as two tests	Internal consistency	No evaluation over time; splitting may not be optimal; underestimates reliability
Interitem	One test administered and items compared	Internal consistency	No evaluation over time

differ in content and difficulty from the beginning to the end. Individuals also may perform differently on these two halves because they are warming up to the test at the beginning and getting tired at the end. A better way is to divide the test by its odd- and even-numbered items. This division is effective if the test items are independent of each other and not arranged in groups of related items.

Interitem Reliability

The fourth method of estimating a test's reliability is similar to split-halves reliability in that only one test is given and a measure of its internal consistency is obtained. However, split-halves reliability indicates the relationship between the test's halves, whereas **interitem reliability** indicates the relationship between the test's items. One source of error in both the interitem and split-halves measures of internal consistency is the extent to which the behavioral content is unevenly sampled within the test. Specifically, the difficulty of the items should be equal. If item difficulty varies, the value of internal consistency estimates of reliability is limited (Anastasi, 1982).

The interitem method of assessing reliability is a solution to the researcher's problem of deciding on a way to split a test into halves. There are many possible ways to split a test, and some splittings will yield better reliability estimates than others, although we usually do not know which ones. Instead of having to decide on one particular splitting (and risk having it be a poor one), suppose we use all possible splittings and average the correlations that result. This would give us a very good assessment of the extent to which the test's items are consistent. Of course, we do not do exactly this because it would be too time-consuming to recalculate test scores and correlations for all possible splittings. However, two statistical procedures allow us to do something like this. The Kuder-Richardson formula, **KR20** (Kuder & Richardson, 1937), and Cronbach's (1970) **coefficient alpha** can be used to evaluate the reliability of items that are scored as correct or incorrect. Coefficient alpha can also be used for instruments, such as personality tests and attitude scales, that are not scored dichotomously but have more than one right answer.

Validity of Tests

Good tests help us make good selection decisions. The most important indicator of a good selection test is a high level of validity. A test can be reliable and standardized adequately yet still not be valid. In one respect, validity refers to the extent to which a test actually measures what it is supposed to measure. An intelligence test must actually measure intelligence and not something else, such as personality. In another respect, validity refers to the use of the test. If we use a mechanical skill test for selecting employees for a particular job, we need to know that the mechanical skill is required on the job. Both the validity of a test to measure the construct it purports to measure and the validity of its use in selection need to be established in any job testing program.

Organizations that develop their own tests must also document the validity of the tests. This may involve the collection of empirical data. If an organization uses a commercial test, validity information most likely will be available from the test developer. Even so, the organization may still need to assess the validity of the test's *use* because the traditional and still largely accepted view is that validity is tied to the situation in which it was established (Anastasi, 1982; Guion, 1965). Research is underway, however, to determine whether evidence of validity can be transported from one organization to another, and the signs are promising. I have more to say about validity and validity generalization in later sections.

Setting Cutoff Scores

To use a test for selection, some score is usually designated as a minimum passing point, that is, as a **cutoff score.** How do we calculate this score? First, we should keep in mind that setting a cutoff score always involves a value judgment. There is no fully objective way to do it. Neither is there a single best way to do it. In fact, we should not spend much time looking for the "real" passing score, because there isn't one (Cascio, Alexander, & Barrett, 1988). However, we can decide where, in a distribution of test scores, to place a "passing" point, and there are procedures to help us do this. One way is to match the test scores of all employees with measures of their performance on the job and then use the test score of the minimally acceptable employee as the passing score. Another way is to have subject matter experts (SMEs) review the test items and decide whether a minimally qualified employee would answer each question correctly. Averaging the SME judgments per item and summing over items yields the cutoff score (Angoff, 1971). This is a popular method of setting cutoff scores, although it is open to criticism because of its subjectivity (Maurer & Alexander, 1992). Various conditions can influence cutoff scores, including the organization's needs. For example, if an organization needs to reduce a large applicant pool, the cutoff score can be set very high so that only a few pass. To do this, the SMEs may be asked to conceptualize a "fully qualified" employee rather than the "minimally qualified" person in their evaluation of test items. This will raise the passing score.

Once a cutoff score has been set, another decision is necessary. Some strategy is needed to decide which one or more of those who pass the test will be hired. There are several ways to do this. The simplest is the top-down method. Starting with the highest scorer, people are selected to fill the open positions.

However, this assumes there is a real difference between people who may score only one or two points apart. Another procedure, the fixed band method, makes no such assumption; rather, it is recognized that small differences in test scores are probably due to measurement error. The decision maker is given a list of those whose passing scores are about the same; thus, any of the group can be selected for the open positions. A related technique, the sliding band method, is useful when there are several open positions and the organization is interested in improving the diversity of its work force. With this procedure, the decision maker selects the highest scorer from the group of equally scoring candidates for the first open position. The "band" of equal scores then can "slide" downward somewhat, so it is possible to fill a second position with someone who was not in the first band (Cascio et al., 1995).

Fairness in Selection Testing

As Guion (1965) observed, unfair discrimination exists when applicants who are equally likely to succeed on the job are *not* equally likely to be hired. If a test is unfair to a protected group, then test unfairness may be a reason for unlawful discrimination. **Test fairness** is actually a statistical concept. It refers to the relationship between test scores and measures of job performance of two different groups. Unfairness is indicated when one group characteristically scores lower on a test than the other group, but a comparable difference is not shown in their job performance. That is, the test is unfair because it underestimates the job performance of those in the lower scoring group.

To determine whether a test is fair, we begin by obtaining test scores and scores on a criterion measure of job performance (such as supervisor evaluations) for each person in a sample. We plot the scores on these two variables on a graph, with the test score on the horizontal axis and the performance score on the vertical axis. The **bivariate distribution** that results probably will show a scattering, such as in figure 5.1*a*. Notice that most of the scores clump in the form of an ellipse oriented in a certain direction. The orientation of this particular distribution indicates that higher test scores are associated with higher performance scores and vice versa, as can be expected from a valid test.

Next, we divide the sample into two groups (such as by gender) and plot the data of each group on another graph. We may find that the scatter of scores in one group has exactly the same shape and orientation and completely overlaps the other group. This would mean that the groups are drawn from the same population and are not different. On the other hand, we may find a difference such as that depicted in figure 5.1*b*. Notice that the distributions are oriented similarly: Higher test scores are associated with higher criterion scores in both groups. However, the distributions do not completely overlap. Group 2 shows both a higher mean test score and a higher mean criterion score than group 1. This might occur if the people in group 2 had more work experience than those in group 1, and if so, the test is *fairly* discriminating on the basis of job ability.

In figure 5.1*c,* the higher mean test score of group 2 is *not* associated with a higher mean performance score. Although their test scores are different, the groups show equal levels of performance; thus, the test underestimates the performance of

Figure 5.1. *The relationship between test scores and measures of performance under two conditions of test fairness. (a) Bivariate distribution of test scores and performance evaluations with groups combined in one sample. Notice that most scores clump in the form of an ellipse. The orientation of the ellipse shows that higher test scores are associated with higher performance (and vice versa). (b) Fair test: Bivariate distributions show a test that discriminates fairly between two groups, as might be expected if members of one group have more job experience than members of the other. (c) Unfair test: Bivariate distributions show two groups that differ on the test but not on job performance, indicating that the test does not predict performance of the groups equally well.*

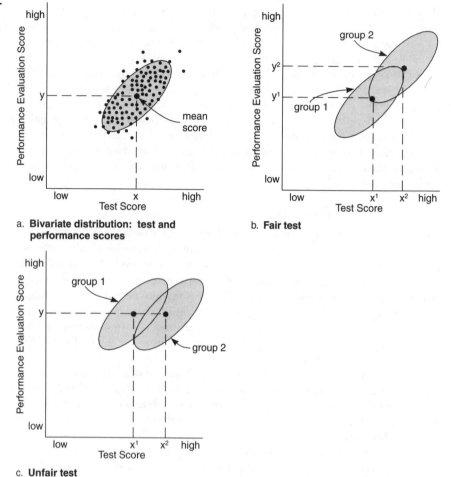

a. **Bivariate distribution: test and performance scores**

b. **Fair test**

c. **Unfair test**

individuals in group 1. If the test is used to select applicants for employment, then members of group 1 will be disadvantaged. Because their test scores are lower, they are less likely to be hired, although they are likely to do the job as well as group 2. This is the idea of test unfairness (Anastasi, 1982).

Assessing the Utility of the Testing Program

How do you know whether a testing program is effective? Psychologists have long been able to assess the effectiveness of selection methods by looking at the numbers hired who could be expected to be successful on the job. In 1939, the **Taylor-Russell tables** were published to aid the personnel specialist in making this assessment. To use the tables, the specialist must calculate (1) the percentage of present employees considered satisfactory, (2) the selection ratio, or percentage of applicants who take the test and pass, and (3) the validity of the test. Then, these data are entered into the tables, and this shows what the test is likely to do in terms of improving the selection process. Improvement is expressed as a *percentage,* not as a dollar figure. However, methodology for translating test effectiveness into dollar amounts also has been available for many years (e.g., Brogden, 1946; Cronbach & Gleser, 1965). This methodology is not often used in the business setting, however, possibly because managers assume that the validity studies are too costly and that the dollar estimates are too difficult to obtain (Boudreau, 1983).

More recently, there has been a renewed effort to assess the effectiveness of selection. Now, the emphasis is on its monetary value. **Utility analysis** is a process by which a selection program is evaluated in terms of actual costs and savings to an organization. The index of **utility** is the standard deviation of performance calculated in terms of dollars (SD_y). Utility can be estimated rather directly in testing for production jobs by considering the units produced by production employees. This is not feasible in programs for selecting nonproduction employees, such as clerks and managers, of course, because these employees do not produce anything that can be counted meaningfully. Schmidt et al. (1979) have proposed that SD_y can be estimated for nonproduction employee testing by using SME judgments. In their study, a panel of supervisors considered the quantity and quality of the average employee's work output and placed a dollar value on it. Following this, they estimated the value of the work done by a poor employee and by an outstanding employee. These quality levels (poor, average, and outstanding) and their associated dollar values were viewed as representing performance at the 15th, 50th, and 85th percentile of a normal distribution of work performance. Recall that the 15th and 85th percentiles are points roughly equal to +/− 1 SD from the mean, which is itself at the 50th percentile. Therefore, the three dollar value estimates provide an assessment of utility (SD_y), or the net monetary worth of the program.

Several times in chapters 3 and 4, I refer to the costs of poor selection and the economy of good selection. Traditionally, I/O psychologists translated the terms *poor* and *good* into validity coefficients and used these as *statistical* evidence of selection effectiveness. However, not long ago, we discovered that managers believe that selection contributes little and is not worth much (Zedeck & Cascio, 1984). The reason for this untoward view, we thought, was that we had been talking statistics rather than dollars. Managers needed to have our validity terms translated into dollars. Therefore, we gave them utility estimates. Utility estimates are supposed to help managers decide how much to invest in the selection and development of human resources (Cascio, 1991). In utility discussions, we try to forecast the costs and benefits of a selection program. However, it is not clear that even this is useful. Latham and Whyte (1994) found that managers were more likely to accept a psychologist's recommendation for investing in a selection program when utility analysis was *not* discussed and only validity information was given. They did not base their decisions on the utility information they were given. What could explain this? Do managers make decisions in some way that is not quite as rational as we thought, or are we still talking statistics?

What is a good test?

A good test is a standardized test. It is administered under exact conditions. Adjustments can be made for testing disabled and older applicants, but as much as possible, the test should be the same for everyone. Standardized tests are scored exactly the same each time. Individual scores are interpreted against those of a standardization sample.

A good test is a reliable test, one that performs in a consistent and predictable way. There are four ways to evaluate reliability: the test-retest, alternate forms, split-halves, and interitem techniques.

Reliability is necessary for validity, and this is the most important feature of a good test. A valid test measures what it is supposed to and it is used for the right purpose. It also is fair.

A good test is easy to use. It has a carefully considered cutoff score and a way to select from among those who pass.

Finally, a good test is economical. It helps the user make the right hiring decision, and this saves money. Utility analysis can show just how economical a test is, and it puts a dollar value on the test.

VALIDATION OF SELECTION TESTS

Some tests *look* as if they measure a particular ability or sample relevant behaviors. Such tests have what is known as **face validity.** Face validity is important insofar as the testee is concerned. A test that appears to ask appropriate questions is generally more acceptable to the person taking the test than one composed of questions that seem irrelevant. Technically, however, face validity is not very important because validity does not depend on the appearance of test items.

Criterion-Related Validity

Validation is a way of testing the test. Either of two general approaches to validation can be used to test the test. Content validation, discussed later in the chapter, determines that the test is logically related to or samples the work activities. The other approach examines the empirical relationship between the test and job performance. Validation strategies in which this empirical method is used give an estimate of the extent to which the test shows **criterion-related validity.** Test scores are correlated with scores on some criterion measure of job success, such as a supervisor's rating. The resulting correlation coefficient, called the **validity coefficient,** indicates the validity of the test, or how well the test score predicts job performance.

Predictive Technique

There are two ways to carry out a criterion-related validity study: the predictive technique and the concurrent technique. In a **predictive validity** study, the test is administered to a group of applicants, called the **validation sample.** Then, the test is put away unscored.[1] Ideally, all applicants are hired. After they have been on the job for awhile, their performance is evaluated. (This evaluation functions as the criterion measure of performance.) At that time also, the tests are scored, and the scores are correlated with the performance ratings. The extent to which these scores and ratings are correlated is the validity coefficient, indicating the ability of the test to predict the criterion measure.

Although the predictive technique provides the best information about the criterion-related validity of a test, true predictive validity studies are not always practical. Usually, there is resistance to hiring a whole group of unweeded applicants. The typical compromise is to use some other procedure, such as an interview, for screening and to include only these screened applicants in the validation sample. Although it solves the practical problem, such a compromise may create another problem. Depending on how effective the screening procedure is, the validation sample that results may have a **restricted range** of abilities. For example, a very good screening device may produce a sample that contains only those who will be relatively successful on the job. Strangely enough, however, it is essential that some potentially *unsuccessful* applicants be included in the validation sample, because we must learn how both they and the successful employees do on the test. A valid test will show high test scores for those who succeed on the job. It will also show low test scores for those who do not succeed. (This will tell us later whom *not* to hire.) However, if we do not include potentially unsuccessful applicants in the validation sample, we will not know whether the test can predict low performance levels. The best strategy for testing the test, given this constraint, is to use a screen that is not very effective. Perhaps, an unstructured interview would do.

Concurrent Technique

An alternative to predictive validation is the concurrent technique. In studies of **concurrent validity,** the organization's present employees make up the validation sample. All those currently doing the job for which the test is being validated are given the test. Their scores are compared to a measure of their performance taken at the same time. The extent to which the test score correlates with the measure of performance indicates the degree of validity. If those who are more successful on the job get high test scores and those who are less successful get low test scores, the test can be accepted as showing good concurrent validity.

In using the concurrent technique, we need to be aware of its shortcomings. For one thing, concurrent studies, like predictive studies, may show a restriction of range. Neither unsuccessful nor highly successful employees are likely to be included in the validation sample. This is because unsuccessful employees probably will have quit or been terminated, and highly successful employees will have moved on to better jobs. Some researchers believe, however, that this problem is no more serious for the concurrent method than for the predictive (Barrett, Phillips, & Alexander, 1981).

Criterion Measure of Performance

A requirement of both predictive and concurrent validation is a good criterion measure of job success. For production jobs, objective productivity can be used. For other jobs, the most readily available measure is the supervisor's rating. We

[1] It is critical that the test not be used to make a selection decision at this point; to do so would interfere with the validity study.

must be cautious in using ratings, because they can contain errors that will distort the validation results. However, if supervisors' ratings are done carefully using an objective procedure, they can be as effective as production measures (Hoffman, Nathan, & Holden, 1991).

If supervisors' ratings are used, they must adequately distinguish between the levels of employee performance. This is important because the ability range of applicants and employees is likely to be restricted. The validation sample probably will be comprised of those who are neither highly successful nor unsuccessful on the job. When a validation study shows that high performers on the job earn high test scores, it is tempting to assume that this linear relationship holds for all ability levels. With an invalid test, however, successful and unsuccessful employees may earn the same score. We can assess this possibility only if we have a criterion measure that discriminates between different levels of employee performance. You will hear more about criterion measures of performance in chapter 7.

Synthetic Validity

Job analysts generally take the view that a job includes a number of different components for which different KSAs are required. These KSAs contribute to overall job performance because they contribute to performance of individual job components. Therefore, one way to use testing in selection is to develop a battery of tests that individually predict performance on the separate job components, that is, that have **job component validity.** These component validities can then be combined or "synthesized" for an overall validity coefficient. This is the approach taken in **synthetic validity** studies (Anastasi, 1982).

Hollenbeck and Whitener (1988) pointed out that the typical criterion-related validity study requires a sample much larger than the small business has available. They proposed a synthetic validity procedure that can circumvent this problem. In this procedure, elements of a job are identified through job analysis. Then, a battery of tests that might predict performance on the different job elements is selected. Each test is given to all employees, regardless of job title, whose jobs include the element to which the test relates. Scores on the individual tests then are correlated with evaluations of performance on the job elements. The overall correlation coefficient of all tests with the performance measures is the estimate of synthetic validity.

Content Validity

Unlike criterion-related methods, **content validation** does not involve collecting empirical data. Rather, the intent is to establish a logical relationship between the contents of the test and the contents of the job. The reasoning is that if the test is a representative sample of the job itself, then a person who can pass it can perform the job. The key element in content validity is representativeness. In the general sense, representativeness refers to sampling. For example, psychological researchers try to choose samples of subjects that represent a given population. Likewise, test validators try to establish that *test content* is a representative sample of the skills and knowledge required on the job. Content validity is shown to the extent that test content can be demonstrated to sample job content.

Content validation depends on a high-quality job analysis. Work activities identified in the job analysis can themselves be used in a test. For example, a typing test samples the work activities of a typist, and it has content validity when used to select typists. A test also may sample the knowledge required on the job. For example, a test used to select fire fighters can contain questions about the proper substances for extinguishing oil and grease fires and about effective ways to enter a burning building. The underlying assumption of the job knowledge test is similar to that of the work sample test: A person who has the necessary knowledge will be able to do the job. However, only if the job analysis is done carefully and thoroughly, is it reasonable to claim that a test has content validity. Otherwise, it is not known that such KSAs are needed on a job.

Construct Validity

A third strategy for assessing test validity combines the reasoning of content and criterion-related validation. **Construct validity** includes both the rational relationship of content validity and the empirical relationship of criterion-related validity. Construct validity describes the extent to which a test measures a theoretical construct or broad trait.

To do a construct validation study, a job analysis is conducted to determine the necessary KSAs. The KSAs are analyzed to identify the underlying trait or construct, and a test is located or developed to measure the construct. Then, special criterion-related studies are used to validate the test. In these studies, scores on the test are correlated with scores on other tests. Some of these other tests are well-accepted measures of the same construct, but others are known to measure very different constructs. For example, suppose a job analysis indicates a need for mechanical comprehension. A test measuring this construct should be compared with other validated tests of the same ability and with tests of some different construct, such as verbal facility. The new test should correlate highly with a previously validated test of the same construct; that is, the scores should *converge* on the existing test. If so, the test is said to have **convergent validity.** If the new test measures *only* this construct, it should not correlate with measures of different constructs. That is, the scores should *diverge* from tests of other constructs, indicating that the test has **divergent validity.** Evidence of both convergent and divergent validity is necessary to show construct validity (Campbell, 1960).

You may wonder why we do not just use the already validated test of the construct and save ourselves a lot of trouble. Currently, construct validation is used mostly by commercial test developers, although there are signs that large organizations are beginning to use it. There are several reasons why they might. One is that an existing test may be too long. Another is that an available test may not by itself thoroughly measure a construct. Research suggests another reason construct validation is useful to an employer. A study was done to show how to replace selection tests that had been validated but also had been exposed to applicants and, therefore, could not be used again. New tests were developed, and with construct validation, they were shown to measure the same construct as the existing test (Turban et al., 1989).

Table 5.3

Validation Strategies: Their Nature, Uses, and Advantages

Validation Method	Technique	Rationale	Advantages
Criterion Related			
Predictive	Test scores of applicants later correlated with performance measure	Empirical: score on test predicts level of performance	Considered the most defensible
Concurrent	Test scores of present employees correlated with performance measure	Empirical: score on test predicts level of performance	Economical and more acceptable than predictive
Synthetic	Identify job components; scores on component tests correlated with performance measures	Both rational and empirical: scores on tests predict job component performance	Useful when samples are too small for routine criterion-related studies
Content	Job analysis; test comprised of work sample or necessary knowledge	Rational: test is sample of job; if high test score then success on job is likely	Appropriate for jobs with few employees or for new jobs
Construct	Job analysis to determine construct; test scores correlated with scores on other validated tests	Both rational and empirical: convergent toward other tests of construct; divergent from tests of other constructs	Economical in some situations; can be used for range of jobs

Validation Study Decisions

What are the advantages of doing one type of validity study instead of another? The answer depends on present needs and the anticipated use of the test. Many psychologists recommend predictive validity studies as providing the most defensible evidence of validity. However, as you can see, predictive validity studies are expensive and may be resisted. Concurrent validity studies, in which current employees are used, are less costly, but the validity evidence they provide is not as clear. In small organizations and with newly developed jobs, neither of these criterion-related techniques may be feasible because it is difficult to get a sample large enough for statistical analyses. Of course, if a criterion-related study is demanded, the problem of small samples can be avoided with a synthetic validity study in which a battery of tests is aimed at predicting performance on job components. However, this means that component tests must be available. A content validity study is another alternative. When there are few employees in the job class, it may be the only route to take. However, a thorough job analysis is absolutely necessary in content validation. Construct validation also requires a job study and careful analysis of the behavioral constructs underlying the KSAs. Construct validation provides evidence of validity by tying the test to a well-established measure. Table 5.3 lists these validation methods for quick reference.

Validity Generalization

So far in this discussion, I have presented test validity as a concept embodying **situational specificity.** That is, test validity is viewed as dependent on the situation in which the test is used. This implies that a validation study needs to be done before a test is used in an organization for the first time, even if it has been validated in another organization, because the *situation* is different. If the new test is used later to select for another job, its validity for that job will have to be established also, again because the situation is different. Part of the reason validities are viewed as situation specific is that validity coefficients for a test used in different organizations or for different jobs *have* varied. Although some of the variance may be due to research errors, until recently it has been widely accepted that there are real differences in the use of a test.

It certainly would be less costly and time-consuming if test validities were not situation specific. Think about how much easier it would be if, instead of having to validate a test that was borrowed from another organization, we could use that company's validity evidence. This is the idea of **test transportability,** which is basic to the research and theory development known as **validity generalization.**

The research on validity generalization uses a statistical procedure known as **meta-analysis,** in which the results from several previous validity studies are combined and analyzed in a new study. The meta-analytic procedure used by Hunter, Schmidt, and Jackson (1982) is based on the assumption that most of the differences in validity coefficients across studies is not due to real situational differences, but to errors in the measurement process. They said that the variation in test validities from organization to organization is largely due to such problems as unreliable criterion measures and restriction in the range of scores of those tested (Hunter et al., 1982; Schmidt & Hunter, 1981a; Schmidt, Hunter, & Raju, 1988). In meta-analysis, statistical corrections for these sources of error are applied. If the corrections can account for most of the variance in the sample of validity coefficients, then it is understood that the variance is not due to real situational differences but to error. This research procedure provides for estimating the true validity coefficient of a test, which then can be generalized. The new coefficient is the corrected mean of the sample of validity coefficients.

Schmidt and Hunter proposed that test validities generalize across organizations and jobs, and their research has provided evidence to support this. In particular, these researchers have found that tests of cognitive or mental abilities are valid across settings. This simply means that the organization in which the job is done is less important than we thought. However, their evidence also indicated that the validities of cognitive ability tests generalize across jobs (Schmidt & Hunter, 1981b). This is surprising. It says that if a test is a good predictor of performance in one job, it is also a good predictor of performance in another *different* job.

Validity generalization has important implications for personnel selection. One is that the time-consuming work required for establishing test validity may no longer be necessary. Future preparation for testing may involve simply analyzing the job and then finding an assortment of tests with good generalized validities (Zedeck & Cascio, 1984). A more important implication relates to the finding that cognitive ability test validities generalize across jobs. I have been discussing test "use" as if it meant that testing for one job is a different use than testing for another job. Validity generalization implies that these are not different uses. It implies that *selection for work* is a single use of a test. As some have proposed (e.g., Tenopyr, 1981), cognitive ability tests may tap into an underlying trait, such as general intelligence, that is required for all jobs. If we assume that the trait is required for all jobs, then a test that measures it should have relevance for any job. If this is true, then in the future, we may need to do nothing more than establish a cutoff score on a test for the job in question.

As our history has shown, new ideas often elicit much response and sometimes a polarization of opinion. Validity generalization is a provocative idea (Schmidt et al., 1988). Some disagree about the research methodology, and modifications of Schmidt and Hunter's procedure have been proposed (e.g., Callender & Osburn, 1980; James et al., 1988; Schmidt, Hunter, & Pearlman, 1982). Some questions need answering before we can know what to make of validity generalization. We first need to better understand the meaning of situational specificity. Does "situation" mean both the tasks and organizational characteristics of the job? It might be that the situation encompasses more than the tasks because the same job does not seem to be the same in different organizations. For example, computer programmers working for a government agency and for a private corporation appear to do different work (Zedeck & Cascio, 1984). Clearly, the final word on validity generalization is not in, and we can expect to hear more about it in the future.

*M*ain *P*oints

Criterion-related validation can be done in a predictive validity study. Test scores earned by a validation sample of job applicants are correlated with a criterion measure of performance taken later. When correlations are high, the test is valid. The concurrent technique is the same except current employees make up the validation sample, and test scores and performance measures are collected concurrently. A synthetic validity study is similar. Scores on a battery of job component tests are correlated with a performance measure.

Content validation is not empirical; it is a way to demonstrate the logical relationship of the test to the job. A job analysis is necessary. Tests are devised from a sample of work activities or of necessary KSAs.

Construct validation requires a job analysis to identify constructs underlying the KSAs. Scores on a test of a construct are obtained and correlated with scores on other tests. The test must show convergence with tests of the same construct and divergence with tests of other constructs.

These techniques have drawbacks. Criterion-related validation depends on a good criterion measure. Content validation requires a well-done job analysis. Construct validation cannot be done unless some other test includes items on the construct in question.

Validity generalization proposes that evidence gathered in one organization or job can be used to support the validity of a test used in another organization or job. Meta-analysis of cognitive ability test validities shows that validity does generalize.

TYPES OF TESTS

Certain basic procedures are required in setting up a selection testing program, whether tests are purchased or developed by the organization (see figure 5.2). A job analysis to determine work activities and KSAs is conducted first. After the job

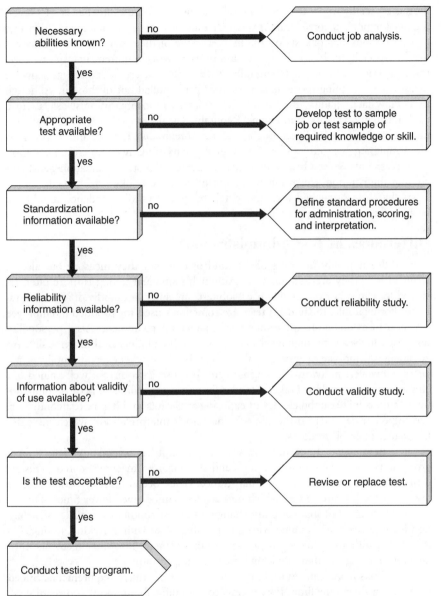

Figure 5.2. *Necessary steps in establishing a testing program.*

Necessary abilities known? — no → Conduct job analysis.

↓ yes

Appropriate test available? — no → Develop test to sample job or test sample of required knowledge or skill.

↓ yes

Standardization information available? — no → Define standard procedures for administration, scoring, and interpretation.

↓ yes

Reliability information available? — no → Conduct reliability study.

↓ yes

Information about validity of use available? — no → Conduct validity study.

↓ yes

Is the test acceptable? — no → Revise or replace test.

↓ yes

Conduct testing program.

analysis, existing tests that assess the required abilities and knowledge need to be identified or plans made for constructing them. Developing a content-valid selection test is one possibility (Schmitt & Ostroff, 1986). There is nothing to say a single test must do it all. Actually, batteries of tests are likely to be more useful because a job usually requires several qualifications that are not well evaluated by one test.

To decide whether to purchase or develop tests, consider what is economical. Usually, it takes less time and is cheaper to purchase a test if one is available.

This is especially true if the organization has few or urgent testing needs. However, the most important consideration is whether an available test is adequate. Although there are thousands of tests on the market, none of them may meet a company's needs, especially if the job is new or has unusual work requirements. In any case, test purchases must be made carefully. Some tests that are advertised as sensitive measures are nothing more than a batch of items pulled out of thin air. Although they show face validity, they can be worthless. The company must ask about a test's reliability, validity, and norms. Reputable test developers will make this information available. In addition, Buros's *Mental Measurements Yearbook* and *Tests in Print* are comprehensive sources that contain evaluations of many commercial tests. Critical assessments written by testing experts, references to other evaluations, and purchasing information are provided by these reference books (Plake et al., 1991). Tests that are not backed with sound reliability and validity evidence should not be accepted.

Differences in Test Administration

Tests differ not only in terms of the kind of behavior they measure but also in terms of how they are administered. Although individual testing is more often reserved for clinical or counseling uses, job tests are sometimes individually administered. For example, **individual tests** are sometimes used for production employee selection to evaluate an applicant's performance on equipment. Also, personality tests used for selecting high-level managers may be administered individually. An advantage of individual testing is that it can be done whenever an applicant appears. However, individual testing is costly because it requires a well-trained test administrator for each test taker. Standardization is more difficult because more administrations increase the chance of exposing applicants to different test conditions. Scoring often depends on the test administrator's interpretations, which increases the chance of error in scores.

In industry, the **group test** is more typical. It has several advantages. First, group tests are usually objective tests and these can be machine scored. This reduces both scoring error and administration costs. Second, many people can be tested at once in a group test, which means a test can be given fewer times. This reduces the chances of inadvertently changing the test conditions. Test standardization is more easily maintained with group testing than with individual testing. On the other hand, group testing is not spur-of-the-moment. Prior arrangements must be made to bring together applicants and test administrator.

Tests have features that imply certain administrative requirements. **Speed tests** have a short time limit. **Power tests** contain difficult questions and require the test taker's full capacity or power, but they have no pressing time limits. Speed tests contain questions that most people could answer if they had enough time. What is tested in a speed test is both accuracy and ability to work quickly. Speed tests are used frequently in industry, especially for testing large groups of applicants. This makes test administration more efficient because the group finishes at the same time, and standardized conditions are easily maintained. When the job requires quick thinking and action, speed tests are especially suitable. For example, some mechanical tests require quick and accurate hand movements.

Pencil-and-Paper and Performance Tests

Certain abilities, such as clerical and mechanical skills, are best assessed with performance tests. A **performance test** is one in which a physical action, such as typing, is evaluated. Typically, the score on a performance test is an index of speed and accuracy, such as the number of errors and the amount of work done in a standard time period. A **pencil-and-paper test** is what it sounds like—a written test. Pencil-and-paper tests are used to test knowledge of information. Usually, they contain multiple-choice or true-false questions, and they can be machine scored.

Increasingly, computers are used to administer pencil-and-paper tests. Questions are stored in a computer file and are presented to job applicants taking the test. Although some differences have been noted between those taking tests manually and those using a video display, computer administration of these tests generally appears to be effective (Newsted, 1985; Silver & Bennett, 1987). This is true at least for power tests; the computer version yields a score very similar to the paper version (Mead & Drasgow, 1993). There may be a problem with presenting speed tests by computer, however. Compared to the paper version, a computerized speed test produces faster but more *inaccurate* responses (Mead & Drasgow, 1993; Van de Vijver & Harsveldt, 1994).

Differences in the Behavior/Trait Measured

Cognitive or Mental Ability Tests

Tests differ in terms of the behavior or trait they measure. Cognitive or mental ability, which reflects educational effects and/or native intelligence, is frequently tested in industry. Both achievement and aptitude tests are used to assess these abilities. What has been learned or achieved through past experience and education is evaluated with an **achievement test.** The test you take for this course is an example. **Aptitude tests** are meant to assess native ability or capacity for learning. Actually, true aptitude tests are difficult to develop. Most actually include items of learned material along with the items on basic capacity. Of course, this is not unreasonable because capacity for learning can depend on previous achievement.

Tests of both general and specific mental abilities have been developed for use in selection. The General Aptitude Test Battery is a general mental ability test developed by the U.S. Department of Labor (1970). The Otis Self-Administering Test of Mental Ability is another general test. It is useful when a moderate level of cognitive ability is required. It does not distinguish well among higher intellectual levels. The Wonderlic Personnel Test is another widely used general mental ability test. Derived from the Otis, the Wonderlic is shorter, takes only a few minutes to administer, and can be used to screen for jobs requiring low or moderate cognitive ability.

Several specific mental ability tests are used, particularly to measure clerical abilities. The Minnesota Clerical Test and the General Clerical Test are examples. Both are speed tests that measure the capacity for quick and accurate perception. Because the tests contain number and name comparison items, the test

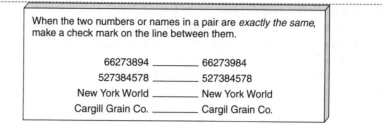

When the two numbers or names in a pair are *exactly the same*, make a check mark on the line between them.

66273894 _____ 66273984

527384578 _____ 527384578

New York World _____ New York World

Cargill Grain Co. _____ Cargil Grain Co.

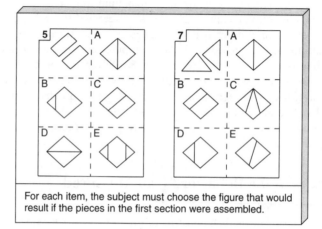

For each item, the subject must choose the figure that would result if the pieces in the first section were assembled.

content is similar to some clerical tasks. (See figure 5.3.) The Minnesota Clerical Test also can function as a test of word processing ability (Silver & Bennett, 1987).

Some special ability tests measure mechanical comprehension. For example, the Revised Minnesota Paper Form Board Test is a pencil-and-paper test used to measure the ability to visualize certain assembly operations. The Bennett Mechanical Comprehension Test is another special ability test suitable for jobs that require an understanding of mechanical principles. Figures 5.4 and 5.5 show sample items from these tests.

Perceptual and Motor Ability Tests

Some specific ability tests focus on perceptual and motor abilities. They measure a range of abilities from gross body coordination to finger dexterity and eye-hand coordination. They are performance tests and are used for jobs requiring mechanical skill. The Purdue Pegboard is an example of such a test. It requires a testee to quickly place pins into holes. Therefore, it functions as an aptitude test of finger dexterity and hand coordination. It is useful in selecting for assembly line jobs. The O'Connor test series also measures perceptual/motor skills. Both forms of this test measure finger dexterity and speed. In one form, the testee places pins into holes by hand; in the other, the task is done with tweezers. Still other tests have been developed to assess aptitudes for work requiring the use of small tools. In one form

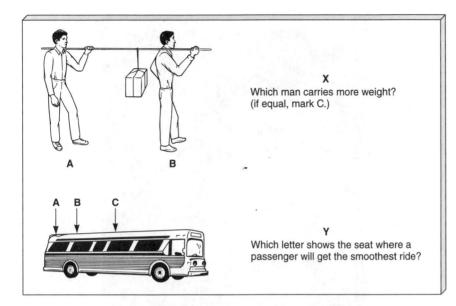

X

Which man carries more weight?
(if equal, mark C.)

A   B

A   B   C

Y

Which letter shows the seat where a
passenger will get the smoothest ride?

Figure 5.5. *Bennett Mechanical Comprehension Test items. This special ability test is suitable for jobs that require a person to understand physical relationships and mechanical principles.*

Sample items from the Bennett Mechanical Comprehension Test. Copyright 1942, 1967–1970, 1980 by The Psychological Corporation. Reproduced by permission. All rights reserved. "Bennett Mechanical Comprehension Test" and "BMCT" are registered trademarks of The Psychological Corporation.

Figure 5.6. *Two forms of the Crawford Small Parts Dexterity Test. In one form, tweezers are used to manipulate small pins in closely spaced holes on a board. In another form, small screws are inserted and screwed into holes.*

of the Crawford Small Parts Dexterity Test, tweezers are used to manipulate small pins in closely spaced holes on a board. In another form, small screws are inserted and screwed into holes with a small screwdriver (see figure 5.6).

What do small parts inspectors, piano tuners, and wine tasters have in common? All have jobs with special perceptual ability requirements. Their jobs demonstrate that work can make special demands on the visual, auditory, and olfactory/gustatory systems. A few tests are available for screening applicants on the basis of these perceptual abilities. For example, simple hearing tests usually require the person to detect tones of varying pitch at low volume.

The visual test with which you are probably most familiar is the Snellen letter chart, a simple test of far visual acuity. This is the *E* chart that you see in optometrists' offices. A testee reads from the chart letters of varying sizes from a specified distance. The score indicates the person's distance vision compared to

that of the normal population. If you have 20/20 vision, you can see from 20 feet what the normal population can see from this distance. If your vision is 20/30, you can see from 20 feet what the normal population can see from 30 feet. The Snellen has some value in selection but it tests distance acuity only. Job demands may require both distance and close acuity, as well as other visual capacities, such as color and depth.

Personality Tests

Personality testing is done by means of projective tests and self-report inventories. In **projective tests,** the person responds to ambiguous stimuli. The assumption is that the test taker projects his or her personality onto the stimuli, and the responses reflect this projection. The most widely known of projective tests are the Rorschach (inkblot) and the Thematic Apperception Test (TAT). In the TAT, people are pictured in ambiguous situations; the testee describes what they are doing (see figure 5.7 for an example). Projective tests are individually administered, and answers must be interpreted by someone trained in clinical psychology. Their use in industry is usually limited to executive selection.

Most personality tests are designed as self-report inventories.[2] A **self-report inventory** is a questionnaire containing personal information items. The Minnesota Multiphasic Personality Inventory (MMPI) is a well-known self-report

[2]Interest tests are similarly constructed as self-report inventories. Usually, they are used for career counseling, because they provide information about the extent to which a person shares interests with others working in various occupations. The Strong-Campbell Interest Inventory is a well-known example.

	M	L
Prefers to get up early in the morning..............................	⠿	■
Doesn't care for popular music..	⠿	⠿
Has an excellent command of English............................	⠿	⠿
Obtains a poorly balanced diet...	■	⠿

Respondent marks the description *most* like him or her (M)
and the description *least* like him or her (L).

Figure 5.8 *An item from the Gordon Personal Inventory. In this personality inventory, a forced-choice response strategy is used. The respondent selects the two descriptions that most resemble and least resemble him- or herself.*

inventory. It contains hundreds of items and measures 11 personality traits. The MMPI was developed for clinical use and is not often used in industry. The California Personality Inventory (CPI) was developed for the normal population. It provides scores on four personality traits. Other general purpose personality tests that are sometimes used include the Sixteen Personality Factor Questionnaire (16PF) and the Gordon Personal Inventory. (An item from the Gordon Personal Inventory is shown in figure 5.8.) Because self-report inventories are pencil-and-paper tests, they can be administered to a group, and they are less expensive than projective tests. Nonetheless, they are used only slightly more often and mainly for executive selection. For example, they may be included in assessment centers (Christiansen et al., 1994).

Intuitively, the idea that different jobs require different personalities is appealing. A salesman, most of us believe, must have certain traits that are not necessary for people in other jobs. If there is any truth in this, it would be reasonable to include a personality test in the selection program. However, those who have tried to use personality tests in selection have not always had good results. Mostly, such tests did not improve selection decisions. Still, the idea of using personality to predict job performance is intriguing.

Not long ago, the interest in personality testing for selection was given a boost when Digman (1990) described how 40 years of research on personality could be consolidated into a five-factor classification. The five factors are (1) extroversion, (2) agreeableness, (3) conscientiousness, (4) emotional stability, and (5) openness. (See table 5.4.) The model is called the Big Five.

The Big Five model provided a new approach to the issue of personality. The NEO Personality Inventory (NEO-PI) was construct-validated specifically to assess the five factors (McCrae & Costa, 1989). New studies and meta-analyses of existing research were done to see if this simpler model could show a valid use of personality in selection. New personality test scores were correlated with performance measures. Finally, the expected relationship was shown. One of the five factors, conscientiousness, clearly showed an ability to predict performance in a range of occupations (Hough et al., 1990; Barrick & Mount, 1991). Another factor, extroversion, also predicted performance in sales and managerial jobs (Barrick & Mount, 1991). Some research showed the job characteristics that were important in the power of personality. Barrick and Mount (1993) found that the amount of autonomy in a managerial job influenced the effect of conscientiousness and extroversion.

*T*able 5.4	The Big Five Personality Factors
Factor Label	**Descriptors**
Extroversion	Sociability; assertiveness; social involvement
Agreeableness	Likability; friendliness
Conscientiousness	Dependability; prudence; self-control
Emotional stability	Emotionality; neuroticism
Openness	Intelligence; independence

Now, there appears to be general agreement that conscientiousness is a valid predictor of work performance. However, some researchers caution that it is premature to broadcast the message that measures of conscientiousness can be included in selection programs. This is because controversy still surrounds the issue of assessing personality for hiring purposes. Questions remain. First, what does it mean when job applicants describe themselves as being conscientious? Does it have anything to do with their frame of reference in answering the test questions? Perhaps, people go by how they think they should present themselves. On test items that relate to work behavior, people may want to answer so as to make a good impression, just as they might in an interview. It may be that applicants taking the test are trying to present themselves as being ideal employment material (Schmit & Ryan, 1993; Schmit et al., 1995). Second, how does the applicant react to being given a personality test when applying for a job? Items on such tests ask for personal information. Applicants may view this as an invasion of privacy and distort their responses or otherwise react negatively (Rosse, Miller, & Stecher, 1994). These questions need to be studied.

Honesty Tests

In some jobs, an important component of performance is the handling of money, and an important selection need is the prediction of employee honesty.

Evaluating honesty has posed difficult problems for selection specialists. A variety of tests have been tried but none so far have been entirely satisfactory. The first to be used was the **polygraph,** or lie detector. This device takes a physiological reading (such as the galvanic skin response) while a series of questions about dishonest behavior are asked. The logic of the test is that the person will respond to the questions at an emotional level, and this can be detected in the physiological measure. However, the polygraph is not valid for selection purposes (Sackett & Decker, 1979). State and federal legislation has made its use unlawful in industry. A second approach is to use pencil-and-paper honesty tests. A number of these have been devised. Usually, they are simply collections of items about actual misbehavior and attitudes toward honesty. These tests present the same difficulty as polygraphs—inadequate evidence of validity (Sackett & Harris, 1984). Ironically, the most serious problem with honesty tests is that they can be faked.

We have been taking a narrow view of employee honesty. Employee theft is only one aspect of antisocial behavior at work. Hogan and Hogan (1989) suggested we would do better to focus on the broader aspects of negative employee behavior, including substance abuse, insubordination, bogus worker compensation claims, and employee theft. Sackett, Burris, and Callahan (1989) found that something of this sort is happening. Researchers have been taking a look at the employee's overall integrity and sense of ethics. Some of these **integrity tests** are personality oriented. They are based on the view that dishonesty is shown in a certain personality profile. Other integrity tests focus on attitudes and feelings about honesty and are more overt in their purpose. Because of this, they might be easy to fake. However, according to one study, this is not necessarily so. Subjects were instructed to try to appear very honest, yet the test was effectively resistant to such score inflation (Cunningham, Wong, & Barbee, 1994).

---

*M*ain

*P*oints

Should tests be developed or purchased? It depends on what needs to be assessed, whether good tests are available, and whether the organization has the capacity to develop and validate a test.

Tests can be speed or power tests, and pencil-and-paper or performance tests. Some are individually administered; others are group administered.

Several good tests are available for assessing cognitive or mental abilities. Some measure general intellectual capacity. Others test for specific mental abilities, such as clerical and mechanical skills. Some performance tests measure perceptual and motor abilities, such as finger dexterity.

Personality tests, either projective or self-report inventories, are sometimes used in executive selection. The Big Five model has spurred efforts to validate personality tests for selection. Conscientiousness has been shown to be a valid predictor of performance. For some jobs, so is extroversion. However, job applicants' reactions to taking personality tests need study.

Honesty tests are needed in selecting for jobs that involve money handling. Integrity tests, which examine a broad area of ethical behavior, are promising.

USING COMPUTERS IN TESTING

Computers can be helpful in the selection testing process in a number of ways. Items can be stored in computer files and then selected in different combinations to produce alternate forms of a test. Computers can be used to score tests and record testee data. As discussed earlier, conventional tests can be administered with computers to provide standardization and save the time of human administrators. Administration of tests by computer is known as **computer-assisted testing.**

With a new methodology, known as **Computer Adaptive Testing (CAT)**, we take a giant step beyond computer-assisted testing. In Weiss and Vale's (1987) enlightening discussion, CAT is described as highly efficient and more precise than any conventional method of testing. The computer *interacts* with the testee to develop and administer a test customized for the individual. It can do this because it contains a bank of questions that have been developed specifically to represent different levels of difficulty on a test. CAT is efficient because it makes the best use of the test taker's responses in selecting items that will constitute the test. The computer uses the person's response to one item to select the next item.

Some of the earliest research on CAT was to develop strategies for the computer to use in interacting with the individual. Weiss and Vale (1987) identified some issues that were addressed. One problem was how to select appropriate items for a test taker. The early CATs contained a bank of test items structured into subtests of different difficulty levels. A branching program was used to select items. That is, if the testee answered the first question correctly, the computer would select the second item from those at the next highest level of difficulty. If the testee answered incorrectly, the second item would be selected from the next lowest level of difficulty.

This early individualized testing had the potential of producing a more precise measure because it provided items appropriate to the individual's ability level. Consider this: In a conventional test, the overall difficulty of items is about the level of the average testee. Therefore, those who have either high or low ability are measured less precisely than those with average ability because there are comparatively fewer items appropriate for them. To measure these individuals more precisely in a conventional test, more items at their ability levels would need to be added, which generally makes the test too long. CAT circumvents this problem. CAT tailors the test to the individual's ability level by providing more items at the appropriate level of difficulty. Fewer items are either too easy or too hard; thus, the test is shorter, and at the same time it is a more precise measure for all levels of ability.

Another problem with the early CAT strategies was that there was no meaningful score. The number of correct answers could not be used, as it is in conventional tests, because each testee is given a different number of questions and questions of different difficulty. There was also no good way to terminate the test. If it was stopped after a certain number of items had been administered, precision of the test was damaged. Giving tests of the same size to all test takers would mean, as it does for conventional tests, that some are not measured as precisely as others.

Teaming CAT methodology with **Item Response Theory (IRT)** provided a way to solve all of these problems. Item Response Theory is actually a group of mathematical models that can be used to describe test items and make inferences about testee responses to them. Most IRT models describe test items in terms of their difficulty. Thus, IRT provides a way to predict how an individual will respond to an item as a function of his or her level of ability. Conversely, it provides a way to estimate the person's level of ability from his or her responses to a set of items that have known levels of difficulty. In other words, if we know how difficult a test is, we can infer an individual's level of ability from his or her correct or incorrect answers on the test.

IRT brings a number of positive features to CAT. It provides a place for starting the test and a means for identifying the best items for the testee. It provides a way to convert a series of test responses into an estimate of the underlying ability level. Finally, it helps the computer program to end a test. Weiss and Vale (1987) discussed each of these features as follows.

An IRT-based CAT starts with an estimate of the test taker's ability level. This estimate is the best guess for someone about whom nothing is known—the mean score or average level of ability in the population. Every item in the computer's test bank has a precise value with respect to its difficulty, because items have been specifically developed to measure a single difficulty level. The computer chooses an item at the average difficulty level and presents it as the first question. When the testee answers the question, the computer compares this bit of information (i.e., correct or incorrect answer) to stored information about the probability that the item would be answered in this way by a person with a known ability level. This stored information is in the form of a probability distribution known as the *item response curve*, which is based on the item's difficulty. By comparing the person's answer to the stored item response curve, the computer gets information about the accuracy of its estimate of the testee's ability level. This allows the computer to generate a new estimate. The new estimate is somewhat closer to the person's "true" ability level. This estimate provides the basis for selecting the second item. The same process is continued with the individual's response to the second and later questions, and a sequence of responses is generated. The sequence is treated similarly to the response to a single item. It is compared to stored sequences of responses at different ability levels. The comparison shows the probability that a person responding in this way has a given level of ability. This process continues, resulting in new estimates that get closer and closer to the person's "true" score of ability.

In selection testing, we want to know whether or not an applicant has passed the cutoff score. IRT gives CAT the ability to end the test as soon as it is clear that the individual's ability level is above or below a cutoff score. It does this by directing the computer to generate a standard error measurement with each new ability level estimate during the testing process. The standard error indicates how likely the ability estimate is to be wrong. As the ability estimate more and more closely approximates the person's "true" score, the standard error gets smaller, and we are more confident of the estimate's accuracy. The computer terminates the test when the combined estimate and standard error are clear of the cutoff score. One implication of this is that the time required for testing depends on how near the individual's true score is to the cutoff score. For applicants with high or low abilities, only a few items are needed to establish that the true score is either above or below the cutoff; thus, testing time is short. The CAT provides a quick but accurate screening of these individuals. For persons with average abilities, more items are needed because a more precise estimate of ability is required to establish that their true scores are either above or below the cutoff (Weiss & Vale, 1987).

In computer-assisted testing, conventional written tests are administered by computer. In contrast, Computer-Adaptive Testing (CAT) creates a way for the computer to customize a test for the individual test taker.

CATs contain a bank of items and a program for selecting items and for assessing the final pass/fail score. Item Response Theory (IRT) helps CAT methodology to do this. Because any testee is likely to have average ability, IRT-based CATs start with a question of average difficulty. The answer is used to make a new ability estimate, and this is used to pick another question. Sequences of answers are compared to stored scoring patterns to estimate the person's true ability. Each new estimate has an identifiable chance of being wrong, or a standard error. When the ability estimate plus or minus the standard error clears the cutoff score, the test is ended.

*C*HAPTER *S*UMMARY

One of the most important selection devices is the psychological test. Depending on its quality, a test can enable the employer to make good assessments of applicants' job potential and high-quality decisions about whom to hire.

A good selection test is standardized: Administration of the test is controlled; scoring is objective; and scores are interpreted against the scores of an appropriate sample. A good selection test is reliable. There are several ways to evaluate a test's reliability including the test-retest, alternate forms, split-halves, and interitem methods. A test must have a cutoff score and a reasonable way to make hiring decisions among applicants who pass. A good test is fair in that it predicts performance equally well for all groups of applicants. In addition, a test must have dollar-value utility. Finally, a good test is valid.

The validity of a test refers to its ability to provide an accurate measurement. This is the most important requirement of testing. There are several ways to assess validity. Criterion-related validity establishes an empirical relationship between test scores and criterion measures of performance. With predictive validation, a criterion-related technique, a sample of applicants is tested to establish the empirical relationship. With concurrent validation, another criterion-related technique, employees are used as the sample. Content validity is based on job analysis and is used to show that the test is valid because it samples the job content. Construct validation, in which both content and criterion-related strategies are used, shows the extent to which a test measures an underlying construct of the KSAs. Test validities obtained in one situation or organization generally have been thought to be specific to that situation. However, research on validity generalization indicates that some validities are generalizable.

I/O psychologists may develop tests or obtain commercial tests. A variety of tests are available, including cognitive or mental ability tests, perceptual and motor ability tests, and personality tests. Others, such as honesty tests, are being studied. Computers are being used to aid conventional testing. Computer-adaptive testing can develop and administer customized tests for individual applicants.

*S*TUDY *Q*UESTIONS

1) What is test standardization, and why is it important?

2) What are the methods of assessing test reliability, and how do they differ?

3) How are cutoff scores decided, and how does the user choose among the passing scorers?

4) What is test fairness, and how is it assessed?

5) What needs to be considered when testing disabled and older applicants?

6) What is the meaning of test utility, and how is it assessed?

7) How are criterion-related validity studies done? What problems can occur in these studies?

8) How does content validation produce evidence of test validity?

9) What is the relationship of convergent and divergent validity to construct validity?

10) What is the major issue underlying the research on validity generalization? Do validities generalize?

11) Distinguish between (a) individual and group tests, (b) speed and power tests, (c) pencil-and-paper and performance tests, and (d) achievement and aptitude tests.

12) How valuable are personality tests in the selection process?

13) Why do we use honesty tests in selection?

14) What is the difference between computer-assisted testing and CAT? How does an IRT-based CAT customize and score a test?

CONSIDER THIS

CASE STUDY

As described in other chapters, Vocational Rehabilitation Services (VRS) runs a sheltered workshop for training their disabled clients in factory work. The organization subcontracts with local manufacturing firms for work projects requiring assembly operations or similar manufacturing tasks.

Routinely, when a new work project comes in, the workshop manager analyzes the work and identifies specific activities and procedures that are needed to accomplish the project. These are written into work orders for the workshop instructors to use in training the clients on the job. In effect, these work orders are instructions on how to perform the job, and they need to be followed exactly for the work to be done properly.

Problem

Recently, VRS has had difficulties with some work projects, apparently because the instructors did not set up the job and do the training as described in the work order. The workshop manager believes that the problem occurred because some instructors have such poor reading skills that they did not understand the work order.

The director of VRS sees this as a problem of personnel selection in that people who are not qualified for the job were hired as workshop instructors. Although most work activities of the instructor's job do not require skill in reading, clearly some do, and this is not being evaluated in the selection procedure. In the past, the organization has hired shop instructors on the basis of an application screening and an unstructured interview. There has never been any specific effort made to determine an applicant's reading ability.

The director is interested in finding a selection procedure that will help VRS select instructors who have the necessary reading skills.

Is there a testing solution to this problem? What would you recommend that the director do?

what's in this chapter?

What is the best way to train someone to do a job? How do you know if you have succeeded? Simple, you say. Just show them how, and then put them on the job and see if they can do it. This is the basic idea, but it is a little more complicated in real-life situations.

In this chapter, you will find several ways to show someone how to do a job. A variety of methods can be used to develop job skills. For example, you can demonstrate a work procedure; tell a trainee the details; provide equipment to practice on; and use a case study. Which is the best method depends on what is being taught, and who is being trained. Different people have different needs for training.

The trainer starts by assessing the need for training. That is, what do employees need to learn? The basic principles of learning and practice are useful in deciding how to structure a program. At the end, trainers do not have to guess at the success of their programs. They can find out if the training worked by using systematic evaluation procedures.

One method frequently used for training employees is the small group discussion. Here, the instructor leads a work group in a discussion of economic problems, and uses a flipchart to present his material.

Chapter 6

Training and
Development
at Work

Contents

In one of his experiments, . . . McGaugh tested the maze-learning ability of two quite different strains of mice. One of the strains was, by heredity, particularly adept at maze learning; the other, particularly stupid at this task. Some animals from each strain were injected with different doses of metrazol after each daily learning trial to see whether there would be an improvement in their ability to retain what they had learned on that trial—and some were not. The findings pleased everyone—presumably even the mice. With the optimal dosage of metrazol, the chemically treated mice were 40 percent better in remembering their daily lessons than were their untreated brothers. Indeed, under metrazol treatment the hereditarily stupid mice were able to turn in better performances. . . .Here we have a "chemical memory pill."

D. Krech

The time will come, perhaps, when humans will have such a memory pill as Krech speculates. Apparently, we have been looking for one. Trainers complain that the principles of learning gleaned from research done in psychological laboratories cannot be used as a *prescription* for employee training programs. True, they cannot. However, we might actually come up with a reasonably good potion for our training ailments by blending the principles of basic learning with other available resources.

Although humans, like animals, have built-in physiological processes that do not require learning, most of what we think and do is acquired and changed through our experiences. That is, our behavior is learned. **Learning** is defined as a relatively permanent change in behavior that results from practice or experience. Research psychologists who study learning want to know what exactly happens in this experience (Wingfield, 1979). Learning and training are not the same, but the difference between them is largely practical. **Training** is a deliberately planned set of *learning experiences* designed to modify some feature of a person's behavior. For example, training can be designed to increase knowledge, improve skill, and/or change attitudes. In learning research, we try to understand the inherent nature of the learning process. In training and education, we try to make learning occur. Training and education differ also. Training tends to be more specific to the type of work that needs to be done, being more oriented to tools and techniques and less aimed at a general foundation of knowledge. Education is oriented toward developing basic, although extensive, knowledge and ability.

To plan and carry out employee training, three questions need to be asked. First, is there a *need* for training? Any of several training needs can exist at work. For example, *new* employees must be trained. All need an orientation to the job. Depending on their experience and previous training, some may need extensive instruction. In addition to training new employees, an organization may need to give refresher training to its present employees. The trainer uses specific techniques, called needs assessment, to determine what training is needed. Second, is learning theory and research useful in training employees? Trainers and educators want to know how to bring about learning. Therefore, they should find basic learning theory and research useful because it can help them arrange training more effectively (Gagne, 1962). For example, they should know that some training activities are good for producing certain kinds of learning but not for others. Different types of activities need to be learned for work. Some may involve perceptual/motor skills, such as driving or operating a power saw. Others involve cognition, such as making judgments or following a sequence of instructions. Do we learn these behaviors through the same learning process? Probably not. Different learning experiences likely are required for each (Houston, 1986). Program developers need to know this in order to custom design their training. Third, how is training designed, carried out, and evaluated? Analytical procedures are available to help in training development. (Job analysis is one.) Effective instructional methods can be borrowed from educational technology for use in training employees. Psychology provides research techniques that can be used for evaluation and to establish that the training does what it is supposed to do. The issues behind these three questions are the thrust of this chapter.

CONDUCTING TRAINING AT WORK: PREPARATION

Experience has taught us that training programs need to be customized to meet specific training needs. They should not be designed specifically to accommodate existing procedures or to match what some other company is doing. Adopting the latest fad may be especially tempting with some types of training. For example, because managerial tasks often seem to be similar across jobs and companies, we may be more willing to accept a general training program for managers than we would be for production employees. Managerial training, however, like all employee training, must be based on an assessment of training needs (Schneier, Guthrie, & Olian, 1988).

Training Needs Assessment

Training and Motivational Needs

Before conducting training, two questions need to be asked: Is there a need for training? If so, what is the nature of this need? Sometimes, when things are not going as well as they should be or when people are not doing what is expected, a need for some intervention is felt. We should not be too quick, however, to assume that the need is for training. A performance problem may occur because employees do not have the necessary knowledge and skill, or it may occur because they lack motivation. Intervention programs often must consider both. However, training and motivational interventions are not interchangeable. Training aims largely to improve ability and knowledge. Thus, training programs are best when a performance problem is due to a lack of ability or skill. Incentive programs are needed for motivational problems in which willingness rather than ability accounts for the discrepancy (see figure 6.1). For example, if employees do not know how to accomplish some aspect of their jobs, they should be trained. However, if something like tardiness is a problem, "teaching" them to come to work on time probably will not help much, because they probably already know how to get to work on time.

Figure 6.1. *The relationship of motivation and ability to training. Training aims largely to improve ability and knowledge. Incentive programs are needed for motivational problems.*

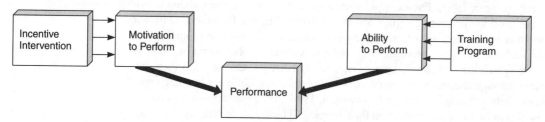

Rather, this problem calls for incentives. We may encounter either or both problems in a needs assessment. Our job is to determine whether a performance discrepancy can be solved by a training program (Wexley, 1984).

Why wait until a performance problem has developed? Why not anticipate future needs and prepare for them? There are three occasions when training needs are likely. One, when new employees are hired, they will not be perfectly matched to their jobs, even with excellent selection. Two, when new jobs are developed or old ones redesigned, present employees will lack the necessary skills for the new work. Three, when a company changes its product or buys new equipment, training will be needed. Some future needs for training also have motivational components; therefore, incentives are needed as well. For example, when a company is planning to buy word-processing equipment, the clerical staff will need training. In addition, employees may react negatively to the new equipment. If so, this reaction should not be ignored.

Sources of Information on Training Needs

Following McGehee and Thayer (1961), most professionals view a **training needs assessment** as a process of getting information about the needs of the organization, the tasks, and the person. Assessment at these three levels provides information that varies in terms of its specificity. Organizational assessment identifies general needs and indicates *where* training is required in the organization. Task or job analysis indicates specifically *what* behaviors need to be improved, and person analysis shows *who* needs to receive training.

Organizational analysis provides general information about such variables as absenteeism, turnover, and accidents. High levels of any of these in a department may indicate a training need. In his review of the research, Latham (1988) found that two themes characterize the thinking on organizational analysis. One is that modern businesses should tie training to the overall business plan or corporate strategy. Training should first be for the benefit of the firm and then for the benefit of the individual. The second theme says that the firm has a social responsibility to minimize loss of employee job skills when technological changes are introduced. Retraining is one way to do this.

Organizational analysis shows the broad outlines of training needs; it is not specific enough to guide instruction. Task and person analyses provide the specifics. Task analysis, discussed in chapter 3 as a type of job analysis, is a method of assessing training needs as well. Task analysis is used to assess the current needs

Table 6.1 Needs Assessment Information

Focus of Assessment	Assessment Levels	Information Sources	Information Obtained
All employees	Task	Job analyses and job descriptions	Description of types of tasks Description of required KSAs Description of career track
New employees	Person	Individual records	Test results, previous training, and experience indicating present capacities
Present employees	Person	Interviews with employee and supervisor Performance evaluations	Employee perceptions of difficulties in job and need for skill development Supervisor perception of needs for improvement and for promotional development Individual performance evaluation
Units or work teams	Organization	Interviews with supervisors and managers	Plans for reorganization, job redesign, or product/procedure change

of a job. The required KSAs give information about the kinds of training needed by anyone who performs the job. When jobs are expected to change and retraining needs are being anticipated, the task analysis is somewhat different. It must be oriented to the future job. One way to analyze future training needs is to use managers' predictions of how jobs are likely to change. To analyze future executive jobs, Hall (1986) proposed a future-oriented job analysis in which anticipated goals of the organization are defined and linked to the executive's tasks.

A **person analysis** describes the difference between what an employee presently can do and what he or she eventually should be able to do. Person analysis is done in a variety of ways. Information about the training needs of new employees can come from selection records, such as test scores or data on previous education and experience. Supervisors are in a position to assess training needs because they see their subordinates' work on a daily basis and conduct periodic performance evaluations. Supervisor information can indicate a need for remedial training for employees whose performance is unsatisfactory or for developing superior employees for promotion. (Table 6.1 summarizes the sources and types of information obtained in needs assessments.) Training needs also can be identified by employees themselves. Survey instruments often are used to solicit employees' self-assessments of training needs. Employees may be able to identify aspects of their jobs with which they have difficulty. However, we need to be careful here because people do not always know what they need to learn.

Training Design

Education design theory is helpful in the development of a training program (Bauman, 1977). Our first step in design is to evaluate the information we have collected

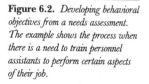

Figure 6.2. *Developing behavioral objectives from a needs assessment. The example shows the process when there is a need to train personnel assistants to perform certain aspects of their job.*

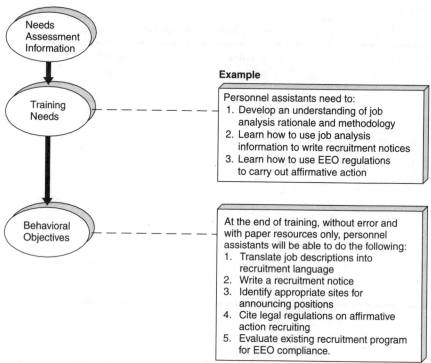

Example

Personnel assistants need to:
1. Develop an understanding of job analysis rationale and methodology
2. Learn how to use job analysis information to write recruitment notices
3. Learn how to use EEO regulations to carry out affirmative action

At the end of training, without error and with paper resources only, personnel assistants will be able to do the following:
1. Translate job descriptions into recruitment language
2. Write a recruitment notice
3. Identify appropriate sites for announcing positions
4. Cite legal regulations on affirmative action recruiting
5. Evaluate existing recruitment program for EEO compliance.

in the needs assessment to determine the exact nature and extent of the **training need.** This need defines the goal and direction of training. A training need indicates the KSAs to be developed. Training programs can be designed to meet more than one training need. An example of a training need is shown in figure 6.2.

In education design, explicit **behavioral objectives** are derived from the more broadly stated training need. They define exactly what changes in knowledge, skill, and ability should take place within a person, and they guide training activities. Well-defined behavioral objectives incorporate measurable post-training **terminal behaviors.** A terminal behavior is the aspect of job performance that training is supposed to produce. It is something that can be seen and measured; it is something that the trainee *does* to show that he or she has acquired a specific knowledge or skill. Behavioral objectives also define conditions and standards for evaluating the extent to which learning occurs. Conditions can include aids that are necessary for performance, such as equipment or reference books. Standards of excellence allow the trainer to evaluate or "grade" the trainee's performance. To establish standards, the training designer must decide what constitutes a successful terminal behavior. Standards define the levels of performance accuracy or quality required. For example, we can stipulate that the terminal performance be error free. Figure 6.2 shows how behavioral objectives are derived for training a group of personnel department employees.

Table 6.2

Behavioral Objectives and Learning Tasks for Training Personnel Assistants

Behavioral Objective	Learning Task
Translate job description information into recruitment language.	Study methods used by organization to analyze jobs and infer employee requirements. Study job descriptions for all jobs presently used. Study terminology used in recent recruitment notices. Using job analysis data, write recruitment statements.
Develop a recruitment notice.	Study recruitment terminology used by the organization. Study job analysis data and other descriptive material. Write a recruitment notice.
Identify appropriate sites for listing position announcements.	Study local labor statistics to determine location of applicant populations. Study community media and directories indicating public posting sites. Study procedures for posting used by organization.

Learning tasks are derived from behavioral objectives. They describe the experiences required to bring about the desired learning. They are specific directions for the instructor. Thus, learning task statements form a bridge between the needs assessment and the instructional phase of the training program. To develop learning tasks, the trainer decides what trainees must do to achieve each behavioral objective. For example, to develop a particular ability, trainees first may need to study a resource document and then practice an administrative procedure (see table 6.2). One or more learning tasks will emerge from each behavioral objective, with complex objectives yielding more learning tasks. When learning tasks have been defined for all behavioral objectives, they are organized into a coherent whole. The trainer is now ready to apply training methods and translate the learning tasks into learning experiences.

*M*ain *P*oints

To prepare for conducting employee training, a trainer must first establish that a training need exists. Not all performance problems can be solved with training. Some training needs can be anticipated, as when new employees are hired or when jobs are changed.

Training needs assessment is conducted by gathering information at the levels of the organization, job, and person. Organizational assessments indicate overall needs and suggest where training might be helpful. Task analysis defines what training is needed for the job. Person analysis identifies individual needs for training.

When a training need is revealed, the process of training design begins. The designer starts with a statement of the training need and from that develops behavioral objectives to be reached in the training program. Behavioral objectives specify what should be learned, and they guide the training. They are phrased in terms of terminal behaviors, or what performance should be shown at the end of training. Learning tasks are drawn out of behavioral objectives, and they determine what the instructor does in training sessions.

USING THE RESEARCH ON LEARNING IN TRAINING DESIGN

Before we take the next step in training design, let us consider what is known about the process of learning. Psychologists have produced a large body of research literature on the nature of learning, and some of it is helpful for trainers to know. Certainly, the literature cannot be used as a list of instructions. It is too general to provide specific answers for training designs. However, it orients the trainer and provides a systematic approach to training that is often missing in common practice (Rasmussen, 1982). In this section, I discuss some learning variables relevant to training. These are practice, motivation, trainee differences, and transfer of training.

Importance of Practice

In order for learning to occur and for material to be retained, practice is essential. For long-term retention, extensive practice is required. Research has made it clear that mere exposure of the trainee to learning material is not an effective training strategy (Houston, 1986). Primarily, practice is repetition of an action or sequence of behaviors. For example, we learn how to change a tire by changing many tires, that is, by repeating the sequence of physical behavior in this operation. Practice is also rehearsal or oral repetition, as when we memorize lines in a play, or go over a train of thought, as in learning law. As these examples suggest, practice can be physical performance or mental activity in which a trainee repeatedly thinks through some material.

Practice contributes to the learning process by actively involving the trainee in the behavior to be learned. Correspondingly, it provides **feedback** about a performance. Feedback gives the trainee information about accuracy and ways to improve. In addition to being informative, practice can be motivating, especially when the trainee is having some success with a task. Accomplishment in acquiring new knowledge and skill is a positive experience and can operate as a reward for continuing practice.

How much practice is enough depends on how long you want new learning to last. Research has shown that long-term retention is aided by overlearning (cf. Schendel & Hagman, 1982). **Overlearning** is the stamping in of a new behavior that is practiced continually, beyond the point at which the behavior is first acquired. Figure 6.3 illustrates this process. Overlearning can account for many long-lasting skills, such as typing or driving.

Section II: Establishing a Strong Work Force

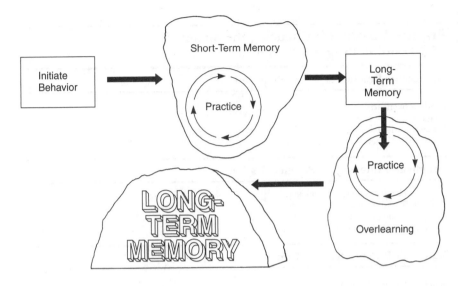

Figure 6.3. *The relationship of practice to learning and memory. Research has shown that overlearning aids long-term memory and leads to long-lasting skills.*

The amount of practice needed depends on how often the ability will be used. If newly learned material is used only infrequently on the job, there will be little opportunity for "natural" practice; therefore, extra practice should be included in the training program. If, however, the learned material is used frequently, opportunities for overlearning will be available on the job; therefore, a trainer needs to be concerned only with the trainee's initial learning of the material. Table 6.3 lists some questions to ask in deciding the amount and form of practice.

Pacing and Content of Practice Sessions

Given that practice is necessary, the next question concerns the design of a practice session. Should trainees have regular, periodic practice throughout training? Should they wait until the end of instruction and have one intense session? These are familiar questions to educators as well as to trainers. College professors often recommend that students study regularly throughout the term. Many students, however, apparently believe it is better to wait until all the material has been covered; that is, until the night before the exam. The issue here concerns the value of **distributed** versus **massed practice**. Before deciding which is better, however, we need to know how much and what kind of material is to be practiced. The concepts of **part** and **whole learning** tell us whether the task should be broken down into its elements and practiced separately or kept whole and practiced all at once.

The best design for a practice session depends on the nature of the learning task. If the task is a simple, coherent whole, then it should be practiced as a whole in a massed session. If it is a complex task, however, or if the training material is extensive and entirely new to the trainee, distributed practice is better. For example, in a program training employees for basic word processing, it was found that two 30-minute training sessions were more effective than one 60-minute massed session (Bouzid & Crawshaw, 1987). In some cases, it is appropriate to

Table 6.3

Practice Variables Influencing the Structure of a Training Program Design

Number of Practice Sessions Required

Need for overlearning?
Frequent practice on the job?
Practice distributed over training?
Intersession or mental practice?

Length and Intensity of Practice Sessions

Practice to be distributed over training?
Number of sessions needed?
Complex or simple tasks?
Importance of order of subtask performance?

Nature of Practice Session Content

Simple task practiced whole?
Practice of complex task elements?
Subtask order practiced whole?
Physical practice or mental practice?

combine these forms of practice. If the activity is a complex set of actions to be performed in *sequence,* then a mixed schedule that combines distributed and massed practice is best. Such tasks as flying an airplane or analyzing research data are complex sets of activities that demand practice of the *elements* as well as the *order* in which the elements are performed. In such cases, we start with distributed practice of the elements followed by massed practice of the whole. A different way to combine distributed and massed practice of a complex activity is for trainees to work in pairs. Each takes half of the task, and together they perform the sequence. Then, they switch roles (Shebilske et al., 1992).

Mental Practice of Physical Tasks

Imagery or **mental practice** is a way of rehearsing in which the procedure for doing a task is mentally performed without the physical movement. Mental practice is helpful in learning perceptual/motor skills, especially if they require many cognitive operations, such as analysis and judgment (Driskell, Copper, & Moran, 1994). Performance can be improved by the alternation of physical and mental practice, especially if the mental practice sessions are short and frequent (Driskell et al., 1994; Richardson, 1967; Zecker, 1982). Mental rehearsal may be more effective as intersessional practice, that is, when it is interspersed between instructional periods. A study of athletic training gives us a clue as to how mental practice helps. Hale (1982) measured the amount of electrical activity in the biceps of experienced weight lifters. When the lifters were told to imagine themselves performing a dumbbell curl, there was more activity in their muscles than when they were told to imagine watching someone performing the curl. Perhaps certain types of mental practice contain elements of physical practice.

Motivation and Learning

Learning psychologists take motivation into account by ensuring that training sessions include reinforcement or rewards. As I discuss in chapter 8, a reinforcer increases the likelihood of a response being repeated. Response repetition or practice is essential for learning to occur. Thus, reinforcement is required in training.

Exactly what is reinforcing varies between individuals. However, certain intrinsic and extrinsic factors are generally rewarding to trainees. Intrinsic motivation refers to the value of the learning task itself. Sometimes, there is joy simply in learning something new. Whether the training experience has an intrinsic value that can reinforce learning depends on the person to some extent. For example, trainees who were encouraged to expect success performed better in training (Eden & Ravid, 1982). Whether the training experience is intrinsically rewarding also depends on the learning tasks, of course. Some simply are not very interesting. In such cases, extrinsic reinforcement outside the task is needed. Extrinsic motivators do not have to be tangible, such as monetary rewards, although they can be. It may be enough for the trainer simply to make a connection between success in training and later on-the-job rewards. Also, the social reinforcement of encouragement or recognition in a training session may be enough.

Feedback and Reinforcement

One way to understand how reinforcement operates on learning is to consider the action-consequence sequence involved in the learning process. The consequence of an action informs the performer about the action. That is, we get feedback from what we do. Feedback produces positive or negative effects on us personally. It also tells us whether we need to modify our action. Therefore, in a learning sequence, an action that results in positive effects is likely to be repeated, and practice of the action will continue. Similarly, because of feedback, an action that has negative effects is likely to be modified (see figure 6.4).

Practically, this suggests that training should include opportunities for practice in which positive outcomes follow accurate performance. In addition, inaccuracies should be communicated to the trainee to encourage changes in performance. Giving trainees information about how they are progressing is helpful, especially to those whose progress is slow (Matsui, Okado, & Inoshita, 1983). Including feedback also keeps the trainer focused on what action or behavior is supposed to be learned. Sometimes, we reinforce a behavior other than the one we mean to develop. A way to avoid this mistake is to incorporate accurate performance feedback into the training sessions. The trainer will need to evaluate trainee behavior and suggest ways to improve.

It seems like an enormous task to give such customized feedback and reinforcement to trainees. Is this really necessary? Research says it is. Some feedback from the trainer is better than none (Karl, O'Leary-Kelly, & Martocchio, 1993), and when a learning task is first started, immediate feedback is better than delayed

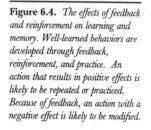

Figure 6.4. *The effects of feedback and reinforcement on learning and memory. Well-learned behaviors are developed through feedback, reinforcement, and practice. An action that results in positive effects is likely to be repeated or practiced. Because of feedback, an action with a negative effect is likely to be modified.*

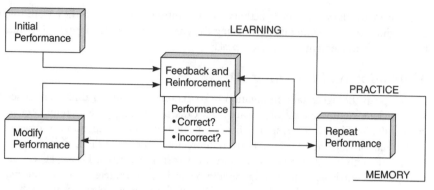

(Mason & Redmon, 1992). However, research also provides a shortcut. The key to reinforcement is frequency: How often must it be given? At first, feedback and reinforcement should be frequent–whenever the correct performance is shown. Later, after the behavior becomes somewhat established, a partial reinforcement schedule can be adopted. In this, the trainer monitors the behavior of trainees and gives reinforcement periodically. For example, reinforcement and feedback can be given after some time has passed, or after the trainee has practiced a certain amount. Partial reinforcement is effective. In one study, for example, subjects who received only occasional reinforcement performed well and reported positive personal reactions to the job itself, seeing it as a varied and enriched activity (Saari & Latham, 1982).

Individual Differences in Trainees

The trainer should consider the capacities and motivation of the trainees in deciding what and how much to cover in a training session. (See figure 6.5.) Several trainee characteristics, such as learning rate, basic abilities, and personality, are likely to interact with instructional strategies (Cronbach & Snow, 1977). For example, training sessions need to be well paced and contain a variety of activities, otherwise some trainees will lose interest.

Trainers need to know about employees' motivation to participate in and learn from training sessions. In general, research has shown that high pretraining motivation improves training performance (cf. Mathieu, Tannenbaum, & Salas, 1992). Motivation to learn may or may not be high, however, depending in part on why the employee is in training. When employees go into training for promotional purposes, they have a different attitude and higher motivation than those who are assigned to training because of poor job performance. When an employee is sent to remedial training, this assignment creates a different reaction which can be detrimental to training performance (Quiñones, 1995).

Existing Trainee Knowledge and Abilities
How does a trainer know a trainee's ability? Surely, the members of a training group will vary. They will; however, if they have been selected for the same job category, it is likely that they will not vary greatly. Further, the needs assessment will provide information on trainee ability.

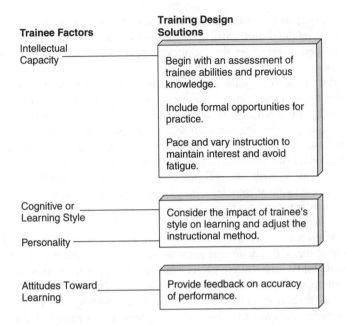

Trainee Factors

Intellectual Capacity

Cognitive or Learning Style

Personality

Attitudes Toward Learning

Training Design Solutions

Begin with an assessment of trainee abilities and previous knowledge.

Include formal opportunities for practice.

Pace and vary instruction to maintain interest and avoid fatigue.

Consider the impact of trainee's style on learning and adjust the instructional method.

Provide feedback on accuracy of performance.

Figure 6.5. *Trainee factors to be considered in planning an effective training program.*

In addition to existing information, the trainer can conduct special assessments. For example, a pretest of what a training program includes can be given to trainees before they are trained. A pretest can show the degree to which trainees already know the material. Using a pretest in assessment is best when training consists mostly of informational content and is designed to increase knowledge of a subject. When the program is geared toward skill development, however, the **miniature training and evaluation** method is more helpful. With this method, a lesson on the task is given and is followed by an evaluation of the trainee's performance on the task. This method detects previously developed skill as well as aptitude and is effective in assessing trainee capacity for a range of manual skills (Siegel, 1983).

Another way to assess trainee abilities is with a **trainability test.** Individuals vary in their **trainability** or capacity to benefit from training, and this will affect the instruction. Two people who have very different intellectual capacities might be taught the same subject matter, but the training methods would differ. More capable trainees can learn new material with fewer formal practice sessions, and some instructional techniques, such as homework or self-instruction, are better suited to them than to less capable trainees. A trainability test is similar to the miniature training and evaluation in that a work sample is used to give a lesson and then to test a trainee's performance. The advantage of trainability tests is that they can predict successful training, even of those who have had no previous training (Robertson & Downs, 1989).

Transfer of Training

The most important goal of employee training is to improve performance on the job. Training is meant to develop behavioral tendencies that are useful when similar situations are encountered on the job (Gagne, 1977). That is, training is meant to be transferred to the work setting. **Transfer of training** occurs when training material is generalized and learning is carried over to the job. Baldwin and Ford (1988) proposed that transfer also includes changes in learning that occur over time while on the job.

Material learned in the past can show either **positive** or **negative transfer** in a current performance situation. For example, knowing how to drive a car will probably help you learn how to drive a truck because some driving abilities will transfer to the new driving situation and retain their usefulness. The hand and foot coordination required in shifting gears is one such ability. However, other driving behaviors will interfere. Zipping around in heavy traffic, a handling style you learned with a small car, will hinder your attempts to handle a large truck. Training programs must maximize positive transfer and minimize negative transfer. It is clearly a waste of time and money for training to develop new skills that are not transferred.

When training transfers, we can detect it in job performance. Baldwin and Ford (1988) proposed that several patterns occur in the transfer and maintenance of a trained ability. They offered a set of hypothetical curves to represent the patterns graphically. (Four of their curves are shown in figure 6.6a–d.) These curves describe certain changes in behavior over time and indicate whether there was effective learning, immediate transfer, and long-term maintenance of the behavior. Three curves show effective learning (figure 6.6a,b,c). Figure 6.6d describes a pattern in which ability is not much greater after than before training. In two of the three curves where there was learning, there also was immediate transfer of the ability (figure 6.6a,c). The other curve describes a situation in which learning gained in training is never used (figure 6.6b). Learning may fail to transfer because of conditions on the job. For example, sometimes newly trained employees arrive back on the job and find that what they have learned is "not done here." If there is transfer, it may or may not persist over time. Two curves show differences in the maintenance of behavior (figure 6.6a,c). In one, the ability is gradually lost, suggesting that it is not often used (figure 6.6a). In the other, the ability declines sharply after a short period (figure 6.6c). This can occur when a supervisor does not support an employee's use of the new ability.

Learning psychologists believe that transfer occurs as a process of **stimulus generalization** and **discrimination** (Houston, 1986). When we learn a behavior in one situation, other situations that are similar tend to elicit the behavior. That is, the *stimulus* for the behavior *generalizes* to other similar stimuli. For example, automotive repair skills learned in vocational school will be used when the individual goes to work in a garage and when the lawn mower breaks down at home because of the similarity of these situations. When we design job training, we should copy or simulate the actual working conditions because the similarity of the job to the training will tend to evoke the trained behavior. To the extent that the relevant conditions of work are simulated, positive transfer can be expected.

Stimulus discrimination is related to generalization. Frequently, what we learn in training is a response contingency: When situation A arises, do X; when situation B arises, do Y. Discrimination between situations A and B is essential for

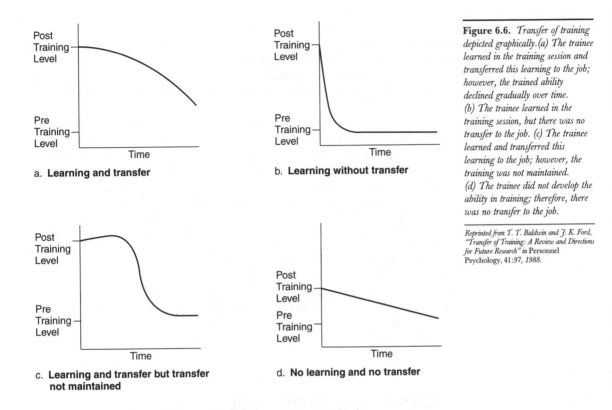

a. **Learning and transfer**

b. **Learning without transfer**

c. **Learning and transfer but transfer not maintained**

d. **No learning and no transfer**

Figure 6.6. *Transfer of training depicted graphically. (a) The trainee learned in the training session and transferred this learning to the job; however, the trained ability declined gradually over time. (b) The trainee learned in the training session, but there was no transfer to the job. (c) The trainee learned and transferred this learning to the job; however, the training was not maintained. (d) The trainee did not develop the ability in training; therefore, there was no transfer to the job.*

Reprinted from T. T. Baldwin and J. K. Ford, "Transfer of Training: A Review and Directions for Future Research" in Personnel Psychology, 41:97, 1988.

correct performance, and the tendency to treat them the same must be suppressed. We must respond differently even though they actually may be quite similar. The ability to see distinctions between two highly similar stimuli and to respond differentially often marks the superior employee. In a practical example, a college recruiter may see a great deal of similarity between one college senior and another, and the recruiter may behave similarly in the interviews. However, the essential element is discrimination between the seniors. If one is superior, the recruiter must behave so as to interest him or her in joining the company.

How does a trainer develop a program that will result in positive transfer? First, the program must be customized to fit the training needs of the organization. Second, training should simulate the relevant aspects of the work for which employees are being trained. A needs assessment that includes a job analysis will help the trainer do this. Trainers may need to impress upon trainees exactly what is most important in the training material and provide reasons or underlying principles of significant material (Fotheringhame, 1986; Salmaso et al., 1983). Third, the trainer can offer a refresher, or relapse prevention session. This can help prevent loss of the newly learned material (Tziner, Haccoun, & Kadish, 1991). Finally, the trainer can recommend that the organization's climate and attitudes toward learning be examined to identify and remove obstacles to transfer that exist in the job (Tracey, Tannenbaum, & Kavenagh, 1995).

Practice is essential in learning. It helps because rehearsing gives feedback on how to improve. Practice can be distributed or massed. Which is best depends on the complexity of the material and whether a sequence is involved. Some material can be practiced as a whole; other material is practiced in parts. Mental practice can improve some skills.

For learning to occur, the person must be motivated. Reinforcement of practice can occur through the intrinsic aspects of work or by extrinsic rewards. Feedback provides for modifications of the behavior. Trainers need to incorporate rewards and feedback in the training. Partial reinforcement is effective for increasing learning and is easy for a trainer to use.

Trainers must consider the trainees when designing a program. Trainees differ in their existing knowledge. A trainer can get information about their abilities from the needs assessment or by testing trainees on a work sample. Trainees also differ in their motivation to learn. Some are in training because they want to advance. Others are sent for remedial help. These trainees differ in motivation and will differ in what they get out of training.

Transfer of training is essential. There are several reasons why it may not occur. Maybe the trainees did not learn, or maybe there were obstacles to using the new learning on the job. Trainers need to do all they can to ensure that transfer occurs.

TRAINING METHODOLOGY

Before we walk into the training room, we should have the session planned. The **lesson plan** is an outline of the content and methodology used in a training session. To structure a lesson plan, we start by mapping out the general organization for the entire training program. We list the learning tasks that were extracted from the behavioral objectives and organize them into an economical and coherent sequence. A number of sequencing patterns can be used to organize this content (see table 6.4). The lesson plan guides the session. Listing the learning tasks helps keep training focused on the objectives. Techniques, materials, and equipment are specified, and a time schedule for covering the training material is included. (Figure 6.7 provides an example.)

Trainees should be considered in the planning stages. The lesson plan should be structured so as to maintain interest and avoid excessive mental or physical fatigue. Alternating complex and simple material, following lectures with discussions or other interactive techniques, and scheduling frequent changes of pace are ways to keep trainees involved. We also need to consider the *trainer*. Sometimes, we find ourselves with a training program and no one to conduct it. In such a situation, there are several solutions. A training staff member can be trained on site or sent off site to obtain training in the subject matter or skill. Qualified trainers

Table 6.4   Sequencing Patterns Used in Ordering Instructional Content of Training Sessions

Sequence Method	Order of Instructional Content
Chronological	From history to current events to future
Climactic	From simple to complex; or from familiar to unknown
Logical	From simple to difficult; from theoretical to practical; or from abstract to concrete
Task order	From the first step to the final step in job operation

Source. A. R. Bauman, *Training of Trainers: Resource Manual.* 1977. U.S. Government Printing Office, Washington, DC.

LESSON PLAN

BEHAVIORAL OBJECTIVE: Use of job description for recruitment.

Learning Task 1: Introduce the nature and use of job analysis.

Time	Method	Materials	Content
9:00 – 9:30	Lecture	Flipchart; Handout - Glossary of terms	Overview of job study techniques; Procedures: Data collection; subject-matter expert panels; Employee qualification statements.
9:30 – 9:40	Question/ Answer period		
9:40 – 10:15	Discussion	Handouts - Sample job analysis, job description	Facilitate discussion of task statement terminology; Discuss inference from tasks to qualification.
10:15 – 10:30	Break		
10:30 – 11:00	Simulation	Paper; Handout - New job analysis	Using new job analysis materials, develop a job description.

Learning Task 2: Translate job description into recruitment notice.

Time	Method	Materials	Content
11:00 – 11:15	Lecture	Flipchart	Purpose of active

Figure 6.7. *A fragment of a lesson plan used in training personnel assistants.*

can be hired specifically to do the instruction. Training can be conducted without an instructor, as when self-instructional materials (such as computer programs) and audiovisual resources are used.

Choosing Training Techniques

One of the most important aspects of lesson planning is the selection of appropriate training techniques. Some training techniques are used to convey information that will increase knowledge; others are used to develop skill. Lectures and reading assignments are economical and effective in presenting large amounts of information. So too, are guided discussion, question-answer sessions, films, and other such audiovisual materials, and computer-assisted instruction. A moment's thought will convince you that these methods are not well suited to skill development, however. Guided practice with feedback, coaching, practice on machine simulators, and demonstrations are better techniques for developing trainee skill. Audiovisual and printed materials can be used if they demonstrate processes or results. For example, some homeowners learn how to do simple electrical wiring by studying the diagrams in "how to" books on home wiring. Such demonstration materials are best combined with practice and feedback sessions, however. To train interpersonal or social skills, the trainer can use such techniques as role play, behavior modeling, and structured experiences.

In lesson planning, we must resist the urge to develop a lesson around a particular technique. Remember, the training objectives dictate the methodology, not vice versa. Rather than ask, "What shall we do in class today?" the trainer should ask, "What do we need to learn today?" In selecting training techniques, the trainer should also consider the formality of the training session, as well as such practical issues as the availability of materials and time. If a technique requires several hours to accomplish, but total training time is less than that, the technique simply cannot be used. In summary, a technique should be appropriate to the learning task, the setting, and the time constraints.

Techniques for Training Knowledge and Skill

Many training techniques have been drawn from adult education, and have been used to train both trainers and employees (Bauman, 1977). Some techniques are quite general and useful for a variety of training content, while others are specialized. For example, the lecture is used to convey information on any subject matter, whereas behavior modeling has been developed primarily for training interpersonal skills, such as employee supervision. Although trainers excel in some methods more than in others, they must be able to use a wide range of techniques. Training programs typically incorporate both informational and skill-building methods. The following are 11 of these techniques listed according to the involvement of the trainee, in order from passivity to activity:

1.   A *lecture,* as you know, is an oral presentation of a topic. A good one is carefully prepared and effective for presenting information or points of view. Lectures can stimulate, inspire, and entertain an audience. They

are useful for opening a topic for discussion and can reach audiences of any size. Variations include a minilecture, which is a short speech. A lecture series is a sequence of lectures extending over several training sessions.

2.   In a *moderated panel discussion,* a small group of experts explore a topic while trainees listen. The moderator keeps the discussion on track. The panel may discuss a topic in depth; provide breadth of information by covering different aspects of an issue; or present alternatives for problem solution. The panel has the advantage of being a less formal method of conveying information, but it requires a thorough moderator to make sure that the discussion is complete.

3.   *Demonstrations* are used when trainers want to present either a method or a result of job performance. Typically, the presentation is accompanied by discussion of what the trainer is doing or what has happened. This technique is particularly good for training psychomotor skills. For example, you can train someone on how to operate a photocopy machine by demonstrating each step.

4.   *Question-answer* sessions are most effective when used as a follow-up to a lecture or panel discussion. Trainees ask questions, typically for clarification. Question-answer sessions are helpful especially for audience participation. If they are announced beforehand as an integral part of the training agenda, they encourage the trainees to pay attention to the lecturer or panel.

5.   A *case study* can be used to present a detailed description of a real or hypothetical problem that employees might encounter on the job. Trainees are asked either individually or as a team to analyze the problem and develop a plan of action to solve it. The case study technique is useful for helping employees learn analytical and problem-solving skills. If used in a group session, it can enhance teamwork.

6.   *Discussion groups* provide an informal way of learning about an issue in a small group. Preparation for the discussion can involve outside reading or some other experience. Discussion groups help members pool their knowledge and answer questions about the issue. However, the trainer must be careful to involve all trainees and keep the discussion focused.

7.   *Role play* is used with a small group of trainees who act out a real or hypothetical situation in front of a larger group. As with the case study method, the situation is detailed for the players. No script is provided. People express their roles as they see fit. Afterward, the problem depicted is discussed in the larger group. Role play is useful for developing interpersonal skills and increasing awareness of social behavior. It is helpful also for stimulating discussion.

8.   *Behavior modeling* is a complex technique for demonstrating and practicing a behavioral process. After the behavior is modeled, trainees rehearse the behavior, and the trainer provides feedback about accuracy and effectiveness. Behavior modeling is a good method for developing interpersonal skills. The trainer can act as a model, or a videotape can present one. With either presentation, the trainee should learn to behave as the model does. The modeling process appears to be enhanced when pertinent points of the modeled behavior are made explicit and closely attached to the model's performance, particularly if these points are not obvious (Mann & Decker, 1984).

9.   *Structured experiences* are exercises that allow trainees to learn interpersonal or communication skills. The structured experience typically focuses on generating certain interactions among the participants. Individuals learn about themselves from observing their own behavior in the group.

10.   In a *simulation,* an experience is devised so as to create the characteristics of a real-life work situation. This may mean developing case study materials in which some work problem, such as conflict, is created. It also may mean using mechanical simulators. For example, pilot training frequently makes use of flight simulators. In all cases of simulation, the trainee interacts with the simulated work situation or equipment and gets feedback from his or her actions.

11.   *Programmed instruction* is a self-instruction technique. Printed materials, such as workbooks, or computer-assisted instruction (CAI) can be used. Programmed instruction is most appropriate for situations in which trainees need to develop individually or to proceed at their own pace. This method is good for presenting factual information.

Techniques for Modifying Attitudinal States

Social psychologists have studied the relationship between attitudes and behavior. Their research indicates that attitudes have a driving effect on thoughts, emotions, and behavior. That is, our attitudes direct our thoughts and color our emotional responses to people, objects, and situations. According to social psychological theory, attitudes are generally consistent with actions (McGuire, 1985). For example, if a trainee's attitude about studying a topic, such as statistics, is positive, then we can expect him or her to be interested in studying statistics. If the trainee's attitude is negative, however, then the tendency is to avoid statistics.

If we, as trainers, must instruct in a subject matter about which trainees feel negatively, then we must try to modify the negative attitude. Research on attitudes suggests a number of ways attitudinal change can occur (McGuire, 1985). One way is through group action. Group discussion of an issue with individuals committing themselves to the group's action can change attitudes and behavior, especially if the group plans a follow-up with individual reports. Self-management training, a specialized technique of this sort, was used successfully in one program

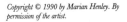

to decrease absenteeism from work. The training consisted of weekly group sessions in which trainees set goals for attendance, made plans for reaching the goals, and monitored their own behavior (Latham & Frayne, 1989). Certain other techniques are useful for improving attitudes and increasing interest in the training content. Behavior modification procedures can be used with individual trainees. If trainees must learn something about which they are fearful, for example, the training program can include help for trainees in coping with their fear. Fearfulness and lack of confidence in some trainees can disrupt training and make it less effective for the entire group.

Site-Specific Training Methods

In the past, training was discussed largely in terms of whether employees were trained *on* the job or *for* the job. This distinction was meant to suggest that training content varied in its specificity. Training on the job was seen as highly job related and training for the job as more general. Actually, training was more clearly distinguished by whether it was conducted at the job site or somewhere else. These historically important methods—apprenticeship, on-the-job training, and vestibule training—are still in use today, although the boundaries between them are less marked now.

Apprenticeship

Apprenticeships combine on-site training with formal education at an off-site location. In general, off-site education is at a university or a vocational school. It provides the theoretical basis of the subject matter. Work-site training provides the necessary application and guided practice.

Apprenticeship has a long history. It was the chief means of education in ancient civilizations. Records of apprenticeship go back as far as 2100 B.C. (Douglas, 1921). Skilled tradesmen and professionals alike were trained as apprentices. In the ancient apprenticeship system, a boy who wanted to enter an occupation was bound over for several years to a master of that trade. At the end of the contract period, the youth became a journeyman and began to earn wages. He continued in this capacity until he was able to set up a shop of his own. This method of education remained essentially unchanged for centuries (Steinmetz, 1967).

The classical apprenticeship continued to be used in workshops in the United States until the beginning of the industrial era (Ghiselli & Brown, 1948). In the eighteenth century, manufacturing methods began to change from handwork to machine processes as a result of increasing development of industrial equipment, such as the steam engine and automatic weaving machinery. This equipment was too expensive for individuals to acquire; therefore, groups of craftsmen began to pool their money and purchase equipment. This was the beginning of the factory. As the factory replaced the small handicraft workshops, fewer skilled craftsmen were needed. As a result, use of the apprenticeship method began to decline. Craftsmen who were employed in factories were paid low wages and they did not function as master trainers. Children were hired to fill most of the labor need. Although they were called apprentices, they received no training.

In a few years, the available supply of trained craftsmen was no longer adequate. Factory managers had to think about training. Needing machinists and being unable to get them, Hoe and Company of New York developed a training program in 1872. Schools also began to address the need for job training. The University of Cincinnati College of Engineering offered a program of cooperative education using the apprenticeship method. Under this plan, apprentices alternated school attendance with factory work assignments (Steinmetz, 1967). These early industrial education efforts were hardly successful, and a major public issue arose in the early 1900s. People questioned who *should* be responsible for vocational education. The Smith-Hughes Act of 1917 attempted to settle the issue by assigning this responsibility to the schools; however, this solution turned out to be inadequate. The schools did not turn out enough workers in any one craft to fill factory demands. Joint action was the next solution. Like the University of Cincinnati program, the new plan was to have schools provide training in the basic aspects of a trade while industry provided practice. The apprentice would be paid by the factory and be guaranteed a job when he became a master of the trade.

A similar method of apprenticeship is used today, although we rely on it considerably less and apply it to fewer occupations. Many professionals, such as physicians and *I/O psychologists,* begin their training with a general university education, continue with an advanced specialized educational program, and finally complete a supervised field internship project. Apprenticeship is also used today in training for the trades, and modern labor unions are favorable toward it. For labor unions, its value goes beyond that of training workers. Union control of the number of apprentices who enter a trade each year prevents flooding of a field by many new entrants and keeps employment high.

On-the-Job Training (OJT)

Another major change in industrial training came with American involvement in World War I. At that time, industrial training was by apprenticeship, which involved low wages and a long-term commitment from apprentices. Few entered apprentice training. Many of those who would have been apprentices went into the military service instead. The labor supply was reduced virtually to untrained people who were willing to work but who had little aptitude for skilled work. In addition, the need for factory workers changed. The war stepped up industrial production, and so industry needed more workers. However, the greatest demand was for semiskilled workers who could run a machine or do a few simple operations. The new jobs created by the war, so different from the complex work of the craftsman, could be taught in a few days. Training did not require a lengthy apprenticeship. Therefore, a new type of training, intensive and short term, was developed. It was conducted entirely on the job and was the forerunner of systematic on-the-job training.

Today, **on-the-job training (OJT)** provides opportunities for a trainee to learn the job by doing it. OJT is used to develop all kinds of skills and abilities, including machine operation, budgeting, supervision, negotiation, and college teaching, to name a few. All levels of employees, from building maintenance staff to the highest paid executive are trained on the job. No special training staff is needed because present employees and supervisors act as trainers. Sometimes, it does not even have the appearance of training: Employees are "shown the ropes" or are given a period of time to "get their feet wet." When OJT is conducted more systematically, training techniques typically include demonstration, guidance with feedback, and question-answer sessions.

The biggest advantage of systematic OJT is that it can have a high level of transfer. Well-planned and executed OJT helps trainees develop only those behaviors used on the job. Thus, the training has the potential of being a complete simulation of the job. It has only the potential, of course, because trainees are sometimes coached incorrectly. Trainees can be deliberately misled, as when present employees are drafted as trainers and resent this. Present employees also can inadvertently teach their own mistakes to new employees. There are other disadvantages as well. For example, materials can be wasted and equipment damaged when untrained workers are put directly to work.

Vestibule Training

During the early years when factory workers were trained on the job, the disadvantages of OJT were revealed. Employers saw that when employees were given work without preliminary instruction, they learned the faults of other employees, consumed the time of others, and created large scrap piles. To correct these faults, industrial trainers developed yet another method of job training, called the vestibule school. **Vestibule training** is on-site training of groups of trainees in a special area removed from the job itself.

A war materials plant installed one of the early vestibule schools. It was located in a room of its own (i.e., a vestibule). The room contained all the machines used on the job. Experienced operators taught three or four trainees at a time. They went over the use of tools and machinery and described the raw materials. In a week, trainees had learned how to operate the plant's machines. On the production line, the new workers were supervised carefully and their errors corrected. In less than three weeks, they reached a high production level. Unfortunately, the training was not always so successful. This method was found to be best for repetitive manufacturing operations. Work requiring a high level of skill and a broad base of knowledge could not be taught adequately in this manner. Although vestibule training may have been adequate as an emergency or war measure, it was not conducive to the needs of peace-time industry (Kelly, 1920).

The success of vestibule training depends on the extent to which an accurate simulation of the job can be produced. Job simulation must include whatever machinery and materials are used on the job. The trainer should be someone who has the job skills and knows effective methods for teaching them. If vestibule training can provide a good simulation of the job, it can avoid the problems of OJT as it was meant to. Unfortunately, vestibule design specifications are not always followed. Often, failure of the training is due to the use of old equipment and low-grade materials in the vestibule. That is, training does not effectively simulate the job. A low level of job simulation in any training program is likely to lead to problems of transfer. In fact, this is the major difficulty with vestibule training.

University Education

Because students are not being prepared for specific jobs but for a life that includes work and other activities, university education is broader and more general than industrial training. University education aims to develop general knowledge and abilities that will be useful in many aspects of life, including work. Written composition and mathematical skills, for example, are likely to be needed in any student's future occupation. Of course, students do specialize their educations to some extent by declaring a major.

Some college majors are more strongly oriented toward a vocation than others. An engineering degree program is an example of a specialized course of study that covers material currently useful in industry. Some students want to know why all university programs are not so specialized and relevant to jobs. Industry also questioned this during those early attempts to get public schools to train workers. However, through experience, organizations discovered that regardless of an individual's preparation, industry itself needed to provide some training (Moore, 1942). Even so, why not make university education more like training? One reason has to do with the durability of the education provided. Consider the depth of study in an educational program. When a program emphasizes depth of study, it usually must neglect breadth and vice versa. (There is not enough time to do it all.) Further, over time, the knowledge and skills gained in any program will become obsolete. Universities have a choice. They can train students to take specific jobs, but the graduates will have little flexibility in terms of the work they can do. Their education also will have to be renewed every few years to prevent **obsolescence.** For example, the information that chemical engineers learn in college goes out of date quickly. For students graduating in 1955, only 75 percent of what they learned in college was still useful after five years (Zelikoff, 1969). On the other hand, universities can offer general education, which is less likely to become obsolete. A general education provides greater flexibility as well, because basic abilities are useful in various jobs. However, graduates will not be specifically prepared for a job.

Business seems to be developing an increasing interest in people with a broad and general education, especially for positions at the executive level. The competencies required of executive managers do not appear to come from a highly specialized education, but from a broad liberal arts background. Some organizations grant leaves of absence to their specialized managers, so they can get a general university education and broaden their perspectives (Saari et al., 1988).

*M*ain
*P*oints

The best training method depends on what needs to be learned. Methods for developing knowledge and skill include such techniques as lecture, discussion, modeling, and simulation. They vary in terms of how actively the trainee is involved.

Historically, people took apprenticeships to learn a trade or profession. This changed to some extent with the advent of the factory. Apprentice training began to be shared by an employer and a school. Today, several trades and professions use apprenticeships.

Other training takes place at work. On-the-job training (OJT), in which an employee is coached by the supervisor or coworkers, was developed because workers needed to be trained more quickly than apprenticeships allowed. Its advantage is high transfer of training. Vestibule training is done at work also, but away from the job. New employees are trained in a vestibule that contains work equipment. This method of training was developed because early efforts to use OJT resulted in too much waste.

Some university majors are oriented toward job training. Usually, university education is more general. As a result, graduates need some training on the job. However, there is less likelihood of skill obsolescence.

TRAINING PROGRAM EVALUATION

Although we may feel confident that a training program works, we need to establish and document that it does. Evaluation is something of a sensitive issue among trainers. Often, if evaluation is done at all, the evaluation measure seems to be *designed* to show only positive effects. Of course, there may be repercussions in finding out the truth. Training can be expensive for the organization. If a training evaluation shows mediocre or negative results, trainers risk losing their jobs. Trainers are only human and are not very enthusiastic about reporting to management that their programs did not work. However, even though neglect of evaluation may protect the training staff from the impact of a failed program, neglect of evaluation also means that trainers get little credit for a *successful* one.

Kirkpatrick (1967) identified four criterion measures of training effectiveness: reaction, learning, behavior, and results. **Reaction measures** indicate the participant's liking for the training. Often, this is the only evaluation of the program. There are problems with this strategy, however. Training may have been enjoyable, but this is not likely the main purpose of the program. Participants may not know whether they learned anything or if what they learned is useful. **Learning**

measures test retention of training material and indicate the extent to which new ability is acquired. Kraiger, Ford, and Salas (1993) identified several ways to measure learning outcomes, depending on whether the training is oriented toward cognitive or skill-based learning outcomes. For example, to assess basic verbal knowledge of information, recognition and recall tests can be used, such as those given in many college courses. In skill-based learning assessment, other methods are needed. For example, a trainee's performance of the skill in a test situation can be systematically observed. Performance measures also can be used to evaluate advanced learning, e. g., to find the point at which a skill becomes automatic.

Kirkpatrick's (1967) learning and reaction measures are internal to the training program in that they are used to assess the extent to which training criteria are met. The other two measures are useful in assessing the validity of the training beyond the training program. **Behavior measures,** such as performance evaluations, indicate the extent to which the training transfers to the job. **Results measures** show whether broad organizational goals, such as reduction of costs or turnover, are attained through training. Results can be assessed by large-scale evaluations, such as utility assessments. For example, a managerial training program was evaluated in terms of dollar estimates of the benefit of providing supervisory skills training (Mathieu & Leonard, 1987).

Training Validity

Training programs are designed around a working hypothesis that training will result in specific changes. A training evaluation study establishes that the hypothesized changes did occur. Thus, training evaluation is meant to assess the validity of training. (Validity, remember, indicates that an instrument or procedure did what it was designed to do.) To evaluate training validity, we must refer back to the needs assessment. The training needs assessment indicates the purpose of the training, or what the program should accomplish. The purpose of training suggests what change is needed and what measures to use to find out if the change occurred. For example, a training need may be for a group of employees to learn certain new material to be applied on the job. Specific performance changes are implied, and assessments of these include both learning and behavior measures.

The overall training purpose also indicates the type of validity that should be established. **Internal validity** refers to the effectiveness of training activities in producing learning. Internal validity is what we usually mean when we refer to **training validity.** On the other hand, **external validity** indicates the extent to which training results can be generalized, and this is an indicator of **transfer validity.** Because we want to establish that trainees learned and that their new learning transferred back to the job, we are interested in both training validity and transfer validity. In fact, to establish external validity, we must first have evidence that the program is internally valid (Goldstein, 1986).

Threats to Validity

To establish validity, we must show that there is a difference in trainee performance and that the difference is due only to the training content. There are many potential reasons, other than the training itself, for training outcomes. Many things

T_able 6.5_	**Threats to Validity: Variables Not a Part of the Training That Can Affect the Outcomes of Training Evaluation**

Threats to Internal Validity

Time-related events and processes	History: specific external events Maturation: personal processes
Experiences of research subjects	Pretesting sensitization: alerting effects Reaction to research design: response to experimental and control groups
Research design and measurement	Biased group assignments: nonrandom Change in instrumentation: different pre- and posttests

Threats to External Validity

	Reactions to testing: testing as part of training versus training without testing

can happen to trainees during the time of training that are not related to the training content. These factors are considered obstacles or threats to the validity of the program. **Threats to validity** are nuisance variables that must be controlled because they can as easily account for training outcomes as the training itself.

Cook and Campbell (1979) described several variables that can function as threats to validity. Some threaten the internal validity of training; that is, they, rather than training, are the source of the learning that is noted. **History** variables are specific outside events that occur during training. Effects of history variables easily can be confused with effects of training. For example, suppose we are conducting a safety training program over the course of a few days, and at some point during this period, a serious accident occurs on the premises. What trainees are learning about safety during the training program may well be affected by their hearing of the accident; thus, the event can influence the training outcome measure. **Maturation** variables are similar to history variables in that they are changes occurring over time; however, they are *processes* that develop rather than specific events. For example, trainees may get tired or bored, or learn from outside experiences during the training period, and these changes can affect training assessment. (These and other threats to validity are listed in table 6.5.)

Some threats to validity occur because of a trainee's personal experience of being a part of an evaluation study. For example, testing a trainee prior to the training program and comparing this to a posttest is a way to determine how much the trainee learned. However, the trainee's performance on the posttest can be influenced because of **pretesting sensitization.** That is, the pretest can alert the trainee to look for material likely to be included in a posttest. Other personal factors that can contaminate training outcomes include employee **reactions to the research design.** Some training validity studies are designed to use experimental and control groups. Employees may perceive their assignment to these groups to be inequitable. Those who are included in a control group may become resentful because they think that their participation is not as important as that of those receiving training. Employees in the experimental group may feel compelled to do well and work harder than they ordinarily would if their training were not being evaluated.

Some obstacles to training validity concern problems of research design and measurement. Training outcome measures can be influenced by **biased group assignments.** Random assignment is the *preferred* method of assigning subjects to groups; however, sometimes volunteers are placed in an experimental group, and other employees are assigned to the control group. When groups systematically differ in this way, the training evaluation is contaminated. Training outcomes also can be affected by changes in the **instrumentation** or methods of pre- and posttesting performance. If one test is used to pretest trainees and a different test is used as the posttest, a difference between the two measures may not be due to the training but because the instruments are not comparable.

If an evaluation study shows a program to have internal validity, the next question is whether it has external validity. For example, can we depend on it to operate effectively with other groups and produce learning that transfers to the job? Threats to external validity are factors that limit the *generalizability* of the evaluation research findings. One threat to external validity exists because testing is included in the evaluation research but not in actual use of the training program. The subject's **reaction to testing** can result in limited generalizability of the training. He or she can become so focused on preparing for tests that performance is changed, often for the better. In a sense, testing has become part of the training program. Later use of the program without testing amounts to a different program, and the learning that occurs may not transfer.

Evaluation Research Designs

The purpose of training evaluation is to establish validity. At least, we should attempt to show internal validity. Depending on the purpose of the training, we also may need to show external validity in terms of transfer and use of the program with other trainees. Evaluation research designs vary in their ability to provide good estimates of validity (Cook & Campbell, 1979). Some of these designs are illustrated in figures 6.8–6.10.

One-Group Testing Designs

The simplest and weakest evaluation of training involves the use of a single post-training test (figure 6.8*a*). The main problems with this design is that there is nothing with which to compare the posttest; therefore, the scores are meaningless. Trainees may have made absolutely no change, or they may have changed because of something other than the training experience. Neither situation can be detected with this design.

In another simple design (figure 6.8*b*), trainees are tested before they go into training. Comparison of the pre- and posttest scores indicates whether any change occurred during the training period. Because of this, the design shows some improvement over the first. However, the possibility cannot be ruled out that a difference between the pre- and posttest is due to threats to validity, such as history

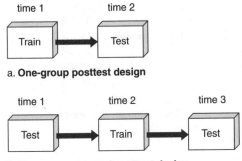

a. **One-group posttest design**

b. **One-group pre- and posttest design**

Figure 6.8. *One-group testing designs for training evaluation. (a) The one-group posttest is a simple but weak design for evaluating training because there is nothing with which to compare the posttest. (b) The one-group pre- and posttest design is an improvement because evaluation of the scores indicate whether any change occurred during training. Both designs present problems because they use only one group of subjects.*

and maturation. Also, because these designs do not use a control group with which to compare the training group, it is not possible to assess whether the training is better than nothing.

Experimental Designs

Training evaluation done with an experimental design using a control group and random assignment of subjects is a considerable improvement over one-group designs, primarily because trainee performance can be compared with that of others who were not trained. A simple but effective experimental design, as shown in figure 6.9*a,* is one in which subjects are randomly assigned to an experimental or a control group. The experimental group is trained, and then both groups are tested. Pretesting is not used in this design; pretesting is not necessary. With random assignment, the two groups may be accepted as being initially the same. Comparison of test scores will indicate whether the experimental group changed as a result of training. A unique advantage of this design is that it controls for the internal and external validity threats due to testing. In addition, random assignment of subjects prevents threats to validity from biased group assignments. Random assignment also prevents history and maturation variables from affecting the groups differently.

Experimental designs can include pretesting if it is desired. For example, as shown in figure 6.9*b,* both the experimental and control groups are pretested, the experimental group is trained, and both groups are posttested. Except for pretesting and the associated threats to validity, this design is the same as the basic experimental procedure, and it has the same advantages. Neither of these designs control all internal validity threats, however. For example, they do not control for differences that can occur in subjects' reactions to being part of a research project. A variation that does provide a way to control this threat is illustrated in figure 6.9*c.* The control group is provided with some activity, other than training, during the time in which the experimental group is being trained. That is, the control group is given a placebo activity. Adverse reactions to being in the control group may be prevented in this way.

The Solomon four-group design retains the advantages of the basic experiment and controls for pretesting threats to validity. As shown in figure 6.9*d,* the Solomon design combines features of the basic experiment with the pretesting design. Subjects are assigned randomly to four groups: an experimental

Figure 6.9. *Experimental designs used in training evaluation. These designs incorporate one or more control groups and random assignment of subjects (a–d). Experimental designs that allow for control groups are the most effective methods of training evaluation. Trainee performance can be compared with that of others who were not trained.*

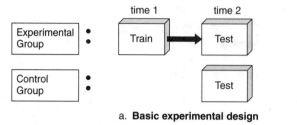

a. **Basic experimental design**

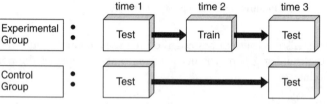

b. **Experimental design with pretesting**

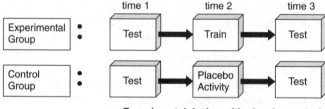

c. **Experimental design with placebo control group**

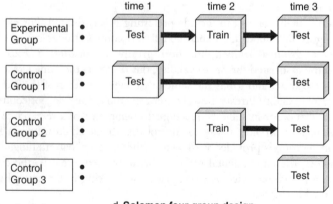

d. **Solomon four-group design**

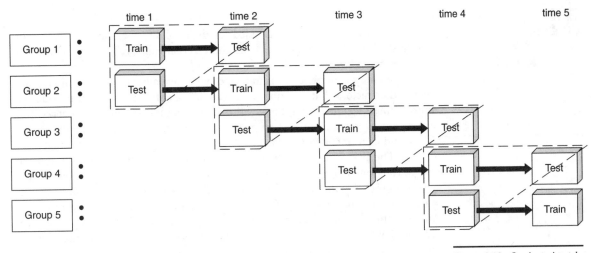

Figure 6.10. *Quasi-experimental design for training evaluation. This complex time series design, in which the testing and training of groups is staggered over a period of time, is useful when controlled experiments are difficult to arrange. The strategy effectively creates experimental and control groups (shown in the dashed outlines). For example, group 2 initially is the control in the experiment in which group 1 is the experimental group; later, group 2 is the experimental group, while group 3 functions as the control.*

group and three different control groups. The experimental group is pretested, trained, and posttested. One control group is given both the pre- and posttests. The second is not pretested but is *trained* and posttested. The third control group gets the posttest only. This design provides the same controls over validity threats that the basic experimental procedure does. In addition, by comparing the pretested groups with those not pretested, the researcher can assess the extent to which pretesting affects the groups receiving training; thus, test sensitization also is controlled.

In some work situations, it is difficult to carry out controlled experiments to evaluate training. There may be company resistance to leaving a whole group of employees untrained, as is necessary if control groups are used. Assigning subjects randomly to groups also can cause complaints. In such situations, **quasi-experimental designs** can be used for training evaluation. For example, a series of pre- and posttests can be given to multiple groups of trainees. By staggering the testing and training of the groups over a period of time, researchers can effectively create experimental and control groups, as shown in figure 6.10. Each group performs as a control group at one time and later as an experimental group when it is trained. That is, the first group of trainees is trained and posttested. Their test scores are compared to the pretest scores of another group that has not yet been trained. At this time, the first group is the experimental group, and the second is the control group. Then, the second group is trained and posttested, and their posttest scores are compared to the pretest scores of a third group waiting to be trained. The second group is now the experimental group, and the third group is its control. Random subject assignment enhances the strategy by ensuring that systematic differences between groups do not occur. Pretest comparisons also can be used to show that the groups were drawn from the same population. This design is vulnerable to pretest sensitization threats, however.

Training programs need to be assessed for their validity. Learning and behavior measures are best for studies of internal and external validity. These measures test for learning and for transfer.

Validity is present when trainee changes actually are due to training and not to other factors that function as threats to validity. A good research design controls these factors. Some known threats to training validity are history and maturation events and processes; pretesting sensitization; biased group assignments; and instrumentation variations.

The best method for a training validity study is the basic experimental design. Random assignment of subjects and use of a control group makes this design resistant to many validity threats. Variations of the method allow the researcher to include pretesting. One allows pretesting of a placebo control group. Another, the Solomon four-group design, uses multiple control groups and provides for control over validity threats. Quasi-experimental designs are useful when there is resistance to other experimental procedures.

SPECIAL TRAINING NEEDS

Compared to the past, companies today are taking more responsibility for conserving and developing the work lives of their employees. Because of the change in perspective, there is more attention given to the needs of trainees. Still, more is needed. Fair employment programs have resulted in better employment for some groups of workers. However, inadequate education frequently has been cited as a major obstacle. Job training can be part of the solution. In this section, I describe some ways that training can meet the special needs of employees.

Multicultural Issues in Training

Equal Opportunity

Because training is a practice that can affect a person's employment opportunities, employers must be able to show that they do not unfairly discriminate in training. This can be done in two ways: (1) Show that the use of training for selection purposes is fair; and (2) show that employees have equal access to training.

For a long time, employers have been using previous education and training to decide whom to hire and promote. Hiring or promoting the more educated applicant is not in *itself* unlawful. However, the educational background must be a valid job qualification, and educational requirements must apply equally to all applicants. The employer must ask, can an employee do the job successfully without the specified education? Are there **protected groups** who would be disadvantaged by unnecessary educational requirements? *Griggs v. Duke Power,* discussed in chapter 3, addressed these issues. The case was brought against an employer who required a high school diploma for a certain job class, a requirement that appeared to operate in a discriminatory fashion. The majority of black applicants for these jobs were disqualified. Griggs argued that this requirement was not necessary because the job could be done by someone who had no diploma. On the basis of evidence presented, the Supreme Court agreed. Duke Power Company was required to stop using this qualification in selecting employees for this job.

The second way to show fair employment practice is to demonstrate that employees have equal access to job training. Because employment decisions can be based on success in training, a company's training programs must be open to all groups of employees, without reference to ethnicity, gender, age, or medical condition. This requirement of equal access can be set aside only in certain instances of affirmative action. For example, in *United Steelworkers of America v. Weber,* the employer was using a temporary affirmative action plan to increase the number of African American employees in the company through a training program. The plan reserved half of the slots in the training program for African American applicants. In a complaint of reverse discrimination, the plaintiff alleged that this constituted discrimination against white workers. Both a district court and a court of appeals agreed that the practice did violate the rights of white employees to equal access to training. However, the Supreme Court reversed the decision, largely because the affirmative action plan was temporary and meant to eliminate racial imbalance in the company (U.S. Office of Personnel Management, 1979).

Multicultural Diversity Training

The modern American work force is diverse in terms of employees' ethnic and cultural backgrounds, as well as their gender, age, and other demographic features. More and more employers are recognizing that such differences do not have to be a problem but can contribute to an organization's success. A national survey of personnel managers found that while most organizations expected to become more diverse, many were unprepared to take advantage of what the increasing diversity offered. Less than one-third had programs in place for making the transition (Hopkins, Sterkel-Powell, & Hopkins, 1994).

Employers who are looking for ways to realize the benefits of a diverse work force are finding that training provides a route. The infusion of new ideas into a work group's activities requires positive attitudes and interpersonal skills. Because many employees have not had an opportunity to work with someone from a different ethnic or cultural group, the necessary knowledge, skills, and attitudes can be developed in training. **Diversity training** is meant to do this. Such programs aim to enhance the trainee's multicultural competence, usually with interpersonal skills training activities that are customized for a diverse group (Garcia, 1995).

Similarly, **cross-cultural training** is useful to businesses that operate in other countries and hire people both from their own and from the host country (Triandis, Feldman, & Weldon, 1974). People from different cultures frequently misunderstand each other's behavior, and interaction problems are commonplace. Misunderstandings and poor interaction are likely to affect employment and retention of workers from both countries, particularly if employees do not receive training on cross-cultural interaction.

Training American employees for overseas work should take account of general cultural issues, as these employees need more than mere skills training. They must make attitudinal adjustments, develop personal support systems, and learn about the host country in a short time. Not many companies provide training that relates to these aspects of job performance, however. Tung (1981) reported that 70 percent of overseas companies have no training program whatsoever. Although there has been little research on the effects of cross-cultural training for overseas employees, there is reason to believe that the rather high failure rate of these employees is due to this lack of preparation (Wexley, 1984).

Trainees with Special Needs

Some workers have special needs that often can be met by training. These individuals include (1) disabled workers; (2) displaced workers; and (3) female employees who have managerial potential.

Qualified disabled workers exhibit the highest rate of unemployment of any group. The rate varies depending on the degree of disability, but it averages about 60 percent. Some 40 percent of working-age men and 70 percent of working-age women are unemployed at any time (Koestler, 1978). Lack of training is the reason most often attributed to high unemployment among the disabled. In the past, disabled children were sent to schools that paid little attention to teaching them job skills, and they received little or no career guidance. The college experience of disabled students is similar. Disabled graduates often have unrealistic expectations and do not know how to seek jobs (Koestler, 1978). Thus, job training programs for disabled workers need to include both job skills training and **work socialization.** Trainees need to learn both how to work and how to be workers. Training should be provided for such essentials as starting work on time and interacting with coworkers and supervisors. Few training programs have been conducted specifically for disabled workers. Most organizations simply include them in routine job training.

People who lose their jobs have special needs that sometimes are addressed with training.[1] First, they may need to have retraining for a different job. This need can develop when the worker's job skills have become obsolete because of technological change or education that has not been renewed. Second, motivational improvement may be needed. Job loss can have a devastating effect, causing the process of searching for a new job to be especially difficult. The person may become so disheartened as to stop searching. Training may help. Eden and Aviram (1993) designed a behavior modeling workshop to study this possibility. The workshop was created to give a boost to the trainee's sense of self-efficacy and to model effective job searching. **Self-efficacy** refers to a person's capacity for coping with demands. People who perceive themselves as efficacious are realistic about their capacities, and they do not overestimate the difficulties they will encounter. They believe in themselves. Eden and Aviram's (1993) workshop was effective. The trainee's self-efficacy improved as a result, and job search behavior increased.

Women in Management

Today in the United States, almost half of the work force is female (Bureau of the Census, 1990). This statistic is somewhat misleading, however. It does not show, for example, that most women work in jobs *traditionally* done by women, such as clerical and service-related occupations. Most women who have managerial jobs are in lower- or middle-level positions. They hold about 40 percent of these positions. However, few executives are female. Less than 5 percent of high ranking managers are women (Gutek, 1993).

---

[1]Organizational downsizing, in which a company reduces the size of the work force by laying off employees, is one reason why employees lose their jobs. Others get fired because of performance problems.

One explanation for the underrepresentation of women at high managerial levels is that women need certain specific abilities that are not acquired in school. These abilities, however, could be acquired in job training. The training method most often suggested is a mentorship. A **mentor** is a higher ranking manager who has experience and is interested in promoting the advancement of the protegé. A mentor could be expected to take a personal interest in developing the woman's potential.

Having a mentor definitely helps managers advance their careers. Studies have found that more promotions and greater earnings come to those who have a mentor (Dreher & Ash, 1990). Women actually are as likely to have a mentor as men are, although they also are more likely to experience barriers in establishing a relationship with a mentor. For example, cross-sex mentorships can carry a sexual connotation that is detrimental (Ragins & Cotton, 1991). Some think that same-sex mentorships are likely to be more beneficial. Dreher and Cox (1996) agree that *certain* same-sex mentorships are more lucrative. They explain, however, that others are not. They noted that some mentors are more helpful than others, and that similarity of the protegé to such a mentor can make the relationship easier to establish. A mentor who is most likely to be helpful in advancing a career is a person who is powerful in the organization. As things stand, that person is most likely to be a white man. Thus, white male managers are more likely to benefit from a mentorship. The researchers found this to be correct; neither women nor minority men were as likely as white men to have a white male mentor. Their mentorships also were less beneficial. This suggests that the best mentor for an ambitious female manager is a white male executive.

Preparing for Special Work

Management Training

Management training is one of the most common formal training programs. Many companies have training for their managerial and supervisory employees. What is actually accomplished with these programs? In a survey of American businesses, Saari et al. (1988) found that companies use a variety of methods in management training, often apparently without having any clear-cut idea about the purpose of this training. Only 27 percent of the organizations surveyed did needs assessments to identify the knowledge and skills managers needed. Maybe this is understandable. Research on management training is not always very helpful in identifying managerial skills and knowledge to be included in training (Wexley & Baldwin, 1986). In the past, most training journal articles were anecdotal and mainly described ways to help managers learn how to deal with specific problems, such as employee discipline (Goldstein, 1980).

To direct the study of management training, an overall theoretical structure is needed, which can describe what a manager does and therefore needs to learn. Mintzberg (1972) offered such a structure. He identified several roles that managers usually perform and described the kinds of work activities that go into these roles. This structure and the work activities can be used to define the kinds of training individual managers need. Some of the roles are interpersonal, such as motivating subordinates and leading task groups. This suggests that the research on motivation and leadership, as discussed in chapters 8 and 10, is useful in assessing managerial training needs and in designing specific training programs. For example, some leadership theorists suggest ways to design training to improve managers' ability to lead (e.g., Fiedler et al., 1984). Some leadership theorists also recognize that a manager must try to motivate the members of his or her task group, and they suggest ways in which a manager can learn how to do this (Yukl, 1989).

Other managerial roles identified by Mintzberg (1972) are informational. The manager needs to be able to obtain information, and use it to make decisions and communicate effectively. What the manager needs to learn in order to do this can be defined from the research on communications and decision making, as discussed in chapter 12. For example, the research on interpersonal interactions can be helpful in describing what a manager needs to learn. Communication skills training has been a popular focus of managerial training programs. Most often, however, this training has taken a personal development approach in which improvement in communication ability is sought indirectly by techniques that purport to increase self-insight. Such training has been criticized as having covert objectives that are unrelated to communications training (Elmes & Costello, 1992; Hargie & Tourish, 1994). Certainly, communications training does not have to be so circuitous. The research can be tapped for methods of identifying communication elements (e.g., Courtright, Fairhurst, & Rogers, 1989) and for ideas on how to incorporate these in a behavior modeling workshop. That is, managers could be trained by observing and practicing the behavior of an effective communicator.

Main Points

Fairness in training means (1) that training used in making selection decisions is not discriminatory, and (2) that employees have equal access to training.

Multicultural issues are important to business because the work force is diverse. To benefit from diversity, some firms are investing in diversity training. This, like cross-cultural training, is meant to improve interpersonal skills in working with members of different ethnic and cultural groups.

Some workers have special needs that can be met by training. Disabled workers are usually underemployed. Job skills training coupled with work socialization probably can help, although few such training programs have been tried. Displaced workers may need training to improve work ability and job seeking skills. They also may need help in dealing with the loss of self-efficacy that can result from delay in finding another job.

Although a number of women have supervisory and middle management jobs, few are executives. The reason usually offered is that they do not have the necessary skill for this work. Mentorships are proposed. Mentors do help managers advance their careers. However, they appear to be more helpful to men, especially white men.

Management training is best designed by using a theoretical structure, such as Mintzberg's, to identify what a manager does. Managerial work is interpersonal, such as leading and motivating subordinates, and informational, such as communicating. Such skills can be developed by training that draws upon the research on leadership, motivation, and communication.

CHAPTER SUMMARY

Every employee training program should be based on a needs assessment in order to provide reason and purpose for the training. Analytical and research techniques are available for gathering information about training needs from a range of sources at the organizational, job, and person levels. Needs assessment is the foundation upon which training goals are based, and behavioral objectives that guide the trainer are derived from these goals.

The psychology of learning should be part of the foundation of training programs as well. From decades of theory and research, we understand a number of variables that are important in the acquisition of new knowledge and skill. These include practice and reinforcement of the new behavior, as well as individual differences between trainees. Of particular significance to job training is the issue of transfer. Positive transfer of new learning to the job is the most important reason why employers train employees.

The experience of educators can be put to use in the training program. Training techniques should be selected carefully. Some techniques are good for conveying informa-tion; others are relevant to skills training; still others are for changing attitudinal states that interfere with learning. These techniques are used in on- and off-site programs, such as apprenticeship and OJT.

Just as training should be designed to meet a real need, so also must it be evaluated. Program evaluation is a process of hypothesis testing. The training designer hypoth-esizes that the training program will accomplish its purpose. Training validation can establish internal and external va-lidity. Depending on the purpose, different criterion mea-sures and research methodologies are appropriate. In any validity study, certain nuisance variables or threats to valid-ity, which contaminate the evaluation research results, are likely to exist. Some research designs are better able to con-trol these threats than others and should be used to evalu-ate training whenever possible.

All employees need some job training. Some require more or special training. Special needs range from work so-cialization for the disabled and retraining for displaced workers, to mentorships for women in management. Man-agerial training is often provided in organizations.

STUDY QUESTIONS

1) How do organizational, task, and person analyses differ? What do these analyses individually contribute to a needs assessment?

2) Describe the way in which behavioral objectives are derived from a training needs assessment. How are behavioral objectives used to guide training?

3) What does practice contribute to the learning process? How much practice is enough, and how should it be scheduled and paced? Does mental practice help?

4) How much and what kind of reinforcement is necessary for learning?

5) What is transfer of training, and why is it important to consider it in training design and evaluation?

6) Name some training techniques that are good for developing (a) physical job skills, (b) interaction skills, and (c) new knowledge of information.

7) How do apprenticeship, OJT, and vestibule training differ?

8) Identify the four criterion measures used in training evaluation research, and describe each.

9) Distinguish between internal and external validity. Identify the threats to validity.

10) What kinds of research designs are used for conducting training evaluation research? What are their strengths and weaknesses?

11) Why is it important to consider equal opportunity issues in training? What is the purpose of diversity training? Who needs cross-cultural training?

12) What are the special training needs of disabled workers? In what ways can displaced workers be helped to find new jobs? What is the best way to advance the careers of managerial women?

13) What does management training accomplish?

CONSIDER THIS

CASE STUDY

As I describe in other case studies, VRS runs a sheltered workshop for disabled clients who are in the process of vocational rehabilitation. Job skills training is conducted by workshop instructors. Work socialization training is provided by rehabilitation counselors. (The agency has the kind of program I recommend in this chapter for disabled workers.)

The agency provides little training for its own employees, however. New employees learn their work on the job through the briefest form of OJT imaginable. They are simply shown around, introduced to coworkers, and told whom to ask if they have any questions. Occasionally, someone is let off work to go to a special educational conference if the agency can afford it. All requests for training must be justified as being relevant to the agency's mission of providing client rehabilitation.

Problem

One of the counselors has made a request to the Executive Director that the agency invest in a diversity training program for the *employees*. In the justification, the counselor noted that not only is the agency's staff becoming more diverse in ethnic and cultural background, so is the agency's client group. The counselor proposed that all employees be included, because most have some contact with the clients and all must work with each other.

The director is considering this request. Because all employees are being included, the training promises to be expensive. Therefore, he must consider carefully.

How would you advise the director? Does VRS need diversity training? Are there potential advantages that the counselor did not mention? Are there cost-cutting measures that could be taken?

what's in this chapter?

Performance evaluation is a topic that makes most people at least a little uneasy. So, why in the world would you be interested in learning about it? First, you probably are or will be an employee; thus, you should know what to expect in terms of having your own performance evaluated and discussed with you. Second, maybe you will need to evaluate the performance of someone else. Supervisors must evaluate how their subordinates are doing. Therefore, they need to learn how to use the methods, and how to prevent biases and errors from creeping in. They also must be able to convey their evaluation to the employee in an effective postappraisal interview. Third, you might someday need to do personnel research, such as test validation. Performance ratings are used as the criterion measure in such research. In this chapter, you will learn about all these aspects of performance evaluation.

Every employee needs to have feedback on how he or she is doing on the job. This feedback is usually given by the supervisor in a private, postappraisal interview.

Chapter 7

Evaluating Job Performance

Contents

Now that Cooper had fallen into the work, it was necessary for them to have little to do with one another in the office. Mr. Warburton used his orderly to send any message he had to give his assistant, and his instructions he sent by formal letter. They saw one another constantly, that was inevitable, but did not exchange half a dozen words in a week. The fact that they could not avoid catching sight of one another got on their nerves. They brooded over their antagonism and Mr. Warburton, taking his daily walk, could think of nothing but how much he detested his assistant.

He had no reason to send in a complaint to headquarters: Cooper did his work very well, and at that time men were hard to get. True, vague complaints reached him and hints that the natives found Cooper harsh. There was certainly a feeling of dissatisfaction among them. But when Mr. Warburton looked into specific cases, all he could say was that Cooper had shown severity where mildness would not have been misplaced and had been unfeeling when himself would have been sympathetic. He had done nothing for which he could be taken to task. But Mr. Warburton watched him. . . . Sooner or later Cooper would deliver himself into his hand.

W. Somerset Maugham*

If we finish Maugham's story "The Outstation," we find that Mr. Warburton finally decided to try to rid himself of Cooper. He based his request for this personnel action on an unsatisfactory rating. In this rating, however, he did not slight the man's job performance. In fact, he said Cooper did his work very well. Rather, he complained that "he couldn't get on with him" and asked that Cooper be transferred. He did this surreptitiously, and when the answer came back—in the negative—he never breathed a word to his subordinate.

How might he have done this more effectively? As you discover in this chapter, Mr. Warburton made a number of mistakes in dealing with his subordinate. These mistakes range from failing to define the exact nature of Cooper's duties and responsibilities, to behaving in such a devious way to request the man's transfer. First, would you say that Cooper does his work well if he cannot get along with his superior and if he treats his own subordinates poorly? The success of many jobs depends on good interpersonal skills. If Cooper's job is one of them, then Mr. Warburton could have based his unsatisfactory rating on Cooper's interpersonal failings. Second, good personnel evaluation should be done openly. Unsatisfactory ratings should be discussed with the employee, and the employee should be encouraged to improve. These issues of personnel evaluation are just as relevant today as they were in the 1920s when Maugham wrote this story.

In this chapter, I discuss the evaluation of job performance. The terms I use, such as *performance appraisal* and *personnel evaluation,* all refer to the need for measuring how well an employee performs on the job. Performance evaluation is a process that begins with a study of the job. Only if we know what activities

*From W. Somerset Maugham, "The Outstation" from *The Casuarina Tree,* in *The Complete Short Stories.* Copyright © A. P. Watt Ltd., London, England. Reprinted by permission of A. P. Watt Ltd. on behalf of The Royal Literary Fund, and W. Heinemann Ltd., London.

constitute the job can we fairly evaluate an employee's success in performing it. The process includes observation and evaluation of an employee's work performance, and it extends into employee counseling because the individual must be given information about needed improvements.

THE USES OF PERFORMANCE EVALUATION

Performance appraisal is a delicate issue. All of us have been evaluated at one time or another, either at work or at school. Sometimes, an evaluation contains things we would rather not hear. You can probably recall an occasion when a professor read a paper of yours and responded critically. You may have reacted defensively. Employees often respond this way. Supervisors are hesitant about performance evaluation because they must take on the role of judge, a role in which they may feel uncomfortable. In spite of these difficulties, performance evaluation is necessary to maintain the vitality of the organization.

Performance evaluation is used to meet basic needs of the organization: to improve the work force and to provide for certain administrative functions. For example, a survey of employers revealed that information obtained from performance evaluation is used to identify the strengths and weaknesses of individual employees, to document personnel decisions, and to develop and evaluate human resource systems, for example, as in training needs assessment (Cleveland, Murphy, & Williams, 1989).

Giving employees information about how they are doing on the job can help them improve in several ways. First, performance evaluation can provide a preview of what is possible in terms of promotion or transfer. Second, performance evaluation must indicate whether the employee has serious deficiencies, and if so, it should outline ways to improve. The most effective feedback includes information on both quantity and quality of performance (Ilgen & Moore, 1987). In spite of our difficulties in receiving it, negative feedback appears to lead to higher levels of performance than positive feedback does (Podsakoff & Farh, 1989).This and other performance evaluation uses are summarized in table 7.1.

Perhaps the most important organizational function of performance evaluation is personnel action. Performance evaluation is used most frequently to reward past performance or justify salary increases and other monetary rewards, such as bonuses (Hall, Posner, & Harder, 1989). It also helps people in all kinds of organizations decide on promotions (Cederblom, 1991). Performance evaluation is also used to decide whether the employee should continue in the job. Effective performance evaluation allows the organization to weed out personnel who are unsatisfactory performers. An alternative to termination is to move the person to another job for which he or she is more suited. Performance evaluation provides the basis for demotion or transfer to another job. One occasion for using performance evaluation in this way is when a company is **downsizing**[1] in order to increase its cost effectiveness. In this case, performance evaluation can be used to identify unsatisfactory and borderline employees for the company to reduce more effectively.

Performance evaluation also is used in personnel research. As discussed in chapter 6, performance evaluation can serve as a diagnostic tool. Training needs assessments include information from performance appraisals about individuals' needs

[1]Several other terms also are used to refer to an organization's effort to shrink and reduce its labor costs, including streamlining, right sizing, and reduction-in-force (RIF).

_T_able 7.1	Purposes of Performance Evaluation
Employee Improvement	Specific job performance feedback
	Career opportunity information
	Goal setting
Decision Making for Administrative Action	Retention of employee
	Reclassification
	Transfer
	Demotion
	Promotion
	Termination
Organizational Research	Evaluation of selection procedures
	Evaluation of training programs
	Evaluation of motivational (incentive) programs
	Development of new employee programs

for training. Most importantly, performance evaluation is the criterion used in the validation of many personnel selection instruments. Recall from chapter 5 that criterion-related validity studies compare test scores with on-the-job behavior as assessed by a performance evaluation instrument. In a similar role, performance evaluation can be used as a behavioral measure to evaluate the success of a training program. You might ask whether the administrative and research uses of personnel evaluation are sometimes at odds. Suppose a supervisor knew an evaluation would be used to provide a raise for a good employee. Would the supervisor provide a more lenient evaluation than if he or she thought the evaluation was part of a selection test validity study? In a validity study, evaluators know they need to be *accurate,* whereas raises depend on positive evaluations; thus, a difference might be expected. In fact, there is evidence that this can occur (Harris, Smith, & Champagne, 1995).

Legal Issues

Fair Employment

Under Title VII of the 1964 Civil Rights Act, any practice that adversely affects employment opportunities of protected groups is unlawful unless it can be shown to be valid. Like selection and training, performance evaluation is used for a number of personnel decisions that may adversely affect equal employment opportunity. Salary increases, promotions, and terminations typically are determined by performance appraisal. For example, a certain level of performance in one job may be required for an employee to move on to a higher job. Notice that the performance evaluation is used as a predictor or selection device in this instance. As such, it is subject to Title VII and, according to the 1978 *Uniform Guidelines,* it should be validated to show that it predicts performance in the higher level job.

Empirical validation of performance appraisal is not easy. Recall from the discussion in chapter 5 that criterion-related validity comes from data showing that a predictor and a criterion measure are strongly correlated. In most cases, criterion-related validation of a performance appraisal used as a *predictor* is simply out of the question because there is no other available measure of performance to be used as the *criterion*. If there is one, we do not know whether *that* measure is valid. Most organizations whose performance appraisal systems have stood up in court have actually used content validation, which is based on a job analysis and a rational, rather than empirical, procedure (Field & Holley, 1982).

Barrett and Kernan (1987) concluded from their review of 51 recent Title VII cases that the courts are no longer interested in deciding on the actual validity of performance appraisal systems. For example, in *Texas Department of Community Affairs v. Burdine* (1981), the Supreme Court decided that it is not necessary to present extensive evidence of validity. The courts are interested, however, in determining whether the system has been used to discriminate unfairly. Employers now need to establish at least some content validity for their appraisal systems and then make sure that decisions made from appraisals are applied evenly to minority and majority employees.

Employment-at-Will

Traditionally, employers have held **employment-at-will rights.** This means that an employee can be terminated whenever the employer chooses. U.S. companies still hold such rights and apparently use them quite freely. It has been observed that some 3 million employees in the private sector get fired each year (Stieber, 1984). The government has limited these rights to some extent. Title VII of the Civil Rights Act made terminations unlawful if they were based on discriminatory practices. Other legislative actions made termination on the basis of medical condition and age unlawful. In addition, employees cannot be terminated because of their union activities.

Some recent court decisions indicate that employers, because of their employment practices, also can limit their own employment-at-will rights. Sometimes, for example, an employee is led to believe that the company will provide essentially permanent employment, terminable only in case of deficient job performance. Then, surprisingly, the employee is terminated, although he or she has received satisfactory performance evaluations for some time. Company behavior of this type may violate the legal principle of "implied covenant of good faith and fair dealing." According to this principle, parties who have established a contract should not unjustly deprive each other of the benefits of the contract. Therefore, if an employer has implied that an employee can remain as long as performance is satisfactory, then an unexpected termination might constitute unjust deprivation or what is commonly known as **wrongful discharge.** The case of *Pugh v. See's Candies* (1981) is an example of this type of claim. Pugh had been an employee for 32 years, coming up through the ranks from a dishwashing job to a vice presidency. He claimed that there had been an implied promise that he would not be terminated without reasonable cause. The implied promise was based on 32 years of satisfactory performance reviews. In the original trial, the court decided that Pugh had no right to sue the employer for a breach of an implied contract and dismissed the case. The appeals court, however, found that the employee could pursue the case on this basis. Although the case was finally decided in favor of the company, the 1981 appeals court decision established something of a precedent. Employees can sue their employers for violating an implied contract that limits the grounds for termination (*SKRSC Update,* 1989).

One attorney has said that the message we should receive from this and other cases is straightforward. If you need to fire someone, you must be ready to show "just cause," that is, you must have a legitimate reason. *Just 'cause* you want to is not a good reason. Performance deficiencies, as shown through an objective appraisal process, are considered by the courts to constitute just cause. Employees must not be misled. If there are serious performance deficiencies, the employee must be warned. The employer is best advised to establish policies and procedures to demonstrate clearly that no contract is being made. Language that misleads by suggesting that employment is *permanent* should be removed from employee handbooks (Schachter, 1984).

Seniority

We have something of a tradition concerning seniority, and labor unions have been instrumental in upholding it. In **seniority systems,** personnel decisions are made on the basis of length of employment rather than on assessments of merit. The advantage is that favoritism or other forms of personal bias tend to be diminished. The relationship between seniority and productivity, however, is questionable. A study of promotions showed that past performance and similarity between the lower and higher level jobs were better predictors of later performance than seniority was (Gordon & Fitzgibbons, 1982).

Seniority systems may have indirect effects on minority and female employees. Because women and minorities have not had full access to employment over the years, they now tend to have less seniority than white male employees. Although this matters little in some personnel decisions, when there is a need for an overall reduction in the work force, these employees tend to be adversely affected by seniority systems. The "last hired, first fired" are more likely to be females and minorities. Seniority systems have a long history, and the issue of their validity in making such personnel decisions has entered the picture only comparatively recently. The courts may be uneasy about upending entrenched seniority systems.

---

*M*ain
  *P*oints

Performance evaluation has three uses: (1) to help employees learn how to improve; (2) to help administrators make good decisions on personnel matters; and (3) to help personnel researchers evaluate the validity of testing and other programs.

Some legal issues are relevant. First, when performance appraisal is used to select employees for personnel actions, such as termination, it must not unfairly discriminate, and it must be valid for such uses. Content validation can show the instrument's validity. Second, the misuse of performance evaluation may be cited in wrongful discharge cases. Employers have employment-at-will rights, but they may compromise their rights by misleading employees about termination. Third, seniority, rather than performance, is sometimes used as the basis of personnel action. Seniority systems are upheld by unions. However, they can have adverse effects on newly hired employees when an organization downsizes.

SOURCES OF EVALUATION

The Evaluators

Who conducts the evaluation of an employee's job performance? Usually, the evaluator is an employee's immediate supervisor. In this chapter, it is most often the supervisor to whom I refer as the evaluator. The supervisor is likely to know the person's work and need little preparation to answer questions about the individual's performance. Because employees view evaluation as part of a supervisor's responsibility, they are more likely to accept evaluation from this source. Research indicates that employees view supervisor evaluations as being more useful than evaluations from others (Herold et al., 1987).

For employees who work independently, the employer may have little personal contact with them and nothing more than indirect evidence of their performance. This is the case with some managerial, technical, and professional employees. For example, your professor's boss probably does not have close day-to-day contact with him or her. With such employees, there are options other than supervisors' evaluations. Assessment by peers, subordinates, and clients can be done. Self-appraisals are an option as well. If employees have close contact with several of these evaluation sources, it is possible to develop an evaluation system combining them.

The procedure in which coworkers are used to perform evaluations is called **peer appraisal.** Reviews of the research literature investigating this technique generally have been positive, and the method appears reasonably unbiased and reliable (Kane & Lawler, 1978). Employees seem generally positive about peer appraisal, although this depends on the purpose of the system and the particular rating received. Employees surveyed in one study felt the system was acceptable when peer evaluations were used for the purpose of performance improvement and when the ratings were satisfying to the ratees (McEvoy & Buller, 1987). However, negative appraisals from peers can have adverse effects on the ease with which group members work together (DeNisi, Randolph, & Blencoe, 1983). Also, some peer appraisals probably are more accurate and easier to do than others. One study showed that peer ratings were more accurate when the peer perceived the ratee to be similar to her- or himself (Fox, Ben-Nahum, & Yinon, 1989).

When employees have little close contact with others, **self-appraisal** is a convenient form of evaluation. Self-appraisal can have advantages for employee development, because the individual can identify his or her own needs for improvements, which may be different from the supervisor's assessments (Harris & Schaubroeck, 1988). However, we should be careful in using self-appraisals. They are more lenient or favorable than supervisor evaluations (Furnham & Stringfield, 1994; Meyer, 1980). Self-appraisals may be affected by personal and cultural attributes. For example, more accurate self-evaluations were obtained from persons with an internal locus of control, high intelligence, and an achievement orientation (Mabe & West, 1982). Some studies have considered whether members of some cultures are more naturally modest and, therefore, less inclined to overrate themselves. The answer to this is not clear. A survey of Taiwanese workers found evidence of modesty. Employees rated themselves less favorably than their supervisors did (Farh, Dobbins, & Cheng, 1991). However, a similar study of mainland Chinese workers found self-appraisals to be more positive than supervisors' ratings (Yu & Murphy, 1993).

The extent of agreement between self-appraisals and evaluations from other sources also appears to depend on the job. Self-appraisals by blue collar and service workers show better agreement with supervisor evaluations than self-appraisals of managerial and professional employees (Harris & Schaubroeck, 1988). The lower agreement of managerial appraisals may be because superiors have less opportunity to observe a manager's job-relevant behavior, or because these individuals have comparatively little information about their peers with whom to compare themselves. In a laboratory test of this idea, subjects were given large amounts of comparative information before they rated themselves. As expected, their self-appraisals were more similar to supervisor appraisals (Farh & Dobbins, 1989). Employee self-appraisals have shown the same effect as a result of improved knowledge of the performance evaluation system (Williams & Levy, 1992). Thus, it may be that the best way to make use of self-appraisal is to train the employee specifically for this task.

Because managers often do not work closely with their superiors, which means that the superior has little information upon which to base an evaluation, another source of evaluation is needed for manager appraisals. Subordinate evaluation is a possibility. Recently, researchers have been interested in finding out if this is an effective strategy for management development purposes. If employees can assess the strengths and weaknesses of their supervisors, then this information can provide **upward feedback** to help managers improve. Researchers have studied subordinate appraisals by comparing them with managers' self-ratings and with ratings done by managers' superiors. The research has shown that subordinates' ratings agree with ratings done by superiors (Riggio & Cole, 1992). Like superiors' ratings, they are less positive than the managers' self-ratings (Furnham & Stringfield, 1994), at least under certain conditions. One study revealed that subordinate raters who were anonymous provided less positive evaluations than those who could be identified (Antonioni, 1994). Although we will have to wait and see, subordinate rating does appear to be a viable alternative.

Performance Information

Production Measures

In jobs in which there is some form of production, a rating is not necessary. An evaluator can collect objective information on the quantity and quality of an individual's work performance and compare this to some standard of productivity in deciding if the individual's performance is satisfactory. The **production measure** can be a count of whatever is produced—number of widgets constructed, boxes packed, letters typed, or deals closed, for example. Information on inaccurate performance, such as the number of errors, complaints, or items returned, also can be included in a production measure.

Production evaluation measures have an obvious advantage. They are *objective* rather than based on someone's subjective estimation of the employee. In fact, they are the kind of measures suggested when subjective evaluations have to be validated (Cascio & Bernardin, 1981). However, production evaluations have some disadvantages. Being results oriented, these measures focus more on the outcomes of performance than on the process of performance. Although this may be perfectly all right for some jobs, in other jobs it allows the evaluation to be influenced by factors that may not be under the control of the employee. Fluctuations in the productivity of work team members, for example, can result in a difference in production. Such effects should be distinguished from production differences that are due to the employee's behavior. Another potential weakness is in the timing of the evaluation. A production record may be based on a period of time that is too short to be representative. For example, researchers studying factory workers found that production levels were stable from one week to the next, but output varied considerably when the interval was longer than this (Rambo, Chomiak, & Price, 1983). A week's production is not always a good estimation of a whole year's work. If this type of production sampling is used in yearly evaluations, assessment will be inaccurate.

Personnel Data

Indirect evaluation evidence can be found in personnel files. Many organizations routinely ask for evidence of good attendance in evaluating job performance. Although some employers include absenteeism and tardiness on a rating form, records of employee attendance can be found easily in personnel files. A trail of personnel actions typically can be found in these files also, such as salary increases, promotions, demotions, and disciplinary actions. However, use of personnel data in evaluation has been criticized. When used as the basis for ratings, influence from irrelevant factors is likely. For example, past personnel actions may unfairly affect present personnel decisions, such as when a present promotion is based on a string of past promotions. Supervisors who participated in the earlier promotion decisions may not treat these data objectively but may bias their evaluations of an employee's later performance. In one study, supervisors who agreed with the initial promotion decision gave evaluations showing positive bias, and those who disagreed showed negative bias (Schoorman, 1988).

Judgmental Measures

Although we can gather personnel data on all employees, it is next to impossible to get production data on all. Some jobs involve very little that can be counted. Even if a count can be taken, it may not be very relevant. For example, suppose we decide to evaluate college professors with a production measure. We might count the number of minutes they spend lecturing, the number of things they write on a chalkboard during lecture, or the number of students to whom they give As. None of these counts measure important aspects of a professor's job. Many jobs are like this. Managerial employees, for example, cannot be evaluated adequately with production measures.

For such jobs, and sometimes even for production jobs, we must rely on human judgments of performance. Such judgments usually relate to the quality of work, although an evaluator can be asked to assess the quantity of work or productivity as well. With judgmental methods, an individual's performance may be compared with that of others in the same job or organizational unit, or the individual may be compared to some absolute standard that is defined for the evaluator. Sometimes, unfortunately, the absolute standard is left undefined, and the evaluator is invited to use his or her own judgment in deciding the standard of comparison.

In the simplest of the judgmental procedures, the evaluator writes a free-form description of the employee's strengths and weaknesses. This **narrative evaluation** is rather like the unstructured letter of reference used in selection in that the evaluator decides what to include. If the evaluator outlines improvements for the employee to make, this can be helpful in giving feedback. The narrative evaluation has a major failing, however. What is included in the evaluation is likely to vary from one evaluator to another and from one employee to another; thus, it is difficult to make comparisons between employees.

There are judgmental procedures that give more standardized information than the narrative. Some of these use a rating scale to make evaluations. Others use checklists or other nonrating techniques for comparing employees. In the next three sections, I discuss these procedures in depth.

*M*ain *P*oints

Most often, the evaluator is the employee's supervisor. The supervisor knows the job and the person's performance. If this is not the case, such as when employees work independently, then the evaluation must come from someone else. Depending on the job, peer-, self-, and subordinate-appraisals may be used. Self-appraisals often are more positive than supervisors' ratings. However, the extent of this leniency varies for people in different jobs. Subordinates' appraisals may be used to provide upward feedback for management development purposes. They tend to agree with appraisals done by the manager's superior.

The information upon which an evaluation is based may be objective or subjective. For some employees, a production measure is possible. Personnel data, such as absenteeism, are available for all employees. For most employees in most jobs, these sources of information are not enough. Instead, human observation and judgment is the source of appraisal information.

APPRAISAL RATING SYSTEMS

The performance rating is the oldest type of formal evaluation. More than 50 years ago, researchers found that most companies that had a formal system, used rating scales for evaluating employees (Starr & Greenly, 1939). The rating scale also is used for a variety of purposes. For example, it is used in survey research, such as job attitude surveys. The rating scale is frequently used as a criterion measure in studies of test validation. In the 1940s, it was almost the *only* criterion measure for this purpose (Tiffin, 1943).

Graphic Rating Scales

With a **graphic rating scale,** employees are rated from low to high on one or more dimensions of job performance. The rater judges the degree to which the employee shows a behavior or has a trait and then uses the scale to express this

Table 7.2   Trait Dimensions Frequently Included on Graphic Rating Scales

Quality of work	Productivity
Accuracy	Economy of materials
Neatness	Economy of time
Initiative	Job knowledge
Job interest	Knowledge of company policies
Dependability	Responsibility
Potential for advancement	Cooperation
Energy	Leadership ability
Judgment	Planning ability
Creativity	Safety

judgment. Such scales can be constructed to evaluate employees on a number of specific dimensions, as well as on overall job performance. For example, a rating scale can be used to evaluate the amount and quality of work accomplished, the extent to which the employee is dependable and shows initiative, and the degree to which he or she can work without supervision. Table 7.2 lists dimensions frequently included on graphic rating scales. When selecting dimensions for a rating scale, a dimension needs to be relevant to the particular job. Scales often are constructed in general terms, without reference to what employees were hired to do. We should not do this, because evaluation of behaviors and traits that are irrelevant to the job is a source of error.

Rating scales differ not only in terms of the dimensions they include but also in terms of their response categories. On a scale from 1 to 10, is 10 high and 1 low, or does 1 mean "best" and 10 "worst"? Until the scale points are defined and labeled, we cannot tell. Assigning points to a scale and defining these points along a positive-negative or high-low continuum is called **anchoring**. Rating scales are anchored with numerical values and verbal designations. The anchors can be simple and located only at the ends of the continuum, such as high–low, or they can be placed at midway points, such as very high–moderately high–moderately low–very low. Table 7.3 shows some examples. In constructing a scale, the rating dimensions should be carefully defined so that raters do not have to guess at what is being asked. Developing detailed anchors will help define the dimension, particularly if anchors are behavioral descriptions of different levels or degrees of the dimension.

Validating the Rating System

An important question to ask about an appraisal rating system is whether the ratings are valid measures of job performance. A statement of validity defines the extent to which the measure truthfully reflects the actual performance variable. A measure should be able to detect when a behavior or trait is present and when it is not. (See figure 7.1.)

Table 7.3   Ways to Anchor a Rating Scale

	Verbal Endpoint Anchors							
Quality of Work	☐	☐	☐	☐	☐	☐	☐	
	High							*Low*

	Verbal and Numerical End- and Midpoint Anchors							
Quality of Work	☐	☐	☐	☐	☐	☐	☐	
	High 7	6	5	4	3	2	1	*Low*

	Verbal End- and Midpoint Anchors			
Quality of Work	☐	☐	☐	☐
	Consistently superior work	*Average quality work*	*Frequent mistakes made*	*Usually not satisfactory*

Figure 7.1. *Relationship between a behavioral variable and its detection by a measurement instrument. A measure is valid only if it can detect both the presence and the absence of a behavior under study.*

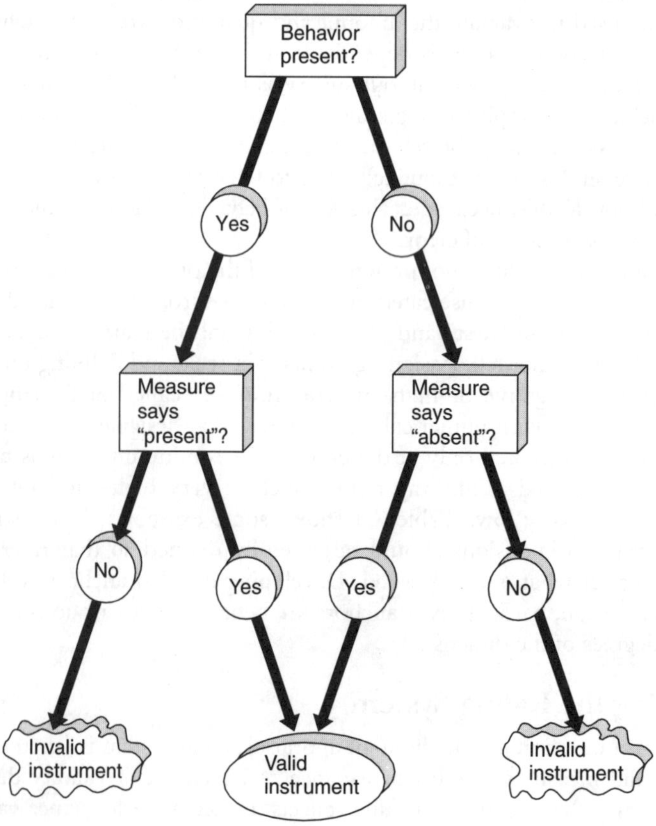

Rating scale validity is conceptually similar to test validity. Recall from the discussion of test validity in chapter 5 that the reliability of an instrument provides some information about its validity. If a measure is not reliable, you may recall, it is not valid either. A good measure of job performance should be able to repeat itself in order to give accurate assessments. If the measure is reliable, it *may* be valid because valid measures are also reliable. Therefore, assessing the reliability of a performance rating instrument and finding a sizable reliability coefficient provides some evidence that the rating is valid. The methods of estimating the reliability of selection methods, discussed in chapters 4 and 5, can be used also for evaluating the reliability of rating instruments. Agreement between raters is one of the most frequently used indicators of rating reliability. Agreement over time (rate-rerate) is used as well.

As mentioned earlier in this chapter, empirical validation of performance appraisal is difficult to do. The major problem is finding another criterion of job performance against which to compare ratings. Recall from chapter 5 that in certain test validation strategies, we compare a test to a valid criterion measure of performance, such as a rating. Now, we are face to face with the question of how to establish the validity of the criterion measure. If we had a **true score** of performance, we would simply correlate the rating with it. If the rating is valid, then we would find it to be highly correlated with the true criterion measure. Unfortunately, true criterion measures are extremely hard to find.

Techniques for computing true scores from independent observations of performance have been devised for use in developing and validating rating scales. One technique uses "expert" ratings as the true performance scores. The experts vary depending on the study, but often they are individuals who have been thoroughly trained to observe behavior and use the rating system (Sulsky & Balzer, 1988). "True" behavior in such studies often is defined by a videotape of actors who perform certain work roles that have been created specifically to demonstrate behavior at specific levels of performance quality. Taped episodes are viewed by experimental subjects and evaluated with a rating scale. The researcher validates the scale by correlating the subjects' ratings with the true scores as they are portrayed in the videotape (Borman, 1978). This method of validating a rating scale is extremely time-consuming, and its adequacy is open to criticism (Barrett & Kernan, 1987; Sulsky & Balzer, 1988). Validation of this kind simply may not be worth the trouble. An easier solution is to base the scale on a job analysis and evaluate its reliability, rather than attempt an empirical validity study.

Rating Errors

Regardless of the technique or scale, judgmental methods always involve subjectivity; therefore, factors irrelevant to performance can bias the evaluation. As I note in the discussion of employment interviews in chapter 4, people vary considerably in their ability to size up someone else. Judgmental errors are commonplace in this regard. Sometimes inaccuracy is due simply to a person's difficulty in judging others, or an error can be due to inadequate information. In some cases, an evaluator has not observed an employee's performance long or closely enough. This occurs when ratings are done by a superior who has little day-to-day contact

Table 7.4

Performance Evaluation Errors Made by Raters

Error	Indicators	Possible Causes
Halo	High intercorrelation of items	Uses knowledge of one item to rate another
Logical	High intercorrelation of items	Rates similar appearing items the same
Proximity	High intercorrelation of adjacent items	Uses knowledge of one item to rate an adjacent item
Leniency	High ratings of all ratees	Has low performance standards; is resistant to giving criticism
Severity	Low ratings of all ratees	Has high performance standards; is resistant to evaluation
Central tendency	Average ratings of all ratees	Is resistant to evaluation; is unable to distinguish between employees
Recency	No indication in rating	Bases rating on most recent behavior
Inadequate knowledge	No indication in rating	Inadequate knowledge of job and/or ratee

with the subordinate. Sometimes, a rater has sufficient contact with the employee, but observations are not recorded. Instead, the rater relies on his or her memory. **Recency error** can occur because the rater bases the evaluation on an inadequate sample of performance behavior—specifically the most recent behavior. The evaluation is overly influenced by recent behavior because it is remembered most clearly.

Some of these errors can be reduced easily. The rating task should be assigned to someone who has close contact with the employee, and employee performance should be periodically recorded in order to establish an adequate behavior sample. As you see in the next sections, however, halo, leniency/severity, and central tendency errors are more difficult to correct. See table 7.4 for a preview of these rating errors.

Halo and Related Errors

One particularly pervasive rating error, known as **halo error,** has been resistant to all kinds of efforts to remove it. Halo error results when an evaluator has difficulty in evaluating ratee characteristics separately. The evaluator resorts to using a general impression to rate specific dimensions. The error occurs when an employee is rated high (or low) on one trait because the rater believes the person is generally high (or low) on other traits. (Notice from this description that halo error can be either positive or negative.) Study of halo error indicates that it coincides with the rater's general impression of the person (Lance, LaPointe, & Stewart, 1994).

Halo error can be viewed as a result of *stimulus generalization*. Recall from the discussion of training transfer in chapter 6 that people learn easily to respond in the same fashion to two similar stimuli. In training, we constantly demand that they do this, in fact. We want trainees to ignore most differences between training conditions and job conditions. If they do not, we have transfer problems. In performance evaluation, however, we expect evaluators to be able to distinguish between what are sometimes small differences between performance dimensions. Raters, however, may be so accustomed to discounting small differences that they fail to make the needed distinctions; thus, one performance dimension is generalized as being the same as another, so they are rated the same. Thus, a halo error occurs.

The research literature indicates that halo error is more likely (1) when the performance dimension is unfamiliar to the rater, (2) when it is not defined, and (3) when it is difficult to observe (Cooper, 1981). This means that whenever the evaluator has little information about the dimension that can show how it is different from some other dimension, then halo is likely. Efforts to minimize the error have been most successful when they have included ways to increase the discriminability of performance dimensions. For example, it is generally agreed that improved definitions and rating scale anchors with behavioral descriptions help reduce halo error.

Another way to reduce halo error is to train raters in how to avoid the mistake. Research has shown that trained raters can reduce halo error, as well as other errors (e.g., Borman, 1979; Latham et al., 1975). However, another problem concerning the relationship between halo error and accuracy then appears. Is a rating more accurate when it contains less halo? Although it might seem so, research has not shown that it always is (Cooper, 1981). "Halo-trained" raters actually may lose accuracy when they begin to treat truly related dimensions as if they are different.

Research on rating accuracy has led to a more careful examination of the meaning of halo. Researchers have found that some performance dimensions, in fact, are highly related; and high similarity in the ratings of these dimensions is not an error. Rather, high correlation between truly related dimensions is **true halo.** From this viewpoint, halo error is an overestimation of true halo. Some statistical procedures for controlling halo error have been criticized because they ignore this distinction and remove not only the halo error but also some true halo (Hulin, 1982; Murphy, 1982). True halo conceivably is important to retain in performance ratings (Nathan & Tippins, 1990). Currently, it appears that the researcher should decide when to apply a correction for halo error, according to whether or not it seems to be a problem.

Two errors that are similar to halo error further complicate the problem of evaluating halo error. A **logical error** is one in which traits are evaluated similarly because they seem logically related. If they actually are not related dimensions, treating them so will look like halo error. If they are related, their high intercorrelation should be expected, and the error is on the part of the developer of the scale who did not distinguish between them. **Proximity error** occurs because of the order of dimensions on a scale. That is, dimensions located next to each other on a rating scale are likely to be evaluated similarly. Logical and proximity errors can result from improperly developed scales. Dimensions that appear to be logically related should be more fully defined, and similar dimensions should be moved apart physically.

Problems of Restricted Range

Leniency and **severity errors** in evaluations occur because raters differ in their expectations of employees in general. Some have high expectations; some have lower expectations. Some raters are easy, and some are harsh. You can see differences in professors in terms of how easy it is to get a good grade from them. Supervisors are like this, too. The lenient rater concentrates ratings at the high or positive end of the rating scale. To this person, all employees are above average. The severe rater concentrates ratings at the low or negative end. To this rater, they are all below average. Neither rater seems to be making logical sense. In fact, however, they are using some abstract standard of what employees are like. **Central tendency error,** also called **average rating error,** is related to leniency and severity errors. It results when all ratings are concentrated in the middle of the scale. The rater who makes this mistake is noted for never using the extreme ends of the rating scale. To this person, everyone looks about average; no one is superior or inferior.

Leniency is a stable response tendency that some raters show whenever evaluations are done (Kane et al., 1995). The tendency to be lenient in ratings is more common than the tendency to be severe (Benedict & Levine, 1988), probably because it is easier to be generous in rating employees. Not inconsequential to the busy supervisor, lenient ratings do not have to be justified to the subordinate. Also, this is due partly to the evaluator's reaction to certain employees. Supervisors are sometimes reluctant to interact with a poor performer. There is evidence that raters delay in evaluating low performers and are more lenient with them than they are with high performers (Benedict & Levine, 1988). Developers of rating systems may inadvertently contribute to this positive bias by requiring documentation of poor behavior but not of good behavior. This makes it easier to evaluate everyone as satisfactory.

Raters who show leniency, severity, or central tendency error have a propensity for concentrating ratings in one section of the rating scale. These errors all produce ratings in which there is a restricted range of differences between dimensions and between ratees. Most importantly, ratings with a restricted range do not differentiate between employees; all employees are evaluated as being essentially the same. Such ratings are not very useful as criteria in validation studies. Test scores cannot be evaluated for their ability to predict high and low performers because ratings that show a restricted range do not distinguish high from low performers.

Comparing Ratings from Different Raters

When raters of two groups of employees use different rating standards, the ratings of the two groups cannot be compared at face value. If one unit has a severe rater and the other a lenient rater or one who sees his or her subordinates as average, the performance of these groups will appear less similar to each other than they actually may be. Similarly, a C from one professor is not necessarily comparable to a C from another, as you know. If ratings must be compared between raters and if the distributions of ratings appear to differ in this way, then some adjustment must be made to allow an accurate comparison.

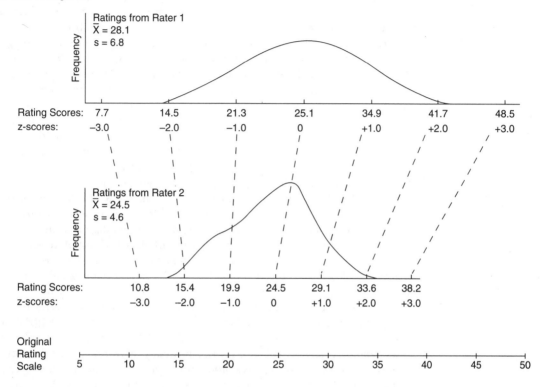

Figure 7.2. *Transformation of ratings to z-scores. The two distributions of ratings from rater 1 and rater 2 occur because the raters used different standards. Individual ratings from the two raters cannot be compared directly. Converting both sets of ratings to z-scores solves this problem because rating scores with the same z-score are comparable.*

A reasonably simple way to salvage the value of the ratings and make them comparable is to convert both sets of ratings to the same scale. A common method of conversion involves computing **z-scores.**[2] The mean and standard deviation of ratings produced by a single rater are calculated, and then each rating score is transformed to a z-score. We find the z-score by subtracting the individual rating score from the mean score and dividing the difference by the standard deviation: $z = \bar{x} - x / s$. The z-score shows where the individual rating is located in the distribution of scores. When all scores are converted for both raters, they are comparable because the z-value is the number of standard deviations away from the mean on a single scale that includes all scores from both raters (see figure 7.2).

Training Raters to Rate

One way to reduce errors in ratings is to teach raters how to avoid making them. Giving supervisors **rater error training** has been effective in various situations (Bernardin, 1978; Bernardin & Walter, 1977; Latham et al., 1975). In the study of rater error training, researchers initially assumed that reduction of rating errors

[2]These z-scores are also called *standard scores.*

would improve the accuracy of ratings. The assumption is reasonable because part of what makes ratings inaccurate is that they contain errors. However, as I note in discussing halo error, raters who are instructed to avoid rating a person the same on different dimensions (which is the typical instruction in halo error training) also produce less accurate ratings. This effect is no longer surprising. Because the raters were careful to avoid giving similar ratings, as they had been instructed, they ignored the true halo between dimensions (Bernardin & Buckley, 1981). Training raters to avoid errors should be done carefully because this training places the rater in a new, but not necessarily more appropriate, frame of mind with respect to making judgments (Hedge & Kavanagh, 1988).

Currently, rater training is changing from a focus on errors to a focus on accuracy. **Accuracy training** has been done in different ways. Some designs attempt to improve the rater's ability to observe work behavior and make decisions about ratings (Hedge & Kavanagh, 1988). In Frame of Reference (FOR) training, the purpose is to establish a common perspective among raters and provide them with a standard for evaluating work behaviors (Bernardin & Buckley, 1981). FOR training can include study of the job, practice and feedback on using a rating scale, and explanations of ratings given by experts (McIntyre, Smith, & Hassett, 1984).

Accuracy training has been compared to error training. A review of research on rater training showed that either can be effective for what it is supposed to improve (Woehr & Huffcutt, 1994). Raters who receive training to avoid errors show less error in their ratings than those who receive only accuracy training. On the other hand, accuracy training appears to be more effective than error training in improving accuracy (Athey & McIntyre, 1987; McIntyre et al., 1984; Pulakos, 1984). FOR training is especially useful in helping raters learn how to produce accurate ratings (Woehr & Huffcutt, 1994). Apparently, FOR training works because it helps raters to develop cognitive prototypes or models of effective employee behavior and to use these to categorize a ratee's performance (Sulsky & Day, 1992).

The need for measures of accuracy to be used in accuracy training brings us back to the problem of finding true scores of performance. Frequently, a group of "experts" is used to generate true scores for studies of accuracy training (Sulsky & Balzer, 1988). A group of individuals developed as experts can provide a reasonably good assessment of performance, if they are well trained and have plenty of time to observe the performance. For example, in one study, a group of I/O psychology graduate students were used as experts. These students had had coursework in performance evaluation, and they viewed a videotaped work performance twice before rating it. Their ratings were more closely related to objective production scores than were those of a nonexpert group (Smither, Barry, & Reilly, 1989).

M_{ain} P_{oints}

Most appraisal systems use graphic rating scales. Rating scales vary in terms of the performance dimensions they include and in how scale anchors are defined.

A rating scale must give a valid assessment of employee performance, especially if the scale is used as a criterion measure. It is difficult to empirically validate a performance rating scale because usually there is no true score available. Reliability assessment and content validation can be used instead.

Judgmental errors are commonplace. Recency error occurs when a rating is based on recent performance only. Halo error occurs when a rater uses a general impression of the ratee rather than actual performance to evaluate specific dimensions. Some of what appears to be halo error instead may be true halo, as when dimensions are naturally associated. Similar to halo error, are proximity and logical errors.

Three rating tendencies—leniency, severity, and central tendency errors—produce distributions that (1) cannot directly be compared between raters, (2) are restricted in range, and (3) give little information about differences between ratees.

Rater error training can help. Raters can learn how to avoid halo and other errors. However, the rater does not always become more accurate. Accuracy training attempts to improve the rater's ability to observe and make use of performance information. Frame of reference (FOR) training is an example.

SPECIAL RATING SCALES

In most discussions of performance evaluation, there are two major themes: how to evaluate, and what to do about all the mistakes. In this section, I describe the rating scales that have been developed specifically to improve evaluation. The earliest effort to deal with the problems of appraisal rating systems was to develop better rating scales. Considerable work has been done in this respect. Several alternatives to the general graphic rating scale are available: the Behaviorally Anchored Rating Scale, the Behavioral Observation Scale, and the Mixed Standard Rating Scale.

Behaviorally Anchored Rating Scale (BARS)

Early study of rating error indicated that improving verbal descriptions of scale anchors made it easier for raters to assess performance. When either anchors or dimensions are ambiguous, raters can interpret them as they see fit. Thus, the ratings may contain error if raters interpret dimensions differently from what the scale developer intended. Carefully describing scale points in behavioral terms is thought to make the rater's task simpler. All the rater will need to do is recognize the description that best fits the employee. The **Behaviorally Anchored Rating Scale (BARS)**, introduced in 1963 by Smith and Kendall, was meant to be a solution to problems of dimension ambiguity.

Flanagan's (1954) critical incidents[3] technique is used to develop a BARS. In the critical incidents study, subject matter experts (SMEs), such as supervisors and job incumbents, describe incidents in which an employee has been very effective on the job and incidents in which the employee has been very ineffective. Thus, the first step in developing a BARS is to identify important aspects of the job and write incidents that describe critical behavior. Typically, SMEs are divided into several groups to do this work. The first group generates critical incidents. The second group extracts the performance dimension from each incident and writes descriptions of high, average, and low levels of performance on each dimension. The behavioral descriptions are mixed together, and a third group sorts them out again into what they believe are the proper sets. A fourth group evaluates these descriptions on a numerical scale and assigns a scale value

[3]As described in chapter 3, the critical incidents technique is a method of job analysis.

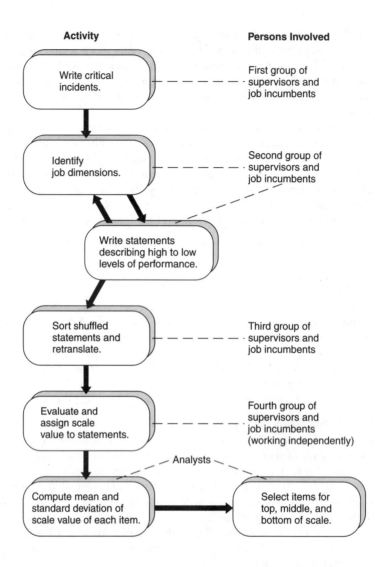

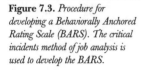

Figure 7.3. *Procedure for developing a Behaviorally Anchored Rating Scale (BARS). The critical incidents method of job analysis is used to develop the BARS.*

Activity

Write critical incidents.

Identify job dimensions.

Write statements describing high to low levels of performance.

Sort shuffled statements and retranslate.

Evaluate and assign scale value to statements.

Compute mean and standard deviation of scale value of each item.

Select items for top, middle, and bottom of scale.

Persons Involved

First group of supervisors and job incumbents

Second group of supervisors and job incumbents

Third group of supervisors and job incumbents

Fourth group of supervisors and job incumbents (working independently)

Analysts

to each. Evaluations are done independently by members of this group; therefore, several numerical values are obtained for each item. These values are combined, and the mean and standard deviation are computed for each item. Only those items that have a low standard deviation—meaning that the evaluators agreed on the scale value of the item—are retained. From these, items are selected that describe behavior at the top, middle, and bottom of the performance scale. These items go directly on the scale, and they define the anchors. (These steps are summarized in figure 7.3.)

Before it is put to use, the scale must be tested. A trial evaluation is conducted in which the new scale is used by two supervisors to rate the same employees. Interrater reliability is assessed by correlating the two supervisors' ratings of

Table 7.5   A BARS for Evaluating Research Analysts on the Dimension of Report Writing

Instructions to Rater: Read the dimension description and then the descriptions of behavior at various points along the scale. Decide which behavior most accurately matches the individual's and check the scale to indicate this. You may mark the scale at any point that seems appropriate, including a point midway between two behavioral descriptions. Use this same procedure for all dimensions.

Dimension: Writing technical reports on research projects.

9	Can be expected to construct well-organized, thorough, and highly accurate reports that need no further explanation
8	Can be expected to present data and discussion that hardly ever need elaboration
7	
6	Can be expected to finish reports on time
5	Can be expected to construct reports that are generally useful but may require explanation
4	Can be expected to submit disorganized reports sometimes
3	Can be expected usually to be late in turning in reports
2	
1	Can be expected to submit reports that typically are incomplete and disorganized

each employee. In addition, the ratings of each dimension across ratees are correlated. These correlations indicate whether or not each dimension measures a unique aspect of performance.

The purpose of this extensive procedure is to develop a scale that describes actions all along the performance dimension, covering a behavioral range from excellent to poor performance. Table 7.5 provides an example of anchors developed for one job dimension. Typically, several job dimensions are included on a BARS, with a specific behavioral description at each anchor point. To use the scale, a rater simply checks the one anchor description that best describes the employee on each dimension. This seems much easier for the rater than using a scale anchored by vague or general terms.

There are some problems with the BARS. First, such scales are time-consuming and difficult to develop. The scale is custom-made for rating employees in a particular job class. Certainly, these constraints will dictate against its development and use by small organizations or for job classes in which there are few employees. Second, it may be that use of the BARS modifies the rater's frame of reference. Some researchers are questioning the value of very specific behavioral anchors. Because raters will have observed behaviors that match the anchor descriptions of some items, but not others, they may assign more importance to the *observed* anchor and bias the rating in the process (Murphy & Constans, 1987; Piotrowski, Barnes-Farrell, & Esrig, 1989).

If the scale has been carefully developed by individuals who are able to define the critical elements of a job accurately, the BARS does have a major

Table 7.6 — Sample BOS Items for Evaluating Job Instructors

	Never		Sometimes		Always
	1	2	3	4	5
1. Maintains contact with supervisors for procedure and equipment update	☐	☐	☐	☐	☐
2. Prepares accurate material for use in classroom presentation and demonstration	☐	☐	☐	☐	☐
3. Keeps instructional equipment clean and in good working order	☐	☐	☐	☐	☐
4. Conducts trainee practice sessions and gives corrective feedback	☐	☐	☐	☐	☐
5. Keeps abreast of developments in training technology and incorporates new techniques as appropriate	☐	☐	☐	☐	☐
6. Provides extra assistance for difficult trainees	☐	☐	☐	☐	☐

advantage in being highly job related. The critical incidents method provides a degree of content validity. Thus, BARS development is useful when an organization needs to validate its appraisal system, as when EEOC compliance is an issue. Another positive aspect of BARS is indirect. Supervisors may complain that developing the scale takes too much time because almost daily records of subordinate behavior are needed. However, their involvement in BARS development can result in their commitment to using the scale (Bernardin, 1977).

Behavioral Observation Scale (BOS)

A second response to the problems of appraisal rating systems is the **Behavioral Observation Scale (BOS)** (Latham & Wexley, 1977). For this rating scale as for the BARS, critical incidents are identified using Flanagan's (1954) method of job analysis. The critical incidents are used to develop behavioral statements describing important aspects of performance. The rater indicates how *frequently* these occur in the employee's behavior. The response categories are defined either numerically or verbally in terms of frequency. Frequency may be a percentage of time, such as "less than 20%, 20%–40%, 40%–60%," or a verbal reference to time, such as "always, sometimes, never." To use the BOS, the rater simply checks the response category that describes how often the behavior is shown. Table 7.6 shows an excerpt from a BOS.

The BOS has considerable intuitive appeal, and some think it may become a "hot item" in performance evaluation methodology (Zedeck & Cascio, 1984). Although there has been relatively little research evaluating it, this method is likely to have some of the same advantages and disadvantages as the BARS. The scale is highly job relevant, but it is also time-consuming and costly to develop.

Mixed Standard Rating Scale (MSRS)

Another device that represents an attempt to construct a better rating scale is the **Mixed Standard Rating Scale (MSRS)** (Blanz & Ghiselli, 1972). In this instrument,

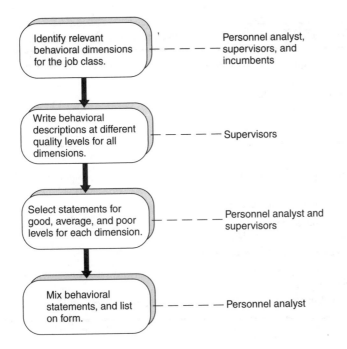

Figure 7.4. *Procedure for developing a Mixed Standard Rating Scale (MSRS). Behavioral descriptions are composed through a critical incidents study.*

Identify relevant behavioral dimensions for the job class. — — — — Personnel analyst, supervisors, and incumbents

Write behavioral descriptions at different quality levels for all dimensions. — — — — Supervisors

Select statements for good, average, and poor levels for each dimension. — — — — Personnel analyst and supervisors

Mix behavioral statements, and list on form. — — — — Personnel analyst

as in the BARS and BOS, behavioral descriptions come from a critical incidents study. These describe good, average, and poor performance. The rater considers each item and indicates whether the employee typically shows behavior that is better, worse, or the same as the description. The rater is not told whether an item indicates good or poor performance or to what dimension it belongs, although sometimes both aspects are apparent.

Developing an MSRS is a complicated procedure. First, supervisors identify as many behavioral dimensions as they believe constitute the job. Then, various levels of performance on each of these dimensions are described. Statements are selected from these descriptions of performance levels to define three specific rating levels: good, average, and poor performance. These become the *standards* against which the ratee's behavior will be compared. Finally, the three standards for each dimension are shuffled or mixed with those for other dimensions and listed on the instrument in random order (the name comes from *mixing* the *standards*). These steps of MSRS development are summarized in figure 7.4.

The MSRS was intended to minimize halo error and leniency, and it does this by using behavioral statements and mixing them on the form. As I discussed previously, ratings of well-defined, specific behaviors are less likely to contain halo error than ratings of ill-defined dimensions (Cooper, 1981). In addition, there may be less of a tendency to rate apparently related dimensions similarly when the dimensions are not placed immediately adjacent to one another. It appears that the method can reduce these types of errors to some extent (Saal & Landy, 1977). The MSRS method is meant to be helpful in identifying careless raters. This is one

Table 7.7

Sample MSRS Items on Two Performance Dimensions

Instructions: Rate each item by selecting and entering the appropriate response from the following:

  + = ratee is better than this statement

  0 = this statement fits the ratee

  − = ratee is worse than this statement

		Rating
1.	Can be counted upon to take the lead in starting and carrying out new projects (I,g)	_____
2.	Writes incomplete reports that contain mistakes (II,p)	_____
3.	Typically does good work on new projects, but requires the lead of another team member to get these started (I,a)	_____
4.	Writes project reports that are usually clear (II,a)	_____
5.	Resists the start-up of new projects and requires constant overseeing to maintain work quality (I,p)	_____
6.	Writes well-documented and accurate project reports (II,g)	_____

Note: Dimension "I" refers to work on new projects, and "II" refers to project reporting. The values, good (g), average (a), and poor (p), refer to job performance. These codes are not included on the actual rating scale.

reason for mixing the items. From the sample listed in table 7.7, note that items are written in such a way that it is illogical for a single ratee to be "better than" the good end of the scale and "worse than" the poor end on the same dimension. Generally, if these kinds of responses are given, the rater is not paying attention. Mixing the items may not be necessary, however. Such errors can be suppressed by simply telling raters that the errors can be detected (Dickinson & Glebocki, 1990).

The MSRS has some problems. Like the BARS and BOS, it is painstaking to develop. If it has many items, which is likely with complex jobs, raters may resist using it. Also, because the items have been mixed, neither the performance dimensions nor the value of each item are readily apparent. Thus, the ratings are not very useful as feedback for employees.

Main Points

One way to improve ratings is to devise a better rating scale. The Behaviorally Anchored Rating Scale (BARS), the Behavioral Observation Scale (BOS), and the Mixed Standard Rating Scale (MSRS) are examples. Each is based on a critical incident study; thus, the evaluation includes only job relevant performance dimensions.

The BARS uses performance descriptors that have assigned values as the scale anchors. To use the BARS, the rater chooses the behavioral anchor on each item that most closely matches the ratee's performance. The BOS is made up of behavioral statements to which the evaluator responds by reporting how frequently the ratee shows the described behavior. In the MSRS, statements describing levels of performance quality are used as standards. The rater indicates whether the ratee behaves the same, better, or worse than the statement describes.

The three scales all have the important advantage of job relevance. However, the process of developing such job specific rating scales is time-consuming.

NONRATING EVALUATION METHODS

Some methods of evaluation that are based on judgments do not use a rating scale format. These methods fall into two categories: checklists and comparisons. With checklist techniques, an evaluator simply checks off the behavioral characteristics that describe an employee's performance. With comparison procedures, one employee is compared to others rather than to some absolute standard of behavior. Because these methods do not use a rating scale, you might suppose that the errors described previously will not be a problem. However, this is not so. These methods, like ratings, use human judgments; thus, they are subject to many of the same errors. For example, recency error, in which the evaluator bases the evaluation on the most recent information, is a potential problem with all nonrating methods.

Checklists

There are two types of checklists: the weighted checklist and the forced-choice checklist. Both present the evaluator with descriptive statements of behavior. They differ in whether the evaluator is required to check a specific number of statements. Forced-choice checklist procedures do not allow the freedom of omitting items. The weighted checklist may.

Weighted Checklist

The **weighted checklist** is particularly easy to use. The evaluator plays the part of reporter, checking those statements that most clearly describe either the best or the typical behavior of the employee. In some variations, the evaluator checks the statements that are least descriptive of the person. The weighted checklist usually allows the evaluator to check as many or as few items as apply. The individual's score is calculated by a personnel analyst who sums the weights of the items checked. Of course, the item weights are not listed on the checklist and presumably the rater is not aware of the actual value of the items. This should curb the tendency toward leniency. If the evaluator does not know the importance of the items, he or she is more likely to report actual behavior.

To develop a weighted checklist, a pool of statements that describe work behavior is generated. These statements can be specific to a particular job or more generally describe employee behavior. Next, the statements are weighted. One frequently used weighting procedure is Thurstone's method of **equal-appearing intervals.** In this, a group of supervisors judge and score each statement as to its desirability in the behavior of a subordinate. Then, the group's mean score per item is calculated. This mean score becomes the weight of the item. The standard deviation of the scores per item is used to assess interjudge agreement. Only those items with small standard deviations are included in the checklist. Items spanning the full range of scale values are included, and each item has a numerical value.

Like many other instruments, the weighted checklist is time-consuming to develop. However, an advantage is that they are easy to use. Checklists are usually acceptable to supervisors. Such errors as leniency and halo do not seem to be problems if the items' values are not apparent. If the items are transparent in the degree to which they indicate desirable qualities, accuracy may be reduced, but then the information becomes available for employee feedback.

Forced-Choice Technique

The **forced-choice checklist** is an attempt to deal with the error that results when evaluators respond to the apparent favorability of a checklist item. (In this error, the rater describes the employee in terms that are generally desirable of employees, rather than in terms of the employee's actual behavior.) Two or more statements describing behavior are grouped together in sets in the forced-choice checklist. The statements in a set are similar in their apparent desirability, but they differ in terms of the extent to which they indicate good or poor work performance. The evaluator is required to select one of two items or two of four items from each set. The evaluator may be asked to select the item that is either most or least like the individual's performance. In sets of four items, both the most and least descriptive items may be required. Some examples are listed in table 7.8.

To develop a forced-choice checklist, employees' scores on a pool of items are correlated with other measures of their job performance. Items are selected according to the extent to which they are associated with good or poor performance, and they are judged as to their desirability. Then, the items are paired on the checklist according to the extent to which they are equally desirable (or undesirable) but different in being associated with good performance. Thus, although two items may appear to be equally positive, they do not equally indicate good performance, and they carry different weights. As with other weighted methods, item weights are not shown on the instrument.

The forced-choice technique has the ability to improve ratings by minimizing leniency. However, lack of information for feedback to employees is a drawback. Another disadvantage is that evaluators may not like it. They may resent being forced to select an item from each item set. In some sets, no item seems to apply to a particular employee, yet the instructions require that one be checked. Raters also tend to resent not knowing when they are giving a good or a poor rating.

Comparison Methods

Sometimes a professor assigns grades on the basis of a "curve." Chances are you know one who does this. In such a case, the professor is not comparing your performance to an absolute standard but to the performance of other students in the class. The rationale is that there is an identifiable distribution in the performance of students, with some doing excellent work, others doing average work, and so forth. Employee comparison methods are similar to this. Employees are compared, not to an absolute standard, but to other employees.

Table 7.8   Forced-Choice Item Samples

Instructions: Following are statements describing various aspects of performance behavior. These statements are grouped in fours. For each group of four, indicate with an "M" the one statement *most* characteristic of the individual, and with an "L" the one *least* characteristic of the individual.

_____ Takes the lead in starting new work projects

_____ Can be relied upon to get a work project done on time

_____ Is cooperative and easy to work with

_____ Shows initiative in obtaining the necessary information and materials to do a project

_____ Takes considerable care with job details

_____ Works diligently until the task is finished

_____ Keeps the work environment clean and well ordered

_____ Is always careful to operate equipment safely

_____ Wastes materials

_____ Withholds project information from coworkers

_____ Is loud and boisterous with coworkers

_____ Keeps a messy, cluttered work area

_____ Displays resistance to changes in procedures

_____ Arrives late and leaves early

_____ Puts off project tasks until the last minute

_____ Spends too much time on insignificant details

Comparison methods were developed in response to a problem that appears when a graphic rating scale is used–the problem of restricted range. Recall that restricted range occurs because of leniency, severity, and central tendency in ratings. Restriction of range limits the usefulness of evaluations because ratees essentially are not differentiated. Comparison methods are based on the assumption that individuals do differ in their performance; therefore, an effective method of evaluation will show this difference.

Rank Order Procedure

With the **rank order comparison,** the evaluator simply thinks of all the employees at once and ranks them from lowest to highest. In a variant of this procedure, the evaluator first selects the best and worst performers, then the next best and worst pair, and so on until all employees have been ranked. Usually, ranking is done in terms of an overall assessment of performance, and an individual's rank is the score. Ranks can be done for different dimensions, but this will increase the time to do the evaluation.

The major advantage of rank ordering is its quick and easy use. Evaluation requires no special forms or instruments and is neither expensive nor time-consuming to develop. Also, supervisors tend to accept it. It does have limitations, however. Little information for feedback is provided. In addition, the distance between the ranks cannot be shown. That is, although one employee can be recognized as more proficient than another, the evaluator has no way of expressing how much more proficient that person is. In like manner, similarities between employees cannot be shown. Two employees may be equally proficient, but with this procedure, one must be ranked higher than the other; no ties are possible. This characteristic of the method can be problematic because we tend to assume that the distance between ranked individuals is equal. In fact, this assumption may be very far from the truth. The employee ranked second may perform just slightly less well than the one ranked first and considerably better than the employee ranked third, but their ranks will not tell us this.

Paired Comparisons

The rank order comparison can require some difficult cognitive processing on the part of the evaluator. A **paired comparison** makes the process simpler. With this procedure, the evaluator compares each employee with every other employee, usually in terms of overall performance. Although the number of comparisons can be large, the processing and decision making required for each is reasonably easy. The evaluator simply decides which of the two being compared is the better and records this decision before comparing the next pair. An employee's score is equal to the number of times he or she was selected as the better performer. The paired comparison method produces a ranking from low scorers to high and has the added advantage of showing the distance between ranks.

The major difficulty with paired comparisons is that they can become tedious. The number of comparisons that will be needed to evaluate all subordinates is computed from the formula: $n (n - 1) / 2$. For a supervisor with eight subordinates, the number of comparisons is not overly burdensome: $8 \times 7 / 2 = 28$. If only an overall evaluation is desired, these 28 comparisons take little time. If several traits are being evaluated by repeating the comparison process, or if the group of subordinates is large, evaluation does become burdensome. There are some computer programs that can make the burden a little lighter. However, if there are many to be evaluated, the task is best divided and given to those who work more closely with particular employees. As mentioned previously, the more accurate evaluations tend to come from evaluators who have close day-to-day contact with employees.

Forced Distribution

When your professor evaluates students on the basis of a curve, the **forced distribution** is being used. The same procedure can be used in employee performance evaluation. With this method, the evaluator sorts the employees into a certain number of categories according to his or her judgment of their work. The form of the distribution can vary, although the normal bell-shaped curve is often used. For example, the evaluator may be asked to evaluate employees according to the following categories: the best 10 percent of the group, the next best 20 percent, the middle 40 percent or average performers, the next lower 20 percent, and the lowest 10 percent or least proficient. The interesting question about the forced distribution as a method of evaluating work performance is, what do the lower categories mean? If the organization has been effective in hiring and retaining few unacceptable employees, we might expect that those judged as falling into the lower levels of the distribution will include some acceptable employees. How many, will depend on the shape of the distribution. Before using the forced distribution, an organization should consider the best curve to use with a select group and the extent to which those categorized at lower levels are likely to have serious performance discrepancies.

The forced distribution method is advantageous when there is a large group of individuals to be evaluated. Typically, an overall evaluation of performance is obtained, although it is possible to repeat the procedure for separate dimensions. Like comparison methods in general and the rank order system in particular, the forced distribution minimizes rater tendencies that result in restricted range. However, for this very reason, it may be resisted by raters who resent being compelled to fit their responses into particular categories.

The weighted checklist is easy to use. The evaluator checks the statements that describe the person's performance. Checklist items are developed from behavioral descriptions and weighted as to their value on the job. Forced-choice checklists are a variation in which an evaluator chooses statements from a set, such as most and least descriptive of the person. Statements in a set are equally desirable, but they have different weights in terms of performance value. Evaluators may react negatively to the forced-choice checklist.

Using the rank order procedure, the evaluator ranks all subordinates at once from best to worst. A ranking of overall performance is quickly done. However, the method yields little feedback, and it cannot show how much difference there is between employees. Paired comparisons are easier. The evaluator compares each employee with every other one and decides who is better. The score is the number of times a person was chosen as the better performer. This method yields a ranking and shows the distance between employees in the ranks. The process is tedious if many must be evaluated.

The forced distribution is like "grading on a curve." The evaluator sorts employees into performance levels using a distribution, such as the normal curve. As it is meant to, the method minimizes rater tendencies that result in a restricted range of scores.

PERSONAL AND DYADIC INFLUENCES

We have already seen that some inaccuracy in evaluation is due to extraneous factors, such as rater tendencies and characteristics of the rating scale. We can expect also that there are other systematic influences due to personal characteristics of raters and ratees, as well as to the nature of their relationship.

Gender and Race Effects

Rater and Ratee Gender

Does the sex of the rater make any difference? Some researchers say it has little effect (Pulakos & Wexley, 1983; Peters et al., 1984; Pulakos et al., 1989). Other researchers, however, have found that male and female raters behave differently and that females are more lenient (London & Poplawski, 1976; Benedict & Levine, 1988). Some have found that female raters give more extreme ratings in that they evaluate good performers more positively and poor performers more negatively (Nevill, Stephenson, & Philbrick, 1983). Others, however, say females are more lenient with poor performers than with good performers (Benedict & Levine, 1988). It might be that the gender of the ratee makes a difference. Maybe raters give better evaluations to ratees of the same sex. There is not much evidence of this, however. In studies in which there was an effect in this direction, it was not a strong one (Pulakos & Wexley, 1983; Pulakos et al., 1989).

Perhaps the ratee's gender is more relevant than the rater's. Some have found that a ratee gender effect can appear in evaluations in certain jobs. For example, in traditionally masculine jobs, males receive higher evaluations, and in traditionally feminine jobs, females receive higher evaluations (e.g., Schein, 1978). Also, researchers have noted that even if the sex of the ratee has no effect on the rating, the person's apparent masculinity or femininity may have an effect, depending on the rater's attitude about women doing the job (Maurer & Taylor, 1994). Ratee gender differences are sometimes shown in the attributions or reasons given for a person's performance. For example, in a sample of highly successful managers, the success of females was attributed less to ability than was the success of males (Greenhaus & Parasuraman, 1993). Other researchers report that a gender effect is shown in the use of the evaluation, such that male ratees receive better ratings than females when the rating is used for making personnel decisions, such as promotions (Dobbins, Cardy, & Truxillo, 1986).

Rater and Ratee Race

If gender makes a difference in performance rating, do you suppose that race of the rater or ratee does, too? A number of studies have been done to address this question. Landy and Farr (1980) reviewed these and found quite mixed results, some indicating racial effects and some not. An interaction of rater and ratee race appeared to be the most consistent finding in the research. That is, raters give better ratings to subordinates of the same race. Later reviewers, in a meta-analysis of studies in which data on the ratings of African American and white raters were available, drew the same conclusion (Kraiger & Ford, 1985). Similarly, subordinates' ratings of their supervisors more closely agreed with the supervisors' self-appraisals if the two were of the same race (Wohlers, Hall, & London, 1993).

The effect of race on the evaluation of a person's performance appears to be indirect and a product of the rater's cognitive processing. For example, in Greenhaus and Parasuraman's (1993) sample of managers, the success of African American managers was attributed by raters as being less due to the manager's ability and more due to help from others, than was the success of white managers. Kraiger and Ford (1985) similarly interpreted the evidence that more positive evaluations are given by same-race raters as being an indication of cognitive processing. They noted that when the proportions of African American and white employees in the sample are about equal, the effect disappears. That is, ratees of the same race as the rater are less likely to receive elevated ratings. They interpreted this in terms of the saliency of race for information processing. They suggested that as the number of individuals possessing a characteristic declines (away from equity), the characteristic becomes more helpful in recalling and processing information about the individuals.

Rater Cognition and Affect

Researchers currently are giving more attention to the rater's cognitive processes in evaluation. There is interest in understanding how raters mentally structure or categorize events and people (Krzystofrak, Cardy, & Newman, 1988). Earlier studies, examining the impact of a rater's level of cognitive complexity, found that cognitively complex raters produce ratings with less halo error and less range restriction (Bernardin, Cardy, & Carlyle, 1982; Schneier, 1977). *Cognitive categorization,* a process in which the behavior of a stimulus person is compared to some cognitive category or prototype, affects the accuracy of ratings. That is, ratees who behave as a rater expects, and who thus fit a cognitive category, are rated more accurately (Mount & Thompson, 1987). Possibly, the category itself also is being reflected in the ratings, rather than simply the person's performance. Results of one study indicated that the attribution of personality traits may function as a categorizing device. Raters inferred personality traits from samples of ratee behavior, and then they used these traits to evaluate the individual (Krzystofrak et al., 1988).

Do you think the rater's mood and feelings about the ratee can influence the evaluation of that person? Some researchers do. Currently, the rater's affective reaction to the ratee is being investigated. In a field experiment, Longenecker et al. (1992) examined some possible antecedents of the rater's emotional affect. They gave executives information about a subordinate's work performance and personality and found that both of these factors independently affected the executive's emotional response. Further, the performance rating produced by the executive also was influenced by the positive or negative information about the person's performance and personality. Longenecker et al. (1992) interviewed executives about what role they thought emotion played in performance evaluation. Almost all of the executives (93.3 percent) said that their personal feelings about a subordinate had the potential for influencing the rating. Other studies have examined the sources and operation of affective reactions to a ratee. For example, Robbins and DeNisi (1994) found evidence that the rater's feeling changes the rating through cognitive processes. That is, the process of gathering and interpreting information about a ratee's performance can modified by the rater's emotional state. The rater appears to pay close attention to information about the ratee that is consistent with the existing affective reaction.

Sometimes evaluations are influenced by characteristics of the rater and by personal attributes of the ratee. There are some gender and race effects in performance appraisal. Also, the rater's own cognitive and affective processes can influence the appraisal.

There is some evidence that male and female raters behave differently. Some researchers find that female raters are more lenient or that they give more variable ratings. There is more evidence that the ratee's gender has an effect. Female ratees may be evaluated less positively if they are performing jobs that are not considered women's work. Also, the reasons underlying ratings may reflect this gender difference.

The race of the rater and ratee has been studied. The most consistent finding is that raters give better evaluations to same-race ratees. However, this effect seems to depend on how salient race is in the evaluator's cognitive processing. Race effects also appear in the attributed basis of a ratee's performance.

Cognitively complex raters give ratings with less error. When ratees perform in ways that fit the rater's cognitive prototype, they are rated more accurately. The rater's affective reaction to a ratee can influence the person's evaluation, possibly through the rater's cognitive process. In observing and judging a person, the rater is more influenced by information that is consistent with the existing affective reaction.

POSTAPPRAISAL INTERVIEW

If we could select an organization at random and examine their files to see how they do performance evaluation, what would we find? Would we find carefully recorded ratings, indicating the evaluation of differences among employees? Would we find evidence that evaluators gave employees feedback about their performance in a considerate manner? Unfortunately, there is a good chance that we would not. We are as likely to find one of two other situations. Both the evaluation and the interview may have been conducted in a ritualized, noninformative fashion, or performance evaluations may have been done but never mentioned to the employees. Although most modern organizations conduct formal evaluations on their employees, some simply file the rating and omit the feedback interview.

Performance Feedback

Throughout this chapter, I have referred to evaluation information being used for feedback to employees. The **postappraisal interview** is the formal occasion in which this feedback is given. Typically, the interview is a private meeting between the supervisor and the subordinate in which the performance evaluation is reviewed.

As people personally experience it, the word *evaluation* often means criticism. We have a definite personal response to criticism: We become defensive. Research indicates that defensiveness increases as the number of criticisms increase

(Kay, Meyer, & French, 1965). Defensiveness affects our behavior. For example, we may find fault with the supervisor. We may reject the feedback rather than incorporate and use it. Of course, supervisors do not remain untouched. Most dislike being in the position of having to give negative information, and they find the appraisal process generally aversive (Longenecker et al., 1992; Napier & Latham, 1986).

Why not omit the feedback? If it is such a painful task for everyone involved, is the postappraisal interview really all that necessary? Maybe the administrative need for performance evaluation could be satisfied if we simply did an evaluation and skipped the feedback interview. Supervisors might be more willing and capable of providing accurate evaluations if they could avoid confronting subordinates with the information. However, even if this is true, *should* we omit feedback? I think not. The purpose of feedback is to inform employees and help them improve. At the very least, they need to know where they stand and that their performance matters to the organization.

The most obvious value of evaluation feedback is its potential as a corrective mechanism. Feedback is necessary for learning a new behavior. It is useful also for keeping learned behavior on track. When our errors are pointed out and we receive suggestions for correcting them, our work performance can be improved. Even interpersonal behavior, such as interaction with customers, can be made more effective by the self-understanding that results from feedback. In a recent study involving bank tellers, subjects increased both their verbal and nonverbal courtesy behavior, such as greeting and smiling, when they were told how they were doing on the job (Elizur, 1987).

Evaluation feedback can be motivational. If the appraisal is done by a capable supervisor whom the subordinate likes, the feedback is more satisfying (Russell & Goode, 1988). If feedback is couched in terms of improvement and goal setting, rather than in terms of criticism, it can provide the impetus for change (Pavett, 1983). Research indicates that subordinates who are more involved in the evaluation process derive more from it. They are more satisfied with the interview and more likely to improve (Burke, Weitzel, & Weir, 1978). Subordinate involvement can be encouraged by having the individual do a self-evaluation and identify goals for the future. Those who participate in setting goals generally have more favorable reactions to an evaluation interview (Meyer, Kay, & French, 1965).

Conducting the Interview

In most organizations, an evaluation and feedback interview are done every six months to a year. Typically, the supervisor begins by citing the subordinate's strengths, then points out weaknesses or needs for improvement, and ends by citing other positive points. When the interview is finished, both the supervisor and the subordinate go away feeling relieved that this unpleasant business is over and done with for another year.

Is this how performance evaluation should be conducted? Actually, it is not the best way. For feedback to be helpful, it should be given more frequently than this (Herold, Linden, & Leatherwood, 1987). The best time to receive feedback on a work behavior is immediately after an action is taken. Coaching an employee on a new task is a day-to-day activity. Although such close monitoring is not required in the case of seasoned employees, they should receive feedback about their work performance more often than every 12 months. Clearly, feedback should be given in a sensitive and considerate manner. Assessment of a person's work has important effects on his or her self-image. Feedback should be specific, detailed, and pertinent to on-the-job actions. That is, feedback should refer to work behavior rather than to personal traits. Further, according to reviews of research, a good performance evaluation interview requires subordinate participation (Ivancevich, 1982; Zedeck & Cascio, 1984). Feedback is more likely to improve performance if goal setting and rewards are part of the feedback process (Balcazar, Hopkins, & Suarez, 1985–1986). The supervisor needs to initiate goal setting, but goals must be acceptable to both parties and relate to actual behavioral accomplishments. In addition, realistic goals that can be attained should be set, although they should be difficult enough to require employee effort. Emphasis on goals changes the performance evaluation from a past orientation to a future orientation and involves the individual in planning for change. Later evaluations should consider what progress has been made toward attaining goals set previously.

Main Points

The postappraisal interview is a private meeting in which feedback from the performance appraisal is given to the employee. This interview is sometimes minimized in actual practice because giving and receiving negative feedback is unpleasant.

Performance evaluation should be done more often than the typical once-a-year practice, and the postappraisal interview should be conducted each time. The interview may be the only means of providing feedback to employees. Therefore, it needs to be done frequently.

Feedback is necessary in learning new behavior. Feedback also can be motivating, especially if it is coupled with setting goals for improvement. The employee should be involved in setting the goals, and later evaluations should consider goal progress.

CHAPTER SUMMARY

The purpose of performance evaluation is threefold. One, it is used for helping employees improve. The postappraisal interview should include feedback for this purpose. Two, it is used for making personnel decisions, such as promotions and terminations. Three, it is used in organizational research, such as selection test validation. When evaluations are used for research, there should be some evidence that they themselves are valid. Content validation may provide this evidence, or true scores may allow empirical validation. How performance evaluation is used has legal constraints. Employment law provides that when performance evaluation is used to make personnel decisions, there must be evidence that this use is fair and valid.

A variety of people, techniques, and instruments are used to conduct performance evaluations. The usual evaluator is an employee's supervisor. Peers, subordinates, and self-evaluations can be used as well. Techniques for conducting evaluations include production measures, records of personnel data, rating scales, and nonrating judgment measures. Production measures base the evaluation on the employee's level of productivity. Personnel data are used as indirect evidence of performance.

Often, what is needed is a judgment of the individual's performance. Judgments are obtained with both rating and nonrating measures. The graphic rating scale is a commonly used instrument, although the frequency and severity of errors that occur with its use make it less than ideal. Some errors appear to occur because of the rater-ratee relationship. Others, such as halo error, are due to the rater's use of the scale. Rater error training, in which raters are taught how to avoid halo and other rating errors, has been suggested as a solution. However, research on error training indicates that it is not always effective in improving the overall accuracy of the evaluation. Accuracy training is now being considered. Some specialized rating scales also have been devised in an effort to reduce rating errors and to improve rating validity. These include the BARS, BOS, and MSRS, all of which are developed from a critical incidents study of the job.

Nonrating methods include checklists and comparisons. Both weighted and forced-choice checklists contain behavioral statements that have different values in the evaluation. Comparison procedures—rank order, paired comparisons, and forced distribution—are based on the idea that a group of employees will differ in their performance levels. Although we can avoid some rater errors with these methods, they have other problems. For example, there may be little information for employee feedback.

Some inaccuracy in performance evaluation is due to personal and interpersonal factors. Research has shown that ratings can be influenced by the gender and race of the rater and ratee. The rater's cognitive process and affective reactions are being studied to discover more about the evaluation process. The rater's affect can influence both the rating and the postappraisal interview.

STUDY QUESTIONS

1) What are the three major uses of information obtained from performance appraisals?

2) In what three ways is performance appraisal subject to the provisions of employment law? What are employment-at-will rights?

3) Who is the most usual evaluator? How good are self-appraisals in comparison with other appraisals?

4) What are the advantages of production measures?

5) What is the value of rating scale anchors?

6) How do you validate a rating scale?

7) What is halo error, and what can be done to prevent it? How is halo error related to "true halo?"

8) What do raters who show leniency, severity, and central tendency have in common?

9) What is the difference between rater error training and accuracy training?

10) Outline the procedures used in developing the BARS, BOS, and MSRS. Compare these scales in terms of their advantages and disadvantages.

11) Some evaluation methods do not use ratings. Identify these methods. What are their limitations?

12) Does the gender and race of a ratee affect his or her performance evaluation?

13) How might the rater's cognitive processes influence a rating?

14) What is the best way to conduct a postappraisal interview?

CONSIDER THIS

CASE STUDY

There are three groups of employees at Vocational Rehabilitation Services: (1) an administrative group, that also includes some accounting and clerical employees; (2) a group of rehabilitation counselors; and (3) a workshop group, including shop supervisors, instructors, and a driver.

The performance evaluation procedure used at VRS is primarily for employee improvement. It is conducted as follows: Each employee is evaluated every six months by his or her supervisor. Supervisors are evaluated by the Executive Director of the agency. The same rating scale is used for all evaluations. (The scale is shown in table 7.9.) To complete the rating, the evaluator is instructed to rate

Table 7.9   VRS Performance Rating Scale

	Inadequate	Adequate	More Than Adequate	Outstanding
Productivity	_____	_____	_____	_____
Quality of Work	_____	_____	_____	_____
Interpersonal Skill	_____	_____	_____	_____
Leadership Ability	_____	_____	_____	_____
Initiative	_____	_____	_____	_____

Explain any "inadequate" or "outstanding" ratings in the space below.

_____

_____

_____

_____

the employee on each performance dimension and to explain any extreme rating (either inadequate or outstanding) with examples of behavior to show that the rating is warranted. Supervisors initiate their subordinates' evaluations by completing the rating and arranging a meeting to discuss it with the subordinate. The discussion is supposed to conclude with the subordinate making a commitment for improvement. These commitments are then reviewed at the next evaluation.

Problem

VRS is planning to review its performance appraisal process. A committee has been established to study the present procedure, rating scale, and postappraisal interview. The committee is interested in discovering better ways to conduct performance evaluation.

How would you advise the committee? Can you think of ways that the process or rating scale could be improved?

$\mathcal{S}$ ection III

In this section, I discuss the emphases of organizational psychology. Here the I/O psychologist studies various aspects of social behavior and contributes to the design and management of effective groups and organizations.

The I/O psychologist's work is done in several ways. First, as I describe in chapters 8 and 9, the emphasis is on the individual employee's work experience. The psychologist studies and describes what motivates people to do good work and how an organization can provide greater opportunities for job satisfaction. The motivation and satisfaction of employees is an important issue not only for establishing a strong work force but also for improving leadership and supervision. Chapter 8 covers theory and research on motivation, and chapter 9 considers the employee's satisfaction in doing the job he or she is hired to do. Leadership, discussed in chapter 10, is critical in preventing and solving problems of human interaction. Leadership is a rich area of study, having captured the interest of scientists from many disciplines over a long period of time. A large body of literature has grown that describes the behavior of a leader at work. Next, in chapter 11, I discuss the social organization of work. The structure of the organization itself affects employees, and what is the best organizational design is a question that has long intrigued social scientists. This, like other areas discussed, is a theory-rich subject. In chapter 12, I continue the discussion of the social aspects of the organization. Communication, group interaction, and conflict are important social dynamics. They are influenced by the structure of the organization. An effective organizational design can go a long way toward managing social interaction.

what's in this chapter?

Most of what we know about work motivation has come from using and researching several different theories of motivation. This chapter is about the theories that are currently under study in the research laboratory and in the workplace.

You will learn all about theories: What a theory is, how it can be useful, why researchers are so interested, and whether there is any reason why managers should be interested.

To start, the historically important theories are reviewed, such as Maslow's need hierarchy. Most of the early theorists thought motivation was all about needs. Later theorists say motivation has more to do with what we think and want, rather than what we need.

In addition to hearing what the theorists have to say, you will also hear what the researchers have to say about the theories. Is it true that people are motivated to self-actualize? Is there any reason to believe that setting a difficult goal will make us work harder? Does money really make the world go 'round?

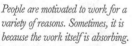

People are motivated to work for a variety of reasons. Sometimes, it is because the work itself is absorbing.

Chapter 8

The Motivation to Work

Contents

The story is about an old man and some young children who played football in front of the old man's house every afternoon after school. The old man didn't like the joyful noises made by the young children as they played football each day. Since he was quite a sage, he thought of a way to reduce their motivation to play in front of his house. One Monday he called the children over to the gate and asked them if they would like to earn a certain sum of money for each game they played. Naturally, the children thought that was a great idea. Then for several weeks the old man paid the children for playing. The next Monday, following their usual excitement, fun, and joy of playing football, the children noticed that the old man was not at the gate with the, now usual and expected, "loot." So they entered the gate and knocked on the old man's door. When he answered the door they inquired why he had not been at the gate to give them their money. His response surprised them. He said that he no longer intended to pay them for playing in front of his house. They responded that if he would not pay, they would not play.

T. C. Mawhinney

At work, as in many realms of everyday life, we are interested in motivation. Often, we are interested in people's motives because, like the old man with the children, we want to change their behavior. Someone does not do what we want, or they do something that we do not want. How do we get them to change? How do we get them to do something else? We try to *motivate* them. We attempt to change the behavior's underlying motive.

What Is Work Motivation?

Motivation refers to the arousal, direction, and persistence of behavior. Specific questions can be framed to focus on each of these three aspects of motivation. We ask about the arousal of behavior when we ask why people do anything at all. We ask about direction when we ask why they do the particular things they do. We ask about persistence when we wonder why they keep on doing those things. In addition to these general questions, which can be asked of any behavior, we can frame questions about work motivation. What about the arousal, direction, and persistence of work behavior? That is, why do people work? Why do they do a particular kind of work? Why do they continue working at the same job year after year, or why do they quit?

Interest in human motivation can be traced as far back as historical records go, and what motivates humans continues to intrigue us. Greek philosophers; medieval writers, such as Saint Augustine; nineteenth-century European philosophers; and Eastern thinkers of many centuries as well as today's psychologists all have proposed more or less complete theories about motivation. Motivation is an issue that regularly captures the attention of college students also. We all ask, "What makes me tick?"

Non Sequitur By Wiley Miller

Philosophers and theologians promoted the earliest position on motivation, that of dualism, which dominated thinking until the present century. In motivational dualism, animal behavior was considered physically motivated primarily through biological drives. Human behavior was thought to have both physical and spiritual determinants, however. Spiritual determinants were the soul, the mind, and the will.

At the end of the nineteenth century, an intellectual revolution deflected motivational theory onto a new track. Two developments were of particular importance: (1) the work of Darwin on evolution and (2) the scientific study of physiology. Darwin's ideas on evolution blurred the previous distinction between animals and humans. He proposed that all animal forms, including the human, evolved from a common ancestor and apparent differences between species occurred through evolutionary change mechanisms. Physiologists of the nineteenth century discovered that they could use the same experimental procedures used by other scientists. In their experiments, behavior appeared to be a consistent, lawful process. Darwin's proposal, that animals and humans have a common background and so they are not so very different, provided physiologists with a rationale. It gave them a basis for doing animal behavior studies and generalizing their findings to human behavior. Animal experimentation revolutionized psychology because it meant that scientific work did not depend entirely on the use of human subjects.

This work came at an opportune time as thinking on the nature of the mind had evolved as well. Some philosophers no longer considered the mind as a spiritual endowment, but rather as something that developed from the lessons of experience. They considered the will to be a part of the mind and to operate as the primary motivator. They believed also that the will was determined through experience. During this time, Descartes attempted to tie the will to physical processes in order to open it up to scientific study. He reasoned in the following way: First, assume that an animal's behavior is motivated by its internal and external environment. Second, assume that we can study animal motivation by manipulating these environmental conditions. Third, assume that animals and

Figure 8.1. *The components of performance according to Heider's analysis of action. "I can" coupled with "I will try" is proposed to induce performance.*

From F. Heider, The Psychology of Interpersonal Relations. *Copyright © 1958 John Wiley & Sons. Inc., New York.*

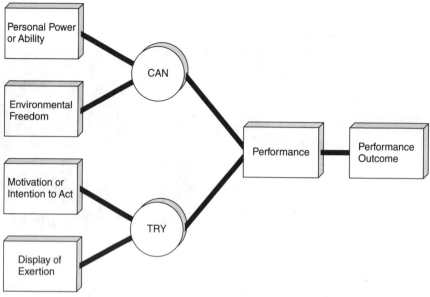

humans are somewhat similar. Then, it stands to reason that we can study human motivation in much the same way as we study animal motivation (Hall & Lindzey, 1957).

Motivation Related to Performance

Although related, being motivated to perform is distinct from learning how to perform. In Heider's (1958) discussion of performance, we can see how the two are connected: Performance is understood as being a case of combining "I can" with "I will try" to produce performance as shown in figure 8.1. Heider's analysis indicates that for any action to be taken, environmental obstacles must not be too great, and the person must have the necessary ability. The psychology of learning enters the picture when we ask how this ability develops. In order to act, the person also must have the "will" to perform and make the necessary effort. Will and effort imply motivation; therefore, the psychology of motivation enters into the analysis of action. We can take another step beyond Heider's analysis and propose that what happens as a result of performance has the potential for modifying both ability and motivation in future performances. This idea is demonstrated in figure 8.2. Many motivation theories include such propositions as these.

Work Motivation Theory

Everybody knows what a theory is: It is speculation that has yet to be proved. It is a nonfact until it is proved. Then it becomes fact. Right? Wrong. It is true that a theory is speculation about aspects of reality, but it is never proved and never becomes fact. We may gain evidence for it, but it is always a theory.

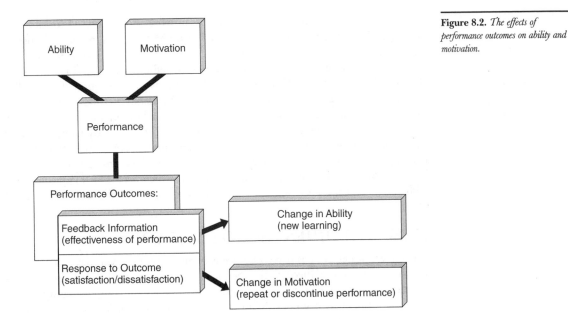

What is a theory, and why would we want one? A **theory** is a creatively constructed set of propositions about some aspect of reality, such as work behavior. A theory has two components: (1) a set of basic assumptions and (2) a set of definitions used to translate these assumptions into elements of real behavior. These are operational definitions. That is, they provide the means for measuring the behavior (Hall & Lindzey, 1957).

What does a theory do for us? First, it can guide research. It can help us make observations that have not been made previously. Its basic assumptions and definitions are used to make predictions that can be tested in studies. In a related fashion, theories are helpful in solving day-to-day work problems. They help us decide what to do, and in this sense, they are very practical. In addition to these important uses, theories also give us a framework within which to incorporate what we already know about behavior, and they tell us what is relevant to study in order to learn more. Altogether, a theory is a guide. Its most important function is to generate new insights. A theory is evaluated more stringently by its ability to predict the future than by its ability to explain what has already happened.

Psychological theories appear in two forms: There are broad and general theories, and there are specific theories with a limited scope. General theories attempt to address any kind of behavioral event. Some theories of motivation are general, in that they cover a full range of motivational issues. Specific theories limit themselves to particular aspects of behavior. Many work motivation theories are specific because they address the motivation to work, and do not claim to say anything about motivation in other realms. We are free, of course, to use either type of theory in our study of work motivation. There are advantages and disadvantages to each. General theories must be interpreted to fit work motivation. Theories developed specifically for the work setting focus directly on this point, but they do not always address all aspects of work motivation.

Motivation theories vary according to whether their central feature is the content of the motivational structure or the process of motivation (Campbell & Pritchard, 1976). Theories that are concerned with identifying the contents of the motivational structure emphasize the needs, drives, or incentives underlying motivated behavior. Process theories are more concerned with the dynamics involved in bringing a person to make an effort or to persist toward some goal. Both of these emphases are desirable in a theory, although equal emphasis may not be necessary. In the following discussion, you will see that some theories are strongly concerned with needs and motives, some are strongly process oriented, and others try to cover both.

NEED THEORIES OF MOTIVATION

The view that behavior is driven by needs is such a part of everyday thinking that we hardly realize it is theoretical. The idea of human needs is rooted in the now-defunct theory of human instincts, which viewed behavior as motivated by inborn impulses. Instinct theory began reasonably. At first, a certain few specific instincts were postulated as providing the motivation for behavior. For example, women were proposed to have a maternal instinct. As the study of behavior advanced, however, it became apparent that these few instincts were inadequate to explain all the behavior that people exhibited. Instead of abandoning instinct theory and taking another approach, however, we simply added more instincts to the list. Each time an observed behavior could not be explained by an existing instinct, a new one was created. Soon, this approach was entirely out of hand. Pages and pages of instincts had been drawn up. The theory was no longer useful to those who wanted to understand and predict behavior (Campbell & Pritchard, 1976).

Not long after the hunt for instincts ended, Henry Murray (1938) took some of the more reputable ones, described them as being learned instead of inherited, and gave them a new name—needs. Thus, the **need theory** of motivation was born. The 20 needs that he proposed still affect our thinking. In fact, some are widely accepted as motivators. For instance, among the 20 are needs for achievement, affiliation, aggression, and nurturance. In spite of its being accepted by many, need theory is subject to the same outgrowth to which instinct theory succumbed. As I discuss in this chapter, research has shown that needs are not always adequate descriptors. We must be careful not to construct new needs to fit each new observation.

Maslow's Need-Hierarchy Theory

Abraham Maslow's (1943, 1970) **need-hierarchy theory** is historically important and has been used by managers and other practitioners to explain behavior. Although attention is given to the process of motivation, this theory focuses primarily on the contents of motivational structure. Maslow proposed that we all have a certain set of needs: (1) *physiological needs,* including those typically considered basic biological drives; (2) *safety needs,* including needs for security and environmental

Section III: Creating an Effective Social Organization

safety; (3) *love needs,* including desires for having friends and for being appreciated; (4) *esteem needs,* including needs for self-confidence and respect from others; and (5) *self-actualization needs,* including needs for self-fulfillment and personal growth.

A **tension-reduction hypothesis** is used to explain the process of motivation. In this, an unsatisfied need creates an uncomfortable state of tension in the person. Tension spurs the individual into action in an effort to reduce the uncomfortable state. Action is maintained until the need is satisfied and the tension is reduced.

Maslow proposed that the individual's need structure is organized so that needs are activated according to a hierarchy, which he described as a pyramid. Physiological needs, being the most essential, form the base of the pyramid. Safety needs form the next level, and so on up the hierarchy with self-actualization at the top. Maslow proposed that the more basic, lower level needs must be satisfied first before any other needs come into play. After these needs are met, the middle level needs begin to motivate behavior. Finally, after all others are satisfied, the need for self-actualization is activated. The systematic progression from basic lower need satisfaction up the hierarchy to self-actualization is the theory's major process element.

In Maslow's view, because the individual is constantly in a state of motivation, an important question concerns what need is being satisfied. He includes a proposition concerning need deprivation to address this question. According to the deprivation-domination proposition, an individual's behavior is dominated by one particular deprived need, and the goal is to satisfy the deprived need. During the time behavior is dominated by the deprived need, all higher needs are deactivated. While higher needs may themselves be deprived, they become inactive and irrelevant when behavior is focused on a lower level need.

Another proposition explains how needs are activated. First, deprivation itself activates the lowest level need. Then, when this need is gratified, the gratification acts as a trigger to activate the next higher deprived need. Thus, satisfaction of a physiological need activates safety needs if they are deprived. Satisfaction of these needs, in turn, triggers love needs and so on until an individual reaches the self-actualization need. If on the way up the hierarchy a lower need becomes deprived, it immediately is reactivated, and the individual moves back down the hierarchy until it is satisfied. Maslow saw **self-actualization** as operating somewhat differently. Unlike lower need satisfaction, efforts to self-actualize motivates more of the same. Only lower need deprivation deactivates it. (See figure 8.3.)

Research and Application

In 1973, Wahba and Bridwell reviewed the research done to test Maslow's theory. They found relatively few studies because the theory is difficult to test. The basic concepts of how needs are activated and gratified cannot be interpreted easily, and measures are hard to devise. For example, how do we operationalize and measure need gratification?

The 30 studies that Wahba and Bridwell found gave only limited support for the theory. Although some studies were poorly designed, even those that were methodologically sound were unable to support the theory. For example, Lawler and Suttle (1972) used a longitudinal design to evaluate the gratification-activation

Figure 8.3. *The relationships among Maslow's concepts of need deprivation, domination, satisfaction or gratification, and activation.*

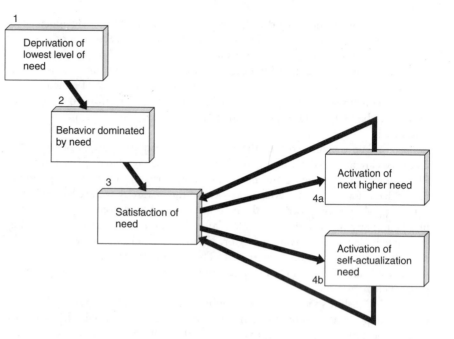

hypothesis, which is a good way to test for the type of behavioral change over time that Maslow predicted. However, there was no real evidence that gratification of one need activated another. Wahba and Bridwell and later reviewers (Campbell & Pritchard, 1976; Korman, 1977) agreed that the propositions of need-hierarchy theory generally are not supported. Although broad groupings of needs have been found, there is no indication that the specific list is accurate. The proposition that need deprivation dominates behavior has not been supported except for self-actualizing behavior. As for this, Wahba and Bridwell suggested that self-actualization actually may be a value about human striving rather than a need.

Given that Maslow's need-hierarchy theory has received so little support, how do we explain the interest it captured in industry? There are at least three ways to explain this. For one thing, Maslow's terms have been publicized to an extent that they are incorporated in our everyday language. Self-actualization is now a word in the dictionary. Secondly, Maslow's ideas have a humanistic appeal, and they make sense to us. The theory treats humans sympathetically and appeals to managers because it explains why some supposed work incentives may not operate as such. The theory says that employees are not simply interested in higher pay. There are other satisfactions at work, such as personal respect. Third, theories that have sweeping implications for work motivation provide a way for managers to make group interventions. Schneider (1985) observed that global perspectives have been more readily adopted by management than individual-oriented theories of motivation because of the type of changes managers are able to make. They must do things that affect large numbers of people rather than single individuals. Theories like Maslow's suggest ways in which they can.

Herzberg's Two-Factor Theory

Herzberg's **two-factor theory** is a need theory, although unlike other theories, the major emphasis is on the outcomes of motivated behavior. Needs are understood as operating to compel behavior; however, there is little concern with identifying them. More effort is made to specify what results from satisfaction of needs. Two-factor theory actually began as a study of job satisfaction. However, the implications for motivation were recognized, and in later work, Herzberg (1966) emphasized the theory's motivational elements.

Two-factor theory was developed empirically. It came mainly from an early study in which groups of engineers and accountants were asked about their jobs. In particular, the researchers wanted to know what kinds of things made them feel especially good or bad about these jobs (Herzberg, Mausner, & Snyderman, 1959). From subjects' responses, Herzberg concluded that there are two kinds of outcomes or factors relating to satisfaction. To explain, he proposed that people have two sets of needs to satisfy, and these needs are associated with the two kinds of outcomes. One set of needs is for a healthy, safe, and secure work environment. These needs are associated with an outcome factor he called the hygiene factor. The hygiene factor is composed of job outcomes that are extrinsic to the actual work a person does. Extrinsic outcomes include pay, job security, relationships with superiors, and physical working conditions. The other set of needs revolve around personal growth and development, and these are associated with the second type of outcome, known as the motivator factor. The motivator factor refers to intrinsic work outcomes, such as achievement, recognition, and responsibility.

Herzberg proposed that the two outcome factors affect motivation in quite different ways. To explain this, he pointed out that people sometimes say they are "not dissatisfied," but they also say that they are "not satisfied." To Herzberg, this meant two processes are operating. One process results in the person being either dissatisfied or not dissatisfied. Herzberg proposed that hygiene factors are effective in dispelling job dissatisfaction; they leave the person feeling "not dissatisfied." The other process can bring satisfaction, but if it is not operating, the person feels "not satisfied." The motivator factors are proposed to result in satisfaction. Their absence leaves the person feeling unsatisfied. (See figure 8.4.) This distinction between performance outcomes is responsible for the two-factor label of this theory. The motivator factor motivates *toward* satisfaction; the hygiene factor motivates *away from* dissatisfaction.

Research and Application

Research specifically testing the two-factor theory has not found much support for it (King, 1970). However, the theory has had considerable attention in industry. The hygiene and motivator factors are used in workplace discussions to describe what people want from their jobs (Khojasteh, 1993). Also, Herzberg's theory, like Maslow's, offers people in business a way to solve performance problems. Quite simply, jobs can be redesigned to make the work more interesting and challenging and to increase responsibility and opportunities for achievement. This method of redesigning, called **job enrichment**, is especially appealing because it promises to motivate high-quality performance. There is more about job enrichment later in this chapter.

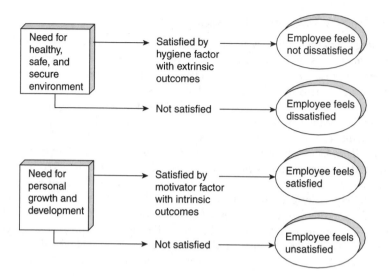

One issue that has captured the attention of researchers is that of intrinsic and extrinsic motivation. It is generally accepted that all jobs involve some combination of extrinsic and intrinsic factors and that these factors are motivating. An interesting question is, how do they combine in motivating behavior? Herzberg's theory implies that they simply add up to determine the level of performance. There is some indication, however, that the relationship may not be additive. For example, if a task is being done because the work is interesting (an intrinsic motivator), what happens if the person gets extra pay (a hygiene factor)? Does it result in still better performance? It would seem so, but Deci (1971, 1972), who posed this question, found that adding extrinsic factors can actually depress performance levels.[1] On the other hand, others point out that under certain conditions extrinsic motivators do not suppress intrinsically motivated behavior. Mawhinney (1990) said that when people are highly motivated by the intrinsic aspects of their work, adding (and subsequently withdrawing) extrinsic rewards does not result in lower performance.

Achievement Theory

In the early 1960s, a researcher was using the Thematic Apperception Test (TAT) to study subjects' responses to certain kinds of ambiguous stimuli (McClelland, 1961).[2] In the study, a theme appeared in the TAT responses that looked like a problem-solving or an achievement process. Individuals showing this pattern seemed to enjoy identifying problems, thinking of solutions, and anticipating obstacles and outcomes. The researcher's interest was piqued because he thought he might be looking at something important in the motivation of work behavior. From this and related studies, McClelland and his associates developed **achievement theory** (Atkinson, 1964; Atkinson & Feather, 1966; McClelland, 1961; McClelland, Atkinson, Clark, & Lowell, 1953). The central feature of this theory is a

---

[1]Such an effect is illustrated in this chapter's opening story about the old man and the children.

[2]Recall from chapter 5 that the TAT is a projective personality test.

Table 8.1   Achievement Theory Predictions of Individuals with a Need to Gain Success or to Avoid Failure

Objective Nature of Achievement			Personal Value of Achievement	
Difficulty of Task	Probability of Success	Value of Outcome	for Person with Need to Gain Success	for Person with Need to Avoid Failure
Difficult	Low	High	Low	High
Moderate	Moderate	Moderate	High	Low
Easy	High	Low	Low	High

need for achievement (nAch). An individual with a high need for achievement wants to have high ability for certain activities. McClelland proposed that these activities are such that (1) there is a standard of excellence, and (2) the person can succeed or fail.

Further study by McClelland's associates suggested that the achievement need is a composite of two related needs: a need to gain success and a need to avoid failure (Atkinson & Feather, 1966). Individuals are thought to have varying amounts of each need, with one being dominant. The dominant need is seen as affecting the individual's assessment of the value that would result from attempting a task. As shown in table 8.1, tasks differ *objectively* in terms of their difficulty and potential reward value. If a task is very easy, the chance of success is high; however, the reward value of doing an easy task is not great. Doing something you know you can do does not give a sense of accomplishment. On the other hand, when the task is difficult, success would be very rewarding, but you are not likely to get this satisfaction because the chance of success is low. For the person whose dominant need is for success, then, a moderately difficult task is the best way to achieve a personally high outcome value. Because the task is only moderately difficult, the probability of successfully obtaining a valuable outcome is not too low. For the person whose need is primarily to avoid failure, the personal outcome value of these task alternatives is different. The easy task is a sure thing. Objectively, success on it may not be worth much, but any avoidance of failure is a personally valuable outcome. The very difficult task is a long shot. Success would be valuable, but success is objectively unlikely. However, hardly anyone would be expected to succeed at this task. A failure would not be considered the person's fault, and *this* is a personally valuable outcome. Feelings of failure are avoided with a difficult task, not because it brings success but because no one expects a successful outcome. The task to be avoided, in this person's estimation, is the moderately difficult one. With the moderately difficult task, the objective chance of failure is low enough for others to expect success, and the personal responsibility for failure is the greatest.

McClelland proposed that high achievers have three characteristics that make them likely to be effective in managerial work. First, high achievers like situations in which they can take personal responsibility for finding solutions to problems. Second, they set moderately difficult achievement goals. Third, high achievers want early, concrete feedback on how they are doing. The business environment provides conditions suitable for high achievers. In business, problems are in abundance; typically, the manager is hired to solve them. Many of these problems are moderately difficult to solve. A manager does not have to wait long before finding out if a solution is successful; that is, feedback is quick. Such conditions are not present in all work environments, however. Consider the work of a scientist, for example. Although problems are readily available, they are difficult and not quickly solved. The scientist often works for long periods with no feedback. According to McClelland, a person with a high need for achievement would find this intolerable.

In later theory development, McClelland (1975; 1977) emphasized the motivation of managers and business entrepreneurs. He proposed that a high need for achievement coupled with a low need for power leads to the success of managers in lower organizational positions and of small business owners. However, high-level managers appear to be motivated differently. To explain, he proposed a *leadership motive pattern*. In this pattern, a person has lower achievement needs, moderate to high needs for power, low need for affiliation, and high needs for personal self-control. A high need for power means that the person is interested in influencing others; a low need for affiliation means that he or she is not worried about being disliked; and high self-control shows a concern with orderly work procedures (McClelland & Burnham, 1976). McClelland proposed that successful high-level managers in large organizations are most likely to exhibit the leadership motive pattern. This is because the work of managers at these levels is more interpersonal than that of managers at lower levels. McClelland believed that influencing the activities of others is more important in high-level jobs than personally doing the work, and a person with a high need for power is more likely to succeed in this than one with a high need for achievement.

Research Evaluation

Achievement theory has been used in several fields of study to organize and advance knowledge of motivated behavior. Eccles (1983) used the theory to study academic performance, for example, and found that the reward value of academic tasks was an important determinant of student achievement. I/O researchers have used the theory to study achievement at work, and theorists have recognized that the need for achievement is a core element of motivation (Locke, 1991). It is well accepted that achievement motivation influences behavior. For example, Steers (1975) found evidence that doing work is more satisfying for persons with a high need for achievement than for those with a low need.

Study of managerial motivation has given some support to McClelland's predictions. First, successful managers at lower organizational levels show the predicted high need for achievement (McClelland & Boyatzis, 1982). Second, there is also support for the predicted relationship between the leader motive pattern and the success of high-level managers in nontechnical positions. However, successful managers in high-level *technical* jobs do not exhibit the leader motive pattern (McClelland & Boyatzis, 1982; Winter, 1979). Cornelius and Lane (1984) studied a sample of technical managers, and they too were unable to show that the leader motive pattern predicted managerial success in technical organizations. Successful low-level managers in these organizations had high needs for affiliation, whereas successful high-level managers had high needs for achievement. Third, an Australian study of small business owners revealed three different patterns of motivation among entrepreneurs (Langan-Fox & Roth, 1995). Some of the study's participants were like the entrepreneurs McClelland described. However, others were more like high-level managers in that they expressed high power and low achievement needs.

$\mathcal{M}_{ain}$ $\mathcal{P}_{oints}$

Some theories say people are motivated because they are trying to satisfy a need.

According to Maslow, workers are motivated by any of five needs, one of which is self-actualization. The process of motivation is from the bottom of a hierarchy upward, with the lowest level need affecting behavior first. Historically, this theory is important because it gives managers ideas about how to motivate employees. However, the research has not supported it.

Herzberg said employees get two kinds of outcomes. One (called the hygiene factor) is extrinsic to the job. It prevents dissatisfaction. The other (the motivator factor) is intrinsic to the job. It brings satisfaction and high performance levels. This theory has not withstood the test of research very well, but it has been used in work settings.

In McClelland's theory, the central feature is need for achievement. The need is expressed when a person strives to solve a problem. Entrepreneurs and some managers are said to be high achievers. McClelland proposed motive patterns to describe managers that vary in the need for achievement. Achievement theory has been used widely. Research on the need for achievement has been supportive; research on the managerial motive patterns has been somewhat less so.

COGNITIVE THEORIES OF MOTIVATION

Some motivation theories give little attention to identifying and describing the operation of specific needs, although they may recognize that an underlying need is being served in behavior. Rather, they concentrate on the cognitive processes of motivation. **Cognitive theories** emphasize that people have thoughts, expectations, and feelings about the actions they take, and about the outcomes of these actions. In this section, we look at some cognitive theories of work motivation.

Expectancy Theory

Expectancy theory is a cognitive theory of work motivation. Vroom's (1964) presentation of **expectancy theory** was meant to provide a way to predict how much effort an individual would put into performing a task. He offered an equation for calculating the motivational force on the person, which could be used to predict the work effort. The equation includes three cognitive components in a multiplicative relationship: Force = Expectancy × Instrumentality × Valence.

Expectancy has two parts. It is a subjective estimate of the likelihood that a particular task can be performed successfully, and it is a subjective estimate of how much effort is required to do it. In other words, we know how likely it is that we can do something if we try, and how hard we would have to try. *Instrumentality* is an assessment of what will happen if we succeed in doing some task. In deciding to take an action, we consider whether a specific level of performance will be instrumental in obtaining an outcome. For any task, we generally can see an array of outcomes that might be obtained. The probability that each outcome actually will result will vary. For example, consider the outcomes of your performance on an exam. What is the likelihood that getting 90 percent of the answers correct will lead to an A? Although it will depend on the class, you might estimate that the chances are high. Now, how likely is that same exam score to result in your obtaining a high-paying job? Probably this outcome is not very likely. These are two instrumentality estimates. **Valence** refers to our emotional response to an anticipated outcome. Some outcomes are highly attractive, some are rather ho-hum, others are repulsive. These varied positive, neutral, and negative feelings about the outcomes of performance are what is meant by valence.

Notice that the components of the force equation have a multiplicative relationship. For motivational force to be greater than zero, all components also must have a value greater than zero. On a behavioral level, this means a person will be motivated only when he or she (1) believes that success on the task is possible (expectancy > 0), (2) perceives that successful performance is likely to lead to a particular outcome (instrumentality > 0), and (3) wants the outcome (valence > 0). Thus, expectancy theory explains why people do not try to do things they believe they cannot do, even if the outcome is very desirable. It also explains why people do not try things that appear to result in undesirable outcomes. These predictions are illustrated in figure 8.5.

Others have elaborated on this view of motivation. Porter and Lawler (1968) extended expectancy theory in three ways. First, they differentiated among the kinds of outcomes available. They noted that some outcomes are rewarding because they are themselves satisfying; thus, they are **intrinsic rewards.**[3] Examples are feelings of accomplishment and of having done something worthwhile. Intrinsic rewards are proposed to be self-administered and immediately satisfying. Other outcomes are valued because they provide the *means* for satisfaction. These are **extrinsic rewards,** and they are administered by others. Extrinsic rewards are the tangibles that employers give, such as pay raises.

Second, Porter and Lawler proposed that effort is due jointly to the subjective value of the reward offered and the expectation that performing at a certain level will result in the reward. Reward value is roughly the same as valence. Effort-reward probability combines aspects of expectancy and instrumentality. It is the extent to which performance is seen as depending on effort and the degree to which the reward is seen as contingent upon performance. Altogether, the meaning is "I can get it if I do it, and I can do it if I try."

Finally, Porter and Lawler (1968; Lawler, 1973) proposed feedback loops to describe how these aspects of motivation develop and change. Through one feedback loop, effort-reward probability is determined by past experience. For example, if you worked hard on your job and then got a pay

---

[3]Intrinsic and extrinsic motivators are concepts common to a number of theories. They are discussed also in connection with Herzberg's theory.

Section III: Creating an Effective Social Organization

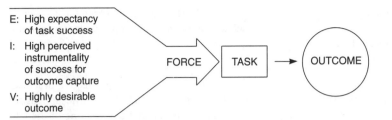

E: High expectancy
   of task success

I: High perceived
   instrumentality
   of success for
   outcome capture

V: Highly desirable
   outcome

Result: High force toward performing the task

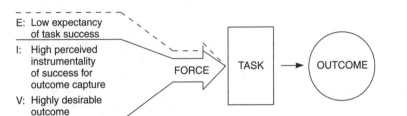

E: Low expectancy
   of task success

I: High perceived
   instrumentality
   of success for
   outcome capture

V: Highly desirable
   outcome

Result: Low force toward performing the task due to perceived task enormity or inadequate personal capacity

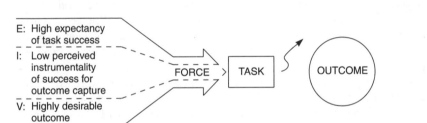

E: High expectancy
   of task success

I: Low perceived
   instrumentality
   of success for
   outcome capture

V: Highly desirable
   outcome

Result: Low force toward performing the task due to perceived low instrumentality of task success for the outcome

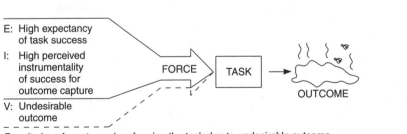

E: High expectancy
   of task success

I: High perceived
   instrumentality
   of success for
   outcome capture

V: Undesirable
   outcome

Result: Low force toward performing the task due to undesirable outcome

raise, you are likely to be more confident in the future that hard work means better pay. A second feedback loop concerns the value of rewards. Porter and Lawler said that we evaluate the rewards we get in terms of equity, comparing the reward to the amount of work done. The evaluation affects our feelings about that particular reward when it is offered again. A third feedback loop explains changes in one's expectation that effort leads to success. Task success or failure affects a person's confidence and expectations about performing similar tasks in the future.

Research Evaluation

Managers and consultants consider some motivational models as effective practical guides for improving employee motivation. Other models have little appeal to practitioners but are interesting to researchers. Expectancy theory is one of the latter. It generated a great deal of research in the early 1970s, and some of the concepts still are interesting to researchers (Schneider, 1985).

In some of the early research, the three components of motivational force were evaluated concurrently. Such studies provide a good test of the proposed multiplicative relationship between the variables. For example, Lawler and Suttle (1973) combined ratings of expectancy, instrumentality, and valence, and compared this combined measure with ratings of effort. In support of the theory, they found that the combined measure predicted effort better than the individual measures did. Dachler and Mobley (1973) also found this result in their study of factory workers.

In studies that evaluate the variables singly, the clearest support is for the predicted effect of instrumentality (Campbell & Pritchard, 1976). For example, employees who perceive high instrumentalities between performance and certain job outcomes also show high performance levels (Gavin, 1970). When experimental subjects are paid on a piece rate, in which work performance is highly instrumental for the outcome of pay, they too become highly productive (Jorgenson, Dunnette, & Pritchard, 1973).

The expectancy variable has been comparatively underresearched. What little research there is, shows mixed results. Some studies found the predicted increase in performance to result from increasing expectations for task success (Arvey, 1972). Others have found the reverse (Harrell & Stahl, 1986). One study's results suggest that the expectancy-performance relationship may actually depend on the person. Miller and Grush (1988) found that subjects who were more aware of their own personal expectations and less attuned to what is expected through social norms behaved as expectancy theory predicts.

Studies of valence have shown mixed results also. However, because of the massive amount of evidence from experimental psychology on the effects of rewards, Campbell and Pritchard (1976) have cautioned us not to be quick in concluding that valence does not affect performance. Most likely, the variable results are due to the ways the concept of valence has been operationalized. For example, some researchers have asked subjects to rate "the importance of pay" and have used this rating as the measure of the valence of work outcomes. Some using this measure have found the predicted effect—that people perform better when pay is more important (Porter & Lawler, 1968) whereas others have not (Jorgenson et al., 1973). Pecotich and Churchill (1981) said that valence is being inaccurately operationalized and that "importance of pay" does not capture its meaning.

In general, research done to test expectancy theory has provided only moderate support for its predictions. Undoubtedly, much of the failure is due to flaws in research designs. A major criticism concerns the use of a design that evaluates differences between subjects instead of a within-subjects design. Expectancy theory is an individual theory with a focus on what happens within the individual. Valence and expectancy in particular are subjectively defined, and there is little reason to suppose that levels of these concepts will be comparable across subjects. This means that research should use a design that allows comparisons between measures taken from the same individuals (Mitchell, 1974). This criticism should be taken seriously. Studies (e.g., Matsui & Ohtsuka, 1978) in which within-subjects designs have been employed show results generally supportive of expectancy theory.

Equity Theory

Adams's (1965) **equity theory** is another cognitive theory of work motivation. In this model, like in expectancy theory, people are viewed as having thoughts, feelings, and opinions that affect their work. Emphasis is on the relationship between these cognitive elements, however.

The concept of cognitive consistency forms the basis of equity theory. This concept was advanced in the late 1950s by such theorists as Festinger (1957) and Heider (1958). Festinger proposed that the relationship between thinking and acting can be either consonant or dissonant. When thoughts and actions are consonant, they are consistent or balanced and stable. When they are dissonant, they are inconsistent or unbalanced and unstable. Turning down an offer for another job is consonant with liking one's present job. However, turning down the offer is dissonant with disliking the present job. **Cognitive dissonance** is an inconsistency in the cognitive structure that produces tension, which in turn motivates action to restore consistency and reduce the tension.[4] How do cognitions become dissonant in the first place? Festinger (1954) said it is because people are continually engaging in cognitive evaluation. They sometimes use objective criteria to evaluate their thoughts and opinions, but often they use another person; hence, it is a social comparison. These comparisons give information about the appropriateness of one's thinking, and they result in feelings of consonance or dissonance.

Adams believed that people make certain kinds of social comparisons at work, and he proposed equity theory to show how social comparisons about pay levels can affect work performance. By causing changes in the consistency of a person's thoughts and feelings about pay, social comparisons can result in changes in motivation and performance.

Adams proposed that the social comparison process begins with the individual's assessment of what he or she puts into the job relative to what is received from it. That is, the person develops a cognitive ratio composed of inputs to the job and outputs from the job. Inputs are things we bring to the job, such as education, experience, and hard work. Outputs are what we derive from the job, such as money, status, and recognition. The **output/input (O/I) ratio** denotes the proportion of job inputs (I) to job outputs (O), and it expresses the extent to which the exchange is felt to be appropriate. When our output is seen as equal to our input, we feel it is a fair exchange. When outputs are greater than inputs, we know we are

[4]Cognitive dissonance incorporates the tension-reduction view of motivation, as do several motivation theories described in this chapter.

Equity Theory Predictions for Consonant and Dissonant Cognitions in Fair, Under-, and Overpayment Conditions

Self-Assessment	Assessment of Other	
	Consonant Comparison	**Dissonant Comparison**
Self fairly paid (O = I)	Other fairly paid (O = I)	Other overpaid (O > I) Other underpaid (O < I)
Self underpaid (O < I)	Other underpaid (O < I)	Other fairly paid (O = I) Other overpaid (O > I)
Self overpaid (O > I)	Other overpaid (O > I)	Other fairly paid (O = I) Other underpaid (O < I)

overpaid, and conversely, when outputs are less than inputs, we feel underpaid. In a second phase of the process, people engage in social comparison. They begin by assessing the O/I ratios of others at work. Then, the person compares his or her self-ratio with the ratios of other significant persons.

The central feature of equity theory is the social comparison. Social comparisons are proposed to affect cognitive consistency and work motivation in certain ways. If the comparison between the self-ratio and the other-ratio is consistent, then the person feels consonant and at ease. If the comparison is inconsistent, dissonance and tension result, and the person will be motivated to reduce the dissonance. Table 8.2 lists the possible social comparisons and their predicted effects on the person's cognitions. Notice that regardless of the actual amount of pay each receive, consonance is predicted whenever the other person has an identical O/I ratio. When both are paid fairly, when both are underpaid, and when both are overpaid, there is consonance and equity. Dissonance and inequity occur whenever the ratio of the other is *different*. When one is fairly paid and the other is not or when one is either overpaid or underpaid and the other is not, there is dissonance.

Adams indicated a number of ways to reduce the tension of dissonance. An individual can quit his or her job, or change the person with whom he or she is making the comparison. The individual also can change his or her own O/I ratio, either through behavioral change or cognitive change. Concerning cognitive change, suppose you feel relatively overpaid because your output is greater than your input (O > I), and your coworker's output is equal to her input (O = I). You can adjust this inequity by rethinking the situation and making a cognitive change. You can tell yourself that you have been underestimating your talents. Thus, your outcome level is deserved (i.e., O = I). You also

Table 8.3   Equity Theory Predictions for Performance Change as a Result of Dissonant Cognitions about Pay

Dissonance	Pay Basis	Quality of Work	Quantity of Work
Underpaid	Hourly	Reduce	Reduce
	Piece rate	Reduce	Maintain or increase
Overpaid	Hourly	Increase	Increase
	Piece rate	Increase	Maintain or reduce

can distort your view of the coworker's ratio; that is, you can decide that you are both actually paid fairly, but she only seems to be less well-paid than you because of some hidden flaw.

Actual behavioral change also can reduce dissonance. Changing one's inputs changes the O/I ratio, and this changes the social comparison. As table 8.3 shows, performance changes can reduce the dissonance of either underpayment or overpayment. Performance can be improved or reduced in terms of changes in its quality or quantity. If an employee has been doing high-quality work but feels that the pay is low compared to others, then reducing the quality of performance will change the ratio and reduce the underpaid dissonance. Simply doing less work will accomplish the same thing under certain conditions. Here, however, the effect depends on whether pay is based on the amount of work done, as with a piece rate or commission, or whether pay is based on time, such as a salary or hourly rate. A salaried employee who decreases the quantity of work changes the O/I ratio and reduces the underpaid dissonance. If, however, an employee is paid on a piece rate, quantity must be maintained while quality is reduced. That is, if you feel underpaid, but your pay depends on the number of widgets you make, you would maintain or increase your production while you decrease the quality of your work. This would improve your O/I ratio. (You would not reduce your quantity because that would further reduce your pay and further reduce your total O/I ratio.)

Research Evaluation

Equity theory has been used to guide the study of pay and motivation, particularly in terms of changes in the quality and quantity of performance. Reviewers of the research have reported that the predicted effects of underpayment on performance are well supported (Campbell & Pritchard, 1976; Goodman & Friedman, 1971). Decreased production among underpaid hourly subjects has been observed as predicted (e.g., Pritchard, Dunnette, & Jorgenson, 1972). Increased production coupled with decreased work quality among underpaid piece rate subjects also has been observed (e.g., Lawler & O'Gara, 1967).

Research has been less supportive of the prediction for overpayment. The design of studies attempting to test overpayment may have been part of the problem, as the operations used in research to induce overpayment dissonance sometimes are questionable. Often, experimental manipulation involves attacks on a person's job qualifications in an effort to lower the perceived inputs. As some critics (e.g., Lawler, 1968) have observed, this is also an attack on self-esteem, and the subject's behavior may actually reflect efforts to repair an injured ego. In spite of this difficulty, some studies have shown support for the overpayment prediction. Increased productivity among overpaid hourly employees has been observed (Pritchard et al., 1972). Decreased quantity plus increased quality among overpaid piece rate employees also has been reported (Goodman & Friedman, 1969). Both of these are consistent with the theory. Some research suggests why the findings on overpayment vary. For example, the sample of managers studied by Summers and DeNisi (1990) reported that they were either underpaid or fairly paid. Almost no one felt overpaid. This may mean that (1) overpayment is not a perceptual reality; (2) feelings of overpayment are continually dispelled by cognitive reevaluation or rethinking; or (3) "payment" includes things that are not being considered in the research. This latter idea is demonstrated by Greenberg (1988) in a study involving nonmonetary payments. It was hypothesized that the status of having a nice office might be counted in determining pay equity. To test this hypothesis, some employees were moved temporarily into offices that were better than their own. By equity theory reasoning, this would create a temporary overpayment condition. During the two weeks of relocation, performance of these employees changed in the direction predicted. They increased their levels of productivity.

Equity theory has some advice for industry. First, performance-pay contingencies should be made explicit, and the process of evaluating performance should be communicated clearly. Employees need to know what inputs lead to what outcomes. Increases in workload, such as those that follow organizational downsizing, should be instituted cautiously. Because they increase the person's input, they also can result in changes in productivity (Ganster & Dwyer, 1995). Second, the company should make an effort to let employees know what their coworkers actually do. People do appear to compare themselves to others, even if the "other" is a generalization of what they believe to be true of those in their own and other companies (Summers & DeNisi, 1990). If people see themselves as being underpaid, even if they actually are not, lower production can result. By communicating complete and accurate information, employers may be able to avoid these performance-pay discrepancies.

Goal-Setting Theory

Locke (1968) initiated the original work on goal-setting theory, although there are others who have contributed to the development of the theory (Locke et al., 1981; Locke & Latham, 1990). Like equity and expectancy theories, **goal-setting theory** is a cognitive theory. Motivation is presented as a cognitive process involving intentions and more or less rational choices of work activities. The theory identifies the contents of the motivational structure, but the greater emphasis is on the process of motivation.

Goals are the central feature of the motivational structure. Locke described goals in basic motivational terms, that is, as providing direction for action and energy for the persistence of behavior. A goal is not a need, although attainment of a goal is expected to fulfill underlying needs (Locke, 1991). Rather, a goal is more like a purpose or intention. Goals are described in terms of their inherent specificity, difficulty, and complexity. Specificity is a goal's clarity or the degree to which it is precisely conceptualized. Goals can be highly specific or very vague. Difficulty refers to how hard or easy it is to achieve the goal. Complexity refers to how internally complicated the goal is. Goals are described also in terms of conflict, or the extent to which work on one goal interferes with or obstructs another. Conflict between or within a person's goals can be caused by pressure exerted by another person (Locke et al., 1994). According to goal-setting theory, goals that differ along these lines have varying effects on performance.

The major proposition of the theory is that certain goal attributes are quite important in motivation. In particular, specific goals are more motivating of high performance than vague ("do your best") goals, and difficult goals are more motivating than easy goals. Goal specificity is proposed to affect the variety of activities in work performance, whereas goal difficulty directly affects the level of performance (Locke et al., 1989).

The process of motivation describes how a goal affects performance. The primary process mechanism in this theory is goal setting. Setting a goal and developing strategies to attain it are proposed to affect both the commitment to reaching the goal and the level of performance. The effect of goal setting on a person's performance is described as occurring through certain cognitive processes, such as the person's expectation that a goal probably can be attained (Locke & Latham, 1990).

The goal-setting process is thought to be influenced by certain other factors, and these factors ultimately have an impact on goal commitment and performance. Some are personal, such as the individual's basic ability to perform the goal-related work. Others are more situational. For example, the source of the goal is proposed to affect goal setting and performance (Locke & Latham, 1990). Sometimes, people set their own goals or participate in setting them. At other times, the goal is created by someone else and assigned to the person. In order to describe the effects of goal origin, Locke defined goal acceptance as the extent to which individual embraces a goal that originated from an outside source. Acceptance and commitment to a goal can occur through participation in the process of goal selection, although participation is not essential. Commitment to an assigned goal can occur because of the influence of authorities and peers, as well as monetary rewards (Locke, Latham, & Erez, 1988). A person who is offered money for performance may become more committed to a goal and more willing to work to reach it. The intensity of the commitment depends on the amount of money offered, with greater amounts producing higher goal commitment and better performance. (See figure 8.6.)

Research and Application

Goal-setting theory continues to excite researchers. Most of the research so far has tested and found support for the predictions about general versus specific goals and difficult versus easy goals. From reviews of many studies, it appears to be well established that specific, difficult goals motivate performance more than vague, easy goals (Locke & Latham, 1990; Schneider, 1985). In fact, the relationship between performance and specific, challenging goals seemed to be beyond doubt to some reviewers (Mento, Steele, & Karren, 1987).

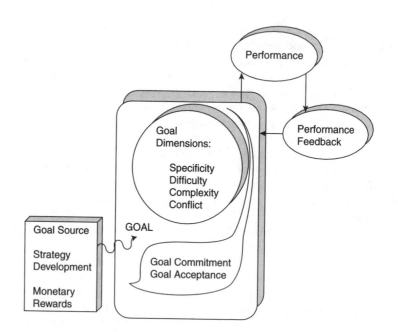

Figure 8.6. *The nature of goals and the process through which goals influence performance. Goal dimensions define the nature of a goal. Certain other factors, such as the goal's source affect aspects of the goal, such as goal commitment. In a feedback loop, goals both affect and are affected by performance.*

In another wave of research testing this theory, possible factors that affect this strong relationship are being explored. One line of study began when Wood, Mento, and Locke (1987) reported that the effects of goals depend on the complexity of the tasks used in the study. From their meta-analysis, they concluded that specific, difficult goals produce better performance on simple tasks (e.g., simple arithmetic problems) than on complex tasks (e.g., supervision). Later studies had similar results. For example, Earley, Connolly, and Ekegren (1989) discovered that assigning specific, difficult goals was surprisingly more detrimental to performance than assigning vague "do your best" goals. However, the tasks they used were complex, involving the prediction of stock prices. Similarly, in a recent field study, difficult goals were associated with poorer performance among professional employees doing complex technical work (Yearta, Maitlis, & Briner, 1995).

Several researchers have attempted to explain why task complexity might have this effect on the goal/performance relationship. One idea is that complex tasks require the development of more and better strategies, and this delays the work on a difficult goal (Chesney & Locke, 1991; Wood & Locke, 1990). Another possibility is that a complex task is a difficult task. *Task* difficulty affects goal commitment, which in turn affects goal attainment (Wofford, Goodwin, & Premack, 1992). It may be that a person has little expectation of completing a task that is complex and difficult, and of achieving the associated goal. Martin and Manning (1995) reported evidence indicating that this is correct. They studied the effects of difficult goals and difficult tasks when subjects also were given information on how well others had performed. They concluded that a person who has a difficult goal needs to have some expectation that success on the task is possible, and they need to be committed to the goal, otherwise, performance suffers.

Goal-setting theory can be applied in the work setting. In fact, goal setting is inherent in many organizations' procedures for employee performance review. Employees undergo evaluation, are given feedback, and goals for improvement are set. In spite of the common use of goal setting for such motivational purposes, there has been little study of these field applications, and most research evaluating the theory's predictions has been done in the laboratory. Yearta et al. (1995) pointed out that there are several reasons to doubt that these laboratory findings generalize directly to the workplace. One is that the workplace is a multiple-goal environment. Controlled lab studies usually investigate single goals. Also, in the real world, employees work toward their goals over an extended period of time; in the laboratory, subjects seldom spend more than an hour working toward a goal. It should be noted, too, that task complexity is relevant to the application of goal setting. The work that many employees do is complex and difficult. Appropriate goal setting for these employees needs to consider the possibility of a negative impact on performance that is due to the assignment of a difficult goal.

Reinforcement Theory

Modern **reinforcement theory** can be traced to Thorndike's (1898) discussion of animal behavior, although many others have contributed to its development (e.g., Hull, 1951; Skinner, 1938; Tolman, 1932). The major premise of the theory is that an action is strengthened or weakened by its own consequence. That is, when a satisfying outcome follows an action, that action is more likely to occur again because of the outcome. An unsatisfying outcome weakens the effect. In this way, the consequences of our actions reinforce our actions. The central motivational concept is **reinforcement,** which is a feature of action outcomes. In reinforcement theory, any action outcome can be reinforcing if the individual needs or wants it. No outcome operates universally as a reinforcer, however; there is always someone for whom it is irrelevant or undesirable. Thus, reinforcement theory is another motivation theory oriented to the individual.

Although needs and motivational driving states are implicit in this theory, there is no concern with identifying the contents of the motivational structure. These are assumed to depend on the individual. The basic idea is that behavior followed by a satisfying outcome will be shown again when similar conditions arise. These "similar conditions" include the need state, as well as the environmental cues that indicate whether satisfaction of the need is possible. Mainly, reinforcement theory is concerned with the motivational process. The theory recognizes that people form associations between their actions and the events that follow these actions, and that they use their memories of associations that occurred in the past to take action in the present situation. These memories and thought processes may but do not necessarily occur consciously. The environment is viewed as affecting behavior, but the person is considered instrumental in taking advantage of what the environment has to offer.

Reinforcement theory can be used to predict effort and choice of tasks. The predicted effects of reinforcement on task performance are summarized in figure 8.7. Three motivational processes are defined: extinction, punishment, and reinforcement. First, if a task is performed and the outcome is neutral (or if there is

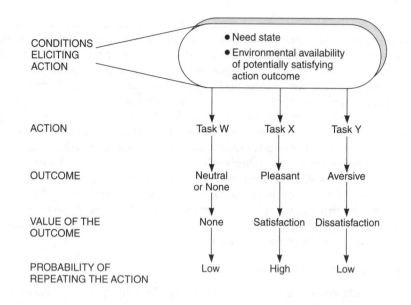

Figure 8.7. *The process by which present activities and outcomes determine the nature of future behavior according to the postulates of reinforcement theory. Behavior followed by a satisfying outcome (e.g., task X) is likely to be repeated again when a similar situation arises.*

CONDITIONS ELICITING ACTION
- Need state
- Environmental availability of potentially satisfying action outcome

ACTION	Task W	Task X	Task Y
OUTCOME	Neutral or None	Pleasant	Aversive
VALUE OF THE OUTCOME	None	Satisfaction	Dissatisfaction
PROBABILITY OF REPEATING THE ACTION	Low	High	Low

no effect), then the outcome has little satisfying value, and the task is not likely to be repeated. This is the process of **extinction** through lack of reinforcement. For example, an employee comes to work early every day, but no one notices. She then begins waiting in the parking lot until time for work. Her behavior was extinguished. Second, if a task is done and the outcome is aversive, a person is not likely to continue this activity either, but for a different reason. The suppressive effect is one of **punishment.** An example is provided by an employee who volunteers to work on the supervisor's special project. The employee is criticized for this by a coworker; therefore, he withdraws from the project. Third, if a person performs a task from which he or she derives a pleasant outcome and high satisfaction, this task is likely to be repeated when the need and conditions arise. This shows the strengthening effect of reinforcement on behavior.

Reinforcement theory also predicts how hard someone will work. An action must have at least an occasional payoff for a person to exert effort, otherwise the behavior is extinguished. Continued effort on a task does not require very frequent reinforcement, however. People often continue work on a task although their behavior is only rarely reinforced. Two processes are proposed concerning the frequency of reinforcement. First, continuous reinforcement is more effective during the initiation of a performance, during which the association between action and outcome is being established. *Continuous reinforcement* is a reinforcement for each correct response. The other process proposed occurs after the behavior has been learned. At this stage, effort can be maintained and even increased by occasional or *partial reinforcement.* In fact, people have been found to work harder when the payoff is risky than when it is secure (Yukl, Wexley, & Seymore, 1972).

Reinforcement schedules are based either on a time interval or on the number of responses. The quantity of time or number of responses required for reinforcement can be fixed or varied. A schedule based on the number of responses

*T*able 8.4	**Schedules of Reinforcement**
Schedule	**Reinforcement Basis**
Continuous	Reinforce every correct response
Partial	Reinforce some but not all correct responses
Fixed interval	Reinforce next correct response after a fixed amount of time has elapsed
Variable interval	Reinforce next correct response after an interval of time that varies in length
Fixed ratio	Reinforce after a fixed number of responses
Variable ratio	Reinforce after a variable number of responses

is called a ratio schedule; that is, it is the ratio of responses to reinforcements. The ratio can be 1 to 1, which constitutes continuous reinforcement. A ratio that is less than 1 to 1 is a partial reinforcement schedule. If the ratio always remains the same, it is a fixed ratio schedule. If the ratio varies, it is a variable ratio schedule. Similarly, reinforcement delivered on a time interval basis can be fixed or varied, producing fixed interval and variable interval schedules. These schedules are listed in table 8.4.

Methods of compensation provide examples of the different reinforcement schedules. A fixed ratio schedule is exemplified by a piece rate or commission pay plan. The rate of pay is fixed, and the amount of earnings depends directly on the amount of work done. For every car sold, or shirt sleeve sewn, a worker gets a fixed amount of money. A variable ratio schedule, in which there is change in the amount of work required for each unit of pay, is used for some service employees, such as waitresses, whose earnings depend largely on tips. Although a certain percentage of the bill is expected for tips, many customers are inexact, and some apply their own rates. A fixed interval schedule is indicated by the monthly or weekly salary. The basis is time, not the amount of work done. Whether we work hard or hardly at all, we get paid the same at a fixed time weekly, monthly, or the like. A variable interval schedule is what faces landowners whose renters are erratic in paying. They do not know whether they will get paid at the time they select to collect the rent, or if it will be two weeks, a month, or an infinity later.

Research and Application

Reinforcement theory has been tested in a wide range of research, and there has been considerable support for its predictions (cf. Houston, 1986). Although this is a broad theory, encompassing all kinds of behavior, it can be applied to motivational problems at work. In fact, as you may have noticed, the other motivation theories incorporate reinforcement concepts, such as rewards or satisfying outcomes. Some researchers have argued that many of the modern theories of work motivation actually can be rewritten in terms of reinforcement theory (Nord, 1969).

Like other theories, reinforcement theory has a message about how to change or modify employees' behavior. **Behavior modification** is a technique, based on reinforcement theory, that can be used to change people's actions by changing their outcomes. The technique has been used in various realms of life, including the work situation.[5] Theoretically, any of the motivational processes can be used to modify behavior. Desired work behavior can be developed by providing rewards. Unwanted work behavior can be extinguished if the existing reinforcer can be identified and removed. Because identifying existing reinforcers is typically difficult, the more usual approach to changing unwanted work behavior is suppression, in which an aversive outcome is added to whatever else is operating. The difficulty with suppression is that it requires a great deal of monitoring. To be effective, the aversive stimulus must be applied each time the unwanted behavior occurs. This makes the process unwieldy for an employer. Because of such problems, the better route to improved employee behavior is to provide rewards for behaviors that are more desirable. For example, both tangible goods and social rewards were used successfully to increase the daily production levels of textile workers (Welsh, Luthans, & Sommer, 1993).

One difficulty in using the theory to guide change programs at work is that it is strongly oriented toward the individual. Interventions must include effective reinforcers; however, reinforcers are individually defined. Also, the reward must be contingent on the behavior that is actually desired. If you want to boost high-quality production, incentives must be offered for quality, not simply for quantity (Skaggs, Dickinson, & O'Connor, 1992). Also because of the emphasis on individual performance, the theory is not easy to translate into programs useful for groups. Much of today's work, however, is done by teams of employees; thus, interventions are needed that are based on a group schedule of reinforcement in which the rewards or incentives are based on the group's productivity rather than on the individual's. The gain-sharing plan used in industry is an example of this (Latham & Huber, 1992).

---

*M*ain *P*oints

Cognitive theories say motivation is due to the expectations, thoughts, and desires that people have.

Expectancy theory uses three subjective processes to describe a person's motivation (1) the expectation of success on a task, (2) the instrumentality of task success for gaining a specific outcome, and (3) the valence of the outcome. Outcomes can yield intrinsic or extrinsic rewards. Research has been mixed, partly because studies have not appropriately tested the theory.

Adams's equity theory shows how pay can motivate. People make social comparisons with others at work, which can cause them to feel fairly or unfairly paid. Feelings of inequity result in performance changes. Research shows the predicted decrease of productivity when the person is underpaid, although it is not clear that overpayment increases productivity.

Locke's goal-setting theory predicts that the goal-setting process motivates performance. When the person is committed to goals that are specific and difficult, high performance results. The research agrees with this prediction in most cases. However, when the task is complex, a difficult goal does not have this effect.

---

[5]Some behavior modification programs are described in the next section.

Reinforcement theory says an action is motivated by its own consequences. We learn from our experiences. Reinforcers are individual; they depend on what the person wants. Desired changes in work behavior can be brought about by rewarding certain actions by means of partial reinforcement. Research support for the theory is substantial.

USING MOTIVATION THEORY AT WORK

In many ways, the theories discussed in this chapter are complimentary, and they can provide a more comprehensive view of that elephantine structure called work behavior if they are taken together. Steers and Porter (1979) made this very point and suggested some ways different theories can be teamed to explain work motivation:

> **Individuals who have particularly strong needs (e.g., *need for achievement*) may also be inclined to make *equity* comparisons with regard to how their peers are being rewarded in relation to the types and amounts of rewards that they themselves are receiving. Not only that, but they will likely be sensitive to what it is that they do that results in "good" responses (from supervisors, peers, the organization, etc.) and thus will likely form ideas (i.e., "*expectancies*") that a certain action (behavior) on their part will, or will not, result in a "good response" (i.e., *reward*) next time [italics added]. (p. 561)**

How might we put these theories to use in the workplace? In general, the theories can provide direction, but the manager must take an active and deliberate role in the program (Steers & Porter, 1979). Beyond this, there are some specific factors to consider. First, a program manager must keep in mind that there are individual differences in what employees need and want out of their work. From reinforcement theory, we know that a work outcome can strengthen a job behavior but only if it is desired by the individual. According to expectancy theory, outcomes vary in their importance to the person. Goal-setting theory says the person must be committed to the goal. Need theories tell us that people differ in the needs they are satisfying at work. Second, a direct connection between productivity and desired outcomes must be established. In both expectancy and reinforcement theories, performance must be perceived as leading to the desired outcome. Goal-setting theory tells us that feedback can provide this connection. Third, opportunities for intrinsic satisfaction should be increased. Several theories suggest that increased employee involvement in the job is needed for greater intrinsic satisfaction. This may involve job enrichment and participation in goal setting. Finally, the nature of the work environment should be considered. All motivation theories tell us to make sure the action is possible; thus, barriers to performance should be removed or minimized.

Intervention Programs

Formal programs that may be useful to managers have been based on the motivation theories. In the 1970s, there was great interest in work motivation programs. For example, Katzell, Bienstock, and Faerstein (1977) found 103 applied motivation programs reported in the professional literature between 1971 and 1975. In this last section, I describe some of these interventions.

Pay Incentive Plans

Employees can be motivated to perform in exchange for monetary rewards. Various pay-for-performance or pay incentive plans have been used. A **pay incentive plan** itemizes the incentives, which can be money, goods, services, and special privileges. The use of monetary incentives to stimulate work performance actually has a long history, although the early schemes for offering incentives were quite simple, usually amounting to no more than a piece rate (Peach & Wren, 1992). Such incentives were offered mostly to blue collar workers. In more recent years, pay incentive plans have been offered to white collar and service workers (Katzell et al., 1977). These latter programs were reported to have good effects on productivity and on absenteeism and tardiness. Pay incentive plans also are being used in the public sector with some success (Deadrick & Scott, 1987; Heneman, Greenberger, & Strasser, 1988; Schay, 1988).

In developing a new incentive plan, we must keep two things in mind. First, we need to verify that the pay items (e.g., bonuses, flexible work hours, and retirement funds) actually operate as incentives. In a discussion of programs that offered innovative work schedules, such as flexible starting and quitting times, Katzell (1980) reported that employees sometimes resisted these changes. Second, we must establish that receiving an incentive is contingent upon the performance it is supposed to motivate, and employees must perceive this contingent relationship. Some items that are commonly included in incentive plans are contingent only on the barest sort of job-related behavior. For example, health plans, vacations, and retirement benefits depend only on the employee's staying with the organization. The employee's level of performance usually has little to do with it. Sometimes, salary increases are contingent in the same sense, as when raises are given routinely after a specified length of time. This situation should be changed either to make benefits contingent on performance, or to remove some items from the incentive plan (e.g., health benefits).

Job Redesign

Pay incentive plans are meant to increase extrinsic motivation. A different approach is to restructure jobs to increase intrinsic satisfaction. **Job redesign** is a motivational change program intended to increase the inherent value of the job. Depending on which theory is used as a foundation, job redesign may aim to (1) provide opportunity to satisfy higher level needs (need-hierarchy theory), (2) increase intrinsic satisfaction with the work itself (two-factor and expectancy theories), (3) increase nonmonetary outcomes (equity theory), (4) provide opportunity for self-set goals (goal-setting theory), and (5) make intangible rewards available (reinforcement theory).

At one time, many jobs were designed so that the number of different operations or tasks was minimized. This was meant to increase productivity. The idea was that operators doing only a few things would become quick, efficient, and more productive in the long run. Later, it was realized that there was a limit to what an operator could do in such repetitive jobs. Social science researchers pointed out that it might be better to make jobs more complex, not less. Complex jobs might be more motivating. Such jobs would include varied work activities, more responsibility for the product, and participation in deciding how to do the job. That is, to improve productivity by creating more motivating jobs, the jobs would have to be more elaborate and interesting. They would have to be enriched.

Job redesign for enrichment can be done in two ways. Both can make the job more interesting and more intrinsically satisfying. A job can be enlarged horizontally. Tasks can be added to reduce repetition and increase variety. A job also can be enlarged vertically. Vertical enlargement gives the employee a chance to plan as well as to carry out the job and to participate in decisions. There is reason to believe that both horizontal and vertical redesign should be done. Lawler (1969) pointed out that horizontal enlargement alone may actually lead to dissatisfaction if employees are overburdened with extra activities that use the same few skills as the original job.

One common feature of an enriched job is increased participation in making decisions about the job. This intervention has long been thought to have good effects on work motivation, and various techniques for increasing participation, such as **quality circles,** have been devised. A considerable body of research has accumulated concerning the effects of participation. This research shows no clear pattern of motivational improvement (Locke & Schweiger, 1979). Sometimes, it leads to greater goal acceptance (Locke et al., 1988). It may depend on the extent of participation. For example, some have investigated employee ownership of the firm. Improvement in product quality and quantity has been reported in firms partly or fully owned by employees (Long, 1980). Employee participation is of interest to organizational theorists, and this issue is discussed further in chapter 11.

Behavior Modification

Programs for behavior modification at work have been developed and tried in organizational settings. For example, Gillen and Heimberg (1980) found reports of 14 behavior modification programs designed to improve the interpersonal skills of applicants in employment interviews. Katzell (1980) discovered several training programs that incorporated behavior modification to improve motivation. Many of these were put together after behavior modification had been reported to be effective in other settings. For example, behavioral techniques had been applied in education to improve pupils' social development, language acquisition, and personal control (Brigham & Catania, 1978).

Probably the best known of the early programs for modifying work performance was the one conducted at Emory Air Freight Corporation ("New Tool: Reinforcement," 1971). Existing performance-reward contingencies were changed by the new program. Specifically, social reinforcement (praise and recognition) was used to reinforce job behaviors that contributed to a new work procedure. The company reported dramatic success and saved thousands of dollars. Some other programs were designed differently, as **token economies.** In these, incidents of the desired behavior are rewarded immediately with tokens that can be exchanged later for goods and services. An old problem—how to get employees to use safety equipment—was tackled with a token economy in one study. The program was found to be effective in bringing factory workers to use ear protection (Zohar, 1980). Other programs have used lottery or gambling devices to conduct the intervention. These have been developed to make various behavior changes. For example, one program was developed to increase courteous behavior in a social service organization (Johnson & Fawcett, 1994). In another successful program aimed at controlling tardiness, playing cards were distributed to employees who came to work on time. At the end of a week, the employee with the best five-card (poker) hand won a $20 prize (Pedalino & Gamboa, 1974). Such programs apparently have been quite successful in improving motivation. Some believe they are more effective than straight pay incentive programs (Evans, Kienast, & Mitchell, 1988).

*M*ain *P*oints

Some formal programs of interventions have been devised. These are based on the motivation theories.

Pay incentive plans, which include monetary and similar incentives, are commonplace. These plans can be effective if the contingency between pay and performance is clear and enforceable. Job redesign is another intervention; it is used to increase intrinsic motivation. The job is enriched with varied and interesting activities and with opportunities to participate in decisions. A third motivational program uses behavior modification. Some of these programs have incorporated social reinforcement of desired behaviors. Others include a "token economy" or a gambling device to initiate changes in employee performance.

CHAPTER SUMMARY

I/O psychologists are interested in motivation because they want to improve work performance. A number of theories are available to help them do this.

Some theories focus on needs as the source of motivation. Need-hierarchy theory offers a list of needs proposed to operate in an orderly fashion. These include the more basic needs, as well as self-actualization. Two-factor theory implies underlying needs but emphasizes performance outcomes. Hygiene and motivator factors are outcomes proposed to affect motivation. There is a good deal of practitioner interest but little research evidence for these two theories. Achievement theory emphasizes the motivating effects of the need for achievement, particularly in managerial work. The need for achievement is supported by research.

Other theories focus on the dynamics of motivation, and all recognize the effects of cognition. According to expectancy theory, the motivational force that drives a person to perform a task is determined by cognitive elements. These include expectations about the likelihood of success, the instrumentality of success for certain outcomes, and the desirability of the outcomes. Equity theory proposes that

people compare their job inputs and outcomes to those of others at work. If the comparison produces feelings of inequity and cognitive dissonance, changes in behavior are predicted. Research shows that the effect sometimes is lowered productivity. Goal-setting theory emphasizes the effects of goals on behavior. Goals both energize and direct behavior. Research supports the proposal that specific and difficult goals are motivating, particularly if the task is not too complex. In reinforcement theory, the primary dynamic of motivation is the strengthening effect of an action's outcome. Reinforcers are satisfying outcomes that result from an action. Considerable research has produced evidence for this theory.

All these theories are used to develop interventions for improving work motivation and performance. Pay incentive plans are based on theories that emphasize the importance of money or other extrinsic rewards in motivating performance. Job redesign is based on theories that emphasize intrinsic satisfactions. Behavior modification programs are based on reinforcement theory and must provide rewarding outcomes for the desired work behavior.

STUDY QUESTIONS

1) What is the purpose of theory? What are the criteria of a useful theory?

2) In what ways do theorists distinguish between the contents of the motivational structure and its process?

3) What are the difficulties of viewing motivation as based on needs?

4) What are the major propositions of Maslow's need-hierarchy theory? Why is this theory important?

5) The tension-reduction hypothesis is used in several theories to describe the dynamics of motivation. What is this hypothesis, and how is it used in the theories described in this chapter?

6) How is two-factor theory similar to and different from other need theories? What are hygiene and motivator factors?

7) What is the nature of the need for achievement? Achievement theory predicts that good managers will show certain need combinations. What are they?

8) What is a cognitive theory of motivation?

9) What are the major propositions of expectancy theory? What are some problems in research purporting to test expectancy theory?

10) How are the concepts of cognitive consistency and dissonance used in equity theory? When are self-other O/I ratio comparisons likely to be experienced as dissonant? How well has equity theory been supported by research?

11) What is the major proposition of goal-setting theory? How does a goal motivate performance? Does it matter if goals are self-set or assigned? What factor affects the goal difficulty-performance relationship?

12) Describe the primary motivational mechanism in reinforcement theory. What is a reinforcer? In what ways can reinforcement theory be used to modify work behavior?

13) How has motivation theory been used in the workplace to devise programs for improving work performance?

CONSIDER THIS

CASE STUDY

Vocational Rehabilitation Services (VRS) is a nonprofit organization that operates a sheltered workshop for people in the community who have disabilities. In the workshop, VRS clients learn to preform light manufacturing and assembly operations. Typically, the work supervisors demonstrate the work to the clients, and then maintain close supervision of them as they work. The clients get training and work experience, and they are paid a piece rate.

The clients vary in the degree and type of disability, although most are physically disabled. A few have mental disabilities. Most are young and have had no previous work experience. All have the capacity for employment. VRS usually has about 25 clients at any one time. They vary in terms of their progress and in the length of time they remain at the workshop. Some stay only a few weeks before they are placed in a job. Others stay as long as a year. At the workshop, the clients work different schedules, depending on their abilities and progress. Some work full time. Others work a half day, either morning or afternoon.

Problem

In addition to the skills training that clients receive, they also are encouraged in other positive employee behaviors, such as punctuality, safety, and cleanliness in the work area. Recently, there has been a problem with the latter. Clients are supposed to clean up the work area at the end of their shift by picking up scraps and trash and putting away tools and unused materials. However, some have not been cleaning at all, and others have been doing a poor job.

The workshop supervisor has reported this problem to the Executive Director. They have been talking about developing motivational interventions, but they need help in devising these.

What would you advise them to do? What interventions based on one or more of the motivation theories discussed in this chapter would you recommend?

what's in this chapter?

For many students, job satisfaction is one of the most important issues. Many I/O psychologists agree. The extent to which people are happy with their jobs has been the subject of thousands of studies.

In this chapter, you will get a glimpse of the research on job satisfaction. You will discover the various aspects of work that can be satisfying or dissatisfying, such as the pay, the supervisor, and the work itself. You will learn what the theorists and researchers think about why some people who do the same jobs seem to have entirely different reactions.

Some seemingly correct assumptions about job satisfaction are being reconsidered in the modern studies. For example, are you sure that satisfied employees are more productive? Do you think a person is more likely to quit a job that is disliked? These are questions of interest to employers, as well as researchers.

What is satisfying about a job?
Sometimes, the work itself is
inherently satisfying.

$\mathcal{C}hapter$ 9

Satisfaction with Work

There are, of course, the happy few who find a savor in their daily job: the Indiana stonemason, who looks upon his work and sees that it is good; the Chicago piano tuner, who seeks and finds the sound that delights; the bookbinder, who saves a piece of history; the Brooklyn fireman, who saves a piece of life.

For the many, there is a hardly concealed discontent. The blue-collar blues is no more bitterly sung than the white-collar moan. "I'm a machine," says the spot-welder. "I'm caged," says the bank teller, and echoes the hotel clerk. "I'm a mule," says the steelworker. "A monkey can do what I do," says the receptionist. "I'm less than a farm implement," says the migrant worker. "I'm an object," says the high-fashion model. Blue collar and white call upon the identical phrase: "I'm a robot." *"There is nothing to talk about,"* the young accountant despairingly enunciates.

Studs Terkel

Are people really so dissatisfied with the work they do? Is it not possible for workers to become happy and prosperous by working hard on a good job? What do people get out of the work they do? The people whom Terkel interviewed often referred to *meaning* in their work when they liked what they did and to lack of meaning when they did not. Although adequate pay, friendly coworkers, and fair supervisors might be mentioned, they emphasized the significance of the work itself. Terkel observed in his introduction to *Working* that the youth of modern society are questioning a "work ethic" in which the individual is subjugated by the job. Young people are asking for meaningful work. Actually, I believe that young people have been asking for meaningful work for some time now, or at least they have been complaining about not having it. Rarely are they heard. In the first part of this century, what people wanted from their jobs was considered so obvious that it hardly warranted research. More recently, job satisfaction has become an intriguing issue not only to researchers but also to people in industry.

History of Job Satisfaction Research

Frederick W. Taylor (1916), one of the pioneers featured in chapter 1, believed that workers' motivation was due largely to their interest in money. He also proposed that the most satisfying situation was one in which a worker could make the most money with the least effort. Both productivity and satisfaction would result, he thought, if workers were given fair wages and work that could be done quickly without excess fatigue. Publications of Taylor's perspective had the effect of directing research attention away from personal satisfaction and toward the work situation. Financial reward was accepted almost without question as the primary satisfier. The "hot topic" of the day was how to design jobs to minimize fatigue, as low productivity was thought to be due to tiring jobs. Studies focused on the impact of varying work hours and giving rest breaks.

The psychologists who conducted the Hawthorne studies were among the first to ask workers about work satisfaction (Roethlisberger, 1941). This research began in the late 1920s and continued over a period of years at the Hawthorne plant of the Western Electric Company. The project actually began as a study of fatigue. The researchers planned to evaluate the effects of different levels of workroom lighting on fatigue and productivity. They hypothesized that increased light would reduce eye fatigue. When the study failed to show the expected effect, the researchers designed another study to evaluate the effects of rest periods on fatigue. When this study failed also, they began to realize that the basic assumptions underlying the research were incorrect. The workers simply did not show the expected responses to changes in their physical environment.

The Hawthorne researchers thought it might be the workers' attitudes about their work that caused their reactions. Workers were interviewed and encouraged to talk about what was important and satisfying to them and what they liked and disliked about their jobs. Most people had mixed reactions to their jobs, and many talked more about social than economic conditions. The researchers' conclusion was that money actually was not very important. Most of us, they said, want the satisfaction that comes from social recognition. People want to be recognized by the boss as someone with good skills and to be an accepted member of the work group. Their conclusion had a major impact on research over the next 20 years. Although Taylor's emphasis on money had been too strong, the interpretation of the Hawthorne studies led to a virtual disregard of pay as a satisfier.

During the 1930s, several large-scale surveys on job satisfaction were done. The surveys were exploratory; their purpose was to discover variables that were associated with job satisfaction. With this approach, researchers took a more open-minded position with respect to the question of what is satisfying to workers.

In 1934, Uhrbrock surveyed employees of a large manufacturing plant. From a sample of more than 4,000 factory workers, foremen, and clerks, he discovered that there was an important difference in attitude, depending on the organizational level of the person's job. Foremen were more positive than clerks, and clerks were more positive than factory workers. Hoppock (1935) also found such a difference. In general, professional and managerial employees were more satisfied with their jobs than were manual laborers. Hoppock speculated that a number of factors make a job satisfying, including social factors, the intrinsic nature of the job, as well as pay and work hours. Next, Hersey (1936) attempted to document the importance of these different factors. He surveyed groups of union and nonunion workers on the importance of 14 policy issues. As you can see in table 9.1, steady employment was important to members of both groups. Adjustment of grievances was meaningful to most union employees. Other issues, such as a chance to show one's initiative, were not important to either group. Probably, some of these responses were due to the times. For example, the importance of steady employment was likely to be a function of the national level of unemployment, which was high in the 1930s.

Interest in job satisfaction grew rapidly from this beginning. Currently, many researchers are interested in the subject and a large body of research exists. Fifteen years ago, Locke (1976) counted more than 3,000 studies! However, the

Table 9.1

Job Satisfaction in the Past: Union and Nonunion Employee Assessments of the Importance of Company Policy Issues

Factor	Employees Rating Factor "Most Important" (%)	
	Union	Nonunion
Employee stocks	05	02
Voice in management	13	06
Fair grievance adjustment	80	24
Chance of promotion	28	47
Steady employment	65	93
Medical, dental benefits	00	06
Safety	57	21
Amount of pay	49	51
Working conditions	49	45
Hours of work	13	23
Supervision	18	38
Methods of pay	00	02
Insurance, pension benefits	18	36
Chance to show initiative	05	06

From R. B. Hersey, "Psychology of Workers" in *Personnel Journal,* 1936, XIV, 291–96. Copyright © 1936. Reprinted with permission of *Personnel Journal,* Costa Mesa, CA. All rights reserved.

literature is filled with disparate findings about the nature and relationships of satisfaction. Some assertions in the literature seemed like obvious truths when they appeared. For example, it seemed clear at one time that satisfied employees were more productive than employees who disliked their jobs. With apparent confidence, Tiffin (1943) said, "The main difference between men and machines is that the productivity of a man is determined very largely by the way he feels about his job and his attitude toward the company that employs him" (p. 313). Now, we find that this relationship is not so clear. Sometimes satisfied workers produce more than dissatisfied workers and sometimes they do not.

Job Satisfaction as a Job Attitude

Job satisfaction is defined as a job attitude and studied along with other attitudinal concepts, such as morale, job involvement, and organizational commitment. Locke (1976) distinguished morale and job involvement from job satisfaction. **Job satisfaction** is an individual's reaction to the job experience, whereas **morale** is about a whole group of workers and includes their general level of satisfaction with the organization. **Job involvement** refers to the degree to which one is absorbed by one's job, which may be either satisfying or dissatisfying depending on the outcome of involvement. The broader concept of **organizational commitment** refers to the extent to which one identifies with and is involved in an organization (Porter et al., 1974). Not only are job involvement, organizational commitment, and job satisfaction conceptually distinct, they also have measurable differences. They are not simply different aspects of one attitude (Brook, Russell, & Price, 1988). Currently, researchers are interested in learning how these attitudes are related. For example, it may be that job satisfaction is brought about by organizational commitment (Vandenberg & Lance, 1992).

If job satisfaction is an attitude, then perhaps social psychologists can tell us something about it from their study of the basic concept of *attitude*. Generally, an attitude is considered to be a cognitive process that structures social perceptions and results in a particular pattern of response (McGuire, 1985). An attitude is not observed; it is inferred from behavior and expressions of emotion. We can think of an attitude as an *emotionally charged idea* that predisposes *action* toward a stimulus. The cognitive component includes perceptions and beliefs about the object, and the affective or emotional component is either a positive or negative feeling. **Job attitudes,** then, can be defined as consistent patterns of thoughts, feelings, and behavior toward some aspect of the job. Like attitudes in general, job satisfaction typically is described in terms of its affective or emotional component. When the affect of the attitude is positive, we call it job *satisfaction;* when it is negative, it is job *dissatisfaction.* We also can talk about job satisfaction in terms of its cognitive component, or the meaning of the work experience. Finally, job satisfaction can be discussed in terms of its behavioral component, or tendency to promote action. The action tendency indicates what people are likely to do, given what they think and feel about their jobs. One action tendency might be to leave a dissatisfying job.

How do job attitudes develop and change? It is likely that people begin to develop attitudes toward work early in life. In fact, some think that a predisposition to be satisfied may be inherited (Arvey et al., 1989). Although this is an intriguing idea, we should be careful about drawing any firm conclusion at this point. The typical research done to examine genetic effects is susceptible to serious threats to validity (Cropanzano & James, 1990). We need to wait and see how this line of research progresses.

Social psychological research indicates that attitudes can develop through early life experiences with the attitude object (McGuire, 1985). In the socialization of children, for example, work is a major part of developing an identity. You may remember as a child being asked, "What are you going to be when you grow up?" and you came up with some occupations you thought you might like. Through socialization, we develop expectations about what certain occupations will be like, and we probably carry these attitudes into our first work experiences. Then, through direct experience, we find out whether a job meets our expectations. As a result, our job attitudes may change. Sometimes, a changed job attitude results in a midlife career change.

THEORIES OF JOB SATISFACTION

A good theory can answer some questions about the source and development of satisfaction. For example, what determines the level of job satisfaction? What are the conditions under which dissatisfaction is likely? Do some aspects of the job operate on satisfaction differently than others? What personal and situational factors are likely to affect job satisfaction? How is job satisfaction related to other aspects of job behavior? In this section, I briefly review some job satisfaction theories.

Recall from chapter 8 that some theories of motivation refer to work-related satisfactions. Need theories include satisfaction concepts in that motivation is defined in terms of our attempts to satisfy basic needs. For example, McClelland (1961) proposed that individuals differ in their need for achievement and that jobs vary in terms of the opportunities they provide for *satisfying* this need. The need fulfillment proposition has strongly influenced the development of job satisfaction theories. With such a perspective, satisfaction depends on the extent to which a job fulfills important needs, such as security and recognition. Cognitive theories of motivation also include satisfaction as part of the motivational process. For example, in equity theory (Adams, 1965), dissatisfaction is an outcome that can motivate behavioral change. Pay inequity is proposed to result in dissonance and dissatisfaction and to drive behavior. Reinforcement theory also includes satisfaction concepts. Reinforcement is viewed as something that brings satisfaction to an existing state of need.

Other theories directly address job satisfaction. Several of these theories contain a **discrepancy hypothesis.** This hypothesis was developed out of research demonstrating that people use cognitive constructs to evaluate what they get from a job. That is, according to the discrepancy hypothesis, the level of satisfaction will be determined by the difference between what is expected and what is experienced. There is considerable research evidence supporting this view of satisfaction (Michalos, 1986).

Locke's Value Discrepancy Theory

Locke (1969, 1976) used the discrepancy hypothesis in his **value discrepancy theory.** He wanted to avoid using a need fulfillment perspective. He thought that satisfaction is more likely to result from the fulfillment of wants or desires than from the fulfillment of deprived needs. That is, what a person considers important or *valuable* has stronger effects on his or her satisfaction. Values can be described in terms of both their content and their intensity or strength. Content refers to *what* is wanted, and intensity refers to *how much* is wanted. The discrepancy hypothesis describes how values operate on satisfaction. Locke's basic proposition is that satisfaction with some factor or aspect of the job is the result of a dual judgment. First, a person judges the job factor in terms of its importance. This judgment reflects the intensity of the value relating to the job factor. Second, the person estimates the discrepancy or difference between how much of the factor is desired and how much is received. Thus, satisfaction with a job factor will depend on the importance of the factor and on the difference between what is desired of it and what is received. Locke further proposed that a factor's importance affects the intensity of the reaction to a discrepancy, and there is evidence that this is correct. That is, when a job factor is very important, a discrepancy matters more and leads to greater dissatisfaction than when the factor is not important (McFarlin & Rice, 1992).

Discrepancy theorists, including Locke, predict that a discrepancy resulting from getting *less* than one wants will lead to dissatisfaction. Consider the job factor of pay. Many of us are not paid as much as we would like, and we feel dissatisfied with this job factor. With other job factors, dissatisfaction can result either when there is not enough or when there is too much of a particular factor. For example, you can be dissatisfied with the temperature of your workroom if it is not warm enough or if it is too hot. For such factors, dissatisfaction is predicted for a discrepancy in *either* direction. There is some support for these discrepancy predictions. First, satisfaction is greater when discrepancies are smaller—or when you get what you expect. Second, negative discrepancies, or getting less than desired, are associated with dissatisfaction on any job factor. Third, a *positive* discrepancy can lead to dissatisfaction on some job factors, such as having more contact with customers than desired (Rice, McFarlin, & Bennett, 1989).

Lawler's Facet Theory

In their early discussion, Lawler and Porter (1967; Porter & Lawler, 1968) included job satisfaction within a motivational framework. Using expectancy theory concepts, they proposed that motivation results from (1) the perceived instrumentality of an action in producing an outcome and (2) the value of the outcome (or rewards). Satisfaction was proposed to result jointly from the rewards and from perceiving these rewards as equitable or fair. In addition, because it yields rewards, performance was seen as an indirect source of satisfaction. As you will see later, viewing work performance as an *antecedent* of satisfaction is radically different. Usually, performance is treated as a *consequence* of satisfaction.

Lawler's (1973) **facet theory** extends this line of thought into a more complete perspective on satisfaction. The primary aim of the facet model is to predict satisfaction with different aspects or facets of the job. Lawler used the discrepancy hypothesis and some of Adams' (1965) motivation theory reasoning to do this. He proposed that the level of satisfaction with a job facet is determined by comparisons between expectations of what *should be* received from the job facet and perceptions of what *is* received. Expectations of what should be received are determined by perceptions of one's input to the job, the inputs and outcomes of others, and the demands of the job. Perception of what actually is received on the job also is determined by equity considerations, specifically by the actual amount one receives compared to the amount others receive.

Satisfaction results when the amount received is the *same* as the amount expected. Dissatisfaction results when one gets *less* than one expects. Lawler proposed that the size of this discrepancy will determine the amount of dissatisfaction. As figure 9.1 illustrates, a number of variables can operate to affect the discrepancy between the amount expected and the amount received. Dissatisfaction with a job facet is more likely when an individual perceives (1) his or her inputs to be high; (2) the job to be demanding; (3) the outcome level to be low; (4) coworkers to have a better input-outcome balance; and (5) coworkers to have greater actual outcomes, particularly if they have similar or less demanding jobs. In the case of positive discrepancies, when *more* is received than should be, Lawler proposed that guilt and discomfort result instead of dissatisfaction. Overcompensation is an example of a positive discrepancy.

In Lawler's theory, the same psychological process operates for all job facets. Importance of the job facet is reflected in the measure of satisfaction, because those facets that are most important will appear as the most or the least satisfactory.

The Social Influence Hypothesis

Given what is known about attitude formation and change, it would not be unreasonable to suppose that job satisfaction is influenced by other people. Social

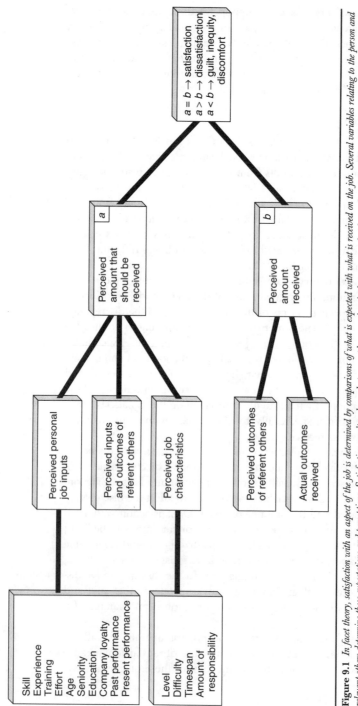

Figure 9.1 In facet theory, satisfaction with an aspect of the job is determined by comparisons of what is expected with what is received on the job. Several variables relating to the person and relevant others determine these expectations and perceptions. Satisfaction results when what an employee receives is the same as what he or she expects. Dissatisfaction results when he or she gets less than expected.

From E. E. Lawler, Motivation in Work Organizations. Copyright © 1973 Brooks/Cole Publishers. Reprinted by permission of the author.

psychologists have shown that attitudes develop in a social context and are molded by reference groups in many cases (Triandis, 1971). Salancik and Pfeffer (1977) have proposed that social influence is an important determinant of job satisfaction. They argue that people do not make the many comparisons for all the different aspects of a job, as discrepancy theorists have suggested. Instead, we take a cognitive shortcut. We simply look to see how others in similar jobs appear to feel. Our perception of their job attitudes influences our own attitudes. That is, when others appear to like a job, then we like it, too. Some laboratory research has supported the **social influence hypothesis.** For example, subjects who heard others evaluate a task positively were themselves more likely to do so when they performed it later (Weiss & Shaw, 1979). Also, satisfaction with various aspects of work is affected by the individual's attachment to a highly cohesive work group (Manning & Fullerton, 1988; O'Reilly & Caldwell, 1985), and cohesive groups provide ample opportunity for social influence.

Landy's Opponent Process Theory

Landy (1978, 1985) observed that satisfaction with a job can change over time even though the job itself has not changed. Most of us have had the experience of no longer liking what we once loved to do. Then, oddly enough, when we are not allowed to do it anymore, we miss it. For example, at first you might really enjoy going to school, and then it becomes commonplace and boring. As graduation draws near, however, you begin to wish that school did not have to end. Landy proposed, in his **opponent process theory,** that this happens because of our internal mechanisms for maintaining a neutral emotional level. That is, we try to smooth out our emotional ups and downs.

To explain this, he used equilibrium concepts drawn from neurophysiology and from opponent process theories of physiological behavior (Solomon & Corbit, 1973). Certain internal bodily processes operate to maintain a homeostatic balance. These balancing processes are opposing in that activation of one counteracts the other. For example, when a high environmental temperature drops suddenly to a low level, the body stops sweating (which reduces internal temperature) and begins shivering (which increases internal temperature). The opposing process is temporarily "locked in" and not disengaged until equilibrium is *surpassed*. Thus, there is a point where the body goes temporarily out of balance in the opposite direction before it returns to equilibrium (Solomon & Corbit, 1973).

Landy viewed job satisfaction as an emotional state that is subject to physiological influences. Emotional balance is a neutral state maintained through opponent processes that counteract the emotional response to a job. He proposed that two different opponent operations come into play: (1) an immediate emotional response and (2) a later reaction after many emotional responses to the job have occurred. The immediate reaction occurs as follows. To start, the person is in an emotionally neutral state. Then a stimulus, such as recognition by one's superior, produces an emotional reaction, which can be either positive or negative. Shortly after this reaction is initiated, emotional neutrality is surpassed, which triggers the opposing response. Because it is opposite to the primary emotion, this opponent process reduces the overall level of emotion. The combination of these two processes produces this experience. The individual first feels a strong emotional effect and then a gradual tapering to an emotionally neutral level. Later, when the stimulus is withdrawn, the individual experiences the opposite emotion before returning to an emotionally neutral state. The opposing process is proposed to become stronger over time; thus, the same stimulus comes to provoke only a slight response. Also, because the opponent process is stronger, withdrawal of a stimulus causes a more extreme "overshooting" of emotional equilibrium. For example, a job that began with high satisfaction but became routine and boring may be grieved for when the person retires.

Main Points

Some theories incorporate a discrepancy hypothesis. In this, job satisfaction results from the difference between what is expected and what is experienced on the job. Locke used this in his theory. He explained that satisfaction depends on how important a job factor is, which determines how much of it is expected. The expectation is compared to how much is received, and this determines the level of satisfaction.

In Lawler's facet theory, satisfaction with various aspects of a job depends on a person's assessment of what a job should provide and what it does provide, compared to what others receive. Dissatisfaction is more likely when the person puts a lot into a demanding job but, compared to others, gets little out of it.

Although people do compare themselves to others, the social influence hypothesis says that they take a shortcut. They simply find out how others feel and adopt that attitude.

Landy's opponent process theory shows how satisfaction changes over time. People's emotional responses to their job experiences are subject to equilibrium processes. A highly satisfying job can become routine and boring through such processes.

MEASUREMENT OF JOB SATISFACTION

Because an attitude is a hypothetical construct, it itself cannot be measured. However, reflections of the attitude in behavior and in reports of thoughts and feelings can be measured. (See figure 9.2.) Researchers have found consistency among the three aspects of an attitude (McGuire, 1985); thus, we can expect that measures of any of the three will provide information about the attitude itself. A variety of measurement instruments can be used in studying job satisfaction. Physiological measures and questionnaires asking about feelings can be used in detecting the affective component of job satisfaction. Questionnaires that access the cognitive component also provide information about the attitude. Whether affective and cognitive measures provide the same kind of information about attitudes is questionable (Moorman, 1993).

Conducting a Satisfaction Survey

Industry has a practical purpose for satisfaction surveys. Arnold and Feldman (1986) cited five ways organizations can use job satisfaction survey data: (1) to diagnose organizational problems; (2) to evaluate the effects of organizational

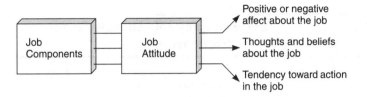

Figure 9.2 *The anatomy of a job attitude. Job attitudes are influenced by components of the job, and they are reflected in behavior, thoughts, and feelings about the job.*

changes; (3) to improve communication with employees; (4) to assess the likelihood of unionization; and (5) to understand absenteeism and turnover. As we will see, the research is not entirely clear on the relationship between satisfaction and some of these variables. Even so, it probably is true that job attitude surveys can provide organizations with useful information in dealing with their human problems.

Given the potential of the satisfaction survey, it is not surprising to find that organizations want to conduct their own studies. A standardized instrument, such as one of those described in the next sections, can be acquired for this purpose, or organizations can develop their own if they prefer. There are some advantages to developing a questionnaire. The instrument can be oriented to the unique features of the organization, and questions of particular interest can be incorporated. However, there are disadvantages, too, because developing a measure is difficult and time-consuming.

To measure job satisfaction accurately, the measurement instrument must be reliable. Recall from the discussion of testing in chapter 5 that reliability refers to the consistency of the results produced with the instrument. When a standardized instrument is used, estimates of reliability are available. When other instruments are used, however, the researcher needs to conduct a reliability study. This is done with the same procedures as are used to evaluate test reliability.

The issue of validity in the measurement of attitudes is a more difficult problem. It may well be that what we *think* we are measuring has little to do with what we *are* measuring. The Hawthorne studies are a case in point. How do we find out if we are measuring job satisfaction and not something else? Locke (1976) has suggested a method of *logical validation*. This procedure integrates all available evidence about an individual's job satisfaction. Talking with survey respondents, pointing out discrepancies in their answers to different questions, and having them explain the meaning of these differences are ways of getting this evidence.

Some general problems of attitude measurement contribute to the difficulty in establishing the reliability and validity of job satisfaction scales. One problem is that questionnaire items may not be interpreted in the same way by all respondents. This is one of the most difficult aspects of developing questionnaires. We simply have no way to ensure that all items will be understood in the same way by every respondent. We can only do our best in carefully developing the instrument.

Triandis (1971) gave some general advice on developing attitude questionnaires. First, the developer needs to decide on the level of inquiry. That is, will the job as a whole or the job components be evaluated? If the company is interested in a quick check on the level of satisfaction, then a single-item questionnaire will probably do. Often, however, the company wants to know about several factors, such as satisfaction with pay, working conditions, management practices, and layoff

Table 9.2 Developing Job Attitude Survey Instruments

Discard	Items referring to the past
	Items that are factual
	Ambiguous items
	Confusing items
	Irrelevant items
	Nondiscriminating items (everyone or no one endorses these)
	Items referring to more than one aspect of the job
Modify	Items containing universals (e.g., always and never)
	Items with unusual or unfamiliar words
	Items with double negatives
	Excessively wordy statements
Keep	Items that one by one cover all job aspects under study
	Clear, simple, and direct statements
	Short items (20 or fewer words)
	Items that can be written as simple sentences
	Items that refer to feelings or reactions to the job

Sources: H. C. Triandis, *Attitude and Attitude Change.* Copyright © 1971 John Wiley & Sons, New York; and A. L. Edwards, *Techniques of Attitude Scale Construction.* Copyright © 1957 Appleton-Century-Crofts, New York.

policies. Once the level of inquiry has been decided, the next step is to develop items. Brainstorming with others about what might be satisfying aspects of the job can result in a large batch of statements or questions. The batch should be screened, and both unclear and factual statements should be discarded. A list of criteria for developing items is shown in table 9.2. It is best to write items that tap into the affective element of the attitude and avoid statements of fact. In this way, the survey is more likely to yield information on how the individual *feels* about the job.

Another issue to decide in constructing a satisfaction survey is the kind of response the survey will solicit. It is possible to use **open-ended questions** in an interview and let the respondent answer in his or her own words. Open-ended questions are useful in an exploratory investigation. However, **closed questions** with predetermined answer categories on a printed form probably will be used because this is less time-consuming to administer. How will the respondent answer these closed questions? A number of different response formats are possible. A checklist is used in some surveys. In others, respondents are asked to reply yes, no, or undecided. A **Likert scale** in which attitude statements are rated from 1 to 5 is used in some surveys.

Standardized Rating Scales

Several **standardized instruments** for measuring job satisfaction are available, and much of the current research is done with one of these. In this section, I describe four well-known standardized instruments that include items covering a range of job factors and sources of satisfaction. These are the Job Descriptive Index, the Minnesota Satisfaction Questionnaire, the Need Satisfaction Questionnaire, and the Faces Scale. There are several advantages to using a standardized instrument.

These rating scales have undergone considerable study and show reasonable levels of reliability and validity. Thus, the user can be more confident that the instrument does what he or she wants it to. In addition, norms for different groups of working people are available to help in analyzing the behavior of the sample. The scales are not absolutely problem free, of course. As Locke (1976) noted, all such surveys, including the ones we design ourselves, assume that the respondent has good self-insight. This is a risky assumption because people are not always aware of their feelings or of the reasons behind them.

Job Descriptive Index (JDI)

A standardized scale that has been used in much of the current research is the **Job Descriptive Index (JDI),** originally developed by Smith, Kendall, and Hulin (1969). This measure shows validity in being correlated with other measures of job satisfaction and demonstrates good reliability (Schneider & Dachler, 1978). Its widespread use has produced norms for several different groups in terms of age, gender, education, and income of the respondents. The JDI response format and some sample items are shown in table 9.3. The six subscales composing the measure contain questions about attitudes toward work, supervision, pay, coworkers, opportunities for promotion, and the job in general. Each subscale can be scored separately to provide component scores, or they can be combined to yield a composite score. Another measure of overall satisfaction, called the Job in General scale, has been developed for use with the JDI subscales. This measure may provide a better global evaluation than the combined JDI subscales (Ironson et al., 1989).

The JDI is open to criticism because descriptive items are mixed with evaluative items. The rationale for including both kinds of items is that the affective and cognitive elements of job attitudes are consistent. If this is a good assumption, then we can expect that the way in which an individual *describes* the job also reflects his or her *feelings* about the job. Even if this is so, however, descriptions of the job provide a less direct measure of affect than evaluations do.

Minnesota Satisfaction Questionnaire (MSQ)

There are two forms of the **Minnesota Satisfaction Questionnaire (MSQ)** (Weiss et al., 1967). The long form includes 100 items about various aspects of the work situation and yields scores that can be compared with norms for several occupational groups. Twenty job factors are represented in these items, including satisfaction with pay, coworkers, supervision, responsibility, social status, and security. The short form includes 20 items and provides an overall measure of job satisfaction. The MSQ uses a five-point Likert rating scale in which the respondent rates each item at some point from very dissatisfied to very satisfied. Sample items from the short form are shown in table 9.4. Notice that the items are constructed so that the respondent describes feelings about the job.

Need Satisfaction Questionnaire (NSQ)

Another satisfaction questionnaire is based on the need fulfillment perspective. The **Need Satisfaction Questionnaire (NSQ)** itemizes several needs that might be satisfied on the job (Porter, 1961). The respondent rates how much satisfaction *should* be available and how much *is* available to meet his or her needs. Table 9.5 shows

Sample Items from the Job Descriptive Index (Revised, 1985). Each Scale Is Presented on a Separate Page

Think of the work you do at present. How well does each of the following words or phrases describe your work? **In the blank beside each word below, write**

__Y__ for "Yes" if it describes your work

__N__ for "No" if it does NOT describe it

__?__ if you cannot decide

WORK ON PRESENT JOB

_____ Routine

_____ Satisfying

_____ Good

Think of the pay you get now. How well does each of the following words or phrases describe your present pay? **In the blank beside each word below, write**

__Y__ for "Yes" if it describes your pay

__N__ for "No" if it does NOT describe it

__?__ if you cannot decide

PRESENT PAY

_____ Income adequate for normal expenses

_____ Insecure

_____ Less than I deserve

Think of the opportunities for promotion that you have now. How well does each of the following words or phrases describe these? **In the blank beside each word below, write**

__Y__ for "Yes" if it describes your opportunities for promotion

__N__ for "No" if it does NOT describe it

__?__ if you cannot decide

OPPORTUNITIES FOR PROMOTION

_____ Dead-end job

_____ Unfair promotion policy

_____ Regular promotions

Think of the kind of supervision that you get on your job. How well does each of the following words or phrases describe this? **In the blank beside each word below, write**

__Y__ for "Yes" if it describes the supervision you get on your job

__N__ for "No" if it does NOT describe it

__?__ if you cannot decide

SUPERVISION

_____ Impolite

_____ Praises good work

_____ Doesn't supervise enough

Think of the majority of the people that you work with now or the people you meet in connection with your work. How well does each of the following words or phrases describe these people? **In the blank beside each word below, write**

__Y__ for "Yes" if it describes the people you work with

__N__ for "No" if it does NOT describe them

__?__ if you cannot decide

COWORKERS (PEOPLE)

_____ Boring

_____ Responsible

_____ Intelligent

Think of your job in general. All in all, what is it like most of the time? **In the blank beside each word or phrase below, write**

__Y__ for "Yes" if it describes your job

__N__ for "No" if it does NOT describe it

__?__ if you cannot decide

JOB IN GENERAL

_____ Undesirable

_____ Better than most

_____ Rotten

Table 9.4   **Sample Items from the Minnesota Satisfaction Questionnaire**

Ask Yourself:	How satisfied am I with this aspect of my job?
Very Sat.	means I am very satisfied with this aspect of my job.
Sat.	means I am satisfied with this aspect of my job.
N	means I can't decide whether I am satisfied or not with this aspect of my job.
Dissat.	means I am dissatisfied with this aspect of my job.
Very Dissat.	means I am very dissatisfied with this aspect of my job.

On My Present Job, This Is How I Feel About . . .

	Very Dissat.	*Dissat.*	*N*	*Sat.*	*Very Sat.*
1) The chance to do something that makes use of my abilities	☐	☐	☐	☐	☐
2) The way company policies are put into practice	☐	☐	☐	☐	☐
3) My pay and the amount of work I do	☐	☐	☐	☐	☐
4) The chances for advancement on this job	☐	☐	☐	☐	☐
5) The freedom to use my own judgment	☐	☐	☐	☐	☐

From D. J. Weiss, et al., *Minnesota Studies in Vocational Rehabilitation: 22 Manual for the Minnesota Satisfaction Questionnaire.* Copyright © D. J. Weiss, R.V. Davis, G.W. England, and L. H. Lofquist.

Table 9.5   **Sample Items from the Need Satisfaction Questionnaire**

On the following pages of Part I will be listed several characteristics or qualities connected with management positions. For each such characteristic, you will be asked to give three ratings:

a. How much of the characteristic is there *now* connected with your management position?

b. How much of the characteristic do you think *should* be connected with your management position?

c. How *important* is this position characteristic to you?

I. Security needs

   a. The feeling of security in my management position

II. Social needs

   a. The opportunity, in my management position, to give help to other people

   b. The opportunity to develop close friendships in my management position

III. Esteem needs

   a. The feeling of self-esteem a person gets from being in my management position

   b. The prestige of my management position *inside* the company (that is, the regard received from others in the company)

   c. The prestige of my management position *outside* the company (that is, the regard received from others not in the company)

From L.W. Porter, "A Study of Perceived Need Satisfaction in Bottom and Middle Management Jobs" in *Journal of Applied Psychology,* 1961, 45, 1–10. Copyright © 1961 by the American Psychological Association.

Figure 9.3 *The Faces Scale. This instrument provides an assessment of overall job satisfaction. A respondent checks the box below the face that expresses his or her general feeling about the job.*

From T. Kunin, "The Construction of a New Type of Attitude Measure" in Personnel Psychology, 8:68–69. Copyright © 1955 Personnel Psychology, Inc., Bowling Green, Ohio. Reprinted by permission.

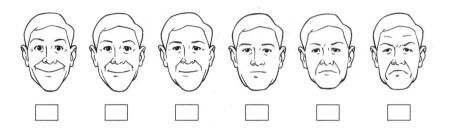

some sample items. Notice that this is an indirect measure inferring satisfaction from need fulfillment. Notice also that the ratings identify discrepancies between what is expected and what is received. This indicates that the NSQ is based on a discrepancy hypothesis. That is, if the individual expects more need satisfaction than the job actually provides, then dissatisfaction is predicted. It is on this theoretical basis that the questionnaire can be criticized. For one thing, the questionnaire provides no good way to show that needs are actually motivating to the respondent (Locke, 1976).

Faces Scale

The fourth measure of job satisfaction is the **Faces Scale** (Kunin, 1955; see figure 9.3). This single-item measure provides an assessment of overall job satisfaction. The scale is unique because the response categories consist of drawings of faces that vary in emotional expression. The drawings have been scaled so that they represent equidistant points along a continuum from positive to negative. A respondent checks the box under the face that best expresses how he or she feels about the job. The Faces Scale is especially useful with illiterate workers or with those who have language difficulties. Further, unlike the other three instruments, this scale is directly focused on the affective or emotional component of the job attitude, making it particularly useful for studies in which job satisfaction is viewed as an emotion.

*M*ain *P*oints

Organizations can make use of information about employee job satisfaction, and some organizations like to do their own satisfaction studies. If they do, the first question is whether to use a standardized instrument, which already has reliability and validity information, or to custom-make an instrument. If the decision is to develop a questionnaire, careful attention must be given to problems in writing understandable questions and to establishing reliability and validity.

Several standardized instruments are available for collecting job satisfaction information. Four well-known ones are described: the Job Descriptive Index (JDI), the Minnesota Satisfaction Questionnaire (MSQ), the Need Satisfaction Questionnaire (NSQ), and the Faces Scale. All four provide a measure of overall job satisfaction. All except the Faces Scale also provide subscales to measure different components of satisfaction. The four measures also vary as to the extent they access affective versus cognitive aspects of job satisfaction.

COMPONENTS OF JOB SATISFACTION

What exactly do we mean when we talk about jobs and satisfaction with jobs? In some studies of job satisfaction, jobs are treated as if they are single uniform entities, and job satisfaction is viewed as a single attitude. Of course, it is likely that jobs and job attitudes are not so simple. If I ask you whether you are satisfied with your job, you will probably give me a qualified answer: "Some aspects of the job are satisfying and others are not." Therefore, to understand satisfaction, we need to consider the components of the job. A job can be defined as an interacting set of tasks, roles, and relationships with others. People are likely to have attitudes about all these aspects of the job, as well as about the job as a whole. Studies have been done to evaluate the components of job satisfaction. In the following sections, we take a close look at satisfaction with (1) the work itself; (2) work interactions, such as supervisor relationships; and (3) the incentives and rewards of the job, such as pay and benefits.

Satisfaction with the Work Itself

Are complex, enriched jobs more satisfying than simple, dull jobs? We have often thought so. Repetitious jobs, in which few abilities are needed, are usually thought to lack meaning and to dissatisfy those who perform them. The nature of the work itself has been a central feature of the research on job satisfaction, and substantial relationships between the content of the job and satisfaction with the job have been reported (Hackman & Oldham, 1976).

The Job Characteristics Model

Some research has been done in an effort to discover what is satisfying about work. One such study found that job enrichment can affect job satisfaction, as well as work performance and employee withdrawal (Hackman & Lawler, 1971). Development of the **Job Characteristics Model** resulted from this study (Hackman & Oldham, 1975, 1976). In this theoretical model, five basic dimensions or characteristics of the job are proposed to affect an individual's psychological states and ultimately lead to changes in satisfaction. As described in table 9.6, the job dimensions are skill variety, task identity, task significance, autonomy, and feedback. The **Job Diagnostic Survey** is an instrument for measuring these dimensions (Hackman & Oldham, 1975). According to the Job Characteristics Model, job dimensions indirectly determine an employee's motivation, performance, withdrawal, and satisfaction because they affect three psychological states (see figure 9.4). The first three dimensions—skill variety, task identity, and task significance—affect the individual's perception of the job as meaningful. The fourth dimension—autonomy—affects feelings of responsibility. The final dimension—feedback—affects knowledge of results. Further, a person's need for personal growth through the job is proposed to moderate the relationship between these job characteristics and employee outcomes, such as satisfaction. The strength of the growth need shows the extent to which growth opportunities on the job are valuable to the individual.

Research has shown moderately strong evidence for the predicted relationship between the five dimensions and job satisfaction (Champoux, 1991; Kelly, 1992; Loher et al., 1985). The main difficulty in supporting the theory as a whole

Figure 9.4 *The Job Characteristics Model. Job dimensions (such as skill variety) are proposed to have specific effects on the employee's psychological states (such as perception of work meaningfulness). These, in turn, determine personal and work outcomes (such as satisfaction). A personal factor—growth need strength—is proposed to modify the relationship between job dimensions and outcomes.*

From J. R. Hackman and G. R. Oldham, "Motivation Through the Design of Work: Test of a Theory." in Organizational Behavior and Human Performance, 6:256. *Copyright © 1976 Academic Press, Inc., Orlando, Florida. Reprinted by permission.*

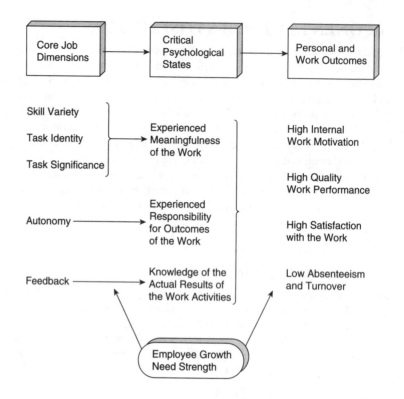

T*able 9.6*

Job Dimensions Measured by the Job Diagnostic Survey

Skill Variety:	the degree to which the job has a variety of tasks and uses many of the employee's skills and abilities
Task Identity:	the degree to which the job involves following a product or process through from beginning to end
Task Significance:	the degree to which the task has meaning or importance
Autonomy:	the degree to which the job allows freedom and discretion in determining work procedures and scheduling
Feedback from the Job:	the degree to which the job has built-in mechanisms by which the individual gets information about work effectiveness

Source: Adapted from J. R. Hackman and G. R. Oldham, Development of the Job Diagnostic Survey. *Journal of Applied Psychology,* 60, pp. 159–170. Copyright © 1975 by the American Psychological Association. Adapted with permission.

is the question of how growth need strength enters the picture. Researchers testing the theory have disagreed most on this point. Some have found that the association between satisfaction and the job dimensions is stronger and less varied among employees with a high growth need than it is for employees with a low growth need (Champoux, 1991; Fried & Ferris, 1987; Loher et al., 1985). This suggests that some employees—those with high growth need strength—will find complex, enriched jobs more satisfying. Other researchers have been unable to show that growth need strength affects behavior in this way (Tiegs, Tetrick, & Fried, 1992). One possibility is that the difficulty lies in viewing growth need strength as a *moderator* of job characteristics. Rather, it may be that it has a direct effect on certain job outcomes (Graen, Scandura, & Graen, 1986; Medcof, 1991). That is, we might expect that employees with high growth need strength would see the job as an opportunity to satisfy the need.

So what *do* employees mean when they say they are satisfied with the work itself? These research results suggest they may mean that the core dimensions of the job are satisfying in that they determine the meaningfulness of the work and/or that the job provides an opportunity for personal growth and development.

Satisfaction with Pay

How can satisfaction with pay be predicted? Is it the absolute value of our earnings that determines whether or not we are satisfied? That is, are we more satisfied with higher wages and less satisfied with lower? To some extent, we are. The wage level itself has been found to predict satisfaction. Employees who receive high wages say they are more satisfied with their pay and are less likely to quit their jobs (Dyer & Theriault, 1976; Gomez-Mejia & Balkin, 1984; Levine, 1993; Rice, Phillips, & McFarlin, 1990). However, other studies indicate that there is more to pay satisfaction than simply how high the wage is. Pay satisfaction can be affected by organizational policies, such as the employer's compensation system. The extent to which pay-setting criteria are clear and consistent makes a difference in how we respond to the size of our paychecks (Dyer & Theriault, 1976; Weiner, 1980). Other compensatory factors, such as benefits, can contribute. For example, the implementation of a flexible benefits program was found to increase employee satisfaction (Barber, Dunham, & Formisano, 1992).

Pay satisfaction is multidimensional. That is, there is more reason to be satisfied (or dissatisfied) than simply the overall amount of wages. Heneman and Schwab (1985) proposed that pay satisfaction is made up of four dimensions: satisfaction with pay level, benefits, pay raises, and the structure and administration of the pay policy. They developed a survey instrument, the **Pay Satisfaction Questionnaire (PSQ),** for evaluating these different aspects of pay satisfaction. (See table 9.7.) The instrument has been evaluated in research, and it appears to be effective in assessing the various components of pay satisfaction (Judge, 1993; Judge & Welbourn, 1994).

Pay satisfaction also can be understood better if we take account of what the person expects in the way of salary. As discussed previously, the discrepancy hypothesis is used by satisfaction theorists, such as Locke (1976) and Lawler (1973), to explain that expectations are relevant to satisfaction. In this view, people are proposed to have a standard or an understanding of how much a fair wage should be. If the wage they receive does not measure up to the standard, they will be dissatisfied. There is evidence to support this proposition. Employees report satisfaction with the amount of their pay when it meets or exceeds their perceptions of what they should be paid (Berkowitz et al., 1987; Dyer & Theriault, 1976). How

*T*able 9.7   Items from the Pay Satisfaction Questionnaire (PSQ)

The statements below describe various aspects of your pay. For each statement, decide how satisfied or dissatisfied you feel about your pay, and put the number in the corresponding blank that best indicates your feeling. To do this, use the following scale:

1	2	3	4	5
Very Dissatisfied	Dissatisfied	Neither Satisfied Nor Dissatisfied	Satisfied	Very Satisfied

1. My take-home pay.   L
2. My benefit package.   B
3. My most recent raise.   R
4. Influence my supervisor has on my pay.   R
5. My current salary.   L
6. Amount the company pays toward my benefits.   B
7. The raises I have typically received in the past.   R
8. The company's pay structure.   S/A
9. Information the company gives about pay issues of concern to me.   S/A
10. My overall level of pay.   L
11. The value of my benefits.   B
12. Pay of other jobs in the company.   S/A
13. Consistency of the company's pay choices.   S/A
14. Size of my current salary.   L
15. The number of benefits I receive.   B
16. How my raises are determined.   R
17. Differences in pay among jobs in the company.   S/A
18. How the company administers pay.   S/A

From H. G. Heneman III and D. P. Schwab, "Pay Satisfaction: Its Multidimensional Nature and Measurement" in *International Journal of Psychology, 20:* 129–141, 1979. Reprinted by permission of International Union of Psychological Science.
Note: L = level, B = benefits, R = raise, S/A = structure/administration.

do people develop their equity standards? Apparently, there are several ways. We can compare our own outcomes with the outcomes of others, such as coworkers or people in other companies who do the same kind of work (Rice, Phillips, & McFarlin, 1990). In addition, internal comparisons may contribute to the development of equity standards (Berkowitz et al., 1987). That is, we may compare our present salary with what we made in the past.

Satisfaction with Supervision

A subordinate's satisfaction with the supervisor may depend on the supervisor's style of leadership. As I discuss in chapter 10, most leadership theory and research has emphasized the effects of leadership on productivity rather than on satisfaction. However, two theories of leadership can be used to understand subordinate satisfaction with the supervisor. Yukl's (1971) discrepancy model and

House's (1971) path-goal theory both address the impact of the supervisor on subordinate satisfaction. Yukl proposed that a subordinate's preference for different types of leader behavior will be used to evaluate what the supervisor actually does. The discrepancy between what is preferred and what is observed determines the employee's satisfaction. Similarly, House proposed that two basic types of leader behavior—showing consideration and initiating task structure—will affect subordinate satisfaction differently, depending on the nature of the work. When the work is clear and unambiguous, a leader who is considerate will be more satisfying. When the work is not clear, a structuring leader will be more satisfying. Although research has not fully supported the prediction that leader structuring is satisfying, there is evidence that leader consideration results in greater satisfaction (Mitchell, 1979).

Other characteristics, such as the supervisor's organizational position and power, can affect subordinate satisfaction. Locke (1970) hypothesized that the relationship between supervisor and subordinate is functional to the extent that the subordinate can realize his or her aims through the supervisor. That is, gaining valuable job outcomes, such as having interesting work or getting a promotion, may depend on a supervisor's upward influence. This, in turn, can modify the subordinate's satisfaction with the supervisor. For example, in a study conducted as a field experiment, the amount of upward influence of a supervisor was manipulated, and ratings of satisfaction with the supervisor were collected from a sample of blue-collar workers (Trempe, Rigny, & Haccoun, 1985). Overall, the power of the supervisor swayed subordinate satisfaction. Subjects were more satisfied when the supervisor was more influential.

There is more than one way to say that you are satisfied (or dissatisfied) with a job. For example, you can say you have enjoyable work and that you like your supervisor, but the pay leaves something to be desired. Many studies address each of these components of job satisfaction.

What is it about the work itself that makes it satisfying? The Job Characteristics Model was devised to answer this question. It identifies the core job dimensions and the psychological processes that affect the job experience. The Job Diagnostic Survey is an instrument for assessing the job dimensions. Most of the model's propositions have been supported by research.

Is pay an important element of job satisfaction? To some people it is. However, how much is required is a relative matter. People seem to have a sense of what a fair wage is. Also, it is not simply how much is earned. Other compensatory factors, such as benefits, are important. The Pay Satisfaction Questionnaire has been devised to assess the elements of pay satisfaction.

An employee's satisfaction with his or her supervisor can be assessed in terms of how the supervisor is preferred or expected to behave compared to how he or she actually does behave. Two leadership theories include this discrepancy hypothesis.

DIFFERENCES BETWEEN PEOPLE: WHO IS SATISFIED?

Dispositional Differences

Recent research suggests that people may be more or less inclined to be satisfied with their jobs because of their personal **dispositions.** This line of investigation appears to have been prompted by studies in which an earlier job attitude was found to predict a later job attitude. Staw and Ross (1985) found that job satisfaction at one time was similar to job satisfaction five years later. Others report that this relationship between earlier and later job satisfaction remains even if the person changes jobs (Gupta, Jenkins, & Beehr, 1992). Staw and Ross (1985) pointed out an interesting implication of such findings: If job satisfaction is *this* stable, then organizational interventions meant to change satisfaction are pointless. Others, however, believe that organizational interventions do have some potential because personal dispositions do not completely overpower situational variables (Gerhart, 1987).

Other research has been done to examine the dispositional factor itself. For example, some reviewers of studies of personality and emotion have concluded that a somewhat stable trait of **negative affectivity** exists in some people (Watson & Clark, 1984). Such people tend to experience more negative emotions and distress, dwelling on the negative aspects of any situation. We might expect these individuals also to be less satisfied with their jobs. Some researchers have reported that they are, but the effect is not strong (Levin & Stokes, 1989). Others have found it strong enough to be detected over time. For example, facets of job satisfaction could be predicted two years after the initial measures were taken (Watson & Slack, 1993). In one study, the influence of positive mood inducement was considered. The researchers hypothesized and found that momentary positive events had less effect on people who showed high negative reactivity (Brief, Butcher, & Roberson, 1995). The results of these studies suggest that negative activity limits people's ability to experience a job as satisfying. This may account for some of the differences between people.

Demographic Differences

A common refrain is that our values are changing, and we are becoming alienated from traditional institutions and ideals. Youth, some think, no longer accepts the Protestant work ethic, and work does not mean what it once did. If we really are less satisfied with our jobs now than we were in the past, national surveys should reveal a general decline in work satisfaction.

National surveys are conducted periodically. Typically, a cross section of workers in different occupations are asked one or two global questions, such as "How satisfied are you in your work?" However, it is difficult to tell whether there has been a change in the national level of job satisfaction, because the surveys are not entirely consistent. Studies evaluating yearly data from 1958 through 1973 (Quinn, Staines, & McCullough, 1974) and from 1972 through 1978 (Weaver, 1980) indicated no substantial change in the nation's overall level of satisfaction. Other studies showed a decline, however (Veroff, Douvan, & Kulka, 1981). A Health, Education, and Welfare report entitled *Work in America* (1973) summarized a number of studies and concluded that there is a decline in work satisfaction. It

Table 9.8 — Average National Work Satisfaction Ratings from 1972 to 1976 by Demographic Variables

Variable	Year of Survey							M^b
	1972	1973	1974	1975	1976	1977	1978	
Race								
White	2.36	2.34	2.38	2.43	2.44	2.37	2.43	2.39
Black	2.09	2.32	2.17	2.34	2.13	2.36	2.01	2.19
Sex								
Male	2.32	2.31	2.35	2.44	2.41	2.33	2.38	2.36
Female	2.28	2.40	2.36	2.40	2.42	2.42	2.39	2.38
Education								
Grade school	2.32	2.22	2.28	2.32	2.32	2.33	2.35	2.31
High school	2.25	2.28	2.38	2.46	2.39	2.38	2.37	2.36
Some college	2.26	2.45	2.35	2.52	2.38	2.36	2.31	2.37
College degree or more	2.44	2.52	2.41	2.37	2.54	2.46	2.49	2.46
Age								
Less than 20	1.43	1.95	2.25	2.08	1.73	2.17	2.14	1.95
20–29	2.06	2.18	2.18	2.24	2.25	2.19	2.67	2.20
30–39	2.37	2.39	2.26	2.48	2.53	2.33	2.35	2.38
40–49	2.36	2.34	2.41	2.48	2.45	2.39	2.43	2.41
50 or more	2.51	2.46	2.55	2.55	2.53	2.55	2.55	2.53
Personal income[a]								
Less than $5,000	–	–	2.23	2.23	2.21	2.21	2.21	2.22
$5,000–$6,999	–	–	2.21	2.47	2.44	2.46	2.14	2.35
$7,000–$9,999	–	–	2.26	2.38	2.37	2.32	2.31	2.33
$10,000–$14,999	–	–	2.42	2.44	2.47	2.35	2.43	2.42
$15,000 or more	–	–	2.58	2.60	2.55	2.48	2.50	2.53
Occupation								
Professional–technical	2.48	2.45	2.48	2.50	2.61	2.46	2.55	2.50
Managerial–administrative	2.51	2.65	2.59	2.64	2.56	2.52	2.55	2.57
Sales	2.24	2.35	2.33	2.71	2.41	1.96	2.48	2.33
Clerical	2.27	2.32	2.25	2.47	2.37	2.33	2.28	2.33
Craftsmen–foremen	2.34	2.19	2.44	2.33	2.56	2.42	2.50	2.39
Operatives	2.13	1.99	2.12	2.15	2.14	2.26	2.18	2.14
Laborers	1.89	2.21	2.29	2.50	2.16	2.36	1.89	2.16
Service	2.20	2.42	2.24	2.42	2.30	2.41	2.31	2.33

From C.N. Weaver, "Job Satisfaction in the United States in the 1970s" in *Journal of Applied Psychology,* 1980, *65,* 364–67. Copyright © by the American Psychological Association. Reprinted by permission.
Note: Respondents were asked to give an overall evaluation of how satisfied they were with the work they do. Mean scores were derived from the following scale: 3 (very satisfied); 2 (moderately satisfied); 1 (a little dissatisfied); or 0 (very dissatisfied).
[a]Not available for 1972 and 1973.
[b]Overall (7-year) mean rating.

was noted that although most working people said that they were satisfied in response to global items, a different picture emerged when they were asked more probing questions. Also, the level of job satisfaction depended on occupational and demographic factors. When job satisfaction data are categorized according to age, ethnicity, occupation, income, and education of the employee, some interesting differences appear, as the mean ratings in table 9.8 show. Workers most satisfied with

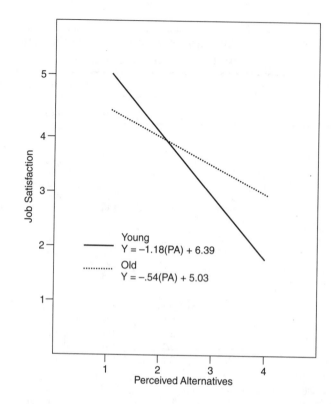

Figure 9.5 *Satisfaction of young and older employees with different perceived work alternatives. The vertical axis of the graph shows mean ratings on job satisfaction items on a 1 to 5 point scale, with larger numbers being more positive. The horizontal axis shows mean ratings of perceived alternatives on a 1 to 4 point scale, with larger numbers indicating more work alternatives. Y is the formula for the regression line. The graph shows that the inverse relationship between alternatives and satisfaction is weaker for older employees.*

From S. B. Pond and P. D. Geyer, "Employee Age as a Moderator of the Relationship Between Perceived Work Alternatives and Job Satisfaction," in Journal of Applied Psychology, 72:555. Copyright © 1987 by the American Psychological Association. Reprinted by permission.

their jobs are older, white, college-educated individuals who have more prestigious occupations and make more money (Weaver, 1980). Thus, the extent to which work satisfaction is actually showing a national decline probably depends on which groups we survey.

Age and Career Stage

The positive association between age and job satisfaction appears to be quite well established. Older workers are more satisfied than younger workers (Rhodes, 1983). Why is this? Do people's values change? Do they become more interested in working as they get older, or do they become more realistic and realize they actually have fewer options? Evidence indicates that people who perceive themselves as having fewer work alternatives are more satisfied with their jobs (Hulin, Roznowski, & Hachiya, 1985). Is there reason to believe that age moderates this relationship? That is, is the impact of having work alternatives different for older than for younger employees? If so, why should it be? One reason may be that the values of older workers have changed during their work lives, and the opportunity for other work may not affect them as strongly as it would a younger worker. This possibility was considered in surveys of white-collar and blue-collar workers, which showed that the effect of available work alternatives on satisfaction does depend on the age of a worker (Pond & Geyer, 1987, 1991). As figure 9.5 shows, there is an inverse relationship between the number of alternatives and the level of satisfaction. Having fewer alternatives is associated with higher satisfaction among both older and younger workers. However, the relationship is weaker for older. Older employees are less affected by the availability of alternatives than younger employees are.

The observed difference in job satisfaction of older and younger workers may not actually be an age difference. It may be due to changes in an employee's career that are associated with seniority or job tenure. Higher income and jobs at a higher organizational level are associated with greater satisfaction, and these are more likely to come to an employee with more seniority. This possibility that older workers are more satisfied because of their career stage has led some researchers to use career development theory to guide satisfaction research. Most career development models propose a three-stage progression of careers: an establishment stage in which the career is being developed, a middle stage in which the career is being advanced, and a final stage in which the career is maintained. In these models, it is assumed that personal needs, expectations, and values are likely to change as an individual moves through the three stages (Kacmar & Ferris, 1989). Perhaps the job evolves into a more meaningful form as the career progresses. The job itself may become intrinsically more satisfying in the final stage, and this may be the reason why people tend to be more satisfied with their work as they get older. Lee and Wilbur (1985) found evidence of this. They classified a sample according to the employee's age, career stage, and job satisfaction. They discovered that younger employees in the early career stage were more dissatisfied. They also noted that younger employees were doing jobs that had fewer intrinsically satisfying dimensions.

Some research has shown a **U-shaped relationship** between age and satisfaction; that is, workers of middle working age are less satisfied than either older or younger employees. Kacmar and Ferris (1989) studied the effects of three different aspects of time on the job—job tenure, organizational tenure, and length of time under one supervisor. They found *both* the often cited linear relationship and a U-shaped relationship between age and satisfaction, depending on the particular facet of satisfaction. In terms of satisfaction with the work itself, a linear relationship appeared in that older workers were more satisfied than younger workers. However, in the case of more extrinsic satisfaction, such as pay and supervision, a U-shaped relationship appeared in that midcareer employees were least satisfied.

Education

The decline in national job satisfaction has been attributed to the increasing numbers of highly educated young people entering the work force. Education is thought to create expectations that cannot be met by work now available to young people. To evaluate this reasoning, we first need to know whether workers are better educated now than they were in the past. Statistics reported by the U.S. Bureau of the Census (1981) indicate that the national level of education has increased steadily since the end of World War II. In 1950, 59 percent of the population had graduated from high school, and 14.8 percent had finished college. In 1980, 80 percent of the population had high school diplomas, and 25 percent had finished college. Secondly, we need to know whether people are likely to be misled about the importance of education at work? Perhaps, they are. Traditionally, we have believed that education leads to a better job. In fact, an education *is* needed for many high level and high paying jobs. Although such jobs have always been comparatively rare, in the past there were fewer educated people to take them. Now, there are more educated people entering the labor force than there are jobs available at high levels. As a result, work that does not actually require a college education is being performed by people with college degrees. That is, many employees are **educationally overqualified** for their jobs.

Lower job satisfaction among young educated workers might be a result of this trend, particularly among those who are overqualified for their jobs. Mottaz (1984) proposed that education helps to develop values for certain dimensions of work, but these dimensions may not be present in the work that is available. His research demonstrated that education can have effects on some work values. Regardless of the organizational levels of their jobs, educated employees assigned more importance to task significance and involvement than their less educated counterparts. Dissatisfaction also was more likely when these intrinsic work values were not realizable, as in a low-level job.

Gender

The large number of women in the labor force represents an important social change in North America. Between 1950 and 1988, the number of women doing paid work increased from 34 percent to 56 percent of all working-age women in the United States (U.S. Bureau of the Census, 1990). In Canada, the proportions of working women increased from 38 percent in 1970 to 57 percent in 1988 (Ministry of Supply and Services, 1990). These figures mean that just under one-half of the total labor force is female. Most working women are concentrated in just a few jobs, however. In the mid-1970s, almost 40 percent of all working women held jobs in just 10 occupations. These occupations were secretary, retail sales worker, bookkeeper, private household worker, elementary school teacher, waitress, typist, cashier, seamstress, and nurse (U.S. Department of Labor, 1975). Not many women have managerial jobs, even in female-dominated fields. For example, few women are school principals, although they teach most of the elementary school children. In the corporate world also, women hold few high-level executive positions (Gutek, 1993).

Evidence indicates that women continue to earn less money than men, and they have fewer promotional opportunities. The U.S. Commission on Civil Rights (1978) gathered data on the extent to which different groups are able to climb a financial ladder as an indication of career development and social mobility. The financial ladder is the extent to which an individual becomes increasingly prosperous through promotions and raises over his or her working life. From these data, it appears that women do not climb the same financial ladder as men. As the curves in figure 9.6 show, the financial ladder does not reach as high for women as it does for men.

Because of these differences, which indicate that work opportunities are more limited for women than for men, it is reasoned that women should be less satisfied with their jobs. However, national surveys do not show a gender difference in job satisfaction (see table 9.8). This surprising result might be explained in several ways. For example, the discrepancy hypothesis can be applied. In this, job satisfaction depends as much on what one expects as on what one receives. Perhaps women are satisfied with their jobs because they expect

Figure 9.6 *The "financial ladder" for female and minority workers compared to majority males. Notice that the curves begin at a lower level and do not reach as high for women and Mexican American men as they do for white men.*

Source: Social Indicators of Equality for Minorities and Women, 1978, p. 57. U.S. Commission on Civil Rights.

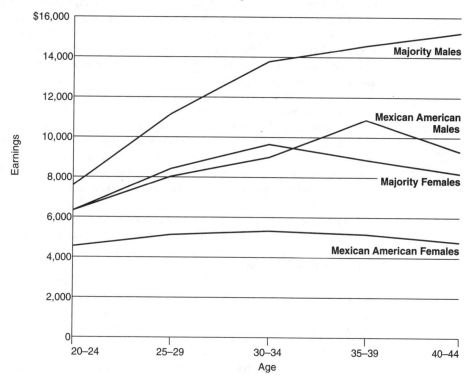

little. Working women as a group receive less from their jobs. If they do not expect much, then their satisfaction would be high. Some evidence points to this (Murry & Atkinson, 1981).

Another explanation of why men and women are equally satisfied with jobs that are quite different is that they have different values. That is, they differ in what they consider to be important at work. By this reasoning, women are satisfied because what they consider valuable is available to them through their jobs. It has been suggested that men value self-direction or autonomy and extrinsic rewards (such as pay and promotions), whereas women value interesting work and social rewards (such as good coworker and supervisor relationships). Research has not shown good evidence for this hypothesis, however. Men's and women's values actually are more similar than this hypothesis suggests (Mottaz, 1986). Over a 20-year period, Veroff et al. (1981) noted that the overall satisfaction of white-collar women declined, and what they valued in their work changed. The ego satisfaction of achievement became more important to women sampled in the later years. Fewer mentioned interesting work as the main satisfaction.

Some researchers believe that there actually are differences, but these are missed in national studies. The overall measures used in many large surveys are too rough and do not include the necessary questions to evaluate the difference between men and women. Miller and Wheeler (1992) found that although women in their sample of managers did not report that they were dissatisfied with the work they did, they were more than twice as likely to leave their jobs as male managers. This suggests that they were dissatisfied in ways that were not reported.

Certain work-related factors may operate differently for men and women. Fricko and Beehr (1992) thought that satisfaction would depend on whether a person's job is congruent with his or her interests. For example, congruence could be assumed if a person gets a job in the field that was studied in college. The researchers recognized also that jobs vary in terms of whether they are done mostly by males or mostly by females, and this might affect a person's opportunities and level of satisfaction. In their study, they looked at the congruence between employees' jobs and their college majors. They found that job satisfaction was higher when there was congruence than when employees were working in another field. The researchers also evaluated the effect of congruence when the employee was working in a field with a high concentration of either males or females. This revealed that both congruence and gender concentration affects job satisfaction. Men and women were more satisfied when their jobs were congruent with their education and when they were working in a same-sex environment. In addition, the study showed that there is a difference between men's and women's satisfaction. The most satisfied employees were men working in male-concentrated fields on jobs that were congruent with their majors in college. The least satisfied were women in female-concentrated fields working on jobs that were *not* congruent with their college majors. (This can be detected by examining the mean scores listed on the graphs in figure 9.7.)

Ethnicity and Culture

National surveys show that the overall level of job satisfaction is significantly lower for black workers than for white workers (Weaver, 1980). (Refer to table 9.8.) Beyond this statistic, very little is known about the job satisfaction of ethnic minorities. There is evidence, however, indicating that work rewards for minority members are quite limited. The U.S. Commission on Civil Rights (1978) reported that unemployment is higher for ethnic minority members. Of those who do have work, the pay is generally lower than for majority members. Thus, there appears to be similar reasons for expecting lower job satisfaction among minority employees, as for female employees.

Education is likely to affect a minority employee's job satisfaction. The U.S. Commission on Civil Rights (1978) reported that the educational level is increasing nationally among ethnic minorities. Ethnic groups differ in terms of the proportions who are college educated, but there has been an increase in all groups since 1960. If education produces high expectations for satisfying work and if these expectations are disappointed in the young person's early career experience, as they may be, given the limitations of jobs available to members of ethnic minorities, then we can expect work satisfaction to be low. Although there has been an attempt in industry to meet affirmative action goals by hiring minority members for high-level positions, educational overqualification exists to some extent (U.S. Commission on

Figure 9.7 *The effects on job satisfaction resulting from gender concentration of the job and congruence between college major and job, for female and male employees. The horizontal axes of these graphs show congruence between job and major, as indicated by low and high median scores. The vertical axes show levels of satisfaction when the job also is male or female concentrated. The graphs demonstrate that job satisfaction is higher for both women and men when they are working in a field congruent with their college majors and in a same-sex environment. As shown by the mean satisfaction scores, the most satisfied employees are men working in a male-concentrated field on congruent jobs. The least satisfied are women in female-concentrated fields on jobs not congruent with their majors.*

From M. A. Fricko and T. A. Beehr, "A Longitudinal Investigation of Interest Congruence and Gender Concentration as Predictors of Job Satisfaction" in Personnel Psychology, 45, 99–117. *Copyright © 1992 Personnel Psychology, Inc. Reprinted by permission.*

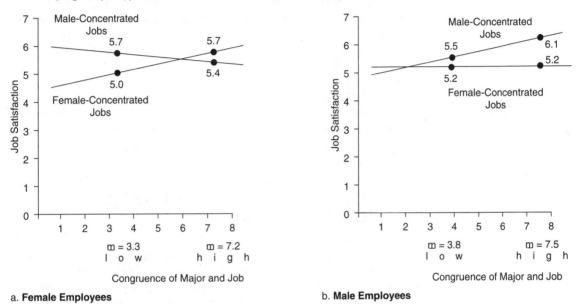

a. **Female Employees**   b. **Male Employees**

Civil Rights, 1978). Specific research has not been done on this question, however, we might speculate that overqualification reduces the level of satisfaction of young workers of all ethnic groups.

If there are individual, group, and subcultural differences in job satisfaction, we may also expect differences among national groups. There is evidence that work is not done the same everywhere. This means that the satisfaction of workers may vary between countries.

Cross-cultural differences in job satisfaction have been reported that are related to the degree of individualism-collectivism. Collectivistic countries, such as Singapore, are oriented toward the group. People are more involved with each other than in individualistic societies, such as the United States, in which individual autonomy is valued. This cultural difference has been proposed to affect job satisfaction, particularly satisfaction with the social aspects of the job. Specifically, it is hypothesized that collectivists are more likely to show high job satisfaction in these areas than individualists. Hui, Yee, and Eastman (1995) evaluated this hypothesis in an analysis of data on employees in 14 different countries. They confirmed the hypothesized relationship. That is, to the extent that a country was collectivistic, the employees were more satisfied with their interpersonal work relationships.

Personal and demographic differences have been studied to see if they explain the differences in job satisfaction. Negative affectivity is an attribute that has been studied. People with high negative affectivity are less satisfied with their jobs.

Demographic factors that affect job satisfaction are age, education, gender, ethnicity, and culture. Older workers are more satisfied than younger workers. This may be due to differences in career progress rather than to age. Education has an effect, possibly because people believe that education will get them better jobs, when in reality it may lead simply to their being overqualified for the jobs available.

Women's work opportunities are more limited than men's. However, according to national surveys, they are no more dissatisfied with their jobs than men are. Researchers have speculated on why this is so. Maybe it is because they expect little or because they get what they want from a job. However, they may be more dissatisfied than they seem. Some research shows that women are dissatisfied in certain jobs, although they may not express it as men do.

THE RELATIONSHIP OF JOB SATISFACTION TO OTHER BEHAVIORS

You might ask why we are interested in job satisfaction. Who cares if people like their jobs? Psychologists consider the quality of life to be important. The study of job satisfaction is one approach to learning about the quality of life. Because we spend so much time at work, many of us believe it ought to be quality time. There are other reasons for studying job satisfaction. For the past 50 years, managers and I/O psychologists alike have assumed that job satisfaction will have important implications for the organization's success. Although research has not revealed the simple, direct relationship that was expected, there has been enough evidence to maintain the belief that satisfaction of employees will affect organizational outcomes. For example, performance and behaviors related to citizenship, such as absenteeism, may be affected.

Satisfaction and Productivity

It seems almost common sense to say that satisfied workers are more productive and that productivity problems are solved by interventions that increase worker satisfaction. Research, however, has failed to show that increasing satisfaction improves performance. Analytical reviews of the early research literature have concluded that there is only a negligible relationship between these variables (Brayfield & Crockett, 1955). Evaluation of later research by means of meta-analysis similarly has indicated that the true correlation is low (Iaffaldano & Muchinsky, 1985).

Currently, there is interest in discovering why better evidence of a relationship between these two variables does not exist. Somehow, it just seems unbelievable that job performance is not related to job attitudes. Some theorists (Lawler & Porter, 1967; Locke, 1970) have suggested that we are looking at the relationship in the wrong way. They proposed that satisfaction does not bring about productivity; rather, productivity causes satisfaction. As shown in figure 9.8, in this theoretical

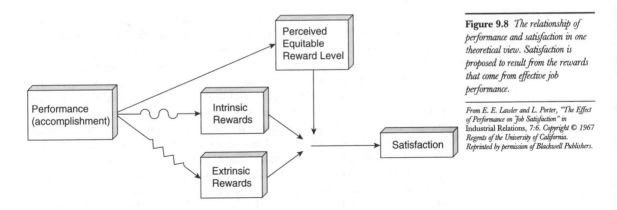

Figure 9.8 *The relationship of performance and satisfaction in one theoretical view. Satisfaction is proposed to result from the rewards that come from effective job performance.*

From E. E. Lawler and L. Porter, "The Effect of Performance on Job Satisfaction" in Industrial Relations, 7:6. *Copyright © 1967 Regents of the University of California. Reprinted by permission of Blackwell Publishers.*

view, satisfaction results from rewards inherent in effective work performance (Lawler & Porter, 1967). The relationship between the two variables is viewed as complex, indirect, and dependent on other personal and situational variables. Under certain conditions, we can expect satisfaction and productivity to be positively associated but not in all situations. In the typical correlational study, these "conditions" are not taken into account; therefore, a low overall correlation is likely to result. Lawler and Porter (1967) suggested two important conditions: Performance must be perceived as instrumental in obtaining rewards, and rewards must be perceived as fair. The results of a lab study gave some support to these predictions. Correlations between performance level and satisfaction were found to be positive when subjects were rewarded appropriately (good performers got a bonus) and negative when they were rewarded inappropriately (poor performers got a bonus) (Cherrington, Reitz, & Scott, 1971).

Personal variables have been proposed to moderate the relationship between satisfaction and performance. For example, Korman (1970) suggested that the individual's level of self-esteem determines the association between satisfaction and performance. That is, self-esteem should promote satisfaction when performance is effective and dissatisfaction when it is not. Although some researchers have reported support for this prediction (Jacobs & Solomon, 1977), others have found that esteem predicts performance and satisfaction directly instead of moderating the relationship between them (Tharenou & Harker, 1984).

Clearly, the idea that satisfaction and productivity are related continues to intrigue us. However, whatever association does exist between these variables is not likely to be as simple and direct as some organizational program designers have been hoping.

Satisfaction and Withdrawal Behavior

Managers are concerned about **employee withdrawal** because it is costly. When people are absent from their jobs, they are not producing, and they may have to be paid for the time they take. When they quit, replacements must be hired and trained. In 1978, Steers and Rhodes estimated that absenteeism costs American industry $26 billion a year. Possibly something could be done about absence and turnover if we could find out the reason for employee withdrawal.

A popular assumption is that job dissatisfaction leads to withdrawal from work. Early research tended to support this position (Brayfield & Crockett, 1955). Dissatisfied workers were somewhat more likely to be absent or to quit than satisfied workers. Later analysis questioned the nature of this relationship, particularly about whether quitting was the same kind of withdrawal as absenteeism and tardiness (Steers & Rhodes, 1978). Porter and Steers (1973) proposed that these are qualitatively different. They said that absenteeism is a spontaneous behavior and probably not due to dissatisfaction. On the other hand, quitting is serious, usually not decided on the spur of the moment, and more likely to reflect dissatisfaction. Thus, researchers should treat turnover and absenteeism as different variables, and recent research has been directed in this way. Incidentally, there are other types of withdrawal from work that might relate to job satisfaction. The use of alcohol and drugs represents a form of withdrawal, as does the kind of idleness characteristic of employees who are said to have "retired on the job."

Absenteeism

In earlier research, the relationship between satisfaction and absenteeism did not appear to be very strong (Muchinsky, 1977). It seemed, however, that important factors were not being taken into account, such as the different components of satisfaction (Terborg et al., 1982). Scott and Taylor (1985) reviewed the research by means of a meta-analysis and concluded that the measures are too general. They thought a stronger relationship could be shown if the frequency and duration of absence were evaluated according to the particular facet of job satisfaction. They found absence frequency to be more strongly related to overall satisfaction, satisfaction with coworkers, and satisfaction with the work itself. Similarly, in another review, Hackett (1989) concluded that individuals who are dissatisfied with the work itself are absent more frequently; and those who are dissatisfied with the job as a whole stay absent longer. Hackett also found an interesting moderator—sex of the employee. Dissatisfaction was more likely to be manifested in absenteeism in women. Hackett discussed this finding in terms of what women might be doing away from work, such as domestic chores. Because there are gender differences in the work experience, however, the greater absenteeism of women might result from dissatisfaction with the work itself. The monotony experienced in doing a repetitive job has been found to decrease job satisfaction and to increase psychological distress in both men and women, and to increase the women's use of sick leave (Melamed, Ben-Avi, Luz, & Green, 1995). Thus, it appears from this research that men and women manifest their dissatisfaction differently; women tend to withdraw by being absent.

Turnover

Traditionally, turnover has been viewed as problematic to organizations. However, it has been pointed out that this is not necessarily so (Dalton, Krackhardt, & Porter, 1981; Mobley, 1982). Some turnover actually may be functional and worth the price the organization must pay. With **functional turnover,** the organization has an opportunity to replace poor performers who quit with those who will perform well. **Dysfunctional turnover** is costly to the organization because good performers quit. An important question for the organization is whether its turnover rate is due to good performers leaving. In general, it looks as if most turnover is func-

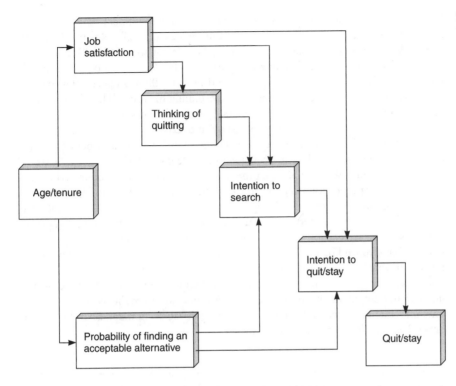

Figure 9.9 *A model of the turnover decision process showing the involvement of job satisfaction. Deciding to quit one's job is viewed as a deliberate cognitive process involving several steps. The process is influenced both by job satisfaction and by the perceived availability of other jobs.*

tional. In their analysis of the research, McEvoy and Cascio (1987) found a negative relationship between turnover and performance. That is, there is more turnover among poor performers.

One factor that may determine an individual's decision to quit is the availability of other jobs, and this depends on the general level of unemployment. Some theorists have considered the condition of the job market. For example, Mobley, Horner, and Hollingworth (1978) proposed a theoretical model that included this variable. Deciding to quit one's job, in their view, is a deliberate cognitive process involving several steps, as shown in figure 9.9. The intention to search for another job is a midrange step in this process influenced both by the level of satisfaction and by the probability of finding an acceptable alternative. Researchers have addressed the question of alternatives in turnover decisions. According to Muchinsky and Morrow (1980), a person is more likely to quit a job he or she dislikes when there are plenty of jobs available than when jobs are hard to find. A meta-analysis of research on satisfaction and turnover provided support for this idea. Dissatisfaction was more predictive of turnover during times of full employment (Carsten & Spector, 1987). Gerhart (1990) further explained this process: A person may *perceive* many work alternatives to exist and decide to search for another job, but if there actually are limited alternatives, this fact can prevent the person from leaving.

Job satisfaction has been found to have a strong negative impact on managers' decisions to search for another job. However, other factors, such as organizational commitment, also affect turnover intentions (Bretz, Boudreau & Judge, 1994;

Naumann, 1993). Job satisfaction and organizational commitment appear to enter into both men's and women's decisions to quit or stay on a job (Rosin & Korabik, 1995). When the person is satisfied and committed, he or she is more likely to stay.

Performance level is likely to figure into the decision to quit or stay, although exactly *how* is not clear. Spencer and Steers (1981) proposed that performance would interact with satisfaction in determining turnover. They found that it did but only in the case of poor performers. Poor performers who were dissatisfied were more likely to quit. Similarly, McEvoy and Cascio (1987) reported that the national level of employment affected turnover rates for good and poor performers, but the effect was odd. They concluded that "either good performers leave in greater proportions than usual when the job market improves, or poor performers leave in greater proportions than usual when the job market worsens" (p. 759).

So, how does this all add up? There appear to be several important variables in determining turnover: performance level, national employment, and job attitudes, such as satisfaction and organizational commitment. They form a complex relationship. Depending on the level of national employment, more poor performers and dissatisfied uncommitted employees leave their jobs. These apparently are not always the same people, however. Dissatisfied employees tend to leave during times of full employment, whereas poor performers are more likely to leave when unemployment is high. Performance level and job satisfaction appear to be two independent reasons why people leave their jobs.

*M*ain *P*oints

People say that satisfied workers are more productive. They also say that workers do not quit if a job is satisfying nor are they often absent from work. Are these truths?

Researchers have not found that job satisfaction helps productivity much, but they may have been going about it in the wrong way. The common assumption—that satisfaction causes productivity, may be wrong. Perhaps it is productivity that brings about satisfaction.

Employee withdrawal, which includes absenteeism and turnover, is associated with job dissatisfaction. The frequency of absence is affected by satisfaction with the work itself. Monotonous jobs lead to job dissatisfaction of both men and women. Women are more likely to be absent from such jobs.

What makes a person decide to quit a job? Job satisfaction and other available jobs. When there are lots of jobs available, a dissatisfied employee is more likely to quit. Other factors are important, though, such as organizational commitment and performance levels. Good performers who are satisfied with their jobs and committed to the organization do not quit, especially when unemployment is high.

CHAPTER SUMMARY

Job satisfaction is a job attitude with cognitive, emotional, and behavioral elements and is thought to affect various aspects of work behavior. Job satisfaction has been included in work motivation theories. Other theories focus directly on job satisfaction. Locke's value discrepancy theory proposes that satisfaction is due to the extent to which there is a discrepancy between what is desired of important job factors and what is received. Lawler's facet theory also considers the discrepancy between what is expected for a job facet and what is received. Expectations are based on perceptions of fairness relative to what others receive. With the social influence hypothesis, a third way in which job satisfaction can be explained, satisfaction results from perceiving others' satisfaction. Finally, Landy's opponent process theory emphasizes the emotional element. Levels of job satisfaction are expected to fluctuate because of changes in stimuli and internal homeostatic processes.

To measure job satisfaction, several standardized instruments are available. The JDI contains items that describe and evaluate satisfaction with different job factors; six subscale scores can be obtained. A Likert scale is used in the MSQ to collect ratings of respondent feelings. The long form has 100 items on 20 job factors. Another questionnaire, the NSQ, contains questions about expectations and perceptions of need fulfillment on the job. Drawings of faces are used in the Faces Scale to depict specific levels of emotional affect and provide a single-item measure of satisfaction.

Job satisfaction is a complex construct, with components relating to different aspects of the job, such as pay, supervision, and the work itself. To understand this construct, we need to discover the nature of an employee's satisfaction with the job as a whole and with these components. Hackman and Oldham's job characteristics model, and the associated Job Diagnostic Survey instrument, provide a way to understand what is satisfying about the work itself. Currently, there is much interest in learning about pay satisfaction. The Pay Satisfaction Questionnaire has been developed for this purpose.

People differ in the satisfaction they derive from their jobs. The effects of personal and demographic variables have been noted. A great deal of research has addressed gender differences. Age and educational differences have been observed. Differences in ethnicity and cultural background can be expected.

Over the course of decades of study, the relationship of job satisfaction to other work behaviors has been found to be much more complex than was first thought. The effect of satisfaction on productivity is not clear. Correlations between the two are not strong, although this may be because important job and person variables are not being considered. Satisfaction affects employee withdrawal, specifically absenteeism and turnover but apparently not by the same process. Other variables, such as organizational commitment, also enter into the relationship.

STUDY QUESTIONS

1) Why should we care about job satisfaction?

2) What is job satisfaction, and how is it different from other job attitudes? How is job satisfaction related to motivation?

3) What is the discrepancy hypothesis?

4) Does "getting more than one wants" lead to dissatisfaction according to Locke's and Lawler's theories?

5) How does job satisfaction develop according to the social influence hypothesis?

6) What are the opponent processes of emotion, and how do they determine the level of job satisfaction, according to Landy?

7) How does one go about developing a job satisfaction questionnaire? What are some problems in establishing the reliability and validity of such measures?

8) Distinguish the JDI, MSQ, NSQ, and Faces Scale. How is the PSQ different from these? What is the Job Diagnostic Survey used for?

9) What does it mean to say that one is satisfied with one's *work*? How does the Job Characteristics Model help to answer this question?

10) Are high-paid employees more satisfied with their jobs? What else is involved in pay satisfaction other than wages?

11) To what extent are attitudes about a supervisor important in job satisfaction?

12) Who is satisfied with their job and who is not?

13) Does being satisfied with the job make a person work harder?

14) What is the effect of job satisfaction on employee withdrawal? What determines whether an employee will search for another job?

CONSIDER THIS

ISSUE

Does work contribute anything to the quality of life in general other than provide enough money for nonwork enjoyment? Does working increase life satisfaction, or is it simply the price we pay to have evenings and weekends to ourselves? If job satisfaction and life satisfaction are related, what is the nature of their relationship? A few people have tried to answer these questions. One indication of life satisfaction is a high level of psychological health, and this also is associated with job satisfaction (Gechman & Weiner, 1975). Unemployment can produce psychological symptoms that clear up when the person goes back to work (Warr, 1983).

We can speculate on how job and life satisfaction are related. Some people have done this. According to a *compensation hypothesis,* a person makes up for job dissatisfaction by increasing nonwork satisfactions. In this way, dreary work-days are made tolerable by having fun during time off. The *spillover hypothesis* says that how you feel about your job generalizes to your life outside of work. This means that a satisfying job can make life more satisfying. It also suggests that a disliked job can cast a shadow over life in general. From a third perspective, called the *segmentation hypothesis,* work and nonwork satisfactions are independent and do not directly affect one another.

Some researchers have tried to find out which view best describes people's actual experience. However, it seems that there are people for whom each is true (Judge & Watanabe, 1994; Kabanoff, 1980).

How is job satisfaction related to life satisfaction in your experience? Do you compensate for dissatisfaction in one realm with satisfying activity in the other? Is there a spillover from work into your personal life? Are job satisfaction and life satisfaction separate processes altogether?

what's in this chapter?

There's quite a history of research on leadership. Scientists from multiple disciplines have studied the topic, and much is known about who the leaders are, how they lead, and what groups do in response.

In this chapter, you will learn about the various ways theorists have described leadership—as a personal trait, as a feature of a work role, and as a means of giving and getting social rewards. Some theorists tell you how to develop leadership skills. Some even have developed leadership training programs for this purpose.

In reality, in this country and in others, positions of leadership are not open to everyone. Women and members of ethnic minorities tradition-ally have had limited access to managerial work in the United States.

Prior to the 1960s, most leadership research focused on white men. Since that time, there has been increasing interest in the experiences of women and ethnic minorities in leadership positions.

Contents

The leader mobilizes the group by dealing first with his lieutenants. It was customary for the Millers [a street corner gang] to go bowling every Saturday night. One Saturday, Sam [the leader] had no money, so he set out to persuade the boys to do something else. Later he explained " . . . I had to show the boys that it would be in their own interests to come with me—that each one of them would benefit. But I knew I only had to convince two of the fellows. If they start to do something, the other boys will say to themselves, 'If Joe does it—or if Chichi does it—it must be a good thing for us too.' I told Joe and Chichi what the idea was, and I got them to come with me. I didn't pay no attention to the others. When Joe and Chichi came, all the other boys came along too."

W. F. Whyte

As old as it is, Whyte's (1937) discussion of the internal interactions of youth gangs highlights some of today's important leadership issues and methods. For one, observation of natural groups and interviews with leaders and members are still common methods of studying leadership behavior. A variety of groups, ranging from children's sports teams to executive planning groups, are studied this way. Whyte's study also focused on informal or emergent leadership, which continues to interest researchers. Finally, several themes appeared in Whyte's study that showed the nature of the leader's role. The leader was important in maintaining the gang's integrity. His role included both group maintenance and task-oriented behavior. These are themes in today's leadership research.

Who are the leaders at work? Suppose you interview someone and ask him or her to name the leaders at the workplace. Any number of individuals might be mentioned: the owner of the business, a manager, a first line supervisor, or a nonmanagerial coworker. Your respondent might say, on second thought, that some of these people are not really leaders but simply fill a managerial position. The point is, leadership at work can be described in terms of both **designated leadership,** in which a formal leader is appointed or elected, and **emergent leadership,** in which someone acts as a leader without having a formal leadership position.

Supervisory, managerial, and executive jobs all include leadership responsibilities. However, management should not be equated with leadership. For one thing, managerial jobs involve other work responsibilities as well as leadership. In addition, not all managers carry out their leadership responsibilities very well. Sometimes an individual occupies a leadership position but shows very little leadership behavior.

Researching Leadership

In previous chapters, I have noted that I/O psychologists often team up with people in other areas of psychology and in other disciplines to learn about work behavior. In this chapter, I discuss another interdisciplinary issue. Leadership has long been studied by social psychologists. Political scientists, military scientists, and sociologists focus on the broader aspects of leadership. Also, some of the recent theory and research on managerial leadership has come from management and administrative science. Leadership, apparently, is on everybody's mind.

Unlike some issues discussed in previous chapters, leadership research is driven by theory. That is, research is done largely to test hypotheses drawn from one or another of the many available theories. Most of this research relies on surveys in which leaders are asked about themselves or subordinates are asked about their supervisors. Responses to survey items are correlated with each other or with other measures, such as ratings of leader effectiveness. The trouble with this type of correlational study of leadership is the same as when questionnaires are used to study group work (see chapter 12). That is, survey procedures ask a respondent to provide data from memory about an interaction process that he or she may not have understood in the first place. A more insidious problem is that questionnaire assessments of leader behavior probably are biased by respondents' ideas about how a good leader *should* behave (Phillips & Lord, 1981). Because of these problems, some researchers have abandoned the questionnaire study in favor of more qualitative research, such as process observation and semistructured interview techniques (e.g., Bryman et al., 1988). These methods put the researcher in more direct contact with the leader. However, process observation and interviews also have limitations. They tend to be subjective and can contain observer biases (Yukl, 1989).

English has many terms for leadership. For example, a leader can be referred to as a director, guide, head, chief, manager, boss, supervisor, instructor, and coach. Leadership theory and research provide us with many, many definitions. Stogdill (1974) noted that we have almost as many definitions of leadership as we have people who write about it. Briefly, leadership has been defined as (1) a personal attribute, (2) a set of behaviors, and (3) a group characteristic. The personal attribute has been described as a personality trait and as a characteristic that relates to social power. As a set of behaviors, leadership has been defined as playing the role, as providing group structure, and as motivating a group toward its goal. As a group characteristic, leadership has been said to be the focus of a group's action, an instrument of the group's goal achievement, and a result of the group's interaction. Stogdill (1974) categorized these definitions into 11 groups. Table 10.1 provides samples. Clearly, there has been a lot of thinking on this subject, yet we do not seem to be resolving our thoughts into a very clear image of leadership. Stogdill's summary of definitions indicated that most of the basic views of leadership present today had published proponents in the 1920s and 1930s. What is the point of this? Bass (1981) said that it is like putting "old wine into new bottles." Instead of thinking of these definitions as right or wrong, Yukl (1989) suggested that we consider them as different perspectives on a highly complex pattern of behavior. Doing so allows us to outline what a leader does. Let us take this advice and define **leadership** as a pattern of behavior in group interaction that affects the group's life and goal achievement. Such a definition is useful in that it does not lock us into thinking of leadership as a specific action that only designated leaders can do. Also, it describes leadership as including two-way influence. That is, the group leader can change the member's behavior, but the member can change the leader's behavior as well.

Table 10.1

Leadership as a Personal Attribute of the Leader

1. *It is an aspect of personality.*
    Leaders have many positive personality traits (1927).
    Leaders have traits that are useful in getting others to perform tasks (1929).

2. *It is the ability to get compliance.*
    Leaders are able to handle members (1921).
    Leaders guide and direct other people (1958).

3. *It is social influence.*
    Leaders cause others to change their conduct (1929).
    Leaders successfully cause change in others (1961).

4. *It is persuasion.*
    Leaders persuade and inspire instead of coerce (1928).
    Leaders influence by persuasion or example (1942).

5. *It is social power.*
    Leaders control the interaction process (1948).
    Leaders have more power than members (1958).

Leadership as Leading Behavior

1. *It is behavior that performs a leadership function.*
    Leaders act in ways that are recognized as being leadership behavior (1953).
    Leaders direct and coordinate work (1967).

2. *It is a behavioral role.*
    Leaders are lifted to their roles by members (1944).
    Leaders play roles defined by reciprocal expectations of leaders and members (1956).

3. *It is behavior that initiates structure.*
    Leaders organize situations (1936).
    Leaders initiate and maintain structure (1959).

Leadership as a Characteristic of Groups

1. *It is the center or focus of group action.*
    Leaders are the center of social movements (1902).
    Leaders focus and release group energy (1927).

2. *It is an instrument of goal achievement.*
    Leaders move the group toward its objective (1928).
    Leaders motivate their groups toward goals (1962).

3. *It is an effect of group interaction.*
    Leaders emerge when groups work on goals (1929).
    Leaders develop through group interaction (1935).

Based on R.M. Stogdill, *Handbook of Leadership: A Survey of Theory and Research.* Copyright © 1974 The Free Press, New York.

LEADERSHIP AS A PERSONAL CHARACTERISTIC

One theory of leadership used to some extent by most people is the **"great man" theory.** This informal theory is rooted in ancient thought and considered seriously in contemporary work. It provides the foundation for the trait and charismatic theories of leadership, which are discussed in the following sections. Quite simply, the "great man" theory says that great leaders are great people. They are leaders because they have abilities and characteristics that cause them to emerge as leaders. Their personal attributes make them appealing to followers. They are the Winston Churchills and John Kennedys of the world.

This is a **univariate theory** in that only one variable is thought important—the personal attributes of the leader. The ""great man" theory does not really specify the characteristics of the great leader. However, it implies that if we knew what they are, we could use them to identify potential leaders. For example, a measure of charismatic behavior might be used to select the right people for leadership positions (Waldman, Bass, & Yammarino, 1990).

The great man theory also implies that leadership is a scarce resource. Apparently, the born leader is not born very often. The international scene is periodically evaluated by some news analyst, and invariably it is discovered that world leaders are in short supply. What can we do about this sorry state of affairs? If leaders are born leaders, as the "great man" theory suggests, then we cannot easily make leaders out of people who were not born that way, and leadership training probably would be a waste of time. Of course, this is a big "if "; leadership may not be such a stable or rare attribute.

Leadership as a Trait

Following directly in the path of the "great man" theory is trait theory. Trait theorists wanted to determine the personal attributes that distinguish leaders from nonleaders, to make it easier to recognize a leader. A broad range of attributes was studied, including (1) demographic factors, such as age, appearance, and socioeconomic status; (2) ability factors, such as scholastic aptitude, practical knowledge, insight, and verbal fluency; and (3) character and personality traits, such as adaptability, introversion/extroversion, dominance, and emotional control. To conduct trait research, some psychologists used a type of *subject-matter expert* panel in which business executives and other supposedly knowledgeable people were asked to identify the traits of a successful leader. Other researchers collected case histories of individuals in high-level positions. Some used **sociometry,** a specialized survey technique, to get information about emerging group leaders (Stogdill, 1948).

The only clear evidence in support of the theory that came from this research related to the leader's capacity, achievement, responsibility, participation, and status. That is, compared to the average group member, the leader has higher intelligence and knows how to get things done. The leader shows more initiative and is more dependable, active, and participative. There was some indication that leaders also are more self-confident, cooperative, and adaptable.

By mid-century, trait theory research was taking a new direction. Researchers were less interested in personality traits and more interested in leader motivation and skill. In addition, they wanted to find out how leader attributes affected group performance. Many studies were being done in work settings. The new studies looked at the leader's initiative, responsibility, task orientation, and need for achievement. They showed that leaders are different from group members in some ways. Leaders were found to be more interested in taking responsibility, pursuing work goals, and getting work done. They were also more persuasive and more willing to accept the consequences of their decisions (Bass, 1981).

The new lines of trait theory research were not able to support a univariate theory of leadership. Rather, over and over again, leader personality traits appeared only as part of a behavioral pattern that included situational variables. Most researchers thought that one important situational variable was the work group's task. For example, a clearly defined and well-structured work project seemed to require a different style of leadership than an ambiguous project involving creative thought. Other situational variables included attributes of group members and aspects of the organization, such as availability of authority. Any of these might be expected to have an impact on the behavior of a leader. The trait research also implied that situational variables may determine the kind of leadership needed (Yukl, 1989). For example, in certain situations, such as when a group needs to do creative work, a good leader's behavior should be moderate. In other situations, the expression of one trait should be balanced by the expression of another. Being task oriented can be balanced by showing concern about how the group is operating. Clearly, it was becoming apparent that the particular characteristics required of a leader depend on situational demands. This evidence formed a root of the situational theories of leadership, which I discuss later in the chapter.

Leadership as a Behavioral Style

The study of traits also led to an expansion of the trait viewpoint. From a new angle, leadership was seen as a *style* of behavior that might reflect several underlying traits. The effectiveness of a leader's style was thought likely to depend on situational factors, such as who the followers were. At the time, during the late 1930s, analysis of world events were bringing many to question whether what happened in Nazi Germany could happen anywhere else given similar leadership. Possibly a particular leadership style could cause followers to behave in ways that other styles did not. The question was, could another leader with Hitler's style cause another Nazi Germany?

In a classic study of leadership, Lewin, Lippitt, and White (1939) proposed to find out whether different group behaviors resulted from different styles of leader behavior. They began by defining the task behaviors that appeared to characterize three known styles: **autocratic, democratic,** and **laissez-faire leadership.** As shown in table 10.2, behaviors that were thought to distinguish leader styles concerned a group's division of labor, work assignments, policy making, and general supervision. Experimental assistants were trained to act out the behavior of each style in leading a group. For example, in playing the part of the autocratic leader, the assistant made all the decisions for the group. He told them what to do and when to do it. This study was important in two ways. First, because the experimental assistants were not known leaders, the study showed that people could be trained in leadership. Therefore, although there might be born leaders, ordinary people could become leaders. Second, the study found that the leader's style did affect the group. You might be surprised to learn that productivity was higher in groups led by an autocratic leader than in groups led by democratic or laissez-faire leaders. However, there was also more discontent in the autocratic leaders' groups. In the democratic groups, work interest was higher and members were more cooperative. As you might expect, nothing much got done in the laissez-faire groups.

Table 10.2	Behavior of Autocratic, Democratic, and Laissez-Faire Leaders
Autocratic Leaders:	Determine all group policy Dictate work techniques and activities one step at a time Assign tasks and work partners Do not participate in the work, except to demonstrate Give "personal" praise and criticism
Democratic Leaders:	Encourage group decision making on policy Explain overall plans and general activities Allow the group to divide tasks and choose work partners Participate, as a member, in the group's work Act objectively in praise and criticism
Laissez-faire Leaders:	Allow the group complete freedom in deciding policy Provide materials and instructions when requested; otherwise take no part in work discussion Do not participate in division of labor Give no appraisal unless requested

Based on K. Lewin, R. Lippitt, and R. K. White, "Patterns of Aggressive Behavior in Experimentally Created Social Climates" in *Journal of Social Psychology,* 10: 271–301. Copyright © 1939 Heldref Publications, Washington, D.C.

Employee-Oriented and Production-Oriented Behavior

Interest in the leader's behavioral style has continued, although we have gone beyond the global concepts of autocratic and democratic leadership. The work of Likert (1961, 1967) and his colleagues at the University of Michigan made an important contribution to our understanding of leadership styles. The Michigan studies established that a leader's style of behavior has identifiable effects on group performance. In one of these studies, the researchers interviewed leaders and members of work groups that were known to be either high or low in productivity. Analysis of the interviews revealed stable differences between the leaders of these groups. Basically, differences reflected the degree to which the leader was personally oriented toward the employees or production. **Employee-oriented leaders** are interested in the group's members. **Production-oriented leaders** are concerned mainly with getting the job done. In this study, leaders of the most productive groups were more employee oriented (Katz, Maccoby, & Morse, 1950). As this type of work continued, researchers became increasingly convinced that the employee-oriented or democratic style would have better effects on a group in the long run. Although autocratic leadership might show short-term improvements in productivity, the effects were thought to be detrimental overall (Likert, 1977).

Consideration and Initiating Structure

Another major research program that focused on leader behavior was undertaken at Ohio State University. From 1946 through the mid-1950s, researchers at Ohio State did surveys and observational studies to try to answer what had become the big question: What exactly do leaders do when they lead? The researchers developed more than 1,800 items to describe different aspects of leader behavior. These items came from people in leadership positions and from members of work groups in numerous organizations. The items referred to such actions as communicating, showing initiative, evaluating, and taking charge (Hemphill, 1949).

Analysis of these surveys resulted in the identification of two basic leadership constructs. The constructs were labeled **consideration** and **initiating structure** (Fleishman, 1967; Halpin & Winer, 1957). Since then, these constructs have been evaluated many times and found to represent reliable aspects of leader behavior. Structuring is production-oriented or task-related behavior, and it includes such behaviors as setting work goals, maintaining standards, defining work procedures, and scheduling activities. In contrast, consideration reflects a leader's interests in group members. A considerate leader cares about members' feelings, respects their ideas, and trusts them.

Leadership measures were developed out of the Ohio State studies. The **Leader Behavior Description Questionnaire (LBDQ)** is used to gather information from group members. Respondents rate items according to how they perceive their leader to behave (Hemphill & Coons, 1957). A similar form, the **Supervisory Behavior Description Questionnaire (SBDQ)** is specifically for leadership in the work setting (Fleishman, 1953). This instrument includes more items referring to initiating structure, particularly with respect to work production. The **Leadership Opinion Questionnaire (LOQ)** was developed for gathering data directly from leaders (Fleishman, 1957). Respondents answer questions about their leadership role and describe how they think a leader should behave. These three instruments give somewhat different evaluations of leadership behavior and make it possible to get information from different informants.

Leader Behavior: A Two-Factor Concept

The findings of the Michigan and Ohio State studies have had an important impact on the way leadership is now conceptualized. In the present way of thinking, leadership behavior falls into one of two categories usually considered as opposites: (1) structuring, autocratic, and production oriented; or (2) considerate, democratic, and people oriented.

One interesting question concerns the relationship between these leader behaviors. It might be that they are true opposites and are endpoints of a single dimension. If so, leaders would tend toward one style or the other. On the other hand, it might be that structuring and consideration are actually different dimensions. If so, a leader could show variable levels of each. He or she might be high on both, low on both, or high on one and low on the other. Currently, the accepted view is that structuring and consideration are different dimensions, and that leaders can exhibit both types of behavior. Depending on a work group's needs, a capable leader may show high levels of both types of behavior, by structuring work tasks and by being considerate of members (see figure 10.1).

Blake and Mouton's (1985) theoretical work shows how leadership behavior can be conceptualized as involving two separate dimensions. In their model, leadership style is couched in terms of concern for people and concern for production. (These are similar to consideration and initiating structure.) Basically, these leadership behaviors are identified as distinct dimensions, and leaders are proposed to vary from low to high on each. Certain styles of behavior are said to

result when the levels of these dimensions are considered (Blake & McCanse, 1991). For example, in the style labeled *team management,* the leader scores high on both dimensions; he or she has an equally high concern for production and people. Another style in which these behaviors are balanced but at a moderate level is termed *middle-of-the-road management.* Other leadership styles emphasize one but not both dimensions. The *country club management style* is largely a people-oriented style. In the *authority-compliance style,* the leader focuses on production issues.

Are both production-oriented and employee-oriented behaviors actually required of a group's leader? Some models, such as Blake and Mouton's, propose that they are. However, other theory and research suggest that group members as well as the leader can contribute to the leadership needs of a group. You will learn in chapter 12 that attention must be given to a group's tasks and to its manner of interacting in order for the group to work effectively. Groups benefit from these behaviors when members as well as leaders exhibit them. Thus, the most appropriate leader behavior may actually depend on the group. If a group contains members who can provide one of these necessities, then the best behavior for the leader might be to provide the other.

Charismatic Leadership

Several decades of research have shown leaders to be mortal human beings who make use of ordinary resources to help ordinary people accomplish sometimes spectacular but more often ordinary things. Still, we cannot let go of the idea that a true leader is one who accomplishes extraordinary feats. Some theories use the concept of *charisma* to describe how people accomplish important work in an organization (Bass, 1985; House, 1977). Two important assumptions are made in the charisma perspective. One is that leadership is essential in getting anything done. It is assumed that nothing much will be accomplished by simply giving a group some resources and turning it loose to do a job. Rather, they need a leader. The second assumption is that a particular kind of leader is needed, especially when the organization must go into previously uncharted territory. They need a charismatic leader. (Of course, these are questionable assumptions.)

What is the **charismatic leader** like? According to theorists who use this concept, a charismatic leader is perceived by followers as a hero who has a gift (Bass, 1985). House (1977) described the charismatic leader as having an extraordinary effect on followers. Followers believe in and are inspired by the leader's mission.

How does the charismatic leader become so influential? Behling and McFillen (1996) found agreement among theorists that the charismatic leader's influence is due to certain personal characteristics. The charismatic leader projects high self-confidence, and dramatizes his or her mission. This leader displays empathy and uses interpersonal skills to give followers a sense of competency and empowerment. Sankowsky (1995) sounded a note of caution, however. He observed that the charismatic may be narcissistic (or overly self-important) and pointed out that this combination of traits can result in a leader who misapprehends business reality and leads the organization into failure.

By itself, the concept of charisma has not received much research attention. However, it is employed as a trait in another recent theory, that of transformational leadership. The research done on transformational leadership indicates that leaders benefit by having a vision that they can convey to their followers (Yukl, 1989). I examine transformational leadership in more detail later.

*M*ain *P*oints

Trait theorists view leadership as a personal characteristic of the leader: A leader is able to lead because of personality and ability traits. Early research attempted to identify the traits of the great leader, without a lot of success. Instead, leadership seemed more clearly to come from the person's behavioral style, and autocratic and democratic behavioral styles were identified and described. A major research undertaking to explore differences in style resulted in the discovery of two important concepts: consideration and initiating structure. These and similar terms are used today to describe leader behavior from many different perspectives.

Traits remain appealing to some theorists. Charisma is one that currently is attracting attention. It is offered as an explanation for visionary leaders in the organization.

LEADERSHIP AS A WORK ROLE RELATIONSHIP

At first, it did not occur to anyone that a leader's situation would make any difference. A leader was a leader no matter what. Then, some situational contingencies were discovered. Organizational and group variables appeared to affect leadership in several ways. One, they might cause changes in the leader's behavior. Two, they might determine whether the leader is able to get a group to perform. Three, they might create conditions that require different leadership behaviors.

Most modern theories of leadership take account of the situation. Some consider situational effects on the leader's role and behavior. Fiedler's (1967) contingency theory is an example. Other theories isolate particular aspects of what a leader must do and then identify situational variables that will affect this function. Normative theories, discussed later, are examples.

Fiedler's Contingency Model

The central postulate of Fiedler's (1967, 1978) **contingency theory** is that group effectiveness depends on an appropriate match between the leader's style and the degree to which the leader has situational control. *Group effectiveness* is defined as the extent to which the group gets its task accomplished. *Leader style* refers both to the leader's behavior and to the motivational foundation of this behavior. *Situational control* is the extent to which the work situation is favorable to the leader.

Leader Style

Fiedler defined two leadership styles. *Relationship-oriented leadership* emphasizes the interpersonal needs of the group and is similar to consideration. *Task-oriented leadership* focuses on the group's task and is similar to initiating structure. Fiedler developed the **Least Preferred Coworker (LPC) Scale** to evaluate leader style. The respondent is asked to think of the person with whom he or she has been least able to work, and to rate the person on an 8-point semantic differential scale. There are 18 pairs of descriptors, such as friendly/unfriendly, cooperative/uncooperative, and pleasant/unpleasant. The favorable pole is scored as 8 and the unfavorable as 1. Scored in this way, the low LPC scorer is the person who describes the least preferred coworker in negative terms. The high scorer describes the coworker in positive terms.

The LPC score is proposed to reflect the leader's values and interests. Fiedler's (1967) research indicated that individuals who score low on the LPC scale actually behave in a task-oriented manner, whereas those who score high are more relationship oriented. In Fiedler's view, both leaders value task success and good relationships, but they differ in terms of which is more important. The low LPC scorer is more concerned with getting the job done. Being so, he or she is annoyed by the least preferred coworker. On the other hand, the high LPC scorer is more concerned with interaction in the group. Although getting the job done is important, it is not everything. Thus, the high scorer can separate work performance from other qualities. The least preferred coworker may be an undesirable work partner, but not undesirable in every sense.

Fiedler's theory has been the most widely researched of any leadership theory, and there has been particular interest in the LPC scale. The items do not look as if they have anything to do with leadership, although as you learned in earlier chapters, face validity is not required for a test to be a valid measure. Reliability is required, however, and studies have evaluated the extent to which individuals' scores at one time consistently predict their scores at another time

(Fiedler, 1973). The research has shown that first and second test administrations are correlated, indicating that the measure is reliable (Bass, 1981). LPC scores also have been found to reflect stable differences in leader behavior (Rice, 1978).

A second question about the LPC scale concerns middle scores. Fiedler gave little attention to the middle LPC scorer in his theory. However, Kennedy (1982) noted that Fiedler's model can be used to predict the middle scorer's performance. Because the LPC score is interpreted in a linear fashion—with increasingly higher scorers performing better when interpersonal work is needed and increasingly lower scorers performing better when a task emphasis is needed—a person scoring in the middle should do moderately well in both situations. Data from natural work groups suggested that they do perform reasonably well in both situations.

Situational Control

According to contingency theory, the priorities that leaders assign to interpersonal and task goals become important in unfavorable situations (Fiedler, 1967). When everything is going well, high- and low-LPC leaders behave similarly. Both show task-oriented and relationship-oriented behavior. However, when the group is stressed, they react differently. The low-LPC leader becomes task oriented, structures all work activities, and controls the group. The high-LPC leader becomes more relationship oriented and is permissive and sharing. Fiedler proposed that each leader's personal goals are endangered in the unfavorable situation; therefore, each reacts in an effort to achieve these goals. The high-LPC leader focuses on group interaction because he or she is motivated primarily by social goals. The low-LPC leader works on the task because he or she is motivated primarily to achieve task success.

What can make the situation unfavorable? Fiedler (1978) specified three variables that define the situation: leader-member relations, task structure, and position power. These factors make things more or less difficult for the leader because they determine the amount of control he or she has. *Leader-member relations* refers to the interpersonal relationship between the leader and the group members. This relationship indicates how well the leader is liked and accepted. It is considered the most important variable, because a leader who has a supportive group can rely on it. *Task structure* is the second most important factor. This refers to the extent to which work goals are clear and procedures can be devised easily. With a structured task, it is easily discernible whether the group has performed well, because the goal and procedures are clear. *Position power* is the social power that comes from organizational rank. Though considered the least important of the three variables, high position power helps a leader to establish and maintain control.

A situation can range from very positive to very negative. The three situational variables define this range, as shown in table 10.3. Situational control is determined first by good or poor leader-member relations, second by a structured or unstructured task, and third by the level of position power. This results in eight levels of control. As the situation becomes less favorable, the leader loses situational control.

The Leader-Situation Match

Fiedler (1966) studied natural work groups in order to identify the best match between leader style and situation. The most interesting finding was that the

Table 10.3   Levels of Situational Control Defined by Three Situational
Variables and the Predicted Effective Leader

Level	Leader-Member Relations	Task Structure	Position Power	Predicted Effective Leader
1	Good	Structured	High	Task
2	Good	Structured	Low	Task
3	Good	Unstructured	High	Task
4	Good	Unstructured	Low	Relationship
5	Poor	Structured	High	Relationship
6	Poor	Structured	Low	Relationship
7	Poor	Unstructured	High	Relationship
8	Poor	Unstructured	Low	Task

Based on material from F. E. Fiedler, *A Theory of Leadership Effectiveness*. Copyright © 1967 The McGraw-Hill Book Companies, Inc., New York.

task-oriented, or low-LPC, leader was more effective when the situation was either the most or the least favorable. When the situation was moderately favorable, the relationship-oriented, or high-LPC, leader was more effective. Fiedler (1967) used these findings to predict the better leader for each level of situational control, as shown in table 10.3.

According to contingency theory, fully positive situations in which all situational variables are high (level 1 in table 10.3), are easy for any leader but particularly for one whose primary interest is task success. The fully negative situation in which all variables are low (level 8), is *difficult* for any leader. However, the task-oriented leader is predicted to be more efficient here because this leader ordinarily gets right down to business and wastes no time trying to repair relationships. The relationship-oriented leader in such a situation would feel compelled to do something about the poor leader-member relations instead of working on the task. When the situation is moderately favorable, what the relationship-oriented leader does naturally is predicted to have a better effect on performance. For example, when leader-member relations are poor, but the task is structured, the leader *should* focus on the group's interpersonal problems. A recent meta-analysis of research showed that there is support for these predictions, in general. That is, high-LPC leaders are better when the situation is moderately unfavorable (levels 4 through 7 in table 10.3), whereas low-LPC leaders are better in the most or least favorable situations (levels 1, 2, and 8) (Schriesheim, Tepper, & Tetrault, 1994).

Descriptive and Normative Leadership Models

Some leadership theories are *descriptive* in that they describe leadership and identify variables that affect leaders. Research on descriptive theories is designed so that leadership is the *dependent* variable. For example, many of Fiedler's studies evaluated the effects of unfavorable group conditions on the leader's behavior. Other leadership theories define the effects of the leader's behavior on other variables,

Table 10.4	The Leader-Member Power Distribution	
Leader Power	**Leader Behavior**	**Member Power**
High	Tells: Leader decides and tells the group the decision.	Low
High	Sells: Leader decides and sells the group on the decision.	Low
Moderate	Consults: Leader decides and asks the group for feedback; or leader asks group for information and then decides.	Moderate
Low	Joins: Leader describes the problem and then joins the group in making the decision.	High

Based on material presented by R. Tannenbaum and W. H. Schmidt, "How to Choose a Leadership Pattern" in *Harvard Business Review*, 34:5–10, 1958.

and research is designed so that leader behavior is the *independent* variable. Group performance and member satisfaction are usually the dependent variables, and the research tests hypotheses about the effects of the leader on the group. These leadership theories are called **normative models**. They make predictions about what behavior is likely to be effective, and they are meant to help the leader lead.

In an early discussion of the power components of leadership, Tannenbaum and Schmidt (1958) proposed a normative theory. First, they observed that the amount of organizational authority available to the leader and to the group members varies systematically. When the leader has more power, the group members have less, and vice versa. Then, the theorists proposed that a leader can deliberately change this power relationship in order to improve group performance. They described actions, shown in table 10.4, by which a leader can either retain or share power. They recommended that the leader assess the situation and decide how to proceed. Aspects of the situation that the leader should consider in deciding what to do include organizational variables, such as time pressure; group member variables, such as motivation; and the leader's own values and attitudes toward the group.

Both descriptive and normative models are useful. We need to know what constitutes and affects leadership. In addition, it would be helpful to know what to do in a particular situation. In the following sections, I review some normative models that focus on particular aspects of the leader's role in the organization.

Vroom and Yetton's Normative Model of Decision Making

The normative model proposed by Vroom and Yetton (1973) specifically addresses the decision-making aspect of the leader's role. (Although decision making is not all that a leader must do, it is a critical part of the leader's job.) It is proposed that a leader can vary the extent to which he or she allows the group to participate in decision making. At one extreme, the leader acts in an autocratic manner and makes the decision alone. The leader acts more moderately when he or she consults the group before making the decision. At the other extreme, the leader shares the problem, and they make a group decision.

The effectiveness of a leader's decision-making behavior is proposed to depend on the situation. Vroom and Yetton (1973) recommended that the leader evaluate the situation to determine the appropriate action to take. Certain aspects of the

Blondie By Young & Drake

group's task should be considered, including the extent to which a high-quality decision is required and whether a decision needs to be acceptable to the group. In addition, the leader should consider his or her own expertise, as well as the motivation of group members and the likelihood that they will accept autocratic behavior.

Vroom and Yetton (1973) translated these situational variables into a series of questions for a leader to use in deciding either to make the decision him- or herself or to share it with group members. By answering yes or no to each question, the leader is tracked through a **decision tree** to behaviors that are likely to have the best outcomes for the situation in question. The decision tree is shown in figure 10.2. Notice that the leader answers seven questions (A through G) about the situation and is led to one of 12 decision points where there is a recommended action. The situational questions refer to the need for decision quality (A and B), a structured task (C), decision acceptability (D and E), and member motivation (F and G). The recommended leader behavior at each decision point is either autocratic (AI and AII), consultative (CI and CII), or group participative (GII). Notice that some decision points indicate that there is only one way to handle the decision. Others cite several options. At some decision points (e.g., 1 and 2), any leader behavior is all right.

When leaders take the recommended actions, are the resulting decisions good ones? Research testing this theory's predictions indicates they are. When leaders adjust their behavior to fit the situation, the decision-making process is more effective and the decisions are better (Ettling & Jago, 1988; Field, 1982; Paul & Ebadi, 1989).

Group members may not agree that the leader's decision-making behavior is effective, however. One study found that leaders' and members' evaluations differed. According to the leaders, the behaviors prescribed by the theory were effective, but the subordinates said they were no more effective than actions that were not prescribed (Field & House, 1990). Similarly, in another study, when subjects took the perspective of the boss, they evaluated the prescribed behavior as being effective. However, when they took the point of view of the group member, they evaluated participative behavior by the leader as more effective than autocratic, whether

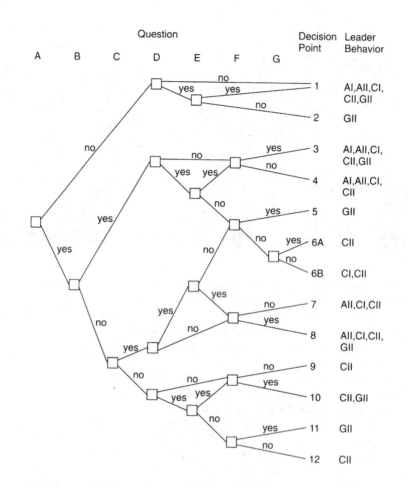

Figure 10.2 *Decision flowchart of leadership action. The questions (A–G) that the leader should ask refer to decision quality (A and B), task structure (C), decision acceptability (D and E), and subordinate motivation (F and G). At each of the 12 decision points, there is a recommended action (leader behavior column). The actions AI and AII are autocratic; CI and CII are consultative; and GII refers to sharing decision making with the group. Some decision points indicate only one way to handle a decision. Other points cite several options of behavior.*

Adapted and reprinted from LEADERSHIP AND DECISION MAKING, *by Victor H. Vroom and Philip W. Yetton, by permission of the University of Pittsburgh Press.* © *1973 by University of Pittsburgh Press.*

or not it was prescribed (Heilman et al., 1984). This may mean that workers are beginning to expect participation as part of their role. Lawler (1985) argued that employees nowadays expect to have a hand in what goes on.

Path-Goal Theory: Motivating Subordinates

House's (1971; House & Dessler, 1974) **path-goal theory** considers the motivation of subordinates an important part of the leader's role. This is another normative model. The purpose is to prescribe leader behavior that will increase worker motivation.

Path-goal theory is based on research in which worker perceptions of the routes or paths to personal goals were considered work motivational factors (Georgopoulous, Mahoney, & Jones, 1957). The reasoning behind this research was that if high productivity is perceived as a path to a valued goal then a worker will be motivated to produce. Path-goal theory also borrows ideas from the expectancy theory of motivation (Vroom, 1964), discussed in chapter 8. Recall that expectancy theory proposed that people are motivated by the availability of routes to a valued goal and by their own beliefs that they can reach the goal. In path-goal theory, the leader is instrumental in these aspects of motivation. He or she can determine the availability and size of rewards and help the subordinate get them. The leader is also in a position to influence the subordinate's perception of appropriate paths to goals. For example, a leader who defines and structures an ambiguous task, lays out the path to task goal accomplishment.

One situational variable that affects a leader's ability to motivate is the degree to which a subordinate's role is ambiguous. Role ambiguity exists whenever job expectations are not clear. Ambiguous roles are undesirable, partly because they provide little information about the paths to success. A structuring leader who clarifies the role can be helpful. However, the appropriate amount of such role clarifying behavior depends on the situation. Leaders who attempt to structure and clarify roles that are already clear to subordinates will be perceived negatively. Here, consideration behavior will be more helpful than structuring. A second variable that influences a leader's ability to motivate subordinates is the extent to which the task is inherently satisfying. When a work group has an unsatisfying task, leader consideration is proposed to have positive effects on both satisfaction and performance. In a way, the considerate leader may offset the effects of the task by providing routes to other satisfactions. A structuring leader in this situation is not expected to improve the group's satisfaction but should improve group performance, because structuring brings the task to a successful finish.

Research has provided only mixed support for the theory (e.g., Dessler & Valenzi, 1977; Schriesheim & DeNisi, 1981). In general, the predictions about leader consideration have been supported more clearly than the predictions about structuring (Mitchell, 1979). However, because of serious problems in the research itself, such as an overreliance on questionnaires, Yukl (1989) noted that the theory has not yet been tested adequately. Podsakoff and his associates would agree. They looked at the research purporting to test the impact of situational variables on a leader's ability to motivate group members. They found several problems, such as use of an inappropriate research design and unreliable measures. For example, crudely constructed questionnaire items are not likely to detect subtle situational influences (Podsakoff et al., 1995).

The first step in understanding leadership was to examine the leader. The next step was to look at the situation surrounding the leader. Fiedler was among the first to take this step. In his contingency theory, he identified situational factors that can make leading easy or difficult. These include leader-member relations, the group's task, and the amount of position power. Whether the combination of these factors result in a difficult situation depends on the leader's style of behavior. Fiedler recommended a match between the leader's style and the situation faced.

Some leadership theories are prescriptive; that is, they tell the leader what to do to reach certain goals. Vroom and Yetton's normative model is an example. The model focuses on decision making as an important task that leaders must perform. The theorists developed a procedure for examining the situation that exists and deciding how to behave in getting the decisions made.

Path-goal theory is a prescriptive theory that tells a leader what to do about motivating group members. By initiating structure and showing consideration, leaders can make desirable goals available, can develop or point out paths to these goals, and can help subordinates reach them.

LEADERSHIP AS A REINFORCING SOCIAL RELATIONSHIP

How do people become leaders? One answer is that they have been reinforced for showing leaderlike behaviors. Reinforcement theory considers leadership to develop in basically the same way as other behavioral patterns develop. Quite simply, leadership action is followed by some reinforcing consequence, causing the action to recur. There is evidence for this view. Bass (1981) found studies showing that leadership behaviors increased when they were rewarded and decreased when they were punished (e.g., Jaffee, 1968). The reinforcers can be both tangible and social. Leaders get monetary rewards, as well as recognition and respect. The group participates in the development of the leader. Social rewards for good leader behavior can come from a leader's interaction with group members.

The group is probably the single most important part of the leader's "situation." Unlike other aspects of the situation, the group is highly similar to the leader. Their roles do not vary greatly. In fact, leaders and followers may sometimes exchange roles. Both leaders and members perform work to get the task done and to maintain the group in good working order. The models presented in this section place a strong emphasis on the exchange between leader and members.

A Social Transaction Perspective

In Hollander's (1958, 1978) **social transaction theory,** leadership is proposed to develop through a process of social exchange. That is, the leader attains and maintains his or her position through interaction with the group. The primary situational variables through which the leader establishes the position are members' perceptions of the leader's qualifications. Members perceive the leader in terms of his or her authority, task competence, and motives. Effective leaders are those who fulfill member expectations, provide valuable resources, and help the group succeed on its task. In exchange, the leader gets rewards from the group. For example, the leader may structure a task and provide information on how to get it done. In exchange, the effective leader earns legitimacy. That is, he or she is "validated" by the group members to occupy the position of leader. Hollander (1958) referred to this validation as *idiosyncrasy credit*. A person earns this credit by convincing the group members that he or she has the ability to lead the group. The leader accumulates idiosyncrasy credit, and this provides the power to further influence the group.

Leader-Member Exchange in the Vertical Dyad

Social transaction theory treats social interaction in a somewhat general sense as occurring between the leader and the group as a whole. Another model uses the idea of social exchange but emphasizes the interpersonal relationships between the leader and individual group members. The **leader-member exchange model,** which is also called the *vertical dyad linkage model,* emphasizes the interaction that occurs between supervisor and subordinate. Because the supervisor and the subordinate are on different levels in the organizational authority hierarchy, they form a vertical dyad. It is proposed that the social exchanges that occur within this vertical dyad will determine the roles, behavior, and outcomes of both parties (Dansereau, Graen, & Haga, 1975; Graen & Cashman, 1975).

The value of this model is its emphasis on the different interactions that can occur between a leader and the group members. Clearly, supervisors do not have the same relationship with all their subordinates. This model points out how the specific relationship affects both the leader's behavior and the group's outcomes. Leaders and members are proposed to engage in two types of exchange, depending on whether the subordinate is part of the supervisor's "in-group." *In-group exchange* has the characteristics of a partnership. The relationship is initiated when the supervisor likes the subordinate and views him or her as capable and motivated (Dockery & Steiner, 1990). Subordinates who are extraverts and who have attitudes similar to the supervisor's attitudes are likely to be in-group members (Phillips & Bedeian, 1994). The social exchange within the in-group dyad allows the subordinate to assume more responsibility and, in return, to receive recognition and support from the leader. The leader benefits from the in-group member's work and receives the member's loyalty and respect. In-group exchange can result in better overall performance and greater worker satisfaction with the leader (Vecchio & Gobdel, 1984). However, members of a supervisor's in-group sometimes receive higher performance ratings than their objective performance would warrant (Duarte, Goodson, & Klich, 1993).

Out-group exchange occurs when the subordinate is *not* a valued partner. In out-group exchange, communication and influence are one way, that is, from the leader to the member. The leader views this subordinate as being neither well qualified nor motivated. The leader behaves in a more directive and authoritative manner, and allows the out-group member little responsibility and influence over the work. As a result, the subordinate shows little loyalty to the leader.

Upward Influence

Leadership has long been conceptualized as a form of downward influence from the leader to the group members. For example, leaders are frequently characterized as being able to persuade members. Both the social transaction and the leader-member exchange models recognize that there also is upward influence from the members. **Upward influence** can change the leader's behavior and help members accomplish goals.

Two issues concerning upward influence are currently being addressed in the research: the goals pursued through upward influence and the strategies used. Subordinates attempt to accomplish two kinds of goals: organizational objectives, such as getting resources; and personal objectives, such as getting approval and personal benefits (Yukl, Guinan, & Sottolano, 1995). A variety of upward influence tactics have been studied. The tactics used appear to depend on the particular goals sought. Ingratiation and personal appeals are used to gain personal benefits.

Assertiveness, rational persuasion, and coalition forming are tactics used to achieve organizational goals, such as increased resources and political support (Ansari & Kapoor, 1987; Kipnis, Schmidt, & Wilkinson, 1980; Yukl et al., 1995). Even upward pressure, such as threats to quit or to complain to a higher authority, is sometimes used to gain personal benefits (Yukl et al., 1995).

Only a few studies have examined the effectiveness of upward influence attempts. Thacker and Wayne (1995) proposed that the particular tactics used will affect both the impression the subordinate makes and the individual's personal goal outcomes, such as in getting a promotion. They found that neither assertiveness nor ingratiation were effective, but rational persuasion did contribute to an impression of promotability. Deluga and Perry (1991) thought that upward influence effectiveness might depend not only on the tactic used but also on whether the person is a member of the supervisor's in-group. They found some evidence of this. In-group members were more likely to report that their influence attempts were effective, and they used different tactics that out-group members. They were less likely to use assertiveness, coalition forming, and appeals to higher authority.

Multiple Linkages in Leadership Effectiveness

In spite of decades of research, we are still not very clear about what makes leaders effective. Following a similar observation, Yukl (1989) undertook the task of integrating and organizing the knowledge that has accumulated over the years. As shown in figure 10.3, leadership is envisioned as a complex interaction process in which a leader expresses certain personal attributes in his or her leader behaviors. These leader behaviors both affect and are affected by the situation. Leader behavior is capable of causing a number of group outcomes or end results, including high productivity and satisfaction. These outcomes occur through the influence of leader behavior on the intervening variables of member motivation and ability. These intervening variables and outcomes also have reciprocal effects on the leader.

The framework itself is an adaptation of Yukl's (1971, 1981) **multiple linkages model,** devised to predict a leader's effect on group productivity. In this model, the concepts of consideration and structuring are used in describing what leaders do. Yukl added the concept of *decision-centralization* to describe the kinds of procedures leaders use to make decisions, that is, whether they retain or share the power to make decisions. In high decision-centralization, the leader retains power and makes the decision alone. In low decision-centralization, the leader shares the decision-making power with the group. Yukl proposed that these leadership behaviors *indirectly* determine the group's productivity. That is, leaders are effective to the extent that they can maximize the members' motivation, the members' skills, and the task role organization. *Task role organization* refers to the efficient use of member skills in task assignments. The group's productivity, then, is determined by the existing levels of member skill and motivation and by the leader's effective use of these resources.

In the multiple linkages model, there are four propositions about how the leader affects members (refer to figure 10.4). First, motivation is proposed to increase when the leader shows high levels of both consideration and structuring. Second, in general, motivation is increased by *low* levels of decision-centralization (or more sharing). Third, task role organization is affected by structuring and decision-

Figure 10.3 *A framework for presenting the components and outcomes of leadership. Leadership is a complex interactive process in which attributes of the leader are expressed in specific managerial behaviors. These behaviors both affect and are affected by situational, group, and outcome variables.*

From Gary Yukl, "Managerial Leadership: A Review of Theory and Research." in Journal of Management, 15:274. Copyright © 1989 Southern Management Association, Lubbock, Texas. Reprinted by permission.

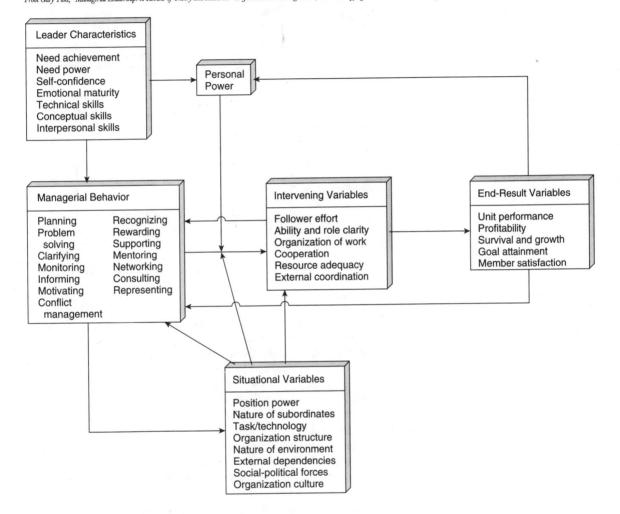

centralization. That is, if the group has little expertise, a leader who behaves in a task-related way and makes the decisions will be helpful. When the group includes skilled and knowledgeable members, however, less of this behavior will be better. Fourth, members' skills are improved by structuring behavior. This occurs mainly when the leader instructs and communicates task-related information to the group.

Yukl proposed that the success of leadership behavior depends on the leader's goal. That is, leadership behavior that results in group productivity is not necessarily the same as behavior that brings about member satisfaction. He predicted different leader behaviors to produce these two group outcomes. To predict the group's satisfaction, Yukl looked at the job satisfaction theory and research

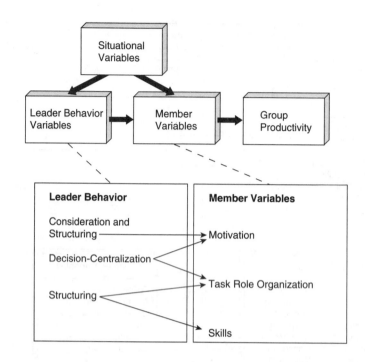

Figure 10.4 *In the multiple linkages model, group productivity is predicted to occur through the effects of leader behaviors on member characteristics. Consideration, structuring, and decision-centralization are important leader behaviors in this respect.*

From Gary Yukl, "Toward a Behavioral Theory of Leadership." in Organizational Behavior and Human Performance, 6:414–40. Copyright © 1971 Academic Press, Inc., Orlando, Florida. Reprinted by permission.

and noted that job satisfaction can be considered a function of the difference between an individual's expectations and experiences. Satisfaction with a leader, then, probably depends on what group members expect and on what the leader actually does. Based on the existing knowledge, Yukl proposed that a member's expectation of leadership is determined by the member's own characteristics. High consideration from a leader is probably expected in all situations. However, the preferred level of leader structuring likely depends on certain motivations of the group member, such as the member's commitment to organizational goals. The preference for decision-making behavior depends on the importance of the decision and on the member's personality. For example, a subordinate who needs to be self-reliant will expect a leader to share power.

The multiple linkages model itself has not been evaluated to a great extent. However, it was constructed largely out of existing research. In fact, Yukl's (1989) framework (shown in figure 10.3) is an adaptation of the model.

*M*ain *P*oints

How do leaders get and hold their positions? Some theorists say they do this by entering into a reinforcing social relationship with the group. In one perspective, the leader makes social transactions with the members. If this is done effectively, the leader earns his or her place in the group. In the related leader-member exchange theory, the social transactions that occur between the leader and particular members of the group are considered the most important. In-group members receive special attention from the leader that out-group members do not receive. In exchange, they provide rewards for the leader. Influence, according to these

Section III: Creating an Effective Social Organization

theories, is not simply downward from the leader to the member. It is upward, also. Group members engage in upward influence to gain organizational and personal benefits, and some of the more effective influence attempts come from in-group members.

A framework for organizing existing knowledge, which is based on Yukl's multiple linkages model, shows that the social interactions between leaders and their group members are central to the group's outcomes.

NEW DIRECTIONS

The study of leadership is branching into new territory. Certainly, research is still being done in an effort to untangle the interrelationship of leader, member, and situational variables. However, some of the more important developments of the current period are those in which we move out of this morass of details and look at leadership from other perspectives. Transformational leadership combines micro- and macro-organizational variables to describe the extraordinary accomplishments of some leaders. The implicit theory approach takes a look at the "insides" of leadership attributions, at how people think about leadership. Here, the startling proposition is made that leadership exists largely in the minds of the followers.

Transformational Leadership

A theory that can be included with the group of models describing leadership as an influential social interaction is **transformational leadership** theory. Bass (1985) used Burns's (1978) work on political leadership to describe ways organizational leaders might bring about major change. The transformational leader has a vision and uses it to transform organizational members. Members are inspired. They come to believe in the importance and value of their work. The leader creates new attitudes and excites followers to aim for higher values and ideals. The transformational leader is said to have influence in every direction—downward with subordinates, laterally with colleagues, upward with superiors, and outward with clients and customers. Thus, this leader can change the culture of the organization.

Transformational leadership includes *charisma*. The personal characteristics and vision of the charismatic leader are proposed to be necessary. Charisma is responsible for the passion and commitment that develops in followers. However, transformational leadership involves more. Bass (1985) described two behaviors that help the leader accomplish transformation. One is *intellectual stimulation,* through which the leader raises the followers' consciousness and gets them to think about old issues in new ways. The other behavior is what Bass called *individualized consideration,* a behavior similar to the Ohio State construct of consideration. In showing individualized consideration, the leader interacts with a group member and attempts to provide support and encouragement to develop and empower the person. Individualized consideration must address the individual's needs, of course. Some group members may not be inspired by a leader's efforts (Yammarino & Bass, 1990).

How is this perspective different from other leadership theory? First, transformational leadership is not simply charismatic leadership, primarily because the transformational leader has an interdependent relationship with group members. Charismatic leadership, which results in follower compliance, keeps followers *dependent* on the leader. Transformational leadership is meant to create follower *independence*. Burns (1978) described the transformation as one through which followers become leaders in their own right. Second, Bass distinguished transformational leadership from social transaction theory. He proposed that followers of the transformational leader are motivated to go beyond the simple transactions in which they and the leader each get something and aim for the leader's goals. However, the use of individualized consideration may make a leader more accessible and open to members' upward influence efforts (Deluga & Souza, 1991). Third, this perspective focuses on the outstanding things that can be accomplished through leadership, rather than the ordinary day-to-day needs of an organization.

As yet, there is little research evaluation of the theory. A survey instrument was developed to provide a measure of leader behavior. Based on qualitative studies in which executives described the characteristics of transformational leaders, Bass (1985) devised the Multifactor Leadership Questionnaire (MLQ). The MLQ contains items describing transformational and transactional leader behavior. Research evaluating the MLQ generally confirmed Bass's view of these as different types of behavior (Bycio, Hackett, & Allen, 1995).

Implicit Theories of Leadership

Many studies have been done with measures, such as the LBDQ, that get information about leaders from group members. In fact, much of what we can say about leadership behavior actually is a description of what subordinates think about leadership. What does this mean, other than that we have inadvertently included the follower's perspective? One answer, according to some researchers, is that these findings actually say more about the subordinate's cognitive structure than about the behavior of the leader (e.g., Phillips, 1984).

Perhaps, our study of leader behavior has been misguided by our research instruments. It is *possible* that subordinates recall what a leader did in the past and then respond to survey questions from their memory of the leader's behavior. This is what we think subjects are doing, of course, when we conduct these studies. However, some research indicates that the respondent does not base the questionnaire response on remembered material. Rather, the person describes a leader prototype, against which he or she has matched the supervisor (Eden & Leviatan, 1975; Rush, Thomas, & Lord, 1977). In other words, survey responses reflect an **implicit theory of leadership** held by the respondent, not the actual behavior of the leader.

According to Lord and his associates, an implicit theory of a leader develops through experience with those in leadership positions (Lord, 1985; Lord, Foti, & Phillips, 1982; Lord, Foti, & De Vader, 1984). They proposed that over time an individual builds up not an accumulation of specific details but an idea or a *cognitive category* of how leaders behave. From this comes a prototype, or cognitive "picture" of what a leader is. The **leader prototype** is a set of characteristics shared by most

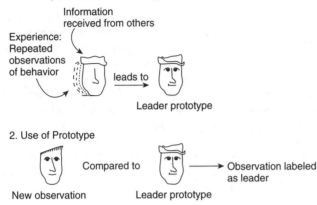

1. Development of Leader Prototype

Information received from others

Experience: Repeated observations of behavior

leads to

Leader prototype

2. Use of Prototype

Compared to

Observation labeled as leader

New observation   Leader prototype

Figure 10.5 *The process of developing and using a leader prototype. Over time, a person makes repeated observations and receives information about leadership behavior from others. Through this experience, the person develops an idea of what a leader is like, that is, a leader prototype. Later, when a new observation is made, it is compared to the leader prototype. If the observed behavior matches the prototype, the observed person is labeled as a leader.*

members of the cognitive category. The person uses the prototype to understand later experiences and to store information about leader behavior (see figure 10.5). For example, the individual compares observations with the leader prototype. If the behaviors match the prototype, then they are labeled like the prototype. That is, if we see someone doing things like our prototype of leadership, we say the person is a leader and store this assessment in our memory. The implication is that when we are asked to describe someone as a leader, we access the prototype and use it in our description.

Some research suggests that people do use an implicit theory to form their perceptions of leadership (e.g., Cronshaw & Lord, 1987; Foti, Fraser, & Lord, 1982; Phillips, 1984). For example, Phillips (1984) found that telling subjects that a person was an effective leader changed their evaluations. Although objectively there was nothing different in the leader's behavior, subjects became more likely to describe the person in terms consistent with the label. Some researchers have begun to explore what goes into the cognitive category (Maurer & Lord, 1991). For example, social power has been identified as one element (Palich & Hom, 1992). We are likely to see more work in this area in the future.

*M*ain *P*oints

Transformational leadership theory is based on macro-organizational concepts, such as political leadership. In this model, as in others, the focus is on an important social interaction. The charismatic leader is seen as having extraordinary influence on the group. The transactions that occur between this leader and the members are said to be transforming. Followers are turned into new people.

Some believe that what we have learned about leadership is actually not about leaders but about followers' conceptions of leadership. That is, we all have an implicit theory of leadership in mind. This implicit theory is built up because we cognitively categorize what we observe people to do in interactions. This results in a mental abstraction called a leader prototype. The prototype is used to define leadership.

TRAINING LEADERSHIP SKILLS

Many theorists have recognized the need for training leaders. Some have developed programs for teaching leadership skills. In their *Managerial Grid,* Blake and Mouton (1978, 1985) provided a training program to help managers assess their people- and task-oriented behaviors and move toward the recommended team-leadership style. Vroom and Yetton's (1973) decision tree is meant to help management trainees learn how to assess and adjust to a situation. Learning to tell the difference between situations that call for shared or directive leadership and learning to behave in these ways are the essentials. Fiedler provided a self-paced, programmed instructional package called *Leader Match* (Fiedler, Chemers, & Mahar, 1976). This program shows trainees how to assess their leadership style with the LPC scale. It is also meant to help trainees learn how to assess and change situational variables to better fit their style.

Instructional Techniques

Most of the procedures used in training other job skills and capacities can be used to train supervisors to lead (see chapter 6). Supervisory and managerial training is often informal. It includes on-the-job training in which the manager learns simply by doing the job. Job rotation also is used as an on-the-job training device. In this procedure, a manager is moved from one position to another in order to gain a broad understanding of the company and a variety of skills. Coaching or mentoring is another commonly used method. Very little controlled research has been done to evaluate the effectiveness of coaching, although considerable anecdotal evidence exists (Bass, 1981). Coaching is thought to be helpful if the coach is someone with whom the new manager can identify and if they have an open and trusting relationship. Coaching is less likely to succeed when the coach allows too little time for the trainee or sees the trainee as a rival.

Formal leadership training workshops are conducted with the variety of methods discussed in chapter 6. Any of the techniques for conveying information may be used, such as lectures, films, and reading assignments. The most frequently used technique is the discussion group. Group discussions are used for going over case studies, for problem solving, and for critiquing written assignments and lecture materials. There is also some use of role play and business games in which a specific management problem is explored and solved. Role playing is used to develop leadership skills by having trainees act out problems and solutions in front of the training group.

Laboratory Training

In the mid-1940s, Kurt Lewin and his associates noticed that students in leadership discussion groups appeared to learn more about leadership by discussing their observations of a group's interactions than by engaging in more formal academic discussions. In fact, their learning could be enhanced if the trainer discarded the formal discussion topic altogether and allowed the group to generate its own material. This was the beginning of what came to be known as **sensitivity** or **laboratory training**. The purpose of laboratory training is to increase the trainees' awareness of their own interpersonal styles. The training is done by having trainees interact in a small group away from the work situation. Trainees are encouraged to experiment with different styles of behavior and to give and receive feedback on the interpersonal effects of these. By trying out different ways of behaving in the protected laboratory setting, the trainee may develop an interpersonal sensitivity that is useful in supervision. The idea behind this training was that an improved awareness of interpersonal dynamics and communication would help the leader's performance.

The laboratory technique caught on, and many organizations enthusiastically provided this training for their managers. Research on laboratory training showed that it resulted in more humanistic attitudes and a better understanding of interpersonal dynamics. Some studies also found that these were stable effects that transferred from the training back to the job (cf. Bunker, 1965). Laboratory-trained managers showed more openness, better communication skill, and more understanding of others. However, most of the research was not able to show that these effects were substantial (Bass, 1981). It appeared also that they depended on the situation that existed on the job. That is, when the trainees went back to jobs that had not changed, they often did not retain the new learning.

Behavior Modeling

Social learning theory (Bandura, 1977) has become the basis for an approach to leadership training. **Social learning theory** recognizes the power of consequences on behavior. Its main proposition is that trainees learn by observing the behavior of models. The **behavior modeling** workshop is designed around specific supervisory problems, such as handling complaints or motivating poor performers. The lessons are usually interpersonal, emphasizing the development of such skills as active listening and responding without defensiveness. The desirable behavior in dealing with each problem is demonstrated by a model, usually in a film or videotape. The lessons to be learned are defined by the trainer, and a group discussion follows the model's demonstration. After the group discussion, trainees role-play the problem and its solution in front of the training group, attempting to duplicate the model's behavior.

Learning through models makes sense. We have long considered that on-the-job training depends on a trainee's ability to reproduce the behavior of a seasoned employee. However, the results of the evaluation research indicate that we do not fully understand the value of behavior modeling. For example, in one well-designed study, Latham and Saari (1979) found good results with behavior modeling. Compared to control groups, trainees showed immediate improvement, and they retained a positive response to training over a period of months. However, another study that used similar methods was unable to show that behavior modeling had significant effects on job behavior, although trainees were favorable toward it (Russell, Wexley, & Hunter, 1984). The different effects of behavior modeling may be due to the way the programs are constructed. For example, in many programs, the model presents only the correct behavior or the right way to do something. It may be that we need also to have the model demonstrate what not to do. In our day-to-day experience, we learn from our own and other people's mistakes.

Given that we believe that leaders are not simply born that way, how can we develop leaders? Some theorists provide prescriptions for behavior that a leader can follow and thus learn how to perform effectively. Others offer formal training programs.

The same basic procedures that are used to train other employees can be used to train people to lead. Many of these techniques are used in informal on-the-job training, such as coaching, and in formal off-site programs, such as case study discussions. Special off-site programs also have been developed for training leaders. These include sensitivity training and behavior modeling.

SPECIAL LEADERS AND SPECIAL SITUATIONS

Prior to the 1960s, the study of leadership was limited largely to the study of white men occupying leadership positions in domestic business organizations. Since that time, it has become increasingly clear that some individuals who play a leadership role are not men, not white, and/or not working in a domestic organization. In the 1970s and 1980s, there was a surge of interest in the experiences of women and minority men in management. The expansion of international business to other countries is beginning to demonstrate that we need also to understand cross-cultural issues better.

Gender Differences in Leadership

Examination of the research on women in management suggests that we have been retreading the route taken in previous study of leadership. We began by looking for feminine traits that might make women effective leaders. We went on to examine differences in the behavioral styles of women and men. More recently, we have been looking into the relationship between the female supervisor and her subordinates.

The first question addressed in the study of gender differences was whether women have the attributes of a leader. Research on sex role stereotypes indicated that men and women were perceived to be opposites. For example, men were seen as competent, and women were seen as expressive. Men were viewed as being managerial material and women were not. In fact, men and managers were described with the same terms, such as having competence and ego strength. Women were described in other terms (Broverman et al., 1972; Schein, 1973). Women were thought to have too little self-confidence and ambition. They seemed to be less task oriented in group interactions (Lockheed & Hall, 1976). In short, the research showed that people saw women as not having the capacities for leadership. People still view women in this way, not only in this country but in others as well (Schein et al., 1996). The usual explanation for the findings of the early research was couched in terms of female socialization. That is, females are brought up from childhood to leave leadership to the men. Any leadership potential that a woman might have was stunted by this upbringing. However, in spite of the findings, women did and still do assume leadership roles, although worldwide their numbers in managerial positions are disproportionately low (Adler, 1993).

In general, then, women are perceived as not having the basic capacities for leadership. However, some are in leadership positions. Why are they exceptions? A recent review of research indicated overall that women leaders are as effective as men (Eagley, Karau, & Makhijani, 1995). There are several views of how leadership is affected by a leader's gender. One view is that leadership actually requires both masculine and feminine characteristics, such as ego strength and expressiveness. Another is that although the leadership role is masculine, some women can perform it because they have learned to act like men.

A number of studies have attempted to show that good leadership requires both masculine and feminine characteristics. However, the findings are not clearly supportive. Most research shows that a manager's role is perceived as masculine, particularly if male subjects are asked. Male and female group members who show masculine gender role characteristics are more likely to emerge as leaders of the group (Goktepe & Schneier, 1989; Kent & Moss, 1994). Studies of students and experienced managers have found that the "good manager" is described in more masculine terms by both men and women. However, female subjects are increasingly less likely to do so (Brenner, Tomkiewicz, & Schein, 1989; Powell & Butterfield, 1989; Schein et al., 1996).

The second view of the gender effect on management is that women have learned to act like men. Some believe that because there are comparatively few women in leadership positions, which makes management a male-dominated domain, the woman manager must adjust in order to survive (Powell & Butterfield, 1989). However, "acting like a man" can help only so much. The woman manager who attempts to succeed by taking on masculine attributes must show enough power to be taken seriously but not enough to violate our cultural stereotypes about aggressive females (Watson, 1988). Several researchers have found that certain masculine traits, such as dominance, do not work for the female manager as they do for the male (e.g., Petty & Bruning, 1980; Watson, 1988). Subordinates tolerate and even support behavior in their male supervisors that they dislike in their female supervisors (Jago & Vroom, 1982). This may be due to the way leadership roles are defined. Research has shown that leadership roles are defined in either masculine terms, such as requiring more task-related ability, or feminine terms, such as involving more interpersonal ability. Men and women are judged more effective when they are "in-role" and less effective when they occupy positions that were defined for the opposite sex (Eagley et al., 1995).

Research that shows a difference in the standards of leadership due to the gender of the leader suggests that leaders are being evaluated by an *implicit theory*. If so, the difference between male and female leaders would be expected to have less to do with actual behavioral differences than with how people think male and female leaders behave. Comparing the research on leader prototypes and gender differences may be helpful in our future understanding of both issues.

Ethnic Minorities in Leadership Roles

Managerial positions traditionally have been closed to members of ethnic minority groups in this country. The situation has improved over the past few decades, and the nonwhite manager is a little more common now than in the past. However, African Americans and other minorities are vastly underrepresented in managerial ranks in even the most open of organizations.

The study of racial differences in leadership has followed a slightly different track than the study of gender differences. There has been some speculation that differences in personal traits can affect leadership success. These speculated trait differences usually are described as being due largely to the impact of the socioeconomic status and subculture of minority members. For example, in one study, individuals who were strongly bicultural (that is, who understand and respond favorably to two different cultures) showed more leadership behavior in mixed cultural groups than subjects who were low on this attribute (Garza et al., 1982). Value differences in subcultures also have been explored. However, the findings are similar to those concerning women managers. Of those who attain high management positions, there appears to be little difference in values that can account for racial differences in managerial success (Watson & Barone, 1976).

Part of the interest in minority leadership centers on the subordinate's reaction to a supervisor of a different race. Like female leadership of male or mixed groups, African American supervision of white or mixed groups has been thought likely to be fraught with difficulty because of adverse subordinate reactions. Actually, however, little is known about the effectiveness of African American managers who supervise white or mixed subordinate groups. Although some research suggests that the interaction of mixed racial groups has improved (Hill & Hughes, 1974), this issue remains relatively unexplored. Part of the difficulty appears to be the scarcity of opportunities for the field study of ethnic minority leaders, as management remains a white domain.

Cross-Cultural Patterns of Leadership

A relevant question, considering the increasing numbers who work in multinational firms, is whether our knowledge of leadership can be transported across national boundaries. Cultural and national influences are strong in many aspects of behavior. We might suppose that they are in leadership as well. If so, it will be important for an overseas company to learn what a host country's people think about leadership. If the company transfers American managers to supervise employees who are native to the host country, then these managers must know what their subordinates expect. If the company intends to develop its host country employees as supervisors, then some thought must be given to training them, which also requires knowledge of their expectations.

Participative management has been studied in other countries. Researchers have found that there are different reactions to this leader behavior. In some countries, workers prefer participation. In other countries, however, they prefer directive leadership. Following an early study in the United States in which employee participation improved group performance (Coch & French, 1948), researchers introduced worker participation in Norway (French, Israel, & As, 1960) and in Puerto Rico (Marrow, 1964). Employees in these countries did not respond favorably. In fact, turnover increased among Puerto Rican workers, apparently because participation was seen as a sign of mismanagement.

More recent studies show that reaction to participative management still varies across countries. One study, set in the Netherlands, found greater satisfaction when there was participative leadership (Koopman et al., 1981). However, a study set in Nigeria found participative management to be unimportant to employees. Employees there performed better under more directive and autocratic supervisors (Ejiogu, 1983). Studies of leadership in India indicate that neither participative nor authoritarian management is very effective. Sinha (cited in Ansari & Kapoor, 1987) proposed a *nurturant-task* leadership style, which combines aspects of people-oriented and task-oriented behavior, to be more appropriate in Indian culture.

Another question is whether other cultures cognitively categorize leader behavior as we do. There is growing evidence that people differ in this respect. Ayman and Chemers (1983) surveyed employees in Iran using a modified version of the Leader Behavior Description Questionnaire. They found that most of the items, on both structuring and consideration, were strongly intercorrelated and appeared to refer to a single form of leadership that the researchers labeled *benevolent paternalism*. In another study, samples from Great Britain, Hong Kong, Japan, and the United States were compared. The researchers used a leadership behavior questionnaire developed in Japan that included items about leader behaviors relating to task accomplishment and effective group maintenance. The results showed two distinct leadership styles, but there were differences between the samples in terms of the specific behaviors that made up the two styles. For example, leaders who were judged by the British sample as showing high levels of people-oriented behavior also did more task-related work than people-oriented leaders in other countries (Smith et al., 1989).

The studies reviewed in this section indicate that the large body of literature that we have accumulated over the years should probably be interpreted as describing a North American style of leadership. Until we have more study of leaders in other countries, we cannot say to what extent and with whom our perceptions of leadership are shared.

---

*M*ain
*P*oints

One way to study leadership is to study those who do most of it. Another way is to study those who might do it. Traditionally, leadership has been closed to women and ethnic minority men in this country.

For the longest time, people believed that women did not have the capacity to be leaders, and researchers attempted to discover why they did not. Most people are still not sure that females have the capacity, but it is becoming obvious that some women are in leadership positions. Current research indicates that overall, both men and women leaders are effective, but they perform different roles. Most leadership positions still are described in masculine terms, and leader behaviors that are effective for men are not always successful when used by women.

Leadership by members of ethnic minorities has received little research attention, as has leadership in other countries. Cross-cultural studies are suggesting that leadership has neither the same meaning nor the same effects in different cultures.

CHAPTER SUMMARY

We find leaders throughout the organization. Some have been designated by their superiors to lead work groups. Others emerge simply because they perform the functions of a leader.

Some people treat leadership as a personal attribute. They believe that great leaders are superior in many ways and that their personal traits reflect this superiority. However, trait research has not found many personal features that all leaders have in common. We learn more about leaders when we look beyond their personal traits and consider leadership as a behavioral style. Research has found that leadership behavior can be described by two factors. One factor includes behavior focused on the group members, as when the leader shows concern about their welfare. This factor is called employee-oriented or consideration behavior. The second factor includes task-related, production-oriented, or structuring behavior.

Research typically finds that effective leadership depends on situational variables, such as a group's task. The most important situational variable is probably the group itself. Some theories consider leadership not simply as a behavioral style but also as a work role that is intimately connected to the group. Fiedler proposed that leaders have a propensity for one behavioral style, but this style may not be appropriate for the group. He believed that the effective style matches the situation. Other theorists have suggested that the leader must adjust to the situation, and that the proper adjustment depends on what part of the leadership role the leader is trying to fulfill. Path-goal theory addresses the leader's role as motivator. Vroom and Yetton focused on the leader as a decision maker.

We need to know how an individual forms a leadership style in the first place. This will help if we want to train or develop a leader. Several theories have addressed this question. Most include mechanisms of social reinforcement. That is, a person learns to lead by being rewarded by others. Social transaction theory describes the leader-group relationship as a social exchange in which both leader and members benefit from each other's actions. The leader-member exchange model emphasizes that the most important of these exchanges are those that take place between the leader and the individual member. In the multiple linkages model, Yukl proposed that the leader gets the group to produce by indirect means, through influencing the members' abilities and motivations.

Some new leadership theories are being developed. One focuses on the exceptional leader—the one that transforms the organization. The transformational leader is one who has charisma and can lead the organization into new territory. A second new theory takes a microscopic look at how followers understand leadership and proposes that we all have an implicit theory of what a leader is and does.

Practically, we need to make full use of our leadership resources. Training for leadership development is one way to do this. Another is to explore the possibility that other, nontraditional leaders might be available. Women and minorities are being studied as they perform leadership roles. We are also beginning to go beyond cultural boundaries and consider how people in other countries both lead and respond to leaders.

STUDY QUESTIONS

1) Who are the leaders in the work organization? How do they get their positions?

2) What is the central idea and the implications of the "great man" theory of leadership?

3) What personal traits do leaders actually have? What is charisma?

4) Describe the two basic styles of leadership behavior.

5) What are some common ways to measure leadership?

6) Distinguish between the low- and high-LPC leader. What are the variables that make up Fiedler's concept of situational control? Which leader is best when the leader's situation is unfavorable?

7) Why is Vroom and Yetton's model called a normative theory? How well has this model been supported in the research?

8) What aspect of the leader's role does path-goal theory address?

9) How does leadership develop?

10) What is the difference between the social exchanges described in social transaction theory and the leader-member exchange model? Who are the in-groups and out-groups described in this latter model?

11) What are the goals and strategies of upward influence?

12) What is the central proposition of Yukl's multiple linkages model? What does he prescribe for the leader who wants to influence group productivity and satisfaction?

13) What does the transformational leader supposedly do and by what means?

14) Describe the operation of an implicit theory of leadership. What does this say about the accumulated body of research on leadership?

15) What is the best way to train a leader?

16) How does a leader's sex affect leadership behavior and effectiveness?

17) What do we know about leadership abilities of members of ethnic minorities in this country?

18) Is leadership understood in other countries as it is in the United States?

CONSIDER THIS

Controversy

As we have taken various routes in our quest to understand leadership, can we now approach the ultimate, undiscussible question? *Is a leader necessary?* We assume so. Why? What can a leader do that responsible group members cannot? Is it a myth that groups need leaders?

Gemmill and Oakley (1992) proposed that it is. They said that leadership functions as a social defense and as a mechanism for maintaining the status quo.

Whenever people are in pain or feel helpless, they develop myths about their need for a great leader who will come and help them out of the mess they are in. Work group members who are uncertain about what to do with an ambiguous task have unpleasant feelings about the uncertainty. They can easily dispel the feelings by projecting them onto the leader role: "What we need here is a leader who can come and tell us what to do."

Gemmill and Oakley (1992) noted that having a leader can result in more than the members bargained for. People give up the burden of responsibility to the leader and learn helplessness. After a time without responsibility, people start to feel alienated. They may realize that this is due partly to the leader role, yet they cannot see that anything really different is possible. Instead, they feel that what

they need is a more powerful, visionary leader who can inspire them out of their apathy. What is not considered is whether they need a leader at all.

Society also contributes to the myth because we want to control the frightening uncertainty of reality. Structures and illusions that have worked in the past are protected. One such illusion is the necessity of leadership. Organizations protect leadership by explaining their successes as being caused by leaders. Companies are said to make it big in the world, not because they have hard-working production employees or incredibly insightful market analysts, but because they have great leaders. Leadership also provides someone to take the blame for organizational dysfunctions, and this in turn preserves the existing organizational structure. The absence or inability of leaders is cited as the cause of business failures. This distracts attention from individual members and allows an organization to remain unchanged.

What do you think? What are the reasons for a leader? Would it help groups to discuss what they want and what they might get from having a leader? Could self-leadership function as well? What would be the results if we declared that leadership is not necessary for group work?

what's in this chapter?

What is the best way to organize? Business managers have been asking this question for a long time, and organizational theorists have been trying to provide them with a good answer.

An organization is made up of people, and the design of an organization structures the relationships between the people. In this chapter, you will learn about important components of organizational structure, such as division of labor and decision-making authority, which some organizational theorists have said are the central focus of a good design. The bureaucracy, the oldest design still in use, is the product of early organizational theorizing. The bureaucracy was meant to be rational, fair, and efficient. Many later theorists have responded to its weaknesses. Some point out its negative effects on workers. Others note that it is good for some situations but not for others. Now, theorists are paying attention to the organization's environment and suggesting ways to meet changing conditions.

In organization development or OD, consultants make use of organizational theory to help organizations modernize and get ready to meet the future. In this chapter, you will learn about strategies and interventions that the consultants use.

Organizations require planning and policy making in order to get information from the environment and keep their products or services up to date. The group that performs this function is made up of top managers in the organization, including the president and vice presidents.

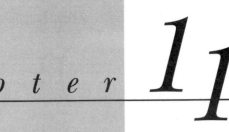

$\mathcal{C}hapter\ 1\!1$

Contents

Designing Effective Work Organizations

H̲e got work in a glass factory. The pay was better, and the work demanded skill. It was piecework, and the more skillful he was, the bigger
wages he earned. Here was incentive. And under this incentive he developed into a remarkable worker.

It was simple work, the tying of glass stoppers into small bottles.
At his waist he carried a bundle of twine. He held the bottle between his
knees so that he might work with both hands. Thus, in a sitting position
and bending over his own knees, his narrow shoulders grew humped
and his chest was contracted for ten hours each day. This was not good
for the lungs, but he tied three hundred dozen bottles a day.

The superintendent was very proud of him, and brought visi-
tors to look at him. In ten hours three hundred dozen bottles passed
through his hands. This meant he had attained machine-like perfection.

Jack London

The *machine-like perfection* described in this Jack London story is a primary aim of the
traditional organization. It is accomplished by having workers do highly simplified
jobs, such as tying stoppers into bottles. The aim, however, is accomplished at a
cost to the employee. Physical strain can result from the repetitive movements and
sustained posture required in such simplified jobs. As some organizational theorists
have noted, this organization also may have effects on workers' psychological
health. For example, it may ask them to be dependent on the organization, to leave
decision making to others, and to do nothing except their own jobs.

In other chapters, I refer to the organization largely as a setting for work
behavior. However, behavior is influenced by the setting; therefore, the organization itself should be examined. In this chapter, I identify the components of organizational structure and discuss several theories describing how organizations might
best be designed. I also examine the organizational change methodology, known as
organizational development (OD).

The Nature of Organization

An **organization** is a group that has a more or less constant membership, a purpose, and a set of operating procedures. **Organizational design** is the formal structure that defines the relationships between the members of the group. This structure specifies appropriate actions and interactions. It also identifies activities
necessary for reaching goals. In other words, organizational design defines the reality of the work situation so that employees know what action to take, when to take
it, and how to relate to others in the group.

All organizations have goals. Some are explicit and included in the organization's **mission statement,** which outlines the purpose and aims of the organization. Other goals are unstated but apparent in the organization's behavior. Because
the most important need of an organization is *survival,* its primary goals concern
output of products or services. These **output goals** are about getting and trans-

forming raw materials into products or services and then placing these in a consumer market. The organization also has secondary goals that relate to its position in society. These **societal goals** are broad aims for how the organization will contribute to society. For example, a company can plan to produce socially valuable products, such as recycled paper, or support a social movement, such as natural resource conservation. Other goals relate to the organization's internal operations. **Operations goals** indicate how the organization will be run. Goals referring to growth, expansion in a market, and reaching certain profit levels are operations goals (Perrow, 1970). The level of effectiveness of an organization might be assessed by evaluating the extent to which it realizes its goals. However, the various goals set by an organization do not contribute equally to its effectiveness. Some goals refer to an organization's operating efficiency, while others are more related to its profit or outcome success. Achievement of a balance of these goals is probably necessary for overall effectiveness (Ostroff & Schmitt, 1993).

THE ELEMENTS OF ORGANIZATIONAL STRUCTURE

The structure of the organization is a guide used to define, allocate, and coordinate work. As such, the structure includes a division of labor, an authority distribution, and a communication system. First, to structure an organization, a plan is developed for allocating work activities. This plan defines jobs, specifies work roles, and establishes work groups. That is, the allocation plan lays out the *division of labor*. Second, power and authority must be distributed in an organization so that the work being done can be coordinated or steered in the right direction. Third, coordination of work involves communication, of course; therefore, the structure also defines the channels of communication.

Organizational structure usually takes the shape of a pyramid in that there are many people at lower levels of the organization, fewer at the middle levels, and often just one at the top. For this reason, the structure is called the **organizational pyramid.** The organization's formal structure is graphically described by the **organizational chart.** A great deal can be learned from an organizational chart. Notice in the chart shown in figure 11.1 that work roles are specified by job and department titles. Authority relationships and communication channels are indicated by the lines that connect supervisors with their subordinates and by the lines that connect peer positions at the same organizational level. For example, the manager of product line A has authority over the plant managers, who have authority over the production employees. *Vertical communication* is conducted along these lines. The 1A and 2A plant managers are peers, and there are *lateral communication* channels between them.

Division of Labor

All organizations have work that must be done, and jobs are defined to divide this work into separate types of activities. This provides the division of labor. Work concerned specifically with an organization's output goals is included in jobs performed by employees making up the **operating core** (see figure 11.2). These employees

Figure 11.1 *An organizational chart depicting the organization's formal structure and work roles defined by job and department titles.*

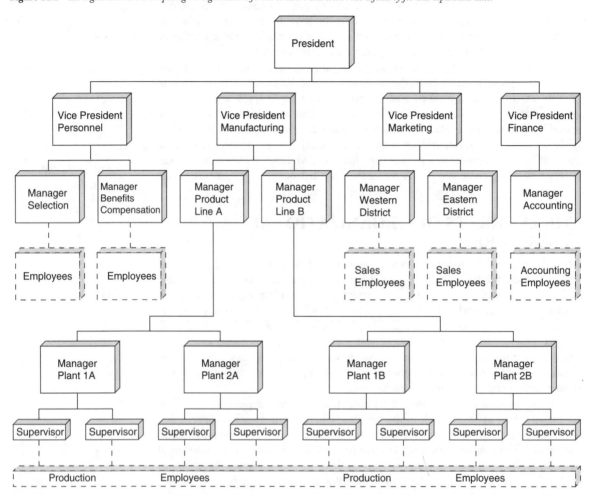

work on transforming raw materials into products or services. Another part of the required work is planning and policy making. Plans and policies are necessary because the organization must be able to get information from the environment, keep its products up to date, and focus on its goals. The group that does this work is the **strategic apex** at the top of the organizational pyramid. This group includes the chief executive officer (**CEO**) who may be the owner of the business. The planning activities of the strategic apex are linked with basic production by **middle management.** Middle management provides coordination of work and a communication link between the strategic apex and the operating core.

Job Specialization

The division of labor is described in terms of **job specialization,**[1] which refers to the simplicity or complexity of the job. In a highly specialized division of labor,

[1]This is *not* the same as the concept of role specialization, which is often used to describe the extent to which an employee is a *specialist* and has a broad knowledge base.

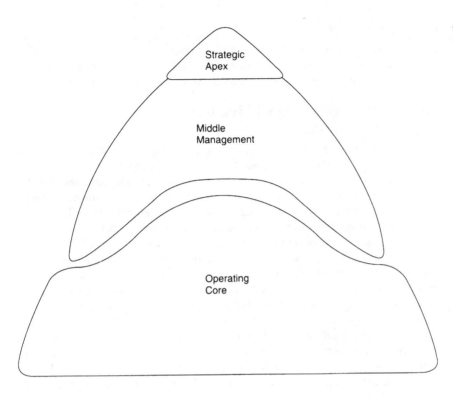

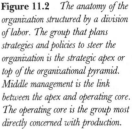

Figure 11.2 *The anatomy of the organization structured by a division of labor. The group that plans strategies and policies to steer the organization is the strategic apex or top of the organizational pyramid. Middle management is the link between the apex and operating core. The operating core is the group most directly concerned with production.*

jobs are narrowly defined so that they are relatively simple and repetitive. An example is the assembly-line operation in which the employee does only one or two simple activities and then passes the product on to the next employee. In a division of labor with low specialization, jobs are broadly defined, varied, and complex. The employee who does them can take more responsibility for the job. For example, a skilled artisan works on a single product from start to finish. A college professor is another whose job is not highly specialized. He or she does a variety of complex tasks, such as research, lecturing, and student counseling. As you will see later in the chapter, organizational theorists have been concerned about the division of labor, particularly about the effects of highly specialized jobs on employee health.

Span of Control

The degree of job specialization determines the need for supervision. When jobs are highly specialized, individual employees have a relatively incomplete understanding of the product or service. For example, a pocket stitcher is not likely to be clear about how the entire garment is constructed. Therefore, careful coordination by a supervisor is necessary in order to keep the work on track when jobs are highly specialized. This is not necessary when the division of labor is not highly specialized, in which jobs are more complex.

Span of control refers to the number of subordinates a supervisor can effectively manage. This number depends on the degree of job specialization. In highly specialized jobs in which employees are dependent on their supervisor, only a small number of subordinates can be managed by one person. In jobs that are less specialized, employees have a better understanding of the work process, and they need less supervision. A supervisor can manage more of these employees. Therefore, one way to increase the span of control is to reduce job specialization. This is done by expanding the job and giving more responsibility to the employee.

Groups of Organizational Members

Horizontal Differentiation

Large organizations are structured so that people doing related work are grouped together in departments. For example, if you are a bookkeeper, you probably work in an office in which others also are doing financial work. **Departmentation** is a way to arrange groups within an organization. It provides for **horizontal differentiation** of the organization by grouping people of different organizational ranks.

An organization can be departmentalized in several ways. *Functional* departmentation is the most common. In this, departments are established according to the type of work being done. For example, departments of finance, engineering, and manufacturing are functional departments. Geographic *location* is another method that is used by companies with branches at distant sites. Departmentation by *product* is used by organizations that produce a varied line of products or services. For example, a company that manufactures leather products, such as shoes and luggage, can departmentalize by these products. Departmentation by *customer* is a related form. Companies that produce men's and women's products often use customer departmentation. Departmentation does not have to be the same throughout the organization. However, at the lowest managerial level, departmentation is usually by function, which means that nonsupervisory employees are grouped according to the work they do. Figure 11.3 illustrates how an organization might departmentalize.

Another aspect of horizontal differentiation is the distinction between *line* and *staff* employees. These terms indicate how *administrative* work is done. All organizations have some administrative work to do. Reporting to government agencies; finding and hiring employees; and taking care of the bank account are some examples. In small organizations, such work is done by the same people who make and market the product. These are **line organizations.** In larger, **line-staff organizations,** special departments perform the administrative work. Line and staff departments within an organization are differentiated by the extent to which they are engaged in profit making. *Line departments* produce and sell consumer goods and services. *Staff departments* contribute only indirectly to profits. Departments of personnel, training, employee relations, and finance are staff departments.

Vertical Differentiation

A second feature of organizational structure that results in employee grouping is **vertical differentiation.** A hierarchy of levels or ranks results from vertical differentiation, and this determines the *height* of the organization. Organizations that are not highly differentiated have a **flat organizational structure.** Those that are highly differentiated have a **tall organizational structure.** The organization depicted in figure 11.3 is tall because it has multiple hierarchical levels.

Job specialization affects vertical differentiation. The number of employees doing basic production and the span of control of their supervisors determine the

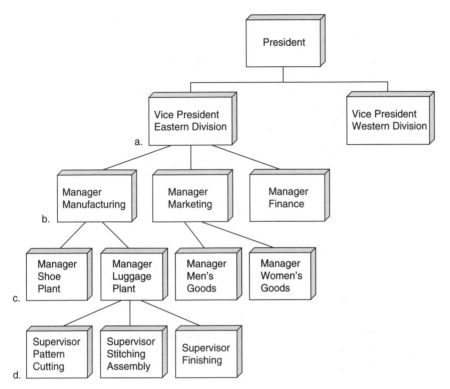

number of hierarchical levels. If there are few operators, a low level of job specialization, and a wide span of control, then the business can be run effectively with just two levels—production employees and a manager. For example, a roofing construction company can be run effectively with two levels: (1) a crew of roofers and (2) the owner who acts as general manager. If there are many operators, highly specialized jobs, and a narrow span of control, then first line supervisors will be needed, and another hierarchical level will be added. If the supervisors' jobs also are highly specialized, then they will require monitoring, and yet another level of management will be needed. This increasing need for work coordination results in a vertically differentiated organization.

Authority and Power in the Organization

Authority is distributed downward from the top of the organization. The distribution is affected by division of labor and vertical differentiation. That is, as levels of management are added to coordinate highly specialized jobs, the distribution of authority shifts somewhat. Although the actual amount of authority available at any one level will vary across organizations, there are two things that can be said about authority in general. First, top management holds more power than anyone else. Middle managers have some power, depending on their organizational rank, but nonsupervisory employees usually have little. Second, the authority distribution is an inversion of the organizational pyramid (see figure 11.4). In tall organizations,

Figure 11.4 *The "inverted pyramid" hierarchy of authority in a tall organization.*

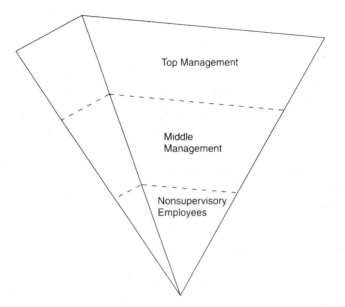

Top Management

Middle
Management

Nonsupervisory
Employees

authority is limited at lower levels. In flat organizations, because there are fewer managerial levels, nonsupervisory employees have considerable power to make decisions about their jobs.

Centralization

Organizational authority is the power to make decisions. Although no employee is absolutely without power, authority is more apparent among managerial employees because they make more decisions than lower level employees. Supervisory power gives the right to direct others and to decide how and when work will be done. Authority also allows an individual to set goals and contribute to the mission of the organization. A person with authority even has the right to decide who else can make decisions.

Centralization and decentralization refer to the amount of decision-making authority at different hierarchical levels. In a **centralized organization,** important decisions are made at the top. Managers at lower levels are allowed little discretion in decision making. In a **decentralized organization,** top management makes policy decisions but delegates other decisions to lower levels. Middle managers in a decentralized organization have considerable discretionary power.

Each way of allocating decision-making authority has advantages and disadvantages. Keeping decisions in the hands of owners or others who are interested in the organization's survival probably is less risky. In addition, decisions made by top-level people may be of higher quality, especially if expert advisors are available. On the other hand, there are reasons for decentralizing. Decentralization may improve employee motivation and behavior. When employees are expected to wait for orders from above, they may react negatively. It also may be more efficient to decentralize an organization that is operating in a changing environment. Employees who are in close contact with the environment may be in the best position to make decisions.

Formalization

Centralization refers to the question of *who* makes decisions. Formalization refers to *how* decisions are made. Formalization is the degree to which standard rules and procedures are used to decide issues. In **formalized organizations,** everything is decided and done "by the book." Work procedures are detailed in written operating manuals. Employees simply follow the manual. In organizations that are not highly formalized, work situations are less predictable. There are few standards that can be applied, and most situations require individual consideration and decision.

If the organization's environment is relatively stable, having a formal set of rules and procedures for making decisions has some real advantages. For example, formalization makes decentralization more acceptable. Decentralization feels less risky to top management when decision-making rules can be written down and given to lower level managers to use in deciding routine issues. However, organizations that exist in changing environments should not rely on formalization. There are too many unique situations in these environments that cannot be anticipated, and it is more efficient to develop the ability of lower level managers to use their own discretion in decision making.

Integration of the Organization

Thus far, you see that the organization is internally differentiated—by a division of labor, an authority hierarchy, and departmentation. However, the organization must have enough *integrity* to operate as a whole. You may wonder how this is possible because the organization now seems like a collection of pieces. Organizations actually are more integrated structurally than they may appear.

The most commonly used method for integrating an organization is the committee. A committee is a group of people from different organizational units who meet periodically to deal with issues that affect all units. When there is a continuing need, the group functions as a **standing committee.** When the need is temporary, it operates as an **ad hoc committee.** A committee is useful when the organization needs to develop a policy that affects the departments, create a solution to a problem, or get widespread commitment on a decision. Committees have disadvantages, however. First, they are slow, partly because they need input from all members and this takes time. Also, committees do not always accomplish what they set out to do.

Organizations periodically need departments to confer on short-term projects, and special task forces or project teams can be created for this purpose. Task forces and project teams are similar to ad hoc committees in being temporary. When the project is finished, the group disbands. The difference between them is the extent to which the work occupies the members' time. Members of committees serve only part time. Task force and project team members work full time on a project. Only when the project is complete do members go back to their regular jobs.

Matrix Organization

Some organizations need many ongoing projects at all times. For example, in research and development (R&D) organizations, special projects are a continuing way of life. When an organization develops such a need, it can be rebuilt as a **matrix organization.** The matrix organization is a new twist on formal structure (see figure 11.5). It departs radically from the traditional organizational pyramid.

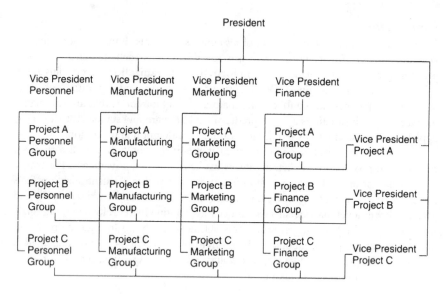

Figure 11.5 *Structure of the matrix organization. Special projects are a continuous way of life for organizations using the matrix structure. Each project team combines experts from different departments. The project team has a manager and the departments have managers; therefore, the employees on these teams report to two bosses.*

However, the matrix organization provides a major gain in integration. Channels of lateral communication that do not exist in the traditional organization become available. The matrix structure is created by using two forms of departmentation to place employees as simultaneous members of a functional department and a project team. The project team is product oriented and is made up of people from different departments who provide expertise relating to every aspect of the work.

The matrix organization is not problem-free, of course. For one thing, the project team and the department each have a manager; thus, each employee reports to two superiors. This can lead to stressful ambiguity and conflict for the employees who are unsure of their roles and responsibilities. Also, conflict occurs between the managers of project teams and departments (Ford & Randolph, 1992; de Laat, 1994). However, the matrix organization does have the advantages of both functional and product departmentation. In functional departments, such as marketing, employees have in-depth understanding of the functional area. Product departments are strong in that employees have breadth and more clarity about the organization's output goals. Combining these strengths results in project teams with both depth and long-range vision. Further, the combined functional and product expertise of the project teams increases the amount of information the organization can handle, which is important to an organization, such as an R&D firm, whose environment is changeable (Ford & Randolph, 1992).

*M*ain *P*oints

Organizations are structured by means of a division of labor. A key factor in division of labor is job specialization, which defines jobs and determines the span of control. Highly specialized jobs are simplified. However, they require close supervision, which limits a supervisor's span of control. Less specialized jobs are more complex, need less supervision, and allow a wider span of control.

Differentiation is an aspect of organizational structure. Through horizontal differentiation, the firm is divided into separate departments. Vertical differentiation provides for distributing authority. In flat organizations, employees have considerable authority; in tall organizations, authority is retained by top management. Authority is needed for decision making. Centralization of authority means that most decisions are made by top managers. In decentralization, authority is delegated. A related concept, formalization, refers to how decisions are made. With high formalization, decisions are made by standard procedures. When formalization is low, decisions are made individually.

Organizations also need integration. Most are integrated by committees that work on issues of common interest. A structure that departs from the typical design and provides high integration is the matrix organization. It operates multiple ongoing project teams, which bring together employees from different departments.

THEORIES OF ORGANIZATION

Business organizations may or may not be effective. Whether an organization survives will depend to a great extent on how it is designed. What is the best way to organize? Many people would like the answer to this question. Since the time when people first began working in groups and sharing the profits of their labor, we have had theories about how to organize. At least there have been some *implicit theories* on this. The message in an implicit theory can be quite simple: "Put one person in charge—the one with the money. This person makes all decisions and gives the orders. Everyone else must obey." The trouble with this simple approach is that it often does not produce an effective organization. Other organizing theories are more complex, and some consider the environment in which the business firm operates.

In this section, I describe how several theorists have envisioned the effective organization, and how they answer the questions about organizing. For example, how will decisions be made? Who will be in control? How will groups be organized? How will interaction and communication be handled? Who will set goals and steer the organization? In other words, organizational theories address the elements of structure that I have just discussed. In so doing, many of the theories offer guidance that recognizes the context and constraints of the organization's environment.

Focus on Organizational Structure

The Bureaucracy

The classical **bureaucracy** is based on the work of several theorists, including Henri Fayol (1949) and Mary Parker Follett (1942) both of whom believed in the need for systematic structuring of employees' work roles. However, Max Weber (1946, 1947) is foremost among the bureaucracy theorists, and it is his organization that is our "traditional" design.[2] In Weber's day, the bureaucratic design represented a definite improvement in organizing. According to Meyer(1982), both capitalism and bureaucracy grew out of movements beginning in the sixteenth

[2]Weber envisioned the use of "bureaus" to hold an organization's written policies and procedures, hence, the term *bureaucracy*.

T*able 11.1*

Characteristics of the Formal Bureaucratic Structure

High Division of Labor	High job specialization Close supervision of work Narrow span of control
High Departmentation	High horizontal differentiation Line-staff organization
Unit of Control	Strict chain of command High vertical differentiation Tall organizational structure
Centralized Decision Making	High formalization Limited delegated power Written rules and procedures Formal, written communication
Limited Communication Channels	Little upward communication Little lateral communication Narrow communication channels

and seventeenth centuries to make European business more rational. Previously, there were centuries of feudalistic organizing in which tenants served landowners, and work was organized by means of nepotism, favoritism, and discrimination. Bureaucracy introduced rational standards and principles of fairness to the organization of work. It also was meant to make the organization more efficient. Weber believed that this design would increase the speed and precision of work activities. In other words, people would know their jobs and be able to work together as smoothly as the parts of a well-oiled machine.

As described in table 11.1, an important feature of the formal bureaucratic organization is a highly specialized division of labor. Weber believed that precision and speed could be gained only if the work was divided into many simplified jobs. His rationale was that simple jobs could be learned and performed quickly. Those doing the same jobs could work in the same physical area to make overseeing easier. High job specialization would require work standardization, of course. Therefore, the best way to do a job would need to be determined, and work procedures would need to be written into procedural manuals. These manuals would be used to train and supervise employees, and ensure that the job is done exactly as it is supposed to be done.

High job specialization has wide-ranging implications for the organization. As discussed previously, specialized jobs are designed according to a central plan of action, but employees know little about this central plan because of their restricted work roles. In fact, in the interest of efficiency, bureaucracy discourages workers from learning anything other than their own jobs. Thus, there is a strong need for employee direction, which results in a limited span of control. Also, most jobs in the bureaucracy are simplified, including supervisory jobs. This calls for a *unity of control* from the top of the organization to the bottom. Finally, the bureaucracy's high job specialization results in high levels of vertical and horizontal differentiation. Between production employees and upper management, there are many levels of authority, and when specialized jobs are grouped physically close together to maximize the span of control, more departments are formed. These have high internal similarity because they have been developed by clustering groups involved in the same type of work. Therefore, the bureaucracy has many functional departments, but each performs a very limited range of activities.

The unity of control that results from this division of labor means that the bureaucracy has a clear chain of command from the top to the bottom of the organization. Delegation of authority is restricted, with just enough power being handed down the chain to do the job. Lower level managers have almost no discretionary power. Situations that they cannot handle with standard operating procedures are referred up to higher management for decision; thus, the bureaucracy is highly centralized. In such an organization, formalization is necessary. When jobs are highly specialized and decision-making power is centralized, exact work procedures and decision rules must be developed to cover all possible situations that can occur. For any problem that arises, a supervisor simply consults the procedures manual. Communication, therefore, is limited to necessary job information and comes from the top down.

Evaluation of the Bureaucracy

Since its introduction, the bureaucratic design has been adopted by a great number of organizations. For some time now, it has been the dominant form of organization in this country. As a result, the bureaucracy[3] has had considerable field testing, and both strengths and weaknesses have been revealed. First, it is recognized as rational and orderly. The formalization of decision rules and work procedures, and the centralization of authority, help to produce clear work roles for employees. Similarly, relationships with customers and clients are made clear and fair. The bureaucracy is a programmed organization in that the same problem is treated in the same manner every time (Pugh, 1966).

Bureaucracies are effective in stable and predictable environments. In changing environments, however, the bureaucracy's formalization and centralization become sources of breakdown. In a world in which technology advances on a daily basis, economic conditions fluctuate, and international issues are relevant, the bureaucracy is sluggish. Written procedures become obsolete. Employees waste time waiting for a decision to come down. Thus, the organization must change to deal with environmental fluctuation (Eisenhardt, 1989; Keck & Tushman, 1993).

An aspect of the bureaucratic design that can make it hard to change is the dependency it demands: Employees are supposed to follow rules and obey orders. This, however, can result in low work motivation. Having to rely on superiors for ordinary decisions can make an individual unwilling to do otherwise, and long-term employees may turn down opportunities to take more responsibility. However, even for employees who are motivated and ambitious, there may be few opportunities for responsible work. The employee at the bottom of the organization can attempt to promote up to a higher level where there is more responsibility and authority. However, such a promotion may require skills and abilities that are not attainable in his or her present simplified job. Further, competition for higher level positions is keen because of the many hopefuls and the few positions (Argyris, 1965).

[3]In the popular use of the term, a bureaucratic organization is one that is caught up in "red tape" and obsessed by rules and regulations. This use of the term indicates a common awareness of a weakness of the design.

In conclusion, we have learned some lessons from our extensive experience with the bureaucracy. One lesson concerns the impact of external conditions. A design that works at one time does not necessarily work at another time or in another place. The bureaucracy is too rigid to function well in a changing environment. A second lesson concerns the impact of structure on people. Organizations can have harmful effects on employees. In the past, social scientists did not fully appreciate the need for organizational designers to consider the person. The human element was ignored as organizational theories focused on designing for efficiency.

Mechanistic and Organic Organizations

Some theorists have considered the business environment in designing the organization. Burns and Stalker (1961) proposed that effective organizational designs can vary, depending on the demands of the environment, from the highly mechanistic at one extreme to the organic at the other. The **mechanistic organization** looks and acts very much like the bureaucracy. It has high job specialization, a strict chain of command, and centralized decision making with formalization. The mechanistic organization is proposed to be effective if the firm's commercial and technological environments are stable. The highly flexible **organic organization** is offered as a more appropriate design in unstable environments. It has low levels of job specialization and comparative freedom in individual work roles. It is decentralized, has little formalization, and channels of authority are not distinctly defined. Committees and project teams are used extensively in the organic organization (Burns, 1963). Table 11.2 contrasts the mechanistic and organic designs.

Burns and Stalker's (1961) discussion pays close attention to the network of interpersonal relationships between individuals in these two organizational designs. The mechanistic organization, like the bureaucracy, has few communication links and little closeness in interpersonal relationships. The strict chain of command means that individuals legitimately can discuss work only with their supervisor or subordinates. On the other hand, organic organizations have an elaborate work-related communication network. Because authority is more widely distributed and because people are not divided into specialized groups, there are many close interpersonal relationships that cut across the organic organization (Shrader, Lincoln, & Hoffman, 1989).

On the surface, it appears that the mechanistic organization is likely to have the same problems as the bureaucracy and that moving toward the organic structure would be a good idea under most modern environmental conditions. Burns and Stalker (1961) looked for organizations that had tried to make such a change. They found some had attempted to change gradually to the organic form by adding new research and development functions to an existing structure. This was not very successful, because of struggles between departments over scarce resources. The new functions were simply absorbed into the existing structure. It may be that gradual change to an organic form is not actually possible, because employees may resist minor changes in responsibility.

What is most important about this theory is the organic design. The proposal that such deliberate flexibility in organizational design not only is sensible but also necessary for businesses operating in unpredictable environments, was revolu-

Table 11.2	Characteristics of the Mechanistic and Organic Forms of Organizational Structure	
Variable	**Mechanistic Organization**	**Organic Organization**
Jobs	Specialized; high role clarity	Not specialized; low role clarity
Span of Control	Narrow	Wide
Authority	Clear channels of authority; strict chain of command	Fuzzy channels of authority; little emphasis on chain of command
Communication	Sparse network	Elaborate network
Departmentation	Mostly functional	Varies
Line-Staff	Extensive use of staff personnel	Often little distinction between line and staff
Decision Making	Centralized; little delegation	Decentralized; high levels of delegation
Integration	Use of policies and procedures	Use of committees and project teams
Environment	Predictable; routine operations	Uncertain; turbulent

tionary at the time. As you will see, many later organizational theorists have incorporated the organic form into their own recommended designs. Discussions of how best to organize now usually contrast the weakness of traditional bureaucratic organization with the potential of the organic organization.

The bureaucracy was developed by early organizational theorists, particularly Weber, who incorporated rationality and order into the design of work organizations. The bureaucratic design is meant to achieve fast and precise machinelike operation. To accomplish this, jobs are highly specialized, and the organization is highly differentiated, both vertically and horizontally. Centralized decision making and formalization means that lower level managers can take "by the book" action, but they have little discretionary power. The bureaucratic design has been used extensively. It works best when the environment is stable. Even so, its rigid structure and control may negatively affect employees' motivation.

Burns and Stalker theorized that effective designs vary depending on the organization's environment. Their mechanistic organization is like the bureaucracy and is effective in stable environments. Organic organizations, with their improved interpersonal networks, are more flexible and appropriate for changing environments. The organic design has greatly influenced the development of organizational thinking.

Focus on Human Relations in Organizations

Beginning in the 1950s, organizational theorists began to be concerned about the impact of the organization on the employee. This concern developed into something of a social movement toward better human relations at work. The human relations movement resulted largely from experience with bureaucratic organizations. Critics of the bureaucracy pointed out that employees have many capacities that ordinarily go unused. If employees are treated well, these capacities might become available to the organization. If employees are treated poorly, however, their capacities may go toward sabotage. Human relations theorists observed that workers were not being treated very well, and they suggested ways for an organization to improve.

McGregor's Theory X and Theory Y

McGregor (1957) proposed that certain assumptions about the nature of human behavior can be seen in the way that any organization is managed and that some of these assumptions are detrimental to organizational success. He presented two managerial approaches—Theory X and Theory Y. In business, McGregor observed, managers are responsible for steering the organization toward its economic mission, and they have to get this done by managing people. When managers take the **Theory X** view of human nature, they motivate and control employees with persuasion, reward, and punishment in order to attain the organization's economic goals. In this style of management, employees are seen as passive, lazy, and rather stupid. They must be made to work because they lack ambition, shirk responsibility, and prefer that others make the decisions. Theory X managers also believe that employees will resist any effort to change them. McGregor proposed that the Theory X approach is not effective.

McGregor (1957) proposed that **Theory Y** is a better approach because it is based on more accurate assumptions about human nature. The Theory Y manager believes that workers are capable and motivated and that they have potential for taking responsibility. The essential task of the Theory Y manager is to provide a means for releasing this potential. McGregor emphasized that the Theory Y perspective does not imply a weak approach to management. Neither does it suggest lowering organizational standards. What it does imply is that obstacles in the way of releasing the potential of employees must be removed, and conditions encouraging their personal growth must be created.

McGregor (1957) believed that organizations that place employees in narrowly defined jobs actually discourage them from developing their abilities and taking responsibility. To break out of the Theory X tradition of management, McGregor recommended gradual decentralization of the organization with more delegation of responsibility to employees. He thought that enlarging jobs at lower organizational levels would help employees accept responsibility. He also suggested allowing employees to participate in decision making. Participation might encourage commitment to organizational goals and, at the same time, satisfy employees' personal needs. Employees must see this "participation" as real, however, and not simply as managerial lip service. As you see in a later section, the extent of managerial support has become an important issue in the success of employee participation.

Theory Z and Japanese Organizations

Since World War II, American behavioral scientists have been interested in Japan, particularly because of its rapid industrialization. In recent years, Japanese business has had a big impact in the United States. Imported Japanese products have cut a swath through the consumer market and are effectively competing with home-produced goods. Since the early 1970s, we have been paying close attention to the Japanese style of organizing (Bhagat & McQuaid, 1982). Mainly, we want to know what they are doing that makes them so successful.

William Ouchi (1981) compared Japanese and American organizations. He found the Japanese organization to be highly paternalistic; that is, it assumes responsibility for employees' lives. In return, employees are committed and loyal to the organization. Employment is for life, and the company becomes part of an individual's personal identity. Jobs tend to be broader and less specialized, and employees participate in decision making through task forces that focus on product quality. Promotion in the Japanese firm is slow, however, often taking many years. In contrast, Ouchi noted, the American organization offers short-term employment, highly specialized jobs, and rapid promotion, but it assumes little responsibility for the employee.

Because of important differences between the two cultures, Ouchi did not recommend the Japanese style for American firms. Instead, he coupled his observations with McGregor's ideas and proposed a **Theory Z** organizational design that combines some of the better features of both the American and the Japanese styles. The Theory Z organization offers long-term employment and moderate job specialization. It is similar to Japanese organizations in that it includes employees in decision making and allows only slow career progress. It is similar to American organizations in not assuming responsibility for the employee.

Researchers doing cross-cultural studies underscore Ouchi's position that differences in the social structures of Japanese and American societies, and in the psychological makeup of Japanese and American workers are important in organizing. These differences can affect the success of imported Japanese-style organizations (Hopkins et al., 1977; Smith, 1984). Some of the difficulties are shown when the Japanese organization is transported wholly to this country. Young (1992) looked into the experiences of manufacturing firms that are using Japanese methods and found that they have not had the success they expected. Part of the problem is that important societal differences are being ignored. Some practices in the Japanese style simply do not have the same result in the two countries. For example, when a U.S. firm adopts the concept of *Kaizen,* or continuous improvement, it also needs to commit to a no-layoff policy. Otherwise, when workers are asked to "strive continuously" to improve productivity and profits, they will recognize that they can work themselves out of a job. That is, as the work force improves and becomes more proficient, fewer workers will be needed to produce the same amount; thus, some will be laid off. Young (1992), like Ouchi (1981), asserted that the Japanese style must be modified for use in the United States.

Argyris's Developmental Model

Argyris (1957, 1964) also contributed to human relations theory. He proposed that the development and health of an organization *mirrors* the development and health of the people in it. This proposition is derived from a particular view of human development. In this view, a person develops from infancy to adulthood through specific growth stages. From stage to stage, the person proceeds from passivity to activity; from dependence to independence; and from being helpless to having many abilities. In the bureaucratic organization, Argyris observed, many employees are treated as *infants*. Nonsupervisory employees are expected to accept their superiors' orders passively. They are expected to use only a few of their abilities in their jobs, and they are discouraged from taking responsibility. Clearly, Argyris concluded, this treatment will have adverse effects on the person and on the organization. Workers will show psychological withdrawal, such as apathy; physical withdrawal, such as absenteeism; and aggression or destructiveness. Further, informal groups will develop to support and protect this behavior (Argyris, 1957).

Although Argyris criticized the bureaucracy, he did not propose to discard it. Rather, he hoped to modernize it. He recommended that the organization be changed in order to minimize employee dependency. Jobs should be enriched, and employees should participate in making decisions that affect their work. He believed this would encourage more personal responsibility. Of course, such changes have to be based on trust in the capacities and motivation of employees, as McGregor (1957) pointed out.

Likert's Organizational Systems

In an effort to explain existing organizations and to suggest a better way to organize, Likert (1961, 1967) proposed four systems of organization. These differ both in managerial behavior and organizational structure. The System 1 organization is similar to the bureaucracy and to McGregor's Theory X management. System 4 is more like Theory Y management. Systems 2 and 3 are in between these extremes.

The System 1 organization is centralized and formalized. It restricts interaction and communication between people at different hierarchical levels. System 1 managers use threats and punishment to motivate subordinates, as Theory X managers do. The employee is treated as if he or she is motivated only to meet basic survival needs.[4] In contrast, managers in **System 4 organizations** show trust and confidence in their employees. This organization is relatively decentralized, and employees participate in the goal-setting process. Communication flows freely in all directions. Employees do not have to "go through channels" because decision authority is delegated to the person who has the relevant information. System 4 is based on a positive managerial strategy that Likert (1967) called the *principle of supportive relationships*. Managers who use this principle try to ensure that employees have positive experiences in all work relationships.

To change to System 4, an organization must increase the level and quality of employee involvement and establish supportive work relationships. Likert proposed that this can be done by means of an *overlapping group structure*. The overlapping group is similar to a project team in that it cuts across the lines of vertical and horizontal differentiation. The overlapping group creates supportive relationships by involving all members in exchanging information and making decisions. As shown in figure 11.6, the groups *overlap* different hierarchical levels through their *linking pin* members. For example, production employees and their supervisor make up a group. The supervisor is a member of another group that includes other supervisors and a manager. The manager, in turn, is the linking pin to yet another group.

---

[4]Likert used Maslow's (1954) need hierarchy to describe employee motivation, as did McGregor and Argyris. Maslow's theory is discussed in chapter 8.

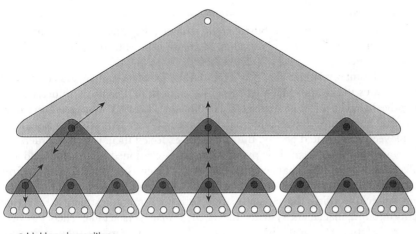

● Linking pin positions
←● Linking pin functions

Figure 11.6 *The overlapping group and the linking pin function in a System 4 organization. Groups overlap different hierarchical levels in the organization because of the linking pin members. Because of their dual membership in groups at different levels, linking pin members tie the organization together.*

From R. Likert, New Patterns of Management. *Copyright © 1961 The McGraw-Hill Companies, Inc., New York. Reprinted with permission.*

Evaluation of Human Relations Theory

Early human relations theory represented a strong reaction to bureaucracy. The primary goal was to deal with some human problems that had arisen in these organizations. At the time, the solution to the problems seemed obvious. Bureaucracies needed to be restructured to improve the treatment of the worker. Human relations theorists offered ways to do this, and they promised to increase organizational effectiveness at the same time. Their recommendations included enriching jobs, increasing worker responsibility, and allowing participation in decision making. However, organizations accepting this advice sometimes ran into trouble. For one thing, high productivity did not always accompany high morale. An organization might be made up of happy workers who were hardly ever busy. In fact, on some occasions, the classical bureaucratic style was more successful in realizing its goals.

Two points can be made concerning our experience with the human relations theories. First, we are still using this approach. One of the most important concepts to come from this work–participation in decision making–has been adopted and tried in many organizations. (I discuss the research on this in a later section.) Also, modern advocates have redefined and repackaged the concept of participation. For example, managers were advised by the human relations theorists to delegate some authority to their subordinates and to include them in decisions. Now, managers are being asked to share responsibility with and "empower" employees, in order to get their commitment to shared goals (Ramsey & Calvert, 1994). Second, the human relations prescriptions appear to have been used to manipulate and exploit. This seems to be the very reverse of what they were meant to do. Possibly, this has occurred because of how the goals were first presented. Although the goal of improving productivity was listed as *secondary* by these theorists, in actuality it can be understood as the primary goal. That is, "humanistic" interventions were offered to management as ways to "make better use" of their human resources in order to increase productivity. In this way, although the theorist may have cautioned against it, the interventions were definite "add ons" (Ramsey & Calvert, 1994).

Experience showed that the bureaucratic structure negatively affects employees, which in turn impairs the organization. Human relations theory was a reaction to this experience.

Human relations theorists explored the problem and suggested more effective ways to operate. McGregor used his concept of Theory X to describe the negative behavior of some managers. He thought Theory Y managers were more effective; they trusted and appreciated their employees. Argyris also noted that employees were treated poorly. Bureaucracies expected them to accept orders and to do nothing more than their own jobs. Argyris cautioned that this had adverse effects and should be changed. In Theory Z, Ouchi said that American firms could adopt some practices of the Japanese organization. However, cultural differences preclude using the Japanese style without some adjustments. Likert described four management systems. In System 1, managers act like Theory X managers. In contrast, those in the more effective System 4 organization are supportive and try to make their employees' work experiences positive.

Although they discussed organizations in somewhat different terms, the four human relations theorists took a major step in the changes they recommended. Each of them recommended enriched jobs, more employee responsibility, and participation in decision making.

Focus on Environmental Contingencies

The trouble with many theories is that they attempt to provide a universal "best design" for all organizations. As organizational thinking advances, however, the organization's context is being considered in proposing effective structures. Currently, organizational theory more frequently takes a *contingency* approach in which environmental variables are specified and related to the organization's effectiveness.

Some theorists limit their discussion of contingencies to the technological aspects of organizational environment. One is Woodward (1965), who proposed that the best structure for an organization is determined by its technology. Her recommendations are based on a study of manufacturing firms. She found that these firms differed in terms of their product, equipment, and method of work. One type of firm was engaged in producing "small batches" of customer-specified products with comparatively simple methods and equipment. Another type was mechanized and engaged in mass producing "large batches" of items via an assembly line. The third used a highly automated "continuous process" method of work with one organizational unit continuing what another had started. (An automobile factory is an example of a continuous process organization.) Woodward concluded that these firms operate in different worlds because of the differences in their technology.

Woodward (1965) proposed that the most effective design for an organization depends on the level of its technological *complexity*. Specifically, she said, firms doing mass production are effective when they are organized as classical bureaucratic or mechanistic organizations. However, small batch and continuous process organizations are less effective when organized in this manner. They need the more flexible organic forms of organization.

Mintzberg's Configurational Theory

Mintzberg (1979; 1983) studied Woodward's (1965) findings and concluded that both work equipment and the general environment are important in designing an effective organization. In his **configurational theory,** Mintzberg (1983) described the organization's work equipment as its *technical system.* The technical system is the machinery that workers in the operating core use to convert raw materials into goods and services. Technical systems range from the simple and easy to understand, to the sophisticated and difficult. They also vary in terms of how much they regulate or control work procedures. In a highly regulating technical system, the equipment defines work procedures; that is, tasks consist of machine operation. In an automated system, the work is completely regulated.

In Mintzberg's (1983) view, two aspects of the outside environment are important in the success of an organization. One is the degree of stability, which refers to the extent to which the environment is stable or dynamic. A dynamic environment is turbulent and unpredictable. The second important feature is the complexity of the *technological knowledge base* in the environment that the organization draws upon. Notice that the technological knowledge base is independent of the organization's technical system. An organization that has a complex technological environment uses knowledge from several advanced fields, but it may or may not need to have a sophisticated technical system. For example, an accounting firm draws upon a complex base of knowledge, but its technical system is relatively simple in that accounting needs little equipment. Conversely, a taxicab company has a fairly complex technical system in the form of its vehicles, but it requires little knowledge of how gasoline engines operate.

Mintzberg (1983) proposed that the three situational variables interact to determine organizational design. That is, the best design depends on (1) the sophistication of the technical system, (2) the complexity of the technological knowledge base, and (3) the stability of the environment. Specifically, he proposed that decentralization is indicated by a sophisticated technical system and a complex technological knowledge base. He said also that the need for adopting either a bureaucratic or an organic structure depends on the extent to which the environment is stable and the technical system is regulating.

Using these relationships and other factors, Mintzberg defined five organizational "configurations" or designs that he thought would operate well in given environments. These are described briefly in table 11.3 and as follows:

1.   The *simple structure,* used by entrepreneurial firms, is centralized but otherwise is an organic organization.
2.   The *machine bureaucracy* is the traditional Weberian bureaucracy; it operates well in a stable environment with a regulating technical system.
3.   The *professional bureaucracy* requires an operating core of expert, professionalized employees because it has a complex technological environment.

Table 11.3

Structural and Environmental Features of Five Organizational Designs

Design Feature	Structural Configuration				
	Simple Structure	**Machine Bureaucracy**	**Professional Bureaucracy**	**Divisionalized Form**	**Adhocracy**
Formalization	Low	High	Low	High	Low
Bureaucratic or organic	Organic	Bureaucratic	Bureaucratic	Bureaucratic	Organic
Distribution of authority	Centralized	Limited horizontal decentralization	Decentralized	Limited vertical decentralization	Selective decentralization
Means of work coordination	Direct supervision	Standardized work	Standardized skills	Standardized outputs	Mutual adjustment
Technical system	Simple; Not regulating	Regulating; Not sophisticated	Not regulating; Not sophisticated	Divisible; Regulating; Not sophisticated	Very sophisticated; Often automated; Varies
Environment	Simple and dynamic	Simple and stable	Complex and stable	Relatively simple and stable	Complex and dynamic

Source: H. Mintzberg, *Structure in Fives: Designing Effective Organizations,* pp. 153, 280–281. Copyright © 1983 Prentice Hall. Reprinted by permission.

4. The *divisional form* is a group of fairly autonomous branches that focus on different markets and are held together by a bureaucratic administrative structure.

5. The *adhocracy* is an organic structure operating by means of project teams in a complex and dynamic environment.

If an organization recognizes its situation and adopts the appropriate one of these designs, will it be more effective than if it did not use the recommended structure? Mintzberg thought so. However, the answer is not yet available. One study was unable to show the proposed effect (Doty, Glick, & Huber, 1993). The researchers speculated that the difficulty may be that Mintzberg did not go far enough, and they suggested that other environmental factors may be important to consider.

Sociotechnical Systems Theory

Research on work technology made it clear that an effective structure depends on situational variables, and this contributed to a change in organizational theorizing. Studies conducted in the 1950s and 1960s at the Tavistock Institute in Great Britain strengthened this redirection of organizational theory, as did the efforts of others to extend von Bertalanffy's (1950) *general systems theory* to work organizations. Both lines of work enter in the development of the **sociotechnical systems theory,** which combines a focus on the technical and the social conditions of work.

The Tavistock research (Trist & Bamforth, 1951; Trist et al., 1963) showed what happens when new technology is introduced without consideration of the people who will use it. The study involved coal mining, an industry that had undergone major technological change. Prior to the 1940s, the British coal industry was organized around small groups of miners working together. This system was known as the *shortwall method* because the mining groups each took a short section of the area to be mined and did all the work. When new mining equipment was introduced, mining was accelerated and work procedures changed. In the resulting *longwall method,* large sections of coal were removed and delivered elsewhere for processing. The immediate effect was the destruction of the small work groups. Low productivity and negative behavior on the part of the miners followed. Thus, introduction of better equipment, ostensibly for improving the organization, actually started a chain reaction of events that reduced effectiveness by disturbing the organization's social relationships. The specific purpose of the Tavistock research was to find a way to reduce these negative effects. One strategy, called the **self-regulating work group,**[5] involved reorganizing the miners into small groups that were given full responsibility for a section of the work. They were made collectively responsible. Their tasks were interdependent and required close social interaction, and jobs were rotated so that all group members could do all jobs. These work groups were unique at the time in that jobs were expanded and the employees took on managerial responsibilities. Essentially, the work which had been organized to accommodate technology was reorganized to meet social demands.

Organizational theorists began to use the language and reasoning of general systems theory (von Bertalanffy, 1950) when it became apparent that both technology and people need to be considered in organizational design (Boulding, 1956; Katz & Kahn, 1966; Rice, 1963). In the systems theory view, the organization is constantly interacting, both internally and externally. Interactions take place through the technological and social subsystems of an organization. Change in any of these subsystems can have effects on others and on the system as a whole. The organization itself interacts with other organizations in the larger environment, and this too can change the system.

Because organizations are open to outside influence from the environment, they are considered to be **open systems.** *Closed* systems are self-controlled and not influenced from the outside, whereas open systems are neither self-controlled nor self-contained. Exchanges with the environment take place when a system is open (Rice, 1963). The processes of exchange are inputs and outputs. *Inputs* are raw materials and financial and human resources. *Outputs* are finished products or services. Systems theory posits that organizations, as open systems, grow and become more elaborate as a result of successful exchanges with the environment (Katz & Kahn, 1966).

There is little research that directly tests the propositions of systems theory in organizations; part of the problem is that the theoretical constructs are difficult to operationalize. It has been a popular model, however, and is used to label many organizational concepts. In fact, Ashmos and Huber (1987) speculated that this may be its undoing; overusing the terminology may actually obscure its value. Systems theory also provides a foundation for much practical advice on organizing. For example, it is the basis for descriptions of the "learning organization," in which a firm learns from its experience or from the consequences of its interactions to be more effective (Kofman & Senge, 1993; McGill & Slocum, 1993).

---

[5]Modern versions of the self-regulating work group often are called *self-managing work teams*.

Some theories concentrate mainly on the impact of environmental factors. In this respect, Woodward's study of manufacturing technology was groundbreaking. She found that organizations using certain technology worked well as bureaucracies, while others with other technology needed organic designs to be successful.

Mintzberg identified three factors relating to technology and environment. One is the sophistication of the technical system or work equipment. The second is the complexity of the technological knowledge base that the organization uses. The third is the stability of the environment. Mintzberg said these variables determine the type of structure an organization must have. He proposed five organizational types ranging from bureaucratic to organic and identified the conditions in which each would work best.

In sociotechnical systems theory development, two lines of work are important. The Tavistock research revealed that social relationships at work can be damaged when new technology is introduced. The self-regulating work group was created to address this. General systems theory can explain why such problems occur. The organization is viewed as an interacting system of equally important social and technical components. The organization also makes exchanges with the environment through inputs of materials and outputs of products.

Focus on Organizational Dynamics

Modern theorists are more likely to consider the organization to be a dynamic interactive system made up of structural, technological, and human components. The organization and its units are considered open to outside influence, and change in response to the environment is the rule, not the exception.

Lawrence and Lorsch's Contingency Model

Lawrence and Lorsch (1967, 1969) were interested in learning *how* effective organizations go about meeting environmental demands. They thought it likely that features of the environment are specifically addressed by certain organizational processes. They defined the concept of *managerial differentiation*[6] as being a critical factor in the organization's operation in this respect. In their theory, differentiation refers to the different thinking styles shown by managers in the various functional departments of an organization. That is, differentiation refers to the variations in managerial approach. The different thinking styles develop because managers must interact with a particular part of the environment—the one that relates to their department's function—and they must become mentally oriented to this "subenvironment." For example, a personnel research department will be oriented toward professional and scientific I/O psychology as its relevant subenvironment. Unlike other managers who are not in human resource departments, this department manager is concerned with issues in I/O psychology, such as finding new ways to evaluate employee performance.

Lawrence and Lorsch proposed that the amount of managerial differentiation needed in an organization depends on two features of the environment:

[6]Notice that differentiation is *not* being used here to describe departmentation and organizational ranking, as I define it earlier.

(1) the *diversity* of relevant subenvironments, and (2) the *uncertainty* of the environment. When the environment contains a diverse group of subenvironments, an organization is more effective if it is highly differentiated with multiple functional departments set up to respond to these subenvironments. Organizations that exist in stable environments can operate effectively with little managerial differentiation. An organization that must interact with an unstable or uncertain environment, however, needs to be highly differentiated.

Managerial differentiation creates a complication. Organizations that exist in uncertain environments or that must respond to diverse subenvironments require differentiation. However, differentiation brings about a general lack of unity in an organization. Therefore, the greater the need for managerial differentiation, the greater the need also for the organization to take steps to recover integration. The need for integration is particularly strong among departments that must interact. Setting up interdepartmental committees is one way to integrate. Another strategy is to develop and apply a particular conflict resolution process. Lawrence and Lorsch found that in effective organizations, conflicts are resolved at the organizational level at which there is relevant information from the environment. That is, those employees who have the specific knowledge should decide the issue.

Galbraith's Information-Processing Model

Galbraith (1973) suggested that we view the organization as a complex and dynamic system for obtaining and processing information from the environment. All organizations need information about the availability of raw materials and markets for finished products, and they need information about how to convert raw materials. The extent to which an organization actually has the information it needs indicates the degree of environmental *uncertainty*. (Notice that in this theory, it is the organization's grasp of the environment that is uncertain. In Lawrence and Lorsch's theory, it is an unstable environment that is uncertain.)

According to Galbraith, environmental uncertainty affects how decisions are made in an organization. For example, in a bureaucratic organization, centralization and formalization provide ways to obtain information and make decisions. These design features are effective as long as the environment itself remains stable and the organization continues to get information about resources and markets. However, when the environment changes, this information quickly becomes outdated, and more and more unique situations appear that cannot be decided by standard operations. Such decisions must be made at higher authority levels; therefore, in the bureaucratic organization, uncertainty increases the workload for management.

An organization can respond to uncertainty in several ways. First, an organization may be able to take control of its environment. For example, a business might purchase a supplier. This stabilizes the environment by making raw materials more reliably available. Second, the organization can make internal changes that affect its ability to respond to its environment. Accumulating *slack resources* is one way for an organization to reduce its uncertainty. That is, during "slack" times, the business can set aside resources, such as extra raw materials, for use during high demand periods. Another internal change is the establishment of work groups that are oriented specifically to the environment. These groups are used to get as much information about the market as possible, and they reduce the need for upper management to make the decisions. Thus, they represent a decentralizing strategy that moves decision making closer to the source of information. Another internal change involves making the communication system more flexible so that information flow is faster. A study of the turbulent microcomputer industry showed that decision making in that industry requires large quantities of up-to-date environmental information (Eisenhardt, 1989). Going through channels in a bureaucratic organization slows down communication, but adding interdepartmental committees or adopting a matrix structure can increase the chances that those who have the information can give it to those who need it.

Uncertainty about Environmental Uncertainty

Theories that consider the organization's environment would be improved by a better definition of environmental uncertainty. Is uncertainty a characteristic of the environment or of the person who perceives the environment? Both views are legitimate, but often it is not clear which is being used. Researchers have attempted to clarify the meaning of environmental uncertainty. For example, Sharfman and Dean (1991) reviewed the theoretical literature and noted that three dimensions of the environment are typically discussed: complexity, instability or dynamism, and resource availability. Complexity is the level of complex knowledge that is required in order for the organization to understand its environment. Recall that Mintzberg (1983) used this dimension of environment in his theory. Instability or dynamism, the dimension used by Lawrence and Lorsch (1967), refers to how fast and unpredictably the environment changes. Resource availability is considered by Galbraith (1973) who focused on what is available to the organization.

Bluedorn (1993) proposed that although these three environmental dimensions often are discussed by theorists as being *in* the environment, in all likelihood, they are in the *perception* of the environment. That is, environmental uncertainty may be the inability of an organization to predict how and how fast the environment will change. Milliken (1987) proposed that we should define uncertainty as an observer's inability to predict one of three aspects of the environment:

1. Uncertainty about the *state* of the environment means that the observer cannot predict how the environment will change.
2. Uncertainty about the *effect* of environmental change means that the observer cannot predict how the organization will fare.
3. Uncertainty about how to *respond* to a changing environment means the observer is unclear about the potential benefits and costs.

Culture Theory

Another development in organizational theory provides a different perspective on organizational dynamics. According to culture theory, organizations have the characteristics of a culture. An organization's **culture** is shown in the basic assumptions and interaction strategies that it has learned to use in coping with both internal issues and the external environment, and that it finds to work well enough to be taught to new organizational members (Schein, 1985). Several indicators suggest that organizations have the features of a culture. First, an organization can be understood as a system of knowledge, beliefs, and values that has evolved over time and is shared by organizational members (Wilkins & Dyer, 1988). These beliefs and values can be about the organization's internal functioning. For example, beliefs about the costs and benefits of absenteeism are part of an organization's culture (Martocchio, 1994). Also, although most research treats culture as an internal factor, it can include values relating to external interactions. Russell and Russell (1992) found entrepreneurial firms to have a culture in which openness to change is valued, which affects their orientation to the environment. The effect can come from the environment, as well. For example, an organization's culture can be determined by characteristics of the industry of which it is a part (Gordon, 1991; Chatman & Jehn, 1994).

Second, organizations are like cultures in that they use language and symbols to express their values and beliefs. For example, an element of organizational culture is shown in the symbols of authority or rewards that are displayed in a company's reception area (Ornstein, 1986). Organizational language includes metaphors and myths. A *metaphor* is a concrete phrase or term that we use to express an abstract idea. For example, Sackmann (1989) found that the managers in one organization used gardening metaphors like "pruning" to refer to necessary reductions, and "planting" and "gathering" to refer to positive people-oriented changes. A *myth* is an extended metaphor used to describe a complex situation in the organization (Pondy, 1983). A myth is not something that is untrue; it is simply an explanation that is not questioned. For example, a study of a community mental health agency found a myth about the positive role of medicating mental health patients. The agency's culture included a belief in the effectiveness of treatment, and the myth—to treat by medicating—was central to this belief (Scheid-Cook, 1988).

Organizational **climate** is not the same as culture, although it is a closely related concept (Ornstein, 1986). Climate has been described as the attitudinal *warmth* of an organization and as the extent to which an organization is supportive of its members. Culture is the more solid and enduring foundation of organizational values and beliefs, which is shown through interactions of groups in the organization. Climate is more changeable and is the expression of culture. Climate also reflects individuals' reactions to the organization. Moran and Volkweln (1992) proposed that climate emerges out of or is created from an organization's culture.

Organizations can be understood as dynamic systems that are open to environmental interaction. Lawrence and Lorsch wanted to know how organizations interact with the environment. They used the concept of managerial differentiation to describe this process. Managerial differentiation is the orientation of managers to relevant environmental areas. How much managerial differentiation an organization needs is dependent on the uncertainty in the environment and the diversity of subenvironments. When an organization increases differentiation, integration declines and integrating strategies need to be added.

Galbraith saw the organization as a system for getting environmental information. Unlike others who use the concept of uncertainty to refer to the outside environment, Galbraith used the term to describe the extent to which an organization has the information it needs. Uncertainty affects an organization's decision-making practices. If it gets the needed information, centralization and formalization are effective. If it gets less than it needs, formalization is not helpful and decisions have to be made individually. Organizations can try to control uncertainty. They can purchase suppliers; accumulate slack resources; and give decision authority to market-oriented work groups.

Those embracing culture theory, view an organization as having characteristics of a culture. It has a shared system of knowledge and values; a language that includes metaphors and myths; and can be described as having a climate.

APPLICATIONS OF ORGANIZATIONAL THEORY

Students sometimes ask me, What is the point of all this theorizing? Does organizational theory have any practical value? In thinking about these questions, I am reminded of the noted psychologist, Kurt Lewin, who observed that "there is nothing so practical as a good theory." I believe he was right. In this section, I discuss two practical uses of organizational theory.

First, notice that organizational theories often are prescriptive. That is, they give advice on how to structure an organization, what precautions to take, and how to remedy a problem. Currently, organizational theory development is moving in the direction of greater complexity, as indicated in table 11.4. Possibly, the theories are converging as well. Most of the current ones focus on the dynamic relationship between an organization and its environment (Bluedorn, 1993). Increasingly, theorists are viewing the organization as an interactive network of people and technology that is responsive to its surroundings. Organizational theorists are offering practical advice on how to deal with one or more aspects of this network.

Employee Participation

One of the most frequently recommended strategies for improving an organization is employee participation. Human relations theorists found bureaucratic employees to be alienated and uninvolved. To reverse this condition, these theorists recommended that employees be included in decision making. Participation was thought likely to increase employee motivation and improve the quality of performance. Similarly, sociotechnical systems theorists recommended employee involvement in decision making. The Tavistock researchers devised the self-regulating work group specifically to give employees responsibility, authority, and control over their work.

To some extent, organizations have taken the advice and have implemented participation programs. Manz (1992) cited reports of more than a thousand firms in the United States that were using self-regulating work teams or similar interventions. Quality circles also have been used to provide employee participation. These are discussion groups in which employees make suggestions about productivity problems and product quality issues.

The question is whether these participation interventions have been effective. Actual experience has not been entirely satisfying. For example, quality circles have been assessed as more likely to fail than to succeed (Leonard, 1983), although they may have a measure of short-term success (Griffin, 1988). Certainly, organizations have found that employee participation has costs as well as benefits. Involv-

Table 11.4	Progression of Organizational Theory Development
Perspective	**Emphasis**
Feudalism	Power relationships between owners and laborers
Bureaucracy	Structure of the formal organization
Human relations theory	Relationships between people and their jobs
Technology theory	Interaction between technology and organizational structures
Sociotechnology theory	Interaction between technology and people
Systems theory	Interaction between organizational units and environment
Configurational theory	Design for environmental and structural contingencies
Organizational dynamics theory	Getting information from the environment
Culture theory	System of shared knowledge and values

ing employees in decision making means that the process takes longer. Also, unless employees are knowledgeable and skilled, the decisions may not be very good. For these reasons, some researchers have suggested that participation is not always a good strategy (Locke & Schweiger, 1979). Still, others have observed that not all of the various interventions are equally good in terms of allowing employees to participate. Participation may have a more or less positive effect depending on how it is handled (Cotton et al., 1988). Some participation programs have produced positive outcomes, but others are so limited they have had little or no effect (Glew et al., 1995; Manz, 1992; Wagner, 1994).

One reason employee participation does not always work is that it is not always acceptable to management. Even when managers publicly endorse the idea, they privately may be resistant to it (Manz, 1992). Acceptance probably depends on the particular decisions employees help to make. Managers are more likely to accept participation when decisions concern the employee's own job than when they concern something of organization-wide importance. A survey of several different companies showed that although most managers said they felt positive about employee participation, in fact, few allowed it (Collins, Ross, & Ross, 1989).

Glew et al. (1995) asked the logical next question. What is the effect when employee participation is not limited but is given a chance? Figure 11.7 shows a framework they thought could help answer this question by showing what to expect when evaluating the success of a participation program. They pointed out that the participation program that management intends may or may not be the one that actually is implemented. The program is likely to be changed by the participants' personalities, abilities, and willingness to participate. In addition, the program can be advanced or constrained by organizational factors, such as a profit-making orientation, the culture of the organization, and even union-management relations. Of primary importance in predicting program success, however, is the question of what the organization expects to get from participation. That is, will both the employees and the organization benefit? Other researchers also have addressed the need to consider managerial motives. In their discussion of quality circles, Bramel and Friend (1987)

Figure 11.7 *A framework of the employee participation process, showing the impact of personal and organizational variables throughout the development and implementation of a participation program.*

From D.J. Glew, A.M. O'Leary-Kelly, R.W. Griffin, and D.D. VonFleet, "Participation in Organizations: A preview of the issues and proposed framework for future analysis" in Journal of Management, 21:395–421. Copyright © 1995 Jai Press, Inc. Reprinted by permission.

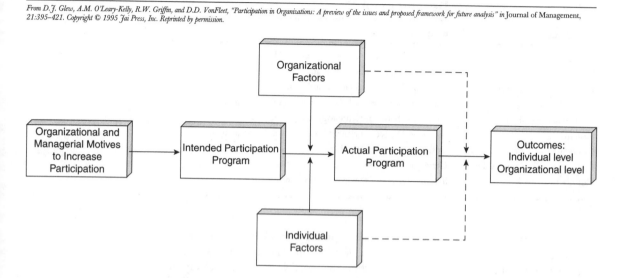

proposed that if an organization's purpose is to exploit workers' creative abilities in solving work problems without sharing the profits that come from the use of their ideas, then this manipulation will become apparent to the members of the group and the participation program will fail. Further, they proposed, if a quality circle evolves into a group that is somewhat autonomous and responsible for making its own decisions, it may fail because middle management undermines it. The expected benefits should be defined at the outset because these motives will direct the development of the program, and they should be taken into account when evaluating its outcomes. Therefore, to successfully implement a participation program, the various individual and organizational factors that can behave as hazards must be recognized.

Environmental Uncertainty and Organizational Innovation

From the early responses to bureaucracy to the modern theoretical models, organizational theorists have recognized that the environment makes demands on the organization. From the start also, theorists have recommended that organizations be sensitive to these demands and be ready to act. Burns and Stalker (1961) made environmental instability the primary force that would bring an organization to change from a mechanistic to an organic structure. Mintzberg (1983) described organizational designs that are intermediate between mechanistic and organic, and recommended these for organizations that need to respond creatively to their environments. Lawrence and Lorsch (1969) observed that managers need to be oriented toward realizing the goals of the organization's relevant subenvironments, especially if the environment is changing. Galbraith (1973) also recognized the need for an organization to be more responsive and creative in dealing with an uncertain environment.

In summary, the recommendation for an organization operating in an uncertain environment is to become more innovative. That is, (1) move toward a more flexible organic structure; (2) increase environmental information seeking and processing; (3) implement employee participation, to increase creativity and to make better use of the human resources; (4) decentralize and move decision making to the organizational members who have the relevant environmental information; and (5) develop an organizational culture and climate that values innovation.

Many firms have accepted this advice and have attempted to become "innovative" organizations in order to be more effective in today's uncertain world. To be effective, of course, the organizational changes should be concentrated on what are the most relevant aspects of the environmental uncertainty. To function as actual innovations, the changes should improve the organization and make it able to meet environmental challenges. The question you should ask is whether the "innovations" have helped make the organization more successful.

Early review of the research literature on innovation found it to be in disarray (Downs & Mohr, 1976). About the only consistent finding was that innovation is associated with uncertainty. That is, more opportunity-seeking and other adaptive organizational behavior is shown when the environment is changing. Damanpour (1991) reviewed the research literature with meta-analytic techniques and found it to be more meaningful than was previously said. He found support for several hypotheses about organizational factors thought likely to produce innovative behavior in response to the environment. For example, he found more innovation when employees are grouped in functional departments and when there are proportionally more professionals or technical experts who can more easily understand new technical ideas. Damanpour (1991) also found that the relationship between such organizational factors and innovativeness was affected by the type of organization. In manufacturing organizations, for example, emphasis on formalization or standardization of work processes actually facilitated innovation; but this was not true in service organizations.

Because managerial reaction was found to be important in determining the fate of employee participation programs, we might anticipate that managers' reactions to innovation are similarly important. Damanpour's (1991) analysis of the research indicated that there is a relationship here. He found that when managers have a favorable attitude toward change, this contributes to an organizational climate that is conducive to innovation. Russell and Russell (1992) also pointed out that innovation requires an organizational culture that includes openness to change. In their study of entrepreneurial organizations, they noted that beliefs in the value of innovation had become part of the organizational culture.

Most organizational theories are prescriptive to some extent. A frequent recommendation is for organizations to allow employee participation in decision making. Many have attempted to incorporate participation, using such techniques as self-managing teams and quality circles. The results have been somewhat disappointing. However, it may be that participation programs have not been well implemented. Managers often are resistant to the idea. It may be better to reconsider the entire process of developing, implementing, and evaluating participation before we decide whether it works.

Organizational theorists recognize that modern firms operate in an uncertain environment and must respond to environmental demands. They have various recommendations for what an organization can do. These recommendations are couched in terms of organizational characteristics and specific environmental conditions. Generally, however, the advice is to be innovative. Most companies need to adopt a flexible organic structure and incorporate decentralizing changes in order to increase participation of employees in addressing the uncertain environment. Many organizations are making an effort to be more innovative. The accumulating research literature indicates some success in making recommended changes.

ORGANIZATIONAL DEVELOPMENT

Given the uncertain environment of most modern organizations, change seems to be necessary for survival. The practical problem, of course, is *how* to change. In the remaining sections of this chapter, you will learn about ways to help organizations make effective changes.

Organizational development (OD) is both a methodology and a guidance system for helping organizations make healthy changes. The theoretical basis for OD varies somewhat depending on the orientation of the person designing the program. Most programs are based on a kind of eclectic model, drawing concepts from several organizational theories (Burke, Clark, & Koopman, 1984). However, a number of OD practitioners take a systems theory viewpoint (Scarpello, 1983) in which organizational problems are understood as problems of the *system*. The changes implemented are meant to have spreading effects throughout the whole organization.

Organizational development is a program of planned interventions. Specifically, OD should improve the internal operations of the organization by opening up communication; decreasing internal destructiveness, such as win-lose conflicts; and increasing creativity in problem solving. It includes the following procedures: (1) diagnosing the organization's current functioning; (2) planning interventions; (3) mobilizing resources to put the plan into action; and (4) evaluating the effects. OD must have the full support of top management. When well done, OD is not simply a patch job focused on lower level employees. It should encompass the whole organization and involve real changes in the way the organization operates (Beckhard, 1969; Bennis, 1969).

OD is initiated by someone in upper management who senses that something is wrong. This person does not have to be the CEO, but he or she must be someone in a high-level position of responsibility who is committed and can provide the funding for the project (Boss & Golembiewski, 1995). A variety of problems can signal a need for OD: (1) difficulties in communication and interaction between departments; (2) problems with organizational planning; (3) unmotivated employees; (4) changes in organizational values, climate, and behavioral norms; (5) having to cope with a merger; and (6) needing to adapt to environmental change. For example, when an organization's environmental niche collapses, the

Dilbert By Scott Adams

organization will cut back its operation in that area. Typically, decisions on how to cut back the labor force are made in the same way that decisions are made about disposing of equipment and buildings. Both are decided in terms of expediency. Often, the only thought about employees is how they might resist this downsizing. However, an OD program can help produce a better solution (Greenhalgh, 1982).

The OD effort is conducted by an **OD change agent.** Frequently, this person is an I/O psychologist who works as an outside consultant. An advantage of using outside consultants is that they are not personally involved in the organization's problem. Early thinking on OD was that an outsider was the *only* person who could do an OD program. Now, however, it is recognized that an insider can conduct OD programs. Increasingly, large organizations are using their own people in OD. One survey found that 53 percent of a sample of OD practitioners were internal consultants (Burke et al., 1984).

Consultants believe that their relationship with the managerial contact person in the organization is important in determining the effectiveness of the OD program. There must be mutual confidence and respect, and frequent communication is necessary (Kellogg, 1984). Personal characteristics of the consultant also can be important in determining OD effectiveness. Successful consultants have been found to be more empathic, sociable, tolerant of ambiguous situations, intuitive, and imaginative (Hamilton, 1988).

The Methodology of OD

OD programs typically incorporate an **action research** design. Action research is a cycle of diagnosis, action, and evaluation used to solve practical problems involving social situations. There are some similarities between action research and the research techniques discussed in chapter 2. Observational and survey techniques are used in both. A field researcher and an action researcher have similar objectives. Both want to find out what might be contributing to an organizational problem. However, the similarity ends there. The field researcher might plan to follow a survey or observational study with an experiment in hopes of determining the cause-effect relationship between certain variables. The action researcher also would like to know the causes of organizational behavior, but the more immediate objective is to *change* the present behavior. Although action research can contribute to the scientific process by identifying common organizational problems and suggesting courses of action (Bartunek, 1983), this is not its main purpose. Action research is a practical method of discovery so that *action* can be taken to change things.

Kurt Lewin (1948) is cited as the originator of action research. In general, Lewin believed that psychology needed to get involved in solving the problems of real life. To do this, he proposed that we learn the general principles of behavior, find out about the particular situation, and then conduct action research. In Lewin's terms, action research is initiated by a social problem and must include educating the participants in solving the problem. Action research is based on the assumption that people both create and change their social reality. Thus, they must be included in the problem-solving process. Action research helps people learn how to change themselves (Peters & Robinson, 1984).

The Action Research Cycle

As depicted in figure 11.8, action research is a repeating cycle that has certain identifiable phases. In the first phase, a problem that reflects a need for organizational change is identified. For example, management may feel that there is too much conflict or that communication is not as fast and efficient as it should be. Next, the OD consultant collects information about the organization's present behavior. The consultant conducts document studies and surveys, interviews key personnel, and observes work operations. The objective is to provide a basis for the OD effort by learning as much as possible about the organization. Initial data analysis should lead to workable hypotheses about interventions and courses of action.

In the third phase of action research, the data are used as feedback to inform the organization about its behavior. The consultant meets with the group of key personnel, communicates the feedback, and then works with the group to diagnose the problem and to plan a program of interventions. This program, which may include such activities as training and goal setting, is implemented in the fourth phase.

After the program has been put into action, evaluation or follow-up is conducted. Follow-up data are analyzed and given to the key personnel group to be used for further diagnosis and possibly the planning of another cycle of action research. The main objective of follow-up is to document the impact of the interventions. However, the evaluation data collection, like the initial data collection, behaves as an intervention in itself. For example, survey questions may give participants ideas that they never had before and, therefore, influence their behavior. This effect is meant to occur as part of the change effort because the consultant encourages the organization to make use of data as they are generated (Schein, 1980).

In order to help in diagnosing organizational problems, the action researcher must have a strong intuitive capacity for selecting out of the many behavioral patterns those variables that are likely to be important in sustaining the problem. This is the "art" of OD. Diagnosis is an aspect of OD in which the consultant may be weak, however, and programs sometimes seem less geared to the organization than to the specific interest and expertise of the consultant. Although the consultant's theoretical perspective will affect the diagnosis, it should not overpower it. A diagnostic perspective that always leads to the same assessment and intervention

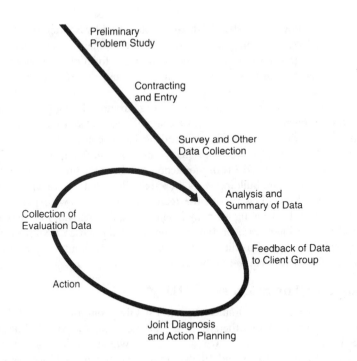

Preliminary
Problem Study

Contracting
and Entry

Survey and Other
Data Collection

Analysis and
Summary of Data

Collection of
Evaluation Data

Feedback of Data
to Client Group

Action

Joint Diagnosis
and Action Planning

is hardly a diagnosis, and it is not likely to be effective in dealing with the organization's real problem (Quinn & McGrath, 1982).

OD Interventions

Although OD consultants do tend to emphasize one or another technique or methodology, there are a variety of interventions that can be used. In Terpstra's (1982) review of the OD literature, he noted some major groups of OD interventions, including survey feedback, training, and team development.

Many OD practitioners emphasize the data collection and feedback phases of action research. That is, they construct what are known as **survey feedback** programs that function as the intervention (e.g., Gavin & Krois, 1983). In these programs, data are collected from employees about their attitudes, values, and perceptions of organizational issues. This information is summarized and presented to key personnel, and often to the employees as well. The survey feedback process is meant to be educational and provide the organization with insight into the views of its employees. It also can function as a catalyst for more effective self-direction.

In many respects, OD is similar to training. It has similar goals, and educational experiences can be included in the program of interventions. Beckhard (1969) described some OD needs that correspond to training needs. For example, there may be a need for individuals to learn new knowledge and skills or develop such abilities as planning and goal setting. A number of experiential learning activities have been devised for these purposes, including some packaged OD programs. Blake and Mouton's (1968) *Grid* includes training in planning, goal setting, and problem solving. Many techniques that I describe in chapter 6 on training are used in OD programs. For example, OD projects often use case study problems to train supervisors in how to solve subordinate-related problems, such as absenteeism (Porras et al., 1982). Training also is used for development of interpersonal skills. Many OD programs have been constructed around a form of sensitivity training to accomplish this. Emphasis is on developing the manager's interpersonal awareness and sensitivity to others.

Teamwork is an important need of organizations facing an uncertain environment. OD practitioners often find that organizations want to improve the interactions of their work teams. **Team building** has become one of the more frequently used OD interventions (French & Bell, 1984). Many of the techniques focus on improving the process of interaction within the team. For example, Eden (1985) described a team-building workshop that addressed a number of teamwork issues. The workshop began with the team exploring its own expectations and problems. It included training for managing conflict, dealing with interpersonal friction, and solving interaction problems. The workshop closed with an activity to make the roles and relationships of team members explicit and to plan the implementation of what was learned in the workshop.

Evaluation: The Success of OD

Some 30 years have passed since the earliest OD programs. Many OD studies have been reported; many others have been done but not reported. The question is, does it work? It appears that we do not know whether it does or not. OD programs reported in the 1960s and 1970s typically were evaluated by means of a research design that was too weak to show whether the program had been successful. Usually, criteria were ill defined, the evaluation was based on subjective measures, and there were few controls over error. Often, the evidence was purely anecdotal (Morrison, 1978). Critics urged that OD researchers use multiple dependent measures over an extensive period of time to determine whether there was a change and whether it was retained. Most programs were followed for less than 24 months, and many included absolutely no measure of retention (Porras & Berg, 1978). In a review of later research, Vicars and Hartke (1984) also found little evidence for the success of OD, but they did find some improvement in the studies. OD studies were using better evaluation techniques than they had in the past.

A potential problem in OD is that behavioral changes are not retained over time. Employees leave OD workshops with new interpersonal and technical knowledge and skill, but they return to organizational settings that have not changed. Usually, in such situations, the new learning is not transferred. As Beckhard (1969) pointed out, this is one reason why OD change programs should be designed to modify the total system. The organizational setting may need to be changed so that new behavior can be transferred and maintained. If an organization accurately conveys a message that the employee behavior will be supported, this should help prevent loss of new learning. For example, obtaining the commitment of supervisors is one way to ensure that employees are encouraged in their new behavior (Boss, 1983).

We might ask consultants what they think distinguishes a successful OD project from an unsuccessful one. Some studies show that consultants can describe OD successes. They mention a genuine interest in the project on the part of management, a clear contract and frequent communication between consultant and client, and an effective feedback process (Burke et al., 1984; Kellogg, 1984). Also,

*T*able 11.5   The Consultant's View of a Successful OD Project

Phase 1: Preliminary Study and Planning

Client-Consultant Relationship:
Genuine interest of client in project
Careful selection of consultant
Client shows readiness for change
Client shows willingness to assume responsibility
Client has available power to use in project

Contracting:
Specific definition of tasks required in project
Clear task agreement—who will do what
Client shows willingness to work with some flexibility
Client shows confidence in consultant
Project involves many hierarchical levels including upper management

Phase 2: Survey Feedback Process

Data Collection:
Use of theoretical model
Access to employees and task information
Access to political information

Feedback:
Consultant effective in communication
Consultant gives careful, sensitive criticism
Consultant and client confident of validity of data
Open, free exchange of information

Phase 3: Diagnosis and Planning

Joint problem solving
Client shows independence in decision making
Development of multiple alternatives
Flexible in testing and deciding on plan of action

Phase 4: Action

Multiple interventions
Limited use of plans with structural change
Client shows responsibility in follow through

Phase 5: Evaluation

Effectiveness assessed
Further action determined

Phase 6: Continuation

Longer, rather than shorter, projects
Long-term projects broken into series of contracts
Later contracts contingent upon success of earlier

Adapted from W.W. Burke, et al., "Improve Your OD Project's Chances for Success" in *Training and Development Journal,* 38:62–68. Copyright © 1984 American Society for Training and Development, Alexandria, Virginia; and D.M. Kellogg, "Contrasting Successful and Unsuccessful OD Consultation Relationships" in *Group & Organization Studies,* 9: 151–176. Copyright © 1984 Sage Publications, Inc., Newbury Park, California.

the organization must assume responsibility for the project if it is to be successful. Evaluation of one action research project showed that groups who were most involved in planning their own survey were more likely to use its results than groups who were less involved (Sommer, 1987). Table 11.5 summarizes the current thinking on the success of OD projects.

*M*ain *P*oints

Organizational development (OD) is a method for helping organizations change. It requires the support of top management and is meant to have spreading effects throughout the organization. It is planned and conducted jointly by organization members and an OD change agent.

OD programs use action research methodology which is oriented toward practical use of the findings. It involves one or more cycles of diagnosing, acting, and evaluating an intervention's effect. Three types of OD interventions are commonly used—survey feedback, training, and team development.

OD research has not yet shown whether or under what conditions OD is successful in helping organizations. The research design is a problem; many reports of success are based on weak or inadequate measures.

*C*hapter *S*ummary

Organizations are structured (1) by a division of labor, (2) by a system for distributing decision-making authority, and (3) by devices for providing integration and unity. An important variable in determining the division of labor and authority distribution is job specialization; highly specialized jobs are simplified and require close supervision. The organization is differentiated horizontally when employees are grouped in separate departments. When they are ranked according to the authority hierarchy, the differentiation is vertical. Organizations are integrated by committees, project teams, and matrix structures.

Organizational theories attempt to answer the question of how to design an effective organization. The bureaucracy is the traditional design. It is characterized by high job specialization, centralized decision making, and formalized operating procedures. Other theories also focus on organizational structure. The mechanistic organization is like the bureaucracy, but the organic organization is a fluid structure that provides more ability to respond to the environment.

After years of experience with the bureaucracy, behavioral scientists began to document its effects on the employee. New theories were offered to improve the organization. Human relations theorists suggested ways to involve employees in the organization. Other theorists focused on technology and environmental change and developed further organizational improvements. Several recommended change to an organic design. Some, such as the sociotechnical systems theorists, emphasized the effects of three variables in their designs—the organization's structure, the person, and the technology. Following this, theorists began to look at other environmental variables, particularly those that might affect the dynamic interaction of the organization with its suppliers and customers. Response to uncertainty in the environment or in the organization's access to environmental information became an important consideration. Other theorists have noticed that organizations look and act like cultures.

Many organizational theories have prescriptive components. For example, organizations often are advised to incorporate employee participation or to change to a more flexible style of operating in order to meet environmental demands. Currently, researchers are asking whether organizations have taken the advice and whether it helps.

Organizations are dynamic structures that must interact with their environment; therefore, they must be able to change. Organizational development is a process and methodology for helping organizations make healthy changes. Through action research, any number of human problems in the organization can be addressed.

*S*TUDY *Q*UESTIONS

1) What kinds of goals do organizations have, and how do these influence the nature of the organization?

2) Define job specialization, and describe how it relates to span of control and vertical differentiation.

3) Describe the forms of departmentation.

4) Distinguish between centralization and formalization.

5) How is the matrix structure different from the traditional organization?

6) Outline the features of the bureaucratic organization.

7) How does the organic organization differ from the mechanistic or bureaucratic organization?

8) What are the similarities of the various human relations theories?

9) How are technology and other features of the environment incorporated into the contingency theories?

10) What is the distinguishing feature of sociotechnical systems theory?

11) How is uncertainty used in the organizational dynamics models?

12) How do culture theorists approach the study of organizations?

13) What advice do organizational theorists give concerning employee-related problems and response to environmental uncertainty? Have organizations taken this advice?

14) Describe the conduct of an OD project. Does OD work?

CONSIDER THIS

CASE STUDY

VRS is a small nonprofit, vocational rehabilitation agency. It has been in operation for 10 years. Its purpose is to provide employment training and referral services for disabled workers in the community. The agency operates a sheltered workshop in which clients are tested for their skills and abilities, given on-the-job training in manufacturing work, coached in effective employee behavior and organizational citizenship, and assisted in their job search.

VRS is a centralized organization. Planning and policy making are done by a community board of directors and the agency's executive director. Internal decisions are made by the executive director, who consults with three department heads if necessary. Supervisors have little discretionary power; mainly, their decisions must follow previously decided operating procedures. An executive assistant is in the process of formalizing these operating procedures in a policy manual.

Problem

The executive director has asked an OD consultant to advise him on a problem within the organization. He is not very clear on exactly what is wrong, but it appears that the agency needs revitalization. There is general apathy among the employees and few signs that anyone is committed to the goals of the organization. Ten years ago when the agency was established, the members were enthusiastic about what they were doing, felt that their work was important, and showed high morale. Now people seem to be just putting in a day's work. The employees' lack of vitality is also affecting the behavior of VRS clients. They, too, are unenthusiastic and lack motivation.

What should the consultant advise?

In this chapter we discover the nature of interaction in the organization by looking at three basic features of groups.

One important feature is communication. This is the foundation of all that goes on at work. Another is the group's internal operations. You will learn how groups are structured and the kinds of functions they perform. You also will learn how they do this interactive work and some problems they face. The third aspect of group interaction is conflict. The way a conflict is managed and resolved is of interest because it has an impact on the goal outcomes and what happens afterward.

At the end of the chapter, collective bargaining, or union-management negotiation, is examined as a special case of between-group interaction and conflict resolution.

Internal cohesiveness provides a group spirit, a feeling of belonging, and a tendency for members to function as a team. In competitive games and at work, performance is enhanced by group cohesiveness.

Chapter 12

The Dynamics
of Interaction

Contents

DBS Arts Library

"Y ou're such a son-of-a———when you get down to work. Well, so-long! I got to fix my horse's hoofs."

I had expected that the man would be struck down. He had used to the Virginian a term of heaviest insult, I thought. I had marvelled to hear it come so unheralded from Steve's friendly lips. . . . Evidently he had meant no harm by it, and evidently no offence had been taken. . . .

The Virginian was looking at his cards. He might have been deaf.

"*And* twenty," said the next player, easily.

The next threw his cards down.

It was now the Virginian's turn to bet, or leave the game, and he did not speak at once.

Therefore Trampas spoke. "Your bet, you son-on-a———."

The Virginian's pistol came out, and his hand lay on the table, holding it unaimed. And with a voice as gentle as ever, . . . he issued his orders to the man Trampas:—

"When you call me that, smile!"

Owen Wister

The narrator in Wister's story observed that although the same words were used on these two different occasions, the words had entirely different meanings, and they caused very different reactions. The narrator concludes that words are meaningless without context. In the modern world of work and leisure, this is a valid conclusion, also. Understanding this truth about communication is necessary for the effective internal operation of an organization and for its contact with the outside environment. International businesses in particular can attest to the fact that the meaning of a communication depends on much more than simply the words uttered. For one thing, communication includes both verbal and nonverbal messages. Communication also is an ongoing process, which means that the communicators' history contributes to the meaning of a message, as it clearly does in this episode of *The Virginian*.

In this chapter, I discuss the issues of interpersonal and intergroup processes. Three components of interaction are considered. First, I examine organizational communication. Next, I look at some larger-scale group dynamics in order to demonstrate how groups interact to reach their work goals. Finally, I discuss the value and problems of conflict, as well as the part it plays in the process of group work.

COMMUNICATION IN THE ORGANIZATION

We can analyze communication at two levels. In **macro-organizational communication,** the focus is on exchanges between the organization and the environment. As discussed in chapter 11, some current organizational theories address the need of the organization to get and use information from the outside environment, especially when the environment is uncertain. The process of exchanging information with suppliers, consumers, competitors, governmental bodies, and professional associations is macro-organizational communication.

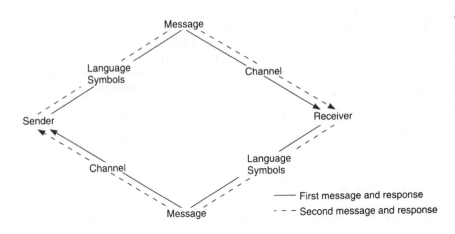

Figure 12.1 *A communication volley, including a feedback loop. The sender's message elicits a response from the receiver. This response provides feedback and allows the sender to evaluate the effectiveness of the original message. The sender's second message takes this evaluation into account.*

In **micro-organizational communication,** which is the emphasis of this chapter, communication within the organization is the subject of interest. At this level, communication is analyzed either interpersonally, such as between supervisor and subordinate, or between groups, such as departments. Micro-organizational communication is the vehicle for work-related interactions throughout the organization. Communication is involved in all aspects of work. All of us spend some part of our workday talking to others, attending meetings, selling, arguing, making calls, or writing letters and reports. Communication also is involved in the introduction of new employees to the organization's operations.

The Elements of Communication

The sender, receiver, language, message, mode, and channel are all elements of the communication process. The *sender* transmits the communication. The *receiver* gets and decodes it. Senders vary in terms of their skills in constructing and sending messages, and receivers vary in their abilities to receive and comprehend messages. The *message* is constructed from the symbols of *language* used in some *mode* of communication and sent through a communication *channel*. Messages are conveyed orally or in writing. **Formal communication** moves through the structured organizational channels. **Informal communication** flows outside the formal organizational structure. Communication is exchanged in *volleys*. That is, messages are sent, and other messages are sent back. Messages often behave as responses or *feedback* to the sender of a message. The feedback message allows the sender to evaluate the effectiveness of the original message. Figure 12.1 illustrates a communication volley.

Communication Language

The language symbols used in a message are both verbal and nonverbal. Generally, these components of a message are consistent, with the nonverbal providing emotional tone to the message and information about the communicator. Although speakers sometimes modify their behavior to make a certain impression on a listener, nonverbal behavior is generally difficult to regulate (DePaulo, 1992). When a speaker says one thing and their body language says something else, we accept the accuracy of the nonverbal language.

Table 12.1	Bureaucratese: Overuse of Institutional Jargon	
Item	**Translation**
We must utilize the utmost caution in proceeding with this projected action.	Let's be careful.
Budgeting constraints should be considered in prioritizing the proposals.	Rank them by how much they cost.
The attached paper, addressing some issues in executive recruitment, is being sent to you with the hope that you will find it stimulating and worthy of being shared with your colleagues.	Are you interested in this? If so, pass it on.
Improve the operational performance capabilities of this equipment.	Make it work better.
It may negatively impact the quality of our decisions.	It may make things worse.
Additional continued interface with this segment of the market is desirable.	Let's meet with them again.

The effectiveness of a communication is the extent to which the intended meaning is received and understood. There are many places in this process in which communication can break down. For example, receivers may not understand the language symbols. Work language provides appropriate symbols and forms for organizational communication. Sometimes, senders get carried away by their ability to manipulate this language and inadvertently compose messages that are incomprehensible. (Table 12.1 provides some humorous examples.) Learning a new work language is part of socialization or becoming adjusted to a new job. When an employee changes jobs, resocialization is required, often including the learning of yet another work language (Chao et al., 1994).

The Mode and Purpose of Communication

Written communication is the *official* means of conveying work-related information. Written messages are tangible. They provide a record of organizational action and can be reviewed and studied. One of the main concerns of the person sending the message should be that the intended receiver actually receives it. The fact that it is written down and sent does not mean that anyone reads or understands it.

Most required interaction at work is through oral communication. In earlier chapters, I describe the interview as a means of making selection decisions and discussing performance appraisals. In a more general sense, the **interview** is a basic mode of communication. The interview is an oral interaction of two or more people who transmit or exchange information (Hunt, 1980).

The interview can be conducted for a variety of purposes. One purpose is to influence job attitudes and behavior. For example, employees are oriented, trained, supervised, and motivated through face-to-face interviews. A second purpose of the interview is to convey information about the values and climate of the organization (Katz & Kahn, 1978). Research has indicated that the quality of the communication itself reflects the nature of the organization's social climate (O'Driscoll &

Evans, 1988). For example, in one study, subordinates reported feeling more social support when they were able to initiate their own interviews with their supervisor (Kirmeyer & Lin, 1987). A third purpose is suggested by Ford and Ford (1995) who proposed that oral communication among high-level managers is the driving force of organizational change programs, such as the OD programs discussed in chapter 11.

Interviews occur daily in the organization, in which employees meet with subordinates, peers, and superiors. They exchange information on what to do on the job, on why a job should be done in a certain way, and on how well they perform. Misinterpretations can arise in these communications, especially when the participants come from different cultural backgrounds. International companies have found that explaining job requirements must be done carefully. A company operating in Japan, for example, found several strategies helpful in making such communications effective, including joking, cooperative complaining, and using mixed Japanese and English expressions (Miller, 1995).

The Flow of Communication

Upward, downward, and lateral communication are features of the direction and flow of organizational communication, and they describe the formal and informal communication channels. Flow of communication is regulated in the organization. There are both explicit and implicit constraints on who can communicate with whom, in what manner, about what subject, and for what purpose.

Formal Communication Channels

The organization's **communication network** is a structure of channels through which information is passed from one individual to another. The network contains the flow of information, and it reflects the formal interaction between organizational members. Several different networks operate in work organizations (see figure 12.2a–d). The *chain* network is a communication pattern that exists in bureaucracies and other organizations in which there is a formal chain of command (figure 12.2a). Information is passed up or down the organizational hierarchy by exchanges between one person and two others—the one above and the one below the person's own position. Depending on its size, the organization may have several communication chains that link upper and lower organizational levels. Although the chain has a two-way capacity, it is used primarily for downward communication. The *wheel* network includes one central person who communicates with each of several others (figure 12.2b). A related pattern, the Y network, includes two central people who pass information to others on the periphery of a grouping (figure 12.2c). In these networks, as in the chain network, the number of open channels is limited, and communication is centralized. People can officially communicate only with certain others. In the *pinwheel* network, all channels are open (figure 12.2d). Everyone communicates with everyone else. The pinwheel exemplifies a decentralized communication structure. Centralized and decentralized networks have different purposes. For example, the decentralized structure can be more effective for creative problem solving, whereas the centralized structure is better for moving information quickly.

The Direction of Communication

Organizational communication varies according to whether its primary purpose is to send information downward, upward, or in horizontal directions. **Downward**

Figure 12.2 Communication networks. a. A chain network is used mostly for communication in organizations in which there are formal lines of authority. b. One central person exchanging information with several others forms a wheel network of communication. c. Y networks develop when two central persons within an organization exchange information and pass it on to other members on the periphery. d. Pinwheel networks allow complete two-way communication in organizations in which all information channels are open.

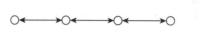

a. **Chain network**

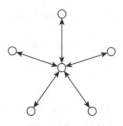

b. **Wheel network**

c. **Y network**

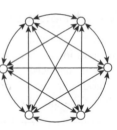

d. **Pinwheel network**

communication carries task-related information to those who perform the work. It also carries information about policies and procedures, and it may be used to give motivational feedback to employees. Horizontal or **lateral communication** occurs between peers. Members of teams and departments must communicate to the extent that their tasks are related. Because authority lines do not have to be crossed, lateral communication typically is quicker than communication up or down the hierarchy.

Upward communication carries information from lower levels of the organization to higher levels. The information may concern the outside environment or internal activities at lower levels of the organization. Management receives feedback about the effectiveness of decisions. Employees have an opportunity to inform superiors about their personal career ambitions and successes, to state opinions and register complaints, and to make suggestions for improvements. Recall from the last chapter that some organizational designs, such as Likert's (1967) linking pin structure, call for improvements in upward communication.

Messages are more likely to be understood when an exchange occurs than when the receiver can make no response. With **one-way communication**, information is sent down from management to employees. Management does not ask for or expect a response. Of course, if there is no upward communication, there is hardly any way to know whether management's message was even received. In **two-way communication**, however, the receipt and acceptance of the message can be verified because a response is expected. Two-way communication allows misunderstandings to be cleared up.

Some problems in organizational design that are discussed in chapter 11, look as if they might be improved by more openness in communication. Human relations theorists, for example, encourage open communication between managers and employees. **Open communication** is the disclosure of personal and/or work-related information. Two central features of the concept are honesty in disclosing information and receptiveness in receiving it. A relationship in which open communication is possible is one in which each person perceives the other to be a good listener who will not respond negatively (Jablin, 1985). In the past, we have rather uncritically accepted the idea that open communication can only benefit the organization. However, it is not always shown to be beneficial. There are situations in which completely honest and open communication can be as destructive as dishonest or misleading communication (McGregor, 1967). Eisenberg and Witten (1987) proposed that under certain conditions open communication would be helpful, such as when organizational members are close, personally able and willing to share, and when the organization need not be concerned about public reactions or keeping operations under cover.

Communication Loss and Distortion

As information is sent down from management to employees through a limited network, such as the chain, it is modified through a process of **filtering**. Middle managers filter information that they receive and pass on. They omit some parts of it and add details to other parts. They send it to some subordinates but not to others. At each level through which a message passes, a manager decides how much of the information needs to be sent on. Obviously, with so much tinkering, the original message changes. Information is lost, and the message may be distorted. How serious is the problem of filtering? Some have reported as much as 80 percent of the information is lost as the message descends from the top to the bottom of an organization, indicating that filtering can be a major problem (Nichols, 1962). However, filtering is often necessary. Communications about organizational policies and procedures may need to be translated into job-relevant language before they are sent to employees.

Filtering occurs in upward communication in largely the same way. Middle management summarizes information from lower levels before sending it to upper management. This may be necessary if the manager's superior does not have the time or technical expertise to review and understand the original message. Employees also may filter information before they send it on to a supervisor. Some information is suppressed when the communication contains bad news or when upper management is not trusted. A common error in upward communication is the omission of important details (Gaines, 1980). Details left out of these messages are often diverted into lateral communication channels. That is, the information that should be given to superiors is communicated only to peers.

The Grapevine: An Informal Network

Much of an organization's communication does not go through formal channels. Instead, it is conveyed by means of a complex informal structure known as the **grapevine**. The grapevine functions as a way of exchanging both nonwork and work-related information. It is a method of communicating information about personal relationships and aspects of the organization, such as the organization's

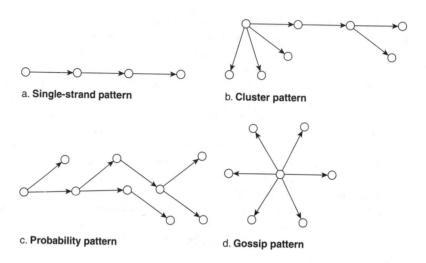

Figure 12.3 *Structural patterns of the grapevine. a. Information is passed by a chain from one person to another. b. A cluster pattern develops when some but not all individuals pass information on. c. In a probability pattern, a person passes information to one or two others who may or may not pass it on. d. The gossip pattern involves one individual who passes on information to many others.*

a. **Single-strand pattern**

b. **Cluster pattern**

c. **Probability pattern**

d. **Gossip pattern**

culture. This informal structure emerges as a task-related channel if formal networks are inefficient. For example, employees who become frustrated with the slowness of formal channels may develop their own informal contacts in high places. Upper management also may deliberately use the grapevine instead of formal channels (Mishra, 1990). Information about policy and procedural changes, about decisions affecting the personnel at large, and about large-scale changes in the organization can be disseminated quickly through the grapevine.

Figure 12.3*a–d* depicts four grapevine patterns that have been identified: the single-strand, cluster, probability, and gossip patterns (Davis, 1953). Most grapevines have only a few people who are central in passing information along, and not everyone is included. Despite what you might think, management is actually more likely to be included than lower level employees. Managers also are more likely to pass on information they receive. In one study, managers were found to receive almost all grapevine information and to pass it on about half the time. Nonsupervisory employees received about half the information and passed it on only about 10 percent of the time (Sutton & Porter, 1968).

Barriers to Communication Reception

Some of the more common problems of communication are those in which the message either is not received at all or is not understood. Hunt (1980) proposed that a message must move through several layers of interference before it is comprehended. These levels of interference include (1) environmental factors, such as noisy working conditions and work activities that compete for the receiver's attention; (2) the relationship between sender and receiver, including how the receiver feels about the sender; (3) the sender's ability to get the meaning across; and (4) the ability and motivation of the receiver to listen or to receive the message.

One reason for poor message reception is the *overloading* of information channels. People use several different behavioral strategies to handle information overloads. Filtering is one. For example, busy managers often decide that a communication sent down to them is not important to subordinates and need not be sent on. Filtering occurs with both oral and written communication, although it may be more apparent with the written. Many managers' in-baskets are filled with written material that goes no farther. A second way to reduce overload is to reroute communications so that responsibility for them is lowered. For example, we may be able to cut down on the number of reports that must be read or meetings that must be attended. Communication overload on one person can be reduced by adding intermediaries, such as assistants, who screen incoming information. If an overloaded person is the hub of a wheel network, it may be possible to add another person to create a Y network or to change the formal channels altogether and adopt a pinwheel network. Finally, we can assign priorities to messages by deciding which need attention and which can wait. Most of us who work in offices have a stack of mail on our desks that we mean to get to eventually.

Assigning a low priority to a communication may have more to do with the style of the message than with its content. If the purpose and meaning of a communication is not immediately clear, the receiver may lose interest. There are many examples of this in our daily in-baskets. We all know people who write long letters and memoranda around a single, sometimes insignificant point. It is irritating to have to wade through a lot of material to get the point of the message. As senders, we can improve our written communications by remembering a few guidelines. In general, it is best to use simple, straightforward language. Limit the length of the message and the number of ideas in it. To some extent, restate important points in different terms. Customize the message according to its purpose and the time and ability of the receiver. Table 12.2 includes two messages. The first memo contains more information, but it is difficult to understand. The points are buried in wordy paragraphs. The second message is sparse and more likely to be read.

*M*ain
*P*oints

Micro-organizational communications are the formal and informal exchanges that occur daily at work. The purpose is to transmit information in order to get work done and to make internal operations more effective.

To analyze communication, consider its elements. The language of a message is both verbal and nonverbal. Comprehension of a special organizational language, or jargon, is usually needed in communication at work. Both written and oral modes are used, although most work communication is oral and takes place in the basic interview. The channels of communication are defined in formal networks that show the acceptable direction of information flow. Downward communication is from supervisors to subordinates and is often one-way with no response expected. Two-way exchanges are possible when upward or lateral communication is acceptable.

Barriers can prevent messages from being received. One reason for poor reception is informational overload. Filtering and assigning attentional priorities are strategies for reducing the overload.

Table 12.2   Two Memoranda Carrying the Same Message

Hollywood Health Corporation
Interoffice Memorandum

MESSAGE 1:

Overly detailed. Essential points are buried in a mass of unimportant information. Unlikely to be read.

To: Dr. Jack Williams, Director
From: Lynn Tennison, Research Associate
Subject: Health Transportation Program

Demographic data were developed and are included in the attached report to determine whether available population characteristics might influence any aspect of the transportation model used in this research evaluation. It also appeared that some of the data would assist us in designing our marketing program for this outreach project. The demographic data presented here are based on the 1980 U.S. Census and cover the 26 census tracts which HHC intends to serve with this new program. The data are presented in tabular form for each tract and are visually displayed in maps indicating which tracts have similar demographic characteristics.

About one-fifth of the families in the targeted area were found to be in the near-poor income category, that is, between poverty and twice-poverty levels. These families were located in the same area as the poverty-level families. Since there are more near-poor than poverty-level families, those census tracts in which the near-poor comprise a significant percentage are far more numerous. In eight tracts, one-quarter to one-third of the population are near-poor. One tract in particular, tract #21, contains more than one-quarter of the total near-poor population.

A strong relationship between family income and car ownership was hypothesized and tested. But, using a simple correlational technique, this relationship could not be substantiated. It was the classic observation that data on number of cars does not necessarily indicate the value or reliability of the vehicles. Poverty families with several drivers in the household may have several old and undependable vehicles. In contrast, higher income families may need only one good, reliable car.

As a supplement to the data on automobile ownership, it was postulated that there may be a discernible relationship between transportation needs and the modes of transportation used by workers in each tract for getting to work. At least three-quarters of the workers in each tract drive themselves to work, and about ten percent in each tract ride to work in another person's car. Bus transportation to work is only a nominal mode with only three tracts exceeding five percent. More workers walk to work than take the bus, but it is still a minor mode of transportation for the area. However, with only five percent of the workers in all 26 tracts walking to work it may help to explain how some people are able to get along without cars. The implication of the finding that almost half of the population have only one car per family (or none) and yet most workers drive to work in their own car is that many families will not have a car available at home for medical or any other transportation need during the working day.

It is hoped that these findings and the statistics included in the attached report will be helpful in directing the marketing effort of the new community health transportation program.

Hollywood Health Corporation
Interoffice Memorandum

MESSAGE 2:

Appropriate level of detail. Only essential points are included. Likely to be read.

To: Dr. Jack Williams, Director
From: Lynn Tennison, Research Associate
Subject: Health Transportation Program

The study for the new community health program is finished. The report is attached. The data in the tables and maps come from the 1980 census. I believe the demographic data are reasonably self-explanatory. However, let me summarize.

Briefly, we found that about one-fifth of the people in our service area fall into the income class in which we are interested. We tried using car ownership as an index of eligibility for the program. However, this does not appear to be useful for this purpose. Information on whether there is a car at home during the workday, which could be used for medical transportation, is a better index of eligibility.

FORMAL AND INFORMAL WORK GROUPS

Almost everyone is involved to some extent in a work group, and the organizational need for work groups is growing. Formal work groups are described largely in terms of their task purpose and their permanence. Temporary work groups include ad hoc committees, task forces, and project teams. Interdepartmental committees are more permanent, as are teams composed of a work supervisor and his or her subordinates. These are a formal part of the organization's structure, and their purpose is to perform needed organizational functions. Other groups at work are informal; that is, they are not officially authorized. Informal groups can stand alone or exist as a subset of a formal group. They can serve a number of personal and/or work-related needs, and they are defined in terms of the members' common interests. Still other groups are extraorganizational; that is, they are composed of employees from several different organizations. These groups are structured around a common theme of interest. Professional groups (e.g., the Society for I/O Psychologists) and most labor unions are like this.

Psychologists study the behavior of groups in lab and field experiments, field observations, and surveys. Groups are often studied in their natural settings, sometimes by means of direct observation. One of the studies done at the Hawthorne Western Electric plant (Roethlisberger & Dickson, 1939) demonstrates one way to observe natural groups. A special observation room—called the bank wiring room—was set up at the plant so that the researcher could observe a small group of employees while they worked. Another way to study natural work groups is to use **participant observation.** In one interesting study, a researcher went to work in a factory and became a member of a small group of machine operators. In this way, he was able to observe the group's social interaction (Roy, 1959–1960). Group process analysis, as discussed in chapter 2, is a *microanalytic* technique developed specifically for observing, recording, and understanding group interaction. Either a participant observer or an outsider can use this technique.

The survey technique is often used to collect data on the attitudes and opinions of group members. The survey is effective when used in this way; however, it has limited value in studying group *interaction*. Unless group members understand the operation of groups, it is unlikely that they can provide good survey data on interaction issues. It is for such reasons that researchers have been criticized for their overuse of questionnaires in group study (cf., Mossholder & Bedeian, 1983). The survey has been devised for the study of individuals. When we use it to study group interaction processes, we are taking a very indirect route. We are asking subjects to tell us what they *think* went on in a group.

Sociometry is a specialized survey technique that can be used for studying the characteristics of groups (Moreno, 1953). In a sociometric study, group members are asked to give information about their personal reactions to other group members. The method is frequently used to study work friendships and informal leadership. Participants can be asked to indicate whom they like, whom they prefer to work with, or whom they wish to have as a leader. When analyzed for a whole group, the data can reveal some relationship patterns. Notice the groupings in figure 12.4. Typically, whatever the question, one or two people get chosen by everyone. These are the "stars." They play central roles in the group.

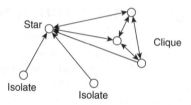

Figure 12.4 *Sociometric analysis is a survey technique used to study relationships among group members. Stars are those who get chosen by many group members. Isolates are chosen infrequently by others. Cliques are subgroups.*

The one or two others who are chosen very infrequently are isolates or fringe members of the group. Pairs, cliques, and other subgroups are revealed also. This type of information is useful for improving interaction within work groups. For example, isolates may need special attention because their capacities are not being used. Cliques can indicate potential conflict in the group.

Goals and Objectives of Work Groups

Whenever a formal work group is established, it is provided with certain human and material resources. Members are assigned, and a leader may be identified. The purpose of the group often is defined. The group may be expected to plan an activity, construct something, decide on a course of action, evaluate a past activity, and/or come up with new ideas. Goal-setting theory, which is discussed in relation to the motivation of individuals in chapter 8, can be used to anticipate the effects of a group's goals on its performance. Goals are proposed to have the effect of mobilizing the group toward accomplishment (Locke & Latham, 1990). However, according to the research, whether or not goals actually have this effect depends on whether the group participated in setting the goals. Groups that set their own goals perform better than groups that have their goals assigned to them (O'Leary-Kelly, Martocchio, & Frink, 1994).

Participative Management

In some organizations, groups of employees plan and make decisions about their work. As discussed in chapter 11, decentralization is a way to include lower level employees in decision making. Delegating authority to work groups of production employees and their supervisor allows for some participation in work decisions, as does establishing project teams.

Specific employee participation strategies have been developed which vary in terms of how much participation is allowed. For example, as discussed in chapter 11, self-regulating work groups allow employees to perform all aspects of a unit of work including managerial tasks. Another method of employee participation is the quality circle. This is a discussion group in which employees generate ideas to solve productivity problems and improve the quality of the work (Munchus, 1983). Although quality circles caught on in this country as a response to the success of Japanese management, they are actually an American invention. The quality circle is based on years of study beginning with Coch and French (1948), who found improvements in productivity as a result of involving workers in decisions. The theoretical foundation of the quality circle was provided by Argyris and other human relations theorists, as discussed in chapter 11.

Success of these groups probably depends on how much autonomy a work group has. Self-managing work groups have considerable authority to control their work, and they are assessed as productive and effective (Campion, Medsker, & Higgs, 1993). However, programs that allow less involvement might be expected to be less motivating and less effective. For example, quality circles have not been shown to be very successful (Lawler & Mohrman, 1985). Bramel and Friend (1987) suggested that the lack of success of quality circles is because of the reason for establishing such groups. They noted that the *image* of the small work group has changed over the years. Sometimes, the work group has been the organization's means of controlling workers. At such times, management is positive about the group. At other times, the work group has been taken as a sign of the rising power of workers, and management has viewed it as unfriendly.

The Purpose of Informal Groups

Informal groups serve personal purposes, not the least of which is to alleviate the boredom and fatigue of routine work. It is not unusual for people in apparently dull jobs to report that they enjoy their work. Roy's (1959–1960) observations of a group of factory workers indicated that the social interaction among members of a work group can make up for the lack of variety in such jobs. He reported that the work group took a number of breaks during the workday in which there was refreshment, horseplay, and work discussion. Like the formal work group, the informal group can provide information about the job and about the organization's mission, policies, and procedures. It can contribute to the organization's success by smoothing the process of getting the daily work done.

The informal group sometimes has negative effects on the organization. For example, the bank wiring room study (Roethlisberger & Dickson, 1939), previously mentioned as an example of field observation, found that the informal work group was effective in getting compliance with its own norms and rules of behavior, even when these directly contradicted the policies of the organization. The group maintained its own productivity at a level lower than management demanded. This occurred through strong informal pressures applied to individuals by other members of the group. "Rate busters" were pressured to decrease their productivity, and "chiselers"–those producing less than the group's rate–to increase their productivity. The primary objective of the group appeared to be resistance to change in the established work routine. Workers seemed to be resistant because they believed that management would take advantage of them by increasing production quotas and not sharing the payoffs (Bramel & Friend, 1987).

Group Processes

Groups perform their work through processes of interpersonal interaction. These processes vary in terms of their benefit to the group. In fact, a group may not be successful in accomplishing its task because its interaction process is faulty. In this section, we look at the processes of group interaction and at the conditions that prevent effective group work.

Communication is the vehicle for group interaction processes. If we observe communication in a group, we will get clues as to what else is going on.

Table 12.3   Codes for Analysis of Communication

Relational Control Message Codes

One-up (↑) messages define or control; one-down (↓) messages request or accept other's definition; one-across (→) messages are neither demanding nor accepting.

Grammatical Forms	Response Forms				
	Support	**Nonsupport**	**Extension**	**Answer**	**Instruction**
Assertion–declarative message	Expresses agreement, approval, or acceptance	Expresses disagreement, disapproval, or nonacceptance	Provides information, continuing topic, discussion	Provides information to question	Gives suggestions or directions
	↓	↑	→	↑	↑
Question–interrogative message	Requests agreement approval, or acceptance	Interrogative form of expressing disagreement, disapproval, or nonacceptance	Requests information on topic of discussion	Interrogative form of giving information to question	Interrogative form of giving suggestions or directions
	↓	↑	↓	↑	↑
Talkover–interruptive message	Interrupts to give agreement, approval, or acceptance	Interrupts to give disagreement, nonapproval, or nonacceptance	Interrupts to give topic information	Interrupts to give information to question	Interrupts to give suggestions or directions
a. Successful–gains conversational floor	↓	↑	↑	↑	↑
b. Unsuccessful–does not gain conversational floor	↓	↑	→	↑	↑

From J.A. Courtwright, G.T. Fairhurst, and L.E. Rogers, "Interaction Patterns in Organic and Mechanistic Systems" in *Academy of Management Journal,* Vol. 32: 773–802, 1989. Reprinted by permission of the Academy of Management, Ada, Ohio.

Communication reflects personal motives and goals, decision procedures, and social influence processes. Observers using group process analysis find that group members communicate their power relationships by the way they interact. For example, one member asks questions and another responds with directives and statements of fact. One person may regularly interrupt another to do this. People also display their relationships by nonverbal messages and by their body position, tone of voice, and eye contact.

    To analyze a group's communication, an observer needs to make note of who talks and in what manner. The observer also needs to notice how others respond. In a procedure that was developed for observing and analyzing conversations, codes were used to indicate the speaker, the grammatical form of the message, and how the message functioned as a response to a previous speaker (Courtright, Fairhurst, & Rogers, 1989). As shown in table 12.3, these aspects of communication demonstrate the message's function. For example, in a conversation about a work procedure, the supervisor interrupts the subordinate and says, "Yes, we should do the job that way." This is a successful interruption or *talkover*

Table 12.4	Behaviors Contributing to the Group Task Function
Task Function	**Description of Observed Behavior**
Initiating	Gets the problem-solving process started by defining the task, suggesting procedures, defining possible goals, and outlining procedures
Giving information and opinions	Provides task-relevant material and data for use in the discussion
Seeking information and opinions	Asks others to contribute task-relevant material
Clarifying and elaborating	Restates comments and adds clarifying information to improve understanding and stimulate further task discussion
Calling for task decision	Tests the group for its readiness to make a decision

by which the supervisor shows support or agreement. Then, the supervisor continues, "We will order the materials, and you can get on it next week." Here, the supervisor uses talkover to give directions. With this coding system, various aspects of group interaction can be studied. For example, Courtright et al. (1989) studied supervisor-subordinate interactions in different organizational designs. They found that communications were more accepting and consultative in the organic organization and more controlling in the mechanistic organization.

Group Functions: Task and Maintenance

In a working group, both verbal and nonverbal behavior of members reveal the group's functions (Weick, 1968). Study of effective groups indicates that a group must perform two functions in order to reach its goals. One function is reflected in task-oriented behavior. The other is shown when a member attempts to maintain or improve the group's interaction process, that is, in maintenance behavior. The formal leader of the group and/or the members perform these functions. Study of groups in natural settings indicates that leaders typically do some, but not all, of this work (Fiedler, 1967). Depending on the situation and the leader's personal tendency, he or she is likely to focus on either the task or the maintenance function. Members of the group may perform the remaining function, or it may be neglected altogether. To the extent that these functions are not adequately performed, we can expect problems in the group.

The **group task function** refers to the formal work goal and is carried out by members who contribute directly to task performance. The nature and extent of task-oriented behavior depends on the particular work assignment. However, in general, members showing task-oriented behavior get the group to generate and evaluate ideas, make decisions, and take task-related actions. Group members who perform this function suggest goals and procedures; seek and give facts and opinions; and clarify and summarize discussions about the task (see table 12.4). The **group maintenance function** refers to the group's internal operations and involves monitoring of the group's process. Groups are more likely to be successful

Table 12.5

Behaviors Contributing to the Performance of the Maintenance Function

Maintenance Function	Description of Observed Behavior
Gatekeeping	Maintains watch over communication in the group; sees that each person has a chance to contribute; and encourages less active members to participate
Harmonizing	Helps disagreeing members deal with their conflict; compromises; uses humor to reduce excessive group tension
Calling for process decision	Draws attention to the group's manner of working; tests for satisfaction with the interaction process

in accomplishing their task when they have the full participation of their members; when group objectives are given a higher priority than personal goals; and when interpersonal conflict within the group is managed effectively. Individuals who perform the group maintenance function make an effort to get members involved in order to meet these criteria. They help the group become more self-aware and deal with friction and interpersonal conflict (see table 12.5).

Problems can occur in the performance of the two group functions. Sometimes groups fail because the task requirements exceed the abilities and motivation of group members. Unstructured and ambiguous tasks are difficult, especially for a group with limited human and material resources. Failure also can occur when a group is distracted and neglects the task function. Sometimes this happens because the group becomes enmeshed in internal problems. For example, people may put their own needs forward and engage the group in satisfying these instead of working on the task. If such *self-oriented behavior* is not handled through group maintenance, it will prevent the group from doing its work. Self-oriented motivations are usually contained in the individual's own "hidden agenda" of personal issues. These personal issues may be about getting power or personal rewards from the group.

Groups can fail to perform their task function because some members do not work. This is called **social loafing.** Social loafing was noted in early studies of group work. Taylor (1911) found some groups to do no more work than an individual working alone. Some recent research has been done to discover the reasons for social loafing. A series of lab experiments indicated that it may have to do with how personally responsible an individual feels for the group's task. Subjects who shared a task with 15 others reported feeling more dispensable, and they used less complex work procedures than those who worked alone or in pairs (Weldon & Mustari, 1988). Others have found that the member's level of satisfaction with the group depends on his or her participation and the feeling of having had an impact on the group (Vanderslice, Rice, & Julian, 1987). These studies suggest that group maintenance needs to include deliberate measures to engage all members in the group's work, especially when there are signs that some have withdrawn.

Behavioral Roles and Group Norms

In the process of interaction, work groups define particular roles that individual members play. A *role* is a set of behaviors that a person is expected to show in a particular situation. The role specifies the particular task activities a work group member should perform and the relationship of the role taker to others in the group. For example, the chair of a committee is expected to open the meeting, keep the group focused on the agenda, and act as referee. A role indicates required behaviors, behaviors that involve some freedom of choice, and behaviors that are unacceptable. The role of your professor probably includes such task activities as lecturing. It may prohibit him or her from establishing close friendships with students.

Sometimes, people have problems with their roles, as I note in the chapter on stress. *Role conflict* occurs when an individual receives discrepant role information. An employee who answers to two bosses may experience role conflict if the bosses expect behavior that is incompatible. When an employee belongs to more than one work group and plays different roles in them, he or she may experience role conflict as well. With *role ambiguity,* an individual does not know the appropriate role to take, which also has been found to function as a stressor.

Roles are specific behavioral prescriptions for individuals; norms are more general guidelines. **Group norms** express the group's values and apply more or less equally to all members. Norms can be about any aspect of work. They can originate from the group's past experience, or they can be introduced into the group from other situations. Internal agreement about group norms appears to improve the group's performance (Argote, 1989).

Norms may or may not be formally recognized. Research indicates that many informal work groups have **productivity norms** that are not recognized by the organization (Lichtman & Lane, 1983). That is, group members are expected to produce a certain amount but no more than this. Another unrecognized group norm concerns the necessity for adhering to established starting and quitting times. In many offices, work does not actually begin in the morning until after employees chat and drink coffee for about 30 minutes. Other work norms concern the amount of acceptable employee theft, the appropriateness of casual dress at work, and the importance of getting to meetings on time.

Norms vary in the extent to which the group allows them to be violated. Because productivity norms seriously affect the entire group, they tend to be vigorously defended. Violation of other norms may be considered less serious. A common norm concerns the wearing of particular clothing at work. For example, commercial airlines employees wear uniforms. If a pilot regularly comes to work in street clothes, this might be serious enough for a reprimand, although perhaps nothing more. Some norms are less important or affect only a few people. The night clerk at the local motel is probably allowed to *sleep* on the job, although the daytime staff are not. Feldman (1984) said that norms are defended to the extent that they serve group needs for survival. If the group can live with the violation, then members do nothing. However, if the violation threatens the group in some serious way, as the violation of productivity norms can, then members apply penalties.

Social Influence

Social influence occurs whenever a person or group causes a change in the behavior, attitudes, opinions, or feelings of another person. We have already seen that work groups can influence their members. They apply pressure to get compliance with group norms, for example. This pressure tends to be coercive; people comply in order to avoid being punished by the group. However, groups also influence their members in less negative ways. For example, a group may become an important reference for a person. Through the process of *identification,* for example, a person may change and become more like the group. Through *assimilation,* the group's position on an issue may become part of the individual's own cognitive structure.

French and Raven (1959; Raven, 1974) proposed that social influence occurs through the use of particular types of social power. They defined **social power** as dependent on either (1) the influence agent's personal characteristics or (2) his or her ability to provide consequences for the influence target.[1] The agent's expertise, attractiveness, and legitimacy in a role relationship are personal characteristics that contribute to power. An agent with *expert power* is one who appears to have superior knowledge and honesty. The target is influenced, not because the message is inherently good, but because it comes from a good source. An agent who has *referent power* is someone whom the target uses as a model. Referent power has special relevance to groups. We want to be like certain others in our groups. We identify with them and adopt their opinions, attitudes, and behavior. An agent who has *legitimate power* has entered into a role relationship with the person who is influenced. The agent has a right to attempt influence, and the target is obliged to comply. The relationship between supervisor and subordinate is an example. There are two types of power that depend on consequences. If an agent has *reward power,* he or she can promise positive consequences for a target who complies with an influence attempt. Punishment for noncompliance can be threatened if the agent has *coercive power.* For example, a supervisor can give rewards, such as recognition, or punishments, such as reprimands. These two types of power depend on the target's belief that the agent can and will apply these consequences.

French and Raven's (1959) model has been criticized for its inconsistent concepts. Power definitions switch back and forth from actual characteristics of an agent to target perceptions of an agent (Patchen, 1974). Also, research on the model has been criticized for its overreliance on weak measures of the power concepts. Usually, studies are done with survey instruments containing a single item for each power. Hinkin and Schriesheim (1989) attempted to solve both problems. They proposed new definitions that make the power bases conceptually consistent. Following French and Raven's example in defining reward and coercive powers as *abilities* of the agent, each of the other powers is redefined as an agent's ability to do something to or for the target. With legitimate power, the agent is able to inspire a feeling of obligation. With expert power, the agent is able to give knowledge. With referent power, the agent can cause the target to feel accepted. The researchers also developed an instrument that contains four items for each power. Table 12.6 lists samples of the items. The instrument has been shown to be a reliable measure of the five power types (Littlepage et al., 1993).

[1]One type of power, informational power, is not social in nature. The influence that occurs is due to the inherent quality of the information contained in the message, not to the person who sends the message.

Table 12.6	**Sample Items from a Measure of Social Power**	
My supervisor can	____ increase my pay level.	(reward power)
	____ give me undesirable job assignments.	(coercive power)
	____ make me feel that I have commitments to meet.	(legitimate power)
	____ give me good technical suggestions.	(expert power)
	____ make me feel valued.	(referent power)

In natural settings, French and Raven (1959) proposed that the powers are used in combination. Research has indicated several relationships between the powers that operate in applied settings. First, having legitimate power means that the agent has reward power. For example, a supervisor who is seen as legitimately holding the position can use rewards to influence subordinates. Second, legitimate power is most important to an influence agent because, at least to some extent, it makes the other powers become available. The supervisor also comes to have expert power because of being in his or her position. Even referent power, in which the supervisor becomes a model for subordinates, becomes available. Third, the use of the different powers has variable outcomes. Performance is influenced most strongly by a supervisor's use of expert and reward powers. Subordinate satisfaction with a supervisor is highest when the supervisor uses expert and referent powers. Together these findings suggest that although a legitimate authority can use any of the powers to influence others, the best strategy is to use those that are strongly related to the legitimate position and that lead to desired outcomes, that is, reward, expert, and referent power (Carson, Carson, & Roe, 1993).

Group Cohesiveness

Internal cohesiveness provides a group spirit and a feeling of belongingness. In cohesive groups, members think in terms of "we," and group goals take precedence over individual goals.

Many researchers have attempted to show that group cohesiveness improves performance. In some early research, for example, internally cohesive groups that were engaged in competitive games were found more likely to win (Sherif, 1966). Because cohesiveness appears to be linked to team performance among competitive sports teams (Widmeyer, Brawley, & Carron, 1992), we might suppose that cohesiveness also is linked to performance in work groups. There is some evidence of this. However, the effect is not as strong in work groups as it is in sports teams. In their meta-analysis, Mullen and Copper (1994) found that cohesiveness and performance were linked. Interestingly, their analysis suggested that the effect may occur in either direction. That is, cohesiveness may bring about better performance, or a successfully performing group may become more cohesive.

Why might there be a relationship between cohesiveness and group performance? Is it because a cohesive group has members who are friendly, so the group is attractive and one could take pride in being a member? Mullen and Copper (1994) considered this question, but they found nothing to indicate that attractiveness of the group is important. Commitment to the group's tasks, however, did increase the cohesiveness-performance effect. The reviewers concluded that efforts to increase productivity by making a group more attractive or by "pumping up" group pride are not likely to be effective.

*M*ain
*P*oints

Much of the important work today is done by groups. Organizations have both formal and informal groups. Goals are assigned to some groups; others develop their own goals. Goals can motivate high performance, particularly if the group sets them. Groups that have more autonomy, such as self-managing work groups, are more effective than groups with less ability to set goals, such as quality circles.

Groups perform their tasks through interaction processes. How well they work can be evaluated in terms of how well they perform two basic functions. The task function refers to task-related work, whereas the maintenance function has to do with the group's internal operation. Both are needed. When they are not performed well, problems appear. An example is social loafing.

Groups define behavioral roles for their members to play. These specify the tasks that members perform. Roles need to be clear and consistent. Group norms also are developed. They are general expressions of what a group values, and they apply to all members. A productivity norm is a common one.

Social influence is a process that affects group performance. Supervisors, for example, can influence the behavior of members of their work groups. Power can come from the person's image as an expert or as a model, or from having access to rewards.

The group's internal cohesiveness also can affect performance. Cohesive groups are generally high performers.

GROUP WORK: PROBLEM SOLVING AND DECISION MAKING

Because the work group's task is the reason for its existence, we might expect that some important aspects of the group's process are about getting the task done. A work group engages in two kinds of task-related activity: problem solving and decision making. In problem solving, the group must generate ideas, gather information, and develop alternative courses of action. Throughout this process, the group also must make decisions. In this section, I examine some ways groups perform task-oriented work and some difficulties they have.

Group Problem Solving

Can groups do anything that individuals cannot? Sometimes we feel that we would be better off without certain of our groups. For example, committees are berated

Section III: Creating an Effective Social Organization

for their slow and bizarre results: "A camel is a horse designed by a committee." Such assessments contain some truth. The literature on creative problem solving indicates that groups do come up with more and higher quality solutions than individuals do (Dennis & Valacich, 1994). (A camel is a better solution to a desert problem than a horse is.)

The effectiveness of a group depends on the nature of its task. Individual work is as good as group work when the task is relatively undemanding, but groups are more effective when the task requires complex problem solving (Johnson et al., 1981). This may be because groups generate more ideas for solving complex problems by pooling their members' resources. Groups can benefit from recognizing and making use of the knowledge and judgment of their more expert members if internal processes allow this (Bottger & Yetton, 1988; Yetton & Bottger, 1982).

Most formal work groups do not use systematic procedures in problem solving. In fact, they may focus almost exclusively on a few potential solutions without fully analyzing the problem (Nutt, 1984). A method that may improve the problem-solving process divides the group's work into three stages and emphasizes **brainstorming** (Maier, 1970). In the first stage of problem solving, the group must attempt to diagnose the problem. Symptoms and possible causes are thoroughly discussed. The major concern is allowing enough time for this. In the second stage, through brainstorming, the group develops a long list of alternative solutions. A risk in this stage is in evaluating alternatives prematurely. The group should pay close attention to its maintenance function at this time and attempt to delay criticism of the ideas generated. In the third stage, the alternatives are evaluated. Each should be given a fair chance and not simply discounted. Sometimes, good ideas look as if they "won't fly" at first. In the end, the group should have a few good solutions from which they select one to put into action.

Group Decision Making

Groups may make more decisions than they are aware of making. Sometimes, decision making is quite deliberate. For example, a group votes to elect a leader or decide on a solution to put into action. At other times, decision making is not so explicit. The group may not even realize that it made a decision. Groups often begin by "deciding" how they will interact and even how they will decide. These "decisions" are not discussed. It is hardly ever the case that someone opens a meeting by asking, "Shall we decide by majority vote, by consensus, or shall we just do what Paul wants?" Instead, decisions about how the group will operate typically are made by default. That is, tradition or someone's personal agenda dictates the group's process. An alert group member can bring such subtle decisions to the attention of the group and enable members to consider whether they are satisfactory. (The group maintenance function is performed through such actions.)

There are several formal procedures for making group decisions. The group can elect a representative and let that person decide for the whole group. Members also can vote, either in public or by secret ballot. In voting, they can use one of several definitions of *majority* to determine whether a vote has carried. Sometimes, a simple majority is used, such as 51 percent of the votes cast. At other times, the decision requires a larger majority, such as a two-thirds vote. A more stringent form of voting is by *consensus* or unanimity of the group. If the group is not unanimous at first, the majority attempts to influence the others to move in their direction. When the group agrees to decide by consensus, it means that each member must be willing to accept and vote for a decision that is not his or her first choice. To the extent that the group initially is split on an issue, consensus seeking will be more time-consuming. Although it may mean more and better deliberation on an issue, there also is a risk that undesirable compromises will be made.

Effective and Ineffective Decisions

How do we know when a decision is a good one? We can wait and see what happens as a result of it, which is the ultimate test. If everything turns out all right, then it was a good decision. Unfortunately, in the organizational setting, feedback about a decision outcome often is very limited. For example, a personnel selection committee can get information about its decisions to hire certain candidates but not about its decisions to reject others. The committee is not certain, therefore, whether it sent away people who would have been a detriment or an asset to the organization.

Certain group characteristics seem to influence the quality of decisions. For example, research has shown that groups with a greater variety of alternatives make better decisions (Wanous & Youtz, 1986), and this variety of alternatives may be more likely in certain groups. Heterogeneous groups, for example, generate more creative solutions than homogenous groups (Hoffman & Maier, 1961). This effect may depend on the way the group is heterogenous, however. Groups whose members differ in rank and status probably will not use all of their member resources. For example, a study of interdisciplinary health care treatment teams showed that heterogeneous groups do not always have the full participation of their members, and the quality of their decisions may suffer as a result (Fiorelli, 1988). In groups with members from physical therapy, occupational therapy, psychology, social services, and medicine, it was found that the high-status physicians made most of the decisions.

Groupthink

The process of group interaction may be responsible for some faulty decisions. Group discussion often results in a polarization of positions (Myers & Lamm, 1976). Although popular wisdom suggests that individual positions become more conservative, research indicates that a change known as the **risky shift** can occur. That is, people become less cautious and more willing to take chances (Clark, 1971).

Janis (1972) studied risky decision making and proposed that certain aspects of the group process are responsible for this effect. He called the interaction pattern **groupthink**. People who are enmeshed in the problems of a highly cohesive group exhibit this style of thinking. Members of the group get so caught up in trying to reach a unanimous decision that they lose sight of their need to evaluate alternate solutions (Janis, 1972; Longley & Pruitt, 1980). Groupthink is proposed likely to occur when (1) the group is homogeneous and insulated from outsiders; (2) members hold each other in high regard; (3) the group leader is directive; (4) the group traditionally has not debated issues; and (5) the group must act fast. Whyte (1989) suggested another factor that leads to such decision fiascoes: the way a question is initially framed. He proposed that groups making risky decisions have looked at their problem as a choice between two losses rather than as a win-lose or a win-win proposition.

Janis (1972) proposed that groupthink is maintained by the group's beliefs about itself and its manner of responding to negative information. For example, such a group believes that its decision cannot be wrong and that it has greater ability to carry out the decision than it actually does have. These false beliefs are maintained by *suppression* of contradictory information. The group scoffs at warnings of potential loss and applies direct social pressure to anyone who expresses doubt.

What can be done to prevent groupthink? Because disagreement is suppressed in such groups, a first step is to encourage members to express any doubts they may have. A strategy for encouraging members in this way involves temporarily breaking the group into two subgroups. One develops a list of alternative solutions and gives it to the other. The second subgroup responds by developing acceptable solutions that are *counter* to these. The subgroups then interact as a group and develop a list of solutions acceptable to both. A recent study found that this method, though legitimizing the expression of differences, was beneficial to groups. Early consensus, which leads to poor decisions, was prevented, and there was strong agreement on the decisions that ultimately were made (Priem, Harrison, & Muir, 1995).

---

*M*ain *P*oints

A major task of work groups is problem solving. Groups are good at this. They develop more creative solutions than individuals, especially with complicated problems. Most groups do not use systematic procedures to do brainstorming, although such procedures could be helpful.

Another major group task is decision making. Groups make many decisions. Some are about the task; others are about the process of interacting. Formal procedures include consensus and majority voting.

Group decisions can be flawed, sometimes because they are risky. A group makes risky decisions when it engages in an interaction pattern called groupthink. In groupthink, the members are so focussed on reaching consensus that they ignore evidence that their actions will lead to failure. To prevent groupthink, members must be encouraged to express their doubts.

CONFLICT IN THE ORGANIZATION

Conflict has been defined in a variety of ways. It is sometimes described as competitive or aggressive behavior. It is said to involve negative interpersonal perceptions and hostile feelings. It is described in terms of what might have caused it, such as scarce resources. Often, it is defined in terms of its win or loss outcomes. However, these descriptions do not reach the core meaning of conflict. Rather, they describe various *manifestations* of an underlying construct. According to Deutsch (1971, 1980), **conflict** is a basic psychological mechanism that centers around incompatible goals. Conflict exists whenever one set of goals, needs, or interests disagree with another set. With this definition, we avoid the problems of confusing conflict with methods of waging and resolving it, and we recognize that its outcomes can be negative or positive.

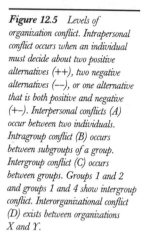
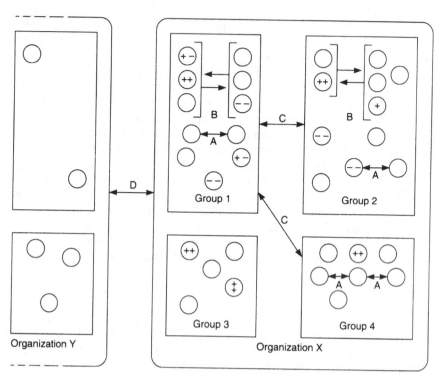

Figure 12.5 *Levels of organization conflict. Intrapersonal conflict occurs when an individual must decide about two positive alternatives (++), two negative alternatives (−−), or one alternative that is both positive and negative (+−). Interpersonal conflicts (A) occur between two individuals. Intragroup conflict (B) occurs between subgroups of a group. Intergroup conflict (C) occurs between groups. Groups 1 and 2 and groups 1 and 4 show intergroup conflict. Interorganizational conflict (D) exists between organizations X and Y.*

Despite the view of some earlier thinkers that conflict is undesirable, our daily lives show that we actively seek conflict. Does this mean we are masochistic? Perhaps it means that conflict is not always destructive and unpleasant. Many of our most valued activities embody conflict, from competitive games to intellectual debates and discussions. We have institutionalized conflict in business, politics, and sports. Conflict is stimulating, arousing, and exciting; and it has positive outcomes. It can be used to energize physical action at work. It provides a channel for solving problems and forms the basis of social change. Conflict also has negative outcomes. Unmet goals, closed communication, and hostile attitudes can result. However, it appears not to be conflict per se that brings about these effects; rather, it is the nature of the conflict and the way it is handled that produce these outcomes. Conflicts about a work group's tasks can be detrimental or helpful to the group depending on the nature of the work. When the group is doing routine work, task-related conflict may simply interfere with getting the work done. However, when the group is doing more difficult work, such as making hard decisions, conflict about the work can actually help the group become more successful (Jehn, 1995).

Conflict can exist at any system level, as demonstrated in figure 12.5. It can be *intrapersonal* or within the individual. For example, a person may have to choose between two positive alternatives, such as two equally good jobs, or between two negative alternatives, such as being laid off or transferred to a bad location. At other levels, conflict can be *interpersonal* or between individuals. If interpersonal conflict occurs between people in a group, or between subgroups, then it is

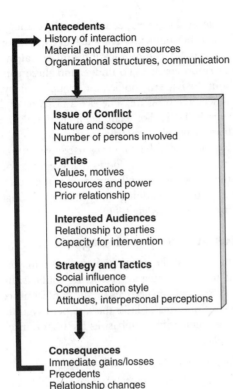

Antecedents
History of interaction
Material and human resources
Organizational structures, communication

Issue of Conflict
Nature and scope
Number of persons involved

Parties
Values, motives
Resources and power
Prior relationship

Interested Audiences
Relationship to parties
Capacity for intervention

Strategy and Tactics
Social influence
Communication style
Attitudes, interpersonal perceptions

Consequences
Immediate gains/losses
Precedents
Relationship changes

Figure 12.6 Important factors in analyzing the conflict process. The analyst needs to follow the development, conduct, and outcomes of the conflict. This requires collecting information about what led to the conflict and about how the conflict is being conducted. Both the antecedents and the conflict determine the consequences. The consequences, in turn, become the background for future conflicts.

intragroup conflict. When one group is in disagreement with another, *intergroup* or *intraorganizational* conflict results. Of course, organizations often are in conflict with one another, forming *interorganizational* conflict. A look at the world news tells us that conflict is *international*. If science fiction writers are right, when we finally make contact with other worlds, we will find that conflict is *interplanetary*.

Observing the Conflict Process

The processes of waging and resolving conflict within a group are similar to those between two groups. Goal relationships affect the internal interaction of group members in much the same way as they do the interaction between groups (Deutsch, 1973, 1980; Tjosvold, 1984). In this discussion, when I refer to **conflict parties,** I mean the persons, factions, or groups who are directly involved. **Interested audiences** are those who are only indirectly involved, but whose presence can influence the conflict's parties. **Third parties** are uninvolved and more or less objective about the conflict.

The development and management of conflict is studied by means of group process observation. The observer records interaction events that identify the players, the issues, and the strategies used to manage the conflict. Figure 12.6 summarizes the kinds of factors that an observer should expect to observe and record. The observer should attempt to determine the parties' motives and values, especially as to what they consider a gain and a loss. Organizational norms about conflict are often carried into work groups. For example, competitiveness may be expected in the organization. The observer should analyze the group's communication to determine whether the conflict reflects such an expectation.

A group's patterns of communication and social influence reflect the strategies it uses to carry on conflict. To understand these patterns, the observer needs information about the issue in conflict, the group's history, and the extent to which the group is under time pressure. The size and scope of the issue can affect the strategy used (Deutsch, 1971). For example, a large, diffuse issue is difficult to manage, as is an issue that people view as a matter of principle. The group's history of interaction also influences the strategies used, as do time pressures on the group. For example, in one study, it was found that giving deadlines to a cooperating group increased their tendency to collaborate. When group members had been working independently, however, adding time pressures brought on competitiveness among them (Carnevale & Lawler, 1986).

Behavioral Styles of Conflict Management

Conflict theory has highlighted the process of conflict management by describing the way individuals behave in waging and resolving conflicts. In the following sections, I consider two theoretical perspectives on the conflict process. One addresses styles of conflict behavior in terms of links that are perceived to exist between the parties' goals. The other perspective emphasizes the importance of the parties' values for each other's goals.

Styles Reflecting the Links Between Goals

According to Deutsch (1973, 1980; Deutsch & Krauss, 1962), the links between the conflicting parties' goals determine whether there is a conflict. The parties may perceive their goals as *independent* or not linked; in this case, there is no conflict. If goals are perceived to be *interdependent*, then there is conflict. Interdependent goals may be linked in one of two ways. When they are linked positively, the parties are moving in the same direction. The striving of one group helps the other. When the goals are negatively linked, the success of one depends on the failure of the other. In this theory, the relationship of goals determines the parties' interaction style. Deutsch proposed that three styles of behavior can result. When goals are independent, behavior is *individualistic;* both persons go their own way. When goals are interdependent, the parties must interact. If they see their goals as positively linked, they behave *cooperatively* for mutual success. If they see their goals as negatively linked, they behave *competitively*.

Deutsch (1973, 1980) described cooperation and competition as styles of conflict management that are expressed in communication, social influence, and problem orientation. **Cooperation** involves open and honest communication. Because their goals are positively linked, the conflicting parties perceive themselves as being similar and as having common interests. They are trusting and, in general, respond helpfully to each other's requests. Their conflict is defined as a mutual problem that can be solved by *collaboration*. They approach their work by using the special talents of each. Persuasion is the predominant method of influence. The social psychological literature indicates that this style of behavior promotes continued interaction, friendliness, trust, and interpersonal attraction (cf. Berscheid & Walster, 1969).

Competition involves misleading or closed communication. Because of their negatively-linked goals, it is in the interest of each party to get, but not give, honest information. Competing parties are suspicious of one another and may show hostility. As competition continues, the scope of the issue expands, and winning may become a matter of general principle. This intensifies the emotion and makes partial gain less acceptable than mutual disaster. The parties begin to believe that only one solution is possible, and each gets ready to impose it on the other. They attempt to influence each other by using threats. There is supportive evidence for this view of competition from the research literature. For example, Sherif (1966; Sherif et al., 1961) reviewed studies indicating that rival groups are distrustful and hostile, and they disrupt one another's goal efforts.

What determines whether groups adopt one or the other of these conflict styles? Deutsch pointed out that features of both the existing relationship and the parties' prior interactions are important in determining the conflict management style. One such characteristic of the existing relationship is the extent of shared membership. That is, do some members belong to both groups? If so, cooperation is possible. However, if there is little membership overlap, then competitive conflict management is more likely (Nelson, 1989). A second aspect of the parties' existing relationship that affects their conflict style is the amount of social power each party has. In many work groups, members have unequal power and status. The group formed by a supervisor and subordinates is an example. Unequal power does not necessarily lead to dominating or competitive behavior. Research indicates that persons with unequal power can and do work cooperatively. Superiors can use their power to promote goal progress that benefits their subordinates as well as themselves (Tjosvold, 1981, 1984). In addition, past interaction and previous wins and losses can determine future conflict behavior. If the parties have cooperated in the past, then they may be able to continue their cooperative behavior in the future. If they have competed, they probably will continue to compete (Keenan & Carnevale, 1989). In fact, an episode of competitive conflict actually may bring about an *escalation* of conflict (Pruitt & Rubin, 1986).

Styles Reflecting the Comparative Value of Goals

Another theory of conflict behavior emphasizes the comparative value of the conflicting parties' goals. In this model, the goal relationship is proposed to be made up of two attitudinal factors, namely, concerns for self and other (Rahim, 1985; Rahim & Bonoma, 1979). *Concern for self* is defined as the extent to which a party is intent upon satisfying its own goals. *Concern for other* is the extent to which a party is interested in satisfying the other's goals. Each party exhibits high or low levels on each of these concerns, as shown in figure 12.7.

These goal concerns provide the basis for five styles of conflict management (Rahim & Bonoma, 1979). *Integrating* behavior is shown when there is high concern both for one's own and for the other's needs. Integrating involves an open exchange of information in which both parties are willing to work out a solution acceptable to both. With a similar style, labeled *compromising,* each party shows moderate concern for itself and the other. Both are willing to accept a partial gain. When one party attempts to smooth over differences, it exhibits *obliging* behavior. There is low self-concern and high concern for the other. The party believes the

Figure 12.7 *A model of organizational conflict. Behavioral styles of the conflicting parties are proposed to be determined by the extent to which each party has a high or low concern for the self and for the other. The resulting interaction styles lead to one of three types of outcomes: positive sum (win/win), mixed (no win/no lose), or zero sum (win/lose or lose/lose).*

Reproduced with permission of the authors and publishers from: Rahim, A., & Bonoma, T.V. "Managing organizational conflict: a model for diagnosis and intervention. Psychological Reports, 1979, 44, 1323–1344. © Psychological Reports. 1979

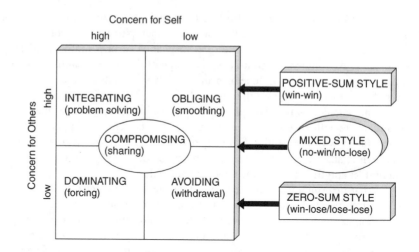

other's needs are greater than its own. *Dominating* behavior is the reverse. A party has high self-concern and ignores the needs of the other. The dominating party forces its position onto the other. Withdrawal from interaction constitutes *avoiding* behavior. The party shows little concern for its own goals or for the other's. As a result, neither party's goals are reached.

Rahim and Bonoma (1979) proposed that each of these behavioral styles is appropriate for certain situations. Integration is best when the issues are complex and coordination is needed. Obliging is appropriate when one party is willing to negotiate for future favors from the other. These two styles are particularly good for dealing with conflict around broad issues of strategic planning. Compromising is effective when the parties' goals are negatively linked and/or when the parties are equally powerful. Dominating is useful when quick action is needed or when a required action is not popular. Avoiding is appropriate when there is a greater risk of loss in confronting the other party than in not dealing with the problem at all.

There are some similarities between Rahim and Bonoma's and Deutsch's models. For example, dominating is like competing in its win-lose orientation. Integrating behavior is similar to cooperation. Compromising behavior has characteristics of both competitive and cooperative behavior. The goal relationships are negative in both cases, but the parties work cooperatively toward a partial gain for each. Also, integrating and compromising are like Deutsch's concepts in that they describe the *interaction* of the conflict parties. However, in discussing the other styles, Rahim and Bonoma switched from this focus on interaction to a focus on the behavior of one party. Dominating, obliging, and avoiding are conflict styles that describe one party's behavior in response to another showing contrasting behavior. That is, one obliges another party who wants its own way. One avoids another who is likely to dominate. One dominates another who yields.

Conflict Outcomes and Interventions

The Outcomes of Conflict

Immediate outcomes of a conflict can be described in terms of the extent to which each of the two parties succeed in reaching their goals, that is, in terms of their wins and losses. Combining these individual outcomes yields an overall total or sum. A **positive-sum outcome** results when both parties win at least partially. A **zero-sum outcome** results when one wins and the other loses. A **negative-sum outcome** occurs when neither party reaches its goals.

Different conflict styles yield outcomes of different value. Deutsch (1973) proposed that competition can result in either zero- or negative-sum outcomes. At best, only one party loses in competition. Often, both lose. With cooperation, one party reaches its goal only if the other also does, which results in a positive-sum outcome. As shown in figure 12.7, Rahim and Bonoma (1979) proposed that both integrating and obliging behavior lead to positive-sum outcomes. Compromising is described as having a mixed outcome, although because both parties accept a partial gain, compromise can also be considered to result in a positive-sum outcome. Dominating indicates a win-lose or zero-sum outcome. Avoiding is predicted to result in a lose-lose or negative-sum outcome.

In addition to specific goal outcomes, there are other effects of conflict. Individuals' emotions are affected by how a conflict is managed, and the interpersonal relationship of the parties can be impaired (Wall & Callister, 1995). Productivity also may be affected. A meta-analysis of research indicated that this depends on the particular task being done (Johnson et al., 1981). For example, cooperation is more effective in increasing productivity when the task is complex and requires problem solving (Johnson & Johnson, 1979). Fallout from the style of conflict management can seriously affect the whole reason for an organization's existence. Tjosvold, Dann, and Wong (1992) noted that customer service is the main purpose of any organization, and argued that the management of conflict within the organization affects how customers are treated.

Another important effect of the conflict management style is the extent to which the conflict is *resolved*. When conflicts are left open, they can flare up in future interaction. Deutsch (1971, 1973) proposed that competition regenerates itself through unresolved conflicts, primarily because of the lingering effects on communication and interpersonal perceptions. If the parties have a history of closed communication, for example, they will have difficulty in becoming cooperative and in communicating openly because of the distrust and suspicion that have been created. With an unresolved conflict, the parties continue to view each other's motives in a negative way.

Tjosvold (1984) found evidence in the research literature for these effects. Several studies showed that cooperative groups continue to evaluate each other in positive terms, whereas groups that have competed remain hostile and continue to devalue each other's accomplishments (e.g., Goldman, Stockbauer, & McAuliffe, 1977; Sherif et al., 1961). Sherif (1966) also found that once a competitive history has developed, the greatest of measures are required to break the parties out of this. Only when it becomes completely clear that one party *cannot* win at the expense of the other are such groups able to collaborate. Recent reviewers have echoed the concerns about the negative effects of conflict. Wall and Callister (1995) observed that unresolved conflicts can produce very unpleasant leftovers.

Intervention: Changing the Level of Conflict

A moderate amount of conflict is helpful in interactions. It can increase creative thought and improve decisions. Thus, there may be times when an increase in conflict is needed. However, because conflict can be harmful, there will be times when it needs to be reduced or when the conflict management style needs to be changed.

Conflict may be created in order to bring about interaction between two parties, such as when groupthink appears to be developing (Priem, Harrison, & Muir, 1995). As defined, conflict does not exist if goals are independent; therefore, organizational interventions that link goals can bring about conflict. For example, the parties may be told that they must interact in reaching their goals. This communication should specify what conflict behavior will be rewarded and what will not be, in order to affect the involved parties' view of their shared goals. If the parties are expected to cooperate and help each other, then this must be expressed (Tjosvold et al., 1992).

In addition to goal independence in which there is actually no conflict, there are *masked conflicts* that on the surface appear to be "no-conflict" situations. For example, conflict may be suppressed, as when a group shows signs of groupthink. In this situation, some members have withdrawn or capitulated to more powerful members of the group. Conflict can be masked also when the issue is small, well contained, and managed effectively by cooperative behavior. Here, the conflict is simply overlooked. This brings up an important caution. We should be careful not to misinterpret effective collaboration. That is, we should not equate conflict only with strife.

Frequently, there is a need for reducing the level of conflict. In some situations, goal relationships are perceived as more interdependent than they actually should be. When two parties behave as if their goals are related, when in fact they are independent, then it is appropriate to intervene by separating the parties and encouraging independent work. To reduce conflict, it may help to dissolve groups that are no longer needed. Also, conflict can be reduced if management defines the nature of the parties' relationship and indicates the extent to which their goals actually are interrelated.

Intervention: Changing the Conflict Management Style

When the conflict is having negative results, a change to a more collaborative interaction style is appropriate. Several have offered ideas on how management or a third party, such as a consultant, can help make this change. Deutsch (1971, 1973) proposed that a strong, resourceful, and benevolent third party can help the conflicting parties become cooperative by (1) removing communication blocks and distortions; (2) narrowing the issue of conflict; and (3) developing rules for interaction. Interventions also can include educating the parties in collaborative interaction and making the links between their goals more apparent. Sherif (1966) found that it was only when groups were given a greater goal—in which it became clear that they all must pull together—that the groups' interaction became more cooperative. Prein (1987) studied intraorganizational conflict and found several strategies that third parties use. For example, through *consultation,* a third party attempts to help the conflicting parties improve their relationship and their interactions while working on the issue. The consultant is supportive and nondirective. Through *authoritative demand,* a third party, such as a work group's superior, can impose a solution on those in conflict.

Conflict within and between groups can be helpful. Often, it is not. The determinant of whether or not conflict is helpful, is how it is managed.

Conflict management is described in two models. In one, Deutsch emphasized goal relationships. He said that when groups' goals are linked in a positive way, they can manage the conflict by cooperating. Cooperation leads to positive outcomes and at least a partial gain for both parties. However, when parties' goals are negatively linked, they interact by competing. Competition leads to negative effects and goal loss for at least one of the parties. In another model, Rahim considered how much one party emphasizes its own goals relative to the goals of the other party. Five conflict styles resulted that vary in these terms. These styles yield a range of outcomes from positive to negative.

How conflict is managed determines goal success. A positive sum outcome means that both parties achieve their goals at least partially. A zero-sum outcome is when one wins and the other loses. A negative-sum outcome means that both fail.

Conflict management also has positive or negative effects on the parties' working relationship and on their future conflict. Negative outcomes are likely to carry over. When groups are not performing successfully, management can attempt to change the level of conflict, or the style of managing the conflict.

A SPECIAL INTERACTION: LABOR-MANAGEMENT NEGOTIATION

Some employees belong to a labor union. **Unions** are worker-oriented organizations that usually draw their members from different employers. Unions are meant to promote the economic and personal interests of their members. In particular, they are concerned with wages, employment opportunities, job security, and working conditions.

American labor unions began as a result of changes that occurred during the eighteenth-century industrial era. Prior to the Industrial Revolution, consumer goods were produced in small workshops by skilled craftsmen. With the advent of mechanized equipment and the birth of the factory, work processes changed markedly. The small shops closed. Many workers were needed in the factory but not necessarily skilled ones. The workplace was organized as a bureaucracy using highly specialized jobs and a strict chain of command. Unskilled laborers, including children, were hired to work at low wage rates and in poor working conditions. By the late 1800s, the average worker did exhausting labor; put in long hours in unhealthy and unsafe workplaces; and received low pay, no benefits, and almost no job security. These working conditions led to the labor union movement. The rationale of the movement was that workers would be more likely to succeed in getting things changed if they approached management as a group.

The labor union is an outside organization that extends itself into a company. A union has a headquarters outside the company and some number of locals. The union *local* is rather like a branch of a company in that it is dispersed from the parent organization. Its internal affairs are handled by officers elected by the local membership. Local union officers represent the union in the workplace and participate in negotiations with management. For example, the *shop steward* handles employee grievances and represents the union on the job. The shop steward and other union officers are employees of the company. However, if the union is large enough, it may employ its own staff centrally to do union business and negotiate with management. Not all employees are unionized, of course. In many companies, there is no union. In some, there is a union but not all employees belong to it; this is called an *open shop*. When a labor contract *requires* employees to join the union, it is called a *union shop*.

The percentage of union members in the U.S. labor force has hovered around 20 percent since the 1940s (U.S. Bureau of the Census, 1975; U.S. Department of Labor, 1986). Most included in this number belong to a union affiliated with the American Federation of Labor-Congress of Industrial Organizations (AFL-CIO). Because of their early development as a vehicle for change in industrial occupations and because of their strength among production employees, we have come to think of labor unions as blue-collar organizations. However, some white-collar workers and professional employees also are unionized. For example, many government employees, elementary and secondary teachers, and college faculty belong to unions.

Employees are likely to be interested in joining a union when they are not satisfied with the extrinsic aspects of their jobs, such as earnings (Hamner & Smith, 1978; Schriesheim, 1978). However, commitment to a union appears to depend also on the extent to which there is conflict with management. One study found that employees who were not satisfied with their jobs and who were actively engaged in union work were unilaterally committed to the union. When individuals were satisfied with their work and union-management relations were positive, they were committed to both the union and the employer (Magenau, Martin, & Peterson, 1988).

Are unions successful in reaching their goals? In some ways, they are. Research shows that collective bargaining has had positive effects on wages. For example, a survey of the salaries of faculty in state universities showed that the average faculty member at unionized institutions earned nearly $5,600 per year more than their nonunionized counterparts (American Association of State Colleges and Universities, 1988–1989). Others also report increases in wages and benefits and improvements in promotions and employee disciplinary policies (Bok & Dunlop, 1970).

Collective Bargaining

A union's most important goal is to protect its members' economic interests and improve working conditions. It does this by negotiating with the employer to develop a **labor contract** covering these issues. The contract usually includes agreements on compensation and benefits, job security, and the rights of management in policy making. The process of negotiating the contract is known as **collective**

bargaining. Collective bargaining begins with each party deciding what issues should be included in the contract and their positions on these issues. Two bargaining teams—representatives of the union and of the employer—negotiate these issues. At the initial stage of negotiation, the teams see if and where they can compromise. Each party comes to the bargaining table with a range of positions on each issue, from what is desired to what is barely acceptable. The initial interactions show whether the parties' positions overlap. If so, it is in this *bargaining zone* that compromises take place (Stagner & Rosen, 1965). If the parties can agree on all issues, they have a tentative labor contract. The contract is then presented to union members who vote either to *ratify* (accept) it or to reject it. If the members reject a tentative contract, negotiations begin again. Ratification of a contract is more likely if members feel that the union represents them well (Martin & Berthiaume, 1995).

Impasse Resolution

Sometimes the union and management teams cannot reach agreement. This is called an *impasse*. In such cases, third party intervention is used to break the impasse. Third parties use strategies that vary according to how formal the intervention is and how binding the resulting judgment is. *Mediation* is the most informal and least binding intervention. The mediator does not impose a decision on the conflicting parties. Rather, he or she helps them compromise and reach their own agreement. Deutsch (1973) described what a mediator does. He or she attempts to reduce the number of issues in conflict, open up communication, and improve the interaction of the parties. Mediation is used more frequently than other methods of impasse resolution (Prein, 1987). When it is successful, it is all that is necessary.

When mediation is not successful, the parties may go to *fact finding*. In this case, a third party gathers information about the disagreement and makes a public recommendation to resolve the conflict. Although the fact finder has no power to impose a resolution, making the recommendation public may result in public pressure on the parties to resolve their conflict. For example, when a conflict involves public services, such as transportation, and union employees are threatening to strike, the publicity may cause both parties to accept the fact finder's recommendation (Kochan, 1980).

Arbitration is both formal and binding. Both parties must accept the arbitrator's decision. Because of this, arbitration is likely to be the last step after both mediation and fact finding have failed to break the impasse. In *conventional arbitration*, the arbitrator can make any settlement that seems appropriate. The final decision may be closer either to the union's position or to management's position. Often, arbitrators make a settlement that is midway between the two. In *final-offer arbitration*, however, a midway decision is not permitted. The arbitrator accepts either the union's final position (or offer) or management's. Further, if the final-offer arbitration is *by package*, the arbitrator must decide on the contract as a whole. That is, he or she must accept the complete offer of either union or management. In final-offer arbitration *by issue*, awards can be split to some extent. The arbitrator can accept the union's final offer on one issue and management's on another. For example, the arbitrator might accept the union's position on wages and management's position on health benefits (Muchinsky, 1990).

Labor unions began early in this century as a result of a movement to improve the low pay and dreadful working conditions of factory workers. Today, a variety of workers belong to unions, including blue-collar, white-collar, and professional employees.

A union has a headquarters and any number of locals. In a union shop, employees must join the union as a condition of employment. In an open shop, they may but are not required to join.

Collective bargaining is the process of negotiating a labor contract. To start, the union and management present their positions. If they can make a deal, a tentative contract is sent to union members for ratification. If they cannot agree, an impasse results. Impasse resolution involves a neutral third party, who may provide mediation, fact-finding, or arbitration. Arbitration is the most binding. Conventional and final-offer arbitration are the strategies used.

CHAPTER SUMMARY

In some jobs, social interaction is the major activity. In almost all jobs, communication and interaction are required. Communication is the transmission and exchange of information. Whether spoken or written, information is conveyed through formal organizational channels of downward, upward, and lateral communication. It is also passed along an informal channel—the grapevine. One of the most important problems in organizational communication is failure to receive or understand the message. This failure can result from a number of factors, including the nature of the message.

Group interaction is studied largely with direct observational procedures, such as group process analysis. Through observation, basic elements of group process can be identified. In group work, certain group functions must be performed. When members do things that contribute to the task or to the effective operation of the group, they perform these functions. Members' actions are often guided by their roles in the group and/or by group norms. All groups have standards and values that are reflected in particular roles and norms. Member behavior also can be determined by the social influence that occurs within the group. Two important work group activities are problem solving and decision making. Faulty decision making can result from groupthink, in which group members fail to think critically.

Conflict is a natural part of human interaction. It can occur both within and between work groups. Two theoretical perspectives provide descriptions of conflict behavior. Following his definition of conflict as an incompatibility between goals, Deutsch identified two behavioral styles that reflect the way goals are linked. When goals are linked positively, conflict is managed by cooperation and has a positive-sum outcome. When goals are negatively linked, the parties compete, and a zero-sum or a negative-sum outcome results. In another view of conflict behavior, the focus is on the parties' interests in achieving their own and the other's goals. Rahim identified several behavioral styles that vary in this respect. For example, integrating includes compromise and results in a positive-sum outcome in which both parties gain. Actual conflict in the organization may need to be increased, decreased, or managed by a different style of behavior. Usually, the problem is one of managing a conflict, and often the parties need to collaborate.

Labor-management negotiation provides a special case of conflict management. Through the process of collective bargaining, teams representing the union and the employer attempt to negotiate an acceptable contract. If they cannot agree, third party intervention is used to break the impasse. Impasse resolution can occur through mediation, fact finding, or arbitration.

STUDY QUESTIONS

1) Describe some uses of the interview as a basic communication mode. What are the advantages of written over spoken communication?

2) Identify the formal and informal communication networks, and describe their use in the organization.

3) What is wrong with one-way communication?

4) By what means is communication in the organization distorted or lost?

5) What kind of work groups are there? What are their purposes? Are they effective?

6) What is the best way to study a group's interaction?

7) How is group communication studied, and what does it tell us?

8) Distinguish between the group's task and maintenance functions.

9) What is a productivity norm? What other norms might groups have?

10) How do people in groups influence each other?

11) How do groups make decisions? What is an effective decision? What is groupthink?

12) What value does conflict have?

13) Identify and distinguish the behavioral styles of conflict management. Under what conditions is cooperation likely to occur?

14) What can be done to intervene in the conflict process?

15) What is collective bargaining?

CONSIDER THIS

CASE STUDY

VRS, the vocational rehabilitation agency described in previous chapters, has a standing committee that meets every Tuesday morning. Members are the executive director, an executive assistant, and the managers in charge of counseling, workshop operations, finance, and contracts.

Under discussion for the past two weeks are ways to improve the workshop. In order to provide basic on-the-job training for its rehabilitation clients, VRS contracts with local manufacturing companies to provide labor for some of the manufacturing work. Usually, this involves assembling small parts or packaging. Once a contract is made, the materials are brought to VRS's workshop where the clients learn to do the work. Then, the products are returned to the company.

The discussion in this week's meeting concerns the deliveries. VRS owns a 10-year-old pick up truck that is used to get materials and return finished goods. Jack, the workshop manager, has pointed out two facts: (1) the truck is starting to need serious repairs, and (2) because the truck's capacity is small, time and money are wasted making numerous trips to and from the company. Jack concludes by proposing that VRS invest the money to buy a new, large-capacity delivery van.

Penny, the finance manager, objects and says that VRS cannot afford this expense. She points out that the cost of repairing the old truck is cheaper than buying a new one. Jack responds that repairing the truck does not deal with the waste of time and money driving back and forth. Penny answers that buying a new vehicle results in other expenses that would equal these labor costs. Jack retorts that this is short-term thinking.

The contracts manager, Connie, interrupts to ask that the group consider other alternatives, such as having the company make some of the larger deliveries.

Jack and Penny ignore Connie's request and continue to debate the costs and benefits of a new vehicle.

Neither the counseling manager nor the executive assistant say anything.

After a few minutes, Eric, the Executive Director, stops the debate. "Okay, let's not get so worked up. I appreciate what you are saying, Penny, but we could probably afford something here. We can shop around for a good price on a van. Maybe, even get one that's a year or so old. Why don't you check into this, Jack. See if you can find something that will meet all our needs."

Problem

What group processes do you observe in this exchange? What are some problems in the interaction? Is the decision a good one?

Section IV

Solving the Human Problems of Work

Part of the reason for the emergence and growth of I/O psychology is the need to identify and solve human problems in the workplace. Today, as in the early years, business managers consult with psychologists to find solutions to human problems that result from environmental, technological, and social sources. These problems affect both the life of the worker and the functioning of the organization. Often, there is a high price to pay.

In this section, chapters 13 and 14 describe how employee health can be harmed at work. Stress is the focus of chapter 13. Some conditions that function as stressors are found to be a part of day-to-day work, and others are brought to work from a stressful home life. Stress affects both the psychological and the physical health of the employee. In chapter 14, other threats to employee health are considered. Employees are exposed, either knowingly or not, to a range of hazards and dangerous substances. Accidents can result, or over time the exposure can cause illness. What can the employer do? Protection and treatment can be provided at work. Both physical and mental health problems appear at work, and modern organizations need to provide employees with assistance in coping with them. Finally, in chapter 15, the issue of work design is addressed. In making arrangements for healthful and effective work performance, design must be considered from three perspectives: time, space, and equipment. In each area, I/O psychologists have developed strategies for creating work designs that solve human problems. Work schedules, workspaces, and machinery can be designed to fit the worker and to avoid problems.

what's in this chapter?

How many people do you know who say their jobs keep them awake at night or give them headaches? How many times have you heard someone say, "This job is killing me!" Some people do lead stressful lives, and the stress may come from the work they do. Some jobs are well known as being stressful.

I/O psychologists are quite interested in work stress. Theorists have attempted to show how something as amorphous as work-role ambiguity might put someone in the hospital. Potential stressors are present in any workplace. Noise, for example, does more than annoy. A heavy workload is not simply fatiguing. It can be emotionally exhausting.

Some people are more stressed because of who they are. Those called Type As are so caught up in succeeding that they sometimes get heart attacks. This is one result of leading a stressful life. There are others. If you do "people work," you can get burned out.

Many believe that certain occupations are more stressful than others. Jobs that have potential for serious outcomes, such as that of the air traffic controller, are thought to be especially stressful.

C hapter 13

Stress and Its
Effects on Work

Contents

Most workers [in the Emergency Medical Service] can identify with me when I describe the state in which I often arrive home after work. My body feels like a car whose driver has one foot on the accelerator and the other on the brake. The result is a feeling of being both completely exhausted and incredibly hyped up!

[Most of us have little] expertise with which to treat the emotional and social components of the patients' problems. The result is that when faced with patients' confusion, anger, hysteria or tears, [we are] likely to feel helpless, inadequate, and ultimately resentful. This anger, in turn, leads some conscientious workers to feel guilty and blame themselves. Others project their anger outward, blaming their coworkers, supervisors, . . . or the patients themselves.

N. K. Graham

Although careers in the Emergency Medical Service (EMS) are exciting, they tend to be short. Graham (1981) noted that many people quit after two to five years of work in this field—"done in, fed up, burned out." Why does this happen? Maybe it is due to the individual who chooses this kind of work. Individuals differ in their vulnerability to stress. Maybe the problem is due to the nature of the job. Occupations differ in terms of their ability to induce stress. Also, organizations vary in their concern about employee stress. Graham states that EMS supervisors are rarely willing to listen to employees' complaints about the stresses of emergency work.

Although stress disorders have been a part of the human health condition for a long time, stress is becoming a serious problem in the modern world. Asterita (1985) looked at the medical literature and concluded that between 75 and 90 percent of all diseases prevalent in the Western world are at least indirectly related to prolonged stress and its physiological impact.

Background of Stress Research

Stress was studied in early clinical research. For example, combat fatigue, the emotional breakdown of men in military combat, was studied in clinical research of the early 1940s. Psychotic behavior, extreme fearfulness, anxiety, ulcers, and hypertension were found to result from this stressful experience. Shock reactions to civilian disasters were studied also in early research, and a symptomatic pattern like combat fatigue was observed (Menninger, 1948). Similarly, living in chronically stressful situations for prolonged periods was found to impair the psychological functioning of an individual. Bettelheim (1943) recorded his own experiences as a prisoner in the Nazi concentration camps at Dachau and Buchenwald in 1938–1939. He described several distinct stages of stress in prisoners. In a late stage, prisoners showed signs of indifference, dissociation of personal identity, regression, and dependency.

Research from animal learning laboratories may have sparked the interest of industrial researchers. For example, a series of animal learning studies conducted in the 1950s, which came to be known as the **executive monkey studies,** spotlighted the potentially stressful effects of work responsibility (Brady, 1958). The experimental design involved an ordinary shock-avoidance training procedure. By learning to operate a lever, animals could avoid receiving shocks. Experimental animals learned this behavior quickly and actually received few shocks. However, they showed considerable emotional behavior, and a number developed stomach ulcers. Ulcers were already being recognized as a stress-related disease, and the researchers conducted other studies to find out exactly what caused this. In the next study, two monkeys were used in a yoked procedure, in which only one, called the executive, was given "work responsibility." Only the executive monkey was able to prevent the shocks because the lever at the executive's position controlled the shocks to both animals. It was reasoned that if the shock itself were the stressor, then both animals would get ulcers. However, if it were the responsibility of being in control, then only the executive monkey would get ulcers. The evidence supported the latter: Only the executive got an ulcer. Brady (1958) drew a direct line between what happened in his lab and what he thought was true in the business world. He concluded that it was the worries of responsibility in the business executive's daily life that caused ulcers.

Later animal research showed that having responsibility did not always produce stress. Lacking control sometimes could produce it as well. Weiss (1968) used two groups of rats that were exposed to the same stimulus—a shock preceded by a warning signal—and arranged it so that only one group could make the response to avoid the shock. This was the "coping" group. The other group was helpless, just as Brady's yoked animal had been. However, in Weiss' study, the helpless animals were more likely to get ulcers. Weiss (1971) explained that Brady's executive monkeys had been misunderstood. He believed that those animals developed ulcers not because of the pressure of being responsible but because they received too little feedback about the effectiveness of their responses. Unlike Brady's animals, Weiss' coping group animals heard a warning signal that was turned off by their avoidance responses. Thus, it was suggested, the coping group received feedback that they could relate to what they had done, and the feedback relieved their stress.

I/O psychologists were relatively slow to begin studying stress. It was not much before the late 1960s that job stress was treated as an I/O research issue. Part of the reason for the delay had to do with the nature of the earlier clinical research. The stressful situations in many of those studies were so obviously extreme that anyone's life would be disrupted. Because ordinary day-to-day life at work presents few disastrous situations, I/O psychologists seemingly would have little reason to study stress (Holroyd & Lazarus, 1982). However, other research, such as the Brady studies, soon began to show that less severe situations could be stressful too. When stress began to look like something that could occur at work on an ordinary day, it became interesting to I/O psychologists.

WHAT IS STRESS?

Hans Selye (1936, 1980), an important theorist in this area of study, defined **stress** in physiological terms as a nonspecific or generalized bodily response. This response results when *any* demand is made on the body, whether it is an environmental condition that we must survive or a demand that we make on ourselves in order to accomplish a personal goal. Further, Selye distinguished between two

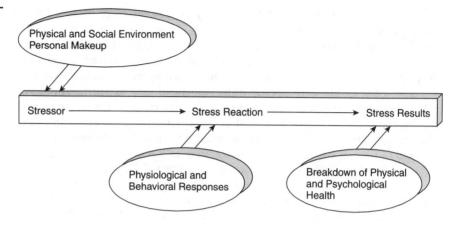

Figure 13.1 *The stress reaction in perspective. Stress is the physiological state produced in a person's body by arousing stimuli. It can result in ill health.*

forms of stress: **Distress** is the response to negative events, and **eustress** (as in euphoria) is the response to positive events. The distinction emphasizes that both positive and negative arousal can constitute physiological stress. The physiological response includes specific changes in the autonomic nervous system and endocrine glands that are triggered by psychological and environmental stimuli (Asterita, 1985). Thus, stress is the physiological state produced in a person's body by an arousing stimulus. However, some researchers refer to it as a **stress reaction** to emphasize that it is a bodily *response* (see figure 13.1 for these terms in perspective).

The conditions that precede and bring about stress are called **stressors.** Any situation, event, or object that makes demands on the body and causes this physiological reaction is a stressor. Stressors can be physical, such as air pollutants. They can be social, such as interpersonal interactions. Our own thoughts and feelings about real or imagined threats can function as stressors. Winston Churchill is credited with once saying, "When I look back on all my worries I remember the story of the old man who said that he had had a lot of trouble in his life, most of which never happened."

Stress that continues over a prolonged period of time shows a variety of consequences or **stress results.** Prolonged stress may lead to a breakdown of both physical and psychological health. For example, stress results include ulcers, psychotic behavior, and burnout. **Burnout,** a term used frequently in discussions of stress, is an identifiable pattern in the behavior of certain individuals indicating extreme fatigue. **Strain** is a stress result often discussed in studies of job stress. A strain is a physiological, psychological, or behavioral sign of ill health.

Stressful Occupations

There is a common belief that certain occupations are inherently stressful. If any of us were asked to name some of the more stressful ones, we could do so. Exciting, high-risk occupations probably would appear on the list, such as firefighter or police officer. We probably would include occupations that have potential for serious outcomes, such as air traffic controller and pilot. Some occupations, such as business executive, would be included because we have heard about the effects of responsibility. With the increasing public awareness of burnout, we might include occupations in the human services, such as nurse, social worker, and teacher. What about blue-collar jobs? Would you include any on your list of stressful occupations? What about construction or transit workers? Some studies recently have examined the experience of urban bus drivers and long-distance truck drivers, and have found evidence of stress due to bad weather and traffic congestion (Evans, 1994; Vivoli et al., 1993).

Managers and Executives

Managers do experience stress. However, the kind of work they do varies, depending on their rank and the nature of their organizations and departments. Therefore, we can expect that some managers will experience more job stress than others. Research indicates that this is so. That is, managerial stress depends on the particular job. In one study, middle-level managers reported more stress than either lower or higher level managers, and they attributed it to work overload and role conflict (Ivancevich, Matteson, & Preston, 1982). Supervisors of blue-collar workers showed more signs of psychological strain than supervisors of administrative employees in the same organization (Axelrod & Gavin, 1980). A more recent study compared executive-level managers in government and business organizations in the United Kingdom. Those in government showed more stress symptoms and dissatisfaction than those in private industry (Bogg & Cooper, 1995).

Executives from different countries have different levels of stress. In one study, the mental health of senior executives from 10 countries (including the United States) was evaluated. Those from economically developing countries (e.g., Brazil and Egypt) showed signs of greater stress than those from developed countries (e.g., Sweden and Germany). The source of this greater stress appeared to be a lack of autonomy in their work responsibilities (Cooper & Hensman, 1985). Some have suggested that lifestyle differences between executives in different countries can account for some of the variance in stress. McCormick and Cooper (1988) compared executives from New Zealand to those from other countries. The very low level of stress reported by the New Zealanders was interpreted as reflecting the relaxed lifestyle in that country. In a similar study, managerial samples from the United States, India, and Japan were questioned. Japanese executives reported more stress in all aspects of life than either the Americans or the Indians (DeFrank, Ivancevich, & Schweiger, 1988). This result confirmed a previous finding that Japanese executives showed more stress symptoms than their international counterparts (Cooper & Arbrose, 1984).

Medical Professionals

Some health care occupations are stressful. A study comparing nurses, physicians, and pharmacists, found nurses to have the highest levels of stress (Wolfgang, 1988). However, the amount of stress experienced by hospital nurses depends on the nursing department or type of care given. Nurses in intensive care units, emergency rooms, and nurseries more often report high levels of stress (Numerof & Abrams, 1984). A variable that appears to be important in determining the stressfulness of health care work is the relationship with patients. The experience of being spurned by patients was found to be involved in burnout among nurses (Mickler & Rosen, 1994). Similarly, personal variables may be important in such occupations. It may be that the stress experienced by most medical professionals results from the interpersonal nature of the work and characteristics, such as the individual's sociocultural background and personality (Lee, 1986). Personal accounts of stress are suggestive in this respect. For example, Lattanzi (1981) described the experience of hospice counselors, pointing out that problems are likely to result from the emotional impact of working with terminally ill patients.

Air Traffic Controllers

Some years ago, the newspapers were filled with reports on negotiations by the air traffic controllers' union. Pay increases were demanded on the basis of this being an extremely stressful occupation. Although an obvious question may be whether a pay increase somehow makes the stress more tolerable, a more important question is whether this job actually is so stressful. From a review of research reporting physiological measurement data, Mohler (1983) concluded that air traffic controllers do experience high levels of distress. One study found that about one-third of its sample was hypertensive, half showed psychiatric problems, and half were heavy drinkers (Rose, Jenkins, & Hurst, 1978). In a more recent study, cross-cultural comparisons also showed the occupation to be stressful, and sources of this stress were described. Shouksmith and Burrough (1988) compared responses of air traffic controllers in New Zealand with those of a Canadian sample reported earlier by McBride, Lancee, and Freeman (1981). The overall level of stress in the job was high in both groups. The participants described their stressors similarly, as being equipment limitations, heavy workload during peak traffic, fear of causing accidents, and poor work environment.

Police Officers

At first glance, police work appears to be highly stressful. Television presents the police officer's job as one that contains built-in danger. Chasing fugitives and apprehending people with weapons seem like the kinds of situations that would cause stress. Research, however, does not always show police jobs to be very stressful. In one survey, police officers' scores on a measure of emotional exhaustion were compared to human service employees' scores previously reported by Maslach and Jackson (1981). The police officers showed lower levels of emotional exhaustion than the human service employees did. Also, their stress appeared to result less from the danger of police work than from inflexible department procedures (Gaines & Jermier, 1983). A study of patrol officers found that the amount of perceived danger on the job correlated with the extent of task variety and significance, suggesting that danger may actually enrich the officers' job (Jermier, Gaines, & McIntosh, 1989).

*M*ain *P*oints

Stress can but does not have to come from a disaster. The way stress currently is defined, as a bodily response to a stressor, indicates that a range of experiences can be stressful, including the workday. Stress can result from positive as well as negative events and can show a variety of consequences, such as strain and burnout.

Several occupations are commonly perceived as being stressful. Some of them are stressful, and others possibly are not. Some that usually are not thought of, such as bus driver, are stressful also. Many occupations are stressful in given situations. Business managers in certain lines of work are stressed, at least in some countries. Medical and health care people, especially nurses, also do stressful work and are vulnerable to burnout. There is evidence to support the common belief that air traffic control is a stressful job. However, surprisingly, there is not much evidence that police work is.

THEORETICAL MODELS OF STRESS

The issue of stress has been studied in several fields, including medicine, clinical psychology, and I/O psychology. Stress research and theory have taken a number of different routes, and this has resulted in some confusing terminology. However, a conceptual richness has come from this cross-disciplinary work. In the following sections, I describe some of the more well-known theoretical models that address the process of stress in general. In later sections, I identify some models that focus on specific aspects of stress, such as Type A behavior.

Selye's General Adaptation Syndrome

Hans Selye (1936, 1946, 1982) was an endocrinologist who devoted most of his career to the study of the physiological process of stress. His theoretical model has taken a position of major importance in current thinking. In this model, Selye proposed that stress is the body's general defensive reaction to a stressor. The underlying physiological basis of stress is the prolonged activation of certain hormonal and nervous system mechanisms. The effects of stress are proposed to vary according to an individual's constitutional makeup. For example, a person who has a stress-vulnerable heart is likely to develop coronary problems, whereas someone with a sensitive stomach will tend to have ulcers.

The **General Adaptation Syndrome** is a concept that Selye used to describe the *process* of stress. The General Adaptation Syndrome is proposed to consist of three more or less distinct phases: (1) the initial alarm reaction, (2) the resistance phase, and (3) the exhaustion phase. During the **alarm stage,** the body mobilizes for action through various hormonal and nervous system changes. For example, adrenaline level and heart and respiratory rates increase. At this point, the individual can cope with the stressor by means of a **fight-or-flight reaction.** The alarm stage is a healthy response to demanding situations. If the stress is relieved, the body returns to its normal state. It is only when stress progresses to the next stage that there are likely to be more serious consequences. During the **resistance stage,** certain superficial signs suggest that the body has returned to normal. For example, heart and respiratory rates have slowed down. However, there are other signs that the body is still in a state of defense. In particular, hormonal levels remain high. Finally, if the stress continues, the person enters the **exhaustion stage.** Bodily processes begin to break down, and illness occurs. If the stress continues without disruption, the person will die.

Note an additional point: Selye believed that our stores of adaptation energy are limited and not fully replaced. He used the analogy of a bank account in which only withdrawals are made; thus, life stress depletes us. "Every biologic activity causes wear and tear; it leaves some irreversible chemical scars, which accumulate to constitute the signs of aging" (1982, p. 11). The message is clear. If you want to stay young looking, keep out of the fast track.

Physiological Processes of Stress

Selye and others who discuss stress have used physiological and biochemical concepts (cf., Asterita, 1985). Because some knowledge of physiological functioning is needed in order to understand these discussions, let us consider some basic facts about the physiology of stress.

First, we should note that the **autonomic nervous system** regulates the visceral systems, such as the cardiovascular and digestive systems, as well as the endocrine glands. It ensures that the internal environment of the body keeps pace with the demands of the external environment. For example, if we need to run, the autonomic nervous system modifies our internal physiology so that we have the energy to do so. Then, it makes the reverse adjustments so that we can calm down and rest. Two subsystems of the autonomic nervous system carry out this dual function by alternating control over the body. The **sympathetic nervous system** provides for the release of energy. When it is in control, there is general body arousal. Heart and respiratory rates increase. Blood is directed away from the viscera to the skeletal muscles. Blood sugar is elevated. Hormones, such as adrenaline, are secreted. In other words, the sympathetic nervous system initiates the body's internal fight-or-flight response. When the threat subsides, the **parasympathetic nervous system** takes over. It provides for an overall slowing down and restoration of the body. Heart and respiratory rates decrease, and blood is redirected to the viscera. Digestion resumes, and sleep occurs. However, the process of slowing down takes some time because hormonal activity has a more prolonged effect than other aspects of sympathetic activation. The endocrine glands secrete into the bloodstream; therefore, hormonal effects, being both general and gradual, continue past the point at which the threat subsides (Schneider & Tarshis, 1980).

Asterita (1985) interpreted Selye's stages in terms of these autonomic processes. The alarm stage of stress corresponds with sympathetic activation, a normal process of energizing the body to react. When the body remains under sympathetic control beyond a certain point, however, the devastating effects of stress appear. During the resistance stage, the autonomic nervous system attempts to maintain a homeostatic balance in the presence of continuing threat. Some bodily processes revert to normal; however, endocrine activity continues. During the exhaustion stage, high blood concentrations of hormones, adrenaline in particular, begin to have adverse effects on the body. Ulcers, lowered resistance to infection, and adrenal failure are likely to result.

The Stressful Life Events Model

Holmes and Rahe (1967; Holmes & Masuda, 1974) agreed with Selye that life events can have physical effects. These researchers set out to identify life events that cause stress reactions. They also wanted to develop a method of gauging the intensity of these reactions. What emerged from their work was the **Stressful Life Events Model.** Briefly, the model posits that a stress reaction occurs whenever an

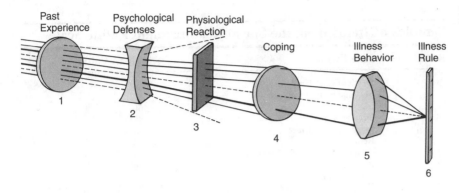

Figure 13.2 *Pathway analysis of the stress process. The pathway includes buffers and filters through which stress events pass. The band of lines represents the set of events that impose on a person at any one time. The bolder the line, the more severe the stress event.*

From R.H. Rahe, et al. "Pathway Analysis of the Stress Process" in Archives of General Psychiatry, *25:331. Copyright © 1971 American Medical Association. Reprinted by permission.*

individual experiences something that requires an adaptive response or coping behavior. The stress-producing event can be positive or negative and involve any aspect of the individual's life, including family and occupation. Life events are proposed to vary in their ability to cause stress. The effects of these events are proposed to be additive, and the overall size of the effect determines the amount of work that the person must do to cope. The concept of **social readjustment** refers to coping or making changes in response to the stress.

Rahe and his associates (1971) proposed a process by which life stress might occur, and they identified changes along the pathway between an initial stressor and ultimate physical illness. As depicted in figure 13.2, the pathway includes buffers and filters with which stressful events are screened. Past experience is the first filter that either augments or lessens the impact of a stressful event. That is, if an event is similar to one in the past that was harmful, then the individual will perceive the event as threatening. The second filter represents psychological defense mechanisms, which are proposed to deflect some stressful occurrences. The third filter is the physiological reaction. Here, the life event is proposed to be transformed into physiological responses. Following this, later filters determine whether the person attempts to cope and/or whether symptoms of illness result.

In conjunction with the model, Holmes and his associates devised the **Social Readjustment Rating Scale** (see table 13.1). Development of this scale began with research in which a *life chart* was used to gather biographical information about subjects' medical histories (Holmes & Masuda, 1974). Holmes and Rahe (1967) believed that stressful life events play a role in causing illness; therefore, medical histories should show this. Using this method in a study of hospitalized patients, researchers found that prior to the onset of their current illnesses the patients had experienced clusters of life events requiring some coping response (Rahe et al., 1971). These events were social and interpersonal incidents involving different aspects of the individual's life. Some events were strongly associated with the onset of disease, whereas others seemed to have only a mild impact. Correlations between these events and illness were used as weights or values for the life events included on the Social Readjustment Rating Scale. Those who scored high on the scale were those with more and more serious life events.

In the 1970s, studies were done to evaluate this theory. Most used some version of the Social Readjustment Rating Scale. The reported results

Table 13.1

Samples of Items from the Social Readjustment Rating Scale

Rank	Life Event	Mean Value
5	Death of close family member	63
6	Personal injury or illness	53
7	Marriage	50
8	Fired at work	47
9	Marital reconciliation	45
10	Retirement	45
11	Change in health of family member	44
12	Pregnancy	40
13	Sex difficulties	39
14	Gain of new family member	39
15	Business readjustment	39
16	Change in financial state	38
17	Death of close friend	37
18	Change to different line of work	36
19	Change in number of arguments with spouse	35

Reprinted with permission from *Psychosomatic Research*, Vol. II, Thomas H. Holmes and Richard H. Rahe, "The Social Readjustment Rating Scale," 1967. Elsevier Science, Inc.

were generally positive and supportive of the model. However, evaluation of the research indicated some serious problems in the measurement and interpretation of life events. Rabkin and Struening (1976) reviewed the research and described its weaknesses. They found that many studies had statistically overestimated the size of the relationship between life events and illness. This occurred because researchers had used inappropriate methods to analyze data from very large samples (e.g., as many as 2500 Ss). Also, the reviewers noted that the rating scale was not a valid or reliable measure. They suggested ways in which the instrument might be invalid. For example, the items may not be relevant to some groups, which could falsely indicate that members of a group have no stressful life events. Rabkin and Struening (1976) concluded that although the life events approach is interesting, the measure and methodology need improvement.

Person-Environment Fit Theory

The **Person-Environment Fit Theory** was developed during the 1970s by French and his associates after years of study on how the social world affects an individual's social adjustment and physical and mental health. This theory is oriented specifically toward stress at work. A central proposition of the theory is that the resources and demands of the work environment may or may not fit the needs, goals, and abilities of the employee. When work demands do not fit the person's abilities and needs, the individual will show signs of strain that will eventually lead to illness. The primary aim of this model is to identify the kinds of conditions likely to result in strain (French, Caplan, & Van Harrison, 1982).

There are four basic concepts in this theory: organizational stress, strain, coping, and social support. *Organizational stress* is defined as the potentially threatening conditions of the job (or *stressors,* in my terms). Important organizational stress conditions include job complexity, workload, role ambiguity, and underuse of abil-

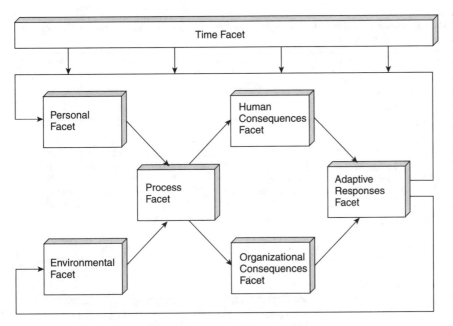

Figure 13.3 *Beehr and Newman's General Facet Model of Stress. More than 150 variables are identified as being related to stress. In this model, these variables are categorized into seven different facets composing the stress process.*

From T.A. Beehr and J.E. Newman, "Job Stress, Employee Health, and Organizational Effectiveness: A Facet Analysis, Model, and Literature Review" in Personnel Psychology, *31:676. Copyright © 1978 Personnel Psychology, Inc., Bowling Green, Ohio. Reprinted by permission.*

ity. However, it is not that the person simply responds to the work environment. The person interacts with the environment. The individual's perception of the stress condition and the extent to which he or she feels personally capable of meeting the demand are important to consider. *Strain* is any unhealthy response that a person makes. Physiological responses, such as high blood pressure, or behavioral characteristics, such as drug use, are evidence of strain. That is, strain encompasses both the long-term results of stress and the immediate stress reaction. *Coping* is defense against stress. Both physiological and behavioral coping mechanisms are used. The normal physiological fight-or-flight response may or may not be an appropriate reaction, depending on the stressor. For example, one cannot always cope by attacking or running away from a threat. In social situations, such as work, this response is often inappropriate, and the energy available for it must be inhibited. Thus, *inhibition* of the fight-or-flight response may actually be an attempt to cope with social stress. *Social support,* the emotional support that comes from interpersonal interaction, is proposed to buffer stress and strain.

A Facet Model of the Job Stress Sequence

Beehr and Newman (1978) developed a model to identify and organize all relevant facets or components of job stress. The **Facet model** incorporates more than 150 variables that either have been studied or were suggested by research as being stress related. These variables are categorized into several different groups or facets. As depicted in figure 13.3, the *personal facet* includes any personal characteristic that can have an impact on how an individual experiences stress. Personality and physical fitness are examples. Personal characteristics are proposed to interact with environmental variables through a *process facet* that involves perception and cognitive evaluation of the stressful situation. The *environmental facet* refers to the

Figure 13.4 *The General Facet Model of Stress showing the influence of time on the stress process. Immediate stress processes are shown as well as long-term human and organizational consequences and long-term adaptive responses.*

From T.A. Beehr and J.E. Newman, "Job Stress, Employee Health, and Organizational Effectiveness: A Facet Analysis, Model, and Literature Review" in Personnel Psychology, *31:676. Copyright © 1978 Personnel Psychology, Inc., Bowling Green, Ohio. Reprinted by permission.*

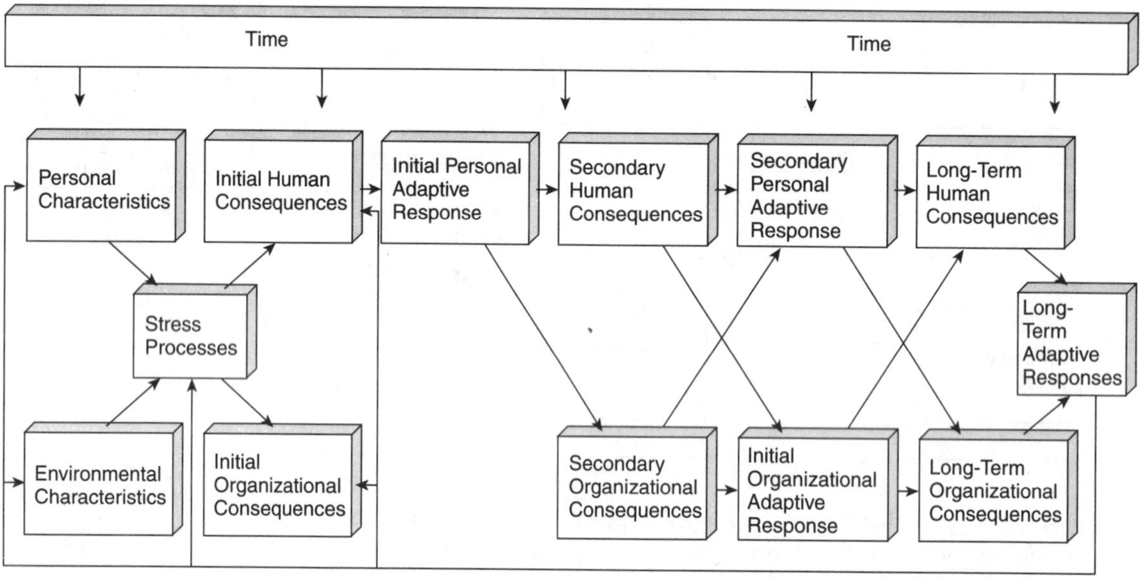

work environment and includes work-role demands, such as role overload; organizational characteristics, such as company size; and external demands, such as customers. Both personal and organizational consequences are proposed to result from the person-environment interaction process. *Human consequences* include effects on psychological functioning, such as anxiety; effects on physical health, such as gastrointestinal problems; and effects on overt behavior, such as drug use and aggression. *Organizational consequences* of stress include such effects as absenteeism, turnover, and productivity losses. *Adaptive responses,* proposed to follow these consequences, represent various attempts to handle the stress. For example, employees can make adaptive responses by seeking social support; organizations can make adaptive responses by changing work schedules; and third parties can make adaptive responses by offering treatment.

Beehr and Newman (1978) added the element of time to these facets of stress to show that stress is a sequential process (see figure 13.4). First, the initial experience of stress is felt, and it has immediate human consequences. Following this, the person makes some *initial* adaptive responses aimed at alleviating the stress. If over time, these initial responses are not successful, secondary consequences to the person and to the organization will occur. Next, the person will make *secondary* adaptive responses. Because the stress problem is now apparent to the organization, organizational adaptive responses are initiated as well. Again, if time does not show these adaptive responses to be successful, then long-term human and organizational con-

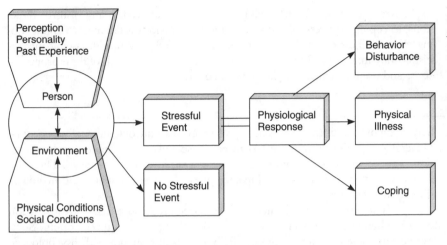

Figure 13.5 *A general perspective on stress. A person-environment interaction determines whether or not a stressful event occurs. The physiological response is connected to the stressful event by a double line to emphasize the intimate relationship between these concepts. The stressful event/response process can result in coping, illness, and/or behavioral disturbance.*

sequences will occur. These can affect the health of both the person and the organization. The consequences are followed by long-term adaptive responses, such as relatively permanent stress management programs. In turn, these adaptive responses may have effects on the stress potential of the person in the future.

A General Perspective on Stress

The theoretical models described are important in current research, and they are typical of the current thinking on stress. In several ways, these theories are complementary. First, they all include a person-environment interaction. Life events are considered stressful only if the person experiences them as such. What determines whether the person will perceive an event as stressful depends on his or her past experience, capabilities, and characteristic ways of viewing and interacting with the world. Second, the theories recognize stress as a physiological phenomenon. The physiological response will depend on (1) whether or not the person perceives a condition as threatening, (2) the manner of coping that is physiologically characteristic of the individual, and (3) the extent to which his or her particular physiological systems and organs are vulnerable. Past learning of coping strategies are likely to affect the physiological response and the particular stress-related illness that may develop.

In the remainder of this chapter, I follow the lead of Beehr and Newman (1978) and discuss stress from the perspective of a facet design. This allows me to discuss the research in a fashion such that a number of important variables can be shown in relation to one another. Using suggestions from the theories discussed, I structure the stress phenomenon as shown in figure 13.5. First, a person-environment interaction determines whether or not a stressful event will occur. The environment consists of both physical and social conditions. Personal variables include perception and cognition, the learning that occurs through experience, and personality. These variables account for some individual differences in how people assess situations as threatening. In figure 13.5, the physiological response is connected to the stressful event by a double line to emphasize that the response is intimately tied to the stressful event. The physiological response may lead in any of three directions: to coping, to stress-related illness, and to behavior disturbance. Without coping efforts, illness and behavioral problems are likely; even with coping mechanisms, they may occur. In the following sections, I consider each of these aspects of stress and use this structure to keep us on target.

<table>
<tr><td>

*M*ain
   *P*oints

</td><td>

Selye's theory outlines the physiological processes and outcomes of stress. The General Adaptation Syndrome has three phases: alarm, resistance, and exhaustion. The alarm phase is an initial fight-or-flight reaction to emergencies. The autonomic nervous system is involved in each phase, because it initiates and maintains the physiological response.

</td></tr>
</table>

The Stressful Life Events Model is based on the idea that a stress reaction occurs whenever a person experiences something that requires coping. Such events can come from any realm of life. The person responds with psychological buffering and filtering processes. The Social Readjustment Scale is an associated measure. Research testing the model has been problematic.

In the Person-Environment Fit Theory, the work environment is featured as a source of stress. Work makes demands that may not fit the person's abilities, and strain can result. Coping is physiological or psychological, and can be aided by social support.

The Facet model draws together all seemingly relevant facets of job stress and relates these in a complex framework. The framework includes personal and environmental precursors, human and organizational consequences, and adaptive responses. Stress is seen as an interactive process that occurs over time.

In general, the theories describe stress as being initiated by a person-environment interaction. A stressful event has an immediate physiological response and can lead to coping and/or illness.

STRESSORS

Several reviewers have attempted to identify and organize the variables that function as stressors. For example, Lazarus and Cohen (1977) classified stressors into three categories: (1) cataclysmic phenomena or sudden, powerful events that affect many people, such as natural disasters; (2) powerful events that affect fewer people, such as family crises; and (3) daily hassles or repetitive problems of daily life, such as work frustrations and commuting. Most of what I discuss in the following sections can be considered daily hassles.

Stressors at work are as varied as they are in other areas of life (see figure 13.6). Some stressors are conditions of the physical work environment. Others are sociopsychological in nature. Relocation and crowding are potential stressors for many people. The job itself can contain stressors, such as work overload and lack of autonomy. The temporal aspects of work, such as time pressures, also can be stressful.

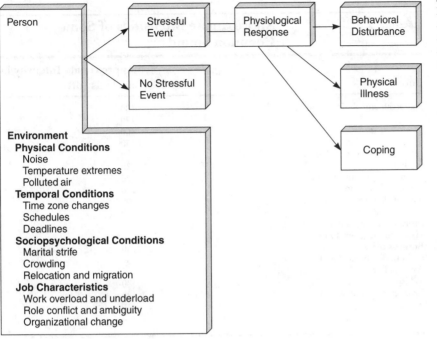

Figure 13.6 *Environmental stressors that affect the worker. These stressors can be physical, temporal, sociopsychological, and/or job-related conditions.*

Diagram boxes and labels:

Person → Stressful Event / No Stressful Event

Stressful Event → Physiological Response

Physiological Response → Behavioral Disturbance, Physical Illness, Coping

Environment
Physical Conditions
 Noise
 Temperature extremes
 Polluted air
Temporal Conditions
 Time zone changes
 Schedules
 Deadlines
Sociopsychological Conditions
 Marital strife
 Crowding
 Relocation and migration
Job Characteristics
 Work overload and underload
 Role conflict and ambiguity
 Organizational change

Physical Stressors

Factors of the physical environment were recognized as stressors when laboratory animals began to show general health effects in response to certain physical conditions imposed by experimental research. Their reactions indicated autonomic nervous system and endocrine involvement. Exposure to noise, for example, was observed to have harmful effects not only on the ear but also on the endocrine glands, indicating that a physiological stress response was involved.

The Effects of Noise

Noise is a psychological concept involving more than perception of sound.[1] Noise is defined as unwanted or undesirable sound. Sounds can be undesirable if they are unpleasant, bothersome, or mask other sounds. Also, sounds can become noise when they are excessively loud. Loudness or **sound intensity** is measured in **decibels** (dB). Table 13.2 lists approximate intensities of some common sounds.

Intense sounds cause hearing loss when the direct physical impact of the sound overstimulates auditory cells. Sometimes, auditory cell exhaustion and the resulting deafness is temporary, and after a period of quietness, hearing returns. However, if auditory cells are damaged, deafness is permanent. The damage may not be widespread; often, only certain frequency ranges are affected. Typically, partial hearing loss is in the high frequency range, which means that high-pitched sounds cannot be heard.

[1]Sound is a perceptual effect produced by wavelike changes in air pressure. The frequency of the wave motion, which is measured in cycles per second or cps, is interpreted as pitch by human sensory mechanisms. The intensity of the air pressure determines the amplitude or height of the wave, and this is interpreted as loudness.

Table 13.2

Approximate Intensities of Some Common Sounds

Sound	Approximate Intensity in decibels (dB)[a]
Spacecraft launch (from 150 ft)	180
	170
	160
	150[b]
Loud thunder, live rock band	140
Hydraulic press	130
Jet engine test control room	120
Woodworking shop	110
Textile plant weaving room	100
Car manufacturing plant, heavy trucks (from 20 ft)	90
Inside car in city traffic, conversation	80
Heavy traffic (from 40 ft)	70
Business office	60
Light traffic (from 100 ft)	50
Average home	40
Whisper	30
Broadcasting studio	20
	10
	0[c]

[a]Decibel is the unit of measurement indicating sound intensity or loudness.
[b]Pain threshold: At approximately 150 dB, the sound begins to be painful to the ear.
[c]Threshold of hearing at 1,000 cps is the lowest intensity of this sound that can be detected.

Beyond the hearing loss caused by loud sounds, does noise operate as a stressor? Research indicates that it does. Physiological effects that are characteristic of the stress reaction appear in subjects who are exposed to high-intensity noise. These include endocrine, cardiovascular, and digestive reactions (McLean & Tarnopolsky, 1977). For example, subjects who were exposed to intense (93 dB) noise while they performed a task showed more vasoconstriction, thus, greater physiological arousal, than a control group working in quieter conditions (Millar & Steels, 1990). Studies of those working in noise at industrial sites also show detrimental health effects, especially cardiovascular problems (Cohen & Weinstein, 1981).

If noise functions as a stressor, we might expect it to impair task performance because energy that ordinarily would be spent on the task would be needed instead to cope with the stress. Whether this is true depends on both the nature of the noise and the complexity of the task. First, intermittent noise is more disruptive than continuous noise. Second, the effect of continuous noise depends on its intensity and on the task. Low-level noise actually seems to improve performance on tasks, such as monitoring, whereas high-level noise disrupts these tasks (Cohen & Weinstein, 1981). Complex tasks are adversely affected by noise. Jobs that require an operator to keep track of two processes at the same time are made more difficult by noise (Broadbent, 1979).

Research indicates that moderate arousal, whatever the source, is more beneficial than either high or low arousal in task performance. This is depicted in

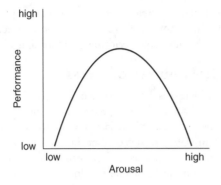

Figure 13.7 *An inverted U relationship: the effect of arousal on performance. Moderate arousal, which is neither too low nor too high, induces the highest task performance.*

figure 13.7. Broadbent (1971) used this "inverted U" arousal concept to explain how noise interferes with work. First, exposure to moderate and high-intensity noise increases an individual's arousal beyond normal. Next, the individual must try to cope with the increased arousal while working on the task. A way to do this is to narrow one's attention and focus on the task while ignoring irrelevant stimuli. As arousal increases, however, the person's attention narrows still more so that even task-relevant cues are ignored. Simple tasks are improved by noise because arousal is raised to a moderate (and beneficial) level. In a complex job, however, the difficulty of the work already has raised the level of arousal. Adding noise is detrimental because it raises arousal too much, and relevant cues are ignored. In complex tasks, noise creates a work overload.

Heat Stress

We can consider either high or low temperature extremes as stressors. However, heat has a more serious potential than cold because we can do less about it. Extremely low temperatures often can be tolerated with insulating clothing. It is more difficult to protect the body from extremely high temperatures. The internal temperature of the human body is maintained at about 98.6°F. This occurs through several homeostatic mechanisms. These include vasoconstriction and dilation, as well as shivering and sweating. External factors also are capable of increasing or decreasing the body's core temperature. Room temperature and such factors as air movement and humidity affect the ability of the body to maintain its core temperature. In heat, high humidity adversely affects body temperature because the cooling effects of sweat evaporation are less (Bell, 1981).

Certain jobs are done in hot surroundings. Industrial plant employees who work with blast furnaces or other heat-producing equipment are exposed to high ambient or room temperatures during the normal work day. Coincidentally, heat stress also can be created when a worker wears protective clothing to guard against hazardous chemical exposure (Taylor and Orlansky, 1993; White, Hodous, & Vercruyssen, 1991). Task performance suffers when temperatures are high (Razmjou & Kjellberg, 1992; Taylor & Orlansky, 1993). The inverted U arousal hypothesis has been used to explain the effects of heat stress on performance. It is believed that heat changes the level of arousal, and arousal affects the individual's attention. When a task load is already heavy, as with complex mental work, the physiological work the body must do to reduce a high core temperature increases the overall workload and makes task performance more difficult (Bell, 1981).

Sociopsychological Sources of Stress

Sometimes the source of stress is other people or aspects of the social environment. Many of us spend eight hours of every work day in close physical proximity of coworkers and customers or clients. In fact, few of us work in our own private rooms or offices. Epstein (1981) observed that the task of managing one's environment becomes increasingly difficult as that environment becomes more populated. Attention and energy ordinarily available for doing work must be diverted to the crowded situation. Resources become scarce. Other people's activities begin to interfere with one's own. Unavoidable and often undesirable interaction with others distracts the individual from work tasks. Violations of personal space cause discomfort. It is through such a process that crowding causes stress. However, it is not simple density that produces stress. Feeling crowded is different from feeling cramped. **Cramping** results when there is too little physical space. **Crowding** is a psychological phenomenon resulting from group processes. You feel *cramped* when your office is overfilled with furniture and boxes of stuff. You feel *crowded* when you share a small office with several other people.

Relocation and Migration

American businesses move their employees around and sometimes send them to establishments outside the country. They also employ many people who have migrated from other countries. For these reasons, we need to consider relocation and migration as stressors at work.

An increasingly ordinary event in the lives of many working people is a **job transfer.** Many transfers are from one organizational unit to another and simply mean moving to another job in the same location. Other transfers involve relocating one's whole life in a move from one region to another or from one country to another. Any relocation is likely to be stressful to some extent. Starting a new job and being unsure about one's skills can arouse stress. Relocation can disrupt nonwork aspects of life as well. The job transfer may mean leaving one's family behind, resulting in loss of the social support the family provided. It also may mean taking the family and subjecting them to new living conditions in another culture. Most people find relocation to be at least somewhat stressful, especially if it means uprooting one's spouse and children (Munton, 1990). Frequent relocation has been shown to be associated with health problems, although the harmful effects depend on whether the person has a choice in the matter and whether the individual likes moving around (Stokols, Shumaker, & Martinez, 1983).

Migration can be both a way of coping and a source of stress. For example, people may cope with the stress of war in their home country by leaving and settling in another country. As a result of the move, they experience other stress. Shuval (1982) observed that the personal resources that a migrant has determines his or her capacity to deal with the stress of migration. Migration may involve educated, ambitious, and adaptable individuals. Conversely, individuals who migrate may be those who have not succeeded in their place of origin and who lack occupational skills. Krau (1981) followed 89 migrants who found it necessary to take up a new occupation. Those who were most successful in making the adjustment had superior personal resources, particularly in terms of self-image and interest in the occupation. Attitudes of resident populations toward a migrant group can range from hostility to acceptance. Even if migrants are accepted, they tend to be low in the community's power hierarchy. This is true even of professionals who migrate (Shuval, 1982).

Job Stressors

A number of job characteristics have been identified as stressors. For example, role demands and the size and nature of the workload are potential stressors (cf. Beehr & Newman, 1978). The Position Analysis Questionnaire (PAQ), a job analysis method described in chapter 3, was used in one study to identify job stressors. Several PAQ descriptors were found to be associated with stress. These included certain manual activities; tasks that require the use of various senses; personally demanding situations; and decision making (Shaw & Riskind, 1983). Organizational constraints or conditions that prevent employees from effectively performing their jobs, such as lacking supplies and equipment, also have been found to be associated with employee anxiety and frustration (Spector, 1987; Spector, Dwyer, & Jex, 1988).

Work Overload

The amount and difficulty of work a person must do can be stressful. **Work overload** and **work underload** are described in both quantitative and qualitative terms. Briefly, a *quantitative overload* is having too much to do. A *qualitative overload* occurs when the work is too difficult. A *quantitative underload* is having too little to do, whereas a *qualitative underload* is work that is too easy. Although few might like to report it, having a work underload can be stressful and can result in illness (Ganster, Fusilier, & Mayes, 1986).

    Work overload has received much attention in research, and the message is clear. Work overloads cause stress. The effects show up in both physiological and psychological measures. For example, hypertension or high blood pressure is associated with higher workloads as are high levels of anxiety and frustration (Cobb & Rose, 1973; Spector, 1987; Spector et al., 1988). Work overload is a source of job stress cited specifically by some occupational groups, including air traffic controllers, hospital nurses, and managers (Ivancevich et al., 1982; Motowidlo, Packard, & Manning, 1986; Shouksmith & Burrough, 1988). Nuclear power plant workers also have been found to show more tension as the amount and difficulty of their work increases (Chisholm, Kasl, & Eskenazl, 1983).

    What job characteristics cause work overload and stress? Anything that creates high attentional demands for an extended time appears to be a factor. Studies of assembly and machine operation tasks in manufacturing plants have indicated that machine pacing of work can be a source of overload, because it determines the demand placed on the operator's attention (Cox, 1985; Smith, 1981). High attentional demand and stress can result from certain pressures as well. Having to pay close attention to accuracy and, at the same time, work fast on difficult machine operations caused psychological strain among factory employees (Martin & Wall, 1989). Work interruptions can increase the attentional demand of a job.

Kirmeyer (1988) found that police dispatchers whose work was frequently interrupted, evaluated their workload as being heavier and said they made more efforts to cope. Similarly, unpredictable interruptions in a computer system's operation was found to cause stress in office workers (Johansson & Aronsson, 1984).

Role Ambiguity and Conflict

An employee's perception of his or her role in the organization can be a source of stress. **Role ambiguity** is present when the work role is unclear; that is, when an employee does not know what is expected in terms of work performance. **Role conflict** exists when task requirements or other aspects of the job are incompatible. If an employee succeeds in one, the other cannot be fulfilled. For example, employees who are expected to do thorough and creative work, and at the same time meet sharp deadlines, often feel role conflict. Role conflict also can occur when the requirements of the job contradict one's personal standards. For example, if employees perceive a product to be inferior, yet know they must sell it, they may feel role conflict.

Such role conditions can cause stress. Role ambiguity has been associated with a number of psychological effects, including job tension, and anxiety and frustration (Kahn et al., 1964; Spector et al., 1988). Role conflict also results in stress. A wide variety of studies have shown this to be true. High levels of role conflict are associated with job tension and anxiety (Chisholm et al., 1983; Hamner & Tosi, 1974), and psychological strain (O'Driscoll & Beehr, 1994). Recent studies have found that role conflict correlates positively with emotional exhaustion in samples of teachers, public service lawyers, and active trade union members (Jackson, Schwab, & Schuler, 1986; Jackson, Turner, & Brief, 1987; Nandram & Klandermans, 1993).

Three categories of work stressors are identified: physical conditions, sociopsychological processes, and job characteristics.

Intense noise causes physiological stress and disrupts performance on complex tasks. High heat levels similarly disturb task performance and overburden the physiological mechanisms that maintain body temperature. The effects of noise and heat typically are interpreted with the inverted U arousal hypothesis. That is, noise and heat increase arousal beyond a level that is helpful to performance. Attention must be divided between the task and coping with the stress.

Relocation can be a stressor if a job transfer is not desired and/or if it uproots the family. In similar ways, migration to another country can create stress, especially if the person must take up a new occupation.

Work overload is a known source of stress. Both physiological and psychological measures show the effects of having too much to do. Overload is cited as an important reason for the stressfulness of several occupations. Certain aspects of work overload create stress. These include time pressure, interruptions, and other factors, such as machine-pacing, that make demands on a worker's attention.

Work role ambiguity and role conflict are known stressors that are associated with psychological strain. Emotional exhaustion has been observed among certain occupational groups who experience role conflict.

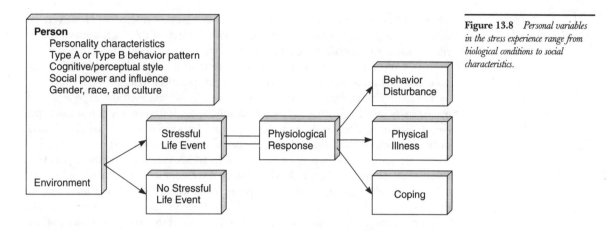

INDIVIDUAL DIFFERENCES IN STRESS VULNERABILITY

Environmental stressors probably affect some people more readily than they do others because of differences in people's susceptibility to stress. Stress theorists suggest that people contribute to their own stress by interpreting environmental conditions as threatening. Research on individual differences has focused on variables that are thought to affect the perception and interpretation of environmental stressors. That is, who is likely to experience a situation as threatening, and what makes them do so? Some personal variables that may be important in this respect are highlighted in figure 13.8.

Male and female employees do not appear to differ in the *amount* of stress they experience or in their particular *manifestations* of stress. In one review, it was concluded that women show more psychological signs of stress, such as anxiety, and men show more physical signs, such as cardiovascular problems (Jick & Mitz, 1985). However, a later meta-analysis of the research found no difference in how stress affected men and women. In the overall analysis and when samples were divided by psychological and physical stress measures, the correlation between stress and sex of the subject was zero (Martocchio & O'Leary, 1989).

Study of racial differences in susceptibility to stress developed out of observations that cardiovascular disorders, particularly hypertension, are prevalent among African Americans. Research and theoretical work has attempted to link the development of cardiovascular disorders to a physiologically based reactivity to stressors. It is reasoned that increases in cardiovascular response to environmental stressors may over time cause permanent changes in the cardiovascular system in any person. Individuals who are by nature physiologically more reactive to stressors might show an initial stress response sooner and sustain cardiovascular changes more quickly than individuals who are not reactive in this way. It is further reasoned that if cardiovascular reactivity is more likely to lead to hypertension, then the higher rate of hypertension among African Americans may indicate that they have a greater vulnerability to stress. In his review of the research, Anderson (1989) noted that there are some fairly stable differences between black and white subjects in terms of stress-induced cardiovascular reactivity. However, he was not able to draw a clear conclusion about the extent to which a racial difference in stress susceptibility is being reflected.

Cultural differences do seem to appear in the experience of work stressors. Using cultural dimensions relating to work practices that had been described by Hofstede (1994), Peterson and his associates (1995) assessed the experiences of managers from 21 countries. They found substantial differences in job stress experience that were due to the manager's cultural background. Two related dimensions were found to distinguish the effects of work overload and role ambiguity. These are (1) power distance, or the extent to which inequality between people is accepted as normal, and (2) individualism, or the extent to which individual versus collective work is emphasized. (High-power-distance countries were identified as those in the Far East and Latin America; low-power-distance countries were mostly Western industrialized nations.) The researchers noted that power distance and individualism together affected the manager's experience of workload and role clarity. They summed up by saying, "Western middle managers are more likely to see the amount they have to do as manageable but to be unsure about how to do it. Middle managers in non-Western countries may believe they know their roles quite clearly but feel they have too much work to do it all well (p. 447)."

Cognitive and Personality Differences

Cognitive style and personality seem likely to affect the way we experience stress. Some theorists, such as Selye, view stress-induced illness as being specific to the way an individual personally perceives and interprets events. There also has been some study of individual personality traits, such as negative affectivity.[2] This is a personal tendency to experience negative emotions, and it has been found to affect a person's response to occupational stressors (Elliott, Chartrand, & Harkins, 1994). Locus of control also is thought to influence the experience of a stressor. Individuals with an internal locus of control are less responsive to stressful job situations than those with an external locus of control (Fusilier, Ganster, & Mayes, 1987). They also benefit more from social support, possibly because internals feel more personally in control of events in their lives than externals do (Cummins, 1989).

People vary in the extent to which they monitor their internal responses to stressors. Some are highly self-focused; others are not. We might reason that highly self-focused individuals, because they pay more attention to their internal stress responses, would also be more likely to take action to cope with a stressor. That is, this personal trait should *buffer* the effect of a stressor. There is probably a limit to this buffering effect, however, depending on what the person expects. If the person expects to be successful in coping, then high self-consciousness should buffer the stress effect. If he or she thinks that coping efforts will not help, then high self-consciousness should actually make things worse (Carver & Scheier, 1981). For example, one factor that affects a person's expectation of success in coping is the extent to which the stressor is a chronic condition. Chronic job stressors, such as work overload, are more difficult to deal with than acute temporary stressors, such as layoffs. Therefore, when an individual is facing a chronic stressor, self-focused attention reminds the person that there is no relief in sight. Frone and McFarlin

[2]Negative affectivity is a dispositional attribute discussed previously as affecting job satisfaction.

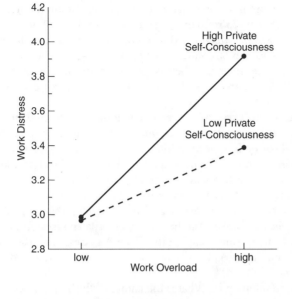

Figure 13.9 *The impact of self-focused attention and workload on job stress. Research by Frone and McFarlin (1989) showed that employees who are highly focused on their internal processes are more stressed by chronic work overload than employees who are less self-conscious.*

From M.R. Frone and D.B. McFarlin, "Chronic Occupational Stressors, Self-Focused Attention and well being: Testing a cybernetic model of stress" in Journal of Applied Psychology, 1989, 74:880. Copyright © 1989 by the American Psychological Association. Reprinted by permission.

Table 13.3   Sample Questions from the Structured Interview on Coronary-Prone Behavior

When you get angry or upset, do people around you know about it? How do you show it?
Do you think you drive harder to accomplish things than most of your associates?
Do you take work home with you? How often?
If you see someone doing a job rather slowly and you know that you could do it faster and better yourself, does it make you restless to watch him? Would you be tempted to step in and do it yourself?
Do you eat rapidly? After you've finished eating, do you like to set around the table and chat, or do you like to get up and get going?

From R.H. Rosenman, "The Interview Method of Assessment of the Coronary-Prone Behavior Pattern" in T. M. Dembroski, et.al., (eds.) *Coronary-Prone Behavior.* Copyright © 1978 Springer-Verlag, Heidelberg, Germany. Reprinted by permission.

(1989) found support for this position in their study of blue-collar workers. Employees who were highly focused on their internal processes were more distressed by chronic work overload than equally overworked employees who were less self-conscious (see figure 13.9). This shows how an individual's characteristic way of perceiving and interpreting events can affect the stress level.

Type A Behavior

The study of **Type A behavior** began when medical researchers Friedman and Rosenman (1959, 1974; Rosenman & Chesney, 1982) saw a connection between certain behavior in their patients and the development of coronary heart disease. These researchers devised a structured interview for observing the verbal and nonverbal behavior of their patients. Table 13.3 lists some of their interview questions. They found that one type of person, whom they labeled Type A, showed signs of being alert, ambitious, competitive, impatient, and aggressive to the point of hostility. Friedman and Rosenman interpreted the abrupt gestures and hurried speech of these patients as reflecting a generally high level of arousal. They concluded that this style of behavior led to coronary heart disease. In others, Friedman and Rosenman saw a contrasting behavioral pattern, which they labeled **Type B.** Type Bs are thought to be easygoing, to run their lives in a less frantic manner than Type As, and to be less likely to develop heart disease (Rosenman et al., 1975).

Research on Type A behavior has addressed several questions. One question is, Does this complex of personal factors actually predict the development of heart disease? It appears to do so. Jenkins's (1974) survey data showed that those scoring high on a Type A measure had more heart attacks than those scoring lower. A research reviewer was not convinced that Type A measures could reliably predict coronary heart disease (Matthews, 1988). Nevertheless, the reviewer concluded, as others have (e.g., Ganster, 1986), that Type A behavior is a risk factor in heart disease. Another reviewer of later research agreed that the cardiovascular system is implicated in the Type A's stress response. Compared to the Type B person, Type As consistently show faster heart rate and higher blood pressure (Lyness, 1993).

A second question is, What is the nature of the Type A behavior pattern? The research indicates that there are two basic dimensions. One relates to impatience, time urgency, and irritability. The other includes achievement and competition (Houston, Smith, & Zurawski, 1986; Spence, Helmreich, & Pred, 1987). It may be that these dimensions do not have the same influence in the development of heart disease. Possibly the impatience-irritability factor has a stronger connection to the development of heart disease than the achievement factor. Some believe that it does (Spence et al., 1987). However, studies also suggest that competitive and achievement oriented behavior is involved in the cardiovascular reactivity that Type As show (Lyness, 1993).

The Type A person appears to be achievement oriented. Several studies have used the **Jenkins Activity Survey** (Jenkins, Rosenman, & Zyzanski, 1979), a pencil-and-paper measure of Type A behavior which includes an achievement scale. Type As' success in business has been reported. In one study, 82 percent of a sample of small business owners scored as Type As on the Jenkins Activity Survey. Those companies that were headed by Type As had a higher return on investments and a better history of sales (Boyd, 1984). Finally, a study of Australian managerial and professional employees showed a link between Type A behavior and occupational level, apparently because of the Type A's self-imposed time commitments. Type A employees appeared to achieve their occupational status at least partly because they devoted their discretionary time to work (Byrne & Reinhart, 1989). That is, they took work home.

A third question is, Do Type As experience more work stress? The research evidence says that they do. For example, Ganster (1986) reviewed laboratory studies indicating that Type As have a generally higher level of arousal and a stronger physiological response to objective stressors. He also found several studies of work stress showing that Type As were more likely than others to report that they *felt* stressed. More recent research showed that compared to Type Bs, Type A workers are more stressed by a heavy workload (Kushnir & Melamed,

1991). It might be that Type As bring this on themselves. Perhaps, because of their achievement orientation, Type As are more likely than Type Bs to seek and find situations that are objectively more stressful (Froggatt & Cotton, 1987). Type As have been found more likely to evaluate job demands as *constituting* a work overload (Kirmeyer, 1988).

Why is Type A behavior interesting to I/O psychologists? There are two reasons. First, the conditions that appear to elicit this behavior, such as opportunities for achievement, are common aspects of the work environment. Thus, certain individuals may show chronic high arousal and develop an associated cardiovascular problem just by being at work. This is something the organization does not want. Second, it looks as if Type A behavior results in high work performance and accomplishment. This, of course, is something that the organization does want (Ganster, 1986).

---

*M*ain *P*oints

Some people, because of their own natures, are more likely to be stressed. Researchers have looked at several personal variables in an effort to discover what makes them vulnerable to stressors. Gender does not differentiate between those who are stressed and those who are not. Race does not seem to, either. Culture may differentiate people. Culture can affect the aspects of work that are experienced as stressful.

Cognition and personality are the most important of the personal variables in describing who is likely to be stressed and who is not. Type A is a complex pattern of behavior that increases stress vulnerability. It produces change in heart rate and blood pressure and can lead to heart disease. Type As are competitive and achievement oriented. Because of this, they make attractive employees. However, they also are more stressed by work, especially by a heavy workload.

THE OUTCOMES OF STRESS

Stress outcomes include a range of behavioral and somatic or bodily changes, such as physical illness, emotional and psychological disturbance, and performance problems. In one sense, we may view these effects as the results of physiologically coping with a stressor. That is, they result from the body's mobilization. Stressors may be kept under control by these physiological coping efforts, and if so, they are effective, although they may have a high cost. For example, responses that over time result in a stomach ulcer probably helped control a stressor prior to the development of the illness. Even the illness itself may get the individual some time away from the stressor (e.g., in the hospital). In the following sections, I consider some behavioral and somatic developments that come about when an individual must live with an existing stressor. Some of these are shown in figure 13.10. At the end of the chapter, I describe some behaviors that may be more effective ways to cope.

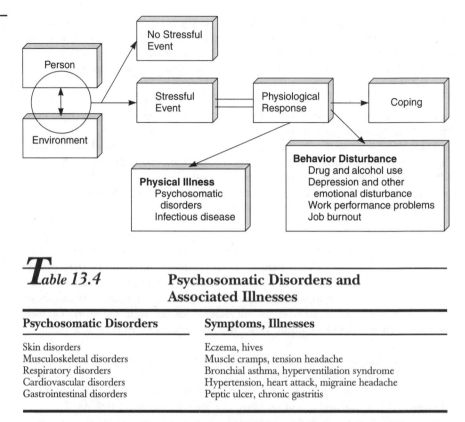

Figure 13.10 *Types of stress results. Note the behavioral and physical disorders that workers can develop when they attempt to live with existing stressful conditions.*

Person

Environment

No Stressful Event

Stressful Event

Physiological Response

Coping

Physical Illness
Psychosomatic disorders
Infectious disease

Behavior Disturbance
Drug and alcohol use
Depression and other emotional disturbance
Work performance problems
Job burnout

$\mathcal{T}$able 13.4   Psychosomatic Disorders and Associated Illnesses

Psychosomatic Disorders	Symptoms, Illnesses
Skin disorders	Eczema, hives
Musculoskeletal disorders	Muscle cramps, tension headache
Respiratory disorders	Bronchial asthma, hyperventilation syndrome
Cardiovascular disorders	Hypertension, heart attack, migraine headache
Gastrointestinal disorders	Peptic ulcer, chronic gastritis

Physical Illness and Behavior Disturbance

Stress can result in a variety of physical illnesses that have either an organic or a psychological basis. Sometimes, following a stressful period, people get colds or flu. This is thought to occur because prolonged sympathetic nervous system activity tends to suppress the immune system. Thus, stress compromises the body's ability to fight infectious disease organisms. Unlike these illnesses, **psychosomatic disorders** do not appear to have an organic basis. Rather, they are physical illnesses that result directly from the wear-and-tear process of prolonged stress. For example, ulcers and coronary heart disease are considered to be psychosomatic. Several categories of psychosomatic disorders have been identified. Some of the more common ones are listed in table 13.4. Physiological processes have been noted in the development of these illnesses. For example, peptic ulcers can develop when an excessive flow of normal digestive fluid is stimulated by stress-induced emotions. In some people, migraine headaches result when pain-sensitive arteries in the head are dilated. Hypertension is probably the most common psychosomatic disorder that can result from a natural process gone awry. In response to stressors, blood vessels leading to visceral organs constrict and blood pressure rises. Vasoconstriction and increased blood pressure remain high and eventually develop into chronic hypertension when emotional strain continues over time (Coleman et al., 1980).

Sometimes prolonged stress leads to behavioral and emotional disturbance, with or without obvious somatic associations. Depression and anxiety are examples, as are irritability, anger, and insomnia. Other behavioral disturbances that may result from stress include drug and alcohol abuse. Although effective in the short term as a way of relaxing and reducing stress, drugs and alcohol used for coping are ineffective in the long run and may themselves become a problem. Other behavioral stress outcomes are work performance problems, such as low productivity, counterproductive work behavior, and burnout.

Job Burnout

In one theoretical model, job burnout is proposed to be a response to stressful work conditions (Cherniss, 1980; Maslach, 1982). Burnout is behavior shown by individuals who work in emotionally demanding situations (Pines & Aronson, 1981). It involves emotional exhaustion, feelings of low personal accomplishment, and depersonalization or callous behavior toward one's clients (Maslach & Jackson, 1981). That is, burnout is feeling emotionally drained and believing that what one does makes no difference. A burned out employee depersonalizes or treats his or her clients as objects. Professionals in "people work" or human service occupations, such as nurses, therapists, social workers, and teachers, are thought most likely to show burnout because of the nature of the work they do. The **Maslach Burnout Inventory,** an instrument used in many studies of burnout, includes three subscales corresponding to the three dimensions of burnout (Maslach & Jackson, 1986).

Research shows that human service employees do experience burnout in response to work stressors (Burke, 1987; Russell, Altmaier, & Van Velzen, 1987). In general, work-role conflict, work overload, and low involvement in decisions contribute to the development of burnout (Jackson et al., 1987). Further, it appears that burnout is a function of the way someone copes. Escapist behavior is a coping mechanism associated with burnout (Leiter, 1991). Similarly, burnout may be more likely when other coping resources are not available at work. For example, a lack of social support is associated with job burnout (Jackson et al., 1987; Leiter, 1988).

Burnout theory was developed to address work in the human services. Common usage of burnout terminology to apply to apathetic or "dropout" behavior among individuals working in occupations other than human service suggests that the concept has been expanded. Is it appropriate to use "burnout" to describe behavior in occupations that involve no actual client contact? Some researchers contend that only certain aspects of the model are useful in describing jobs in general. Gardner (1987) argued that although people in other jobs can show emotional exhaustion, depersonalization is irrelevant outside the human service professions. Evans and Fischer (1993) agreed, reporting that depersonalization did not appear in the responses of computer company employees, although the other two components did.

Perhaps a better way of understanding the burnout process is to first view emotional exhaustion as a response to stressors, such as work overload and role conflict. Then, depersonalization can be seen as a defense against emotional exhaustion (Maslach, 1982). Depersonalization is not the only possible way of coping with emotional exhaustion, but in the human services, it may be available when other coping strategies are not (Ashforth & Lee, 1990; Lee & Ashforth, 1990). In their discussion of the research, Cordes and Dougherty (1993) pointed out that the human service

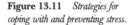
Figure 13.11 *Strategies for coping with and preventing stress.*

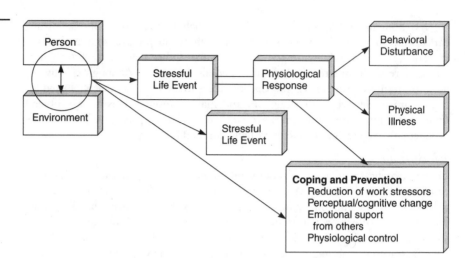

employee's socialization may legitimize and thus contribute to the use of depersonalization. For example, years ago when I worked as a clerical employee in a welfare office, I was told by the social workers that for my own peace of mind, I should not get too involved with the clients, that I must not "take their problems home with me."

Coping with Stress

The results of uncontrolled stress are serious and costly to the individual and the work organization. Although some stressors can be removed, it is not likely that we will ever live in a stress-free world. What does seem necessary is that we learn how to cope effectively with the stress we experience. There are ways to improve working conditions, reduce work stressors, and help individuals become more effective in preventing and coping with stress (see figure 13.11).

Individual strategies for coping include cognitive and behavior modification to help a person learn new ways of understanding existing conditions. People who are effective in coping with stress often say that they do this by trying to get a new perspective on the situation (Gilbert & Holahan, 1982). Coping strategies also include activities designed to control physiological and emotional reactions. Relaxation, meditation, biofeedback, and physical exercise are examples. Another coping strategy involves social interaction—getting help and emotional support from others. Any of these activities can be useful at work. Most organizational stress interventions are aimed at helping employees develop their own individual capacities to resist stress (Murphy, 1986).

Reducing Work Stressors

Sometimes, the most direct way to deal with stress is to change the source of the problem, that is, to remove the stressor. Stressful physical conditions often can be modified so that they are no longer harmful. It is often possible to substitute safe equipment and materials for harmful ones. As I note in chapter 15, if employees work in hazardous environments, they can be provided with protective clothing. Similarly, personal protection from excessive noise can be provided, or it may be possible to isolate the stressor if it cannot be removed. Noisy and heat-producing equipment can sometimes be relocated to insulated compartments or rooms.

Workload stressors can be modified by job redesign or by employee reassignment. Jobs change over time, with tasks being added or dropped, often in a rather haphazard manner. Sometimes, the change is deliberate as when an organization downsizes and a person's workload is increased by tasks previously done by someone else. Periodic job analysis, with an eye on the job relationships within a unit, can show how to reallocate tasks and modify the workload. Role conflict and ambiguity can be addressed in job analysis and employee training. Work responsibilities should be made clear, and employees whose jobs have changed, such as downsizing survivors, need to be instructed on what is expected of them. Sometimes work stressors are difficult to remove, however. Job redesign and other changes within the organization can *themselves* produce stress. This is less likely if employees are forewarned to expect changes and if they have some influence in the decision, particularly as to how the change will affect their future (Ashford, 1988).

Obtaining Social Support

In coping with stress, many of us find it helpful to talk over our problems with family members, friends, and people at work. **Social support** is an exchange of resources that takes place between at least two people, often members of the same social network (Shumaker & Brownell, 1984). Social support can be helpful in coping with stress (Cohen & Wills, 1985). One way social support is helpful is to provide a buffer against the stressor, or enable the person to resist. For example, in a survey of nurses, social support was found to buffer the effect of a patient's death and to help the nurse cope with this experience (McIntosh, 1991).

What do distressed individuals get from social support? They can get specific information and guidance for dealing with a stressful situation or for preventing stress. They also get emotional support and encouragement (Denton, 1990; Greenglass, 1993). Apparently, however, women are more capable of making use of social support than men are. Greenglass (1993) found that women, but not men, used social support from the work supervisor to both solve and prevent stress problems. Both women and men benefit from social support provided by family members and friends. Studies have found that people get different kinds of help from different supporters. Supervisors can provide social support that is instrumentally useful on the job, as well as emotionally helpful (Eastburg et al., 1994; Greenglass, 1993). Coworkers often are helpful with objective job problems, for which they can provide facts and opinions, and with career development concerns (Burke, Weir, & Duncan, 1976). Interviews with supervisors revealed that subordinates also can be important sources of emotional support (Erera, 1992).

Several researchers have considered what happens at work when an individual does not have social support. For example, it has been found that lacking supportive work relationships can contribute to the development of psychological strain and job burnout (Burke, 1987; Jackson et al., 1986; Jayaratne & Chess, 1984; Leiter, 1988). In particular, supervisory support may be needed (Russell et al., 1987). For example, after nursing supervisors were trained in how to give positive feedback, nurses in their units showed reduced levels of emotional exhaustion (Eastburg et al., 1994). Similarly, police dispatchers who received support from their supervisors reported less tension in coping with a heavy workload than dispatchers with less support (Kirmeyer & Dougherty, 1988). However, the impact of social support also appears to depend on the individual. For example, supervisor support has been found to be more helpful for persons showing Type B behavior, an internal locus of control, and an extraverted personality (Cummins, 1989; Eastburg et al., 1994; Greenglass, 1988).

Stress Management Programs

Many organizations today have stress management activities and programs for their employees. Undoubtedly, some of these have resulted from the public attention to stress at work. In addition, it is likely that the increase is partly due to the impact of successful Worker's Compensation claims for stress-related illnesses. It is becoming apparent that employers must provide help for employees in coping with job stress.

Most **stress management programs** do not make changes in the work situation. Rather, they take an individual-oriented approach and teach employees how to help themselves cope with work. Individual-oriented activities are appealing because they are inexpensive and can easily be incorporated in other employee assistance programs (Murphy, 1986). Work-site stress management programs include a variety of techniques. Most have training for relaxation and for increasing self-awareness. They may include biofeedback, meditation, and/or cognitive restructuring. These techniques are usually included in general employee health programs, and they are discussed in chapter 14.

A number of employers offer physical fitness programs. These programs are based on the belief that physical exercise can reduce stress and its effects. Exercise may reduce the physiological stress reaction in any of three ways. One, exercise may have a protective effect by decreasing the individual's normal level of sympathetic nervous system response, that is, by reducing such stress indicators as rapid heart rates. Two, because most stressful situations do not actually allow the individual to engage in fight-or-flight behavior, exercise during episodes of stress may allow the person to work off the energy produced by the stress response. Three, engaging in physical exercise may bring on a state of relaxation (Falkenberg, 1987).

How effective stress management interventions are, is not known. Most work-site programs are not monitored over the long term. The research on these programs has problems. It has most often relied on self-report measures with no control group. However, Murphy (1986) concluded his review by saying that stress management programs look hopeful. They are being received positively by employees, and there appear to be some improvements in employee health.

---

*M*ain
*P*oints

Physical illness can result from a stressful experience. Sometimes, stress makes the body vulnerable to disease organisms. At other times, the illness is psychosomatic.

Stress reactions can bring about psychological or behavioral disturbances. These problems can occur as a result of how the person copes with stress. The main feature of job burnout is emotional exhaustion. This may be a result of coping with the stress of doing "people work" by depersonalizing the client. Burnout is observed mostly in human service occupations.

Coping with work stress can start with the removal of stressors. This may involve workplace changes or job redesign. Most formal stress management programs are oriented toward helping workers individually learn how to cope. Social support can help a stressed employee cope in that it provides information and help in solving problems, as well as emotional support and encouragement.

CHAPTER SUMMARY

Stress is recognized as a serious problem in today's world. From events of catastrophic proportions to small irritations in daily life, a range of stressors take their toll in heightened arousal, physical illness, and behavior disturbance. It is increasingly clear that stress occurs at work, often as a result of working conditions and job characteristics.

Several theories of the process and components of stress have been advanced. Selye's General Adaptation Syndrome presents stress as a process involving physiological changes that progress over three stages. The Stressful Life Events Model attempts to identify the kinds of events that function as stressors. The Person-Environment Fit Theory focuses on the extent to which work demands and resources match the needs and abilities of the employee. The Facet model attempts to organize the variables of stress, from causes to consequences.

A range of work conditions can induce physiological stress. The stressors can be physical, such as noise. They can be elements of the job, such as work overload. They also can be sociopsychological in nature, such as relocation.

People are likely to differ in their vulnerability to stressors. The research does not show a very clear picture of how they differ. However, there may be some identifiable cultural differences. The Type A pattern of behavior has been proposed to account for some differences in how individuals react to stress. Research supports the proposition that Type A behavior poses an actual risk of stress-related disease. The Type A person also shows a different response to work stressors than the Type B person.

Stress may result in organic disease, psychosomatic disorders, and a variety of behavioral disturbances, including problems of work performance. Job burnout is a disturbance that appears most likely to affect people in human service occupations, although the emotional exhaustion component of burnout may appear in others. There are a number of remedies for the problems of stress at work. Physical stressors can be removed, or workers can be protected from them. Jobs can be redesigned. Employees can be provided with social support. Some organizations have stress management programs, which may include physical exercise.

STUDY QUESTIONS

1) Define stress, stressor, stress results, and strain.

2) Are some occupations more stressful than others? If so, why?

3) Describe the three stages of Selye's General Adaptation Syndrome. What are the physiological processes that underlie these stages?

4) Identify the basic propositions of the Stressful Life Events Model. According to this model, who is likely to develop a stress-related illness?

5) Define the following Person-Environment Fit Theory terms: organizational stress, strain, coping, and social support.

6) What are the facets in Beehr and Newman's Facet model of job stress? How is this theory helpful in understanding the process of coping with stress at work?

7) Using the arousal hypothesis, explain how physical working conditions operate to cause stress.

8) Certain characteristics of jobs have been found to operate as stressors. Identify these stressors.

9) Are there differences in the stress experienced by men and women, different racial or cultural groups, and people with different personalities?

10) What is Type A behavior? Does it actually cause heart disease? Would an organization be interested in hiring a Type A person?

11) What kinds of physical illness and behavioral disturbance can result from stress? Who is likely to suffer from job burnout? What are the components of burnout?

12) What can be done to help people cope with stress? How does social support help?

CONSIDER THIS

CASE STUDY

At Vocational Rehabilitation Services (VRS)[3] an unusual personnel problem has developed. Vince, who is the head of Rehabilitation Counseling, is reporting the problem to the Director of VRS.

"Eric, I'm worried about Julie," Vince began, "She has been acting so strangely lately, I just don't know what's wrong with her.

"She's been acting like she doesn't care anymore. You know she's been with us a long time. And, she was always a good counselor. But, now, well, I just don't know. . . ." Vince trailed off, shaking his head.

"What does she do?" Eric asked.

"It's more like what she doesn't do. She's just so . . . so uninterested, these days. She used to care a lot about the clients. I know she did. She was always very involved with them. In fact, I used to worry that she was too involved. Now, though, she's just the opposite. She couldn't care less. She treats them . . . , well, badly. She doesn't really try to help. She acts like . . . , I don't know, . . . She acts like it's their fault."

"Have you said anything to her?"

---

[3]VRS has been described previously in case studies at the end of several chapters.

"Yes. I have. I told her she was being too rough on her cases, that she was treating them like baggage. I also pointed that she's not keeping up."

"Did that help?"

"No. Not really. First, she said she didn't feel like she was accomplishing anything. Then, she said she couldn't try anymore, that they don't appreciate it. Finally, she shrugged it all off, said that's just the way it is, can't help it."

Vince continued. "I don't know. All of us are overworked. You know that. Especially these last few months. All the counselors have heavy caseloads. I mean, Julie has no more work than anyone else."

"What have you thought about doing?" Eric asked.

"I don't know. I hate to let her go. I need all the counselors. With the client load that we have right now, I can't really spare anyone. And, to try to hire a new counselor right now. . . . I don't see how I can spare the time to find someone and get them up and running."

"Okay. Well, let me think about this." Eric said. "You keep me posted on anything new that happens."

Problem

The Director must decide what to do to solve the problem. Can you help? What would you say is the nature of the problem that VRS faces? What steps should the director take? Should he get help for the counselor? Should she be discharged because of her poor job performance? Should anything else be done?

People take health problems to work with them, and while they are at work they pick up others. Because of this easy transit between work and home, it is not always easy to tell what caused a problem, especially if it is a mental health problem or a physical illness that developed over a long time.

In this chapter, you will learn about injuries and illnesses that occur at work. You will learn about some of their causes, such as workplace hazards and alcohol and drug abuse. You also will learn what employers do to prevent employee health problems. Health and safety law requires some interventions. Others are made because accidents and illnesses are costly. It is worth the employer's money to clean up hazards and institute health promotion and employee assistance programs.

Respiratory disease can result from exposure to toxic substances at the workplace. Here, an industrial nurse assists a worker in a test of breathing capacity.

Chapter *14*

Contents

*Employee
Health
Problems and
Organizational
Interventions*

I now recalled all the quiet mysteries which I had noted in the man. I remembered that he never spoke but to answer; . . . that for long periods he would stand looking out, at his pale window behind the screen, upon the dead brick wall; I was quite sure he never visited any refectory or eating house; while his pale face clearly indicated that he never drank beer, . . . or tea and coffee even, like other men; that he never went anywhere.

Revolving all these things, and coupling them with the recently discovered fact, that he made my office his constant abiding place and home, and not forgetful of his morbid moodiness; revolving all these things, a prudential feeling began to steal over me. My first emotions had been those of pure melancholy and sincerest pity; but just in proportion as the forlornness of Bartleby grew and grew to my imagination, did that same melancholy merge into fear, that pity into repulsion. . . . What I saw that morning persuaded me that the scrivener was the victim of innate and incurable disorder. I might give alms to his body; but his body did not pain him; it was his soul that suffered, and his soul I could not reach.

Herman Melville

The narrator of this story, an attorney, describes his scrivener[1] Bartleby as developing a mental health problem. At first, the employee is a careful and conscientious writer. Then, gradually he exhibits signs of a disturbance. His work performance begins to decline; he refuses to accept any additional assignments; and he spends most of his time staring out the window at the brick wall. The attorney does what most employers would do initially: He tries to get him to change. He reasons, pleads, and finally threatens to fire him. The problem only gets worse. Ultimately, Bartleby does no work at all, and he takes up residence in the office. The attorney pays him off and tells him to go. Bartleby refuses to leave. Finally, in a last desperate effort to get rid of this haunted being, the attorney moves his office to another building and leaves Bartleby behind.

Although the problem described admittedly is severe and the solution extreme, it is an example of the kind of distressing situation that can develop in the workplace. We may not expect to find individuals with extremely severe mental disorders at work; however, it is likely that many employees have mild psychological problems. Also, most physical health problems have psychological components. The source of these problems can be the work setting or other areas of life outside the work environment. Whatever the source, they can emerge at work and become challenges for the employer.

In chapter 13, you saw how stress can affect the health of an employee. In this chapter, you discover that there are other threats to employee health and well being. Some health problems result from exposure to hazards and toxic substances. Accidents and occupational illnesses may be caused by an employee's involuntary or unknowing exposure to workplace hazards. Other health problems are due to

[1]A scrivener is a writer or copier of documents. Modern technology has made this occupation obsolete.

the employee's knowing use and abuse of substances that are not part of the work environment. The person's work is likely to be impaired by any of these problems, and the employer may need to help get the problem under control. I conclude this chapter with a description of some health programs that organizations use to help employees handle these problems.

MENTAL HEALTH PROBLEMS AT WORK

Anxiety and depression are common psychological problems that are likely to affect employees and the work they do. As discussed in chapter 13, anxiety and depression can be part of the response to a stressor. In this chapter, I describe research showing that they are present in a range of employee health problems. Anxiety and depression can develop as a result of difficult and hazardous work conditions, although they also are problems that develop in the nonwork realm of an employee's life. Whatever their source, they can interfere with productivity and affect interactions in the organization; thus, they may require the employer's attention.

Anxiety and Depression

For many people, anxiety is a fairly infrequent occurrence and results from a specific aversive condition that can be identified. However, some people go through life with constant anxiety. It may be free floating and not really specific, or it may be attached to particular events that most of us do not find very serious. Although there are differences in terms of how severe the disorder is, anxiety is not an unusual problem. In fact, in the United States, it is the most common of the psychiatric disorders. There also appear to be societal differences in the incidence of anxiety. For example, in some countries, business executives report high anxiety levels (Cooper & Arbrose, 1984). High anxiety can have some serious consequences for both the employee and the organization.

A person with a serious anxiety disorder evaluates ordinary life events as threatening. Often, the person responds with avoidance rather than with effective coping skills. Because the avoidance behavior brings immediate relief from tension, it is maintained. In the long run, however, avoidance is maladaptive because it does nothing about the threatening event (Coleman et al., 1980). With other anxiety disorders, a person may respond to a threatening situation, not with avoidance, but by exaggerating previously useful behaviors to the point that they are maladaptive. For example, compulsive behaviors can interfere with work and may even physically endanger a person who is performing a hazardous job (Jenkins & Baggett, 1992).

Depression is an affective or mood disorder experienced in different degrees, from mild to severe. It is a common problem in our society. Depression can result from drug and alcohol abuse, physical illness, and anxiety disorders (Aneshensel & Huba, 1984). Depression can be a problem of employees who have high job demands, such as work overload and role conflict (Bromet et al., 1988). However, work also can make things better. Being employed and having job security can improve a person's psychological well-being (Kuhnert & Palmer, 1991; Winefield & Tiggemann, 1990).

Although mild depression may actually be somewhat adaptive in that it provides the time for physical and psychological repair, severe depression is not good. The severely depressed person slows down mentally and physically and loses enthusiasm. Work activities do not seem worth the effort. The person shows little interest in interpersonal relationships, withdraws, and spends time mulling over past mistakes. Not surprisingly, self-esteem suffers (Coleman et al., 1980). We might guess that Melville's Bartleby suffered from severe depression.

*M*ain
   *P*oints

Anxiety and depression are two psychological problems that occur at work. Often, they are part of a complex response to stressful and hazardous work conditions. In general, they are the two most frequently diagnosed psychiatric disorders.

Anxiety and depression range in severity from mild to severe. An anxious person perceives situations and events as threatening when objectively they may not be severe. High anxiety often leads to behavior that is avoidant or otherwise maladaptive. Depression is a mood disorder that can occur with substance abuse and physical illness. Work can be part of the problem in developing depression. It also can help lift depression. Although mild depression may not be harmful, severe depression is not healthy and can lower self-esteem.

WORK-RELATED INJURIES AND ILLNESSES

Although they are likely to include psychological aspects, most of the reported employee health problems are primarily physical. In this section, I discuss three such categories of physical health problems: (1) injuries received in work accidents; (2) illnesses caused by exposure to toxins at work; and (3) musculoskeletal injuries caused by the physical trauma of daily work.

Accidents at Work

As there are occupations that are more *stressful* than others, so also are there occupations that are more *hazardous* than others. Work accident rates vary by industry, because employees are exposed to different hazards. For example, meat packing is a high-risk industry, with butchers, meat cutters, and packers all showing high rates of accidents (Conroy, 1989). Table 14.1 shows the way industries differ in terms of accidental deaths and injuries. Agriculture, mining, construction, and transportation have relatively more fatal accidents than other industries. Notice in table 14.1 that for every 100,000 workers in mining, there were 27 deaths, and in agriculture there were 26. The *type* of accident varies across industries. Many injuries in agriculture and forestry are likely to result from working with machinery, such as chain saws (Slappendel et al., 1993) and fence post drivers (Miller, 1992). Construction workers are likely to be injured in falls. Transportation workers, not surprisingly, are involved in more motor vehicle accidents (National Safety Council, 1988).

We can look at the work accident rate in a number of ways. For example, we can look at the severity of the accident. **Accident severity** is described in terms

Table 14.1 — Deaths, Injuries, and Rates of Work Accidents in 1994 by Industry

Industry Division	Workers (000)	Deaths	Percent Change from 1993	Deaths Per 100,000 Workers	Disabling Injuries[b]
All industries	122,400	5,000	—[a]	4	3,500,000
Agriculture[b]	3,400	890	+7	26	140,000
Mining, quarrying[b]	600	160	+6	27	20,000
Construction	6,200	910	+3	15	300,000
Manufacturing	18,100	690	−1	4	590,000
Transportation and public utilities	6,100	740	−1	12	260,000
Trade[b]	28,100	450	+1	2	800,000
Services[b]	41,300	640	+3	2	860,000
Government	18,600	520	−1	3	530,000

Note: National Safety Council estimates are based on data from the Bureau of Labor Statistics, National Center for Health Statistics, state vital statistics departments, and state industrial commission.
[a]Change less than 0.5 percent.
[b]Agriculture includes forestry, fishing and agricultural services. Mining includes oil and gas extraction. Trade includes wholesale and retail trade. Services include finance, insurance, and real estate.

of fatalities and injuries. Financial costs of lost wages, property damage, and medical expense sometimes are used to evaluate accidents as well. Also, we can compare the work accident rate to the rates of accidents occurring elsewhere to see how safe the workplace is. The National Safety Council (1991) reported that 10,500 deaths occurred in work accidents in 1990, which averaged to a little less than one every hour. Even more deaths occurred in nonwork accidents that year. Two every hour were killed at home, and five every hour were killed in highway accidents. These statistics suggest that the workplace is actually relatively safe.

So, you ask, if the workplace is so safe, then why are we concerned? Although the workplace is *comparatively* safe, work accidents are still a serious problem in terms of the actual numbers of deaths and injuries. As table 14.1 shows, 5,000 people were killed in work accidents in 1994. Although this indicates a decrease in deaths since 1990, there were more disabling injuries. In 1994, 3.5 million disabling injury accidents occurred, compared to 1.8 million in 1990 (National Safety Council, 1991; 1995). For these people and their families, the work accident picture is grim.

Occupational Disease

The rates for death and disability from **occupational disease** may be as high as the rates for accidents. It is difficult to estimate these statistics for a number of reasons. First, it is difficult to disentangle work-related causes from nonwork causes. For example, if someone develops lung cancer, is it because of exposure to radiation at the uranium mine where the person works, or is it because of a long-standing smoking habit? The answer is not obvious. Another reason for the difficulty in assessing these diseases is their slow development. Often, the illness does not appear until years after the worker was exposed to the hazard. Thus, the link to the work situation is difficult to establish. Even in cases in which the work site is identified as a contributor to the illness, the *degree* to which the work environment contributed may be difficult to determine. This is the problem in diagnosing cancers and cardio-vascular diseases that have developed over time.

In spite of the difficulty, research has identified a large number of occupational diseases (U.S. Bureau of Labor Statistics, 1985). Skin diseases are frequently reported, although the incidence depends on the particular industry (see table 14.2). Lung diseases that result from breathing various particles have been responsible for the deaths of workers. Black lung disease, caused by breathing coal dust, and brown lung disease, which results after long exposure to cotton dust, are two such diseases. Workers who handle asbestos materials have a high risk of developing asbestosis, another respiratory disorder.

Like accident rates, the rates of occupational illness vary across industries, indicating again that workers are exposed to varied health hazards. Data presented by the National Safety Council (1995) show that the manufacturing industry, in general, has high rates of illness. By examining table 14.2, you can see that workers in manufacturing report high incidences of repetition trauma disorders. Also, they report skin diseases, and they are more likely than workers in other industries to have a respiratory ailment due to toxic substances. The agricultural industry reports the highest incidence of skin disease. Many poisonings occur in agriculture. These illnesses may be due to the use of pesticides. A study investigating South American farmers' use of pesticides found a major health problem due to pesticide poisoning. Undoubtedly, part of the problem is the imprudent use of these substances, as protective equipment is not always used while applying pesticides (Grieshop & Winter, 1989).

Causes of Occupational Illness

Toxic substances are categorized in terms of their effects on the human body (Asfahl, 1984). **Systemic poisons** damage vital organs. For example, lead poisoning, which can develop from chronic exposure to leaded gasoline, has been shown to damage the central nervous system. **Carcinogens** are substances that cause cancer. Toxic agents that have been associated with occupational cancer include certain pesticides, hardwood dusts, asbestos, and ionizing radiation (National Safety Council, 1987).

Irritants damage the skin or the respiratory system. Irritating dusts cause a variety of lung diseases. Long-term exposure to a lung irritant results in tissue scaring that gradually reduces lung functioning. The health impact in such cases develops over many years and is not likely to be immediately apparent. **Asbestosis,** the lung disease that results from breathing asbestos fibers, at one time was believed to affect only workers who had actively worked with the material on the job, such as those who install it or remove it from buildings.[2] However, studies in occupational medicine have shown that workers in a variety of jobs show evidence of lung damage that seems to be related to exposure to asbestos insulation. For example, firefighters are exposed to burning and charred buildings that contain asbestos. Studies have found that veteran firefighters, with years of such exposure, now show greater than expected rates of lung scarring and reduced lung functioning. Others who are even more passively exposed than firefighters, such as custodians, also have shown signs of developing lung disease (Raloff, 1990).

[2]Asbestos has been used for insulating and fireproofing buildings and equipment.

Table 14.2 Number and Incidence of Occupational Illnesses in 1993 by Industry and Type of Illness

Occupational Illness	Private Sector[a]	Agriculture[a,b]	Mining[b]	Construction	Manufacturing	Trans. and Pub. Util.	Trade[b]	Finance[b]	Services
Number of Illnesses (in Thousands)									
All Illnesses	***482.1***	***5.8***	***1.7***	***8.7***	***299.6***	***20.7***	***49.1***	***21.1***	***75.5***
Disorders associated with repeated trauma	302.4	1.1	0.7	2.3	227.0	11.1	22.5	14.4	23.3
Skin diseases, disorders	60.2	2.7	0.1	2.2	30.8	2.8	4.4	0.9	16.3
Respiratory conditions due to toxic agents	24.2	0.3	0.1	0.8	10.1	2.0	3.0	1.5	6.4
Disorders due to physical agents	20.1	0.5	0.1	0.8	11.3	1.1	3.2	0.4	2.8
Poisoning	7.6	0.1	(c)	0.3	3.8	0.3	1.5	(d)	1.4
Dust diseases of the lungs	2.7	0.1	0.6	0.2	0.9	0.3	(d)	(d)	0.6
All other occupational diseases	64.3	1.1	0.2	2.1	15.8	3.1	14.3	3.7	24.7
Incidence Rate (per 10,000 Full-Time Workers)									
All Illnesses	***61.1***	***54.2***	***26.3***	***20.8***	***167.2***	***37.9***	***23.8***	***34.7***	***32.9***
Disorders associated with repeated trauma	38.3	10.3	11.2	5.4	126.7	20.3	10.9	23.7	10.2
Skin diseases, disorders	7.6	25.4	1.7	5.4	17.2	5.1	2.1	1.5	7.1
Respiratory conditions due to toxic agents	3.1	2.5	0.9	2.0	5.6	3.7	1.5	2.5	2.8
Disorders due to physical agents	2.5	4.4	1.1	1.9	6.3	2.0	1.5	0.7	1.2
Poisoning	1.0	0.2	0.4	0.8	2.1	0.5	0.7	(d)	0.6
Dust diseases of the lungs	0.3	0.5	8.7	0.4	0.5	0.5	(d)	(d)	0.3
All other occupational diseases	8.2	9.9	2.4	5.0	8.8	5.6	6.9	6.1	10.8

Source: Bureau of Labor Statistics, U.S. Department of Labor. Components may not add to totals due to rounding.

[a]Private sector includes all industries except government, but excludes farms with less than 11 employees.

[b]Agriculture includes forestry and fishing, mining includes quarrying and oil and gas extraction; trade includes wholesale and retail, finance includes insurance and real estate.

[c]Fewer than 50 cases.

[d]Data not reported or do not meet publication guidelines.

We live in a world in which entirely new chemicals—substances that never before existed—are being produced daily. Many of these are meant to serve quite benign purposes, such as to clean and preserve materials and equipment we use every day. In this way, these substances are likely to be in our homes and office buildings. The **sick-building syndrome** is a term used to describe sudden episodes of employee illness that result from toxic conditions found in some of the newest office buildings. The problem is indicated by a sharp increase in the incidence of particular symptoms, such as eye and throat irritations, headaches, dizziness, nausea, and skin rashes. Sick-building syndrome can affect employees who have just moved into a new building, particularly one that does not have windows that can be opened. The problem appears to result from two factors: (1) the presence of hazardous chemicals that have been used in manufacturing the building's furnishings, such as carpets, upholstery, and draperies and (2) the use of a closed air recirculation system for climate control. Chemical fumes that escape from the furnishings are recirculated by a closed air conditioning system, as are such airborne disease organisms as viruses and bacteria, which can contribute to the problem by increasing employees' exposure to colds and flu (*SKRSC*, 1990).

Repetition Injury Disorders

Not all health problems are caused by toxic substances or accidents. The equipment and the design of a job can have some health consequences as well. For example, prolonged operation of video display terminals or computer monitors sometimes results in eyestrain, apparently because of a change in visual accommodation. Overaccommodation or temporary nearsightedness can result when an operator stays at the computer for a long time (Shahnavaz & Hedman, 1984).

One class of health problems affects the musculoskeletal system of the body. Like occupational illness, these musculoskeletal problems develop slowly because of exposure to inherently hazardous conditions. Like accidents, they involve injuries. Note that table 14.2 includes "disorders associated with repeated trauma." **Repetition trauma disorder** is related directly to the nature of the work required by a job, and it develops because of the many slight injuries that occur from repeated performance of the same physical action. Study of these problems began when Japanese scientists discovered the existence of a cervicobrachial, or neck and upper limb, disorder. The disorder develops in keyboard operators and others who do handwork on a machine for long continuous periods while maintaining a rigid posture and arm position. This disorder appears to be due to an accumulation of minor injuries that result from the continuous arm and hand movements, and by the muscle work involved in maintaining a static body posture over several hours at a time (Maeda, Horiguchi, & Hosokawa, 1982; Nakaseko, Tokunaga, & Hosokawa, 1982).

More recent studies indicate that repetition trauma is experienced by employees in a wide range of jobs and can affect the person's back as well as neck and shoulders. Musculoskeletal pain experienced by employees can originate in either the upper or the lower back or the extremities, including the arms and wrists (Bru, Mykletun, Sveback, 1994). Work may cause physical trauma in any of these areas. For example, welders were found to have shoulder trauma resulting from the extended periods of static work and posture required by this job (Törner et al., 1991). Jobs that require sustained body posture while operating equipment that vibrates also have been found to cause lower back pain. For example, crane operators and helicopter pilots reported lower back pain as a result of static posture and machine vibration (Burdorf & Zondervan, 1990; Bongers et al., 1990).

What can be done about the serious problem of employee injury and illness? As you will see in a later section of this chapter, a variety of interventions have been devised to handle employee health problems. Some of these are meant to control accidents and employee exposure to unhealthy work demands.

---

*M*ain *P*oints

Injuries and illnesses can occur when workers are exposed to hazardous and unhealthy work conditions. Several industries have comparatively high accident rates, including agriculture, construction, and transportation. Accidents often involve hazardous equipment and vehicles. Although the workplace is relatively safe, accidental death and impairment of employees is serious and expensive.

Occupational disease can be work related. However, because it often develops over a long time period the cause may be difficult to specify. Some industries, such as manufacturing, show high illness rates, especially of repetition trauma and skin disorders. Skin disorders and poisonings of agricultural workers suggest hazardous use of pesticides. Toxic substances encountered at work include systemic poisons, carcinogens, and skin and lung irritants. Asbestosis is a lung disease resulting from breathing asbestos fibers.

Musculoskeletal disorders, such as repetition trauma, develop slowly in response to an accumulation of slight injuries received over time while doing a job. Long periods of sustained body posture and repeated movements or use of vibrating equipment can cause repetition trauma in the person's back, neck, and/or extremities.

PROBLEMS RESULTING FROM SUBSTANCE ABUSE

Some drugs are used for medicinal purposes. Others have largely recreational uses. Over-the-counter and prescribed drugs, such as pain medication and tranquilizers, are examples of medicinal drugs. Recreational drugs include such substances as alcohol and nicotine. Any drug has the potential of being misused, regardless of its primary purpose. The terms *dependence* and *addiction* are used to talk about the psychological and physiological need for a drug. We think of addiction as having occurred when withdrawal symptoms, such as headaches or intense craving, result from withholding the substance. **Substance abuse** refers to the excessive use of a substance, with or without dependence. Substance abuse is a problem at many workplaces.

Alcohol Abuse

Alcohol is America's favorite recreational drug and has been for a long time. In the late 1700s, Americans consumed great quantities of alcoholic beverages when economic and agricultural conditions promoted the distillation of an abundance of whiskey. In the 1830s, economic conditions changed, a temperance movement got underway, and abstinence was encouraged as the way to improve the labor force

(Gomberg, 1982). From the 1870s until the early 1940s, in the United States and in most of the industrialized world, consumption of alcohol declined steadily. There were some exceptions to this trend. For example, in industries in which workers lived in work camps away from home, such as railroad construction, mining, and logging, alcohol was used heavily (Strauss, 1976). In general, however, alcohol use declined. The decade of the 1940s was the driest this country had seen in more than a century. In the 1950s, alcohol consumption began to rise again (Sulkunen, 1976).

Historically in the United States, fewer women than men drank. Those who did, drank less than their male counterparts. These patterns persist today (Johnson, 1982). Those who use alcohol or drugs at work also are more likely to be men, especially men under the age of 30 (Hollinger, 1988). Part of the gender difference may be due to differences in social roles. For example, our society has been intolerant of the female alcoholic, although we accept some alcohol use by women. It may be that we are becoming more tolerant of female alcohol users; in the 1970s, about two-thirds of the women in this country drank at least occasionally (Gomberg, 1982).

Behavioral Effects of Alcohol Use

Legal intoxication is defined in terms of **blood alcohol content (BAC)** rather than the amount of alcohol consumed. This takes into account the fact that the physiological impact of alcohol depends on the physical size of the person. Legal intoxication has been defined by the laws of several states as 0.10 percent BAC.

Although there is a fairly high rate of **alcoholism,** I do not wish to overstate this problem. Most who drink are not alcoholic. However, working while under the influence of alcohol is problematic, whether or not the employee is an alcoholic. Alcohol is a depressant drug, and it has the effect of reducing the quality of performance. Whatever the activity, we do it less well when we are intoxicated than when we are sober. Even at blood alcohol levels considerably lower than 0.10 percent BAC, work performance is adversely affected. As BAC approaches 0.10 percent, the range of behavioral processes that are disrupted expands. Features of industrial tasks, such as perceptual processes, motor control, and communication are impaired (Hahn & Price, 1994). Complex cognitive processes, such as those involved in managerial strategic planning, are affected also (Streufert et al., 1993).

Intoxication is associated with accident behavior (Shain, 1982), possibly because consuming alcohol increases the errors that are made in work performance. For example, experienced pilots operating a flight simulator while under the influence of alcohol made a number of serious errors in performing the simulated trip. Even at 0.025 percent BAC, errors were made, and they increased as BAC levels increased (Billings et al., 1991). The use of alcohol diminishes our perceptual and cognitive capacities. These diminished capacities are more consequential when we are doing work that is risky, such as vehicle and industrial equipment operation. Drinking and operating machinery is a dangerous combination.

Work-Related Risk Factors

Although many alcohol problems are due to nonwork influences and are imported to the workplace, there is a possibility that work-related factors contribute to alcohol abuse. There are two perspectives on how this can occur and there is research support for both. In one view, work strains due to stress bring about problem drinking. In the other view, drinking is a behavior that is regulated by norms. Regarding this

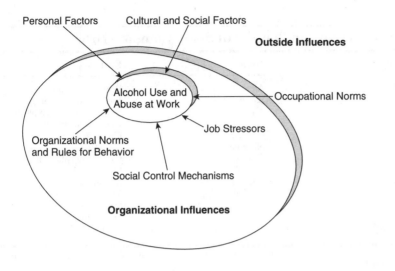

Figure 14.1 *Influences on the use and abuse of alcohol at work.*

Personal Factors

Cultural and Social Factors

Outside Influences

Alcohol Use and Abuse at Work

Occupational Norms

Organizational Norms and Rules for Behavior

Job Stressors

Social Control Mechanisms

Organizational Influences

latter perspective, recall from chapter 11 that organizations function in many ways as cultures do, with social norms and other social control mechanisms to regulate behavior. These influences are depicted in figure 14.1. Norms for alcohol consumption are present in the work organization. Some occupational groups, such as construction workers, and some white-collar organizational units, such as administrative departments, have been found to have norms *promoting* alcohol use (cf. Trice & Sonnenstuhl, 1988). The nature of an organization's norms for drinking often can be detected from the number of business meetings that include alcohol and from after-work socialization among coworkers. Social drinking among coworkers tends to legitimize alcohol use and make drinking on the job easily concealed. Individuals who report working under the influence of alcohol also report that they frequently engage in after-work drinking with coworkers (Hollinger, 1988). The amount of social control that exists in the organization also influences the use of alcohol. That is, when work performance is not very visible to coworkers or when there is little supervision, no one may notice that alcohol is being used at work. Under such conditions, workers are more likely to drink on the job (Ames & Janes, 1987).

Drug Abuse

The definition of **drug abuse** traditionally has depended on the extent to which a particular drug is regulated by society. Substances that are considered unacceptable for use are regulated, and they are what we mean when we talk about drugs. Substances of which we approve, such as medicines, or of which we are ambivalent, such as alcohol and nicotine, are described differently. Thus, drug abuse refers to the use of such regulated substances as opium, marijuana, and cocaine. Table 14.3 describes a number of these substances. The incidence of use depends on the drug. More people use marijuana than other regulated drugs. In 1987, it was reported that 10 percent of the population used marijuana and 3 percent used cocaine. Compared to alcohol and tobacco use, however, these rates are low. In the United States, 59 percent of the population drink and 32 percent smoke (Rosen, 1987).

*T*able 14.3

Classification and Sources of Some Common Drugs

Class	Drug	Sources
Sedative	Alcohol	Beer, wine, spirits
	Barbiturates	Seconal, methaqualone
Stimulant	Amphetamines	Benzedrine, methamphetamine
	Cocaine	Coca plant, synthesized
	Caffeine	Coffee, tea, cola
	Nicotine	Tobacco
Narcotic	Opiates	Opium, morphine, heroin
	Methadone	Synthesized
Hallucinogen	Cannabis	Marijuana
	Mescaline	Wild mushroom
	LSD	Synthesized
	PCP	Synthesized
Antianxiety	Tranquilizers	Valium

Note: Some sources listed are trade names. Several drugs do not have naturally occurring sources, but are synthesized in chemical laboratories.

The user's experience is used to classify drugs. Drugs can calm, or stimulate the user, or they can produce perceptual distortions. **Sedatives** and **narcotics** have calming effects. Barbiturates are sedatives. Used sparingly, they reduce tension and induce sleep. Excessive use produces sluggishness, confusion, and memory loss. Long-term use can disturb motor coordination and cause depression. Opium and the opium derivatives, including morphine and heroin, are narcotics. All opiates have been used for medical and for recreational purposes. Comparatively, opiate abuse is not severe (Greene & Dupont, 1974). Amphetamines are **stimulants.** Forms of the drug were used by soldiers in World War II to overcome fatigue while on duty. Since then, civilians such as night workers and truckers, have used them for the same purpose (Jarvik, 1967). Amphetamines mimic the physiological stress response. The drug pushes the body toward greater use of its own resources: Blood pressure and muscular tension increase, and both appetite and sleep are suppressed. Amphetamine abuse can cause brain damage (Ellinwood, 1971). The **hallucinogens** are used largely for recreation. They produce hallucinationlike experiences, typically involving vision. Cannabis, found in marijuana, is a mild hallucinogen. It can have various and even contradictory effects. Tension reduction, increased feelings of well-being, sensory enhancement, and negative experiences, such as depression and anxiety, have been reported.[3] Cannabis has negative effects on work performance. It adversely affects reaction time and impairs tracking and visual performance in vehicle operation (Moskowitz, 1976).

Is employee substance abuse an expensive problem for industry? Some national statistics say that it is. More than 40 percent of serious industrial accidents involve alcohol or drugs. Alcohol and drug abuse is believed to cost industry billions of dollars each year in lost work time, low productivity, and health and accident insurance (Cowan, 1987). The costs are large enough to suggest that something needs to be done. There are several directions that might be taken, from modifying work stressors to sending individuals for treatment. Some firms take a shortcut to a drug-free workplace by firing those using drugs.

[3]Cannabis also is noted for increasing the user's interest in food. For this reason, marijuana has been used medicinally by cancer patients whose appetite is dangerously suppressed by chemotherapy.

The U.S. government considers the problem of workplace drug use to be serious. The Drug-Free Workplace Act of 1988 defines requirements for employers who are federal contractors and federal grant recipients. Briefly, the act specifies that such employers must notify their employees that possessing or using drugs at work is prohibited and must specify the actions that will be taken against them if they use drugs at work. The employer also needs to establish a drug-free awareness program and assistance for employees. Finally, the employer must impose the sanctions, which may include termination, on any employee who is convicted of a drug use violation occurring in the workplace.

Detection of Drug Use

The success of any intervention depends on the employer's ability to detect drug and alcohol use and identify the users. The first step, before instituting any **drug testing program,** is to determine whether there are signs of drug or alcohol use among employees. Certainly, overt use of drugs and alcohol *at* the workplace is a sign. Personnel data can point to a problem that is more covert. For example, compared to nonusers, substance abusers are absent and tardy more often, take more sick leave, and are involved in more accidents (Cowan, 1987). Employers who investigate and find such indicators of employee drug use *before* instituting the drug testing program actually get better results in terms of reduced accidents and illnesses (Feinauer & Havlovic, 1993).

The usual method of detecting drug and alcohol use in industry is **urinalysis.** A urine test, however, may not be the best method. Testing can be costly, particularly if a precise technology is used. Probably, however, the greatest concern about urinalysis is its accuracy. For one thing, it is less capable of detecting alcohol intoxication than other tests, such as the **breathalizer.** Also, urinalysis is affected by the **cross-reactivity** of certain over-the-counter drugs which can cause a test to appear positive for an illegal drug. Another aspect of its inaccuracy has to do with the length of time that drug metabolites remain in the body. Some drugs are detectable long after the period of intoxication. The drug from a single marijuana cigarette can be detected in the urine for as long as 120 hours after it was smoked, and cocaine can be detected for 25 hours after use (Rosen, 1987). This means that detection of a substance in the urine does not necessarily prove that the person is presently intoxicated by the drug (Cowan, 1987; Rosen, 1987). Even so, some have found that job performance is impaired hours after a drug has been used and when the user no longer feels the effect (Leirer, Yesavage, & Morrow, 1991).

Prior to implementation of a drug testing program, the organization must consider the possibility of negative employee reactions. The strongest reaction is to **random drug testing** in which a group of employees are randomly selected and tested without prior notice. Employees partly object to random testing because they perceive it as being arbitrary and not based on any reasonable suspicion of drug use. In addition, the arbitrary timing of testing is offensive (Hartstein, 1987). Employees are less negative toward testing if they expect it and if they know that the consequence of detection is getting help rather than getting fired (Stone & Kotch, 1989).

Use of Domesticated Drugs

A drug is domesticated if it is incorporated into a society's way of life. In the domestication process, the drug comes to be seen as reasonably safe, and many people begin and continue to use it. Even if **domesticated drugs** are found later to be harmful, their continued use often is sanctioned (Gilbert, 1976). Domesticated drugs in our society include caffeine and nicotine, and possibly alcohol as well. Domesticated drug use in the American workplace is about as old as industry itself. The smoke-filled boardroom and the office coffeemaker are images of white-collar work. The question about domesticated drugs is whether they lead to employee health problems and increase employer costs.

Caffeine is contained in coffee, tea, chocolate, cola drinks, and many over-the-counter medicines, such as headache remedies. Many people are physically dependent on caffeine. Should we care? Perhaps not. Caffeine is apparently benign when used moderately. Being a stimulating drug, caffeine produces some of the same effects as other stimulants. It increases blood pressure, basal metabolism, and muscular tension, and interferes with sleep. Its short-term effects on work performance are positive. For example, physically hard work can be done for longer periods when caffeine is consumed. Caffeine also increases alertness on vigilance tasks. However, withdrawal symptoms such as drowsiness, irritability, and headache can occur when a person stops using caffeine (Gilbert, 1976).

Tobacco is the only source of nicotine. Since 1964, when the American public was warned of the health dangers of this domesticated drug, the percentage of smokers has declined. Still, there are a very large number who use the drug. In this country, about 30 percent of the population smokes (Rosen, 1987).[4] Nicotine is a stimulant. It increases the level of physiological arousal: Heart rate and blood pressure rise, the adrenal glands are stimulated, and appetite is suppressed (Russell, 1976). If you are a smoker, you may find these effects surprising. Although physiologically it is a stimulant, nicotine is *subjectively* tranquilizing. As you may know, smokers are less irritable when they can smoke (Gilbert, 1979; Sommese & Patterson, 1995).

Does nicotine affect work performance? In some tasks it may have a positive effect. In vigilance and reaction tasks, nicotine improves performance, possibly because of the general physiological arousal it induces (Waller & Levander, 1980). Information processing appears to be quicker, and memory for task details is sometimes better when smokers are allowed to smoke (Peeke & Peeke, 1984; Wesnes & Warburton, 1984). Hand tremor is a harmful effect of long-term tobacco use. Tremors impair performance in tasks requiring fine motor control. Withdrawal from nicotine addiction impairs performance and causes psychological effects, such as depression (Sommese & Patterson, 1995).

Because it increases the user's risk of physical illness, tobacco use is an employee health problem that generates costs for the employer. For example, those who smoke are sick with colds more often than their nonsmoking counterparts (cf. Parkes, 1987). They take more sick leave and use more health insurance benefits. The health care of nonsmokers who work with smokers is another possible cost. Coincidentally, smoking also increases the costs of building maintenance. Walls and draperies in the workplace of smoking employees get dirty faster and must be cleaned more often because of smoke residue deposits.

[4]According to a report from the Center for Disease Control, about 35 percent of American high school students were smoking in 1995, up from 28 percent in 1991.

Substance abuse is a problem of excessive use of alcohol and regulated drugs. Alcohol has a long history in the United States and presently is used by a large proportion of the population. Legal intoxication is defined by many state laws as 0.10 percent BAC. Some workers drink on the job. Drinking impairs work performance, even if the drinker is not intoxicated. Errors in performance have been observed at blood alcohol levels much lower than 0.10 percent. Although problem drinking often originates outside of work, workplace norms can contribute to alcohol abuse.

Drug abuse refers to the excessive use of regulated drugs. More people use marijuana than other regulated drugs. There are fewer marijuana users than alcohol or tobacco users. Regulated drugs are classified as sedatives and narcotics, stimulants, or hallucinogens. These drugs have different effects on the user. Abuse can cause very negative effects. Drug testing programs usually involve urinalysis, which may not always be accurate. Urinalysis is not as good in detecting alcohol as the breathalyzer. Urinalysis results can be affected by cross-reactive medications. Random drug testing is often resisted by employees.

Domesticated drugs are those that have society's approval. Many people are addicted to caffeine, although the health result may be minor, and work performance is not harmed. Nicotine use may improve work performance. However, because it increases the person's risk of illness, smoking is an employee health problem that can generate high costs for the employer.

PERSPECTIVES ON INTERVENTION

The workplace is an appropriate setting for intervening in the development of employee problems. Although not all employee problems originate from poor working conditions, work-site programs can help both those that do and those that do not.

In the past, a *restorative* approach was taken in dealing with problems of mental health, just as it was in dealing with physical illness. That is, nothing was done until a person became ill, at which time treatment was given to restore normal health. A different way to intervene is to take the public health approach, in which prevention is the point.

In the public health perspective, prevention is interpreted rather broadly. The aim of **primary prevention** is to take the first basic steps and remove unhealthy conditions in order to prevent disease and promote health. This can be accomplished through activities that are either physical, psychosocial, or sociocultural in nature. For example, physical primary prevention might include exercise and health education programs focused on avoiding stress-related disorders. Psychosocial primary prevention might involve helping employees learn to recognize the hazardous conditions they are likely to encounter on the job. Sociocultural primary prevention considers the community of which employees are a part. For example, workplace activities might be developed that encourage the growth of supportive groups within the organization. In **secondary prevention,** emphasis is on early treatment. Detecting illness and other signs of developing problems, and then getting help for those affected are secondary prevention efforts. At this level of intervention, organizations need to obtain information about (1) high-risk groups, (2) hazardous conditions that are likely to harm the employee's well-being, and (3) treatment resources that are available.

Work-site activities and interventions can be developed to accomplish both primary and secondary prevention. An organization should begin by asking whether work conditions are the source of employee health problems. In this chapter and in chapter 13, I want to emphasize that this is a necessary step. Whether problems are physical, psychological, or behavioral in nature, a good intervention program begins by removing hazards and modifying stressful work. Secondary prevention involves training people to recognize employee problems and to do something about them. If supervisors are trained to notice aversive conditions and to recognize signs of problems in employee performance, they can become intermediaries in the prevention process. Some work-site interventions are designed to help the employee work more effectively with conditions that are not easily modified. These interventions include training to change attitudes, reduce anxiety, and break habits, such as smoking. Referral programs that integrate community resources with those of the organization can be developed to address other problems, such as alcoholism.

PREVENTING INJURIES AND ILLNESSES

The **Occupational Safety and Health Act** was passed in 1970 to ensure safe and healthful conditions for people at work. A new federal agency was formed at the same time, the **Occupational Safety and Health Administration (OSHA).** OSHA is supposed to make sure that employers maintain a safe workplace, as provided by the Occupational Safety and Health Act. OSHA does this by requiring that employers monitor their own establishments and report any accident or work-related illness that involves lost work time. In response to reports and complaints of hazards, OSHA also conducts work-site inspections and may require an employer to modify conditions that appear hazardous. The act covers job-related illnesses, as well as accidents, although OSHA's emphasis has been largely on accidents. An exception is the recent emphasis on AIDS and other infectious diseases. OSHA has proposed a set of standards for protecting health care workers from exposure to infectious diseases (SKRSC, 1989).

OSHA regulates the use of some hazardous substances, although at present, standards have not been developed to control all the problems I mentioned. One OSHA requirement is that employees be informed about the dangers of substances they encounter on their jobs. Hazardous chemicals need to be identified and their physical risks determined. Employees must be given information about safe use of a substance, and they need protective clothing and equipment (SKRSC, 1990).

Most full-time employees are covered by **Worker's Compensation** insurance, which provides benefits to employees injured in work accidents. Benefits are provided also when workers develop health problems from exposure to toxic substances on the job. In some cases, employees may be compensated for psychological as well as for physical problems. Although Worker's Compensation regulations

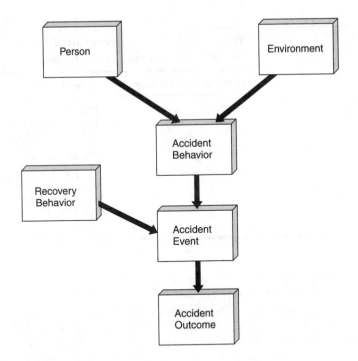

Figure 14.2 *The accident sequence. The accident process begins when a person behaves unsafely in the presence of an environmental hazard.*

previously required that both the illness and its cause be physical in nature, more recent evaluations indicate that this is no longer the case. Worker's Compensation review boards are accepting stress claims if the stress disorder can be shown to have been caused by work (Schachter et al., 1988).

Interventions to Reduce Workplace Hazards

Research has shown that accidents occur when a person behaves unsafely in the presence of an environmental hazard (see figure 14.2). If accidents are viewed in this way—as based on an interaction—then it should be possible to intervene in accident development by changing either the hazard or the human. In fact, although it might be better to change both, most safety programs emphasize one or the other. (Table 14.4 lists examples.) In this section, I discuss ways to control hazards. In the next section, I review some efforts made to encourage safe behavior.

Interventions meant to reduce the danger of the workplace fall into three general categories. First, action can be taken to remove existing hazards. Sometimes, however, this is not possible. Instead, safety measures are developed to alert workers to hazards or to protect workers from them.

Hazardous Conditions

Hazards are conditions that interact with human behavior in an unfavorable way. Any aspect of work that interferes with or disrupts effective work behavior is considered a hazard. Hazards can include dangerous equipment and work demands, and even certain aspects of the physical work setting, such as lighting. Poor lighting

Table 14.4

Interventions to Prevent or Reduce Accidental Injuries and Illnesses

Direction of Change	Intervention
Person	Improve job skills
	Improve safety knowledge
	Change antisafety attitudes
	Correct sensory deficits
	Provide rest pauses
Environment	Improve warning signals
	Provide protective gear
	Improve lighting
	Install machine guards
	Improve job design

produces a temporary deficiency in vision and permits other hazards to be hidden. Jobs differ in the extent to which they include hazards and objective risks. A job's risk level is a predictor of accidents in that people in more hazardous jobs have more accidents (Hansen, 1989). What kinds of jobs are objectively risky? Certainly, work activities that involve the use of power tools and vehicles or make excessive demands on someone's physical capacity are hazardous. Some of these hazards can be removed by adding guards and other safety devices, by exchanging dangerous tools for safer ones, or by redesigning hazardous equipment. For example, in an effort to reduce the musculoskeletal stress that mail carriers experience, alternate mailbags were designed that redistributed the mailbag weight. Experimental testing of the new designs showed that the alternate mailbags produced less fatigue (Bloswick et al., 1994).

Warning Signs and Signals

With many safety efforts, we try to prevent accidents and occupational illness by providing warning signals. Warning signs are posted in buildings wherever there is potential danger. "Watch Your Step," "Caution–Door Opens Out," and "Wet Floor" are familiar examples.

The effectiveness of warning signals first depends on their being noticed. Do people pay attention to signs they see at work? They may not. Part of the problem is that warnings are not always effectively designed and placed. Cunitz (1981) described two criteria for designing warnings. One, the message should identify the nature and severity of the hazard. It also should tell people what they should do and not do. Two, the signal should capture people's attention. It should be located in the right place. When posting instructions for operating a machine, it is best to list the safety instructions first, before the operating procedures (Wogalter et al., 1987). In addition, effective messages must be delivered through an attention-getting sensory mode. A series of lab and field experiments showed that voice warnings are superior to printed hazard signs (Wogalter & Young, 1991). Auditory signals have an imperative quality that make them good attention-getters. For this reason, alarm bells and sirens are noticeable even in noisy workplaces.

Personal Protection

Sometimes, the only thing that can be done about an adverse environmental state is to protect the worker. Safety clothing and other protective devices are meant to reduce accidents and illnesses by shielding the worker from existing hazards. They include safety glasses and face shields, hardhats, safety shoes, and gloves. Devices for hearing protection are available, including earplugs, earcaps, and helmets. These vary in their ability to protect against intense noise and in their acceptability to workers who must wear them. Hearing protectors may be unacceptable to a worker because they impair the person's ability to locate sounds in the environment (Mershon & Lin, 1987).

Because of the number of lung diseases that can result from airborne toxins, it is important to provide respiratory protection for employees who work with substances of suspected risk. Adequate respiratory protection may be provided with air-purifying devices, which filter out pollutants. These include disposable dust masks that filter out comparatively large particles, such as from paint and welding solder. Other devices include face masks with attached filtering chambers. The chambers contain purifying granular material. When air-purifying devices cannot reduce the contaminant to a safe level or when the atmosphere is oxygen deficient, a separate air system must be used. Atmosphere-supplying respirators are available for this. The user carries the air supply in a tank on his or her back with a breathing tube connecting the tank to a full-face mask (Asfahl, 1984).

Interventions to Modify Unsafe Behavior

Safety programs can be aimed at modifying the human element. Sometimes, it seems easier to get a person to change than to do something about hazardous conditions. Such safety programs generally are meant to increase a person's knowledge of safety and motivation to behave safely.

Effective work procedures are safe work procedures. Safety precautions included as a routine part of the job are more likely to be practiced in all circumstances than safety measures tacked on as an afterthought. Maier and Verser (1982) provided an example. Because electricians sometimes must do wiring with the power off and sometimes with the power on, they should be trained to perform their jobs using procedures appropriate for *live* wires. Then, if they fail to turn off the power in cases in which they meant to, it will not matter because the procedure they learned is safe for either circumstance.

Motivational Interventions

Some safety efforts are meant to motivate safe work behavior or to modify an attitude about danger. Sometimes, they are directed toward increasing worker acceptance and use of personal protection.

Workers may resist using equipment provided for their own protection. A protective device may not be comfortable to wear and may actually interfere with performing the job. However, even with reasonably comfortable equipment that does not adversely affect performance, workers may resist. This resistance is thought to stem from aspects of social interaction and attitudes, such as being concerned about what others think. Both social influence and personal convenience can affect the use of safety equipment. Subjects doing a chemical laboratory task used instructions that included a directive to wear a safety mask and gloves. They were more likely to comply when the protection was close at hand and when the work partner also used the equipment (Wogalter, Allison, & McKenna, 1989).

Whenever protective devices are needed, training on their use should be made an integral part of job training. In addition, special incentives for using them need to be offered. For example, in a program designed to increase the use of eye protection among shipyard workers, supervisors were trained to give social reinforcement to workers who used the protective device (Smith, Anger, & Uslan, 1978). In another incentive program for encouraging personal protection, workers in a textile mill were given tangible rewards for wearing earplugs.[5] Prior to the intervention, only about a third of the workers were using the protection. After two months in the program, 90 percent of the employees were using earplugs while they worked (Zohar & Fussfeld, 1981).

Some programs have been devised to include employees in discussing and setting goals for safety. These motivational programs have had positive effects on accident rates. In one manufacturing company, employees participated in identifying the critical safety behaviors of their jobs and in setting goals for safety improvement. An overall reduction of the plant's accident rate resulted (Cooper et al., 1994). In other programs, small groups are used to modify unsafe behavior. As discussed in chapter 6, employee training may require that an interfering attitude about the subject matter be changed first. Attitudes about safe behavior provide a good example of this need. An effective way to change attitudes is through group discussion and goal setting with individual commitment and group follow-up. A safety program designed for pizza deliverers used the group method and increased safe driving practices. Employees met in small groups, in which they talked about seat belt use and other driving habits. In addition, they received feedback on their behavior, and they made personal commitments to improve in specific ways (Ludwig & Geller, 1991). Clearly, workers can do something about accident and illness reduction. Worker participation programs suggest that we might need to ask them.

*M*ain *P*oints

OSHA is a federal agency that oversees workplace compliance with health and safety law. This law is meant to protect workers from hazards and toxic conditions. Worker's Compensation provides benefits for workers who are injured or made ill at work.

Some workplace safety interventions are meant to remove or modify dangerous equipment and hazardous conditions of the work setting. Other interventions are made when hazards are difficult to remove. Posting warning signs and providing signals to alert workers to hazards is one way. Auditory signals are good for getting workers' attention. Providing personal protection, such as masks and earplugs, is another way to make workers safer while they work among hazards.

Workplace interventions also can be oriented toward modifying the unsafe behavior of workers. Some programs use group methods to motivate safety and change risky attitudes. Such methods can be used to decrease worker resistance to using personal protection while on the job. They also can be used to get people to set goals and commit themselves to behaving more safely.

---

[5]Textile mill machinery is noisy enough to cause hearing loss.

Section IV: Solving the Human Problems of Work

Sally Forth By Greg Howard & Craig MacIntosh

INTERVENTIONS FOR IMPROVING PERSONAL CONTROL

Employee health problems can be understood as reflecting the specific difficulties we have in coping with daily life. In one theoretical view, handling life's challenges requires two personal responses: coping and resting. (Stoyva & Anderson, 1982). In the coping phase, an individual actively works to resolve a problem. In the resting phase, the person stops to relax. Both behaviors are necessary, although we can expect people to differ in their abilities to perform them. For some people, the major problem is an inability to cope effectively. They need to learn better ways to meet challenges. The anxiety-prone individual who engages in avoidance behavior is one such person. Others are deficient in knowing how to relax and rest. This may describe the Type A person who always seems to be busy. Many of the techniques that are used in work-site programs are meant to assist distressed employees in learning to relax more effectively. These techniques include relaxation training and physical exercise. Techniques for developing coping skills, such as anxiety management training, are sometimes available to employees.

Handling Anxiety and Depression

The primary need of individuals with severe anxiety or depression is for improved coping skills. Because many anxieties are overreactions to ordinary events, treatment should help the person learn to distinguish between serious and minor threats. Also, the person may need to unlearn maladaptive avoidance responses and learn more effective actions.

     Systematic desensitization is a useful psychological intervention. It is best for helping people unlearn avoidance behavior when a problem involves an identifiable anxiety arousing stimulus. This behavioral technique is based on the idea that fears are learned responses to objects and events, and contradictory responses can be used to inhibit these reactions (Wolpe, 1969). Systematic desensitization is a procedure that combines relaxation and counterconditioning to accomplish such change. First, the individual is thoroughly trained in a relaxation technique. Second, stimuli that bring on anxiety are identified and ordered in a hierarchy from mildly to extremely arousing. Then, the client and the therapist go over the hierarchy one item at a time, while the person practices relaxation (Deffenbacher & Suinn, 1988).

Several **cognitive behavioral interventions** are used to help in developing coping skills. Social problem-solving training has been used to treat people with depression. The purpose of the technique is to help the individual learn more effective ways to handle social stressors. Training begins with activities to encourage a positive attitude toward solving interaction problems. Then a number of cognitive skills, such as defining problems, generating alternate solutions, making decisions, and implementing solutions, are practiced (Nezu & Perri, 1989). Rational restructuring is another cognitive behavioral intervention. It is used to strengthen a person's ability to assess situations accurately. When something is labeled as threatening, although objectively it is not, then a reasonable way to intervene is to help the person change the *labeling* process. Those who suffer from anxiety are likely to misinterpret benign conditions, and rational restructuring is designed to help them (Goldfried, 1988).

Relaxation Training

Most work-site health intervention programs include **relaxation training** for reducing tension (Ivancevich & Matteson, 1986). Various physical and mental strategies to change an individual's response to stressful conditions are used in relaxation training. These strategies include biofeedback, meditation, and progressive relaxation. With all of these techniques, the idea is to learn how to relax at will. Relaxation training is most helpful to people who have tension headaches, insomnia, and chronic anxiety (cf. Stoyva & Anderson, 1982). These techniques also may help to reduce coronary risk factors, such as high blood pressure (Patel et al., 1985).

In some relaxation training, precise instruction is given on how to reach the proper mental state. **Biofeedback,** however, involves little from a trainer. Electronic equipment is used to monitor internal processes and to feed back this information to trainees in order for them to learn how to control their reactions. Any of several physiological processes can be monitored, such as heart rate, blood pressure, and brainwave patterns. Stress-related psychosomatic disturbances, such as migraine headaches, can be reduced with biofeedback training. Blood pressure can be lowered as well (Patel et al., 1985). Biofeedback is probably best used in an integrated program that includes verbal relaxation training, because not all people are able to learn through this method. Verbal methods are richer in terms of instructing trainees on how to initiate the relaxation response.

Progressive relaxation is the most frequently used of the verbal methods. Training begins with the construction of a relaxation image. The image comes from a real moment in a person's life that he or she remembers as being very calm and relaxed. The second step is instruction in deep muscle relaxation. The individual learns how to focus mentally on muscle groups and to contract and relax them alternately. The third step is to develop an association between the relaxation image and the physical relaxation. The individual learns how to use the image to invoke the relaxation response. Practice continues until complete relaxation can be achieved with the relaxation image alone (Deffenbacher & Suinn, 1988).

Type A Intervention

In earlier discussions of how to change Type A behavior, Friedman and Rosenman (1974) suggested that the Type A person stop making "things to do" lists and remove the clock from the workplace. These actions might help prevent the feeling of being behind schedule. By themselves, however, such procedures may not be very useful in modifying Type A behavior. For one thing, Type A behavior has been strongly reinforced in the past; therefore, the person is likely to see his or her responses as the *only* way to be (Suinn, 1978). However, some researchers believe that Type A people have difficulty both with coping and with the recovery process (Cameron & Meichenbaum, 1982; Suinn, 1978). Therefore, the Type A person might benefit from interventions that combine coping skills training with relaxation. **Anxiety management training** is one such procedure. A person is trained to pay attention to internal indicators of anxiety arousal and to react to these by initiating a *relaxation* response instead of the usual anxious response. In this sense, relaxation is used as an active way to cope with anxiety. Some have had success in using anxiety management training to change the physiological correlates of Type A behavior (Suinn & Bloom, 1978), especially if the method is combined with a cognitive behavioral intervention (Kelly & Stone, 1987).

Health Promotion Programs

Some programs are not oriented toward identifying employees with specific problems but are more generally aimed at increasing health and wellness. The goals of **health promotion programs (HPPs)** are to enhance employee health and indirectly contribute to the organization's mission. Health promotion programs focus most strongly on primary prevention. Many companies have programs that include exercise and fitness, nutrition and weight control, drug and alcohol abuse prevention, stress management, and smoking cessation (Sonnenstuhl, 1988).

The purpose of biofeedback and progressive relaxation training procedures is to improve the person's physiological state by using *mental* strategies. With physical exercise, the idea is to accomplish this change with *physical* strategies. As discussed in chapter 13, some employers have developed physical fitness programs for employees because they believe that fitness reduces stress. Can gross physical activity, such as exercising, improve psychological health? Some believe that it can. Falkenberg (1987) concluded from a review of the research that the effects of exercise on anxiety and depression depend on the type of exercise and the length of time the person has been doing it. Long-term, vigorous exercise, such as jogging, is associated with reduced anxiety and depression (see also, Dishman, 1982). Of course, the hard part is getting those of us who need it most to do the physical exercise. Harrison & Liska (1994) investigated the reasons people give for not exercising. They found that employees who are at risk for health problems, such as those who are overweight or smoke, are most likely to perceive work- and family-related barriers to participation in fitness programs, such as long work hours and family responsibilities. This suggests that employers may need to remove some barriers if they want high-risk employees to benefit from fitness programs.

Smoking Cessation

Because of the proliferation of information on the health effects of smoking, many people have been motivated to quit. Because nicotine is addictive, however, this is not easily done. Some smokers get help from smoking cessation programs at work. Such programs may address the person's motivation to quit smoking. It appears that those who have intrinsic reasons for quitting, such as concerns about health and self-control, are more likely to be successful than those with extrinsic reasons (Curry, Wagner, & Grothaus, 1990).

Procedures used to help smokers quit are concerned primarily with getting them through the withdrawal period. Withdrawal can bring about irritability, anxiety, mood swings, low stress tolerance, and craving for tobacco (Fagerstrom, 1983; Sommese & Patterson, 1995). Typically, work-site programs include persuasive materials designed to change the person's attitude about tobacco and to develop intrinsic motivation for quitting. There usually are discussion and goal-setting meetings, self-monitoring, and social support resources. In group meetings, commitments to reduce nicotine intake and dates for complete abstention are set. Evidence indicates that these programs can help employees quit smoking (Malott et al., 1984).

Smoking cessation programs need to give more attention to the problem of relapse, because it is the rule rather than the exception. Smokers who have quit with the help of a smoking cessation program have been shown to have a 50 to 75 percent chance of starting again within a year (Krantz, Grunberg, & Baum, 1985). Of course, it may be that program participants are those who are more addicted to nicotine and have the hardest time stopping. However, even those who quit on their own have some probability of relapse. Relapse is a major problem in the treatment of other drug addictions as well. The graph in figure 14.3 shows that individuals who stop using alcohol and heroin have relapse characteristics similar to those of smokers (Hunt, Barnett, & Ranch, 1971). Drug abuse interventions, including smoking cessation, should be oriented toward building coping skill and self-efficacy in order to avoid relapse. Withdrawal from an addiction requires self-management skills, especially when the person is exposed to situations in which the substance would ordinarily be used. If these skills are not well developed and if the person lacks confidence, then relapse can be expected (Marlatt, 1985).

Employee Assistance Programs

Sooner or later most supervisors have to deal with a subordinate whose physical or psychological problems affect his or her work. Discharging the employee may not be a good solution because the person may be someone—such as a senior or high-level employee—in whom the company has a great deal invested. Usually, the supervisor tries to counsel the employee. However, this probably will not be effective for a number of reasons. One, the employee may have a serious problem and need professional help. Two, the supervisor is probably not skilled in counseling. Three, the supervisor's time and energy is taken away from his or her own work responsibilities (Roman, Blum, & Bennett, 1987).

Some employee health programs are meant mainly to take over the supervisor's counseling role. These programs vary in terms of how much treatment is

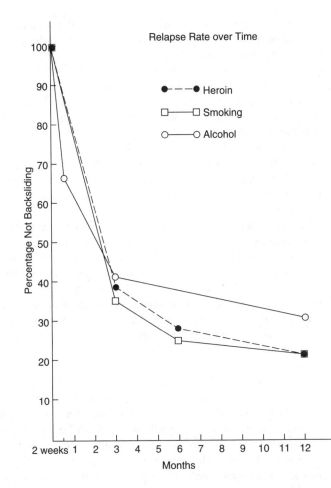

Relapse Rate over Time

● – –● Heroin
□———□ Smoking
○———○ Alcohol

Percentage Not Backsliding

2 weeks 1 2 3 4 5 6 7 8 9 10 11 12

Months

Figure 14.3 *Relapse rates after treatment for drug dependence. Notice that individuals who quit using heroin, alcohol, and tobacco have similar relapse characteristics.*

From W.A. Hunt, L.W. Barnett, and L.G. Ranch, "Relapse Rates in Addiction Programs," in Journal of Clinical Psychology, 27. Copyright © 1971 by Clinical Psychology Publishing Co., Inc., Brandon, VT 05733. Reprinted by permission.

given at the work site. Some organizations employ counselors to do this work. Other organizations depend on **referral programs** in which employees are sent to community agencies, such as hospitals, clinics, and mental health care centers.

The foundation of the modern approach to employee health is found in the counseling programs of the 1940s, which specifically addressed the problem of alcoholic employees. The main thrust of the alcoholism program was to help supervisors recognize problem drinkers among their subordinates and get them to join Alcoholics Anonymous (AA). Supervisors were trained to use **constructive confrontation,** a disciplinary strategy by which employees are motivated to do something about their own problems (Trice & Beyer, 1984; Sonnenstuhl, 1988).

Employee assistance programs (EAPs) include primary as well as secondary prevention, although their main purpose is to intervene in the performance deterioration that occurs because of employee problems. It is reasonable for an employer to expect quality performance from workers and demand that behavior impairing this performance be changed. In the early alcoholism programs, threat of job loss was considered an important impetus to behavioral change, and it still is. The manager of one EAP was quoted as saying, "I've seen marriages go, yachts go and gold club memberships go, but when it comes to the paycheck, it's an important motivator" (Kasabian, 1983).

A key feature of the modern EAP is the use of job performance criteria in identifying troubled employees. Supervisors are trained to play a detection and referral role. They do not attempt to diagnose an employee's problem. Rather, they are instructed to approach problems solely in terms of performance deficiencies. The kinds of behavior that supervisors believe to indicate performance problems include decreased productivity, apathetic or irritable behavior, and absenteeism (Bayer & Gerstein, 1990). If there are no signs of a performance deficiency, then a personal problem is not a concern of the employer. However, defining a problem as a *performance* problem gives the supervisor an appropriate basis for motivating the employee to change.

The EAP often endorses the supervisor's use of constructive confrontation in motivating the employee to improve his or her work performance. Currently in constructive confrontation, the supervisor presents an employee with evidence of the performance deficiency, advises the person of the consequences of continued poor performance, and offers to refer him or her to the EAP to get help with any personal problem that may be causing the performance decrement (Roman et al., 1987). Some clinical psychologists, however, believe that constructive confrontation is unnecessarily punitive and that it is difficult for supervisors to use (Sonnenstuhl, 1988).

EAP Structure

Employees with a range of problems including alcohol and drug abuse, work stress, marital and family difficulties, and legal and financial troubles are referred by supervisors or may approach the EAP on their own. Some of the most common problems among employees are marital and family difficulties. Employee assistance programs attempt to help by providing **family counseling** at the workplace or, by referral, obtaining help from private therapists, university programs that train counselors, community mental health agencies, or religious organizations (Trice & Beyer, 1984).

EAPs are structured so as to provide both primary and secondary prevention. They make assessments of at-risk populations, help supervisors identify troubled employees, counsel and refer employees to appropriate outside treatment, and monitor employee progress. Table 14.5 summarizes what is needed in developing an EAP. First, the purpose of the program should be defined, and both labor and management support for it should be established. Second, procedures for conducting the EAP need to be specified, including ways to maintain confidentiality, manage work-site programs, make referrals, and monitor employee progress. Third, an EAP should be staffed so as to link the organization effectively with economical outside services. Some clinical knowledge will be helpful to the EAP staff in evaluating community resources, although knowledge of the needs and constraints of the workplace may be an even more important consideration (Roman et al., 1987). Fourth, the program must be publicized. Training supervisors in how to use an EAP specialist for advice and help, and promoting positive attitudes about EAP referral are part of this effort (Trice & Beyer, 1984). Employees need to know about the resources of the EAP. EAPs are designed to encourage voluntary self-referrals,

_T_able 14.5	The Structure of an Employee Assistance Program

Structural Component	Developmental Activities
EAP statement of policy	Determine rationale and orientation of program
	Establish commitment of management and labor
Specific operating procedures	Determine procedures for
	Maintenance of confidentiality
	Acceptance of cases: self- or supervisor-referral
	Management of work-site interventions
	Referrals to outside sources
	Follow-up of cases
Staffing and location	Determine necessary expertise of program staff
	Establish program location to maintain confidentiality
	Identify outside referral sources
	Determine availability of health insurance benefits
Promotion of program	Construct plans for publicity
	Instruct supervisors and employees in program use
	Plan strategies for evaluating treatment services

yet many employees are unaware of the EAP where they work or do not know what it offers (Steele & Hubbard, 1985). To be successful in attracting the voluntary participation of employees who need its help, an EAP must be publicly supported by top management. One study showed that employees' confidence in their EAP, which determined their willingness to use it, depended on their belief that management was supportive of the program (Milne, Blum, & Roman, 1994).

Alcoholism Treatment

Reduction of alcohol abuse continues to be an important feature of employee assistance programs. Treatment begins when a supervisor recognizes the signs of alcohol abuse in an employee's work behavior and refers him or her to the EAP. Help for the alcohol abuser is available through inpatient and outpatient treatment programs and through such self-help groups as Alcoholics Anonymous. These are not workplace interventions. However, the organization can obtain such treatment for alcoholic employees from community service agencies. Treatment of severe alcoholism involves crisis intervention and detoxification; medical and psychiatric inpatient care; outpatient counseling; and postrecovery care (Renner, 1976).

Psychosocial and behavioral treatment techniques are used with individuals and groups on an outpatient basis. Individual treatment of alcoholism includes techniques developed for treating anxiety disorders, such as relaxation training and systematic desensitization. These techniques appear to be most appropriate for drinkers who show high levels of tension and anxiety (Litman, 1976). Some alcoholic treatment is based on behavior modification theory. In this, emphasis is on changing the behavior itself, rather than on any supposed source of the problem. Intervention involves interfering with the reinforcement of drinking by giving reinforcement for other less harmful behaviors. Controlled drinking becomes a possibility with behavior modification because an individual learns to distinguish appropriate from inappropriate occasions for drinking and develops strategies for limiting consumption

Table 14.6　　　　The Twelve Steps of AA

1.　We admitted we were powerless over alcohol–that our lives had become unmanageable.

2.　We came to believe that a Power greater than ourselves could restore us to sanity.

3.　We made a decision to turn our will and our lives over to the care of God as we understood him.

4.　We made a searching and fearless moral inventory of ourselves.

5.　We admitted to God, to ourselves, and to another human being the exact nature of our wrongs.

6.　We were entirely ready to have God remove all of these defects of character.

7.　We humbly asked Him to remove our shortcomings.

8.　We made a list of all persons we had harmed and became willing to make amends to them all.

9.　We directed amends to such people wherever possible, except when to do so would injure them or others.

10.　We continued to take personal inventory and when we were wrong, promptly admitted it.

11.　We sought through prayer and meditation to improve our conscious contact with God, as we understood Him, praying only for knowledge of His Will for us and the power to carry that out.

12.　Having had a spiritual awakening as the result of these steps we tried to carry this message to alcoholics and practice these principles in all our affairs.

The Twelve Steps are reprinted with permission of Alcoholic Anonymous World Services, Inc. Permission to reprint this material does not mean that AA has reviewed or approved the contents of this publication, nor that AA agrees with the views expressed herein. AA is a program of recovery from alcoholism–use of the Twelve Steps in connection with programs and activities which are patterned after AA, but which address other problems, does not imply otherwise.

(Baekland, Lundwall, & Kissin, 1975). For individuals whose alcohol problem is not yet severe, controlled drinking is a good outcome (Rosenberg, 1993). In fact, for some, controlled drinking may be a better goal than total abstinence. Total abstinence is difficult and is likely to result in treatment dropout (Litman, 1976).

Alcoholics Anonymous is a well-known self-help organization for alcoholic rehabilitation. An informal group therapy approach with strong religious overtones is the foundation of AA. Table 14.6 lists the twelve-step program. The aim of AA is total abstinence. However, the emphasis of the program is on remaining sober one day at a time, and member assistance is available 24 hours a day in reaching this goal. AA is thought most likely to help middle-class people who are guilt prone, externally oriented, and sociable (Baekland et al., 1975).

Main
Points

To handle anxiety and depression, the individual may need to have better coping skills and techniques for relaxing. Systematic desensitization is used to help control anxiety. Cognitive behavior interventions, such as social problem solving and rational restructuring, can help a person learn to cope with social stressors and assess threats. Relaxation techniques include biofeedback training and progressive relaxation. Type A intervention may include both coping skills and relaxation training methods.

Health promotion programs are not for treatment. They are for enhancing employee health. They may include exercise or physical fitness and smoking cessation. A weakness in fitness programs is that they may not encourage employ-

Section IV: Solving the Human Problems of Work

ees who most need the training. Work-site smoking cessation programs can assist employees through withdrawal, but relapse is a problem.

Employee assistance programs help employees with various problems. Counseling may be available at the work site or, through referral, from community sources. Employees may volunteer for treatment or be referred by supervisors. Supervisors may use constructive confrontation to motivate an employee to get help. EAPs traditionally have helped alcoholics. Treatment is through referral to outside resources, such as medical clinics or Alcoholics Anonymous. Behavior modification can be used to accomplish controlled drinking.

CHAPTER SUMMARY

This chapter has two parts. First, the discussion of employee health is concluded, and second, interventions used to help employees with health problems are described.

Anxiety and depression are factors in many employee health problems including work-related stress. These psychological disorders affect work performance and may require action on the part of an employer. Anxious or depressed employees can be offered special training to help them learn how to cope and control the sources of their difficulties.

Working conditions contribute to some employee health problems. Work accidents result in injuries. A number of occupational diseases develop from toxic chemicals and hazardous particles, such as asbestos, used in the workplace. Some industries, such as agriculture, transportation, and manufacturing have comparatively high rates of accidental injury and occupational illness. Performance of some jobs lead to musculoskeletal distress.

Abuse of alcohol and drugs create other employee health problems. Even if a substance is not used at work, its effects can carry over to the workplace. Drug and alcohol use, at levels lower than intoxication, have adverse effects on work performance. Organizations have launched drug testing programs to determine the extent of substance abuse among their employees. The use of domesticated drugs, such as nicotine, can incur costs to the employer, as well as the individual.

Organizations attempt to remedy employee health problems by means of primary and secondary preventive measures. In compliance with federal law on workplace health and safety, some interventions are directed toward reducing accidental injury and occupational illness. Safety programs include hazard removal, and the provision of warning signals and personal protection. Other safety programs attempt to modify human behavior by increasing safety knowledge and/or improving motivation. Safety programs have been based on attitude change strategies, including worker participation in small groups. Health promotion programs are meant to improve the general health of employees and include activities through which employees can increase their physical fitness and break unhealthy habits. The employee assistance program is an effort to intervene in the development of a range of physical and psychological health problems. An EAP staff can provide assistance or can refer employees to outside resources. Alcoholism treatment typically is provided.

STUDY QUESTIONS

1) How do anxiety and depression affect work performance and employee behavior?

2) How dangerous is the workplace in comparison to other accident sites? What are some hazardous industries, and why would you say they are dangerous?

3) What is an occupational disease, and what kinds of substances or conditions cause such diseases?

4) Is repetition trauma disorder an injury or an illness?

5) What are the effects of alcohol use on work behavior? When is alcohol use likely to get out of hand? What work-related variables can affect alcohol use by employees?

6) What kinds of drugs do employees use? How is drug use at work detected, and what are the problems in detection?

7) Is the use of domesticated drugs harmful? Should we be concerned about employees who use these drugs at work?

8) Distinguish between primary and secondary prevention.

9) What does OSHA do? What is the purpose of Worker's Compensation?

10) What kinds of hazards can be found in the workplace? What can you do to reduce the chance of accidents and illness in the workplace if you cannot remove the hazards?

11) Identify some interventions that help employees control anxiety and relieve depression. What procedures might be helpful to the Type A person?

12) What is the purpose of the health promotion program? Do physical fitness programs help? What kinds of difficulties do work-site smoking cessation programs face?

13) What is an EAP and how is one structured? What kinds of services do EAPs provide? What is constructive confrontation?

14) What kind of help is available for alcohol abusers?

CONSIDER THIS

CASE STUDY

A situation exists at Vocational Rehabilitation Services (VRS)[6] that may be an employee health problem. Employees in the Counseling Department reported the situation to the VRS director.

The issue is smoking on the premises. About one-third of the employees and clients smoke. VRS has no policy on smoking, and people have been smoking freely at work. However, some nonsmokers have complained about working with smokers. Illness symptoms due to second-hand smoke have been reported. Also, some employees and clients have talked about the danger of smoking in the workshop where chemicals are sometimes used.

The counselors who brought the issue to the attention of the director suggested that VRS initiate a smoking ban. Smokers would be allowed to smoke only outside the building during their scheduled breaks. The ban would apply to employees and clients alike.

The counselors pointed out that most employees and clients would not resist such a ban because most do not smoke, and many would welcome it. Some smokers would dislike and might even resist the smoking ban. However, the counselors described evidence from a recent study of a work-site smoking ban[7] which showed that smokers do sometimes accept a ban. VRS smokers would need to have a lot of information about the smoking ban. They would need to know that it affected everyone and that there were very good reasons for it. They would need to be assured that VRS was concerned about the smokers and the inconvenience of the ban for them.

The counselors suggested that this kind of information be used in developing material for announcing the smoking ban and getting acceptance from the smokers. They offered to develop the material for the director to use in announcing the ban. They would identify health reasons for the ban and suggest ways for the director to show that VRS knows how hard it is for smokers to work without smoking.

Problem

The director must decide what to do. He can deny the request for a smoking ban. If so, he will need another way to address the nonsmokers' concerns, or he can institute a smoking ban. He can adopt the counselors' suggested method of announcing and promoting the smoking ban, or he can come up with something else. He is concerned about the distress a ban will cause employees and clients who smoke. What should he do?

---

[6]There is more information about VRS in the cases described in other chapters.

[7]The study is fully described in Greenberg, J. (1994). Using socially fair treatment to promote acceptance of a work site smoking ban. *Journal of Applied Psychology, 79*, 288–297.

Suppose you want to start up a business. Where do you begin? Of course, you have to know what product or service you will offer. You also need to figure out what work is involved in producing that product or service. Then you have to decide if you will employ someone to do the work and whether they will need any equipment. Of course, if you do hire people, you will need to have a place for them to work, and you'll have to tell them when to come to work and how long to stay.

This chapter is about designing all these aspects of work. First, you will learn about time schedules. Next, you will discover how to set up a workspace. Then, you will learn about designing work systems that use either ordinary tools or very sophisticated machines, such as computers and robots.

Clerical employees do most of the computer work in the modern organization. Although managers are often enthusiastic about computerization of the office, they use computers least.

$$C\ h\ a\ p\ t\ e\ r\ \mathit{15}$$

Contents

*Designing the
Work
Environment*

Finally someone said we were going on the floor, and we descended from the sixteenth floor to the first. We were in groups of six by then, all following Miss Cooper doggedly. . . . Miss Cooper said I had to work on the special sale counter, and showed me a little book called *The Stage-Struck Seal*, which it seemed I would be selling. I had gotten about halfway through it before she came back to tell me I had to stay with my unit.

I enjoyed meeting the time clock, and spent a pleasant half-hour punching various cards standing around, and then someone came in and said I couldn't punch the clock with my hat on. So I had to leave, . . . and I went and found out my locker number, which was 1773, and my time-clock number, which was 712, and my cash-box number, which was 1336, and. . . . And that was my first day.

My second day was better. I was officially on the floor. I stood in a corner of a counter, with one hand on *The Stage Struck Seal,* waiting for customers.

Shirley Jackson

In this short story, Jackson tells of her experience as a temporary sales clerk at a department store during one holiday season. In describing these two days of employment, she draws attention to some important aspects of how work is designed. Work requires time, space, and tools as well as a person. The typical organization is comprised of multiple work groups using equipment in a work space on a time schedule. In this final chapter, I first examine the temporal and physical aspects of work, and then I discuss the design of equipment and tools for work.

ARRANGING TIME FOR WORK

Temporal working conditions include the schedule of working hours and the length of the work period. If the work period averages about eight hours a day for a five-day workweek, the employee is considered full time. If the work period is less, then the worker is part time.

Traditionally, business has taken the hopeful position that the amount of time employees spend at work equals the amount of time they actually work. Many supervisors make a great effort to get people to their workstations and to keep them there. However, an employee's mere presence does not guarantee that work is being done. There is a difference between nominal and actual working hours. *Actual hours* are those spent working. **Nominal hours** are clock hours in which the employee is physically present. Nominal hours include actual hours, breaks, and time spent in nonwork activities, such as personal chores and idling. Anecdotal evidence indicates that all employees engage in some amount of nonwork activity while on the job. It has been proposed that people adjust their actual productive hours, up or down, according to the number of hours they are present on the job. In fact, according to Parkinson's (1957) "law," work tends to expand to fill the time allowed for it. If this is true, then perhaps no more work is done in a nine-hour day than in an eight-hour day. Therefore, hiring part-time or temporary help during rush periods, such as holiday seasons, may be cost effective.

Fixed and Flexible Working Hours

The standard business schedule is 8 A.M. to 5 P.M. These are conventional starting and quitting times for many workers. A variation of this schedule is **flextime** or flexible working hours. With flextime, an employee is allowed to start and end the workday at times other than the conventional eight to five. The number of work hours remains the same, but the employee decides when the workday starts and ends. The employer determines a *core period* in which all employees must be present. Two flexible bands of time for arrival and departure also are established. For example, with a core period of 9:30 A.M. to 3:00 P.M., one band may extend from 6:30 A.M. to 9:30 A.M. and the other from 3:00 P.M. to 6:00 P.M. Employees then choose their arrival and departure times within these bands to schedule an eight-hour day.

Many employers think that flextime can benefit both the organization and the employee. A review of the research suggested that flextime does not impair performance on the job, but neither does it improve it (Dunham, Pierce, & Castaneda, 1987). Flextime does reduce absenteeism, however (Dalton & Mesch, 1990; Ronen & Primps, 1980). It is thought to help when work encroaches on employees' personal lives. Medical appointments, getting the car serviced, shopping, and attending children's school events can more easily be scheduled when there is flexibility in work hours. Commuting is easier as well. Most workers respond favorably to flextime because of this freedom (Ralston, 1989).

The Compressed Workweek

Since midcentury, we have considered the **standard workweek** to be eight hours a day, five days a week. Prior to the 1950s, however, the workweek was longer than this. Many workers put in ten to twelve hours per day, six days a week. Even now, sixty or so hours a week are not unusual for self-employed and professional people, to "moonlighters" who have two jobs, and to working women who also carry a full load of household duties.

An alternate work schedule that has become popular over the past 10 to 15 years is the **compressed workweek.** In this, employees work ten to twelve hours each day for three or four days a week. Frequently called the "4/40" (4 days/ 40 hours), the compressed workweek is thought to have advantages for both employers and employees. As far as organizational needs are concerned, the compressed workweek does not appear to be ineffective, and work performance may actually be improved (Dunham et al., 1987). The primary advantage to employees is the leisure and personal time of a three-day weekend. Employees are generally positive about the compressed workweek (Dunham et al., 1987; Pierce & Dunham, 1992). Its primary disadvantage is the long fatiguing workday. The problem is likely to depend on how long the workweek is. Workers on a 5-day 60-hour schedule showed several signs of fatigue in their performance (Rosa & Colligan, 1988).

Part-Time Work

A growing trend in business is the use of part-time employees, usually at about half time. One estimate indicates that some 19 million American workers are doing part-time work (Nardone, 1986). The service and retail trade industries, in particular, rely heavily on part-time workers. Most of us have had part-time jobs at one time. You may have one now. College students and other young workers make up a large segment of the group of part-time employees. Part-time work is also attractive to many working mothers, disabled and older workers, and retired people who want to work. In fact, surveys indicate that two-thirds of all part-time workers are women, and most male part-time workers are either under 24 or over 62 years of age (Nardone, 1986). Part-time work is attractive also to people who simply want time to pursue other interests.

Reduced work hours have potential advantages to the organization. The proportion of *actual* working hours may be increased in this way. Some jobs, such as those involving creative thinking, may be done just as efficiently on a part-time schedule as on a full-time schedule. Some sedentary data entry jobs might be improved by reduced hours because what is physiologically difficult in a long shift is not necessarily difficult in a short one. However, there are potential drawbacks to part-time employment. Work tradition favors full-time employees. In part-time jobs, employees often get lower pay and fewer fringe benefits. They also get less training and fewer opportunities for promotion (Rotchford & Roberts, 1982).

There are several different ways of arranging part-time work. The work may be temporary or permanent, seasonal or year round, the main occupation or a secondary job. On the basis of his review of the research, Feldman (1990) proposed that worker satisfaction with these arrangements depends on the needs of the person and the type of work. He believed that certain employees gravitate toward part-time jobs of a particular type. For example, flexible scheduling may be an important factor for young student workers and for working mothers, and both groups are likely to be interested in temporary part-time jobs. A later survey of part-time workers showed that married women with children were more likely than student workers to have permanent part-time jobs (Feldman & Doerpinghaus, 1992).

Shift Work

Many organizations operate beyond the standard business day, and some maintain two or three shifts for 24-hour operation. Certain services, such as hospitals, fire and police departments, and public utility companies, require 24-hour operation. Some manufacturing and transport operations are done around the clock also. The workshifts are scheduled in various ways. Because day work is scheduled for a standard eight hours, two more eight-hour shifts can be added easily. A typical three-shift schedule includes a day shift from 7 A.M. to 3 P.M., an evening shift from 3 P.M. to 11 P.M., and a night shift from 11 P.M. to 7 A.M. A variation, which includes a compressed workweek, allows two 12-hour shifts for 24-hour operation, with employees working three to four days a week (Pierce & Dunham, 1992).

The task of assigning workers to one or another of these shifts brings up the question of whether the assignment should be permanent or change periodically. In a **fixed shift** system, employees are either day workers or night workers. However, working at night produces a private life out of synchrony with the rest of the world. The night worker is sleeping when others are working. One solution to this is to use a **rotating shift** system. The rotating shift spreads the burden around because all employees work all shifts at various times. Having employees share the night work is thought at least to limit the inconvenience. Shifts can be rotated forward or backward. In **forward rotation,** workers rotate to a *later* shift, such as from an evening shift to a night shift. In **backward rotation,** they change to an earlier shift, such as from an evening shift to a day shift.

The Night Shift

Is there any reason, other than inconvenience, for limiting night work? There is some evidence that says so. Night shifts and long work hours, both of which can be expected to cause fatigue, are associated with performance problems. People who work at night tend to be less productive and to make more errors (Gannon, Norland, & Robeson, 1983). Performance decrements appear at different rates across the shift, which may reflect decreasing physiological arousal as the night progresses (Craig & Condon, 1984). Also, there are more accidents on night shifts than on day shifts, especially during the last three hours of the work period (Levin, Oler, & Whiteside, 1985). More motor vehicle accidents occur among working truck drivers on night runs. In general, accident rates are higher in the late half of the truck driver's shift than in the early half, although the relationship between fatigue and accidents is complex and may involve personal variables, such as age of the driver (Hamelin, 1987; McDonald, 1984). Sleep disturbance is common among night workers, even among those who are on permanent night shifts. Security guards, for example, were found to experience more sleep problems and depression than other workers (Alfredsson et al., 1991). The fatigue of night work appears to accumulate, and the night worker takes longer to recover on off days (Totterdell et al., 1995). However, it may be that some of these adverse effects can be avoided if the worker is given a choice in the shift assignment. Some studies have reported that night workers are no worse off than day workers when the employee freely chooses the shift. Barton (1994; Barton & Folkard, 1991) found that nurses who chose to work on fixed night shifts were *not* different from day or rotating shift workers on several measures of fatigue and health.

Rotating Shifts

Although rotating shifts are more democratic, they also have more adverse effects on workers than fixed shifts do. Workers on rotating shifts have the same kinds of difficulties that night workers generally do, but the problems are more severe among rotating shift workers (Dunham, 1977). Typically, workers have difficulty adjusting to the changes in their sleep/wake cycles (Paley & Tepas, 1994; Wolinsky, 1982). Figure 15.1 shows that the fatigue of night work on rotating shifts takes longer to overcome on rest days (Totterdell et al., 1995). Wilkinson (1992) reviewed research on shiftwork and found that permanent or slowly rotating shifts are better because workers are more capable of adapting. Fixed shifts appear to cause less stress than rotating shifts (Jamal & Baba, 1992). Workers experience less difficulty and are more favorable toward *forward* rotation, especially if shifts do not rotate too quickly (Barton & Folkard, 1993; Knauth & Kiesswetter, 1987). Choice is important, also. Shiftwork, whether fixed or rotating, is more tolerable when the individual can choose the hours of work (Barton et al., 1993).

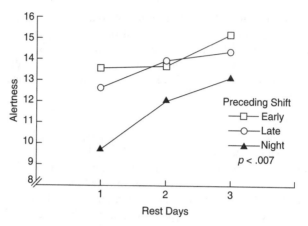

Figure 15.1 *Recovery from the effects of work on various shifts. A sample of nurses working early, late, and night shifts showed variations in the length of rest time required to recover. Measures of alertness taken during the rest period were lowest for night shift workers.*

From P. Totterdell, et al., "Recovery from Work Shifts: How Long Does It Take?" in Journal of Applied Psychology, 80:43–57. Copyright © 1995 by the American Psychological Association. Reprinted by permission.

*M*ain
*P*oints

Temporal working conditions include the schedules of work and the length of the work period. Flextime is a variation of the standard day schedule that reduces absenteeism. Within limits, flextime allows workers to choose when they arrive at and leave work.

The length of the workweek can vary. The compressed week is a variation of the standard week. Rather than working eight hours a day for five days a week, employees put in ten to twelve hours a day for three or four days a week. Many people work less than full time. Some part-time jobs are temporary. Others are permanent.

Shift work is done by workers in many industries that operate 24 hours a day. Typically three eight-hour shifts are run. Workers may be assigned to a fixed day or night shift, or they may rotate through all shifts. Rotation can be forward or backward.

Research shows that night work results in more performance errors, fatigue, and sleep disturbance. The effects are less pronounced if the employee freely chooses night work. Rotating shifts have more severe effects for the night worker, apparently because the worker does not have time to adapt. Research shows that workers are better off with fixed or forward rotating shifts that change slowly.

DESIGNING THE SPACE FOR WORK

The physical features and spatial arrangement of the workplace are central to the design of work. In designing workspace, questions such as the following need to be asked. Where will employees do their tasks? Will they stand at counters or tables, or will they sit at desks? Will they need extra light?

The Physical Environment

Noise, lighting, and atmospheric conditions, such as temperature and humidity, are important aspects of the physical environment of work. A long history of

Section IV: Solving the Human Problems of Work

research and anecdotal evidence indicates that physical working conditions can affect personal comfort, health, and job performance. Their impact is complex, however, and likely to depend on the person. For example, although some workers can maintain good performance in spite of noisy and poorly lighted surroundings, others cannot.

Workplaces are hardly ever too quiet. The problem is too much noise, but how much is too much? The Occupational Safety and Health Administration (1980) has guidelines to help answer this question. OSHA begins by noting that the ear is not equally sensitive to all sound frequencies. High-frequency noise sounds louder to us than equally intense low-frequency noise. Thus, people can tolerate more low-frequency than high-frequency noise. The **decibel A (dBA) scale** of sound intensities take this into account; intensities are weighted according to human sensitivities. OSHA uses the dBA scale to determine acceptable levels of noise. (Refer to table 13.2 for examples of sound intensities on the dBA scale.) OSHA's guidelines consider both the loudness and the duration of noise exposure. The concept of **noise dose** is used to specify this. Noise intensities greater than 90 decibels constitute a *partial noise dose*. This is fairly loud. For example, a heavy truck 20 feet away has a noise intensity of about 90 dBA. The acceptable limit of noise exposure over an eight-hour day must average no greater than 90 dbA. When intensities are high, exposure time must be less. This can be done by rotating workers out of the noise, providing ear protection, or controlling the noise with sound-absorbing materials.

Illumination

The basic issue in workplace illumination is the amount of light needed. For work performed outside during daylight hours, sunlight is a good source that requires nothing more than shading the eyes from glare. For work done at night or inside a building, light must be provided. In these situations, we need to know how much is enough.

Good general lighting throughout the workplace is a beginning in any illumination plan. General lighting is best provided by indirect light sources and light-colored walls and floors. Lights placed over work areas focus attention on the work material. The optimal level of light for work depends on the task. For example, visual tasks involving small materials require more light. Lighting also depends on the amount of time that someone spends doing visual work and on the extent to which the visual work is critical to overall performance. Further, individual differences in people affect the optimal level of light. For example, the visual ability to focus on close work declines as a person ages. Increasing the light in the work area can help to counteract this decrement.

Lighting that is too intense also can cause performance problems. For example, inspection tasks need spotlighting; however, if the light is too bright, it may wash out surface details and make flaws more difficult to detect (Faulkner & Murphy, 1973). Intense spotlights also can interfere with vision in the periphery of the work area. If peripheral visibility is important on the job, then the intensity of spotlights must be reduced and the level of general lighting raised (Martin & Graveling, 1983).

Proper illumination for computer work can be a problem if the operator works with both paper and screen displays simultaneously, as those doing data entry usually do. It is difficult to get the right amount of light in each area if only one light source is being used. Reading the screen of a **video display terminal VDT** is easier if the general light level is low, because the contrast between the screen background and characters is better. However, reading paper material is easier if general light is bright. The solution? Reduce general lighting and add a desk lamp.

Glare is another problem of lighting design. Glare is a bright spot in the visual field that is more intense than the light level to which the eye is adapted. Glare may be simply uncomfortable, or it may be temporarily blinding. The effects become more severe as the bright spot gets closer to the direct line of sight. For example, meeting a car along a dark highway is visually harsh because the headlights are in the direct line of sight. There are two types of glare. **Direct glare** comes from a light source in the field of vision. A window or a bare light bulb over a worktable can produce direct glare. Direct glare is minimized by increasing general light and shielding the light sources. **Reflected glare** occurs when light rays are bent by a glossy surface. Many different kinds of polished surfaces are capable of creating reflected glare, including VDT screens, high-gloss paint, polished floors, and equipment made of shiny metal and glass. Reflected glare can be reduced by using textured surfaces, such as flat paint on walls and crinkle finishes on machinery.

Arranging Workspaces

The three-dimensional volume of space in which work is done is called the **workspace envelope.** As demonstrated in figure 15.2, the envelope is defined by the operator's reach and measured as sweeping arcs through space. Workspace design is mainly a case of deciding where things should go within the workspace envelope. For the work system to function well, work surfaces and seating need to fit the operator, and control devices must be placed so that the operator can reach them. A number of factors affect the operator's reach: the kind of movements required in performing the task; the physical size and fitness of the operator; and whether the operator is sitting or standing.

One of the difficulties in designing the human into the system results from the range of differences in people. How do we make the workspace fit the user when people vary so much? The first steps in handling this problem is to find out who the users are and how much they actually do differ. **Anthropometry** is a special area of study that provides basic information on human physical dimensions and guidance on how to use these dimensions in workspace design. Various body measurements have been collected from many national groups of men and women, yielding two types of anthropometric data. **Static data** are the fixed structural dimensions of the body, such as stature and shoulder height (see table 15.1 for some other examples). Each measured dimension is described in terms of the mean value (the 50th percentile) and the lower and upper extremes (5th and 95th percentiles). These values describe the smallest, average, and largest people measured. **Dynamic data** describe the needs and characteristics of the body as it moves through space, yielding such dimensions as the amount of space required in close working quarters. Dynamic measurement has resulted in the definition of two important design concepts: clearance and reach. **Clearance** specifies the amount of space required for work. *Head room, leg room,* and *elbow room* are common terms referring to clearance. **Reach** is the ability of a worker to reach and manipulate controls (Pheasant, 1986).

Section IV: Solving the Human Problems of Work

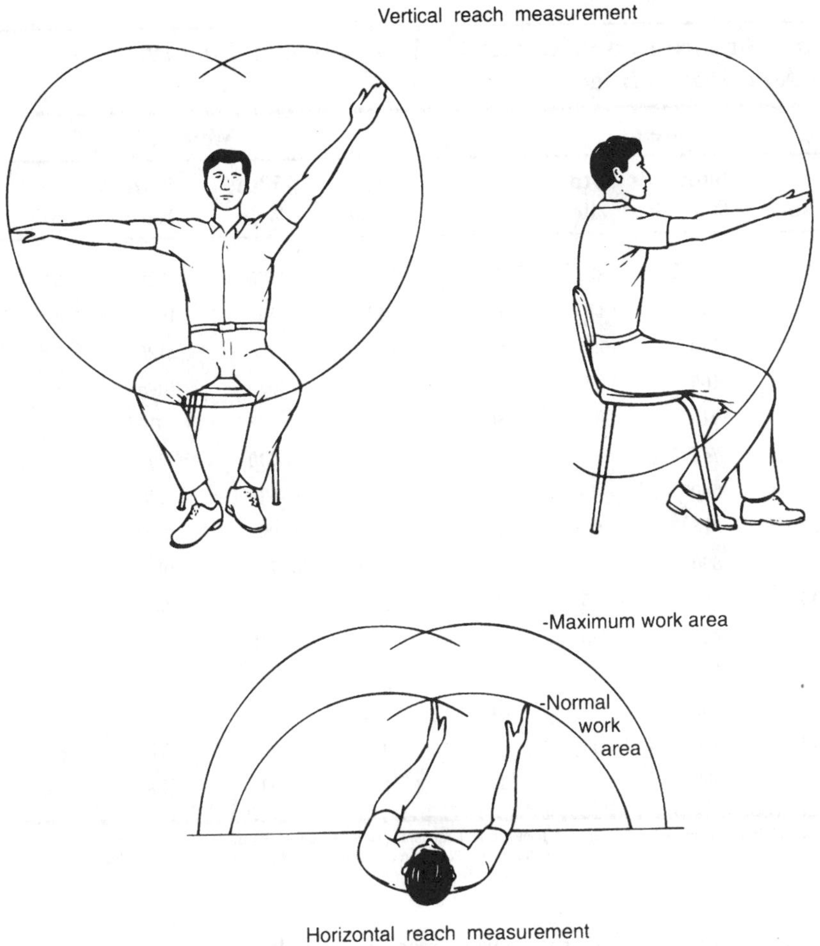

Vertical reach measurement

Figure 15.2 *Measuring reach to determine the workspace envelope. Horizontal and vertical arcs through space define the envelope.*

-Maximum work area

-Normal work area

Horizontal reach measurement

To determine workspace dimensions, anthropometric data are used in one of three design strategies. **Design for a range** is the appropriate strategy to use when work equipment and furniture need to be adjustable. This strategy should be adopted whenever possible because adjustments allow a better fit for a greater number of users. The adjustable chair is an example. It can be positioned to fit a large range of body sizes. **Design for the average** is used when it is either very costly or not possible to make equipment adjustable. The dimensions of the equipment are based on those of the average person in order to minimally inconvenience the largest number of users. Many features of stores are designed in this way, such as display and checkout counters. **Design for the extremes** is used when minimum distances are critical. This strategy is necessary for designing clearance and reach within the workspace envelope. The dimensions of the largest user determine clearance, because space usable by this person will be usable by all smaller users. For example, vehicle cabs should have enough clearance for the largest driver. In contrast, reach requirements in the workspace envelope should be determined by measurements

Table 15.1

Static Anthropometric Data Collected from a Survey of American Adults

Dimension	Men				Women			
	5th %ile	50th %ile	95th %ile	SD	5th %ile	50th %ile	95th %ile	SD
1. Stature	1640	1755	1870	71	1520	1625	1730	64
2. Eye height	1595	1710	1825	70	1420	1525	1630	63
3. Shoulder height	1330	1440	1550	67	1225	1325	1425	60
4. Elbow height	1020	1105	1190	53	945	1020	1095	47
5. Hip height	835	915	995	50	760	835	910	45
6. Knuckle height	700	765	830	41	670	730	790	37
7. Fingertip height	595	660	725	39	565	630	695	40
8. Sitting height	855	915	975	36	800	860	920	36
9. Sitting eye height	740	800	860	35	690	750	810	35
10. Sitting shoulder height	545	600	655	32	510	565	620	32
11. Sitting elbow height	195	245	295	31	185	235	285	29
12. Thigh thickness	135	160	185	16	125	155	185	17
13. Buttock–knee length	550	600	650	31	525	575	625	31
14. Buttock–popliteal length	445	500	555	33	440	490	540	31
15. Knee height	495	550	605	32	460	505	550	28

From S.T. Pheasant, *Bodyspace: Anthropometry, Ergonomics and Design.* Copyright © 1986 Taylor & Francis Ltd., London, England. Reprinted by permission.
Note: Dimensions are in millimeters. Percentiles refer to the distribution of the population, with the 5th and 95th representing the smallest and the largest of the subjects.

taken from the user with the shortest reach because larger users can reach what smaller ones can (Pheasant, 1986).

Work Surfaces and Chairs

The workspace envelope can include several work surfaces. In planning the space for a work surface, such as a counter or table, two horizontal reach zones are important. One is the **maximum work area.** This is the distance reached by a fully extended arm. Work equipment controls that get only occasional use may be positioned at maximum reach, but those that get heavy use should not be because sustained arm extension is hard on the elbow. The **normal work area,** the other reach zone, encompasses the distance reached by the forearm when the upper arm hangs straight down in its natural position. As shown in figure 15.2, the normal work area is defined by a comfortable sweeping movement of the upper arm around the shoulder joint. Most of the work should be contained within the normal work area.

The proper height of a work surface depends on the stature of the worker; on whether the person sits or stands to do the work; and on the type of task being performed. For most work, the surface height should be set so that the upper arm

Section IV: Solving the Human Problems of Work

hangs naturally from the shoulder, with the elbow bent and the forearm dropped slightly below horizontal. This principle varies, however, according to task demands. For example, fine detailed work requires a higher surface than work done with large materials. In general, standing work surfaces should be higher than seated work surfaces. For seated work, the best height of a work surface depends on the height of the seat.

Seating and work surfaces should be designed simultaneously because the design of one will influence the other. Seating also must be designed to meet particular task requirements. For example, seating in vehicle cabs must satisfy different needs for body support and posture than seating in front of a computer or at a drafting table. In the design of seating, several dimensions of the chair are important, including its depth, width, and overall height. Anthropometric data, such as hip and thigh measurements, are used in planning these seat dimensions (refer to table 15.1). The best seat height for many work activities is slightly lower than the distance from the user's knee to the floor. If the seat is much higher than this, pressure on the underside of the thigh results in discomfort. Seats that are too high should be lowered, or the person should use a footrest. When a seat is much too low, the user may have difficulty in sitting down and getting up. Seats that are too low should be raised, although armrests will help. Armrests must not interfere with an operator's ability to move close to the worktable, however.

Some of us spend almost all of our work time sitting down. In many sedentary jobs, the major physical activity is a precise, rapid, and repeated hand response. Usually, a single body posture is maintained throughout the entire workshift on such sedentary jobs. For example, some assembly workers maintain a single, unbalanced posture in which the torso is bent forward. Sewing machine operators have been observed to be almost completely immobile throughout the day. Keyboard operators typically adopt a very limited number of postures. In all these work activities, muscle fatigue and pain result from postural immobilization (Laville, 1985). The problem may go beyond simple fatigue, however. As described in chapter 14, there is evidence that postural immobilization and repetitive arm movements injure the muscular structure of the neck and shoulders. Such problems appear to be on the increase, possibly because of changes in jobs brought about by the increasing mechanization of the workplace (McPhee, 1982). Improving the work surface and seating for sedentary work should help. In one study, an adjustable table and a better chair were evaluated positively by VDT users (Shute & Starr, 1984). The table allowed separate adjustments to be made in the height and angle of the keyboard and screen; and the chair allowed lower overall heights to accommodate shorter people and had a shallower seat than conventional chairs.

Designing Workspaces for Disabled Workers

Disabled workers should be considered in workspace design. One reason is the general improvement of workspaces. Pheasant (1986) noted that the disabled employee often can be a kind of "barometer" to faulty designs and can identify design deficiencies that other people simply tolerate. In addition, qualified disabled workers have a right to work. It is frequently the case that a disabled person can perform a job when the workspace is adjusted to allow him or her access to the work equipment.

In the past, there was almost no anthropometric data that could be used to create better workspace designs for those with physical disabilities. This bleak picture is changing as methods have been developed for measuring the movement abilities of disabled subjects (e.g., Rahimi & Malzahn, 1984), and static and dynamic measurements have been published. For example, the size of the workspace envelope required for certain disabled workers has been studied. Rozier (1977) evaluated work surface requirements of below- and above-elbow amputees who work with a prosthesis. He found that the normal work surface area of these workers was considerably smaller than that of the average able-bodied operator. Some research indicates that we need to evaluate work surface design for disabled workers even when the upper extremities are not affected. In one study, subjects with motor dysfunction in the lower limbs were limited in their upper limb capacities as well (Nowak, 1989). In another study, the posture adopted by a group of paraplegic workers while performing a manual task was compared to that of a control group of able-bodied subjects. The posture of the paraplegic subjects appeared to cause physiological strain that did not occur in the control subjects (Do, Bouisset, & Moynot, 1985).

*M*ain *P*oints

Workspace design must consider the physical environment. Noise must be controlled. OSHA has standards for defining acceptable noise levels. Lighting must be provided. Depending on the task and the worker, spotlighting may be needed. Glare is a problem to be controlled.

Information on the user of a workspace is needed in design. Anthropometric data are used along with three design strategies to determine workspace dimensions. These strategies are design for a range; design for the average; and design for the extremes.

To design worktables, maximum and normal work surface areas need to be defined. These areas and the needed height of the table depend on the task, the worker's stature, and whether the worker stands or sits while working. For seated work, the work surface and chair should be designed together, because the dimensions of one depend on those of the other.

Well-designed seating and surfaces for sedentary work can reduce the muscular fatigue of this work. Disabled workers have unique workspace needs. Studying these needs can benefit all workers.

DESIGNING EFFECTIVE WORK SYSTEMS

In the past, work equipment and machinery were designed by engineers alone. Because the focus of engineering was on the development of the machine, there was little attention given to the user. Typically, if equipment designers gave any thought to the operator, it was merely to suppose that the person would have to make some adjustments in order to use the machine. In the early days of the machine age, this approach perhaps was acceptable because usually no great danger resulted from ignoring the human in equipment design. However, as equipment became more sophisticated, serious errors and accidents occurred, often because the machinery made demands that human operators could not meet. This early experience made clear the fact that the person must be considered as part of the work system if it is to operate safely and effectively. This is the point at which the psychologist enters the picture.

For some time now, psychologists have applied their knowledge and research skills to the design of equipment and work systems. Many who do this work are called engineering psychologists. The primary goal of engineering psychology[1] is to ensure that the human is included in equipment and work system designs. Engineering psychology has long been considered a sister field of I/O psychology because of its emphasis on the worker and the physical conditions of work.

Engineering psychologists use the scientific methods of observation and experimentation, as well as some special I/O techniques, such as job and task analysis. As noted in chapter 1, the time and motion study, involving carefully timed and analyzed observations, was one of the earliest applied research methodologies. The point of these early studies was to increase work efficiency. Modern techniques of work system analysis go way beyond the time and motion study. For example, one method includes analysis of a model of the job, observation of actual work, and interviews with job incumbents and supervisors. Descriptions of tasks, equipment, and work environment result from this analysis. The demands of the system on the worker also are identified. These include the perceptual, decision-making, and physical demands of the job (Rohmert, 1985b). I/O psychologists are often hired to do this type of study not only because of their understanding of human behavior but also because they can analyze tasks, jobs, and work systems, as well as do research in the field setting on the psychology of the worker. The inclusion of I/O and engineering psychologists in system analysis and development provides for humanizing the design of technology and work systems.

The Nature of Human-Machine Systems

The term **human-machine system** is used to describe the relationship between the human operator and the work equipment. The **machine** in the human-machine system is any equipment an operator uses to do the work. To many people, the term *machine* conjures up visions of large metal things with moving parts animated by electrical or internal combustion engines. Some machines are like this. Others—sewing machines, typewriters, film projectors, and computers—are not like this but are machines nonetheless. Others also do not easily fit the description yet are considered as the machine element in work systems. Ovens, boilers, scales, cameras, elevators, and metal detectors are some examples. Some machines are called "tools," such as drills, saws, mixers, floor polishers, staplers, and paper shredders.

Over the long history of human work, machines have been created and used to extend our abilities and overcome our limitations. People can carry heavy loads; however, even heavier loads can be moved with wheels. That is, the human's capacity is amplified or made stronger by the machine element. In addition to *amplification,* machinery contributes to human work in other ways. The machine can be *complementary* by filling in where the human is only partially capable. Such devices as infrared sensors complement the human eye in an area in which we have no vision.

[1]The field is known also as human engineering, human factors, and ergonomics. Europeans refer to the field as ergonomics. In the United States, we call it either engineering psychology or human factors.

Replacement is the third way machinery is used. Some machines substitute for humans by doing things the human can do. Replacement can be a contribution if it frees us to do other things. This is the idea behind **automation.** In these three ways, technology provides us with the capacity to reach beyond our limits and do otherwise impossible things (Rohmert, 1985a).

General Systems Theory Perspective

The theoretical foundation for much of the thinking on human-machine system design is **general systems theory** (von Bertalanffy, 1950). This theory is useful in describing the nature of interactive structures of many different types, and it has been applied to a range of organized systems, including social organizations. The *whole* of the system is addressed, including the organizational fabric that ties the system's elements together. In this respect, the theory is similar to the gestalt principle. **Gestalt psychology,** which addresses human perception, considers psychological wholes to exist beyond the sum of their parts. Both gestalt and general systems theory view the interaction of the elements of a system as producing an event that can be understood only by analyzing the dynamic process itself. That is, if we want to understand how a human perception is formed, or how a human-machine system runs, we must look at their processes and internal interactions.

General systems theory describes the development and life of a system in *dynamic* terms. First, the unique nature of a system results from its continual adaptation to both internal and external demands. Second, changes in one component of a system affect other components and the system as a whole. That is, the work system develops out of the *interactions* and *exchanges* that occur between the human and machine components. Third, the components are linked through their exchange of things, such as information. There are two exchange processes: **inputs** and **outputs.** *Within* a component, an internal **conversion process** occurs after input and before output.

All these dynamic processes exist in the human-machine work system. Input to the human is information sent by machine display instruments. Input to the machine is information sent by the operator through control devices. Further, each type of input has its corresponding output. That is, information to the human comes through the output of the machine, and the machine receives information through the output of the human. Both human and machine have internal conversion processes. In conversion, the input is used to make decisions and plan action. The input-conversion-output process is a repeating cycle of interaction, as shown in figure 15.3.

Most importantly, general systems theory identifies the specific vulnerability of a system to malfunction. A work system performs well only when its components' interactions are effective. Mistakes and accidents occur at the links between components. That is, mistakes and accidents occur during the interaction of the human and the machine, or during input and output. This vulnerability must be considered in design, and special attention should be given to strengthening the links between the system's components. Effectively allocating work functions, considering human needs and capacities, and training the operator can improve the system by making these links stronger.

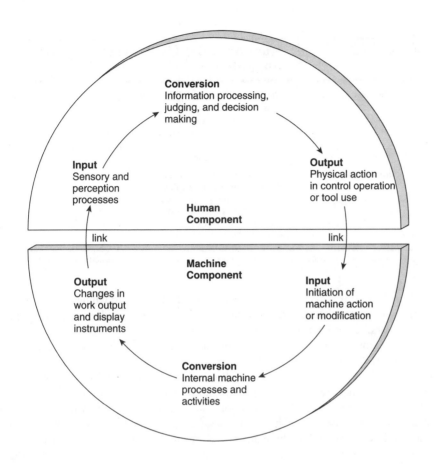

Figure 15.3 *The input-conversion-output cycle of a human-machine work system. The human and the machine are linked at two points in the cycle. Information comes to the human through the output of a machine, and the machine receives information through the output of the human. Both humans and machines engage in internal conversion processes to use this input information to determine their output.*

In the figure:

Conversion
Information processing, judging, and decision making

Input
Sensory and perception processes

Output
Physical action in control operation or tool use

Human Component

link

link

Machine Component

Output
Changes in work output and display instruments

Input
Initiation of machine action or modification

Conversion
Internal machine processes and activities

Allocation of Work Functions

To develop a work system, we begin by defining its purpose or mission. What is the system supposed to do? Next, we identify and describe the specific work functions that need to be performed in order to accomplish this mission. Then, these work functions are allocated as either human or machine tasks. Task analysis is used to identify the required work functions. Knowledge of human behavior is essential in allocating the functions.

Function allocation is the process of deciding who or what is going to do what part of the work task. This is probably the designer's most important decision because it establishes the framework for the entire work system. As a guide to function allocation, Fitts (1951) published lists of work activities that appeared to be better performed either by a human or by a machine. More elaborate lists have been published since then. Table 15.2 shows one. Briefly, these lists indicate that humans are more efficient in tasks that require cognitive powers, such as interpreting sensory stimuli, reasoning, evaluating, and making decisions. Humans are also more flexible, creative, and capable of learning. Some functions have to be performed by humans because machines cannot do them. For example, we do not have machines that can

Table 15.2	Work Activities List Used in Function Allocation[a]
Humans Are Best at:	Detection of a range of different sensory stimuli
	Sensory detection in noise or clutter
	Recognition of unusual stimuli
	Deciding how to respond to unusual situations
	Generalizing and drawing conclusions from complex data
	Creative problem solving
Machines Are Best at:	Sensory detection of extreme stimuli (e.g., ultraviolet light)
	Rapid mathematical calculations
	Storing and quickly retrieving large amounts of information
	Long-term repetitive activity
	Long-term monitoring
	Applying high levels of physical force

[a]These lists were first known as the Fitts lists and later as the MABA–MABA lists (i.e., "men are best at, machines are best at").

replace their own parts, and most cannot start themselves. Machines have greater capacity in terms of sheer force and stamina. They are better at long-term and repetitious work, especially because they do not suffer fatigue and boredom.

Sometimes, work functions are allocated with little or no attention to humans. Tasks that a *machine* does well are given to the machine, and the person is assigned whatever is left over. Although this may be convenient to designers, it is likely to be a mistake. Clearly, machines and people do not necessarily have opposite capacities. Sometimes both and sometimes neither can perform a particular work function. Also, some functions *should* be performed by the operator even though they could be done by machines. For example, interesting tasks need to be assigned to the human because they make the job more satisfying. In general, allocation of functions needs to be well thought out, particularly in terms of its human impact. If there is a choice, the designer should weigh the value of assigning a function to the machine or the human in terms of the total system operation. Certainly, utilitarian and cost considerations should be made. However, allocation to a machine is not always less expensive, especially when mistakes and accidents are counted (Price, 1985).

Work systems are described in terms of interaction loops, as figures 15.3 and 15.4 illustrate, and they are distinguished by the extent to which the loop fully controls the system. A **closed-loop system** is self-regulatory, with each interaction leading into the next to complete the loop. Such a system turns itself on, performs the necessary functions, and then turns itself off. Human-machine systems are closed-loop systems because the operator's role is to regulate the system. Most work is done by closed-loop human-machine systems.[2]

Figure 15.4 demonstrates the processes involved in a familiar closed-loop human-machine system—a driver and a vehicle—and shows the "microscopic" nature of systems analysis. The driver initiates the system by manipulating certain controls (e.g., ignition). This control action provides input to the car, and this input is used to guide the vehicle's conversion process. In turn, the car displays information about the start-up process in display units built into the dash. This machine

[2]An open-loop system is not self-controlled. A commonly cited example is the automatic fire sprinkler system found in many modern commercial buildings. It has the ability to activate itself, but intervention from outside the system, usually from the fire department, is required to turn it off.

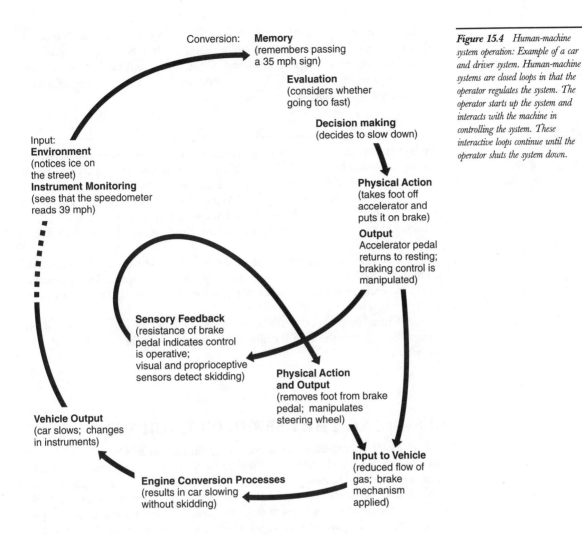

Conversion:

Memory
(remembers passing
a 35 mph sign)

Evaluation
(considers whether
going too fast)

Decision making
(decides to slow down)

Input:
Environment
(notices ice on
the street)
Instrument Monitoring
(sees that the speedometer
reads 39 mph)

Physical Action
(takes foot off
accelerator and
puts it on brake)

Output
Accelerator pedal
returns to resting;
braking control is
manipulated)

Sensory Feedback
(resistance of brake
pedal indicates control
is operative;
visual and proprioceptive
sensors detect skidding)

**Physical Action
and Output**
(removes foot from brake
pedal; manipulates
steering wheel)

Vehicle Output
(car slows; changes
in instruments)

Engine Conversion Processes
(results in car slowing
without skidding)

Input to Vehicle
(reduced flow of
gas; brake
mechanism
applied)

Figure 15.4 Human-machine system operation: Example of a car and driver system. Human-machine systems are closed loops in that the operator regulates the system. The operator starts up the system and interacts with the machine in controlling the system. These interactive loops continue until the operator shuts the system down.

output provides input to the driver about the state of the machine (e.g., fuel level). The initiation completes the first loop. In a miniloop within the system, the driver receives direct feedback about the state of the vehicle through auditory and tactual sensation (e.g., engine noise and vibration). To begin a second loop, the driver uses this information to decide what to do next (e.g., operate the controls) to back out of the garage. The loops continue in this fashion until the system is shut down (i.e., parked at work).

The number of functions allocated to a human in a closed-loop system varies, depending on the type of work. The person may perform almost all work functions. This is the case when a worker uses nothing more than a few tools to do a job. For example, college teaching jobs often are done with such tools as a word processor, copying machine, and telephone, but most of the work is done personally by the instructor. Other work systems are shared more equally by the machine and the person. A dental hygienist's job, in which the work includes both mechanical and personal contributions, is an example. Still other work systems are designed so that the machine does almost all the work, with the human functioning as regulator of the system. This describes an increasing number of jobs in which an operator simply monitors machines.

*M*ain *P*oints

The human-machine system involves interaction between a worker and any equipment or tools used in the work. Machines contribute to work by amplifying or complementing human abilities and by replacing the human through automation.

General systems theory is used to guide work system design. The theory emphasizes that interactions between the human and the machine are most important. Interaction processes are input and output. Errors and accidents occur during these interactions.

Function allocation is the process of deciding whether the human or the machine will perform a task. Lists of human and machine capabilities are available to help the designer decide. Tasks assigned to the human should be significant, not merely what is left over.

Closed-loop work systems are self-regulating, usually because of the human who initiates the action, maintains interaction with the machine, and turns the system off.

DESIGNING THE USER INTO EQUIPMENT

The psychologist contributes to system design in two areas. One is the design of machine displays for informational input to the worker. The psychologist uses his or her knowledge of human perception and cognition to help design displays that an operator can use safely and effectively. The other area is the human output to the machine. The operator responds to machine displays by making decisions and operating controls. The psychologist works on this aspect of system design by using his or her knowledge of human cognition and physical ability to help design control devices. In this section, first, I discuss machine displays that are effective in providing information. Then, I take up the issue of control design.

Effective Machine Displays

A basic aim in designing machine displays is to attract the operator's attention. Several design features are important in this. For example, attention is influenced by the manner in which information is transmitted. Some information *sources* are simply more noticeable than others, such as sounds. Task variables also can influence attention, particularly the use of the information and the size of the operator's attentional workload. Some information should not be displayed because it is not used and can contribute unnecessarily to the demands on the operator's attention. Other information has important uses and must be displayed to ensure that the operator will notice it. Information that is needed on the job will draw the worker's attention.

Machine displays conceivably can be directed to any of the human senses; however, most human-machine systems use visual and auditory signals. To decide the **sensory modality** of the display, the designer must consider the type of information, its attentional demand, and the number and nature of other messages being sent at the same time. When messages are long, complex, abstract, and sequential, or when they must be retained for future reference, visual displays are better than auditory displays. Visual messages also are useful when the auditory sense is overloaded, either by too many messages or by noise. When the message is short, simple, or demanding of attention, auditory displays are better. Auditory signals are an option when visual signals are not feasible, as when information must be conveyed in the dark. Auditory signals are preferable when the operator is moving around or using other displays. With our sense of hearing, we can detect a sound signal from afar without having to be oriented toward the source. Because of this, auditory signals are especially effective for warnings (Oborne, 1987).

For a message to be sent, machine information first must be translated into something humans can perceive and understand. That is, it must be appropriately coded. Codes vary by sensory modality and by the degree to which they are realistic or symbolic. For example, a factory whistle is an auditory code used to symbolize quitting time. Many visual codes use written language and other symbols. The word *on* painted on a switch and lighted arrows on elevators are examples. There are some guidelines for effective coding. First, the coded signal must be *detectable* by a human sense. Second, the coded signal must be *discriminable* so that the receiver can distinguish it from other signals. Third, the code must be *meaningful* in terms of what it represents. Fourth, use of the code must be *standardized*. It would be very confusing if "O" meant "switch on" with one machine and "switch off" with another (McCormick & Sanders, 1982). The information must be coded to suit any existing **population stereotype.** This refers to what people expect or understand something (such as "O") to mean.

Visual Displays

Many visual displays carry static or unchanging information. Hallway signs and printed materials, such as safety instructions, are examples. Other visual displays carry dynamic material that must be updated frequently. **Dynamic visual displays** come in a variety of forms (see figure 15.5). They can be circular or semicircular dials, or vertical or horizontal scales. Some show an entire range of numbers; others have a small window over one section of the scale. In some displays, the pointer moves over a fixed scale. In others, the scale moves around a fixed pointer. Both quantitative and qualitative information can be displayed. **Quantitative displays** give numerical information and are used when a precise reading is needed. The speedometer in a car is an example. **Qualitative displays** are used when information about ranges, rather than exact values, is needed. You do not have to know the temperature of a car's engine, but you do need to know whether it is cold or hot. Qualitative displays also are used to indicate whether a machine is on or off and to give emergency information. For example, engine temperature gauges typically have a red danger zone to indicate overheating.

Location of visual displays is a critical concern in setting up a workspace. Display devices must be positioned so that an operator can read them without having to

Figure 15.5 *Quantitative and qualitative visual displays. Quantitative displays give precise numerical information. Qualitative displays exhibit ranges rather than exact values.*

Quantitative Displays
4:03p
Open window digital display, moving scale
0
10
20
30
40
50
60
70
80
Semicircular dial, moving pointer
5
4
6
3
7
2
0
1
Circular dial, moving pointer
8
7
6
5
4
Open window over vertical scale, fixed pointer
1
2
3
Horizontal scale, moving pointer
Qualitative Displays
RECHARGE
NORMAL
Circular dial, fixed pointer
NORMAL
COLD
HOT
Semicircular dial, moving pointer
HOT
COLD
Vertical scale, moving pointer

take extra steps. This may seem obvious, but in practice, displays are sometimes placed so that the operator must lean over or get up in order to read them. When the workspace envelope is limited in size, prime locations should be given to displays that get frequent use and/or give important information. Warning lights that have to be placed at a distance should be bright and flashing when they are on. When quantitative displays (such as clocks) have to be placed at a distance from the operator, increasing their size will help. When several qualitative displays need to be checked at the same time, it is easier if they are grouped and oriented so that their pointers are aimed in the same direction to indicate a "normal" reading. A quick sweeping glance at the group will provide an adequate check reading because any that deviate from normal will stand out. Notice in figure 15.6 how quick it is to identify the dial with the pointer away from normal.

The touch sensory mode can be used as a substitute for vision. A number of tactual display devices have been developed for the visually handicapped. **Braille printing** is one example. A **tactual graph** is another. Both can be used to code informational input to the operator. Data from ordinary graphs can be translated into a tactual graph by embossing techniques that produce raised lines and dots.

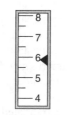

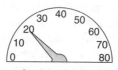

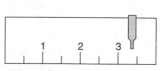

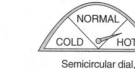

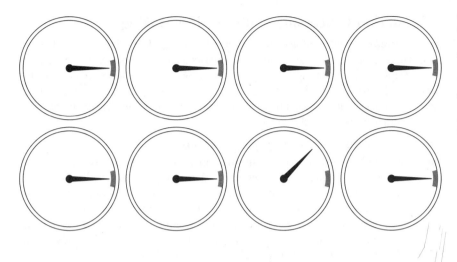

Figure 15.6 *Placement of similar dials to facilitate check reading. Normal on these dials is indicated by the dark band on the right side of each dial. A quick glance at the group will provide an adequate check reading because the one that has deviated from the normal is readily apparent.*

Subjects without sight can easily read these graphs by touch when the data curves and the x and y axes are marked. The trouble is in adding the grid. A grid makes the task of locating points easy in the visual graph; however, the added detail leads to confusion in the tactual graph. A raised grid attached to the back of the graph has been found effective (Lederman & Campbell, 1982). A single-sided graph that includes a lightly defined grid and heavier superimposed data curves also works (Aldrich & Parkin, 1987).

Auditory Displays

Buzzers, bells, whistles, and human voices are auditory displays. They are good for warnings and emergency information, and they can be used with visual displays to capture attention and convey a message. Auditory displays can improve performance when they are used in conjunction with visual displays (Colquhoun, 1975). Except for voices, auditory displays are clearly limited in the amount of information they can carry. To develop an effective auditory warning system, the designer must determine exactly what information is essential to convey and keep the amount included at a bare minimum. When multiple auditory alarms with various meanings are installed in a work system, users typically are unable to distinguish between them. A study of hospital alarms demonstrated this point. Hospital staff and nurses were able to identify the meaning of only about half of the alarms used (Momtahan, Hetu, & Tansley, 1993).

Because voice communication is as rich as written words, **synthesized speech** is being evaluated as an auditory alternative to the visual display. Synthesized voice displays have good potential, especially when there is visual overload. At the present time, however, intelligibility is a problem. Performance that is based on information from synthetic speech is slower and less accurate than performance based on natural speech (Ralston et al., 1991). Researchers are attempting to find ways to make synthesized speech more understandable. There is also work being done to improve listener reception of synthesized speech. Messages are better understood when subjects are given context information and if the message is slowed down and repeated (Marics & Williges, 1988).

Information Processing and Decision Making

As an operator receives information input, processing of that information begins. Informational processing blends into the decision-making and planning phases of thought and action. Although perception and aspects of attention are part of this phase, emphasis is on cognition. It is important for the equipment designer to understand how information processing proceeds and what cognitive factors might affect the operator's decisions and actions.

Serial and Parallel Processing of Information

One way to look at how we process information is to consider the manner in which attention and other cognitive resources are used in task performance. In some work situations, we must concentrate on one source of information and use our cognitive resources to perform one task at a time. This is called **serial processing** of information. In other work situations, we must divide our attention between two sets of information. Cognitive resources also are divided and the information is received and processed simultaneously. This is **parallel processing** of information.

Triesman's (1969) **channel model** can be used to show what we do in serial and parallel processing. According to this theory, our attention and processing depend on the "channel" or aspect of the environment from which we obtain information. Environmental channels are determined by the sensory mode receiving the information. For vision, space is a channel. When information sources are located in physically different *places,* they are in different visual channels. For hearing, pitch is a channel. Speakers with low-pitched voices occupy different channels than speakers with high-pitched voices. According to the channel model, two pieces of information that come to one of our senses along different channels require focused attention and serial processing. However, if two sets of information come through the same channel at the same time, then we *must* process them in parallel. For example, if two people with similar voices are speaking at once, we find it difficult to listen only to one. If we are to understand anything they are saying, we must divide our attention between the two speakers and process their messages in parallel.

Whether efficiency is improved with parallel or serial processing depends on the nature of the task. If two inputs require different responses, then the task is easier when the information sources are separated so as to elicit serial processing. However, when two inputs call for the same response, then parallel processing actually makes the work easier (Wickens, 1984). If parallel processing is desired, then the trick is to direct the informational input to the operator through the same channel. This is not always easily done. An example is provided by the "head-up display" used in an aircraft. This is a device for projecting landing instrument information onto the front window of the airplane. Its purpose is to improve the pilot's use of instrument information while he or she is looking out the window for other landing cues during bad weather. Moving the information source up from its usual position below the window was thought likely to help the pilot monitor the instrument information and the view out the window simultaneously with divided attention and parallel processing. Because the information from both sources occur at the same time and require the same response, placing them in the same channel seemed appropriate. Actually, however, the visual distance between the *close up* view of the head-up display and the *far* view out the window operates to keep these sources of information in *different* channels. That is, the eye accommodated to read the projected instrument display cannot see the distant ground, and vice versa. This means that attention is not divided, and the information is not processed in parallel as intended.

Cognitive Workload

Modern work systems rely heavily on the operator to make quick and accurate decisions. In decision making, parallel processing usually is not possible. Deciding is a procedure of selecting discrete responses, and these operations have to be done one at a time, that is, in serial fashion. Serial processing, of course, is time-consuming, and the operator may be unable to decide as quickly as the system demands. Therefore, in designing the decision requirements of a system, the overall **cognitive workload** of the operator must be considered (Wickens, 1984). Cognitive workload depends on the number and complexity of the operator's tasks. It can be estimated by assessing the demands of the system's machinery, by the operator's self-ratings, or by observations of how busy the operator is. Cognitive workload also depends on *who* is doing the work. Individuals differ in their abilities to handle cognitive work. Trained and experienced operators are more capable than inexperienced or untrained operators of handling a heavy workload. For example, to a novice, driving seems to require too many operations at once, but after practice, the driver becomes able to handle this workload.

Vigilance work can be described as a problem of cognitive overload. A **vigilance task** is one in which a worker monitors some display or process in order to detect signals, signs, or objects that appear infrequently and unpredictably. Examples of vigilance tasks are found in the work of night watch personnel, radar and sonar operators, refinery maintenance workers, and quality control inspectors. On the surface, vigilance tasks look as if there is very little to be done. An operator can spend an entire work shift "watching nothing happen," and vigilance has been characterized as boring, monotonous work. However, because workload is defined in terms of the amount and complexity of the work, vigilance actually may be a case of cognitive *overload*. Vigilance can be highly demanding of an operator's attention.

Signal detection theory defines the types of accurate and inaccurate responses that a person monitoring a machine display or work process can make. Accurate detection of a signal depends on the signal appearing and being recognized for what it is. This correct response is called a *hit* in signal detection terminology. Another correct response is that in which the nonsignal is recognized as such. There are two types of incorrect response. A *miss* occurs when the observer fails to detect a signal that does appear. A *false alarm* occurs when the observer misperceives a nonsignal for a signal. These four responses are summarized in table 15.3.

Vigilance tasks vary in terms of how a signal is defined and whether there is more than one category of signal. In some situations, a signal is "no change." Either target events occur or nothing happens. This is the situation that the power plant monitor faces. In other types of work, nonsignal *noise* is present. For example, certain blips (signals) on a radar screen must be distinguished from similar ones (noise). The quality control inspector has a vigilance job with more than one type of signal. He or she must identify items that are flawed in any way (signals) from acceptable items (nonsignals).

Table 15.3	Four Responses in Signal Detection			
	Stimulus	**Response**	**Response Accuracy**	**Common Term**
	Signal	Signal	Correct acceptance of signal	Hit
	Signal	Nonsignal	Incorrect rejection of signal	Miss
	Nonsignal	Signal	Incorrect acceptance of nonsignal	False Alarm
	Nonsignal	Nonsignal	Correct rejection of nonsignal	–

Vigilance has been the subject of research inquiry for almost 50 years. Mackworth (1950) originally studied the performance of radar operators in World War II and noted that their performance declined as the workshift wore on. Since then, a large number of laboratory studies have been done, also showing that vigilance performance deteriorates over time. Numerous factors that contribute to the performance decrement have been identified, such as distractions and the person's motivation (cf. Mackie, 1987). The decrement has been proposed to be due to the operator's loss of perceptual sensitivity over the workshift, which occurs because maintaining concentration is highly fatiguing (Broadbent, 1971). Does vigilance in field settings show the same decrement over time, as is shown in laboratory research? There is not much evidence that it does. However, Wiener (1987) suggested that the lack of evidence for the decrement in some jobs may be because managerial intervention has prevented it. Inspection workers are rotated on and off the inspection job throughout the day. Therefore, the vigilance task has a short duration. Also, most inspectors do other things as well as inspection. These are two courses of action that research suggests will solve vigilance problems.

Main Points

Whether to use visual or auditory displays depends on the kind of message, its importance, and whether other messages are sent at the same time. Visual displays are best if a message is long, complex, or needs to be kept. Auditory displays are good for short, important messages and warnings. Auditory and visual message codes vary by how realistic or symbolic they are.

Visual displays can present static or dynamic material. The message can be quantitative or qualitative. To arrange displays, those that are used frequently or have important information must get prime locations. Some displays use touch instead of vision.

Auditory displays use voices and other sounds, including synthesized speech. These displays are limited in the amount of information they can convey.

Information-processing occurs through either focused attention and serial processing or divided attention and parallel processing. The channel through which information is conveyed determines the processing. Information that comes through different channels is processed serially. When two sets of information come through one channel, parallel processing is required.

Cognitive workload is increased by use of attention and cognitive resources for information processing. Vigilance may constitute a heavy cognitive workload because of the heavy demand on attention.

WORKING WITHOUT AND WITH MACHINES

Human output in a system's operation occurs through physical work and machine control. These actions, which can be physically great or small, allow an operator to act on his or her decisions in operating a system. Thus, the operation of controls represents the second interface between human and machine. As such, control operation is another link in which the system is vulnerable to error. Controls, like displays, need to be designed with the human user in mind. In this section, I examine the nature of physical work and the design of some tools and control devices.

All human work is physical in nature to some degree. A task can require only the slightest physical activity, as in pressing a button, or it can require the strength of the whole body, as in maneuvering and lifting a load. In the act of physical work, basic movements are combined in a response pattern, such as moving back and forth, bending, straightening, and rotating. Some movements are discrete, such as flipping a switch. Others form a chain of actions, such as lifting, carrying, and placing a box. Still others require immobilizing the body for an extended time. (See table 15.4 for further descriptions of movements.)

Handling Materials by Hand

Loading and unloading vehicles, handling baggage at the airport, lifting and stacking boxes in storage, and moving furniture are examples of **manual materials handling**. This is hard physical work. It can result in a variety of strains and injuries, including lacerations, bruises, cardiovascular strain, and back injury (National Institute for Occupational Safety and Health, 1981). Although one of the major advantages of machines is their capacity to handle and move materials, we still do a great deal of this work by hand. Often, lifting, loading, and moving materials are done without even the slightest technological aid to make the work easier. A study showed that attaching handles to boxes makes the moving task easier and less energy consuming (Drury et al., 1989), yet most boxes do not have handles.

Lifting is part of almost all manual materials handling, and it is an activity that is physically fatiguing. Even for workers experienced in doing lifting tasks, the work can have excessive physiological costs in terms of energy consumption (Mital, Foononi-Fard, & Brown, 1994). In addition, it can cause injury, particularly if it is done incorrectly. What is the correct way to lift? Typically, we are advised not to bend over to pick up an object—which is our natural tendency—because this puts strain on our backs. Rather, we should squat, grasp the object, and then rise by using our leg muscles. Lifting in this way results in less pressure on the lower back (Ekholm, Arborelius, & Nemeth, 1982). However, the extent to which leg lifts can be executed more safely than back lifts depends on the size of the object. If it is too large to be grasped between the knees, then extending the arms around it will again strain the back. Some

*T*able 15.4   Types of Hand and Foot Work Movements

Movement	Description	Examples
Positioning	Moving hand or foot from one place to another	Reaching for door handle
Manipulating	Handling controls or tools	Turning door handle and manipulating ignition key
Sequencing	Making step-by-step movements in order	Turning ignition key, pressing gas pedal, and releasing hand brake
Continuous adjustment	Moving a multiposition control constantly	Turning steering wheel, pressing gas pedal
Static adjustment	Maintaining a specific position	Holding gas pedal at one level
Repeating	Doing the same movement over and over again	Manipulating gear shift lever to change gears

From M.S. Sanders and E.J. McCormick, *Human Factors in Engineering and Design*, 6th ed. Copyright © 1986 The McGraw-Hill Companies, Inc., New York. Reprinted by permission.

research indicates that leg lifts actually consume more energy than back lifts, because of the added cost of raising the weight of the body from the squat position (Garg & Saxena, 1979). Further, Oborne (1987) pointed out that requiring the person to change from the natural back lift tendency to some other method in order to lift heavy loads is simply another example of how we ask the human to adjust to the environment instead of adjusting the environment to the human.

Use of Hand Tools

The physical feature most symbolic of work is the hand. Many types of work belong almost exclusively to the hand, and this is reflected in our language. Notice the many terms and expressions—*handwork, handles, handling, doing it by hand, handy, lending a hand,* and *not lifting a finger.* Much of the world's work is still done with hand tools. In the hand-tool work system, the major functions are allocated to the human. The tool or "machine" element plays a somewhat minor role. Even so, effective design of tools can improve performance in this work system. Poor tool design can cause inefficiency and worker injury.

Hand Differences

Hand dimensions vary according to the person's gender and age. Women's hands are generally smaller than men's, and older people have less flexibility in their hands than younger people. There also are some racial differences in hands. Evaluation of women's hand dimensions in one study showed that Hong Kong Chinese women have smaller hands than British and American women, but they have larger hands than Japanese women (Courtney, 1984).

An individual difference that is often neglected by designers of tools and controls is *handedness.* Most tool handles and control arrangements are designed for right-handed users. Left-handed operators are expected to adjust. Adjustment is not

Section IV: Solving the Human Problems of Work

easy, however. Research indicates that neither left- nor right-handed people perform as well with the nondominant hand as with the dominant hand (Garonzik, 1989). Probably, a slight performance decrement is not important in most situations. Also, there are fewer left-handed people; the incidence is generally thought to be no greater than 29 percent (Hardyck & Petrinovich, 1977). In work systems that have high demands for quick and accurate responses, however, the performance difference that results from requiring the operator to work with the nondominant hand may be critically important.

Tool Handle Design

Hands can be injured by tools that are improperly designed. A number of **cumulative-effect hand traumas** have been found to occur from the use of tools at work. These are repetition trauma disorders (discussed in chapter 14). They result when a worker sustains repeated minor injuries from using a tool over a long period of time. Hand traumas include *tenosynovitis,* which is caused by repeated injury of the tendons in the palm of the hand. With *carpal tunnel syndrome,* a related disorder, the nerve in the wrist is injured. Both conditions result from work requiring the wrist to be held in a bent position.

Some tools have been redesigned as a result of research on hand injuries. One design feature that has received considerable study is the handle that requires a *bent wrist.* For example, conventional pliers with straight handles require the wrist to be bent when they are used, and a cumulative-effect trauma, such as carpal tunnel syndrome, can result from long-term use. A tool with a bent handle is used with a *straight* wrist and prevents this trauma. Several bent-handle designs have been developed. In one early study, redesigned pliers with bent handles were compared with conventional straight-handle pliers. Only 10 percent of workers using the bent handle developed signs of tendon trauma, although more than 60 percent of the workers using the conventional pliers did (Tichauer, 1978). Many ordinary tools, such as axes, hammers, and brooms, have since been redesigned to incorporate bent handles. Workers using bent-handle tools can perform well with no loss of efficiency (Schoenmarklin & Marras, 1989).

The purpose of the tool affects its design needs. For example, tools used to make thrusting motions should be designed to allow a perpendicular thrust of the hand *against* the handle. Lug wrenches, which are used to remove flat tires, are designed this way. Tools that are gripped and turned can be designed in either of two ways, depending on what they are supposed to do. Cylindrical handles turn on their own axis (e.g., a screwdriver). These are good for work requiring precision but not much physical force. Other handles turn on a perpendicular axis and are meant to be used with force. For example, certain wrenches provide a T-shaped handle for gripping and turning on the perpendicular axis. This is an energy-efficient design. Figure 15.7 *a–d* illustrates some tool designs that incorporate these movements.

Machine Control Devices

Control devices provide the means for an operator to communicate with and command a machine or tool. Thus, controls should be designed to enhance the operator's ability to use the equipment without making errors. To accomplish this, a design must make it easy for the operator to locate and identify control devices. The operator's

Figure 15.7 *Handle designs to fit tool use. Perpendicular (a) and parallel (b) designs for thrusting motions. For gripping and turning motions, on the handler's own axis (c) and on the perpendicular axis (d).*

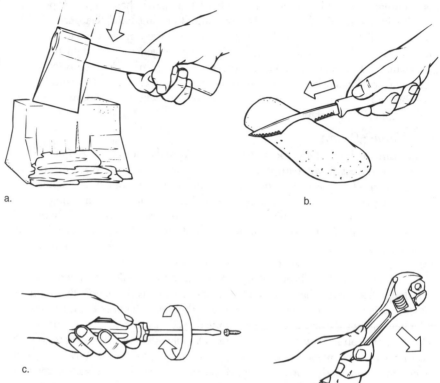

a.

b.

c.

d.

expectations should be considered as well. The concept of population stereotype refers to the fact that people have stable expectations not only about the meanings of signs but also about how controls are supposed to operate. Sometimes, errors occur because a person expects a device to operate in a different fashion than it does. For example, one common population stereotype is that you loosen things (such as screws and lids) or reduce their level (such as intensity or volume dials) by turning them *counterclockwise*. This will be our first approach with a new item. A device or knob that turns in the opposite direction can be exasperating. Many studies have been done to identify the control movement expectations of people in the Western world. What do people in the Eastern world expect? If they have different ideas about how things operate, then we are likely to have trouble using each other's equipment. Studies of Chinese and American samples indicate that there are important differences in how controls are expected to operate (Courtney, 1988; Hsu & Peng, 1993).

Types of Controls

Basic control devices are the knob, the push button, and the pedal. Other devices are variations of these, such as handwheels, dials, cranks, levers, and switches. Two factors are important in designing controls: (1) the need for discrete versus continuous control operations, and (2) the preference for linear versus rotary devices. **Discrete controls** are useful when just a few adjustment positions are needed. The on-off switch is a discrete control with two positions. The automobile windshield wiper is another discrete control. **Continuous controls** are more useful when many different settings are needed. Room light dimmer controls and a vehicle's gas and brake pedals are examples. Continuous controls are needed also when the speed of a response is more important than an exact setting. For example, when you must slam on the brakes, it is important that you be fast, but you do not have to depress the brake pedal to an exact point. The gas and brake pedals also are linear controls. **Linear controls** move in a straight line. Toggle switches and push buttons are linear because they move in a short straight line. **Rotary controls** are knobs that move in a circular pattern, such as radio dials, oven controls, and steering wheels (Kantowitz & Sorkin, 1983).

Feedback in Control Operations

The operator must be able to find the control device and not confuse it with other controls. Coding and labeling are needed in this respect. Typically, we use visual codes because controls are easily labeled with written words and symbols. A sound signal can be added to inform the operator that a control has been activated. Tactual coding can be used for control identification, as many controls are operated by the bare hand. The shape, size, and texture of knobs and levers can be recognized by touch alone. Controls also provide the operator with kinesthetic information because of the resistance built into them. Control resistance not only helps the operator manipulate the device but also allows him or her to identify the control. The resistance acts as a "label." You can tell the difference between a car's clutch and its brake because of the difference in the resistance of the pedals.

Closed-loop human-machine systems are closed by virtue of the feedback information exchanged by the two system components. Input to the human via machine displays provides feedback on the results of previous control actions or machine adjustments. Other feedback loops do not involve machine displays. Some of what we do in operating a machine is based on the immediate personal feedback we get from the control operation. We get immediate visual feedback when we look to see that we are turning a knob in the right direction. We also get auditory feedback when we hear the sounds that accompany a machine's start-up. We get kinesthetic feedback from the resistance we feel in operating a control device. These are *sensory feedback loops.* (Refer to figure 15.4 to see an example.) Such feedback provides a way to monitor work progress. Sometimes, adjustments must be made quickly in order to avert accidents or system failure. The sensory feedback loop can provide the quickest information for this, and the design of human-machine systems should take it into account.

Human work is done sometimes with equipment and sometimes without. Although machines have superior ability to lift and move materials, much of this work is done manually. Heavy lifting is physically taxing and can cause injury.

Much work is done with hand tools. Certain tool handle designs cause cumulative hand traumas, such as carpal tunnel syndrome. The work purpose of a

*M*ain
*P*oints

tool and its potential for causing injury, as well as the user's dominant hand, must be considered in hand tool design.

Human output in human-machine systems occurs through physical action and control operations. Knobs, dials, and pedals are common control devices. Controls can be discrete or continuous, and linear or rotary.

In control design, we must remember that users must locate and operate controls easily. Expectations of how things work should be considered, and control devices need to be labeled. Control knobs can be identified by touch. Control resistance gives kinesthetic information. Such sensory feedback is useful in operating equipment.

SPECIAL MACHINES

Science fiction writers long have imagined that computers and robots would be instrumental in space exploration and, at the same time, the source of some frightening problems. For example, in some stories, robots are portrayed very much like humans, even to the point of having human emotions. Computers are described as highly efficient brains, made lifelike by natural-sounding synthesized voices. In some science fiction, computers are particularly fearsome because they make their own decisions and use robots to carry out these decisions. The combination of computer and robot can result in humanlike automatons of immense strength and cunning. At the present time, the space program does use computers and robots. However, work in space is not the primary use of this machinery. Most computers and robots are used in down-to-earth business and industry. Although the problems with them may be unnerving, they are not quite what they are in science fiction.

Computers

Computer information is sent to an operator through static displays, such as printouts, and by dynamic visual and auditory displays. Synthesized speech is currently being studied for its potential as an auditory display. However, the most commonly used dynamic display is through the computer monitor or the video display terminal. Control devices for most computers are a **keyboard** and a cursor-positioning device, such as a **mouse.**

The greatest difference between offices of today and those of 40 years ago is the computer. Computers were first introduced to office work in the early 1950s. By the early 1980s, there were some 15 million computer terminals in offices in the United States alone. In the 1990s, computer work has become part of the work that a majority of American workers do on a day-to-day basis.

The office computer is historically linked to the typewriter. The typewriter was one of the first office technologies, along with the duplicator and the telephone. When the computer became more efficient in word processing than the typewriter, it began to replace the typewriter in the office (Stewart, 1985). The computer is much more than a high-class typewriter, however. Basically, it is an *information-processing machine* that extends our ability on some tasks, such as storing information. It complements our abilities in some areas in which we are inefficient. For example, the computer can perform arithmetic operations quickly and without error. Computer technology is being added to many human-machine systems to provide this type of assistance. In other systems, computers are used to replace the human. They play the central "starring" role in data collection and analysis and in communications. Psychologists and other scientists use computers to do research, develop theoretical models, and write books and articles. In some restaurants, waiters register their customers' orders by means of a hand-held computer. Travel agents use their computers to communicate with other computers and make travel and lodging reservations. Secretaries use computers to produce letters and reports, and maintain filing systems. Accountants use them to record, project, and maintain financial resources. Hospitals use them to run medical equipment. Law enforcement agencies use them to analyze evidence.

Because of their information-processing capacities, computers are now being used to perform some work previously thought to be uniquely human. For example, new computer technology and programming have resulted in the development of computer-based "intelligent" or expert systems. **Expert systems** are programmed procedures for problem solving and decision making. Expert systems have been developed for making medical diagnoses; analyzing and interpreting research data; diagnosing mechanical malfunctions; and planning business operations. In addition, job applicants are tested and new employees are trained by computers. In general, the work that an expert system can do is the work that human experts can do. Human experts have a body of knowledge and know how to use it to solve problems. To develop an expert system, computer scientists compile the knowledge and methods of human experts and then translate this information into computer language (Chignell & Peterson, 1988).

Human Problems in Computer Use

People sometimes are enthusiastic about using computers on their jobs. Those who believe that a computer will improve their performance are more likely to welcome this equipment (Davis, 1993). However, workers may react negatively to computers. Part of the reason may be the poor allocation of functions that is typical of the human-computer system. That is, the important work is allocated to the computer. The operator ends up doing only simple tasks or monitoring. In some systems, the operator spends the entire workshift at the keyboard entering data. In other jobs, the person's role is that of machine monitor. If the same kind of work was done after computerization as before, the computer can improve the quality of the job for the person (Long, 1993). However, if the person's role is reduced by computerization, an unsatisfying job can result.

Clerical employees do the most computer work. Managers, although often expressing enthusiasm for computerization of the office, use computers least, and those that do use computers do not find that they enhance job quality (Long, 1993). Some think the reason managers do little computer work is that using a keyboard is too much like clerical work (Swartz, 1986). However, one reason managers cite is that it is difficult to skim material on a VDT screen. Other employees also say that reading from a VDT screen is not as easy as reading from paper, and lab studies have shown that VDT reading is slower (Gould & Grischkowsky, 1984). Researchers have found that this is due to the poor image quality of the material displayed on a VDT and that VDT reading speed is as fast as reading from paper when the displayed material is of high quality (Gould et al., 1987; Jorna & Snyder, 1991).

THE WIZARD OF ID

Brant parker and Johnny hart

Robots

The unique feature of robots, distinguishing them from many other new technologies, is their versatility. They can be programmed for a number of different tasks, from materials handling to precision work with small tools, and they can be reprogrammed (Shenkar, 1988). Robots function as hands and arms and operate in a humanlike manner, although they hardly resemble human beings (see figure 15.8). The robot arm has joints and a variety of "finger" levers or clamps, depending on the task it will perform. Essentially, the **robot** is a mechanical manipulator. It is usually automated by computer equipment. However, it is possible to view an extender that a human wears to enhance strength, as a robot. Such a device is a manipulator, but it is controlled by a human rather than a computer (Kazerooni, 1990). Eventually, speech controls will operate robot arms, and work is underway to develop equipment that can recognize human speech (Newell et al., 1991; Noyes, Haigh, & Starr, 1989).

Although computers have affected white-collar jobs in the modern world, robots have more of an impact on blue-collar jobs. Robots usually do repetitive work involving fixed procedures in manufacturing operations. They have been developed to work on the assembly line, performing such activities as welding and spray painting. They are used also in loading and transporting materials and finished products. An advantage of robots is their ability to perform heavy and dangerous work (Lambrinos & Johnson, 1984).

In this and in other countries, such as Japan, computer controlled robots are beginning to be an integral part of **automated factories.** The automobile industry is currently undergoing robotization. The number of workers that will be replaced by robots is not clear. However, some forecasters predict that as many as 8 million workers might be replaced by the year 2000 and that almost all factory workers will be replaced by the year 2025 (Ayers & Miller, 1982). Although more recent predictions are less extreme, robotization is still likely to result in a serious displacement problem (Shenkar, 1988).

One answer to the concerns about worker displacement is that a new industry will be created to design, sell, and service robots. However, if predictions of the numbers displaced are accurate, the jobs provided by this new industry will

Figure 15.8 An industrial robot.

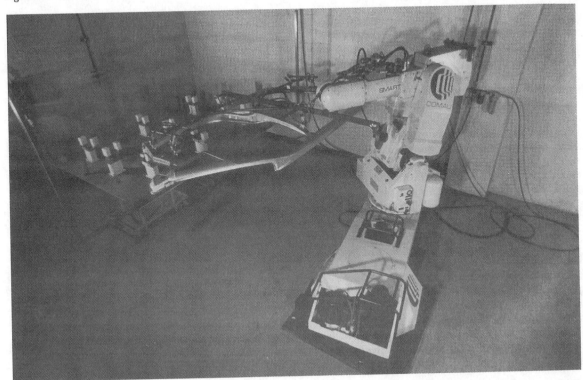

not be enough (Shenkar, 1988). Also, workers who are transferred as a result of robotization will need retraining for their new jobs. For some younger people who would like to move into another line of work, job transfer may be a plus, but it may not be considered desirable by older workers. Further, robotization, like computerization, is likely to result in task allocation in which the human's job includes more machine monitoring and troubleshooting.

*M*ain *P*oints

Computers are information processing machines. They amplify and complement human abilities, or they replace the human. They are central to office work. Expert systems do work once thought to be uniquely human.

Workers are likely to accept a computer if it improves performance, or they may react negatively if adding a computer causes job quality to decline. Some employees resist computers because VDT screens are hard to read.

Robots are mechanical manipulators controlled by a computer. They can be programmed to do a variety of work, usually in manufacturing. They are central in the move toward automated factories. The potential problem is massive displacement of blue-collar workers.

CHAPTER SUMMARY

The theme of this chapter is work design. Design is considered in three ways: (1) in the scheduling of work, (2) in arranging the workspace, and (3) in designing work equipment and human-machine systems. In each aspect of design, the worker must be considered.

The temporal conditions of work affect the performance of the worker and the functioning of the work system. Therefore, the scheduling of work hours should be done carefully. Some plans vary starting and quitting times. Others vary the length of the workweek by increasing the number of hours worked per day. One important schedule variation is shiftwork. The difficult part of shiftwork is night work, and the difficulty is severe with rotating shifts.

Workspaces must be designed and arranged to fit the user. Engineering psychologists have developed design strategies that emphasize the human use of equipment and space. These design strategies and anthropometric data have been helpful in designing the worker into the workspace. Work surfaces and chairs should be adjustable to the extent possible. The designer also needs to think about the physical environment of work, particularly the needs to control noise and provide illumination.

Central to the design of human-machine work systems is the fact that people and machines differ in what they can and should do. Function allocation is the process of deciding what tasks each will perform in a work system. Ideally, machines should be allocated work that humans cannot do well.

General systems theory emphasizes that effective work systems depend on the interactions between the system's components. Two interactions—input and output—link the human and the machine. Input from the machine to the human depends on effective displays. Displays vary in the kinds of information they convey and in the human sense used to detect the signal. Most designs rely on visual and auditory displays. Control devices provide the means for the operator to interact with the machine. They are coded so that the operator can locate them, with visual, auditory, and/or tactual labels, and their operation provides feedback.

Physical activity is the major work in some jobs, such as manual materials handling. Certain physical activities and poorly designed equipment and tools can result in problems, such as lifting injuries and repetition trauma. Using computers and robots can be an answer to some work needs. Robots can do physical work, and computers can do information processing. However, the use of these machines can result in other potentially serious problems. Many blue-collar workers may be replaced by robots, and many white-collar workers may do more menial tasks or machine monitoring.

STUDY QUESTIONS

1) What are some new ways to schedule a workday and a workweek? If an organization must operate around the clock, what is the best way to schedule shift work?

2) Identify the three strategies for designing workspaces, and specify when each is needed.

3) How high should a work surface be? What is the best design for work seating?

4) What is a machine, and what is its purpose in human work?

5) Outline general systems theory. How is it helpful in analyzing human-machine systems?

6) In effective function allocation, when should a work task be assigned to the human?

7) What is the difference between open-loop and closed-loop systems?

8) When is it better to use the visual modality rather than the auditory to convey a message? What kind of information can be conveyed by auditory displays?

9) What is the difference between serial and parallel processing?

10) Why is vigilance difficult?

11) What kinds of hand injuries can result from tool use, and what causes them?

12) Describe the different kinds of control devices.

13) What human problems may occur because of computer and robot use?

CONSIDER THIS

CONTROVERSY

What happens when the computer shuts down? Do people revert to "manual" and pick up the work themselves. Do they use their own cognitive abilities in place of the computer's, or do they sit around helplessly and wait for the computer to come back up? They probably do the latter, wouldn't you say?

This is a performance problem that has developed as a result of using automated equipment. It is called the "out-of-the-loop" performance decrement, and it is being studied in research.[3]

As you learn in this chapter, humans play an important role in closed-loop human-machine systems because they use their superior information processing abilities to control the machine. When this human role is given over to a computer, we have automated the system. We also have designed the human *out* of the loop.

What are the effects of replacing the human? Complacency is a likely result. Maybe people sit around and wait for the computer, because what they do doesn't matter much. After all, in many cases, nothing results from automation failure except a little lost time. However, what if it is more than a little lost time? What if the automated equipment is flying an airplane?

Another reason that workers may not go to manual when a system fails is that they have forgotten how. When skills are not used, they are lost. In addition, some workers may never have developed the manual skills in the first place. If they were trained on the automated equipment, they may never have learned the underlying manual skills. To make the problem even more serious, research is finding that those who do not have the manual capacities to operate the system are also less effective in monitoring and may be unaware of impending malfunction (Endsley & Kiris, 1995).

Here's the controversy. Are we asking for trouble by training workers and educating students to rely on computerized equipment? Are we doing the future generation a disservice by teaching school children computer operation and allowing them to do their homework assignments on computers? Should we instead require kids to learn how to solve the problems with their own brains?

---

[3]For example, see Endsley, M. R., & Kiris, E. O. (1995). The out-of-the-loop performance problem and level of control in automation. *Human Factors, 37,* 381–394.

Appendix

Graduate Programs in Industrial/Organizational Psychology

The following is a list of graduate programs in I/O psychology in the United States and Canada. The programs are classified according to the state or province in which they are located and the level of the degree(s) they offer. This list is taken from *Graduate Training Programs in Industrial/Organizational Psychology and Related Fields,* Arlington Heights, IL: Society for Industrial and Organizational, Inc., 1992. Other programs, called organizational behavior (OB) programs, are similar in content to I/O programs but are not listed in this appendix. OB programs are usually offered by business departments, whereas I/O programs are offered by psychology departments. More information about all these programs can be obtained from the *Graduate Training Programs* publication.

Location	University	Degree(s)
Canada		
Alberta	U. of Calgary	Doctoral, Masters
British Columbia	U. of British Columbia	Doctoral
Ontario	Queen's	Doctoral
	U. of Western Ontario	Doctoral
	U. of Waterloo	Doctoral
United States		
Alabama	Auburn	Doctoral
	U. of Alabama	Doctoral, Masters
California	California State, San Bernardino	Masters
	California State, Long Beach	Masters
	California State, Sacramento	Masters
	California School of Professional Psychology	Doctoral
	Claremont Graduate School	Doctoral
	San Francisco State	Masters
	San Jose State	Masters
	U. of California, Berkeley	Doctoral
Colorado	Colorado State	Doctoral
	U. of Colorado, Denver	Masters
Connecticut	U. of Connecticut	Doctoral
	U. of Hartford	Masters
	U. of New Haven	Masters
D.C.	George Washington	Doctoral

Location	University	Degree(s)
Florida	Florida International	Doctoral
	Florida Tech	Masters
	U. of Central Florida	Masters
	U. of South Florida	Doctoral
	U. of West Florida	Masters
Georgia	Georgia Institute of Technology	Doctoral
	U. of Georgia	Doctoral
	Valdosta State College	Masters
Illinois	DePaul	Doctoral
	Illinois Institute of Technology	Doctoral
	Illinois State	Masters
	Northern Illinois	Doctoral
	Southern Illinois	Masters
	U. of Illinois, Urbana-Champaign	Doctoral
Indiana	Indiana, Purdue	Masters
	Purdue	Doctoral
Iowa	Iowa State	Doctoral
Kansas	Kansas State	Doctoral, Masters
Kentucky	Western Kentucky	Masters
Louisiana	Louisiana State	Doctoral
	Tulane	Doctoral
Maryland	U. of Baltimore	Masters
	U. of Maryland	Doctoral
Massachusetts	Springfield College	Masters
Michigan	Central Michigan	Doctoral, Masters
	Michigan State	Doctoral
	U. of Michigan	Doctoral
	Wayne State	Doctoral

Location	University	Degree(s)	Location	University	Degree(s)
Minnesota	U. of Minnesota	Doctoral	Ohio	Bowling Green State	Doctoral
	Mankato State	Masters		Ohio State	Doctoral
Mississippi	U. of Southern	Doctoral		Ohio	Doctoral
	Mississippi			Wright State	Doctoral, Masters
Missouri	U. of Missouri,	Doctoral		U. of Akron	Doctoral, Masters
	St. Louis			Xavier	Masters
Nebraska	U. of Nebraska,	Doctoral, Masters	Oregon	Portland State	Doctoral, Masters
	Omaha		Oklahoma	U. of Tulsa	Doctoral, Masters
New Jersey	Fairleigh Dickinson	Masters	Pennsylvania	Carnegie Mellon	Doctoral
	Montclair State	Masters		Pennsylvania State	Doctoral
	Stevens Institute	Doctoral		West Chester	Masters
	of Technology		South Carolina	Clemson	Masters
New York	City U. of New York	Doctoral, Masters	Tennessee	Middle Tennessee State	Masters
	Columbia	Doctoral		U. of Tennessee	Doctoral
	Fordham	Doctoral	Texas	Lamar	Masters
	New York	Doctoral, Masters		Rice	Doctoral
	Rensselaer Polytechnic	Masters		Texas A&M	Doctoral
	Institute			U. of Houston	Doctoral
	SUNY, Albany	Doctoral		U. of North Texas	Doctoral, Masters
North Carolina	Appalachian State	Masters	Virginia	George Mason	Doctoral, Masters
	East Carolina	Masters		Old Dominion	Doctoral
	North Carolina State	Doctoral		Radford	Masters
	U. of North Carolina	Masters		Virinia Tech.	Doctoral
			Wisconsin	U. of Wisconsin	Masters

Glossary

A

Accident severity: the extent to which an accident has serious detrimental effects.

Accuracy training: training to improve a rater's ability to evaluate job performance by improving observation and evaluation skills.

Achievement test: a mental ability test used to evaluate what someone has learned.

Achievement theory: a work motivation theory proposed by McClelland and Atkinson that emphasizes the individual's need to accomplish meaningful work goals.

Action research: a method of study and analysis that involves diagnosis, action, and evaluation in OD projects.

Activity process analysis: a technique of direct observation used for studying the process of a work activity.

Ad hoc committee: a temporary group of employees formed to deal with a specific organizational issue.

Adverse impact: a discriminatory effect of a selection procedure on a person's employment opportunity.

Affirmative action: a positive stance taken in recruitment to speed up equality in employment; meant to improve recruitment of women and minorities and may involve hiring quotas.

Age Discrimination in Employment Act (ADEA): federal measure making it unlawful to consider age in selection decisions.

Alarm stage: the first stage in Selye's model of stress; corresponds to the physiological fight-or-flight response.

Alcoholism: alcohol abuse; usually involves loss of control over drinking.

Alternate forms: a method of assessing test reliability in which scores on two versions of the same test are correlated.

Americans with Disabilities Act: a law passed in 1990 that provides equal employment opportunity for qualified disabled employees.

Anchoring: the process of defining points on a graphic rating scale; numerical or verbal labels can be used.

Anthropometry: measurement of human physical dimensions; a specialty within engineering psychology.

Anxiety management training: technique that combines relaxation and coping skills instruction to relieve anxiety.

Applied psychology: fields of psychology in which basic psychological knowledge and research methods are used to learn about and solve practical problems.

Apprenticeship: a traditional method of training in which general education is combined with on-site job training.

Aptitude test: a test of native (innate) ability or capacity for learning.

Army Alpha: a written test developed by psychologists during World War I for classifying army inductees.

Army Beta: a nonlanguage test developed by psychologists for classifying army inductees during World War I.

Asbestosis: an occupational disease caused by long-term exposure to asbestos.

Assessment center: a selection technique in which assessors observe and evaluate a group of applicants working on activities that simulate the job.

Autocratic leadership: a style of behavior in which the leader is directive and controlling.

Automated factories: manufacturing plants operated mainly by machinery, including robots.

Automation: the use of machines to replace human workers in an occupation or at a workplace.

Autonomic nervous system: the homeostatic system that regulates the internal environment of the body.

Average rating error: a rater error in which ratings are concentrated in the middle of a scale; also called central tendency error.

B

Backward rotation: a schedule in which workers are regularly changed from a later workshift to an earlier one.

Behavioral Consistency Method: a job application procedure in which samples of personal history are obtained.

Behavioral objectives: explicit statements of what KSAs will be developed in training; derived from training goals.

Behavioral Observation Scale (BOS): a performance rating scale in which dimensions are described in behavioral terms; response categories are frequencies.

Behaviorally Anchored Rating Scale (BARS): a performance rating scale in which dimensions and scale points are described in behavioral terms; rater checks the best descriptor.

Behavior measure: a criterion measure of training performance that indicates the extent to which training is transferred to the job.

Behavior modeling: a method of leadership training based on social learning theory in which trainees learn by observing others.

Behavior modification: a technique, based on reinforcement theory, used to improve motivation and performance.

Biased group assignments: a threat to the internal validity of a training program due to systematic differences between trainees placed in experimental and control groups.

Biodata: personal or biographical information used to develop items for biographical inventories.

Biofeedback: a relaxation training procedure in which feedback about internal bodily processes is provided with electronic equipment.

Biographical inventory: an application, containing personal information items, that can be scored; developed like a weighted application blank.

Bivariate distribution: a distribution obtained by plotting scores on one variable on the horizontal axis and scores on another variable on the vertical axis of a graph.

Blood alcohol content (BAC): the amount of alcohol in the blood, used to set legal intoxication levels.

Bottom-line concept: used in adverse impact assessments; the final step in selection; the number of applicants hired.

Braille printing: a tactual display used to convey printed material to visually handicapped users.

Brainstorming: a method of creative problem solving; includes procedures for enhancing idea generation and solution evaluation.

Breathalizer: a test for detecting alcohol use.

Bureaucracy: the classical organizational design in which there is a specialized division of labor, centralized authority, and formalization.

Burnout: a behavioral disturbance resulting from prolonged stress; individual shows extreme fatigue and discouragement.

Bypassing: communications sent by a route outside the accepted channels, as by going around a supervisor.

C

Carcinogen: a substance that can cause cancer.

Career development: a training program in which employees learn the paths and decision points in developing an occupation.

Causal network: a view of human behavior as being caused by more than one factor or source of influence.

Centralized organization: an organization in which most decisions are made by top management.

Central tendency error: a rater error in which ratings of employees are concentrated in the middle of a scale.

Central tendency measures: descriptive statistics that indicate the average behavior of a group of subjects.

CEO: chief executive officer or head of a company.

Channel model: information-processing model used to design tasks for either serial or parallel processing; proposed by Triesman.

Charismatic leadership: a style of behavior through which a visionary leader inspires followers to accomplish great things.

Chilling effect: a *Uniform Guidelines* term used to describe a discriminatory stance that some companies take to discourage certain job applicants.

Civil Rights Act: original legislation passed in 1964 making employment discrimination on the basis of race, religion, national origin, and sex unlawful; 1991 Act supports and amends some provisions.

Clearance: the amount of workspace required by a worker; an anthropometric measure.

Climate: the psychological or social atmosphere of an organization.

Closed-loop system: a self-controlled work system in which each interaction leads to the next to complete a loop.

Closed questions: test or questionnaire items in which answers are chosen from a predetermined set of responses.

Coefficient alpha: Cronbach's procedure for assessing interitem reliability of tests; provides an index of internal consistency.

Cognitive behavioral interventions: techniques used in developing coping skills to relieve depression and anxiety.

Cognitive dissonance: a theoretical concept referring to inconsistency or imbalance in cognitions; proposed to result in tension.

Cognitive style: a person's characteristic pattern of thinking.

Cognitive theory: theoretical emphasis on the effects of thoughts, beliefs, and expectations in determining behavior.

Cognitive workload: the amount and complexity of the mental work involved in a job.

Collective bargaining: the process of negotiating a labor contract between a union and an organization.

Communication network: a structure of channels in the organization through which information is passed.

Comparable worth: the view that equal pay should be provided for jobs that have equal value.

Competition: a conflict management style involving negative behavior designed to defeat the other party.

Compressed workweek: a schedule of ten to twelve hours a day for three or four days a week.

Computer Adaptive Testing (CAT): using computers to develop and administer a customized test for each testee.

Computer-assisted testing: using computers to administer a conventional test.

Concurrent validity: a form of criterion-related validity in which current employees are used as the validation sample.

Configurational theory: an organizational theory proposed by Mintzberg in which effective organizational structures are proposed depending on the technical environments in which they exist.

Conflict: a psychological construct involving incompatible goals.

Conflict parties: the persons, factions, or groups who are directly involved in a conflict.

Consideration: a leadership style in which a leader shows concern for the welfare of group members; similar to employee-oriented behavior.

Constructive confrontation: a procedure used by supervisors to motivate employees to deal with problems, such as alcoholism; informing an employee of the consequences of the problem.

Construct validity: assessment of the extent to which a test measures a theoretical construct or trait; incorporates evidence of convergent and divergent validity.

Content adequacy: the extent to which a measure samples important aspects of a behavior.

Content validity: assessment of test validity based on evidence that the test samples the job content.

Contingency theory: Fiedler's leadership theory in which a leader's effectiveness is seen as depending on the leader's style and amount of control over the situation.

Continuous controls: control devices with many different settings, such as a radio tuning knob.

Contrast error: a judgment error in which the evaluation of one person is unduly affected by the evaluation of another person.

Control group: the group of subjects not exposed to experimental manipulation; compared with the experimental group.

Control resistance: force built into a control that can be detected by the kinesthetic senses; gives feedback about control operation.

Convergent validity: an aspect of construct validity in which a test of a construct is shown to converge toward an accepted test of the same construct.

Conversion processes: a concept used in systems design referring to the internal processes of converting input into output.

Cooperation: a conflict management style involving behavior that helps both conflicting parties to reach their goals.

Correlation: the degree of association between two variables; expressed as a value between -1.00 and +1.00.

Covariance: relationship between two variables that systematically occur and change together.

Cramping: having too little space because of too many objects in the surroundings.

Criterion measure: a measure of work behavior, such as a supervisor's rating, used in evaluating the validity of a test or other instrument or procedure.

Criterion-related validity: assessment of the soundness of a test based on empirical evidence that it predicts a criterion measure of job performance.

Critical incidents: specific worker behaviors cited as important to job success or failure; used in job analysis and in developing performance rating scales.

Cross-cultural differences: differences in the behavior of people from different countries.

Cross-cultural training: training to improve employees' abilities in interacting with people from other countries.

Cross-reactivity: a problem in drug testing in which use of over-the-counter drugs causes a urinalysis to appear positive for a regulated drug.

Crowding: having too little space because of too many people in the surroundings.

Culture: the shared knowledge, beliefs, and values of an organization that have developed over time; represents how an organization approaches its problems.

Cumulative-effect hand trauma: a disorder caused by repeated slight injury from long-term use of poorly designed hand tools.

Current employee referrals: a method of recruiting applicants by accepting referrals from employees.

Cutoff score: the score on a test designated as the minimum passing score.

D

Decentralized organization: an organization in which many decisions are made by lower level managers and employees.

Decibel: the unit of measure of sound intensity or loudness.

Decibel A (dBa) scale: a scale of sound intensities weighted according to human sensitivities.

Decision tree: a device for deciding an issue; the user answers an ordered series of questions and arrives at a recommended action.

Democratic leadership: a style of behavior in which the leader shares decision making with the group.

Departmentation: a procedure for dividing organizational members into groups.

Dependent variable: the variable hypothesized to respond to changes in the independent variable; the variable measured in an experiment.

Descriptive statistics: indices, such as mean and standard deviation, that summarize and describe the behavior of subjects.

Designated leader: a formally appointed or elected leader.

Design for a range: a design strategy taking account of differences in people; used to design adjustable equipment.

Design for the average: an equipment design strategy in which the dimensions of the average operator are used.

Design for the extremes: a design strategy taking account of the smallest or largest user; used in determining clearance and reach requirements.

Direct glare: glare due to a light source in the field of vision.

Direct observation: an observational method in which the researcher records subjects' overt behavior.

Discrepancy hypothesis: theoretical statement that job satisfaction depends on the difference between what is desired and what is experienced on the job.

Discrete controls: control devices having few settings, such as an on-off switch.

Disposition: a personal propensity or tendency.

Distress: a stress response to negative events.

Distributed practice: short study or rehearsal sessions that are spread over a period of time.

Divergent validity: an aspect of construct validity in which a test of a construct is shown to differ from a test measuring a different construct.

Diversity training: Training designed to increase employees' cross-cultural understanding and ability to work with diverse coworkers.

Domesticated drugs: drugs that are socially accepted for common use, such as caffeine and nicotine.

Downsizing: an overall reduction in the number of people an organization employs.

Downward communication: messages sent by superiors to subordinates.

Drug abuse: excessive use of a regulated drug.

Drug testing program: an organizational program for detection of drug use.

Dynamic data: anthropometric measurements of the space required for the body to move.

Dynamic visual displays: dials and scales on equipment through which changing information is conveyed visually.

Dysfunctional turnover: turnover that is costly to the organization, as when good performers quit.

E

Educationally overqualified: an employee who has more education than his or her job requires.

Emergent leader: a person who performs the leadership role without being appointed or elected as leader.

Employee assistance program (EAP): an organizational program for helping employees with personal problems.

Employee-oriented leadership: a style of behavior shown by a leader who is concerned about the followers' welfare.

Employee withdrawal: forms of retreat from work, such as absenteeism and turnover.

Employment-at-will rights: the rights traditionally held by employers to decide on questions of hiring and termination.

Engineering psychology: a related field concerned with the study and design of human-machine systems (also called human factors).

Equal-appearing intervals: a procedure used for developing weights for performance statements to go on a weighted checklist evaluation; uses supervisor judgments.

Equal Employment Opportunity Commission (EEOC): federal agency established in 1972 to monitor employers' compliance with Title VII of the Civil Rights Act.

Equal Pay Act (EPA): a federal law that regulates compensation practices; requires employees who do the same job to be paid the same.

Equity theory: a motivation theory proposed by Adams that emphasizes the effects of cognitive inconsistency between pay and performance in motivating change.

Equivalence: an indication of the extent to which two forms of a test measure the same behavioral dimension.

Eustress: stress induced by positive events.

Executive monkey studies: early research demonstrating the impact of stressful work on physical health.

Exhaustion stage: the third stage of stress in Selye's model in which bodily processes break down.

Expectancy theory: a motivation theory proposed by Vroom that emphasizes the effects of expectations about work performance in determining motivation.

Experiment: a research technique that allows a researcher to control the conditions to which subjects are exposed and test hypotheses about cause-effect relationships.

Experimental group: the subjects to whom the experimental condition is exposed.

Expert systems: computer programs produced by compiling and translating the information a human expert uses in making decisions.

External consulting: work in which a professional provides expert services on a contract basis.

External validity: the extent to which the results of a training program evaluation can be generalized to other situations and trainees.

Extinction: a concept used in reinforcement theory to indicate performance loss through lack of reinforcement.

Extrinsic rewards: tangible outcomes of work performance, such as pay; concept used in motivation research.

F

Faces Scale: a standardized job satisfaction survey instrument in which drawings of faces are used as response categories.

Facet model: a theoretical model proposed by Beehr and Newman; various components of job stress are organized in sequence.

Facet theory: Lawler's job satisfaction theory; satisfaction with a job component is determined by perceptions of equity and discrepancies between what is expected and what is received.

Face validity: having the appearance of being well founded as when test items look as if they measure a particular content.

Fact-finding methods: informal procedures for exploring and studying a problem at work.

Factor comparison: a job evaluation method in which jobs are assessed as to the extent that they contain the elements of value present in benchmark jobs.

Family counseling: therapeutic activity, often included in EAPs, that is meant to help employees with marital and family problems.

Feedback: information given about previous performance.

Field experiment: a study conducted in a practical work setting, such as a business, by means of the experimental method.

Fight-or-flight reaction: physiological arousal that provides the body with energy to respond to a threat; corresponds to the alarm stage in Selye's stress model.

Filtering: a process of reducing and/or modifying organizational communications.

Fixed shifts: workshift assignments that do not rotate.

Flat organizational structure: an organization having little vertical differentiation or few levels.

Flextime: a flexible work schedule that allows employees some control over their starting and quitting times.

Forced-choice checklist: a nonrating performance evaluation method containing sets of performance statements from which the evaluator must choose.

Forced distribution: a nonrating performance evaluation in which employees are distributed among predetermined categories ranging from high to low.

Formal communication: informational exchange through the official channels of an organization.

Formalized organization: an organization that uses written rules and standard procedures; "going by the book."

Forward rotation: a schedule in which workers are regularly changed from an earlier workshift to a later one.

Four-fifths rule of thumb: informal method of evaluating differences in selection ratios of different groups in adverse impact assessments.

Function allocation: the assignment of required tasks to the person or the machine in a human-machine system.

Functional turnover: turnover that is good for the organization, as when poor performers quit.

G

General Adaptation Syndrome: a theoretical model proposed by Selye describing stress as a general physiological response occurring through three stages of severity.

General systems theory: a theoretical model proposed by von Bertalanffy that emphasizes the interactions between all components of a system.

Gestalt psychology: a school of psychology in which the psychological whole is viewed as greater than the sum of its parts.

Goal: a purpose or intention; the central concept in goal-setting theory.

Goal-setting theory: Locke's theory of work motivation; emphasizes a process of developing commitment to work goals.

Grapevine: an informal communication network.

Graphic rating scale: a performance evaluation instrument in which employees are rated from high to low on one or more dimensions.

"Great man" theory: an informal theory of leadership in which great leaders are seen as having superior attributes.

Griggs v. Duke Power Company: 1971 Supreme Court case defining practices that constitute employment discrimination.

Group maintenance function: a group's need to maintain itself in good working order; performed by members who pay attention to the interactions.

Group norms: general guidelines for the behavior of group members that express the group's values.

Group process analysis: a technique of direct observation for studying interpersonal or group phenomena.

Group task function: refers to a group's formal goal; carried out by members who contribute directly to task performance.

Group test: a test administered to a group of individuals.

Groupthink: a construct describing the thought processes that impair decision making in highly cohesive groups.

H

Hallucinogens: drugs that have hallucinationlike effects, such as cannabis; used largely for recreation.

Halo error: a judgment or rating effect in which the evaluator assumes an association between two traits that does not exist.

Hawthorne studies: early field experiments done at the Hawthorne plant of the Western Electric Company; noted for unexpected finding that social conditions affect work.

Hazard: an environmental condition that interacts negatively with human behavior to cause an accident.

Headhunter: a recruitment agent.

Health promotion programs (HPPs): organizational programs to increase the general health of employees, such as fitness programs.

Hiring quota: affirmative action plan for hiring disproportionate numbers of females and minorities.

History: a threat to internal validity due to specific outside events that can be confused with training effects during training evaluation.

Horizontal differentiation: results from dividing an organization into groups, such as departments.

Human-machine system: a work system composed of a worker and equipment or tools.

Human relations movement: emphasis on the social conditions of work; resulted in the development of organizational psychology.

I

Implicit theory of leadership: the view that leadership is a reflection of a follower's thoughts.

In-basket exercise: an assessment center activity in which the candidate handles routine materials that might accumulate on an executive's desk.

Independent variable: the variable that the researcher manipulates and controls in an experiment; hypothesized to have a causal effect.

Individual differences: an emphasis of research that aims to discover how people are different rather than how they are similar.

Individual test: a test administered to one person at a time.

Industrial/organizational (I/O) psychology: an applied psychology; the study of human behavior at work.

Inferential statistics: mathematical procedures used for testing hypotheses and inferring relationships between variables.

Informal communication: informational exchange that takes place outside formal organizational channels.

Information technology: computerized equipment that makes it possible to process large amounts of information.

In-house consultant: a professional hired as an employee to provide expert advice.

Initiating structure: a behavioral style in which a leader focuses on accomplishing a task; similar to production-oriented leadership.

Inputs: the information displayed or raw materials received by one component of a system from another in human machine systems.

Instrumentation: a threat to internal validity in training due to differences in the instruments used for pre- and posttesting.

Integrity test: a test assessing honest and ethical employee behavior.

Interested audience: comparatively uninvolved persons whose presence may affect the behavior of parties in conflict.

Interitem reliability: a method of assessing test reliability in which the consistency of the items is evaluated.

Internal consistency: an indication of the extent to which a test measures the same behavior across items.

Internal validity: the extent to which training activities are effective in producing the learning desired in a training program.

Interrater reliability: an index showing the extent to which evaluators agree in their assessments.

Interview: a basic mode of communication in which information is transmitted or exchanged.

Intrinsic rewards: performance outcomes that have inherent satisfactions, such as feelings of accomplishment.

Introspective method: a process of self-examination used by some researchers as a research perspective.

Irritants: toxic substances that damage the skin or respiratory system.

Item Response Theory (IRT): a theoretical model used in Computer Adaptive Testing to evaluate test responses as a function of a testee's level of an underlying trait tested by the item.

J

Jenkins Activity Survey: a pencil-and-paper measure of the Type A behavioral pattern.

Job: a group of positions in which employees perform identical or similar tasks.

Job analysis: a job study; methods for doing a job study.

Job attitude: a consistent pattern of thoughts, feelings, and behavior toward some aspect of the job.

Job Characteristics Model: theoretical model by Hackman and Oldham in which job dimensions are proposed to affect job satisfaction and other employee outcomes.

Job component validity: the ability of a test to predict performance on a component of the job rather than on the whole job.

Job Descriptive Index (JDI): a standardized instrument in which items describing and evaluating the job are used to measure job satisfaction.

Job Diagnostic Survey: instrument used to measure job dimensions, such as task significance, described in the Job Characteristics Model.

Job element method: a job analysis technique used to identify the KSAs that distinguish a superior from a marginally acceptable worker; uses an SME committee.

Job enrichment: redesign of a job to include more variety and interesting tasks, or order to increase the intrinsic value of the job.

Job evaluation: a method for deciding compensation levels in which the intrinsic worth of a job determines its monetary value.

Job family: a group of related jobs.

Job involvement: degree to which an employee is absorbed by his or her work; a job attitude.

Job redesign: an applied motivation program; the job is changed to increase the inherent value of work activities.

Job satisfaction: an individual's reaction to the job experience; a job attitude.

Job specialization: the extent to which an organization's division of labor is based on simplified work procedures.

Job transfer: a relocation in which an employee moves to another job or organizational unit.

K

Keyboard: the control device for typewriters, calculators, and most computers.

KR20: the Kuder-Richardson formula for assessing interitem reliability of tests; provides an index of internal consistency.

KSAs: knowledges, skills, and abilities; job analysis terminology referring to job requirements.

L

Laboratory training: sensitivity training used to improve leadership behavior.

Labor contract: an agreement between a union and management outlining the conditions of employment and the rights of employees.

Laissez-faire leadership: a style of leader behavior in which followers are given complete freedom.

Lateral communication: messages exchanged by peers or individuals on the same organizational level.

Leader Behavior Description Questionnaire (LBDQ): a measure of leadership style used to gather information from group members.

Leaderless group discussion: an assessment center activity in which a group of candidates work together without having assigned roles.

Leader-member exchange model: a theoretical perspective in which leadership is described as resulting from the interaction of two individuals on different levels of an organization's hierarchy, such as supervisor and subordinate.

Leader prototype: a cognitive category describing a type of leader; used to cognitively classify and store information about leaders.

Leadership: a pattern of behavior shown in group interaction that affects the group's life and goal achievement.

Leadership Opinion Questionnaire (LOQ): a measure of leader behavior used to gather information directly from leaders.

Learning: process of acquiring behavior through the lessons of experience.

Learning measure: a criterion measure of performance in training; assesses trainee's acquisition of the training material.

Learning tasks: the learning experiences required to bring about the desired KSAs in a trainee; derived from behavioral objectives.

Least Preferred Coworker (LPC) Scale: Fiedler's measure of leadership style in which respondents rate the person with whom they are least able to work.

Legal intoxication: the level of blood alcohol content that defines intoxication by law; in many states it is 0.10 percent BAC.

Leniency error: a rater error in which ratings are concentrated at the high end of the scale.

Lesson plan: outline of content and methodology used in a training session.

Likert scale: a rating scale allowing a graded response to a questionnaire item; respondent marks a point along a continuum from favorable to unfavorable.

Linear controls: control devices, such as toggle switches, that move in a straight line.

Line organization: an organization in which those involved in profit making also perform administration tasks.

Line-staff organization: a complex organization with separate departments for administration and profit making.

Logical error: a rater error in which the rater evaluates two dimensions similarly because they appear logically related.

M

Machine: the mechanical or equipment component of a human-machine system.

Macro-organizational communication: informational exchange between an organization and important segments of its environment, such as consumers.

Manual materials handling: moving of work materials and products by hand.

Maslach Burnout Inventory: a measure of job burnout; includes subscales on emotion and burnout behavior proposed to occur in human service work.

Massed practice: study taking place in one long session.

Matrix organization: a formal structure incorporating project teams and functional departments that overlap.

Maturation: a threat to internal validity due to personal developmental processes taking place during training evaluation.

Maximum work area: the total usable work surface area defined by the reach of a fully extended arm.

Mechanistic organization: a highly specialized, centralized, and formalized organization; similar to the bureaucracy.

Mental practice: rehearsal of a learning task with mental imagery.

Mentor: someone at a higher organizational level who shows interest in an employee's development; used in executive training.

Meta-analysis: a statistical procedure in which the results of many separate studies are combined and analyzed.

Micromotion study: an observation technique in which a work process is filmed and analyzed; used in engineering psychology.

Micro-organizational communication: informational exchange within the organization, such as between departments.

Middle management: supervisory and managerial employees who function as a link between the strategic apex and operating core of an organization.

Miniature training and evaluation: a procedure for assessing trainees' existing knowledge and trainability.

Minnesota Satisfaction Questionnaire (MSQ): a standardized job satisfaction questionnaire that uses a Likert scale for rating job factors; includes long and short forms.

Mission statement: a written description of the purpose and goals of an organization.

Mixed Standard Rating Scale (MSRS): a performance rating scale in which an employee's typical behavior is rated better, the same, or worse than the behavioral descriptors.

Morale: the general level of satisfaction of a group of employees.

Motivation: a construct referring to the source of behavior; addresses the arousal, direction, and persistence of behavior.

Mouse: a control device moved along the work surface to position the computer cursor.

Multiple hurdles: a series of selection procedures through which job applicants are evaluated.

Multiple linkages model: Yukl's theory of leadership; describes how a leader interacts with group members to influence their productivity and satisfaction.

N

Narcotics: drugs used for inducing sleep and relieving pain, such as the opiates.

Narrative evaluation: a performance evaluation in which a supervisor writes a free-form description of an employee.

Need for achievement (nAch): the central concept of the achievement theory of motivation; a desire to accomplish meaningful work goals.

Need-hierarchy theory: Maslow's motivation theory in which a hierarchy of biological and acquired needs are proposed to drive behavior.

Needs assessment: an approach to problem solving in which analytical and fact-finding techniques are used to assess a need.

Need Satisfaction Questionnaire (NSQ): a standardized job satisfaction instrument using ratings to infer satisfaction of needs.

Need theory: an approach to motivation that emphasizes the operation of needs; from earlier theory on instincts.

Negative affectivity: the tendency to experience unfavorable emotions.

Negative correlation: an association in which two factors vary in opposite directions.

Negative-sum outcome: a conflict outcome in which both parties lose.

Negative transfer: carry over of training material that interferes with performance on the job.

Noise: sound that is undesired or unpleasant.

Noise dose: the acceptable level of noise exposure determined by OSHA; should average no more than 90 dbA per day.

Nominal hours: the hours than an employee is physically present at work; includes time spent on work and nonwork activities.

Normal work area: the work surface area defined by the reach of the forearms.

Normative model: a theoretical perspective on leadership that prescribes leader behavior likely to be effective in different situations.

Nuisance variables: extraneous variables that must be controlled in an experiment to prevent them from affecting the relationship between independent and dependent variables.

O

Observational methods: research techniques in which behavior is recorded as it occurs naturally; includes surveys.

Observer effect: a problem of observational research in which the observer's presence influences the subject's behavior.

Obsolescence: the loss of job qualifications because skills are based on out-of-date equipment or methods.

Occupational disease: a physical illness caused by exposure to toxins or hazardous working conditions.

Occupational Safety and Health Act: legislation passed in 1970 to ensure safe and healthful working conditions.

Occupational Safety and Health Administration (OSHA): federal agency formed to enforce work safety standards.

OD change agent: an external or internal consultant who conducts an OD program.

One-way communication: transmission of messages in which no response is expected; usually downward communication.

On-the-job training (OJT): training in which the individual learns by doing the job at the job site.

Open communication: the honest exchange of personal and/or work-related information.

Open-ended questions: test or questionnaire items in which the respondent answers in his or her own words.

Open systems: a systems theory view of organizations as being influenced by the outside environment.

Operating core: the group of employees who perform the basic production or service work.

Operational definitions: specific operations that define or allow the experimenter to manipulate the independent variable and measure the dependent variable.

Operations goals: internal objectives concerning how an organization runs its daily activities.

Opponent process theory: Landy's theory in which job satisfaction is proposed to be an emotional state subject to the physiological process of homeostasis.

Organic organization: a flexible organization that has low job specialization, low formalization, and a decentralized decision-making structure.

Organization: a group of people who have a common purpose and a set of operating procedures.

Organizational analysis: a needs assessment in which broad measures, such as turnover, are used to indicate general needs for training.

Organizational chart: a graphic description of an organization's formal structure.

Organizational commitment: the extent to which an employee identifies with and is involved in the organization.

Organizational design: the formal structure that regulates the behavior of members of an organized body.

Organizational development (OD): a methodology or set of interventions used for helping organizations make healthy changes.

Organizational pyramid: an organizational structure with many people at the bottom, few in the middle, and one at the top.

Output goals: the central goals of an organization, referring to its products and services.

Output/input (O/I) ratio: an equity theory concept expressing the relationship between what one brings to a job and what one gets out of it.

Outputs: the physical work, control processes, or products of a work system.

Overlearning: an ingraining process of learning through continued practice beyond initial acquisition.

P

Paired comparison: a nonrating performance evaluation in which each subordinate is compared with every other subordinate.

Parallel processing: a cognitive process in which attention is divided between two tasks that are performed simultaneously.

Parasympathetic nervous system: a branch of the autonomic nervous system that stimulates body repair and restoration.

Participant observation: a technique for studying natural groups in which the researcher is a member of the group.

Part learning: practice of the elements of a learning task in separate study sessions.

Path-goal theory: a normative theory of leadership proposed by House; focuses on the leader's role as motivator.

Pay incentive plan: a program of interventions to improve work motivation; based on theories emphasizing extrinsic rewards.

Pay Satisfaction Questionnaire (PSQ): instrument used to measure employees' levels of satisfaction with pay level, raises, benefits, and pay policies.

Peer appraisal: performance evaluation conducted by a coworker.

Pencil-and-paper test: a written test usually with a machine-scorable answer sheet.

Percentile: the percentage of a standardization sample that scored at or below a given raw score.

Performance test: a test evaluating some physical action.

Person analysis: training needs assessment performed at the level of the individual employee.

Person-Environment Fit Theory: French's theoretical model of job stress; proposes that work demands not suited to a person's abilities or needs will induce stress.

Personnel selection: a multiphasic process of hiring; involves job analysis, recruitment, and evaluation of applicants.

Point system: a job evaluation method in which jobs are assigned monetary points to the extent they contain certain factors of value.

Polygraph: lie detector test; has been used as an honesty test.

Population stereotype: a stable expectation or understanding held by a group of people about how something operates or what certain symbols mean.

Position: a set of work tasks performed by one person.

Position Analysis Questionnaire PAQ: a worker-oriented job analysis instrument using job elements as items.

Positive correlation: an association in which two factors vary in the same direction.

Positive-sum outcome: a conflict outcome in which both parties win at least partially.

Positive transfer: carry over of training material that contributes to performance on the job.

Postappraisal interview: a meeting of rater and ratee in which the performance evaluation is discussed.

Power test: a test with difficult questions requiring the testee's full capacity.

Predictive validity: the extent to which a measure predicts future performance; a form of criterion-related validity using applicants as the validation sample.

Pretesting sensitization: a threat to internal training validity due to the effects of testing trainees before training them.

Primary prevention: health program interventions that change hazardous or unhealthy conditions to prevent illness.

Production measure: a performance evaluation consisting of a count of whatever the employee does or produces on the job.

Production-oriented leadership: a style of behavior shown by a leader concerned with getting the task done.

Productivity norm: an expectation in work groups that a certain level of productivity will be maintained.

Program evaluation: assessment of the effectiveness of work programs by means of experimental research.

Progressive relaxation: a verbal method of relaxation training involving mental images and deep muscle contraction.

Projective test: an individually administered personality test in which ambiguous stimuli are used as items.

Protected group: a group of people protected by law, such as those under the age of 18.

Proximity error: a rater error in which dimensions located close to each other on an instrument are evaluated similarly.

The Psychological Corporation: the first successful consulting firm, established in 1921 by Cattell.

Psychosomatic disorder: physical illness that appears to be due to prolonged stress.

Punishment: an aversive stimulus applied to suppress behavior; not the same as negative reinforcement.

Q

Qualitative display: a visual display containing information about the general range or states of a machine's functioning.

Quality circle: a discussion group in which production employees come up with ideas for improving the product.

Quantitative display: a visual display containing specific numerical information for precise readings of a machine's operation.

Quasi-experimental design: research design retaining some features of control present in an experiment; used in field studies, such as training evaluation.

R

Random drug testing: a drug detection program conducted at unannounced times with randomly selected employees.

Rank order comparison: a nonrating performance evaluation in which employees are classified from best to worst.

Rater error training: instruction for raters on how to avoid making errors in performance evaluation.

Reach: the space limitation due to a worker's physical dimensions; an anthropometric measure.

Reaction measure: a training criterion measure; assesses trainee's liking for the training program.

Reaction to research design: a threat to internal validity of training due to reactions of subjects assigned to experimental or control groups in training evaluation.

Reaction to testing: a threat to the external validity of training due to subject responses to pre- and posttesting.

Realistic job preview: a method of recruitment and selection in which an applicant is given accurate job information in an interview or work sample.

Recency error: a rater error that occurs because evaluation is based on the employee's most recent behavior.

Referral programs: health programs that refer troubled employees to outside resources for treatment.

Reflected glare: glare caused by light rays that are bent and sent back from glossy surfaces.

Rehabilitation Act: a federal measure making it unlawful to discriminate against qualified disabled applicants and employees.

Reinforcement: the extent to which a performance outcome is experienced as satisfying in some way.

Reinforcement theory: a theory used to study learning and motivation; emphasizes that action is strengthened or weakened by its own consequence.

Relaxation training: a health intervention in which the employee is taught to use physical or mental strategies, such as meditation, to reduce anxiety.

Reliability: the extent to which measurements or evaluations of a person are consistent.

Reliability of judgments: agreement or consistency in the evaluations of applicants or employees across raters.

Repetition trauma disorder: a musculoskeletal ailment due to the cumulative effect of repeated, slight injuries.

Resistance stage: the second stage of stress in Selye's model; includes signs that the body remains in a state of defense.

Restricted range: a characteristic of a distribution in which scores or ratings are concentrated in one area of the scale.

Results measure: a training criterion measure; indicates long-range training effects on the organization.

Risky shift: a change of opinion in the direction of a less cautious position as a result of group interaction.

Robot: a mechanical manipulator used in industry that may be operated by a computer and a video camera.

Role ambiguity: unclear job expectations.

Role conflict: incompatible job expectations.

Rotary controls: control devices that move in a circular pattern, such as a radio volume knob.

Rotating shifts: workshift assignments in which employees alternate in working the day, evening, and night periods.

S

Scattergram: a graphic display of data using two scores from each subject; the extent and direction of "scatter" demonstrate the correlation between the scores.

Scientific management: a technique developed by Frederick Taylor for systematic problem solving at work.

Secondary prevention: health program interventions for detecting problems and arranging treatment.

Sedatives: drugs used for inducing sleep and relieving pain, such as barbiturates.

Selection ratio: the proportion of applicants who pass a selection hurdle compared to the number considered; used in adverse impact assessments.

Self-actualization: a concept proposed by Maslow to describe the motivation for self-fulfillment and personal growth.

Self-appraisal: a performance evaluation in which an employee assesses his or her own performance.

Self-efficacy: the capacity for coping with personal demands.

Self-regulating work group: an organizational intervention in which employee groups are given responsibility and control of the work.

Self-report inventory: a pencil-and-paper personality test.

Seniority system: a plan in which personnel decisions are based on length of employment; usually a union-management agreement.

Sensitivity training: a technique of experience-based training in which individuals learn interpersonal skills.

Sensory modality: the mode of sensation (e.g., vision) important in display design.

Serial processing: cognitive work in which attention is focused on one source of information and tasks are done one at a time.

Severity error: a rater error in which employee ratings are concentrated at the low end of a scale.

Sick-building syndrome: physical illness caused by chemical fumes and disease organisms that are recirculated in buildings with closed ventilation.

SIOP (Society for Industrial and Organizational Psychology): division 14 of the American Psychological Association.

Situational interview: a selection interview in which "what if" questions from a critical incidents study are asked.

Situational specificity: the view that test validity depends on the condition or situation in which a test is used.

SME committee: a group of job-knowledgeable persons, such as incumbents; used in a job analysis.

Social influence hypothesis: the proposition, in job satisfaction research, that job attitudes change because of the impact of other people.

Social learning theory: a theory proposed by Bandura describing the process of learning through observation of others.

Social loafing: idleness among group members; what members do who contribute little to the group's task.

Social power: the ability to cause change in another person.

Social readjustment: concept used in the Stressful Life Events Model to describe an individual's response in coping with stress.

Social Readjustment Rating Scale: a measure of the extent to which a person is at risk for stress from recent life events.

Social support: tangible and emotional care given by other people to help one cope with stress.

Social transaction theory: a theory of leadership proposed by Hollander in which a leader attains his or her position through social exchanges with group members.

Societal goals: an organization's objectives for contributing to society, such as conservation of natural resources.

Sociometry: a specialized survey technique used for studying groups; group members are asked about their personal reactions to other members.

Sociotechnical systems theory: an organizational theory proposing that technology affects the social structure of the organization.

Sound intensity: the loudness of a sound or the amplitude of a sound wave.

Span of control: the number of subordinates that a supervisor can manage effectively.

Speed test: a test with easy questions and a time limit.

Split-halves: a method of assessing test reliability; a test is given twice, split in half, and scored as two tests.

Stability: an index of reliability; the extent to which a test is consistent over time.

Standardization sample: the group used to generate test norms; the group must be similar to those being tested.

Standardized instrument: a well-researched measure that has reliability and validity, procedures for administration and scoring, and norms for comparative purposes.

Standard workweek: consists of eight hours a day for five days a week.

Standing committee: a more or less permanent group of employees formed to deal with continuing organization-wide issues.

Static data: in anthropometry, the fixed physical dimensions of the body, such as stature.

Statistical method: an approach to research in which many people are studied and information is evaluated with mathematical procedures.

Stimulants: drugs used for energizing or increasing physiological arousal, such as amphetamines.

Stimulus discrimination: an aspect of training transfer; a response contingency in which either of two responses is evoked by distinctions in the stimuli.

Stimulus generalization: an aspect of training transfer; a response contingency in which a learned response is evoked in new situations that resemble the training stimulus.

Strain: a physiological, psychological, or behavioral sign of ill health resulting from stress.

Strategic apex: the small group of top managers who develop plans for steering the organization.

Strength: the requirements for force in using equipment.

Stress: a physiological response of the body to environmental or personal demands.

Stressful Life Events Model: theoretical model of Holmes and Rahe; identifies the kinds of personal experiences that lead to stress.

Stress management programs: individually oriented programs for helping employees learn how to cope with stress.

Stress reaction: the body's physiological response to a stressor.

Stress results: the consequences of prolonged stress; includes breakdown of physical and psychological health.

Stressor: a condition, event, person, or object that causes stress in an individual.

Structured interview: use of specific questions to guide and control an interview.

Substance abuse: excessive use of alcohol or regulated drugs.

Supervisory Behavior Description Questionnaire (SBDQ): a measure of supervisory style as seen by subordinates; similar to the LBDQ.

Survey: an observational research method in which questionnaires are used and participants provide self-reports; best for studying internal states.

Survey feedback: an OD intervention emphasizing the feedback of survey data to organizational members.

Sympathetic nervous system: a branch of the autonomic nervous system that stimulates general body arousal and energy.

Synthesized speech: an auditory display in which machine-produced human language is used to convey information.

Synthetic validity: an indication of overall test validity based on a synthesis of job component validities.

System 4 organization: a theoretical design proposed by Likert for an organization; uses an overlapping group structure and supportive managers.

Systematic desensitization: a health intervention that combines relaxation and counterconditioning to help a person unlearn avoidance responses and reduce anxiety.

Systemic poison: toxic substances that damage vital organs.

T

Tactual graph: a data graph with raised lines and dots that can be detected by touch; used by the visually handicapped.

Tall organizational structure: an organization that is highly differentiated vertically, with many levels or ranks.

Task analysis: a method of job analysis in which observational research is used to identify the activities of a job; also a training needs assessment at the level of the job.

Taylor-Russell tables: tables showing the expected proportion of satisfactory employees hired with personnel tests having a given validity.

Team building: an OD technique emphasizing the development of interaction skills in teamwork.

Tension-reduction hypothesis: used in motivation theory; proposes that behavior is driven by the discomfort of a deprived need.

Terminal behavior: required performance that training is supposed to produce; part of a behavioral objective.

Test fairness: extent to which a test is capable of predicting the performance of two groups equally well.

Test norms: distribution of test scores obtained from a standardization sample; used to interpret scores of test takers.

Test reliability: ability of a test to obtain consistent scores from a testee; ability of a test to predict itself.

Test-retest: method of assessing test reliability; a test is given twice and the scores are correlated.

Test standardization: control over the administration, scoring, and interpretation of tests.

Test transportability: the view that evidence of test validity obtained in one situation can be generalized when the test is used in another situation.

Theory: a set of definitions and propositions that describe some aspect of reality; used to guide research.

Theory X: McGregor's theoretical perspective on traditional management in which employees are viewed negatively.

Theory Y: McGregor's theoretical perspective on modern management in which employees are assumed to be motivated and capable.

Theory Z: a theoretical style of organizing proposed by Ouchi in which features of Japanese and American organizations are combined.

Third parties: uninvolved persons who are more or less objective about a conflict; may help in resolution.

Threats to validity: nuisance variables that can as easily account for training outcomes as the training itself unless they are controlled.

Time and motion studies: early research done by Taylor and the Gilbreths in which work was studied by observing the timing and movements of task actions.

Title VII: section in the Civil Rights Act that addresses employment discrimination.

Token economy: a behavior modification program using tokens to provide immediate reinforcement; tokens are exchanged for goods and services.

Trainability test: a test capable of assessing someone's ability to be trained for a job.

Training: a planned learning experience meant to change specific KSAs.

Training need: drawn from training needs assessment; the nature and extent of learning required; indicates the training goal or purpose.

Training needs assessment: evaluation of the need for training; performed at organizational, task, and person levels.

Training validity: the internal validity of a training program.

Transfer of training: generalization of learned material from one situation to another; carry over of learning from training to the job.

Transfer validity: a form of external validity; the extent to which training transfers to the job.

Transformational leadership: a perspective on leadership; describes a visionary leader who can inspire followers to make major changes in an organization.

True halo: the actual similarity between dimensions on a performance rating scale; not an error.

True score: the actual level of job performance; estimates are used to validate performance evaluation methods.

t-test: an inferential statistics technique for evaluating the difference between experimental and control groups, as between their means.

Two-factor theory: Herzberg's motivation theory; focuses on the motivating effects of two groups of performance outcomes called the hygiene and motivator factors.

Two-way communication: the exchange of information between two or more people.

Type A behavior: a style of aggressive behavior proposed to result in coronary heart disease.

Type B behavior: a style of relaxed behavior proposed to be less likely to result in heart disease than Type A behavior.

U

Unfair discrimination: employment decisions in which applicant characteristics, such as race and gender, are inappropriately considered.

Uniform Guidelines on Employment Selection Procedures: document describing the government's position on employment discrimination; outlines ways for employers to evaluate their selection practices.

Union: an employee-oriented organization that promotes the economic interests of its members.

Univariate theory: a theoretical model proposing only one variable is necessary to explain the behavior in question.

Upward communication: messages sent by subordinates to superiors.

Upward feedback: use of subordinate performance evaluation in the development of supervisors and managers.

Upward influence: in social exchange theory, the effort of a group member to influence the leader's behavior.

Urinalysis: a urine test often used in drug testing programs to detect drug use.

U-shaped relationship: a bivariate distribution that, when plotted on a graph, yields a curve that looks like a *U.*

Utility: an estimate of the monetary value of a selection procedure.

Utility analysis: an assessment of selection programs in terms of their monetary costs and savings.

V

Valence: a concept used in motivation theory referring to an individual's emotional reaction to a performance outcome.

Validation sample: the group of subjects used in conducting validity studies.

Validity: the ability of an instrument or procedure to perform as intended, as in selection, testing, or training.

Validity coefficient: the correlation coefficient obtained by correlating test scores with criterion measures; indicates the test's ability to predict performance.

Validity generalization: the extent to which tests that are valid in one situation also are valid in other situations.

Value Discrepancy Theory: Locke's job satisfaction theory proposing that satisfaction is determined by the discrepancy between what is desired and what is received.

Variability measures: descriptive statistics that indicate the extent to which subjects' scores differ from each other.

Vertical differentiation: a result of dividing the organization by grouping employees into levels or ranks.

Vestibule training: on-site job training of groups of trainees in a special area removed from the actual job.

Video display terminal (VDT): the most commonly used display of computer information.

Vigilance task: a job composed of monitoring activities.

W

Weighted application blank: an application containing personal data items that can be scored like test items.

Weighted checklist: a nonrating performance evaluation; the evaluator checks off the statements that describe an employee's behavior.

Whole-job ranking: a job evaluation method in which all jobs in an organization are ranked by their overall value.

Whole learning: practice of an entire learning task or sequence in the same study session.

Worker's Compensation: insurance paid for by employers to provide benefits to employees sustaining work-related injuries or illnesses.

Work overload: having too much to do or having work that is too difficult; often cited as a cause of job stress.

Work socialization: the process of learning the social realities of work and how to be an employee.

Workspace envelope: the three dimensions of space comprising the work area; important in the arrangement of machine controls.

Work underload: having too little to do or having work that is too easy.

Wrongful discharge: an employment termination judged to violate the employee's rights.

Z

Zero-sum outcome: a conflict outcome in which one party wins and the other loses.

z-score: a transformed score; used when widely varying performance ratings from different evaluators must be compared.

References

A

Aamodt, M. G., Bryan, D. A., & Whitcomb, A. J. (1993). Predicting performance with letters of recommendation. *Public Personnel Management, 22,* 81–90.

Adams, J. S. (1965). Inequity in social exchange. In L. Berkowitz (Ed.), *Advances in experimental social psychology* (Vol. 2). New York: Academic Press.

Adcock, C. J. (1964). *Fundamentals of psychology.* Middlesex: Penguin.

Adkins, C. L., Russell, C. J., & Werbel, J. D. (1994). Judgments of fit in the selection process: The role of work value congruence. *Personnel Psychology, 47,* 605–623.

Adler, N. J. (1993). An international perspective on the barriers to the advancement of women managers. *Applied Psychology: An International Review, 42,* 289–300.

Alderfer, C. P. (1977). Organization development. *Annual Review of Psychology, 28,* 197–224.

Aldrich, F. K., & Parkin, A. J. (1987). Tangible line graphs: An experimental investigation of three formats using capsule paper. *Human Factors, 29,* 301–309.

Alfredsson, L., Akerstedt, T., Mattsson, M., & Wilborg, B. (1991). Self-reported health and well-being amongst night security guards: A comparison with the working population. *Ergonomics, 34,* 525–530.

American Association of State Colleges and Universities. (1988–1989). *National faculty salary survey by discipline and rank in state colleges and universities.* Washington, DC: American Association of State Colleges and Universities.

American Psychological Association. (1992). Ethical principles of psychologists and code of conduct. *American Psychologist, 47,* 1597–1611.

Ames, G., & Janes, C. R. (1987). Heavy and problem drinking in an American blue collar population. *Social Science and Medicine, 25,* 949–960.

Anastasi, A. (1982). *Psychological testing,* (5th ed.). New York: Macmillan.

Anderson, N. B. (1989). Racial differences in stress-induced cardiovascular reactivity and hypertension: Current status and substantive issues. *Psychological Bulletin, 105,* 89–105.

Aneshensel, C. S., & Huba, G. J. (1984). An integrative causal model of the antecedents and consequences of depression over one year. In J. R. Greenley (Ed.), *Research in community and mental health* (Vol. 4.) Greenwich, CT: JAI Press.

Angoff, W. H. (1971). Scales, norms, and equivalent scores. In R. L. Thorndike (Ed.), *Educational Measurement* (pp. 508–600). Washington DC: American Council on Education.

Ansari, M. A., & Kapoor, A. (1987). Organizational context and upward influence tactics. *Organizational Behavior and Human Decision Processes, 40,* 39–49.

Antonioni, D. (1994). The effects of feedback accountability on upward appraisal ratings. *Personnel Psychology, 47,* 349–356.

Argote, L. (1989). Agreement about norms and work-unit effectiveness: Evidence from the field. *Basic & Applied Social Psychology, 10,* 131–140.

Argyris, C. (1957). *Personality and organization.* New York: Harper & Row.

Argyris, C. (1964). Being human and being organized. *Trans-Action, 1,* 3–6.

Argyris, C. (1965). *Organization and innovation.* Homewood, IL: Irwin.

Arnold, H. J., & Feldman, D. C. (1986). *Organizational behavior.* New York: McGraw-Hill.

Arvey, R. D. (1972). Task performance as a function of perceived effort-performance and performance-reward contingencies. *Organizational Behavior and Human Performance, 8,* 423–433.

Arvey, R. D., Bouchard, T. J., Segal, N. L., & Abraham, L. M. (1989). Job satisfaction: Environmental and genetic components. *Journal of Applied Psychology, 74,* 187–192.

Arvey, R. D., Miller, H. E., Gould, R., & Burch, P. (1987). Interview validity for selecting sales clerks. *Personnel Psychology, 40,* 1–12.

Asfahl, C. R. (1984). *Industrial safety and health management.* Englewood Cliffs, NJ: Prentice-Hall.

Ash, P., & Kroeker, L. P. (1975). Personnel selection, classification, and placement. *Annual Review of Psychology, 26,* 481–508.

Ashford, S. J. (1988). Individual strategies for coping with stress during organizational transitions. *Journal of Applied Behavioral Science, 24,* 19–36.

Ashforth, B. E., & Lee, R. T. (1990). Defensive behavior in organizations: A preliminary model. *Human Relations, 43,* 621–648.

Ashmos, D. P., & Huber, G. P. (1987). The systems paradigm in organization theory: Correcting the record and suggesting the future. *Academy of Management Review, 12,* 607–621.

Asterita, M. F. (1985). *The physiology of stress.* New York: Human Sciences Press.

Athey, T. R., & McIntyre, R. M. (1987). Effect of rater training on rater accuracy: Levels-of-processing theory and social facilitation theory perspectives. *Journal of Applied Psychology, 72,* 567–572.

Atkinson, J. W. (1964). *An introduction to motivation.* Princeton: Van Nostrand.

Atkinson, J. W., & Feather, N. T. (1966). *A theory of achievement motivation.* New York: Wiley.

Axelrod, W. L., & Gavin, J. F. (1980). Stress and strain in blue-collar and white-collar management staff. *Journal of Vocational Behavior, 17,* 41–49.

Ayers, R. V., & Miller, S. M. (1982, May-June). Industrial robots on the line. *Technology Review*, 35–46.

Ayman, R., & Chemers, M. M. (1983). Relationship of supervisory behavior ratings to work group effectiveness and subordinate satisfaction among Iranian managers. *Journal of Applied Psychology, 68,* 338–341.

B

Baekeland, F., Lundwall, L., & Kissin, B. (1975). Methods for the treatment of chronic alcoholism: A critical appraisal. In R. J. Gibbins et al. (Eds.), *Research advances in alcohol and drug problems* (Vol. 2). New York: Wiley.

Bailey, J. R., & Ford, C. M. (1994). Of methods and metaphors: Theater and self-exploration in the laboratory. *Journal of Applied Behavioral Science, 30,* 381–396.

Balcazar, F. E., Hopkins, B. L., & Suarez, Y. (1985–1986). A critical, objective review of performance feedback. *Journal of Organizational Behavior Management, 7,* 65–89.

Baldwin, T. T., & Ford, J. K. (1988). Transfer of training: A review and directions for future research. *Personnel Psychology, 41,* 63–105.

Bandura, A. (1977). *Social learning theory*. Englewood Cliffs, NJ: Prentice-Hall.

Barber, A. E., Dunham, R. B., & Formisano, R. A. (1992). The impact of flexible benefits on employee satisfaction: A field study. *Personnel Psychology, 45,* 55–75.

Barber, A. E., & Roehling, M. V. (1993). Job postings and the decision to interview: A verbal protocol analysis. *Journal of Applied Psychology, 78,* 845–856.

Barnes, R. M. (1940). *Motion and time study* (2nd ed.). New York: Wiley.

Baron, R. A. (1993). Interviewers' moods and evaluations of job applicants: The role of applicant qualifications. *Journal of Applied Social Psychology, 23,* 253–271.

Barrett, G. V., & Kernan, M. C. (1987). Performance appraisal and terminations: A review of court decisions since *Brito v. Zia* with implications for personnel practices. *Personnel Psychology, 40,* 489–503.

Barrett, G. V., Phillips, J. S., & Alexander, R. A. (1981). Concurrent and predictive validity designs: A critical reanalysis. *Journal of Applied Psychology, 66,* 1–6.

Barrick, M. A., & Mount, M. K. (1991). The Big Five personality dimensions and job performance: A meta-analysis. *Personnel Psychology 44,* 1–26.

Barrick, M. R., & Mount, M. K. (1993). Autonomy as a moderator of the relationships between the Big Five personality dimensions. *Journal of Applied Psychology, 78,* 111–118.

Barton, J. (1994). Choosing to work at night: A moderating influence on individual tolerance to shift work. *Journal of Applied Psychology, 79,* 449–454.

Barton, J., & Folkard, S. (1991). The response of day and night nurses to their work schedules. *Journal of Occupational Psychology, 64,* 207–218.

Barton, J., & Folkard, S. (1993). Advancing versus delaying shift systems. *Ergonomics, 36,* 59–64.

Barton, J., Smith, L., Totterdell, P., Spelten, E., et al. (1993). Does individual choice determine shift system acceptability? *Ergonomics, 36,* 93–99.

Bartunek, J. M. (1983). How organization development can develop organizational theory. *Group & Organization Studies, 8,* 303–318.

Bass, B. M. (1965). *Organizational psychology*. Boston: Allyn & Bacon.

Bass, B. M. (1981). *Stogdill's handbook of leadership: A survey of theory and research* (Rev. Ed.). New York: Free Press.

Bass, B. M. (1985). *Leadership and performance beyond expectations*. New York: Free Press.

Bauman, A. R. (1977). *Training of trainers: Resource manual*. Washington, DC: U.S. Government Printing Office.

Baxter, J. C., Brock, B., Hill, P. C., & Rozelle, R. M. (1981). Letters of recommendation: A question of value. *Journal of Applied Psychology, 66,* 296–301.

Bayer, G. A., & Gerstein, L. H. (1990). EAP referrals and troubled employees: An analogous study of supervisors' decisions. *Journal of Vocational Behavior, 36,* 304–319.

Bazar, J. (1994). Vietnamese psychologists meet challenges of a changing society. *Applied Psychology: An International Review, 5* (3), 1,3.

Becker, T. E., & Colquitt, A. L. (1992). Potential versus actual faking of a biodata form: An analysis along several dimensions of item type. *Personnel Psychology, 45,* 389–406.

Beckhard, R. (1969). *Organization development: Strategies and models*. Reading, MA: Addison-Wesley.

Beehr, T. A., & Newman, J. E. (1978). Job stress, employee health, and organizational effectiveness: A facet analysis, model, and literature review. *Personnel Psychology, 31,* 665–699.

Behling, O., & McFillen, J. M. (1996). A syncretical model of charismatic/transformational leadership. *Group & Organization Management, 21,* 163–191.

Bell, P. A. (1981). Physiological, comfort, performance, and social effects of heat stress. *Journal of Social Issues, 37,* 71–94.

Bellows, R. M. (1954). *Psychology of personnel in business and industry,* (2nd Ed.). New York: Prentice-Hall.

Benac, N. (1995). Clinton: `Mend, don't bend' affirmative action. *San Francisco Examiner,* July 19, Section A, pp. 1, 9.

Benedict, M. E., & Levine, E. L. (1988). Delay and distortion: Tacit influences on performance appraisal effectiveness. *Journal of Applied Psychology, 73,* 507–514.

Bennis, W. G. (1969). *Organization development: Its nature, origins, and prospects*. Reading, MA: Addison-Wesley.

Berkowitz, L., Fraser, C., Treasure, F. P., & Cochran, S. (1987). Pay, equity, job gratifications, and comparisons in pay satisfaction. *Journal of Applied Psychology, 72,* 544–551.

Bernardin, H. J. (1977). Behavioral expectation scales versus summated scales: A fairer comparison. *Journal of Applied Psychology, 62,* 422–427.

Bernardin, H. J. (1978). Effects of rater training on leniency and halo errors of student ratings of instructors. *Journal of Applied Psychology, 65,* 60–66.

Bernardin, H. J., & Buckley, M. R. (1981). Strategies in rater training. *Academy of Management Review, 6,* 205–212.

Bernardin, H. J., Cardy, R. L., & Carlyle, J. J. (1982). Cognitive complexity and appraisal effectiveness: Back to the drawing board? *Journal of Applied Psychology, 67,* 151–160.

Bernardin, H. J., & Walter, C. S. (1977). Effects of rater training and diary keeping on psychometric error in ratings. *Journal of Applied Psychology, 62,* 64–69.

Berry, L. M. (1990, April). *Careers of I/O psychology alumni: Part II. Working with an I/O master's degree*. Paper presented to the convention of the Western Psychological Association, Los Angeles.

Berscheid, E., & Walster, E. H. (1969). *Interpersonal attraction.* Reading, MA: Addison-Wesley.

Bettleheim, B. (1943). Individual and mass behavior in extreme situations. *Journal of Abnormal and Social Psychology, 38,* 417–452.

Bhagat, R. S., & McQuaid, S. J. (1982). Role of subjective culture in organizations: A review and directions for future research. *Journal of Applied Psychology Monograph, 67,* 653–685.

Billings, C. E., Demosthenes, T., White, T. R., & O'Hara, D. B. (1991). Effects of alcohol on pilot performance in simulated flight. *Aviation, Space, & Environmental Medicine, 62,* 233–235.

Binning, J. F., Goldstein, M. A., Garcia, M. F., & Scattaregia, J. H. (1988). Effects of preinterview impressions on questioning strategies in same- and opposite-sex employment interviews. *Journal of Applied Psychology, 73,* 30–37.

Blackler, F. (1988). Information technologies and organizations: Lessons from the 1980s and issues for the 1990s. *Journal of Occupational Psychology, 61,* 113–127.

Blake, R. R., & McCanse, A. A. (1991). *Leadership dilemmas—Grid solutions.* Houston: Gulf Publishing.

Blake, R. R., & Mouton, J. S. (1968). *Corporate excellence through Grid organization development.* Houston: Gulf.

Blake, R. R., & Mouton, J. S. (1978). *The new Managerial Grid.* Houston: Gulf.

Blake, R. R., & Mouton, J. S. (1985). *The Managerial Grid III: The Key to Leadership Excellence* (3rd ed.). Houston: Gulf Publishing Company.

Blanz, F., & Ghiselli, E. E. (1972). The mixed standard scale: A new rating system. *Personnel Psychology, 25,* 185–199.

Bloswick, D. S., Gerber, A., Sebesta, D., Johnson, S., et al. (1994). Effect of musculoskeletal fatigue and metabolic load. *Human Factors, 36,* 210–218.

Bluedorn, A. C. (1993). Pilgrim's progress: Trends and convergence in research on organizational size and environments. *Journal of Management, 19,* 163–191.

Bogg, J., & Cooper, C. (1995). Job satisfaction, mental health, and occupational stress among senior civil servants. *Human Relations, 48,* 327–341.

Bok, D., & Dunlop, J. (1970). *Labor and the American community.* New York: Simon & Schuster.

Bongers, P.M., Hulshof, C. T., Dijkstra, L., Boshuizen, H. C., et al. (1990). Back pain and exposure to whole body vibration in helicopter pilots. *Ergonomics, 33,* 1007–1026.

Boring, E. G. (1950). *A history of experimental psychology.* New York: Appleton-Century-Crofts.

Boring, E. G., & Lindzey, G. (Eds.). (1932). *A history of psychology in autobiography* (Vol. II). New York: Appleton-Century-Crofts.

Borman, W. C. (1978). Exploring upper limits of reliability and validity in performance ratings. *Journal of Applied Psychology, 63,* 135–144.

Borman, W. C. (1979). Format and training effects on rating accuracy and rater errors. *Journal of Applied Psychology, 64,* 410–421.

Borman, W. C. (1982). Validity of behavioral assessment for predicting military recruiter performance. *Journal of Applied Psychology, 67,* 3–9.

Boss, R. W. (1983). Team building and the problem of regression: The Personal Management Interview as an intervention. *Journal of Applied Behavioral Science, 19,* 67–83.

Boss, R. W., & Golembiewski, R. T. (1995). Do you have to start at the top? The Chief Executive Officer's role in successful organization development efforts. *Journal of Applied Behavioral Science, 31,* 259–277.

Bottger, P. C., & Yetton, P. W. (1988). An integration of process and decision scheme explanations of group problem solving performance. *Organizational Behavior & Human Decision Processes, 42,* 234–249.

Boudreau, J. W. (1983). Effects of employee flows on utility analysis of human resource productivity improvement programs. *Journal of Applied Psychology, 68,* 396–406.

Boulding, K. (1956). General systems theory—The skeleton of science. *Management Science, 2,* 197–208.

Bouzid, N., & Crawshaw, C. M. (1987). Massed versus distributed word processor training. *Applied Ergonomics, 18,* 220–222.

Boyd, D. P. (1984). Type A behavior, financial performance and organizational growth in small business firms. *Journal of Occupational Psychology, 57,* 137–140.

Brady, J. V. (1958). Ulcers in the "executive" monkey. *Scientific American, 199,* 95–100.

Bramel, D., & Friend, R. (1987). The work group and its vicissitudes in social and industrial psychology. *Journal of Applied Behavioral Science, 23,* 233–253.

Bray, D. W. (1982). The assessment center and the study of lives. *American Psychologist, 37,* 180–189.

Bray, D. W., & Campbell, R. J. (1968). Selection of salesmen by means of an assessment center. *Journal of Applied Psychology, 52,* 36–41.

Bray, D. W., Campbell, R. J., & Grant, D. L. (1974). *Formative years in business: A long-term AT&T study of managerial lives.* New York: Wiley.

Brayfield, A. H., & Crockett, W. H. (1955). Employee attitudes and employee performance. *Psychological Bulletin, 52,* 396–424.

BRE exam preparation manual. (1977). Washington, DC: U.S. Civil Service Commission, Bureau of Recruiting and Examining.

Brenner, O. C., Tomkiewicz, J., & Schein, V. E. (1989). The relationship between sex role stereotypes and requisite management characteristics revisited. *Academy of Management Journal, 32,* 662–669.

Bretz, R. D., Boudreau, J. W., & Judge, T. A. (1994). Job search behavior of employed managers. *Personnel Psychology, 47,* 275–301.

Brief, A. P., Butcher, A. H., & Roberson, L. (1995). Cookies, disposition, and job attitudes: The effects of positive mood-inducing events and negative affectivity on job satisfaction in a field experiment. *Organizational Behavior & Human Decision Processes, 62,* 55–62.

Brigham, T. A., & Catania, A. C. (1978). Introduction: The behavior analysis technology. In A. C. Catania & T. A. Brigham (Eds.), *Handbook of applied behavior analysis: Social and instructional processes.* New York: Irvington.

Broadbent, D. E. (1971). *Decision and stress.* New York: Academic Press.

Broadbent, D. E. (1979). Human performance and noise. In C. M. Harris (Ed.), *Handbook of noise control.* New York: McGraw-Hill.

Brogden, H. E. (1946). On the interpretation of the correlation coefficient as a measure of predictive efficiency. *Journal of Educational Psychology, 37,* 65–76.

Bromet, E. J., Dew, M. A., Parkinson, D. K., & Schulberg, H. C. (1988). Predictive effects of occupational and marital stress on the mental health of a male workforce. *Journal of Organizational Behavior, 9*, 1–13.

Brooke, P. P., Russell, D. W., & Price, J. L. (1988). Discriminant validation of measures of job satisfaction, job involvement, and organizational commitment. *Journal of Applied Psychology, 73*, 139–145.

Broverman, I. K., Vogel, S., Broverman, D. M., Clarkson, F. E., & Rosenkrantz, P. S. (1972). Sex role stereotypes: A current appraisal. *Journal of Social Issues, 28*, 59–78.

Bru, E., Mykletun, R. J., & Sveback, S. (1994). Assessment of musculoskeletal and other health complaints in female hospital staff. *Applied Ergonomics, 25*, 101–105.

Bruning, J. L., & Kintz, B. L. (1977). *Computational handbook of statistics* (2nd ed.). Glenview, IL: Scott, Foresman.

Brush, D. H., & Owens, W. A. (1979). Implementation and evaluation of an assessment-classification model for manpower utilization. *Personnel Psychology, 32*, 369–383.

Bryman, A., Bresnen, M., Beardsworth, A., & Keil, T. (1988). Qualitative research and the study of leadership. *Human Relations, 41*, 13–30.

Bunker, D. R. (1965). The effect of laboratory education upon individual behavior. In E. H. Schein & W. G. Bennis (Eds.), *Personal and organizational change through group methods.* New York: Wiley.

Burdorf, A., & Zondervan, H. (1990). An epidemiological study of low-back pain in crane operators. *Ergonomics, 33*, 981–987.

Burke, R. J. (1987). Burnout in police work: An examination of the Cherniss model. *Group & Organization Studies, 12*, 174–188.

Burke, R. J., Weir, T., & Duncan, G. (1976). Informal helping relationships in work organizations. *Academy of Management Journal, 19*, 370–377.

Burke, R. J., Weitzel, W., & Weir, T. (1978). Characteristics of effective employee performance review and development interviews: Replication and extension. *Personnel Psychology, 31*, 903–919.

Burke, W. W., Clark, L. P., & Koopman, C. (1984). Improve your OD project's chances for success. *Training & Development Journal, 38*, 62–68.

Burns, J. M. (1978). *Leadership.* New York: Harper & Row.

Burns, T. (1963). Industry in a new age. *New Society, 18*, 17–20.

Burns, T., & Stalker, G. M. (1961). *The management of innovation.* London: Tavistock.

Buros, O. K. (Ed.). (1978). *The eighth mental measurements yearbook.* Lincoln, NE: University of Nebraska, Buros Institute of Mental Measurements.

Burrington, D. D. (1982). A review of state government employment application forms for suspect inquiries. *Public Personnel Management Journal, 11*, 55–60.

Bycio, P., Hackett, R. D., & Allen, J. S. (1995). Further assessments of Bass's (1985) conceptualization of transactional and transformational leadership. *Journal of Applied Psychology, 80*, 468–478.

Byrne, D. G., & Reinhart, M. I. (1989). Work characteristics, occupational achievement and the Type A behaviour pattern. *Journal of Occupational Psychology, 62*, 123–134.

C

Callender, J. C., & Osburn, H. G. (1980). Development and test of a new model for validity generalization. *Journal of Applied Psychology, 65*, 543–558.

Cameron, R., & Meichenbaum, D. (1982). The nature of effective coping and the treatment of stress related problems: A cognitive-behavioral perspective. In L. Goldberger & S. Breznitz (Eds.), *Handbook of stress: Theoretical and clinical aspects.* New York: Free Press.

Campbell, D. T. (1960). Recommendations for APA test standards regarding construct, trait, and discriminant validity. *American Psychologist, 15*, 546–553.

Campbell, J. P., & Pritchard, R. D. (1976). Motivation theory in industrial and organizational psychology. In M. D. Dunnette (Ed.), *Handbook of industrial and organizational psychology.* Chicago: Rand McNally.

Campion, M. A., Campion, J. E., & Hudson, J. P. (1994). Structured interviewing: A note on incremental validity and alternative question types. *Journal of Applied Psychology, 79*, 998–1002.

Campion, M. A., Medsker, G. J., & Higgs, A. C. (1993). Relations between work group characteristics and effectiveness: Implications for designing effective work groups. *Personnel Psychology, 46*, 823–850.

Campion, M. A., Pursell, E. D., & Brown, B. K. (1988). Structured interviewing: Raising the psychometric properties of the employment interview. *Personnel Psychology, 41*, 25–42.

Carnevale, P. J., & Lawler, E. J. (1986). Time pressure and the development of integrative agreements in bilateral negotiations. *Journal of Conflict Resolution, 30*, 636–659.

Carroll, S. J., Jr., & Nash, A. N. (1972). Effectiveness of a forced-choice reference check. *Personnel Administration, 35*, 42–46.

Carson, P. P., Carson, K. D., & Roe, C. W. (1993). Social power bases: A meta-analytic examination of interrelationships and outcomes. *Journal of Applied Social Psychology, 23*, 1150–1169.

Carsten, J. M., & Spector, P. E. (1987). Unemployment, job statisfaction, and employee turnover: A meta-analytic test of the Muchinsky model. *Journal of Applied Psychology, 72*, 374–381.

Carver, C. S., & Scheier, M. F. (1981). *Attention and self-regulation: A control theory approach to human behavior.* New York: Springer-Verlag.

Cascio, W. F. (1976). Turnover, biographical data, and fair employment practice. *Journal of Applied Psychology, 61*, 576–580.

Cascio, W. F. (1991). *Costing Human Resources: The Financial Impact of Behavior in Organizations* (3rd ed.). Boston: Kent.

Cascio, W. F., Alexander, R. A., & Barrett, G. V. (1988). Setting cutoff scores: Legal, psychometric, and professional issues and guidelines. *Personnel Psychology, 41*, 1–24.

Cascio, W. F., & Bernardin, H. J. (1981). Implications of performance appraisal litigation for personnel decisions. *Personnel Psychology, 32*, 211–226.

Cascio, W. F., Outtz, J., Zedeck, S., & Goldstein, I. L. (1995). Statistical implications of six methods of test score use in personnel selection. *Human Performance, 8*, 133–164.

Cascio, W. F., & Silbey, V. (1979). Utility of the assessment center as a selection device. *Journal of Applied Psychology, 64*, 107–118.

Cash, T. F., & Kilcullen, R. N. (1985). The aye of the beholder: Susceptibility to sexism and beautyism in the evaluation of managerial applicants. *Journal of Applied Social Psychology, 15,* 591–605.

Cederblom, D. (1991). Promotability ratings: An underused promotion method for public safety organizations. *Public Personnel Management, 20,* 27–34.

Cederblom, D., Pence, E. C., & Johnson, D. L. (1984). Making I/O psychology useful: The personnel administrator's view. *The Industrial-Organizational Psychologist, 21*(3), 9–17.

Champoux, J. E. (1991). A multivariate test of the Job Characteristics Theory of Work Motivation. *Journal of Organizational Behavior, 12,* 431–446.

Chao, G. T., O'Leary-Kelly, A. M., Wolf, S., Klein, H. J. et al. (1994). Organizational socialization: Its content and consequences. *Journal of Applied Psychology, 79,* 730–743.

Chatman, J. A., & Jehn, K. A. (1994). Assessing the relationship between industry characteristics and organizational culture: How different can you be? *Academy of Management Journal, 37,* 522–553.

Cherniss, C. (1980). *Professional burnout in human service organizations.* New York: Praeger.

Cherrington, D. L., Reitz, H. J., & Scott, W. E., Jr. (1971). Effects of reward and contingent reinforcement on satisfaction and task performance. *Journal of Applied Psychology, 55,* 531–536.

Chesney, A. A., & Locke, E. A. (1991). Relationships among goal difficulty, business stategies, and performance on a complex management simulation. *Academy of Management Journal, 34,* 400–424.

Chignell, M. H., & Peterson, J. G. (1988). Strategic issues in knowledge engineering. *Human Factors, 30,* 381–394.

Chisholm, R. F., Kasl, S. V., & Eskenazl, B. (1983). The nature and predictors of job related tension in a crisis situation: Reactions of nuclear workers to the Three Mile Island accident. *Academy of Management Journal, 26,* 385–405.

Christiansen, N. D., Goffin, R. D., Johnston, N. G., & Rothstein, M. G. (1994). Correcting the 16PF for faking: Effects on criterion-related validity and individual hiring decisions. *Personnel Psychology, 47,* 847–860.

Clark, R. D., III. (1971). Group-induced shift toward risk: A critical appraisal. *Psychological Bulletin, 76,* 251–270.

Cleveland, J. N., Murphy, K. R., & Williams, R. E. (1989). Multiple uses of performance appraisal: Prevalence and correlates. *Journal of Applied Psychology, 74,* 130–135.

Cobb, S., & Rose, R. M. (1973). Hypertension, peptic ulcer, and diabetes in air traffic controllers. *Journal of the American Medical Association, 224,* 489–492.

Coch, L., & French, J. R. P. (1948). Overcoming resistance to change. *Human Relations, 1,* 512–532.

Cohen, S., & Wills, T. A. (1985). Stress, social support and the buffering hypothesis. *Psychological Bulletin, 98,* 310–377.

Cohen, S., & Weinstein, N. (1981). Nonauditory effects of noise on behavior and health. *Journal of Social Issues, 37,* 36–70.

Coleman, J. C., Butcher, J. N., & Carson, R. C. (1980). *Abnormal psychology and modern life* (6th ed.). Glenview, IL: Scott, Foresman.

Collins, D., Ross, R. A., & Ross, T. L. (1989). Who wants participative management? *Group & Organization Studies, 14,* 422–445.

Colquhoun, W. P. (1975). Evaluation of auditory, visual and dual mode displays for prolonged sonar monitoring in repeated sessions. *Human Factors, 17,* 425–437.

Conroy, C. (1989). Work-related injuries in the meatpacking industry. *Journal of Safety Research, 20,* 47–53.

Cook, T. D., & Campbell, D. T. (1979). *Quasi-experimentation: Design and analysis issues for field settings.* Chicago: Rand McNally.

Cooper, C. L., & Arbose, J. (1984). Executive stress goes global. *International Management, 15,* 42–48.

Cooper, C. L., & Hensman, R. (1985). A comparative investigation of executive stress: A ten-nation study. *Stress Medicine, 1,* 295–301.

Cooper, M. D., Phillips, R. A., Sutherland, V. J., & Makin, P. J. (1994). Reducing accidents using goal setting and feedback: A field study. *Journal of Occupational & Organizational Psychology, 67,* 219–240.

Cooper, W. H. (1981). Ubiquitous halo. *Psychological Bulletin, 90,* 218–244.

Cordes, C. L., & Dougherty, T. W. (1993). A review and an integration of research on job burnout. *Academy of Management Review, 18,* 621–656.

Cornelius, E. T., & Hakel, M. D. (1978). *A study to develop an improved enlisted performance evaluation system for the U.S. Coast Guard.* Washington, DC: Department of Transportation, United States Coast Guard.

Cornelius, E. T., & Lane, F. B. (1984). The power motive and managerial success in a professionally oriented service industry organization. *Journal of Applied Psychology, 69,* 32–39.

Cotton, J. L., Vollrath, D. A., Froggatt, K. L., Lengnick-Hall, M. L., & Jennings, K. R. (1988). Employee participation: Diverse forms and different outcomes. *Academy of Management Review, 13,* 8–22.

Coulton, G. F., & Feild, H. S. (1995). Using assessment centers in selecting entry-level police officers: Extravagance or justified expense? *Public Personnel Management, 24,* 223–254.

Courtney, A. J. (1984). Hand anthropometry of Hong Kong Chinese females compared to other groups. *Ergonomics, 27,* 1169–1180.

Courtney, A. J. (1988). Chinese response preferences for display-control relationships. *Human Factors, 30,* 367–372.

Courtright, J. A., Fairhurst, G. T., & Rogers, L. E. (1989). Interaction patterns in organic and mechanistic systems. *Academy of Management Journal, 32,* 773–802.

Cowan, T. R. (1987). Drugs and the workplace: To drug test or not to test? *Public Personnel Management, 16,* 313–322.

Cox, T. (1985). Repetitive work: Occupational stress and health. In C. L. Cooper & M. J. Smith (Eds.), *Job stress and blue collar work.* New York: Wiley.

Craig, A., & Condon, R. (1984). Operational efficiency and time of day. *Human Factors, 26,* 197–205.

Crant, J. M., & Bateman, T. S. (1990). An experimental test of the impact of drug-testing programs on potential job applicants' attitudes and intentions. *Journal of Applied Psychology, 75,* 127–131.

Cronbach, L. J. (1970). *Essentials of psychological testing.* New York: Harper & Row.

Cronbach, L. J., & Gleser, G. (1965). *Psychological tests and personnel decisions* (2nd ed.). Urbana: University of Illinois Press.

Cronbach, L. J., & Snow, R. E. (1977). *Aptitudes and instructional methods.* New York: Irvington.

Cronshaw, S. F., & Lord, R. G. (1987). Effects of categorization, attribution, and encoding processes on leadership perceptions. *Journal of Applied Psychology, 72,* 97–106.

Cropanzano, R., & James, K. (1990). Some methodological considerations for the behavioral genetic analysis of work attitudes. *Journal of Applied Psychology, 75,* 433–439.

Cummins, R. (1989). Locus of control and social support: Clarifiers of the relationship between job stress and job satisfaction. *Journal of Applied Social Psychology, 19,* 771–788.

Cunitz, R. J. (1981). Psychologically effective warnings. *Hazard Prevention, 17,* 5–7.

Cunningham, M. R., Wong, D. T., & Barbee, A. P. (1994). Self-presentation dynamics on overt integrity tests: Experimental studies of the Reid Report. *Journal of Applied Psychology, 79,* 643–658.

Curry, S., Wagner, E. H., & Grothaus, L. C. (1990). Intrinsic and extrinsic motivation for smoking cessation. *Journal of Consulting and Clinical Psychology, 58,* 310–316.

D

Dachler, H. P., & Mobley, W. H. (1973). Construct validation of an instrumentality-expectancy-task-goal model of work motivation: Some boundary conditions. *Journal of Applied Psychology, 58,* 397–418.

Dalton, D. R., Krackhardt, D. M., & Porter, L. W. (1981). Functional turnover: An empirical assessment. *Journal of Applied Psychology, 66,* 716–721.

Dalton, D. R., & Mesch, D. J. (1990). The impact of flexible scheduling on employee attendance and turnover. *Administrative Science Quarterly, 35,* 370–387.

Damanpour, F. (1991). Organizational innovation: A meta-analysis of effects of determinants and moderators. *Academy of Management Journal, 34,* 555–590.

Dansereau, F., Graen, G., & Haga, W. (1975). A vertical dyad linkage approach to leadership within formal organizations. *Organizational Behavior and Human Performance, 13,* 46–78.

Darley, J. G. (1968). 1917: A journal is born. *Journal of Applied Psychology, 52,* 1–9.

Davis, F. D. (1993). User acceptance of information technology: System characteristics, user perceptions and behavioral impacts. *International Journal of Man-Machine Studies, 38,* 475–487.

Davis, K. (1953). Management communication and the grapevine. *Harvard Business Review, 31,* 43–49.

Davis, K. R., & Sauser, W. I. (1991). Effects of alternative weighting methods in a policy-capturing approach to job evaluation: A review and empirical investigation. *Personnel Psychology, 44,* 85–127.

Davis, K. R., & Sauser, W. I. (1993). A comparison of factor weighting methods in job evaluation: Implications for compensation sysems. *Public Personnel Management, 22,* 91–106.

Deadrick, D. L., & Scott, K. D. (1987). Employee incentives in the public sector: A national survey of urban mass transit authorities. *Public Personnel Management, 16,* 135–143.

Deci, E. L. (1971). The effects of externally mediated rewards on intrinsic motivation. *Journal of Personality and Social Psychology, 18,* 105–115.

Deci, E. L. (1972). The effects of contingent and non-contingent rewards and controls on intrinsic motivation. *Organizational Behavior and Human Performance, 8,* 217–229.

Deffenbacher, J. L., & Suinn, R. M. (1988). Systematic desensitization and the reduction of anxiety. *Counseling Psychologist, 16,* 9–30.

DeFrank, R. S., Ivancevich, J. M., & Schweiger, D. M. (1988). Job stress and mental well-being: Similarities and differences among American, Japanese, and Indian managers. *Behavioral Medicine, 14,* 160–170.

de Laat, P. B. (1994). Matrix management of projects and power struggles: A case study of a R&D laboratory. *Human Relations, 47,* 1089–1119.

Deluga, R. J., & Perry, J. T. (1991). The relationship of subordinate upward influencing behaviour, satisfaction and perceived superior effectiveness with leader-member exchanges. *Journal of Occupational Psychology, 64,* 239–252.

Deluga, R. J., & Souza, J. (1991). The effects of transformational and transactional leadership styles on the influencing behavior of subordinate police officers. *Journal of Occupational Psychology, 64,* 49–55.

Denenberg, V. H. (1976). *Statistics and experimental design for behavioral researchers: An introduction.* New York: Wiley.

DeNisi, A. S., Randolph, W. A., & Blencoe, A. G. (1983). Potential problems with peer ratings. *Academy of Management Journal, 26,* 457–464.

Dennis, A. R., & Valacich, J. S. (1994). Group, sub-group, and nominal group idea generation: New rules for a new media? *Journal of Management, 20,* 723–736.

Denton, T. C. (1990). Bonding and supportive relationships among Black professional women: Rituals of restoration. *Journal of Organizational Behavior, 11,* 447–457.

DePaulo, B. M. (1992). Nonverbal behavior and self-presentation. *Psychological Bulletin, 111,* 203–243.

Dessler, G., & Valenzi, E. R. (1977). Initiation of structure and subordinate satisfaction: A path analysis test of path-goal theory. *Academy of Management Journal, 20,* 251–259.

Deutsch, M. (1971). Conflict and its resolution. In C. G. Smith (Ed.), *Conflict resolution: Contributions of the behavioral sciences.* Notre Dame, IN: University of Notre Dame Press.

Deutsch, M. (1973). *The resolution of conflict.* New Haven: Yale University Press.

Deutsch, M. (1980). Over fifty years of conflict research. In L. Festinger (Ed.), *Four decades of social psychology.* New York: Oxford University Press.

Deutsch, M., & Krauss, R. M. (1962). Studies in interpersonal bargaining. *Journal of Conflict Resolution, 6,* 52–76.

Development Dimensions International. (1977). *1977–1978 catalog.* Pittsburg, PA: Development Dimensions International.

Dickinson, T. L., & Glebocki, G. G. (1990). Modifications in the format of the mixed standard scale. *Organizational Behavior & Human Decision Processes, 47,* 124–137.

Dictionary of Occupational Titles (4th ed., Rev.). (1991). Washington, DC: U.S. Government Printing Office.

Digman, J. M. (1990). Personality structure: Emergence of the five-factor model. *Annual Review of Psychology, 41,* 417–440.

Dinesen, I. (1942). Sorrow acre. In *Winter's tales.* New York: Random House.

Dipboye, R. L. (1982). Self-fulfilling prophecies in the selection/recruitment interview. *Academy of Management Review, 7,* 579–587.

Dipboye, R. L., & Macan, T. H. (1988). A process view of the selection-recruitment interview. In R. Schuler, V. Huber, & S. Youngblood (Eds.), *Readings in personnel and human resource management.* New York: West, 217–232.

Dishman, R. K. (1982). Contemporary sport psychology. In R. L. Terjung (Ed.), *Exercise and sport sciences reviews,* (Vol. 10). New York: Franklin Institute Press.

Do, M. C., Bouisset, S., & Moynot, C. (1985). Are paraplegics handicapped in the execution of a manual task? *Ergonomics, 28,* 1363–1375.

Dobbins, G. H., Cardy, R. L., & Truxillo, D. M. (1986). Effect of ratee sex and purpose of appraisal on the accuracy of performance evaluations. *Basic and Applied Social Psychology, 7,* 225–241.

Dockery, T. M., & Steiner, D. D. (1990). The role of the initial interaction in leader-member exchange. *Group & Organization Studies, 15,* 395–413.

Dorfman, D. (1982, June 20). Professional headaches. *San Francisco Chronicle.*

Doty, D. H., Glick, W. H., & Huber, G. P. (1993). Fit, equifinality, and organizational effectiveness: A test of two configurational theories. *Academy of Management Journal, 36,* 1196–1250.

Dougherty, T. W., Turban, D. B., & Callender, J. C. (1994). Confirming first impressions in the employment interview: A field study of interviewer behavior. *Journal of Applied Psychology, 79,* 659–665.

Douglas, P. H. (1921). *American apprenticeship and industrial education.* New York: Columbia University Press.

Downey, R. G., Knight, P. A., & Saal, F. E. (1987). Undergraduate programs in I/O psychology: A response to Peters. *The Industrial-Organizational Psychologist, 24*(3),49–52.

Downs, G. W., & Mohr, L. B. (1976). Conceptual issues in the study of innovation. *Administrative Science Quarterly, 21,* 700–714.

Doyle, K. O., Jr. (1974). Theory and practice of ability testing in ancient Greece. *Journal of the History of the Behavioral Sciences, 10,* 202–212.

Drakeley, R. J., Herriot, P., & Jones, A. (1988). Biographical data, training success and turnover. *Journal of Occupational Psychology, 61,* 145–152.

Dreher, G. F., & Ash, R. A. (1990). A comparative study of mentoring among men and women in managerial, professional, and technical positions. *Journal of Applied Psychology, 75,* 539–546.

Dreher, G. F., & Cox, T. H., Jr. (1996). Race, gender, and opportunity: A study of compensation attainment and the establishment of mentoring relationships. *Journal of Applied Psychology, 81,* 297–308.

Dreiser, Theodore. (1917). *Sister Carrie.* New York: Horace Liveright.

Driskell, J. E., Copper, C., & Moran, A. (1994). Does mental practice enhance performance? *Journal of Applied Psychology, 79,* 481–492.

Drury, C. G., et al. (1989). Symmetric and asymmetric manual materials handling: I. Physiology and psychophysics. *Ergonomics, 32,* 467–489.

Duarte, N. T., Goodson, J. R., & Klich, N. R. (1993). How do I like thee? Let me appraise the ways. *Journal of Organizational Behavior, 14,* 239–249.

Dunham, R. B. (1977). Shift work: A review and theoretical analysis. *Academy of Management Review, 2,* 626–634.

Dunham, R. B., Pierce, J. L., & Castaneda, M. B. (1987). Alternative work schedules: Two field quasi-experiments. *Personnel Psychology, 40,* 215–242.

Dunnette, M. D., & Borman, W. C. (1979). Personnel selection and classification systems. *Annual Review of Psychology, 30,* 477–526.

Dyer, F. N., & Hilligoss, R. E. (1980). Using an assessment center to predict field performance of Army officers and NCO's. *JSAS Catalog of Selected Documents in Psychology, 10,* ms. 2163.

Dyer, L., & Theriault, R. (1976). The determinants of pay satisfaction. *Journal of Applied Psychology, 61,* 596–604.

E

Eagley, A. H., Karau, S. J., & Makhijani, M. G. (1995). Gender and the effectiveness of leaders: A meta-analysis. *Psychological Bulletin, 117,* 125–145.

Earley, P. C., Connolly, T., & Ekegren, G. (1989). Goals, strategy development, and task performance: Some limits on the efficacy of goal-setting. *Journal of Applied Psychology, 74,* 24–33.

Eastburg, M. C., Williamson, M., Gorsuch, R., & Ridley, C. (1994). Social support, personality, and burnout in nurses. *Journal of Applied Social Psychology, 24,* 1233–1250.

Eberhardt, B. J., & Muchinsky, P. M. (1982). An empirical investigation of the factor stability of Owens' Biographical Questionnaire. *Journal of Applied Psychology, 67,* 138–145.

Eccles, J. (1983). Expectancies, values, and academic behaviors. In J. T. Spence (Ed.), *Achievement and achievement motives.* San Francisco: Freeman.

Eden, D. (1985). Team development: A true field experiment at three levels of rigor. *Journal of Applied Psychology, 70,* 94–100.

Eden, D., & Aviram, A. (1993). Self-efficacy training to speed reemployment: Helping people to help themselves. *Journal of Applied Psychology, 78,* 352–360.

Eden, D., & Leviatan, U. (1975). Implicit leadership theory as a determinant of the factor structure underlying supervisory behavior scales. *Journal of Applied Psychology, 60,* 736–741.

Eden, D., & Ravid, G. (1982). Pygmalion versus self-expectancy: Effects of instructor- and self-expectancy on trainee performance. *Organizational Behavior and Human Performance, 30,* 351–364.

Edwards, A. L. (1957). *Techniques of attitude scale construction.* New York: Appleton-Century-Crofts.

Eisenberg, E. M., & Witten, M. G. (1987). Reconsidering openness in organizational communication. *Academy of Management Review, 12,* 418–426.

Eisenhardt, K. M. (1989). Making fast strategic decisions in high-velocity environments. *Academy of Management Journal, 32,* 543–576.

Ejiogu, A. M. (1983). Participative management in a developing economy: Poison or placebo? *Journal of Behavioral Science, 19,* 239–247.

Ekholm, J., Arborelius, U. P., & Nemeth, G. (1982). The load on the lumbo-sacral joint and trunk muscle activity during lifting. *Ergonomics, 25,* 145–162.

Elizur, D. (1987). Effect of feedback on verbal and non-verbal courtesy in a bank setting. *Applied Psychology: An International Review, 36,* 147–156.

Ellinwood, E. H. (1971). Assault and homicide associated with amphetamine abuse. *American Journal of Psychiatry, 127,* 90–95.

Elliott, T. R., Chartrand, J. M., & Harkins, S. W. (1994). Negative affectivity, emotional distress, and the cognitive appraisal of occupational stress. *Journal of Vocational Behavior, 45,* 202–222.

Elmes, M. B., & Costello, M. (1992). Mystification and social drama: The hidden side of communication skills training. *Human Relations, 45,* 427–445.

Endsley, M. R., & Kiris, E. O. (1995). The out-of-the-loop performance problem and level of control in automation. *Human Factors, 37,* 381–394.

Epstein, Y. M. (1981). Crowding stress and human behavior. *Journal of Social Issues, 37,* 126–144.

Erera, I. P. (1992). Social support under conditions of organizational ambiguity. *Human Relations, 45,* 247–264.

Ettling, J. T., & Jago, A. G. (1988). Participation under conditions of conflict: More on the validity of the Vroom-Yetton model. *Journal of Management Studies, 25,* 73–83.

Evans, B. K., & Fischer, D. G. (1993). The nature of burnout: A study of the three-factor model of burnout in human service and non-human service samples. *Journal of Occupational & Organizational Psychology, 66,* 29–38.

Evans, G. W. (1994). Working on the hot seat: Urban bus operators. *Accident Analysis & Prevention, 26,* 181–193.

Evans, K. M., Kienast, P., & Mitchell, T. R. (1988). The effects of lottery incentive programs on performance. *Journal of Organizational Behavior Management, 9,* 113–135.

F

Fagerstrom, K. (1983). Tolerance, withdrawal and dependence on tobacco and smoking termination. *International Review of Applied Psychology, 32,* 29–52.

Falkenberg, L. E. (1987). Employee fitness programs: Their impact on the employee and the organization. *Academy of Management Review, 12,* 511–522.

Farh, J., & Dobbins, G. H. (1989). Effects of comparative information on the accuracy of self-ratings and agreement between self- and supervisor ratings. *Journal of Applied Psychology, 74,* 606–610.

Farh, J., Dobbins, G. H., & Cheng, B. (1991). Cultural relativity in action: A comparison of self-rating made by Chinese and U.S. workers. *Personnel Psychology, 44,* 129–147.

Faulkner, T. W., & Murphy, T. J. (1973). Lighting for difficult visual tasks. *Human Factors, 15,* 149–162.

Fayol, H. (1949). *General and industrial management.* London: Pitman and Sons.

Feinauer, D. M., & Havlovic, S. J. (1993). Drug testing as a strategy to reduce occupational accidents: A longitudinal analysis. *Journal of Safety Research, 24,* 1–7.

Feldman, D. C. (1984). The development and enforcement of group norms. *Academy of Management Review, 9,* 47–53.

Feldman, D. C. (1990). Reconceptualizing the nature and consequences of part-time work. *Academy of Management Review, 15,* 103–112.

Feldman, D. C., & Doerpinghaus, H. I. (1992). Patterns of part-time employment. *Journal of Vocational Behavior, 41,* 282–294.

Feltham, R. (1988). Validity of a police assessment center: A 1–19-year follow-up. *Journal of Occupational Psychology, 61,* 129–144.

Festinger, L. (1954). A theory of social comparison processes. *Human Relations, 7,* 117–140.

Festinger, L. (1957). *A theory of cognitive dissonance.* Evanston, IL: Row, Peterson.

Fiedler, F. E. (1966). The effect of leadership and cultural heterogeneity on group performance: A test of the contingency model. *Journal of Experimental Social Psychology, 2,* 237–264.

Fiedler, F. E. (1967). *A theory of leadership effectiveness.* New York: McGraw-Hill.

Fiedler, F. E. (1973). The contingency model—A reply to Ashour. *Organizational Behavior and Human Performance, 9,* 356–368.

Fiedler, F. E. (1978). The contingency model and the dynamics of the leadership process. In L. Berkowitz (Ed.), *Advances in experimental social psychology* (Vol. 11). New York: Academic Press.

Fiedler, F. E., Bell, C. H., Chemers, M. M., & Patrick, D. (1984). Increasing mine productivity and safety through management training and organization development: A comparative study. *Basic & Applied Social Psychology, 5,* 1–18.

Fiedler, F. E., Chemers, M. M., & Mahar, L. (1976). *Improving leadership effectiveness: The Leader Match concept.* New York: Wiley.

Field, H. S., & Holley, W. H. (1982). The relationship of performance appraisal system characteristics to verdicts in selected employment discrimination cases. *Academy of Management Journal, 25,* 392–406.

Field, R. G. (1982). A test of the Vroom-Yetton normative model of leadership. *Journal of Applied Psychology, 67,* 523–532.

Field, R. H. G., & House, R. J. (1990). A test of the Vroom-Yetton model using manager and subordinate reports. *Journal of Applied Psychology, 75,* 362–366.

Finkle, R. B. (1976). Managerial assessment centers. In M. D. Dunnette (Ed.), *Handbook of industrial and organizational psychology.* Chicago: Rand McNally.

Fiorelli, J. S. (1988). Power in work groups: Team member's perspectives. *Human Relations, 41,* 1–12.

Fitts, P. M. (Ed.). (1951). *Human engineering for an effective air-navigation and traffic-control system.* Columbus, OH: Ohio State University.

Fitzgerald, L. F. (1980). *The incidence and utilization of assessment centers in state and local governments.* Washington, DC: International Personnel Management Association.

Flanagan, J. C. (1954). The critical incident technique. *Psychological Bulletin, 51,* 327–358.

Fleishman, E. A. (1953). The description of supervisory behavior. *Journal of Applied Psychology, 37,* 1–6.

Fleishman, E. A. (1957). The leadership opinion questionnaire. In R. M. Stogdill & A. E. Coons (Eds.), *Leader behavior: Its description and measurement.* Columbus: Ohio State University Bureau of Business Research.

Fleishman, E. A. (1967). Performance assessment based on an empirically derived task taxonomy. *Human Factors, 9,* 349–366.

Fletcher, C. (1987). Candidate personality as an influence on selection interview assessments. *Applied Psychology: An International Review, 36,* 157–162.

Follett, M. P. (1942). In L. Urwick et al. (Eds.), *The collected papers of Mary Parker Follett.* New York: Harper & Row.

Ford, J. D., & Ford, L. W. (1995). The role of conversations in producing intentional change in organizations. *Academy of Management Review, 20,* 541–570.

Ford, R. C., & Randolph, W. A. (1992). Cross-functional structures: A review and integration of matrix organization and project management. *Journal of Management, 18,* 267–294.

Fotheringhame, J. (1986). Transfer of training: A field study of some training methods. *Journal of Occupational Psychology, 59,* 59–71.

Foti, R. J., Fraser, S. L., & Lord, R. G. (1982). Effects of leadership labels and prototypes on perceptions of political leaders. *Journal of Applied Psychology, 67,* 326–333.

Fox, S., Ben-Nahum, Z., & Yinon, Y. (1989). Perceived similarity and accuracy of peer ratings. *Journal of Applied Psychology, 74,* 781–786.

Freedman, D. (1995, May 15). Affirmative action under 3-way review. *San Francisco Examiner,* Section A, p. 7.

French, J. R. P., Jr., Caplan, R. D., & Van Harrison, R. (1982). *The mechanisms of job stress and strain.* New York: Wiley.

French, J. R. P., Jr., Israel, J., & As, D. (1960). An experiment on participation in a Norwegian factory. *Human Relations, 13,* 3–19.

French, J. R. P., Jr., & Raven, B. (1959). The bases of social power. In D. Cartwright (Ed.), *Studies in social power.* Ann Arbor, MI: Institute of Social Research.

French, W. L., & Bell, C. H., Jr. (1984). *Organization development: Behavioral science interventions for organization improvement,* (3rd ed.). Englewood Cliffs, NJ: Prentice-Hall.

Fricko, M. A., & Beehr, T. A. (1992). A longitudinal investigation of interest congruence and gender concentration as predictors of job satisfaction. *Personnel Psychology, 45,* 99–117.

Fried, Y., & Ferris, G. R. (1987). The validity of the job characteristics model: A review and meta-analysis. *Personnel Psychology, 40,* 387.

Friedman, M., & Rosenman, R. H. (1959). Association of specific overt behavior pattern with blood and cardiovascular findings. *Journal of the American Medical Association, 169,* 1286–1296.

Friedman, M., & Rosenman, R. H. (1974). *Type A behavior and your heart.* New York: Knopf.

Froggatt, K. L., & Cotton, J. L. (1987). The impact of Type A behavior pattern on role overload-induced stress and performance attributions. *Journal of Management, 13,* 87–98.

Frone, M. R., & McFarlin, D. B. (1989). Chronic occupational stressors, self-focused attention, and well-being: Testing a cybernetic model of stress. *Journal of Applied Psychology, 74,* 876–883.

Furnham, A., & Stringfield, P. (1994). Congruence of self and subordinate ratings of managerial practices as a correlate of supervisor evaluation. *Journal of Occupational & Organizational Psychology, 67,* 57–67.

Fusilier, M. R., Ganster, D. C., & Mayes, B. T. (1987). Effects of social support, role stress, and locus of control on health. *Journal of Management, 13,* 517–528.

G

Gagne, R. M. (1962). Military training and principles of learning. *American Psychologist, 17,* 83–91.

Gagne, R. M. (1977). *The conditions of learning* (3rd ed.). New York: Holt, Rinehart & Winston.

Gaines, J., & Jermier, J. M. (1983). Emotional exhaustion in a high stress organization. *Academy of Management Journal, 26,* 567–586.

Gaines, J. H. (1980). Upward communication in industry: An experiment. *Human Relations, 33,* 929–942.

Galbraith, J. (1973). *Designing complex organizations.* Menlo Park, CA: Addison-Wesley.

Gallois, C., Callan, V. J., & Palmer, J. M. (1992). The influence of applicant communication style and interviewer characteristics on hiring decisions. *Journal of Applied Social Psychology, 22,* 1041–1060.

Gannon, M. J., Norland, D. L., & Robeson, F. E. (1983). Shift work has complex effects on lifestyles and work habits. *Personnel Administrator, 28*(5), 93–97.

Ganster, D. C. (1986). Type A behavior and occupational stress. *Journal of Organizational Behavior Management, 8*(2), 61–84.

Ganster, D. C., & Dwyer, D. J. (1995). The effects of understaffing on individual and group performance in professional and trade occupations. *Journal of Management, 21,* 175–190.

Ganster, D. C., Fusilier, M. R., & Mayes, B. T. (1986). Role of social support in the experience of stress at work. *Journal of Applied Psychology, 71,* 102–110.

Garcia, M. H. (1995). An anthropological approach to multicultural diversity training. *Journal of Applied Behavioral Science, 31,* 490–504.

Gardner, A. (1987). Depersonalization: A valid dimension of burnout? *Human Relations, 40,* 545–560.

Garg, A., & Saxena, U. (1979). Effects of lifting frequency and technique on physical fatigue with special reference to psychophysical methodology and metabolic rate. *American Industrial Hygiene Association Journal, 40,* 894–903.

Garonzik, R. (1989). Hand dominance and implications for left-handed operation of controls. *Ergonomics, 32,* 1185–1192.

Garza, R. T., Romero, G. J., Cox, B. G., & Ramirez, M. (1982). Biculturalism, locus of control, and leader behavior in ethnically mixed small groups. *Journal of Applied Social Psychology, 12,* 237–253.

Gaugler, B. B., Rosenthal, D. B., Thorton, G. C., & Bentson, C. (1987). Meta-analysis of assessment center validity. *Journal of Applied Psychology, 72,* 493–511.

Gaugler, B. B., & Rudolph, A. S. (1992). The influence of assessee performance variation on assessors' judgments. *Personnel Psychology, 45,* 77–98.

Gavin, A. T. (1977). *Guide to the development of written tests for selection and promotion: The content validity model* (technical memorandum 77-6). Washington, DC: Personnel Research and Development Center, U.S. Civil Service Commission.

Gavin, J. F. (1970). Ability, effort, and role perception as antecedents of job performance. *Experimental Publication System, 5*(190A), 1–26.

Gavin, J. F., & Krois, P. A. (1983). Content and process of survey feedback sessions and their relation to survey responses: An initial study. *Group & Organization Studies, 8,* 221–247.

Gechman, A. S., & Wiener, Y. (1975). Job involvement and satisfaction as related to mental health and personal time devoted to work. *Journal of Applied Psychology, 60,* 521–523.

Gemmill, G., & Oakley, J. (1992). Leadership: An alienating social myth? *Human Relations, 45,* 113–129.

Georgopoulous, B. S., Mahoney, G. M., & Jones, N. W., Jr. (1957). A path-goal approach to productivity. *Journal of Applied Psychology, 41,* 345–353.

Gerhart, B. (1987). How important are dispositional factors as determinants of job satisfaction? Implications for job design and other personnel programs. *Journal of Applied Psychology, 72,* 366–373.

Gerhart, B. (1990). Voluntary turnover and alternative job opportunities. *Journal of Applied Psychology, 75,* 467–476.

Ghiselli, E. E., & Brown, C. W. (1948). *Personnel and industrial psychology.* New York: McGraw-Hill.

Ghiselli, E. E., & Brown, C. W. (1955). *Personnel and industrial psychology.* New York: McGraw-Hill.

Gilbert, D. G. (1979). Paradoxical tranquilizing and emotion-reducing effects of nicotine. *Psychological Bulletin, 86,* 643–661.

Gilbert, L. A., & Holahan, C. K. (1982). Conflicts between student/professional, parental, and self-development roles: A comparison of high and low effective copers. *Human Relations, 35,* 635–648.

Gilbert, R. M. (1976). Caffeine as a drug of abuse. In R. J. Gibbins et al. (Eds.), *Research advances in alcohol and drug problems* (Vol. 3). New York: Wiley.

Gillen, R. W., & Heimberg, R. G. (1980). Social skills training for the job interview: Review and prospectus. *Progress in Behavior Modification, 10,* 183–206.

Gilmore, D. C., Beehr, T. A., & Love, K. G. (1986). Effects of applicant sex, applicant physical attractiveness, type of rater and type of job on interview decisions. *Journal of Occupational Psychology, 59,* 103–109.

Glew, D. J., O'Leary-Kelly, A. M., Griffin, R. W., & Van Fleet, D. D. (1995). Participation in organizations: A preview of the issues and proposed framework for future analysis. *Journal of Management, 21,* 395–421.

Goktepe, J. R., & Schneier, C. E. (1989). Role of sex, gender roles, and attraction in predicting emergent leaders. *Journal of Applied Psychology, 74,* 165–167.

Goldfried, M. R. (1988). Application of rational restructuring to anxiety disorders. *Counseling Psychologist, 16,* 50–68.

Goldman, M., Stockbauer, J. W., & McAuliffe, T. G. (1977). Intergroup and intragroup competition and cooperation. *Journal of Experimental Social Psychology, 13,* 81–88.

Goldstein, I. L. (1980). Training in work organizations. *Annual Review of Psychology, 31,* 329–372.

Goldstein, I. L. (1986). *Training in organizations: Needs assessment, development, and evaluation* (2nd ed.). Monterry, CA: Brooks/Cole.

Gomberg, E. S. L. (1982). Historical and political perspective: Women and drug use. *Journal of Social Issues, 38,* 9–23.

Gomez-Mejia, L. R., & Balkin, D. B. (1984). Faculty satisfaction with pay and other job dimensions under union and nonunion conditions. *Academy of Management Journal, 27,* 591–602.

Goodman, P. S., & Friedman, A. (1969). An examination of quantity and quality of performance under conditions of overpayment in piece rate. *Organizational Behavior and Human Performance, 4,* 365–374.

Goodman, P. S., & Friedman, A. (1971). An examination of Adams' theory of inequity. *Administrative Science Quarterly, 16,* 217–288.

Gordon, G. G. (1991). Industry determinants of organizational culture. *Academy of Management Review, 16,* 396–415.

Gordon, M. E., & Fitzgibbons, W. J. (1982). Empirical test of the validity of seniority as a factor in staffing decisions. *Journal of Applied Psychology, 67,* 311–319.

Gorlin, H. (1982). An overview of corporate personnel practices. *Personnel Journal, 61,* 125–130.

Gotcher, J. M. (1992). Assisting the handicapped: The pioneering efforts of Frank and Lillian Gilbreth. *Journal of Management, 18,* 5–13.

Gould, J. D. et al. (1987). Reading from CRT displays can be as fast as reading from paper. *Human Factors, 29,* 497–517.

Gould, J. D., & Grischkowsky, N. (1984). Doing the same work with hard copy and with cathode-ray tube (CRT) computer terminals. *Human Factors, 26,* 323–337.

Graen, G., & Cashman, J. F. (1975). A role making model of leadership in formal organizations: A developmental approach. In J. G. Hunt & L. L. Larson (Eds.), *Leadership frontiers.* Kent, OH: Kent State University Press.

Graen, G. B., Scandura, T. A., & Graen, M. R. (1986). A field experimental test of the moderating effects of growth need strength on productivity. *Journal of Applied Psychology, 71,* 484–491.

Graham, N. K. (1981, January). Done in, fed up, burned out: Too much attrition at EMS. *Journal of Emergency Medical Service,* 24–29.

Graves, L. M., & Karren, R. J. (1992). Interviewer decision processes and effectiveness: An experimental policy-capturing investigation. *Personnel Psychology, 45,* 313–340.

Greenberg, J. (1988). Equity and workplace status: A field experiment. *Journal of Applied Psychology, 73,* 606–613.

Greene, M. H., & Dupont, R. L. (1974). Heroin addiction trends. *American Journal of Psychiatry, 131,* 545–550.

Greenglass, E. R. (1988). Type A behavior and coping strategies in female and male supervisors. *Applied Psychology: An International Review, 37,* 271–288.

Greenglass, E. R. (1993). The contribution of social support to coping strategies. *Applied Psychology: An International Review, 42,* 323–340.

Greenhalgh, L. (1982). Maintaining organizational effectiveness during organizational retrenchment. *Journal of Applied Behavioral Science, 18,* 155–170.

Greenhaus, J. H., & Parasuraman, S. (1993). Job performance attributions and career advancement prospects: An examination of gender and race effects. *Organizational Behavior & Human Decision Processes, 55,* 273–297.

Grieshop, J. I., & Winter, D. M. (1989). Agricultural pesticide accidents and prevention in Ecuador. *Accident Analysis and Prevention, 21,* 394–398.

Griffin, R. W. (1988). Consequences of quality circles in an industrial setting: A longitudinal assessment. *Academy of Management Journal, 31,* 338–358.

Guion, R. M. (1965). *Personnel testing.* New York: McGraw-Hill.

Gupta, N., Jenkins, G. D., & Beehr, T. A. (1992). The effects of turnover on perceived job quality: Does the grass look greener? *Group & Organizational Management, 17,* 431–44.

Gutek, B. A. (1993). Changing the status of women in management. *Applied Psychology: An International Review, 42,* 301–311.

H

Hackett, R. D. (1989). Work attitudes and employee absenteeism: A synthesis of the literature. *Journal of Occupational Psychology, 62*, 235–248.

Hackman, J. R., & Lawler, E. E., III. (1971). Employee reactions to job characteristics. *Journal of Applied Psychology, 55*, 259–286.

Hackman, J. R., & Oldham, G. R. (1975). Development of the job diagnostic survey. *Journal of Applied Psychology, 60*, 159–170.

Hackman, J. R., & Oldham, G. R. (1976). Motivation through the design of work: Test of a theory. *Organizational Behavior and Human Performance, 16*, 250–279.

Hahn, H. A., & Price, D. L. (1994). Assessment of the relative effects of alcohol on different types of job behaviour. *Ergonomics, 37*, 435–448.

Hakel, M. D. (1986). Personnel selection and placement. *Annual Review of Psychology, 37*, 351–380.

Halachmi, A. (1992). The brave new world of information technology. *Public Personnel Management, 21*, 533–553.

Hale, B. D. (1982). The effects of internal and external imagery on muscular and ocular concomitants. *Journal of Sport Psychology, 4*, 379–387.

Hall, C. S., & Lindzey, G. (1957). *Theories of personality*. New York: Wiley.

Hall, D. T. (1986). Dilemmas in linking succession planning to individual executive learning. *Human Resource Management, 25*, 235–265.

Hall, J. L., Posner, B. Z., & Harder, J. W. (1989). Performance appraisal systems: Matching practice with theory. *Group & Organization Studies, 14*, 51–69.

Halpin, A. W., & Winer, B. J. (1957). A factorial study of the leader behavior descriptions. In R. M. Stogdill & A. E. Coons (Eds.), *Leader behavior: Its description and measurement*. Columbus: Ohio State University Bureau of Business Research.

Hamelin, P. (1987). Lorry drivers' time habits in work and their involvement in traffic accidents. *Ergonomics, 30*, 1323–1333.

Hamilton, E. E. (1988). The facilitation of organizational change: An empirical study of factors predicting change agents' effectiveness. *Journal of Applied Behavioral Science, 24*, 37–59.

Hamner, W. C., & Smith, F. J. (1978). Work attitudes as predictors of unionization activity. *Journal of Applied Psychology, 63*, 415–421.

Hamner, W. C., & Tosi, H. (1974). Relationship of role conflict and role ambiguity to job involvement measures. *Journal of Applied Psychology, 59*, 497–499.

Hansen, C. P. (1989). A causal model of the relationship among accidents, biodata, personality, and cognitive factors. *Journal of Applied Psychology, 74*, 81–90.

Hardyck, C., & Petrinovich, L. F. (1977). Left–handedness. *Psychological Bulletin, 84*, 385–404.

Hargie, O. D. W., & Tourish, D. (1994). Communication skills training: Management manipulation or personal development? *Human Relations, 47*, 1377–1389.

Harrell, A., & Stahl, M. (1986). Additive information processing and the relationship between expectancy of success and motivational force. *Academy of Management Journal, 29*, 424–433.

Harris, M. M., & Schaubroeck, J. (1988). A meta-analysis of self-supervisor, self-peer, and peer-supervisor ratings. *Personnel Psychology, 41*, 43–62.

Harris, M. M., Smith, D. E., & Champagne, D. (1995). A field study of performance appraisal purpose: Research-versus administrative-based ratings. *Personnel Psychology, 48*, 151–160.

Harrison, D. A., & Liska, L. Z. (1994). Promoting regular exercise in organizational fitness programs: Health-related differences in motivational building blocks. *Personnel Psychology, 47*, 47–71.

Hartstein, B. A. (1987). Drug testing in the workplace: A primer for employers. *Employee Relations Law Journal, 12*, 577–604.

Harvey, R. J., Friedman, L., Hakel, M. D., & Cornelius, E. T., III. (1988). Dimensionality of the Job Element Inventory, a simplified worker-oriented job analysis questionnaire. *Journal of Applied Psychology, 73*, 639–646.

Harvey, R. J., & Lozada-Larsen, S. R. (1988). Influence of amount of job descriptive information on job analysis rating accuracy. *Journal of Applied Psychology, 73*, 457–461.

Health, Education, and Welfare Special Task Force. (1973). *Work in America*. Cambridge, MA: MIT Press.

Hedge, J. W., & Kavanagh, M. J. (1988). Improving the accuracy of performance evaluations: Comparison of three methods of performance appraiser training. *Journal of Applied Psychology, 73*, 68–73.

Heider, F. (1958). *The psychology of interpersonal relations*. New York: Wiley.

Heilman, M. E., Hornstein, H. A., Cage, J. H., & Herschlag, J. K. (1984). Reactions to prescribed leader behavior as a function of role perspective: The case of the Vroom-Yetton Model. *Journal of Applied Psychology, 69*, 50–60.

Hemphill, J. K. (1949). The leader and his group. *Journal of Educational Research, 28*, 225–229.

Hemphill, J. K., & Coons, A. E. (1957). Development of the Leader Behavior Description Questionnaire. In R. M. Stogdill & A. E. Coons (Eds.), *Leader behavior: Its description and measurement*. Columbus: Ohio State University Bureau of Business Research.

Heneman, H. G., III, & Schwab, D. P. (1985). Pay satisfaction: Its multidimensional nature and measurement. *International Journal of Psychology, 20*, 129–141.

Heneman, R. L., Greenberger, D. B., & Strasser, S. (1988). The relationship between pay-for-performance perceptions and pay satisfactions. *Personnel Psychology, 41*, 745–759.

Herold, D. M., Liden, R. C., & Leatherwood, M. L. (1987). Using multiple attributes to assess sources of performance feedback. *Academy of Management Journal, 30*, 826–835.

Hersey, R. B. (1936). Psychology of workers. *Personnel Journal, 14*, 291–296.

Herzberg, F. (1966). *Work and the nature of man*. Cleveland: World Publishing.

Herzberg, F., Mausner, B., & Snyderman, B. (1959). *The motivation to work* (2nd ed.). New York: Wiley.

Hill, W. H., & Hughes, D. (1974). Variations in leader behavior as a function of task type. *Organizational Behavior and Human Performance, 11*, 83–96.

Hinkin, T. R., & Schriesheim, C. A. (1989). Development and application of new scales to measure the French and Raven (1959) bases of social power. *Journal of Applied Psychology, 74*, 561–567.

Hoffman, C. C., Nathan, B. R., & Holden, L. M. (1991). A comparison of validation criteria: Objective versus subjective performance measures and self- versus supervisor ratings. *Personnel Psychology, 44,* 577–600.

Hoffman, L. R., & Maier, N. R. F. (1961). Quality and acceptance of problem solutions by members of homogeneous and heterogeneous groups. *Journal of Abnormal and Social Psychology, 62,* 401–407.

Hofstede, G. (1994). Management scientists are human. *Management Science, 40,* 4–13.

Hogan, J., & Hogan, R. (1989). How to measure employee reliability. *Journal of Applied Psychology, 74,* 273–279.

Hoiberg, A., & Pugh, W. M. (1978). Predicting navy effectiveness: Expectations, motivation, personality, aptitude, and background variables. *Personnel Psychology, 31,* 841–852.

Hollander, E. P. (1958). Conformity, status, and idiosyncracy credit. *Psychological Review, 65,* 117–127.

Hollander, E. P. (1978). *Leadership dynamics: A practical guide to effective relationships.* New York: Free Press.

Hollenbeck, J. R., & Whitener, E. M. (1988). Criterion-related validation for small sample contexts: An integrated approach to synthetic validity. *Journal of Applied Psychology, 73,* 536–544.

Hollinger, R. C. (1988). Working under the influence (WUI): Correlates of employees' use of alcohol and other drugs. *Journal of Applied Behavioral Science, 24,* 439–454.

Holmes, T. H., & Masuda, M. (1974). Life change and illness susceptibility. In B. S. Dohrenwend & B. P. Dohrenwend (Eds.), *Stressful life events: Their nature and effects.* New York: Wiley.

Holmes, T. H., & Rahe, R. H. (1967). Social readjustment rating scale. *Journal of Psychosomatic Research, 11,* 213–218.

Holroyd, K. A., & Lazarus, R. S. (1982). Stress, coping, and somatic adaptation. In L. Goldberger & S. Breznitz (Eds.), *Handbook of stress: Theoretical and clinical aspects.* New York: Free Press.

Hopkins, M. E., Lo, L., Peterson, R. E., & Seo, K. K. (1977). Japanese and American managers. *Journal of Applied Psychology, 96,* 71–72.

Hopkins, W. E., Sterkel-Powell, K., & Hopkins, S. A. (1994). Training priorities for a diverse work force. *Public Personnel Management, 23,* 429–435.

Hoppock, R. (1935). *Job satisfaction.* New York: Harper.

Hough, L. M., Eaton, N. K., Dunnette, M. D., Kamp, J. D., & McCloy, R. A. (1990). Criterion-related validities of personality constructs and the effect of response distortion on those validities. *Journal of Applied Psychology, 75,* 581–595.

House, R. J. (1971). A path-goal theory of leader effectiveness. *Administrative Science Quarterly, 16,* 321–338.

House, R. J. (1977). A 1976 theory of charismatic leadership. In J. G. Hunt & L. L. Larson (Eds.), *Leadership: The cutting edge.* Carbondale, IL: Southern Illinois University Press.

House, R. J., & Dessler, G. (1974). Path-goal theory of leadership: Some post-hoc and a priori tests. In J. G. Hunt & L. L. Larson (Eds.), *Contingency approaches to leadership.* Carbondale, IL: Southern Illinois University Press.

Houston, B. K., Smith, T. W., & Zurawski, R. M. (1986). Principal dimensions of the Framingham Type A scale: Differential relationships to cardiovascular reactivity and anxiety. *Journal of Human Stress, 12,* 105–112.

Houston, J. P. (1986). *Fundamentals of learning and memory* (3rd ed.). New York: Academic Press.

Howard, A. (1984). I/O careers in industry. *The Industrial-Organizational Psychologist, 21*(4), 46–54.

Howard, A. (1990). *The multiple facets of industrial-organizational psychology: Membership survey results.* Arlington Heights, IL: Society for Industrial and Organizational Psychology.

Howard, A., & Lowman, R. L. (1985). Should industrial/ organizational psychologists be licensed? *American Psychologist, 40,* 40–47.

Hsu, S., & Peng, Y. (1993). Control/display relationship of the four-burner stove: A reexamination. *Human Factors, 35,* 745–749.

Huffcutt, A. I., & Arthur, W. (1994). Hunter and Hunter (1984) revisited: Interview validity for entry-level jobs. *Journal of Applied Psychology, 79,* 184–190.

Hui, C. H., Yee, C., & Eastman, K. L. (1995). The relationship between individualism-collectivism and job satisfaction. *Applied Psychology: An International Review, 44,* 276–282.

Hulin, C. L. (1982). Some reflections on general performance dimensions and halo rating error. *Journal of Applied Psychology, 67,* 165–170.

Hulin, C. L., Roznowski, M., & Hachiya, D. (1985). Alternative opportunities and withdrawal decisions: Empirical and theoretical discrepancies and an integration. *Psychological Bulletin, 97,* 233–250.

Hull, C. L. (1951). *Essentials of behavior.* New Haven, CT: Yale University Press.

Hunt, G. T. (1980). *Communication skills in the organization.* Englewood Cliffs, NJ: Prentice–Hall.

Hunt, W. A., Barnett, L. W., & Ranch, L. G. (1971). Relapse rates in addiction programs. *Journal of Clinical Psychology, 27,* 455–456.

Hunter, J. E., & Hunter, R. F. (1984). Validity and utility of attenuation predictions of job performance. *Psychological Bulletin, 96,* 72–98.

Hunter, J. E., Schmidt, F. L., & Jackson, G. B. (1982). *Meta-analysis: Cumulating research findings across studies.* Beverly Hills, CA: Sage.

I

Iaffaldano, M. T., & Muchinsky, P. M. (1985). Job satisfaction and job performance: A meta-analysis. *Psychological Bulletin, 97,* 251–273.

Ilgen, D. R., & Moore, C. F. (1987). Types and choices of performance feedback. *Journal of Applied Psychology, 72,* 401–406.

Ironson, G. H., Smith, P. C., Brannick, M. T., & Gibson, W. M. (1989). Construction of a job in general scale: A comparison of global, composite, and specific measures. *Journal of Applied Psychology, 74,* 193–200.

Ivancevich, J. M. (1982). Subordinates' reactions to performance appraisal interviews: A test of feedback and goal-setting techniques. *Journal of Applied Psychology, 67,* 581–587.

Ivancevich, J. M., & Matteson, M. T. (1986). Organizational level stress management interventions: A review and recommendations. *Journal of Organizational Behavior Management, 8,* 229–248.

Ivancevich, J. M., Matteson, M. T., & Preston, C. (1982). Occupational stress, Type A behavior, and physical well-being. *Academy of Management Journal, 25,* 373–391.

J

Jablin, F. M. (1985). Task/work relationships: A life-span perspective. In M. L. Knapp & G. R. Miller (Eds.), *Handbook of interpersonal communication.* Beverly Hills, CA: Sage.

Jackson, S. (1966). My life with R. H. Macy. In S. E. Hyman (Ed.), *The Magic of Shirley Jackson.* NY: Farrar, Straus, and Giroux.

Jackson, S. E., Schwab, R. L., & Schuler, R. S. (1986). Toward an understanding of the burnout phenomenon. *Journal of Applied Psychology, 71,* 630–640.

Jackson, S. E., Turner, J. A., & Brief, A. P. (1987). Correlates of burnout among public service lawyers. *Journal of Occupational Behaviour, 8,* 339–349.

Jacobs, R., & Solomon, J. (1977). Strategies of enhancing the prediction of job performance for job satisfaction. *Journal of Applied Psychology, 62,* 417–427.

Jaffee, C. L. (1968). Leadership attempting: Why and when? *Psychological Reports, 23,* 939–946.

Jago, A. G., & Vroom, V. H. (1982). Sex differences in the incidence and evaluation of participative leader behavior. *Journal of Applied Psychology, 67,* 776–783.

Jamal, M., & Baba, V. V. (1992). Shiftwork and department-type related to job stress, work attitudes and behavioral intentions: A study of nurses. *Journal of Organizational Behavior, 13,* 449–464.

James, L. R., Demaree, R. G., Mulaik, S. A., & Mumford, M.D. (1988). Validity generalization: Rejoinder to Schmidt, Hunter, and Raju (1988). *Journal of Applied Psychology, 73,* 673–678.

Janis, I. L. (1972). *Victims of groupthink.* Boston: Houghton Mifflin.

Jarvik, M. E. (1967). The psychopharmacological revolution. *Psychology Today, 1*(1), 51–58.

Jayaratne, S., & Chess, W. A. (1984). The effects of emotional support on perceived job stress and strain. *Journal of Applied Behavioral Science, 20,* 141–153.

Jehn, K. (1995). A multimethod examination of the benefits and detriments of intragroup conflict. *Administrative Science Quarterly, 40,* 256–282.

Jenkins, C. D., Rosenman, R. H., & Zyzanski, S. J. (1979). *Jenkins Activity Survey.* New York: Psychological Corporation.

Jenkins, F. H., & Baggett, J. C. (1992). Compulsive personality traits affecting aeronautical adaptability in a naval aviator: A case report. *Aviation, Space, & Environmental Medicine, 63,* 529–532.

Jenkins, C. D. (1974). Behavior that triggers heart attacks. *Science News, 105,*402.

Jermier, J. M., Gaines, J., & McIntosh, N. J. (1989). Reactions to physically dangerous work: A conceptual and empirical analysis. *Journal of Organizational Behavior, 10,* 15–33.

Jick, T. D., & Mitz, L. F. (1985). Sex differences in work stress. *Academy of Management Review, 10,* 408–420.

Johansson, G., & Aronsson, G. (1984). Stress reactions in computerized administrative work. *Journal of Occupational Behavior, 5,* 159–181.

Johnson, D. F., & White, C. B. (1980). Effects of training on computerized test performance in the elderly. *Journal of Applied Psychology, 65,* 357–358.

Johnson, D. W., & Johnson, R. T. (1979). Type of task and student achievement and attitudes in interpersonal cooperation, competition, and individualization. *Journal of Social Psychology, 108,* 37–48.

Johnson, D. W., Maruyama, G., Johnson, R., Nelson, D., & Skon, L. (1981). The effects of cooperative, competitive, and individualistic goal structures on achievement: A meta-analysis. *Psychological Bulletin, 89,* 47–82.

Johnson, M. D., & Fawcett, S. B. (1994). Courteous service: Its assessment and modification in a human service organization. *Journal of Applied Behavior Analysis, 27,* 145–152.

Johnson, P. B. (1982). Sex differences, women's roles and alcohol use: Preliminary national data. *Journal of Social Issues, 38,* 93–116.

Jorgenson, D. O., Dunnette, M. D., & Pritchard, R. D. (1973). Effects of the manipulation of a performance-reward contingency on behavior in a simulated work setting. *Journal of Applied Psychology, 57,* 271–280.

Jorna, G. C., & Snyder, H. L. (1991). Image quality determines differences in reading performance and perceived image quality with CRT and hard-copy displays. *Human Factors, 33,* 459–569.

Judge, T. A. (1993). Validity of the dimensions of the Pay Satisfaction Questionnaire: Evidence of differential prediction. *Personnel Psychology, 46,* 331–355.

Judge, T. A., & Watanabe, S. (1994). Individual differences in the nature of the relationship between job and life satisfaction. *Journal of Occupational & Organizational Psychology, 67,* 101–107.

Judge, T. A., & Welbourne, T. M. (1994). A confirmatory investigation of the dimensionality of the Pay Satisfaction Questionnaire. *Journal of Applied Psychology, 79,* 461–466.

K

Kabanoff, B. (1980). Work and nonwork: A review of models, methods, and findings. *Psychological Bulletin, 88,* 60–77.

Kacmar, K. M., & Ferris, G. R. (1989). Theoretical and methodological considerations in the age-job satisfaction relationship. *Journal of Applied Psychology, 74,* 201–207.

Kahn, R. L., Wolfe, D. M., Quinn, R. P., Snoek, J. D., & Rosenthal, R. A. (1964). *Organizational stress: Studies in role conflict and ambiguity.* New York: Wiley.

Kane, J. S., Bernardin, H. J., Villanova, P., & Peyrefitte, J. (1995). Stability of rater leniency: Three studies. *Academy of Management Journal, 38,* 1036–1051.

Kane, J. S., & Lawler, E. E., III. (1978). Methods of peer assessment. *Psychological Bulletin, 85,* 555–586.

Kantowitz, B. H., & Sorkin, R. D. (1983). *Human factors: Understanding people-system relationships.* New York: Wiley.

Karl, K. A., O'Leary-Kelly, A. M., & Martocchio, J. J. (1993). The impact of feedback and self-efficacy on performance in training. *Journal of Organizational Behavior, 14,* 379–394.

Kasabian, C. (1983, April 3). How firms help troubled workers. *San Francisco Examiner,* Section E, p. 1, 9.

Katz, D., & Kahn, R. (1966). *The social psychology of organizations.* New York: Wiley.

Katz, D., & Kahn, R. L. (1978). *The social psychology of organizations* (2nd ed.). New York: Wiley.

Katz, D., Maccoby, N., & Morse, N. C. (1950). *Productivity, supervision and morale in an office situation.* Ann Arbor, MI: University of Michigan, Institute for Social Research.

Katzell, R. A. (1980). Work attitudes, motivation, and performance. *Professional Psychology, 11,* 409–420.

Katzell, R. A., & Austin, J. T. (1992). From then to now: The development of industrial-organizational psychology in the United States. *Journal of Applied Psychology, 77,* 803–835.

Katzell, R. A., Bienstock, P., & Faerstein, P. H. (1977). *A guide to worker productivity experiments in the United States, 1971–75.* New York: New York University Press.

Kay, E., Meyer, H., & French, J. R. P. (1965). Effects of threat in a performance appraisal interview. *Journal of Applied Psychology, 49,* 311–317.

Kazerooni, H. (1990). Human-robot interaction via the transfer of power and information signals. *IEEE Transactions on Systems, Man, & Cybernetics, 20,* 450–463.

Keck, S. L., & Tushman, M. L. (1993). Environmental and organizational context and executive team structure. *Academy of Management Journal, 36,* 1314–1344.

Keenan, P. A., & Carnevale, P. J. (1989). Positive effects of within-group cooperation on between-group negotiation. *Journal of Applied Social Psychology, 19,* 977–992.

Kellogg, D. M. (1984). Contrasting successful and unsuccessful OD consultation relationships. *Group & Organization Studies, 9,* 151–176.

Kelly, J. E. (1992). Does job re-design theory explain job re-design outcomes? *Human Relations, 45,* 753–774.

Kelly, K. R., & Stone, G. L. (1987). Effects of three psychological treatments and self-monitoring on the reduction of Type A behavior. *Journal of Counseling Psychology, 34,* 46–54.

Kelly, R. W. (1920). *Training industrial workers.* New York: Ronald Press.

Kennedy, J. K. (1982). Middle LPC leaders and the contingency model of leadership effectiveness. *Organizational Behavior and Human Performance, 30,* 1–14.

Kent, R. L., & Moss, S. E. (1994). Effects of sex and gender role on leader emergence. *Academy of Management Journal, 37,* 1335–1346.

Khojasteh, M. (1993). Motivating the private vs. public sector managers. *Public Personnel Management, 22,* 391–401.

King, N. (1970). Clarification and evaluation of the two-factor theory of job satisfaction. *Psychological Bulletin, 74,* 18–31.

Kipnis, D., Schmidt, S. M., & Wilkinson, I. (1980). Intraorganizational influence tactics: Explorations in getting one's way. *Journal of Applied Psychology, 65,* 440–452.

Kirk, R. E. (1968). *Experimental design: Procedures for the behavioral sciences.* Belmont, CA: Brooks/Cole.

Kirkpatrick, D. L. (1967). Evaluation of training. In R. L. Craig & L. R. Bittel (Eds.), *Training and developmental handbook.* New York: McGraw-Hill.

Kirmeyer, S. L. (1988). Coping with competing demands: Interruption and the Type A pattern. *Journal of Applied Psychology, 73,* 621–629.

Kirmeyer, S. L., & Dougherty, T. W. (1988). Work load, tension, and coping: Moderating effects of supervisor support. *Personnel Psychology, 41,* 125–139.

Kirmeyer, S. L., & Lin, T. (1987). Social support: Its relationship to observed communication with peers and superiors. *Academy of Management Journal, 30,* 138–151.

Kissler, G. (1985). Practicing I/O psychology as a component in a large company. *The Industrial-Organizational Psychologist, 22(2),* 16–25.

Klimoski, R., Friedman, B., & Weldon, E. (1980). Leader influence in the assessment of performance. *Personnel Psychology, 33,* 389–401.

Klimoski, R. J., & Strickland, W. J. (1977). Assessment centers—Valid or merely prescient? *Personnel Psychology, 30,* 353–361.

Kluger, A. N., & Colella, A. (1993). Beyond the mean bias: The effect of warning against faking on biodata item variances. *Personnel Psychology, 46,* 763–780.

Knauth, P., & Kiesswetter, E. (1987). A change from weekly to quicker shift rotations: A field study of discontinuous three-shift workers. *Ergonomics, 30,* 1311–1321.

Kochan, T. A. (1980). *Collective bargaining and industrial relations.* Homewood, IL: Irwin.

Koenker, R. H. (1974). *Simplified statistics.* Totowa, NJ: Littlefield, Adams.

Koestler, F. A. (1978). *Jobs for handicapped persons: A new era in civil rights.* Public Affairs Committee.

Kofman, F., & Senge, P. M. (1993). Communities of commitment: The heart of learning organizations. *Organizational Dynamics, 22(2),* 5–22.

Koopman, P. L. et al. (1981). Content, process, and effects of participative decision making on the shop floor: Three cases in the Netherlands. *Human Relations, 34,* 657–676.

Korman, A. K. (1970). Toward an hypothesis of work behavior. *Journal of Applied Psychology, 54,* 31–41.

Korman, A. K. (1977). *Organizational behavior.* Englewood Cliffs, NJ: Prentice-Hall.

Korman, A. K., Greenhaus, J. H., & Badin, I. J. (1977). Personnel attitudes and motivation. *Annual Review of Psychology, 28,* 175–196.

Kraiger, K., & Ford, J. K. (1985). A meta-analysis of ratee race effects in performance ratings. *Journal of Applied Psychology, 70,* 56–65.

Kraiger, K., Ford, J. K., & Salas, E. (1993). Application of cognitive, skill-based, and affective theories of learning outcomes to new methods of training evaluation. *Journal of Applied Psychology, 78,* 311–328.

Krantz, D. S., Grunberg, N. E., & Baum, A. (1985). Health psychology. *Annual Review of Psychology, 36,* 349–384.

Krau, E. (1981). Immigrants preparing for their second career: The behavioral strategies adopted. *Journal of Vocational Behavior, 18,* 289–303.

Krech, D. (1969). Psychoneurobiochemeducation. *California Monthly, 79.* Reprinted in R. V. Guthrie (Ed.). (1971). *Psychology in the world today: An interdisciplinary approach* (2nd ed.). Reading, MA: Addison-Wesley.

Krzystofiak, R., Cardy, R. L., & Newman, J. (1988). Implicit personality and performance appraisal: The influence of trait inferences on evaluations of behavior. *Journal of Applied Psychology, 73,* 515–521.

Kuder, G. F., & Richardson, M. (1937). The theory of the estimation of test reliability, *Psychometrika, 2,* 151–160.

Kuhnert, K. W., & Palmer, D. R. (1991). Job security, health, and the intrinsic and extrinsic characteristics of work. *Group & Organization Studies, 16,* 178–192.

Kuna, D. P. (1976). The concept of suggestion in the early history of advertising psychology. *Journal of the History of the Behavioral Sciences, 12,* 347–353.

Kunin, T. (1955). The construction of a new type of attitude measure. *Personnel Psychology, 8,* 65–77.

Kushnir, T., & Melamed, S. (1991). Work-load, perceived control and psychological distress in Type A/B industrial workers. *Journal of Occupational Behaviour, 12,* 155–168.

L

Lambrinos, J., & Johnson, W. G. (1984). Robots to reduce the high cost of illness and injury. *Harvard Business Review, 62*(3), 24–28.

Lance, C. E., LaPointe, J. A., & Stewart, A. M. (1994). A test of the context dependency of three causal models of halo rater error. *Journal of Applied Psychology, 79,* 332–340.

Landy, F. J. (1978). An opponent process theory of job satisfaction. *Journal of Applied Psychology, 63,* 533–547.

Landy, F. J. (1985). *Psychology of work behavior.* Homewood, IL: Dorsey.

Landy, F. J. (1992). Hugo Munsterberg: Victim or visionary? *Journal of Applied Psychology, 77,* 787–802.

Landy, F. J., & Farr, J. L. (1980). Performance rating. *Psychological Bulletin, 87,* 72–107.

Langan-Fox, J., & Roth, S. (1995). Achievement motivation and female entrepreneurs. *Journal of Occupational and Organizational Psychology, 68,* 209–218.

Latham, G. P. (1988). Human resource training and development. *Annual Review of Psychology, 39,* 545–582.

Latham, G. P., & Frayne, C. A. (1989). Self-management training for increasing job attendance: A follow-up and a replication. *Journal of Applied Psychology, 74,* 411–416.

Latham, G. P., & Huber, V. L. (1992). Schedules of reinforcement: Lessons from the past and issues for the future. *Journal of Organizational Behavior Management, 12,* 125–149.

Latham, G. P., & Saari, L. M. (1979). Application of social learning theory to training supervisors through behavioral modeling. *Journal of Applied Psychology, 64,* 239–246.

Latham, G. P., Saari, L. M., Pursell, E. D., & Campion, M. A. (1980). The situational interview. *Journal of Applied Psychology, 65,* 422–427.

Latham, G. P., & Wexley, K. N. (1977). Behavioral observation scales for performance appraisal purposes. *Personnel Psychology, 30,* 255–268.

Latham, G. P., Wexley, K. N., & Pursell, E. D. (1975). Training managers to minimize rating errors in the observation of behavior. *Journal of Applied Psychology, 60,* 550–555.

Latham, G. P., & Whyte, G. (1994). The futility of utility analysis. *Personnel Psychology, 47,* 31–46.

Lattanzi, M. E. (1981). Coping with work-related losses. *Personnel and Guidance Journal, 59,* 350–351.

Laville, A. (1985). Postural stress in high-speed precision work. *Ergonomics, 28,* 229–236.

Lawler, E. E. (1968). Equity theory as a predictor of productivity and work quality. *Psychological Bulletin, 70,* 596–610.

Lawler, E. E. (1969). Job design and employee motivation. *Personnel Psychology, 22,* 426–435.

Lawler, E. E. (1973). *Motivation in work organizations.* Belmont, CA: Brooks/Cole.

Lawler, E. E. (1985). Education, management style, and organizational effectiveness. *Personnel Psychology, 38,* 1–26.

Lawler, E. E., & Mohrman, S. A. (1985). Quality circles after the fad. *Harvard Business Review, 85,* 65–71.

Lawler, E. E., & O'Gara, P. W. (1967). Effects of inequity produced by underpayment on work output, work quality, and attitudes toward work. *Journal of Applied Psychology, 51,* 403–410.

Lawler, E. E., & Porter, L. W. (1967). The effect of performance on satisfaction. *Industrial Relations, 7,* 20–28.

Lawler, E. E., & Suttle, J. L. (1972). A causal correlation test of the need hierarchy concept. *Organizational Behavior and Human Performance, 7,* 265–287.

Lawler, E. E., & Suttle, J. L. (1973). Expectancy theory and job behavior. *Organizational Behavior and Human Performance, 9,* 482–503.

Lawrence, P. R., & Lorsch, J. (1967). *Organization and environment.* Cambridge, MA: Harvard University Press.

Lawrence, P. R., & Lorsch, J. W. (1969). *Organization and environment: Managing differentiation and integration.* Homewood, IL: Irwin.

Lazarus, R. S., & Cohen, J. B. (1977). Environmental stress. In I. Altman & J. F. Wohlwill (Eds.), *Human behavior and environment* (Vol. 1). New York: Plenum.

Lederman, S. J., & Campbell, J. I. (1982). Tangible graphs for the blind. *Human Factors, 24,* 85–100.

Lee, C. (1986). Professionals in medical settings: The research evidence in the 1980s. *Journal of Organizational Behavior Management, 8,* 195–213.

Lee, R., & Wilbur, E. R. (1985). Age, education, job tenure, salary, job characteristics, and job satisfaction: A multivariate analysis. *Human Relations, 38,* 781–791.

Lee, R. T., & Ashforth, B. E. (1990). On the meaning of Maslach's three dimensions of burnout. *Journal of Applied Psychology, 75,* 743–747.

Leirer, V. O., Yesavage, J. A., & Morrow, D. G. (1991). Marijuana carry-over effects on aircraft pilot performance. *Aviation, Space, & Environmental Medicine, 62,* 221–227.

Leiter, M. P. (1988). Burnout as a function of communication patterns: A study of a multidisciplinary mental health team. *Group & Organization Studies, 13,* 111–128.

Leiter, M. P. (1991). Coping patterns as predictors of burnout: The function of control and escapist coping patterns. *Journal of Occupational Behaviour, 12,* 123–144.

Leonard, J. (1983). Can your organization support quality circles? *Training & Development Journal, 37,* 67–72.

Levin, I., & Stokes, J. P. (1989). Dispositional approach to job satisfaction: Role of negative affectivity. *Journal of Applied Psychology, 74,* 752–758.

Levin, L., Oler, J., & Whiteside, J. R. (1985). Injury incidence rates in a paint company on rotating production shifts. *Accident Analysis and Prevention, 17,* 67–73.

Levine, D. I. (1993). What do wages buy? *Administrative Science Quarterly, 38* 462–483.

Levine, E. L., Ash, R. A., & Bennett, N. (1980). Exploratory comparative study of four job analysis methods. *Journal of Applied Psychology, 65,* 525–535.

Levy-Leboyer, C. (1992). The chicken and the egg: Which came first? *Applied Psychology: An International Review, 42,* 52–54.

Lewin, K. (1948). Action research and minority problems. In G. W. Lewin (Ed.), *Resolving social conflicts.* New York: Harper.

Lewin, K., Lippitt, R., & White, R. K. (1939). Patterns of aggressive behavior in experimentally created social climates. *Journal of Social Psychology, 10,* 271–301.

Lichtman, R. J., & Lane, I. M. (1983). Effects of group norms and goal setting on productivity. *Group & Organization Studies, 8,* 406–420.

Likert, R. (1961). *New patterns of management.* New York: McGraw-Hill.

Likert, R. (1967). *The human organization.* New York: McGraw-Hill.

Likert, R. (1977). Past and future perspectives on system 4. *Proceedings of the Academy of Management* Ada, OH: Northern Ohio University Academy of Management.

Litman, G. K. (1976). Behavioral modification techniques in the treatment of alcoholism: A review and critique. In R. J. Gibbins et al. (Eds.), *Research advances in alcohol and drug problems* (Vol. 3). New York: Wiley.

Littlepage, G. E., Van Hein, J. L., Cohen, K. M., & Janiec, L. L. (1993). Evaluation and comparison of three instruments designed to measure organizational power and influence tactics. *Journal of Applied Social Psychology, 23,* 107–125.

Locke, E. A. (1968). Toward a theory of task motivation and incentives. *Organizational Behavior and Human Performance, 3,* 157–189.

Locke, E. A. (1969). What is job satisfaction? *Organizational Behavior and Human Performance, 4,* 309–336.

Locke, E. A. (1970). Job satisfaction and job performance: A theoretical analysis. *Organizational Behavior and Human Performance, 5,* 484–500.

Locke, E. A. (1976). The nature and causes of job satisfaction. In M. D. Dunnette (Ed.), *Handbook of industrial and organizational psychology.* New York: Wiley.

Locke, E. A. (1991). The motivation sequence, the motivation hub, and the motivation core. *Organizational Behavior and Human Decision Processes, 50,* 288–299.

Locke, E. A., Chah, D., Harrison, S., & Lustgarten, N. (1989). Separating the effects of goal specificity from goal level. *Organizational Behavior and Human Decision Processes, 43,* 270–287.

Locke, E. A., & Latham, G. P. (1990). *A theory of goal setting and task performance.* Englewood Cliffs, NJ: Prentice-Hall.

Locke, E. A., Latham, G. P., & Erez, M. (1988). The determinants of goal commitment. *Academy of Management Review, 13,* 23–39.

Locke, E. A., & Schweiger, D. M. (1979). Participation in decision-making: One more look. In B. M. Staw (Ed.), *Research in organizational behavior* (Vol. 1). Greenwich, CT: JAI Press.

Locke, E. A., Shaw, K. N., Saari, L. M., & Latham, G. P. (1981). Goal setting and task performance: 1969–1980. *Psychological Bulletin, 90,* 125–152.

Locke, E. A., Smith, K. G., Erez, M., Chah, D., & Schaffer, A. (1994). The effects of intra-individual goal conflict on performance. *Journal of Management, 20,* 67–91.

Lockheed, M. E., & Hall, K. P. (1976). Conceptualizing sex as a status characteristic: Applications to leadership training strategies. *Journal of Social Issues, 32,* 111–124.

Loher, B. T., Noe, R. A., Moeller, N. L., & Fitzgerald, M. P. (1985). A meta-analysis of the relation of job characteristics to job satisfaction. *Journal of Applied Psychology, 70,* 280–289.

London, J. (1911). The apostate. In A. Calder-Marshall (Ed.). (1966). *The pan Jack London.* London: Pan Books.

London, M., & Poplawski, J. R. (1976). Effects of information on stereotype development in performance appraisal and interview contexts. *Journal of Applied Psychology, 61,* 199–205.

Long, R. J. (1980). Job attitudes and organizational performance under employee ownership. *Academy of Management Journal, 23,* 726–737.

Long, R. J. (1993). The impact of new office information technology on job quality of female and male employees. *Human Relations, 46,* 939–961.

Longenecker, C. O., Jaccoud, A. J., Sims, H. P., Jr., & Gioia, D. A. (1992). Quantitative and qualitative investigations of affect in executive judgment. *Applied Psychology: An International Review, 41,* 21–41.

Longley, J., & Pruitt, D. G. (1980). Groupthink: A critique of Janis's theory. In L. Wheeler (Ed.), *Review of personality and social psychology* (Vol. 1.) Beverly Hills, CA: Sage.

Lord, R. G. (1985). An information processing approach to social perceptions, leadership and behavioral measurement in organizations. In B. M. Staw & L. L. Cummings (Eds.), *Research in organizational behavior* (Vol. 7). Greenwich, CT: JAI Press.

Lord, R. G., Foti, R. J., & De Vader, C. L. (1984). A test of leadership categorization theory: Internal structure, information processing, and leadership perceptions. *Organizational Behavior and Human Performance, 34,* 343–378.

Lord, R. G., Foti, R. J., & Phillips, J. S. (1982). A theory of leadership categorization. In J. G. Hunt, U. Sekaran, & C. Schriesheim (Eds.), *Leadership: Beyond establishment views.* Carbondale, IL: Southern Illinois University Press.

Lowry, P. E. (1992). The assessment center: Effects of varying consensus procedures. *Public Personnel Management, 21,* 171–183.

Lowry, P. E. (1994). Selection methods: Comparison of assessment centers with personnel records evaluations. *Public Personnel Management, 23,* 383–395.

Ludwig, T. D., & Geller, E. S. (1991). Improving the driving practices of pizza deliverers: Response generalization and moderating effects of driving history. *Journal of Applied Behavior Analysis, 24,* 31–44.

Lupton, D. E. (1988). A consultant's view of being a consultant. Part III: The national consulting firm. *The Industrial-Organizational Psychologist, 25*(2), 39–44.

Lyness, S. A. (1993). Predictors of differences between Type A and B individuals in heart rate and blood pressure reactivity. *Psychological Bulletin, 114,* 266–295.

M

Mabe, P. A., & West, S. G. (1982). Validity of self-evaluation of ability: A review and meta-analysis. *Journal of Applied Psychology, 67,* 280–296.

Macan, T. H., & Dipboye, R. L. (1988). The effects of interviewers' initial impressions on information gathering. *Organizational Behavior & Human Decision Processes, 42,* 364–387.

Macan, T. H., & Dipboye, R. L. (1994). The effects of the application on processing of information from the employment interview. *Journal of Applied Social Psychology, 24,* 1291–1314.

Mackie, R. R. (1987). Vigilance research—Are we ready for countermeasures? *Human Factors, 29*, 707–723.

MacKinnon, D. W. (1962). The nature and nurture of creative talent. *American Psychologist, 17*, 484–495.

Mackworth, N. H. (1950). *Researches on the measurement of human performance* (medical council special report series 268). London: His Majesty's Stationery Office.

Maeda, K., Horiguchi, S., & Hosokawa, M. (1982). History of the studies on occupational cervicobrachial disorder in Japan and remaining problems. *Journal of Human Ergology, 11*, 17–29.

Mael, F. A. (1991). A conceptual rationale for the domain and attributes of biodata items. *Personnel Psychology, 44*, 763–792.

Magenau, J. M., Martin, J. E., & Peterson, M. M. (1988). Dual and unilateral commitment among stewards and rank-and-file union members. *Academy of Management Journal, 31*, 359–376.

Mager, R. F., & Pipe, P. (1970). *Analyzing performance problems.* Belmont, CA: Fearon.

Maier, N. R. F. (1952). *Principles of human relations: Applications to management.* New York: Wiley.

Maier, N. R. F. (1970). *Problem solving and creativity in individuals and groups.* Belmont, CA: Brooks/Cole.

Maier, N. R. F., & Verser, G. C. (1982). *Psychology in industrial organizations* (5th ed.). Boston: Houghton Mifflin.

Malott, J. M. et al. (1984). Co-worker social support in a worksite smoking control program. *Journal of Applied Behavior Analysis, 17*, 485–495.

Mann, R. B., & Decker, P. J. (1984). The effect of key behavior distinctiveness on generalization and recall in behavior modeling training. *Academy of Management Journal, 27*, 900–909.

Manning, F. J., & Fullerton, T. D. (1988). Health and well-being in highly cohesive units of the U.S. Army. *Journal of Applied Social Psychology, 18*, 503–519.

Manz, C. C. (1992). Self-leading work teams: Moving beyond self-management myths. *Human Relations, 45*, 1119–1140.

Marics, M. A., & Williges, B. H. (1988). The intelligibility of synthesized speech in data inquiry systems. *Human Factors, 30*, 719–732.

Marlatt, G. A. (1985). Relapse prevention: Theoretical rationale and overview of the model. In G. A. Marlatt & J. R. Gordon (Eds.), *Relapse prevention: Maintenance strategies in the treatment of addictive behaviors.* New York: Guilford Press.

Marrow, A. J. (1964). Risks and uncertainties in action research. *Journal of Social Issues, 20*, 5–20.

Martin, B. A., & Manning, D. J., Jr. (1995). Combined effects of normative information and task difficulty on the goal commitment-performance relationship. *Journal of Management, 21*, 65–80.

Martin, J. E., & Berthiaume, R. D. (1995). Predicting the outcome of a contract ratification vote. *Academy of Management Journal, 38*, 916–928.

Martin, R., & Graveling, R. A. (1983). Background illumination and its effects on peripheral visual awareness for miners using cap lamps. *Applied Ergonomics, 14*, 139–141.

Martin, R., & Wall, T. D. (1989). Attentional demand and cost responsibility as stressors in shopfloor jobs. *Academy of Management Journal, 32*, 69–86.

Martocchio, J. (1994). The effects of absence culture on individual absence. *Human Relations, 47*, 243–262.

Martocchio, J. J., & O'Leary, A. M. (1989). Sex differences in occupational stress: A meta-analytic review. *Journal of Applied Psychology, 74*, 495–501.

Maslach, C. (1982). *Burnout: The cost of caring.* Englewood Cliffs, NJ: Prentice-Hall.

Maslach, C., & Jackson, S. E. (1981). The measurement of experienced burnout. *Journal of Occupational Behavior, 2*, 99–113.

Maslach, C., & Jackson, S. E. (1986). *The Maslach Burnout Inventory.* Palo Alto, CA: Consulting Psychologists Press.

Maslow, A. H. (1943). A theory of human motivation. *Psychological Review, 50*, 370–396.

Maslow, A. H. (1954). *Motivation and personality.* New York: Harper.

Maslow, A. H. (1970). *Motivation and personality* (2nd ed.). New York: Harper & Row.

Mason, M. A., & Redmon, W. K. (1992). Effects of immediate versus delayed feedback on error detection accuracy in a quality control simulation. *Journal of Organizational Behavior Management, 13*, 49–83.

Mathieu, J. E., & Leonard, R. L. (1987). Applying utility concepts to a training program in supervisory skills: A time-based approach. *Academy of Management Journal, 30*, 316–335.

Mathieu, J. E., Tannenbaum, S. I., & Salas, E. (1992). Influences of individual and situational characteristics on measures of training effectiveness. *Academy of Management Journal, 35*, 828–847.

Matsui, T., & Ohtsuka, Y. (1978). Within-person expectancy theory predictions of supervisory consideration and structure behavior. *Journal of Applied Psychology, 63*, 128–131.

Matsui, T., Okado, A., & Inoshita, O. (1983). Mechanism of feedback affecting task performance. *Organizational Behavior and Human Performance, 31*, 114–122.

Matthews, K. A. (1988). Coronary heart disease and Type A behaviors: Update on and alternative to the Booth-Kewley and Friedman (1987) quantitative review. *Psychological Bulletin, 104*, 373–380.

Maugham, W. S. (1924). The outstation. In *The Casuarina Tree.* New York: Doubleday.

Maurer, S. D., & Fay, C. (1988). Effect of situational interviews, conventional structured interviews, and training on interview rating agreement: An experimental analysis. *Personnel Psychology, 41*, 329–344.

Maurer, S. D., Howe, V., & Yee, T. W. (1992). Organizational recruiting as marketing management: An interdisciplinary study of engineering graduates. *Personnel Psychology, 45*, 807–833.

Maurer, T. J., & Alexander, R. A. (1992). Methods of improving employment test critical scores derived by judging test content: A review and critique. *Personnel Psychology, 45*, 727–762.

Maurer, T. J., & Lord, R. G. (1991). An exploration of cognitive demands in group interaction as a moderator of information processing variables in perceptions of leadership. *Journal of Applied Social Psychology, 21*, 821–839.

Maurer, T. J., & Taylor, M. A. (1994). Is sex by itself enough? An explanation of gender bias issues in performance appraisal. *Organizational Behavior & Human Decision Processes, 60,* 231–251.

Mawhinney, T. C. (1990). Decreasing intrinsic "motivation" with extrinsic rewards: Easier said than done. *Journal of Organizational Behavior Management, 11,* 175–191.

Mayfield, E. C., & Carlson, R. E. (1966). Selection interview decisions: First results of a long-term research project. *Personnel Psychology, 19,* 41–53.

McBride, A., Lancee, W., & Freeman, S. (1981). The psychosocial impacts of a labour dispute. *Occupational Psychology, 54,* 125–134.

McClelland, D. C. (1961). *The achieving society.* Princeton: Van Nostrand.

McClelland, D. C. (1975). *Power: The inner experience.* New York: Irvington-Halsted-Wiley.

McClelland, D. C. (1977). Entrepreneurship and management in the years ahead. In C. A. Bramlette, Jr. (Ed.), *The individual and the future of organizations.* Atlanta: Georgia State University, College of Business Administration.

McClelland, D. C., Atkinson, J. W., Clark, R. A., & Lowell, E. L. (1953). *The achievement motive.* New York: Appleton-Century-Crofts.

McClelland, D. C., & Boyatzis, R. E. (1982). Leadership motive pattern and long-term success in management. *Journal of Applied Psychology, 67,* 737–743.

McClelland, D. C., & Burnham, D. (1976, March-April). Power is the great motivator. *Harvard Business Review, 25,* 159–166.

McCormick, E. J. (1976). Job and task analysis. In M. D. Dunnette (Ed.), *Handbook of industrial and organizational psychology.* Chicago: Rand McNally.

McCormick, E. J. (1979). *Job analysis: Methods and applications.* New York: American Management Association.

McCormick, E. J., Jeanneret, P. R., & Meacham, R. C. (1972). A study of job characteristics and job dimensions as based on the Position Analysis Questionnaire (PAQ). *Journal of Applied Psychology, 56,* 347–368.

McCormick, E. J., & Sanders, M. S. (1982). *Human factors in engineering and design,* (5th ed.) New York: McGraw-Hill.

McCormick, I. A., & Cooper, C. L. (1988). Executive stress: Extending the international comparison. *Human Relations, 41,* 65–72.

McCrae, R. R., & Costa, P. T., Jr. (1989). Rotation to maximize the construct validity of the factors in the NEO Personality Inventory. *Multivariate Behavioral Research, 24,* 107–124.

McDaniel, M. A., Schmidt, F. L., & Hunter, J. E. (1988). Job experience correlates of job performance. *Journal of Applied Psychology, 73,* 327–330.

McDaniel, M. A., Whetzel, D. L., Schmidt, F. L., & Maurer, S. D. (1994). The validity of employment interviews: A comprehensive review and meta-analysis. *Journal of Applied Psychology, 79,* 599–616.

McDonald, N. (1984). *Fatigue, safety, and the truck driver.* London: Taylor & Francis.

McEvoy, G. M., & Buller, P. F. (1987). User acceptance of peer appraisals in an industrial setting. *Personnel Psychology, 40,* 785–797.

McEvoy, G. M., & Cascio, W. F. (1987). Do good or poor performers leave? A meta-analysis of the relationship between performance and turnover. *Academy of Management Journal, 30,* 744–762.

McFarlin, D. B., & Rice, R. W. (1992). The role of facet importance as a moderator in job satisfaction. *Journal of Organizational Behavior, 13,* 41–54.

McGehee, W., & Thayer, P. W. (1961). *Training in business and industry.* New York: Wiley.

McGill, M. E., & Slocum, J. W. Jr. (1993). Unlearning the organization. *Organizational Dynamics, 22* (2), 67–78.

McGregor, D. (1967). *The professional manager.* New York: McGraw-Hill.

McGregor, D. M. (1957). The human side of enterprise. In *Adventure in thought and action: Proceedings of the fifth anniversary convocation of the School of Industrial Management, M.I.T.* Cambridge, MA: MIT Press.

McGuire, W. J. (1985). Attitudes and attitude change. In G. Lindzey & E. Aronson (Eds.), *Handbook of social psychology* (3rd ed., Vol. II). New York: Random House.

McIntosh, N. J. (1991). Identification and investigation of properties of social support. *Journal of Organizational Behavior, 12,* 201–217.

McIntyre, R. M., Smith, D. E., & Hassett, C. E. (1984). Accuracy of performance ratings as affected by rater training and perceived purpose of rating. *Journal of Applied Psychology, 69,* 147–156.

McLean, E. K., & Tarnopolsky, A. (1977). Noise, discomfort and mental health: A review of the socio-medical implications of disturbance by noise. *Psychological Medicine, 7,* 19–62.

McPhee, B. (1982). Deficiencies in the ergonomic design of keyboard work and upper limb and neck disorders in operators. *Journal of Human Ergology, 11,* 31–36.

Mead, A. D., & Drasgow, F. (1993). Equivalence of computerized and paper-and-pencil cognitive ability tests: A meta-analysis. *Psychological Bulletin, 114,* 449–458.

Medcof, J. W. (1991). A test of a revision of the job characteristics model. *Applied Psychology: An International Review, 40,* 381–393.

Meglino, B. M., Denisi, A. S., & Ravlin, E. C. (1993). Effects of previous job exposure and subsequent job status on the functioning of a realistic job preview. *Personnel Psychology, 46,* 803–822.

Meglino, B. M., DeNisi, A. S., Youngblood, S. A., & Williams, K. J. (1988). Effects of realistic job previews: A comparison using an enhancement and a reduction preview. *Journal of Applied Psychology, 73,* 259–266.

Melamed, S., Ben-Avi, I., Luz, J., & Green, M. S. (1995). Objective and subjective work monotony: Effects on job satisfaction, psychological distress, and absenteeism in blue-collar workers. *Journal of Applied Psychology, 80,* 29–42.

Melville, H. (1856). Bartleby. In *The piazza tales.* Reprinted in E. Current-Garcia & W. R. Patrick (Eds.). (1964). *American short stories,* (Rev. Ed.). Chicago: Scott, Foresman.

Menninger, W. C. (1948). *Psychiatry in a troubled world.* New York: Macmillan.

Mento, A. J., Steel, R. P., & Karren, R. J. (1987). A meta-analytic study of the effects of goal setting on task performance: 1966–1984. *Organizational Behavior and Human Decision Processes, 39,* 52–83.

Mershon, D. H., & Lin, L. (1987). Directional localization in high ambient noise with and without the use of hearing protectors. *Ergonomics, 30,* 1161–1173.

Meyer, H. H. (1980). Self-appraisal of job performance. *Personnel Psychology, 33,* 291–295.

Meyer, H. H., Kay, E., & French, J. R. P., Jr. (1965). Split roles in performance appraisal. *Harvard Business Review, 43,* 123–129.

Meyer, M. W. (1982). "Bureaucratic" versus "profit" organization. *Research in Organizational Behavior, 4,* 89–125.

Michalos, A. C. (1986). Job satisfaction, marital satisfaction, and the quality of life: A review and preview. In F. M. Andrews (Ed.), *Research on the quality of life.* Ann Arbor, MI: University of Michigan Institute for Social Research.

Mickler, S. E., & Rosen, S. (1994). Burnout in spurned medical caregivers and the impact of job expectancy training. *Journal of Applied Social Psychology. 24,* 2110–2131.

Millar, K., & Steels, M. J. (1990). Sustained peripheral vasoconstriction while working in continuous intense noise. *Aviation, Space, & Environmental Medicine, 61,* 695–698.

Miller, J. G., & Wheeler, K. G. (1992). Unraveling the mysteries of gender differences in intentions to leave the organization. *Journal of Organizational Behavior, 13,* 465–478.

Miller, K. (1992). Causes of accidents with post-drivers and their remedies. *Applied Ergonomics, 23,* 101–104.

Miller, L. (1995). Two aspects of Japanese and American co-worker interaction: Giving instructions and creating rapport. *Journal of Applied Behavioral Science, 31,* 141–161.

Miller, L. E., & Grush, J. E. (1988). Improving predictions in expectancy theory research: Effects of personality, expectancies, and norms. *Academy of Management Journal, 31,* 107–122.

Milliken, F. J. (1987). Three types of perceived uncertainty about the environment: State, effect, and response uncertainty. *Academy of Management Review, 12,* 133–143.

Milne, S. H., Blum, T. C., & Roman, P. M. (1994). Factors influencing employees' propensity to use an employee assistance program. *Personnel Psychology, 47,* 123–145.

Ministry of Supply and Services. (1990). *Women in Canada: A Statistical Report* (2nd ed.). Ottawa: Author.

Mintzberg, H. (1972). *The Nature of Managerial Work.* New York: Harper Collins Publishers.

Mintzberg, H. (1979). *The structuring of organization.* Englewood Cliffs, NJ: Prentice-Hall.

Mintzberg, H. (1983). *Structure in fives: Designing effective organizations.* Englewood Cliffs, NJ: Prentice-Hall.

Mishra, J. M. (1990). Managing the grapevine. *Public Personnel Management, 19,* 213–228.

Mital, A., Foononi-Fard, H., & Brown, M. L. (1994). Physical fatigue in high and very high frequency manual materials handling: Perceived exertion and physiological indicators. *Human Factors, 36,* 219–231.

Mitchell, T. R. (1974). Expectancy models of job satisfaction, occupational preference and effort: A theoretical, methodological and empirical appraisal. *Psychological Bulletin, 81,* 1053–1077.

Mitchell, T. R. (1979). Organizational behavior. *Annual Review of Psychology, 30,* 243–281.

Mobley, W. H. (1982). *Employee turnover: Causes, consequences, and control.* Reading, MA: Addison-Wesley.

Mobley, W. H., Horner, S. O., & Hollingworth, A. T. (1978). An evaluation of precursors of hospital employee turnover. *Journal of Applied Psychology, 63,* 408–414.

Mohler, S. R. (1983). The human element in air traffic control: Aeromedical aspects, problems, and prescriptions. *Aviation, Space, and Environmental Medicine, 54,* 511–516.

Momtahan, K., Hetu, R., & Tansley, B. (1993). Audibility and identification of auditory alarms in the operating room and intensive care unit. *Ergonomics, 36,* 1159–1176.

Moore, Herbert. (1942). *Psychology for business and industry* (2nd ed.). New York: McGraw-Hill.

Moorman, R. H. (1993). The influence of cognitive and affective based job satisfaction measures on the relationship between satisfaction and organizational citizenship behavior. *Human Relations, 46,* 759–776.

Moran, E. T., & Volkwein, J. F. (1992). The cultural approach to the formation of organizational climate. *Human Relations, 45,* 19–47.

Moreno, J. L. (1953). *Who shall survive?* Beacon, NY: Beacon House.

Morrison, P. (1978). Evaluation in OD: A review and assessment. *Group & Organization Studies, 3,* 42–70.

Moskowitz, H. (1976). Cannabis and experimental studies of driving skills. In R. J. Gibbins et al. (Eds.), *Research advances in alcohol and drug problems* (Vol. 3). New York: Wiley.

Mossholder, K. W., & Bedeian, A. G. (1983). Group interactional processes: Individual and group level effects. *Group & Organizational Studies, 8,* 187–202.

Motowidlo, S. J., Packard, J. S., & Manning, M. R. (1986). Occupational stress: Its causes and consequences for job performance. *Journal of Applied Psychology, 71,* 618–629.

Mottaz, C. (1984). Education and work satisfaction. *Human Relations, 37,* 985–1004.

Mottaz, C. (1986). Gender differences in work satisfaction, work-related rewards and values, and the determinants of work satisfaction. *Human Relations, 39,* 283–384.

Mount, M. K., & Thompson, D. E. (1987). Cognitive categorization and quality of performance ratings. *Journal of Applied Psychology, 72,* 240–246.

Muchinsky, P. (1977). Employee absenteeism; A review of the literature. *Journal of Vocational Behavior, 10,* 316–340.

Muchinsky, P. (1990). *Psychology applied to work* (3rd ed.). Pacific Grove, CA: Brooks/Cole.

Muchinsky, P. M., & Morrow, P. C. (1980). A multidisciplinary model of voluntary employee turnover. *Journal of Vocational Behavior, 17,* 263–290.

Mullen, B., & Copper, C. (1994). The relation between group cohesiveness and performance: An integration. *Psychological Bulletin, 115,* 210–227.

Mullins, T. W. (1982). Interviewer decisions as a function of applicant race, applicant quality and interviewer prejudice. *Personnel Psychology, 35,* 163–174.

Munchus, G., III. (1983). Employer-employee based quality circles in Japan: Human resource policy implications for American firms. *Academy of Management Review, 8,* 255–261.

Münsterberg, H. (1903). Psychology in the system of knowledge. *Psychological Review Monograph, 4.*

Münsterberg, H. (1910). The market and psychology. Originally published as chapter 7 of *American Problems.* New York: Moffat, Yard. Reprinted in D. Mankin, R. E. Ames, Jr., & M. A. Grodsky (Eds.). (1980). *Classics of industrial and organizational psychology.* Oak Park, IL: Moore.

Münsterberg, H. (1914). *Psychology: General and applied*. New York: Appleton.

Münsterberg, H. (1915). *Business psychology*. Chicago: LaSalle Extension University.

Munton, A. G. (1990). Job reloaction, stress and the family. *Journal of Organizational Behavior, 11,* 401–406.

Murphy, K. R. (1982). Difficulties in the statistical control of halo. *Journal of Applied Psychology, 67,* 161–164.

Murphy, K. R., & Constans, J. I. (1987). Behavioral anchors as a source of bias in rating. *Journal of Applied Psychology, 72,* 573–577.

Murphy, L. R. (1986). A review of organizational stress management research: Methodological considerations. *Journal of Organizational Behavior Management, 8,* 215–227.

Murray, H. A. (1938). *Explorations in personality*. New York: Oxford University Press.

Murry, M. A., & Atkinson, T. (1981). Gender differences in correlates of job satisfaction. *Canadian Journal of Behavioral Sciences, 13,* 44–52.

Myers, D. G., & Lamm, H. (1976). The group polarization phenomenon. *Psychological Bulletin, 83,* 602–627.

N

Nakaseko, M., Tokunaga, R., & Hosokawa, M. (1982). History of occupational cervicobrachial disorder in Japan. *Journal of Human Ergology, 11,* 7–16.

Nandram, S. S., & Klandermans, B. (1993). Stress experienced by active members of trade unions. *Journal of Organizational Behavior, 14,* 415–431.

Napier, N. K., & Latham, G. P. (1986). Outcome expectancies of people who conduct performance appraisals. *Personnel Psychology, 39,* 827–837.

Nardone, T. T. (1986). Part-time workers: Who are they? *Monthly Labor Review, 109,* 13–19.

Nathan, B. R., & Tippins, N. (1990). Effects of observers' performance expectations on behavior ratings of work groups: Memory or response bias? *Journal of Applied Psychology, 75,* 290–296.

National Institute for Occupational Safety and Health. (1981, March). *Work practices guide for manual lifting* (PB82-178998). Cincinnati: National Institute for Occupational Safety and Health.

National Institute of Drug Abuse. (1978, March 17). *Drug abuse statistics in 1977*. Washington, DC: U.S. Government Printing Office.

National Safety Council. (1987). *Accident facts, 1987 edition*. Chicago: National Safety Council.

National Safety Council. (1988). *Accident facts, 1988 edition*. Chicago: National Safety Council.

National Safety Council. (1991). *Accident facts, 1991 edition*. Chicago: National Safety Council.

National Safety Council. (1995). *Accident facts, 1995 edition*. Itasca, IL: National Safety Council.

Naumann, E. (1993). Antecedents and consequences of satisfaction and commitment among expatriate managers. *Group & Organization Management, 18,* 153–187.

Neidig, R. D., & Martin, J. C. (1979). *The FBI's management aptitude program assessment center. Research report no. 2: An analysis of assessor's ratings* (technical memorandum 79–2). Washington, DC: Office of Personnel Management.

Nelson, R. E. (1989). The strength of strong ties: Social networks and intergroup conflict in organizations. *Academy of Management Journal, 32,* 377–401.

Nevill, D. D., Stephenson, B. B., & Philbrick, J. H. (1983). Gender effects on performance evaluation. *Journal of Psychology, 115,* 165–169.

Newell, A. F., Arnott, J. L, Dye, R., & Cairns, A. Y. (1991). A full-speed listening typewriter simulation. *International Journal of Man-Machine Studies, 35,* 119–131.

Newsted, P. R. (1985). Paper versus on-line presentations of subjective questionnaires. *International Journal of Man-Machine Studies, 23,* 231–247.

New tool: "Reinforcement" for good work. (1971, December 18). *Business Week,* 76–77.

Nezu, A. M., & Perri, M. G. (1989). Social problem-solving therapy for unipolar depression: An initial dismantling investigation. *Journal of Consulting and Clinical Psychology, 57,* 408–413.

Nichols, R. G. (1962). Listening is good business. *Management of Personnel Quarterly, 4,* 4.

Nord, W. B. (1969). Beyond the teaching machine: The neglected area of operant conditioning in theory and practice of management. *Organizational Behavior and Human Performance, 4,* 375–401.

Nowack, E. (1989). Workspace for disabled people. *Ergonomics, 32,* 1077–1088.

Noyes, J. M., Haigh, R., & Starr, A. F. (1989). Automatic speech recognition for disabled people. *Applied Ergonomics, 20,* 293–298.

Numerof, R. E., & Abrams, M. N. (1984). Sources of stress among nurses: An empirical investigation. *Journal of Human Stress, 10,* 88–100.

Nutt, P. C. (1984). Types of organizational decision processes. *Administrative Science Quarterly, 29,* 414–450.

O

Oborne, D. J. (1987). *Ergonomics at work* (2nd ed.). New York: Wiley.

Occupational Safety and Health Administration. (1980). *Noise control: A guide for workers and employers* (3048). Washington, DC: U.S. Department of Labor.

O'Driscoll, M. P., & Beehr, T. A. (1994). Supervisor behaviors, role stressors and uncertainty as predictors of personal outcomes for subordinates. *Journal of Organizational Behavior, 15,* 141–155.

O'Driscoll, M. P., & Evans, R. (1988). Organizational factors and perceptions of climate in three psychiatric units. *Human Relations, 41,* 371–388.

O'Leary-Kelly, A. M., Martocchio, J. J., & Frink, D. D. (1994). A review of the influence of group goals on group perfomance. *Academy of Management Journal, 37,* 1285–1301.

O'Reilly, C. A., & Caldwell, D. F. (1985). The impact of normative social influence and cohesiveness on task perceptions and attitudes: A social information processing approach. *Journal of Occupational Psychology, 58,* 193–206.

Ornstein, S. (1986). Organizational symbols: A study of their meanings and influences on perceived psychological climate. *Organizational Behavior and Human Decision Processes, 38,* 207–229.

Osburn, H. G., Timmreck, C., & Bigby, D. (1981). Effect of dimensional relevance on accuracy of simulated hiring decisions by employment interviewers. *Journal of Applied Psychology, 66,* 159–165.

Ostroff, C., & Schmitt, N. (1993). Configurations of organizational effectiveness and efficiency. *Academy of Management Journal, 36,* 1345–1361.

Ouchi, W. (1981). *Theory Z: How American business can meet the Japanese challenge.* Reading, MA: Addison–Wesley.

Owens, W. A. (1968). Toward one discipline of scientific psychology. *American Psychologist, 23,* 782–785.

Owens, W. A. (1976). Background data. In M. D. Dunnette (Ed.), *Handbook of industrial and organizational psychology.* Chicago: Rand McNally.

Owens, W. A., & Schoenfeldt, L. F. (1979). Toward a classification of persons. *Journal of Applied Psychology Monograph, 65,* 569–607.

P

Painter, N. I. (1995). The same old white-male superiority line, fixed up. *San Francisco Examiner,* April 11, Section A, p. 17.

Paley, M. J., & Tepas, D. I. (1994). Fatigue and the shiftworker: Firefighters working on a rotating shift schedule. *Human Factors, 36,* 269–284.

Palich, L. E., & Hom, P. W. (1992). The impact of leader power and behavior on leadership perceptions: A LISREL test of an expanded categorization theory of leadership model. *Group & Organization Management, 17,* 279–296.

Parkes, K. R. (1987). Relative weight, smoking, and mental health as predictors of sickness and absence from work. *Journal of Applied Psychology, 72,* 275–286.

Parkinson, C. N. (1957). *Parkinson's law and other studies in administration.* Boston: Houghton Mifflin.

Patchen, M. (1974). The locus and basis of influence in organizational decisions. *Organizational Behavior and Human Performance, 11,* 195–221.

Patel, C. et al. (1985). Trial of relaxation in reducing coronary risk: Four-year follow-up. *British Medical Journal, 290,* 1103–1106.

Paul, R. J., & Ebadi, Y. M. (1989). Leadership decision making in a service organization: A field test of the Vroom-Yetton model. *Journal of Occupational Psychology, 62,* 201–211.

Pavett, C. M. (1983). Evaluation of the impact of feedback on performance and motivation. *Human Relations, 36,* 641–654.

Peach, E. B., & Wren, D. A. (1992). Pay for performance from antiquity to the 1950s. *Journal of Organizational behavior, 12,* 5–26.

Pecotich, A., & Churchill, G. A. (1981). An examination of the anticipated-satisfaction and importance valence controversy. *Organizational Behavior and Human Performance, 27,* 213–226.

Pedalino, E., & Gamboa, V. U. (1974). Behavior modification and absenteeism: Intervention in one industrial setting. *Journal of Applied Psychology, 59,* 694–698.

Peeke, S. C., & Peeke, H. V. S. (1984). Attention, memory, and cigarette smoking. *Psychopharmacology, 84,* 205–214.

Peiró, J. M., & Munduate, L. (1994). Work and organisational psychology in Spain. *Applied Psychology: An International Review, 43,* 231–274.

Peres, S. H., & Garcia, J. R. (1962). Validity and dimensions of descriptive adjectives used in reference letters for engineering applicants. *Personnel Psychology, 15,* 279–296.

Perrow, C. (1970). *Organizational analysis: A sociological approach.* Belmont, CA: Wadsworth.

Peters, L. H. (1985). Undergraduate programs in I/O psychology: Survey results. *The Industrial-Organizational Psychologist, 23*(1), 37–39.

Peters, L. H., O'Connor, E. J., Weekley, J., Pooyan, A., Frank, B., & Erenkrantz, B. (1984). Sex bias and managerial evaluations: A replication and extension. *Journal of Applied Psychology, 69,* 349–352.

Peters, M., & Robinson, V. (1984). The origins and status of action research. *Journal of Applied Behavioral Science, 20,* 113–124.

Peterson, M. F., Smith, P. B., Akande, A., Ayestaran, S., et al. (1995). Role conflict, ambiguity, and overload: A 21-nation study. *Academy of Management Journal, 38,* 429–452.

Petty, M. M., & Bruning, N. S. (1980). A comparison of the relationships between subordinates' perceptions of supervisory behavior and measures of subordinates' job satisfaction for male and female leaders. *Academy of Management Journal, 23,* 717–725.

Pheasant, S. T. (1986). *Bodyspace: Anthropometry, ergonomics and design.* London: Taylor & Francis.

Phillips, A. P., & Dipboye, R. L. (1989). Correlational tests of predictions from a process model of the interview. *Journal of Applied Psychology, 74,* 41–52.

Phillips, A. S., & Bedeian, A. G. (1994). Leader–follower exchange quality: The role of personal and interpersonal attributes. *Academy of Management Journal, 37,* 990–1001.

Phillips, J. (1984). The accuracy of leadership ratings: A cognitive categorization perspective. *Journal of Applied Psychology, 33,* 125–138.

Phillips, J. S., & Lord, R. G. (1981). Causal attributions and perceptions of leadership. *Organizational Behavior and Human Performance, 28,* 143–163.

Pierce, J. L., & Dunham, R. B. (1992). The 12-hour work day: A 48-hour, eight-day week. *Academy of Management Journal, 35,* 1086–1098.

Pines, A., & Aronson, E. (1981). *Burnout: From tedium to personal growth.* New York: Free Press.

Piotrowski, M. J., Barnes-Farrell, J. L., & Esrig, F. H. (1989). Behaviorally anchored bias: A replication and extension of Murphy and Constans. *Journal of Applied Psychology, 74,* 823–826.

Plake, B. S., Conoley, J. C., Kramer, J. J., & Murphy, L. U. (1991). The Buros Institute of Mental Measurements: Commitment to the tradition of excellence. *Journal of Counseling & Development, 69,* 449–455.

Podsakoff, P. M., & Farh, J. (1989). Effects of feedback sign and credibility on goal setting and task performance. *Organizational Behavior and Human Decision Processes, 44,* 45–67.

Podsakoff, P. M., MacKenzie, S. B., Ahearne, M., & Bommer, W. H. (1995). Searching for a needle in a haystack: Trying to identify the illusive moderators of leadership behaviors. *Journal of Management, 21,* 423–470.

Pond, S. B., & Geyer, P. D. (1987). Employee age as a moderator of the relationship between perceived work alternatives and job satisfaction. *Journal of Applied Psychology, 72,* 552–557.

Pond, S. B., & Geyer, P. D. (1991). Differences in the relation between job satisfaction and perceived work alternatives among older and younger blue-collar workers. *Journal of Vocational Behavior, 39,* 251–262.

Pondy, L. R. (1983). The role of metaphors and myths in organization and the facilitation of change. In L. R. Pondy, P. J. Frost, G. Morgan, & T. Dandridge (Eds.), *Organizational symbolism.* Greenwich, CT: JAI Press.

Porras, J. I. et al. (1982). Modeling-based organizational development: A longitudinal assessment. *Journal of Applied Behavioral Science, 18,* 433–446.

Porras, J. I., & Berg, P. O. (1978). Evaluation methodology in organization development: An analysis and critique. *Journal of Applied Behavioral Science, 14,* 151–173.

Porter, L. W. (1961). A study of perceived need satisfaction in bottom and middle management jobs. *Journal of Applied Psychology, 45,* 1–10.

Porter, L. W., & Lawler, E. E. (1968). *Managerial attitudes and performance.* Homewood, IL: Dorsey.

Porter, L. W., & Steers, R. M. (1973). Organizational work and personal factors in employee turnover and absenteeism. *Psychological Bulletin, 80,* 151–176.

Porter, L. W., Steers, R. M., Mowday, R. T., & Boulian, P. V. (1974). Organizational commitment, job satisfaction, and turnover among psychiatric technicians. *Journal of Applied Psychology, 59,* 603–609.

Powell, G. N., & Butterfield, D. A. (1989). The "good manager": Did androgyny fare better in the 1980s? *Group & Organization Studies, 14,* 216–233.

Prein, H. (1987). Strategies for third party intervention. *Human Relations, 40,* 699–719.

Premack, S. L., & Wanous, J. P. (1985). A meta-analysis of realistic job preview experiments. *Journal of Applied Psychology, 70,* 706–719.

Price, H. E. (1985). The allocation of functions in systems. *Human Factors, 27,* 33–45.

Priem, R. L., Harrison, D. A., & Muir, N. K. (1995). Structured conflict and consensus outcomes in group decision making. *Journal of Management, 21,* 691–710.

Prien, E. P. (1977). The function of job analysis in content validation. *Personnel Psychology, 30,* 167–174.

Primoff, E. S. (1975). *How to prepare and conduct job element examinations* (technical study 75–1). Washington, DC: Personnel and Development Center, U.S. Government Printing Office.

Pritchard, R. D., Dunnette, M. D., & Jorgenson, D. O. (1972). Effects of perceptions of equity and inequity on worker performance and satisfaction [monograph no. 1]. *Journal of Applied Psychology, 56,* 75–94.

Pruitt, D. G., & Rubin, J. Z. (1986). *Social conflict: Escalation, stalemate, and settlement.* New York: Random House.

Pugh, D. S. (1966). Modern organization theory: A psychological and sociological study. *Psychological Bulletin, 66,* 235–251.

Pugh v. See's Candies, Inc. (1981). Cal. App. 3d.

Pulakos, E. (1984). A comparison of rater training programs: Error training and accuracy training. *Journal of Applied Psychology, 69,* 581–588.

Pulakos, E. D., & Schmitt, N. (1995). Experience-based and situational interview questions: Studies of validity. *Personnel Psychology, 48,* 289–308.

Pulakos, E.D., Schmitt, N., Whitney, D., & Smith, M. (1996). Individual differences in interviewer ratings: The impact of standardization, consensus discussion, and sampling error on the validity of a structured interview. *Personnel Psychology, 49,* 85–102.

Pulakos, E. D., & Wexley, K. N. (1983). The relationship among perceptual similarity, sex, and performance ratings in manager-subordinate dyads. *Academy of Management Journal, 26,* 129–139.

Pulakos, E. D., White, L. A., Oppler, S. H., & Borman, W. C. (1989). Examination of race and sex effects on performance ratings. *Journal of Applied Psychology, 74,* 770–780.

Q

Quinn, R. E., & McGrath, M. R. (1982). Moving beyond the single-solution perspective: The competing values approach as a diagnostic tool. *Journal of Applied Behavioral Science, 18,* 473–476.

Quinn, R. P., Staines, G. L., & McCullough, M. (1974). *Job satisfaction: Is there a trend?* (Manpower research monograph no. 30). Washington, DC: U.S. Department of Labor.

Quiñones, M. A. (1995). Pretraining context effects: Training assignment as feedback. *Journal of Applied Psychology, 80,* 226–238.

R

Rabkin, J. G., & Struening, E. L. (1976). Life events, stress, and illness. *Science, 194,* 1013–1020.

Ragins, B. R., & Cotton, J. L. (1991). Easier said than done: Gender differences in perceived barriers to gaining a mentor. *Academy of Management Journal, 34,* 939–951.

Rahe, R. H., Pugh, W. M., Erickson, J., Gunderson, E. K. E., & Rubin, R. T. (1971). Cluster analysis of life changes. I. Consistency of clusters across large Navy samples. *Archives of General Psychiatry, 25,* 330–332.

Rahim, M. A. (1985). A strategy of managing conflict in complex organizations. *Human Relations, 38,* 81–89.

Rahim, A., & Bonoma, T. V. (1979). Managing organizational conflict: A model for diagnosis and intervention. *Psychological Reports, 44,* 1323–1344.

Rahimi, M., & Malzahn, D. E. (1984). Task design and modification based on physical ability measurement. *Human Factors, 26,* 715–726.

Raloff, J. (1990, June 16). More jobs linked to asbestos hazards. *Science News, 137,* 373.

Ralston, D. A. (1989). The benefits of flextime: Real or imagined? *Journal of Organizational Behavior, 10,* 369–373.

Ralston, J. V., Pisoni, D. B., Lively, S. E., Greene, B. G., et al. (1991). Comprehension of synthetic speech produced by rule: Word monitoring and sentence-by-sentence listening times. *Human Factors, 33,* 471–491.

Rambo, W. W., Chomiak, A. M., & Price, J. M. (1983). Consistency of performance under stable conditions of work. *Journal of Applied Psychology, 68,* 78–87.

Ramsey, V. J., & Calvert, L. M. (1994). A feminist critique of organizational humanism. *Journal of Applied Behavioral Science, 30,* 83–97.

Rasmussen, R. V. (1982). Team training: A behavior modification approach. *Group & Organization Studies, 7,* 51–66.

Raven, B. H. (1974). The comparative analysis of power and power preference. In J. T. Tedeschi (Ed.), *Perspectives on social power*. Chicago: Aldine.

Razmjou, S., & Kjellberg, A. (1992). Sustained attention and serial responding in heat: Mental effort in the control of performance. *Aviation, Space, & Environmental Medicine, 63*, 594–601.

Reilly, R. R., Brown, B., Blood, M. R., & Malatesta, C. Z. (1981). The effects of realistic previews: A study and discussion of the literature. *Personnel Psychology, 34*, 823–834.

Reilly, R. R., & Chao, G. T. (1982). Validity and fairness of some alternative employee procedures. *Personnel Psychology, 35*, 1–62.

Rendero, T. (1980). College recruiting practices. *Personnel, 57*, 4–10.

Renner, J. A., Jr. (1976). Alcoholism in the community. In A. W. Burgess and A. Lazare (Eds.), *Community mental health: Target populations*. Englewood Cliffs, NJ: Prentice–Hall.

Rhodes, S. R. (1983). Age-related differences in work attitudes and behavior: A review and conceptual analysis. *Psychological Bulletin, 93*, 328–367.

Rice, A. K. (1963). *The enterprise and its environment*. London: Tavistock.

Rice, R. W. (1978). Construct validity of the least preferred co-worker score. *Psychological Bulletin, 85*, 1199–1237.

Rice, R. W., McFarlin, D. B., & Bennett, D. E. (1989). Standards of comparison and job satisfaction. *Journal of Applied Psychology, 74*, 591–598.

Rice, R. W., Phillips, S. M., & McFarlin, D. B. (1990). Multiple discrepancies and pay satisfaction. *Journal of Applied Psychology, 75*, 386–393.

Richardson, A. (1967). Mental practice: A review and discussion. *Research Quarterly, 38*, 95–107.

Riggio, R. E., & Cole, E. J. (1992). Agreement between subordinate and superior ratings of supervisory performance and effects on self and subordinate job satisfaction. *Journal of Occupational & Organizational Psychology, 65*, 151–158.

Roback, A. A. (1952). *History of American psychology*. New York: Library Publishers.

Robbins, T. L., & DeNisi, A. S. (1994). A closer look at interpersonal affect as a distinct influence on cognitive processing in performance evaluations. *Journal of Applied Psychology, 79*, 341–353.

Roberson, M. T., & Sundstrom, E. (1990) Questionnaire design, return rates, and response favorableness in an employee attitude questionnaire. *Journal of Applied Psychology, 75*, 354–357.

Robertson, I. T., & Downs, S. (1989). Work-sample tests of trainability: A meta-analysis. *Journal of Applied Psychology, 74*, 402–410.

Robinson, D. D. (1981). Content-oriented personnel selection in a small business setting. *Personnel Psychology, 34*, 77–88.

Robinson, D. D. (1987). A consultant's view of being a consultant: Part II. *The Industrial-Organizational Psychologist, 24*(4), 43–52.

Roethlisberger, F. J. (1941). *Management and morale*, chapter 2. Cambridge, MA: Harvard University Press. Reprinted as The Hawthorne Experiments. In D. Mankin, R. E. Ames, Jr., & M. A. Grodsky (Eds.). (1980). *Classics of industrial and organizational psychology*. Oak Park, IL: Moore.

Roethlisberger, F. J., & Dickson, W. J. (1939). *Management and the worker*. Cambridge, MA: Harvard University Press.

Rohmert, W. (1985a). Ergonomics and manufacturing industry. *Ergonomics, 28*, 1115–1134.

Rohmert, W. (1985b). AET—A new job-analysis method. *Ergonomics, 28*, 245–254.

Roman, P. M., Blum, T. C., & Bennett, N. (1987). Educating organizational consumers about employee assistance programs. *Public Personnel Management, 16*, 299–312.

Ronen, S., & Primps, S. B. (1980). The impact of flexitime on performance and attitudes in 25 public agencies. *Public Personnel Management Journal, 9*, 201–207.

Rosa, R. R., & Colligan, M. J. (1988). Long workdays versus restdays: Assessing fatigue and alertness with a portable performance battery. *Human Factors, 30*, 305–317.

Rose, R. M., Jenkins, C. D., & Hurst, M. W. (1978). Health change in air traffic controllers: A prospective study. I. Background and description. *Psychosomatic Medicine, 40*, 142–165.

Rosen, T. H. (1987). Identification of substance abusers in the workplace. *Public Personnel Management, 16*, 197–207.

Rosenberg, H. (1993). Prediction of controlled drinking by alcoholics and problem drinkers. *Psychological Bulletin, 113*, 129–139.

Rosenman, R. H. et al. (1975). Coronary heart disease in the Western Collaborative Group Study: Final follow-up experience of 8.5 years. *Journal of the American Medical Association, 233*, 872–877.

Rosenman, R. H., & Chesney, M. A. (1982). Stress, Type A behavior, and coronary disease. In L. Goldberger & S. Breznitz (Eds.), *Handbook of stress: Theoretical and clinical aspects*. New York: Free Press.

Rosin, H., & Korabik, K. (1995). Organizational experiences and propensity to leave: A multivariate investigation of men and women managers. *Journal of Vocational Behavior, 46*, 1–16.

Ross, S. (1995, April 1). Study: Affirmative action doesn't work against white men. *San Francisco Examiner*, Section B, p. 2.

Rosse, J. G., Miller, J. L., & Stecher, M. D. (1994). A field study of job applicants' reactions to personality and cognitive ability testing. *Journal of Applied Psychology, 79*, 987–992.

Rotchford, N. L., & Roberts, K. H. (1982). Part-time workers are missing persons in organizational research. *Academy of Management Review, 7*, 228–234.

Roy, D. F. (1959/1960). Banana time. *Human Organization, 18*, 158–168.

Rozier, C. K. (1977). Three-dimensional work space for the amputee. *Human Factors, 19*, 525–533.

Rush, M. C., Thomas, J. C., & Lord, R. G. (1977). Implicit leadership theory: A potential threat to the internal validity of leader behavior questionnaires. *Organizational Behavior and Human Performance, 20*, 93–110.

Russell, C. J., Mattson, J., Devlin, S. E., & Atwater, D. (1990). Predictive validity of biodata items generated from retrospective life experience essays. *Journal of Applied Psychology, 75*, 569–580.

Russell, D. W., Altmaier, E., & Van Velzen, D. (1987). Job-related stress, social support, and burnout among classroom teachers. *Journal of Applied Psychology, 72*, 269–274.

Russell, J. S., & Goode, D. L. (1988). An analysis of managers' reactions to their own performance appraisal feedback. *Journal of Applied Psychology, 73*, 63–67.

Russell, J. S., Wexley, K. N., & Hunter, J. E. (1984). Questioning the effectiveness of behavior modeling training in an industrial setting. *Personnel Psychology, 37,* 465–481.

Russell, M. A. H. (1976). Tobacco smoking and nicotine dependence. In R. J. Gibbins et al. (Eds.), *Research advances in alcohol and drug problems* (Vol. 3). New York: Wiley.

Russell, R. D., & Russell, C. J. (1992). An examination of the effects of organizational norms, organizational structure, and environmental uncertainty on entrepreneurial strategy. *Journal of Management, 18,* 639–656.

Ryan, A. M., & Lasek, M. (1991). Negligent hiring and defamation: Areas of liability related to pre-employment inquiries. *Personnel Psychology, 44,* 293–319.

Ryan, T. A., & Smith, P. C. (1954). *Principles of industrial psychology.* New York: Ronald Press.

Rynes, S. L., & Boudreau, J. W. (1986). College recruiting in large organizations: Practice, evaluation, and research implications. *Personnel Psychology, 39,* 729–757.

S

Saal, F. E., & Landy, F. J. (1977). The mixed standard rating scale: An evaluation. *Organizational Behavior and Human Performance, 18,* 19–35.

Saari, L. M., Johnson, T. R., McLaughlin, S. D., & Zimmerle, D. M. (1988). A survey of management training and education practices in U.S. companies. *Personnel Psychology, 41,* 731–743.

Saari, L. M., & Latham, G. P. (1982). Employee reaction to continuous and variable ratio reinforcement schedules involving a monetary incentive. *Journal of Applied Psychology, 67,* 506–508.

Sackett, P. R., Burris, L. R., & Callahan, C. (1989). Integrity testing for personnel selection: An update. *Personnel Psychology, 42,* 491–529.

Sackett, P. R., & Decker, P. J. (1979). Detection of deception in the employment context: A review and critical analysis. *Personnel Psychology, 32,* 487–506.

Sackett, P. R., & Harris, M. M. (1984). Honesty testing for personnel selection: A review and critique. *Personnel Psychology, 37,* 221–246.

Sackett, P. R., & Wilson, M. A. (1982). Factors affecting the consensus judgment process in managerial assessment centers. *Journal of Applied Psychology, 67,* 10–17.

Sackmann, S. (1989). The role of metaphors in organization transformation. *Human Relations, 42,* 463–485.

Saks, A. M. (1994). A psychological process investigation for the effects of recruitment source and organization information on job survival. *Journal of Organizational Behavior, 15,* 225–244.

Salancik, G. R., & Pfeffer, J. (1977). An examination of need satisfaction models of job satisfaction. *Administrative Science Quarterly, 22,* 427–456.

Salmaso, P., Baroni, M. R., Job, R., & Peron, E. M. (1983). Schematic information, attention, and memory for places. *Journal of Experimental Psychology: Learning, Memory, and Cognition, 9,* 263–268.

Sanchez, J. I., & Levine, E. L. (1989). Determining important tasks within jobs: A policy-capturing approach. *Journal of Applied Psychology, 74,* 336–342.

Sankowsky, D. (1995). The charismatic leader as narcissist: Understanding the abuse of power. *Organizational Dynamics, 23,* 57–71.

Scarpello, V. (1983). Who benefits from participation in long-term human process interventions? *Group & Organization Studies, 8,* 21–44.

Schachter, V. (1984, July 19). Rightful termination: The answer to wrongful discharge liability. Paper delivered at the Bay Area Personnel Association, San Francisco.

Schachter, V. et al. (1988). *Update '88: Significant developments in labor and employment law and litigation.* San Francisco: Schachter, Kristoff, Ross, Sprague & Curiale.

Schay, B. W. (1988). Effects of performance-contingent pay on employee attitudes. *Public Personnel Management, 17,* 237–250.

Scheid-Cook, T. L. (1988). Mitigating organizational contradictions: The role of mediatory myths. *Journal of Applied Behavioral Science, 24,* 161–171.

Schein, E. H. (1980). *Organizational psychology* (3rd ed.). Englewood Cliffs, NJ: Prentice–Hall.

Schein, E. H. (1985). *Organizational culture and leadership.* San Francisco: Jossey-Bass.

Schein, V. E. (1973). The relationship between sex role stereotypes and requisite management characteristics. *Journal of Applied Psychology, 57,* 95–100.

Schein, V. E. (1978). Sex role stereotyping, ability, and performance: Prior research and new directions. *Personnel Psychology, 31,* 259–268.

Schein, V. E., Mueller, R., Lituchy, T., & Liu, J. (1996). Think manager—think male: A global phenomenon? *Journal of Organizational Behavior, 17,* 33–41.

Schendel, J. D., & Hagman, J. D. (1982). On sustaining procedural skills over a prolonged retention interval. *Journal of Applied Psychology, 67,* 605–610.

Schmidt, F. L., Caplan, J. R., Bemis, S. E., Decuir, R., Dunn, L., & Antone, L. (1979). *The behavioral consistency method of unassembled examining* (technical memorandum 79–21). Washington, DC: U.S. Office of Personnel Management.

Schmidt, F. L., & Hunter, J. E. (1981a). Two pitfalls in assessing fairness of selection tests using the regression model. *Personnel Psychology, 35,* 601–607.

Schmidt, F. L., & Hunter, J. E. (1981b). Employment testing: Old theories and new research findings. *American Psychologist, 36,* 1128–1137.

Schmidt, F. L., Hunter, J. E., McKenzie, R. C., & Muldrow, T. W. (1979). Impact of valid selection procedures on work-force productivity. *Journal of Applied Psychology, 64,* 609–626.

Schmidt, F. L., Hunter, J. E., & Pearlman, K. (1981). Task differences as moderators of aptitude test validity in selection: A red herring. *Journal of Applied Psychology, 66,* 166–185.

Schmidt, F. L., Hunter, J. E., & Pearlman, K. (1982). Progress in validity generalization: Comments on Callendar and Osburn and further developments. *Journal of Applied Psychology, 67,* 835–845.

Schmidt, F. L., Hunter, J. E., & Raju, N. S. (1988). Validity generalization and situational specificity: A second look at the 75% rule and Fisher's z transformation. *Journal of Applied Psychology, 73,* 665–672.

Schmit, M. J., & Ryan, A. M. (1993). The Big Five in personnel selection: Factor structure in applicant and nonapplicant populations. *Journal of Applied Psychology, 78,* 966–974.

Schmit, M. J., Ryan, A. M., Stierwalt, S. L., & Powell, A. B. (1995). Frame-of-reference effects on personality scale scores and criterion-related validity. *Journal of Applied Psychology, 80,* 607–620.

Schmitt, N. (1977). Interrater agreement in dimensionality and combination of assessment center judgments. *Journal of Applied Psychology, 62,* 171–176.

Schmitt, N. (1991). Report on efforts to revise SIOP's licensure position. *The Industrial-Organizational Psychologist, 29,* 33–50.

Schmitt, N., & Ostroff, C. (1986). Operationalizing the "behavioral consistency" approach: Selection test development based on a content-oriented strategy. *Personnel Psychology, 39,* 91–108.

Schneider, A. M., & Tarshis, B. (1980). *An introduction to physiological psychology* (2nd ed.). New York: Random House.

Schneider, B. (1985). Organizational behavior. *Annual Review of Psychology, 36,* 573–611.

Schneider, B., & Dachler, H. P. (1978). A note on the stability of the job descriptive index. *Journal of Applied Psychology, 63,* 650–653.

Schneier, C. E. (1977). Operational utility and psychometric characteristics of behavioral expectation scales: A cognitive reinterpretation. *Journal of Applied Psychology, 62,* 541–548.

Schneier, C. E., Guthrie, J. P., & Olian, J. D. (1988). A practical approach to conducting and using the training needs assessment. *Public Personnel Management, 17,* 191–205.

Schoenmarklin, R. W., & Marras, W. S. (1989). Effects of handle angle and work orientation on hammering: I. Wrist motion and hammering performance. *Human Factors, 31,* 397–411.

Schonpflug, W. (1993). Applied psychology: Newcomer with a long tradition. *Applied Psychology: An International Review, 42,* 5–30.

Schoorman, F. D. (1988). Escalation bias in performance appraisals: An unintended consequence of supervisor participation in hiring decisions. *Journal of Applied Psychology, 73,* 58–62.

Schriesheim, C. A. (1978). Job satisfaction, attitudes toward unions, and voting in a union representation election. *Journal of Applied Psychology, 63,* 548–552.

Schriesheim, C. A., & DeNisi, A. S. (1981). Task dimensions as moderators of the effects of instrumental leadership: A two-sample replicated test of path-goal leadership theory. *Journal of Applied Psychology, 66,* 589–597.

Schriesheim, C. A., Powers, K. J., Scandura, T. A., Gardiner, C. C., & Lankau, M. J. (1993). Improving construct measurement in management research: Comments and a quantitative approach for assessing the theoretical content adequacy of paper-and-pencil survey-type instruments. *Journal of Management, 19,* 385–417.

Schriesheim, C. A., Tepper, B. J., & Tetrault, L. A. (1994). Least preferred co-worker score, situational control, and leadership effectiveness: A meta-analysis of contingency model performance predictions. *Journal of Applied Psychology, 79,* 561–573.

Schuman, H., & Kalton, G. (1985). Survey methods. In G. Lindzey & E. Aronson (Eds.), *Handbook of social psychology* (Vol. I). New York: Random House.

Scott, K. D., & Taylor, G. S. (1985). An examination of conflicting findings on the relationship between job satisfaction and absenteeism: A meta-analysis. *Academy of Management Journal, 28,* 599–612.

Scott, W. D. (1914, May). How suggestion works on the prospect's brain. Originally published in *Advertising & Selling.* Reprinted in D. Mankin, R. E. Ames, Jr., & M. A. Grodsky (Eds.). (1980). *Classics of industrial and organizational psychology.* Oak Park, IL: Moore.

Selye, H. (1936). A syndrome produced by various nocuous agents. *Nature, 138,* 32.

Selye, H. (1946). The general adaptation syndrome and the diseases of adaptation. *Journal of Clinical Endocrinology, 6,* 117–230.

Selye, H. (Ed.). (1980). *Selye's guide to stress research* (Vol. 1). New York: Van Nostrand Reinhold.

Selye, H. (1982). History and present status of the stress concept. In L. Goldberger & S. Breznitz (Eds.), *Handbook of stress: Theoretical and clinical aspects.* New York: Free Press.

Shaffer, G. S., Saunders, V., & Owens, W. A. (1987). Additional evidence for the accuracy of biographical data: Long-term retest and observer ratings. *Personnel Psychology, 39,* 791–809.

Shahnavaz, H., & Hedman, L. (1984). Visual accommodation changes in VDU-operators related to environmental lighting and screen quality. *Ergonomics, 27,* 1071–1082.

Shain, M. (1982). Alcohol, drugs and safety: An updated perspective on problems and their management in the workplace. *Accident Analysis and Prevention, 14,* 239–246.

Shani, A. B., & Sena, J. A. (1994). Information technology and the integration of change: Sociotechnical system approach. *Journal of Applied Behavioral Science, 30,* 247–270.

Sharfman, M. P., & Dean, J. W. (1991). Conceptualizing and measuring organizational environments: A critique and suggestions. *Journal of Management, 17,* 681–700.

Shaw, J. B., & Riskind, J. H. (1983). Predicting job stress using data from the position analysis questionnaire. *Journal of Applied Psychology, 68,* 253–261.

Shebilske, W. L., Regian, J. W., Arthur, W., & Jordan, J. A. (1992). A dyadic protocol for training complex skills. *Human Factors, 34,* 369–374.

Shenkar, O. (1988). Robotics: A challenge for occupational psychology. *Journal of Occupational Psychology, 61,* 103–112.

Sherif, M. (1966). *In common predicament: Social psychology of intergroup conflict and cooperation.* Boston: Houghton Mifflin.

Sherif, M., Harvey, O. J., White, B. J., Hood, W. R., & Sherif, C. W. (1961). *Intergroup conflict and cooperation: The robber's cave experiment.* Norman, OK: University of Oklahoma Press.

Shouksmith, G., & Burrough, S. (1988). Job stress factors for New Zealand and Canadian air traffic controllers. *Applied Psychology: An International Review, 37,* 263–270.

Shrader, C. B., Lincoln, J. R., & Hoffman, A. N. (1989). The network structures of organizations: Effects of task contingencies and distributional form. *Human Relations, 42,* 43–66.

Shumaker, S. A., & Brownell, A. (1984). Toward a theory of social support: Closing conceptual gaps. *Journal of Social Issues, 40*(4), 37–55.

Shute, S. J., & Starr, S. J. (1984). Effects of adjustable furniture on VDT users. *Human Factors, 26,* 157–170.

Shuval, J. T. (1982). Migration and stress. In L. Goldberger & S. Breznitz (Eds.), *Handbook of stress: Theoretical and clinical aspects.* New York: Free Press.

Siegel, A. I. (1983). The miniature job training and evaluation approach: Additional findings. *Personnel Psychology, 36,* 41–56.

Silver, E. M., & Bennett, C. (1987). Modification of the Minnesota Clerical Test to predict performance on video display terminals. *Journal of Applied Psychology, 72,* 153–155.

Skaggs, K. J., Dickinson, A. M., & O'Connor, K. A. (1992). The use of concurrent schedules to evaluate the effects of extrinsic rewards on "intrinsic motivaion": A replication. *Journal of Organizational Behavior Management, 12,* 45–83.

Skinner, B. F. (1938). *The behavior of organisms.* New York: Appleton-Century-Crofts.

SKRSC. (1989, June-July). *Update: Current development in employee relations law and litigation.* Newsletter available from Schachter, Kristoff, Ross, Sprague, and Curiale, 505 Montgomery St., San Francisco 94111.

SKRSC. (1990). *The environmental & workplace safety reporter,* Vol.1(1). Newsletter available from Schachter, Kristoff, Ross, Sprague, and Curiale, 505 Montgomery St., San Francisco 94111.

Slappendel, C., Laird, I., Kawachi, I., Marshall, S., et al., (1993). Factors affecting work-related injury among forestry workers: A review. *Journal of Safety Research, 24,* 19–32.

Smith, J. E., & Hakel, M. D. (1979). Convergence among data sources, response bias, and reliability and validity of a structured job analysis questionnaire. *Personnel Psychology, 32,* 677–692.

Smith, M. J. (1981). Occupational stress: An overview of psychosocial factors. In G. Salvendy & M. J. Smith (Eds.), *Machine pacing and occupational stress.* London: Taylor & Francis.

Smith, M. J., Anger, W. K., & Uslan, S. S. (1978). Behavioral modification applied to occupational safety. *Journal of Safety Research, 10,* 87–88.

Smith, P. B. (1984). The effectiveness of Japanese styles of management: A review and critique. *Journal of Occupational Psychology, 57,* 121–136.

Smith, P. B., Misumi, J., Tayeb, M., Peterson, M., & Bond, M. (1989). On the generality of leadership style measures across cultures. *Journal of Occupational Psychology, 62,* 97–109.

Smith, P. C., & Kendall, L. M. (1963). Retranslation of expectations: An approach to the construction of unambiguous anchors for rating scales. *Journal of Applied Psychology, 47,* 149–155.

Smith, P. C., Kendall, L. M., & Hulin, C. L. (1969). *Measurement of satisfaction in work and retirement.* Chicago: Rand McNally.

Smither, J. W., Barry, S. R., & Reilly, R. R. (1989). An investigation of the validity of expert true score estimates in appraisal research. *Journal of Applied Psychology, 74,* 143–151.

Solomon, R. L., & Corbit, J. D. (1973). An opponent process theory of motivation: II. Cigarette addiction. *Journal of Abnormal Psychology, 81,* 158–171.

Sommer, R. (1987). An experimental investigation of the action research approach. *Journal of Applied Behavioral Science, 23,* 185–199.

Sommese, T., & Patterson, J. C. (1995). Acute effects of cigarette smoking withdrawal: A review of the literature. *Aviation, Space, & Environmental Medicine, 66,* 164–167.

Sonnenstuhl, W. J. (1988). Contrasting employee assistance, health promotion, and quality of work life programs and their effects on alcohol abuse and dependence. *Journal of Applied Behavioral Science, 24,* 347–363.

Spector, P. E. (1987). Interactive effects of perceived control and job stressors on affective reactions and health outcomes for clerical workers. *Work and Stress, 1,* 155–162.

Spector, P. E., Dwyer, D. J., & Jex, S. M. (1988). Relation of job stressors to affective, health, and performance outcomes: A comparison of multiple data sources. *Journal of Applied Psychology, 73,* 11–19.

Spence, J. T., Helmreich, R. L., & Pred, R. S. (1987). Impatience versus achievement strivings in the Type A pattern: Differential effects on students' health and academic achievement. *Journal of Applied Psychology, 72,* 522–528.

Spencer, D. G., & Steers, R. M. (1981). Performance as a moderator of the job-satisfaction-turnover relationship. *Journal of Applied Psychology, 66,* 511–514.

Stagner, R., & Rosen, H. (1965). *Psychology of union-management relations.* Belmont, CA: Wadsworth.

Starr, R. B., & Greenly, R. J. (1939). Merit rating survey findings. *Personnel Journal, 17,* 378–384.

Staw, B. M., & Ross, J. (1985). Stability in the midst of change: A dispositional approach to job attitudes. *Journal of Applied Psychology, 70,* 469–480.

Steele, P. D., & Hubbard, R. L. (1985). Management styles, perceptions of substance abuse, and employee assistance programs in organizations. *Journal of Applied Behavioral Science, 21,* 271–286.

Steers, R. M. (1975). Effects of need for achievement on the job performance-job attitude relationship. *Journal of Applied Psychology, 60,* 678–682.

Steers, R. M., & Porter, L. W. (1979). *Motivation and work behavior* (2nd ed.). New York: McGraw-Hill.

Steers, R. M., & Rhodes, S. R. (1978). Major influences on employee attendance: A process model. *Journal of Applied Psychology, 63,* 391–407.

Steinmetz, C. S. (1967). The evolution of training. In R. L. Craig & L. R. Rittel (Eds.), *Training and development handbook.* New York: McGraw-Hill.

Stewart, T. (1985). Ergonomics of the office. *Ergonomics, 28,* 1165–1178.

Stieber, J. (1984). Most U.S. workers still may be fired under the employment-at-will doctrine. *Monthly Labor Review, 107,* 34–38.

Stogdill, R. M. (1948). Personal factors associated with leadership: A survey of the literature. *Journal of Psychology, 25,* 35–71.

Stogdill, R. M. (1974). *Handbook of leadership: A survey of theory and research.* New York: Free Press.

Stokols, D., Shumaker, S. A., & Martinez, J. (1983). Residential mobility and personal well-being. *Journal of Environmental Psychology, 3,* 5–19.

Stone, D. L., & Kotch, D. A. (1989). Individuals' attitudes toward organizational drug testing policies and practices. *Journal of Applied Psychology, 74,* 518–521.

Stoyva, J., & Anderson, C. (1982). A coping-rest model of relaxation and stress management. In L. Goldberger & S. Breznitz (Eds.), *Handbook of stress: Theoretical and clinical aspects*. New York: Free Press.

Strauss, R. (1976). Problem drinking in the perspective of social change, 1940–1973. In W. J. Filstead, J. J. Rossi, & M. Keller (Eds.), *Alcohol and alcohol problems: New thinking and new directions*. Cambridge, MA: Ballinger.

Streufert, S., Pogash, R. M., Gingrich, D., Kantner, A., et al. (1993). Alcohol and complex functioning. *Journal of Applied Social Psychology, 23*, 847–866.

Suinn, R. M. (1978). The coronary-prone behavior pattern: A behavioral approach to intervention. In T. M. Dembroski et al. (Eds.), *Coronary-prone behavior*. New York: Springer-Verlag.

Suinn, R., & Bloom, C. (1978). Anxiety management for Type A persons. *Journal of Behavioral Medicine, 1*, 25–35.

Sulkunen, P. (1976). Drinking patterns and the level of alcohol consumption: An international overview. In R. J. Gibbins et al. (Eds.), *Research advances in alcohol and drug problems* (Vol. 3). New York: Wiley.

Sulsky, L. M., & Balzer, W. K. (1988). Meaning and measurement of performance rating accuracy: Some methodological and theoretical concerns. *Journal of Applied Psychology, 73*, 497–506.

Sulsky, L. M., & Day, D. V. (1992). Frame-of-reference training and cognitive categorization: An empirical investigation of rater memory issues. *Journal of Applied Psychology, 77*, 501–510.

Summers, R. J. (1995). Attitudes toward different methods of affirmative action. *Journal of Applied Social Psychology 25*, 1090–1104.

Summers, T. P., & DeNisi, A. S. (1990). In search of Adam's Other: Reexamination of referents used in the evaluation of pay. *Human Relations, 43*, 497–511.

Sutton, H., & Porter, L. W. (1968). A study of the grapevine in a governmental organization. *Personnel Psychology, 21*, 223–230.

Swartz, J. (1986, September). Computers: Executives love 'em, but they don't use 'em. *APA Monitor*, 8.

T

Tagalakis, V., Amsel, R., & Fichten, C. S. (1988). Job interview strategies for people with a visible disability. *Journal of Applied Social Psychology, 18*, 520–532.

Tannenbaum, R., & Schmidt, W. H. (1958). How to choose a leadership pattern. *Harvard Business Review, 36*, 95–101.

Taylor, F. W. (1911). *The principles of scientific management*. Reprinted (1967). New York: Norton.

Taylor, F. W. (1916, December). The principles of scientific management. Originally published in *Bulletin of the Taylor Society*. Reprinted in D. Mankin, R. E. Ames, Jr., & M. A. Grodsky (Eds.). (1980). *Classics of industrial and organizational psychology*. Oak Park, IL: Moore.

Taylor, H. C., & Russell, J. T. (1939). The relationship of validity coefficients to the practical effectiveness of tests in selection: Discussion and tables. *Journal of Applied Psychology, 23*, 565–578.

Taylor, H. L., & Orlansky, J. (1993). The effects of wearing protective chemical warfare combat clothing on human performance. *Aviation, Space, & Environmental Medicine, 64*, 1–41.

Taylor, S. H. (1989). The case for comparable worth. *Journal of Social Issues, 45*, 23–37.

Taylor, S. H. (1990, April). *Characteristics and careers of I/O psychology alumni*. Paper presented at the convention of the Western Psychological Association, Los Angeles.

Tenopyr, M. L. (1981). The realities of employment testing. *American Psychologist, 36*, 1120–1127.

Tenopyr, M. L., & Oeltjen, P. D. (1982). Personnel selection and classification. *Annual Review of Psychology, 33*, 581–618.

Terborg, J. R., Lee, T. W., Smith, F. J., Davis, G. A., & Turbin, M. S. (1982). Extension of the Schmidt and Hunter validity generalization procedure to the prediction of absenteeism behavior from knowledge of job satisfaction. *Journal of Applied Psychology, 67*, 440–449.

Terkel, S. (1974). *Working*. New York: Avon.

Terpstra, D. E. (1982). Evaluating selected organization development interventions: The state of the art. *Group & Organization Studies, 7*, 402–417.

Texas Department of Community Affairs v. *Burdine* (1981). 450 U.S. 248.

Thacker, R. A., & Wayne, S. J. (1995). An examination of the relationship between upward influence tactics and assessments of promotability. *Journal of Management, 21*, 739–757.

Tharenou, P., & Harker, P. (1984). Moderating influence of self-esteem on relationships between job complexity, performance, and satisfaction. *Journal of Applied Psychology, 69*, 623–632.

Thorndike, E. L. (1898). Animal intelligence. *Psychological Monograph, 2*, no. 8.

Thorton, G. C., III, & Zorich, S. (1980). Training to improve observer accuracy. *Journal of Applied Psychology, 65*, 351–354.

Tichauer, E. R. (1978). *The biomechanical basis of ergonomics*. New York: Wiley.

Tiegs, R. B., Tetrick, L. E., & Fried, Y. (1992). Growth need strength and context satisfactions as moderators of the relations of the job characteristics model. *Journal of Management, 18*, 575–593.

Tiffin, J. (1943). *Industrial psychology*. New York: Prentice-Hall.

Tjosvold, D. (1981). Unequal power relationships within a cooperative or competitive context. *Journal of Applied Social Psychology, 11*, 137–150.

Tjosvold, D. (1984). Cooperation theory and organizations. *Human Relations, 37*, 743–767.

Tjosvold, D., Dann, V., & Wong, C. L. (1992). Managing conflict between departments to serve customers. *Human Relations, 45*, 1035–1054.

Tolliver, L. (1983). Social and mental health needs of the aged. *American Psychologist, 38*, 316–318.

Tolman, E. C. (1932). *Purposive behavior in animals and men*. New York: Appleton-Century-Crofts.

Törner, M., Zetterberg, C, Anden, U., Hansson, T., et al. (1991). Workload and musculoskeletal problems: A comparison between welders and office clerks (with reference also to fishermen). *Ergonomics, 34*, 1179–1196.

Totterdell, P., Spelten, E., Smith, L., Barton, J., & Folkard, S. (1995). Recovery from work shifts: How long does it take? *Journal of Applied Psychology, 80*, 43–57.

Tougas, F., & Beaton, A. M. (1993). Affirmative action in the work place: For better or for worse. *Applied Psychology: An International Review, 42*, 253–264.

Tracey, J. B., Tannenbaum, S. I., & Kavenagh, M. J. (1995). Applying trained skills on the job: The importance of the work environment. *Journal of Applied Psychology, 80,* 239–252.

Trempe, J., Rigny, A., & Haccoun, R. R. (1985). Subordinate satisfaction with male and female managers: Role of perceived supervisory influence. *Journal of Applied Psychology, 70,* 44–47.

Triandis, H. C. (1971). *Attitude and attitude change.* New York: Wiley.

Triandis, H. C., Feldman, J. M., & Weldon, D. E. (1974). Designing preemployment training for the hard to employ: A cross-cultural psychological approach. *Journal of Applied Psychology, 59,* 687–693.

Trice, H. M., & Beyer, J. M. (1984). Employee assistance programs: Blending performance-oriented and humanitarian ideologies to assist emotionally disturbed employees. In J. R. Greenley (Ed.), *Research in community and mental health: A research annual* (Vol. 4). Greenwich, CT: JAI Press.

Trice, H. M., & Sonnenstuhl, W. J. (1988). Drinking behavior and risk factors related to the work place: Implications for research and prevention. *Journal of Applied Behavioral Science, 24,* 327–346.

Triesman, A. (1969). Strategies and models of selective attention. *Psychological Review, 76,* 282–299.

Trist, E. L, & Bamforth, K. W. (1951). Some social and psychological consequences of the longwall method of goal-getting. *Human Relations, 4,* 3–38.

Trist, E. L., Higgin, G. W., Murray, H., & Pollock, A. B. (1963). *Organization choice.* London: Tavistock.

Tullar, W. L., & Barrett, G. V. (1976). The future autobiography as a predictor of sales success. *Journal of Applied Psychology, 61,* 371–373.

Tullar, W. L., Mullins, T. W., & Caldwell, S. A. (1979). Effects of interview length and applicant quality on interview decision time. *Journal of Applied Psychology, 64,* 669–674.

Tung, R. L. (1981). Selection and training of personnel for overseas assignments. *Columbia Journal of World Business, 16,* 68–78.

Turban, D. B., Sanders, P. A., Francis, D. J., & Osburn, H. G. (1989). Construct equivalence as an approach to replacing validated cognitive ability selection tests. *Journal of Applied Psychology, 74,* 62–71.

Tziner, A., Haccoun, R. R., & Kadish, A. (1991). Personal and situational characteristics influencing the effectiveness of transfer of training improvement strategies. *Journal of Occupational Psychology, 64,* 167–177.

U

Uhrbrock, R. S. (1934). Attitudes of 4430 employees. *Journal of Social Psychology, 5,* 365–377.

Uniform guidelines on employee selection procedures. (1978). In *Federal Register, 43*(166), 38290–38309.

U.S. Bureau of the Census. (1975). *Historical statistics of the United States,* bicentennial ed., part I. Washington, DC: U.S. Government Printing Office.

U.S. Bureau of the Census. (1981). *Statistical abstract.* Washington, DC: U.S. Government Printing Office.

U.S. Bureau of the Census (1990). Statistical Abstract of the United States. *The National Data Book.* Washington, DC: Author.

U.S.Bureau of Labor Statistics. (1985). *Annual survey.* Washington, DC: Author.

U.S. Commission on Civil Rights. (1978). *Social indicators of equality for minorities and women.* Washington, DC: U.S. Government Printing Office.

U.S. Department of Labor (1970). *General Aptitude Test Battery: Section III. Development.* Washington, DC: U.S. Government Printing Office.

U.S. Department of Labor. (1972). *Handbook for analyzing jobs.* Washington, DC: U.S. Government Printing Office.

U.S. Department of Labor. (1975). *Handbook on women workers* (bulletin 197). Washington, DC: USDOL, Employment Standards Administration, Women's Bureau.

U.S. Department of Labor. (1986). *Employment and earnings,* (33 [1]). Washington, DC: U.S. Government Printing Office.

U.S. Office of Personnel Management. (1979). *Equal employment opportunity court cases.* Washington, DC: Office of Intergovernmental Personnel Programs.

V

Vandenberg, R. J., & Lance, C. E. (1992). Examining the causal order of job satisfaction and organizational commitment. *Journal of Management, 18,* 153–167.

Vanderslice, V. J., Rice, R. W., & Julian, J. W. (1987). The effects of participation in decision-making on worker satisfaction and productivity: An organizational simulation. *Journal of Applied Social Psychology, 17,* 158–170.

Van de Vijver, F. J. R., & Harsveldt, M. (1994). The incomplete equivalence of the paper-and-pencil and computerized versions of the General Aptitude Test Battery. *Journal of Applied Psychology, 79,* 852–859.

Varca, P. E., & Pattison, P. (1993). Evidentiary standards in employment discrimination: A view toward the future. *Personnel Psychology, 46,* 239–258.

Vecchio, R. P., & Gobdel, B. C. (1984). The vertical dyad linkage model of leadership: Problems and prospects. *Organizational Behavior and Human Performance, 34,* 5–20.

Veres, J. G., Lahey, M. A., & Buckly, R. (1987). A practical rationale for using multi-method job analyses. *Public Personnel Management, 16,* 153–157.

Veroff, J., Douvan, E., & Kulka, R. A. (1981). *The inner American: A self-portrait from 1957 to 1976.* New York: Basic Books.

Vicars, W. M., & Hartke, D. D. (1984). Evaluating OD evaluations: A status report. *Group & Organization Studies, 9,* 177–188.

Viswesvaran, C., Barrick, M. R., & Ones, D. S. (1993). How definitive are conclusions based on survey data: Estimating robustness to nonresponse. *Personnel Psychology, 46,* 551–567.

Viteles, M. S. (1926). Psychology in industry. *Psychological Bulletin, 23,* 631–680.

Vivoli, G., Bergomi, M., Rovesti, S., Carrozzi, G. et al. (1993). Biochemical and haemodynamic indicators of stress in truck drivers. *Ergonomics, 36,* 1089–1090.

von Bertalanffy, L. (1950). The theory of open systems in physics and biology. *Science, 111,* 23–29.

Vroom, V. H. (1964). *Work and motivation.* New York: Wiley.

Vroom, V. H., & Yetton, P. W. (1973). *Leadership and decision making.* Pittsburgh: University of Pittsburgh Press.

W

Wagner, J. A. III. (1994). Participation's effects on performance and satisfaction: A reconsideration of research evidence. *Academy of Management Review, 19,* 312–330.

Wahba, M. A., & Bridwell, L. G. (1973). Maslow reconsidered: A review of research on the need hierarchy theory. *Proceedings of the Thirty-third Annual Meeting of the Academy of Management,* 514–520.

Waldman, D. A., Bass, B. M., & Yammarino, F. J. (1990). Adding to contingent-reward behavior: The augmenting effect of charismatic leadership. *Group & Organization Studies, 15,* 381–394.

Wall, J. A., & Callister, R. R. (1995). Conflict and its management. *Journal of Management. 21,* 515–558.

Waller, D., & Levander, S. (1980). Smoking and vigilance: The effects of tobacco smoking on CFF as related to personality and smoking habits. *Psychopharmacology, 70,* 1331–1336.

Walsh, J. P., Weinberg, R. M., & Fairfield, M. L. (1987). The effects of gender on assessment center evaluations. *Journal of Occupational Psychology, 60,* 305–309.

Wanous, J. (1977). Organizational entry: Newcomers moving from outside to inside. *Psychological Bulletin, 84,* 601–618.

Wanous, J. P., & Youtz, M. A. (1986). Solution diversity and the quality of group decisions. *Academy of Management Journal, 29,* 149–159.

Warr, P. B. (1983). Work, jobs, and unemployment. *Bulletin of the British Psychological Society, 36,* 305–311.

Watson, C. (1988). When a woman is the boss: Dilemmas in taking charge. *Group & Organization Studies, 13,* 163–181.

Watson, D., & Clark, L. A. (1984). Negative affectivity: The disposition to experience aversive emotional states. *Psychological Bulletin, 96,* 465–490.

Watson, D., & Slack, A. K. (1993). General factors of affective temperament and their relation to job satisfaction over time. *Organizational Behavior & Human Decision Processes, 54,* 181–202.

Watson, J. G., & Barone, S. (1976). The self-concept, personal values, and motivational orientations of black and white managers. *Academy of Management Journal, 19,* 36–48.

Weaver, C. N. (1980). Job satisfaction in the United States in the 1970's. *Journal of Applied Psychology, 65,* 364–367.

Weber, M. (1946). Bureaucracy. In H. Gerth & C. W. Mills (Eds.), *From Max Weber: Essays in sociology.* New York: Oxford University Press.

Weber, M. (1947). *The theory of social and economic organization.* Glencoe, IL: Free Press.

Webster, E. G., Booth, R. E., Graham, W. K., & Alf, E. F. (1978). A sex comparison of factors related to success in Naval Hospital Corps School. *Personnel Psychology, 31,* 95–106.

Weick, K. E. (1968). Systematic observational methods. In G. Lindzey & E. Aronson (Eds.), *Handbook of social psychology* (Rev. Ed.). Reading, MA: Addison-Wesley.

Weiner, N. (1980). Determinants and behavioral consequences of pay satisfaction: A comparison of two models. *Personnel Psychology, 33,* 741–757.

Weiss, D. J., Dawis, R. V., England, G. W., & Lofquist, L. H. (1967). *Manual for the Minnesota Satisfaction Questionnaire* (Minnesota Studies in Vocational Rehabilitation, Vol. 22). Minneapolis: University of Minnesota Industrial Relations Center.

Weiss, D. J., & Vale, C. D. (1987). Adaptive testing. *Applied Psychology: An International Review, 36,* 249–262.

Weiss, H. M., & Shaw, J. B. (1979). Social influences on judgments about tasks. *Organizational Behavior and Human Performance, 24,* 124–140.

Weiss, J. M. (1968). Effects of coping responses on stress. *Journal of Comparative and Physiological Psychology, 65,* 251–260.

Weiss, J. M. (1971). Effects of coping behavior with and without a feedback signal on stress pathology in rats. *Journal of Comparative and Physiological Psychology, 77,* 22–30.

Weldon, E., & Mustari, E. L. (1988). Felt dispensability in groups of coactors: The effects of shared responsibility and explicit anonymity on cognitive effort. *Organizational Behavior and Human Decision Processes, 41,* 330–351.

Welsh, D. H. B., Luthans, F., & Sommer, S. M. (1993). Managing Russian factory workers: The impact of U.S.-based behavioral and participative techniques. *Academy of Management Journal, 36,* 58–79.

Wernimont, P. F., & Campbell, J. P. (1968). Signs, samples, and criteria. *Journal of Applied Psychology, 52,* 372–376.

Wesnes, K., & Warburton, D. M. (1984). The effects of cigarettes of varying yield on rapid information processing. *Psychopharmacology, 82,* 338–342.

Wexley, K. N. (1984). Personnel training. *Annual Review of Psychology, 35,* 519–551.

Wexley, K. N., & Baldwin, T. T. (1986). Management development. *Journal of Management, 12,* 277–294.

White, M. K., Hodous, T. K., & Vercruyssen, M. (1991). Effects of thermal environment and chemical protective clothing on work tolerance, physiological responses, and subjective ratings. *Ergonomics, 34,* 445–457.

Whyte, G. (1989). Groupthink reconsidered. *Academy of Management Review, 14,* 40–56.

Whyte, W. F. (1937). *Street corner society.* Chicago: University of Chicago. Selection reprinted in H. Proshansky & B. Seidenberg (Eds.). (1966). *Basic studies in social psychology.* New York: Holt, Rinehart & Winston.

Wickens, C. D. (1984). *Engineering psychology and human performance.* Columbus: Merrill.

Widmeyer, W. N., Brawley, C., & Carron, A. V. (1992). Group dynamics in sport. In T. S. Horn (Ed.), *Advances in Sport Psychology* pp. 124–139. Champaign, IL: Human Kinetics.

Wiener, E. L. (1987). Application of vigilance research: Rare, medium, or well done? *Human Factors, 29,* 725–736.

Wiesner, W. H., & Cronshaw, S. F. (1988). A meta-analytic investigation of the impact of interview format and degree of structure on the validity of the employment interview. *Journal of Occupational Psychology, 61,* 275–290.

Wilkins, A. L., & Dyer, W. G., Jr. (1988). Toward culturally sensitive theories of culture change. *Academy of Management Review, 13,* 522–533.

Wilkinson, R. T. (1992). How fast should the night shift rotate? *Ergonomics, 35,* 1425–1446.

Williams, J. R., & Levy, P. E. (1992). The effects of perceived system knowledge on the agreement between self-ratings and supervisor ratings. *Personnel Psychology, 45,* 835–847.

Winefield, A. H., & Tiggemann, M. (1990). Employment status and psychological well-being: A longitudinal study. *Journal of Applied Psychology, 7,* 455–459.

Wingfield, A. (1979). *Human learning and memory: An introduction.* New York: Harper & Row.

Winter, D. G. (1979). *Navy leadership and management competencies: Convergence among tests, interviews and performance ratings.* Boston: McBer.

Wister, O. (1902). *The Virginian: A Horseman of the Plains.* Macmillan Company.

Woehr, D. J., & Huffcutt, A. I. (1994). Rater training for performance appraisal: A quantitative review. *Journal of Occupational & Organizational Psychology, 67,* 189–205.

Wofford, J. C., Goodwin, V. L., & Premack, S. (1992). Meta-analysis of the antecedents of personal goal level and of the antecedents and consequences of goal commitment. *Journal of Management, 18,* 595–615.

Wogalter, M. S., Allison, S. T., & McKenna, N. A. (1989). Effects of cost and social influence on warning compliance. *Human Factors, 31,* 133–140.

Wogalter, M. S., Godfrey, S. S., Fontenelle, G. A., Desaulniers, D. R., et al. (1987). Effectiveness of warnings. *Human Factors, 29,* 599–612.

Wogalter, M. S., & Young, S. L. (1991). Behavioural compliance to voice and print warnings. *Ergonomics, 34,* 79–89.

Wohlers, A. J., Hall, M., & London, M. (1993). Subordinates rating managers: Organizational and demographic correlates of self/subordinate agreement. *Journal of Occupational & Organizational Psychology, 66,* 263–275.

Wolfgang, A. P. (1988). Job stress in the health professions: A study of physicians, nurses, and pharmacists. *Behavioral Medicine, 14,* 43–47.

Wolinsky, J. (1982, December). Beat the clock. *APA Monitor.*

Wollack, S. (1994). Confronting adverse impact in cognitive examinations. *Public Personnel Management, 23,* 217–224.

Wolpe, J. (1969). *The practice of behavior therapy.* New York: Pergamon.

Wood, R. E., Mento, A. J., & Locke, E. A. (1987). Task complexity as a moderator of goal effects. *Journal of Applied Psychology, 72,* 416–425.

Wood, R. E., & Locke, E. A. (1990). Goal setting and strategy effects on complex tasks. In B. M. Staw & L. L. Cummings (Eds.), *Research in Organizational Behavior* (Vol. 12, pp. 73–109. Greenwich, CT: JAI Press.

Woodward, J. (1965). *Industrial organization: Theory and practice.* Oxford: Oxford University Press.

Wooten, W. (1993). Using knowledge, skill and ability (KSA) data to identify career pathing opportunities: An application of job analysis to internal manpower planning. *Public Personnel Management, 22,* 551–563.

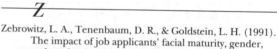

Yammarino, F. J., & Bass, B. M. (1990). Transformational leadership and multiple levels of analysis. *Human Relations, 43,* 975–995.

Yearta, S. H., Maitlis, S., & Briner, R. B. (1995). An exploratory study of goal setting in theory and practice: A motivational technique that works? *Journal of Occupational and Organizational Psychology, 68,* 237–252.

Yetton, P. W., & Bottger, P. C. (1982). Individual versus group problem solving: An empirical test of a best member strategy. *Organizational Behavior and Human Performance, 29,* 307–321.

Yoder, D. (1945). New horizons in industrial employee relations. *Public Personnel Review, 6,* 28–32.

Young, S. M. (1992). A framework for successful adoption and performance of Japanese manufacturing practices in the United States. *Academy of Management Review, 17,* 677–700.

Yu, J., & Murphy, K. R. (1993). Modesty bias in self-ratings of performance; A test of the cultural relativity hypothesis. *Personnel Psychology, 46,* 357–363.

Yukl, G. (1971). Toward a behavioral theory of leadership. *Organizational Behavior and Human Performance, 6,* 414–440.

Yukl, G. (1981). *Leadership in organizations.* Englewood Cliffs, NJ: Prentice-Hall.

Yukl, G. (1989). Managerial leadership: A review of theory and research. *Journal of Management, 15,* 251–289.

Yukl, G., Guinan, P. J., & Sottolano, D. (1995). Influence tactics used for different objectives with subordinates, peers, and superiors. *Group & Organiation Management, 20,* 272–296.

Yukl, G., Wexley, K. N., & Seymore, J. D. (1972). Effectiveness of pay incentives under variable ratio and continuous reinforcement schedules. *Journal of Applied Psychology, 56,* 19–23.

Z

Zebrowitz, L. A., Tenenbaum, D. R., & Goldstein, L. H. (1991). The impact of job applicants' facial maturity, gender, and academic achievement on hiring recommendations. *Journal of Applied Social Psychology, 21,* 525–548.

Zecker, S. G. (1982). Mental practice and knowledge of results in the learning of a perceptual motor skill. *Journal of Sport Psychology, 4,* 52–63.

Zedeck, S., & Cascio, W. F. (1984). Psychological issues in personnel decisions. *Annual Review of Psychology, 35,* 461–518.

Zelikoff, S. B. (1969). On the obsolescence and retraining of engineering personnel. *Training & Development Journal, 23,* 3–14.

Zohar, D. (1980). Promoting the use of personal protective equipment by behavior modification techniques. *Journal of Safety Research, 12,* 78–85.

Zohar, D., & Fussfeld, N. (1981). A system approach to organizational behavior and modification: Theoretical considerations and empirical evidence. *International Review of Applied Psychology, 30,* 491–505.

*P*hotograph *Credits*

Name Index

Jenkins, G. D., 286
Jermier, J. M., 420
Jex, S. M., 433
Jick, T. D., 435
Johansson, G., 434
Johnson, D. F., 127
Johnson, D. L., 24
Johnson, D. W., 397, 405
Johnson, M. D., 262
Johnson, P. B., 458
Johnson, R. T., 405
Johnson, W. G., 512
Jones, A., 100
Jones, N. W., Jr., 318
Jorgenson, D. O., 248, 251
Jorna, G. C., 511
Judge, T. A., 283, 297, 300
Julian, J. W., 392

K

Kabanoff, B., 300
Kacmar, K. M., 289
Kadish, A., 169
Kahn, R., 17, 359
Kahn, R. L., 380, 434
Kalton, G., 56, 57
Kane, J. S., 201, 210
Kantowitz, B. H., 509
Kapoor, A., 322, 333
Karau, S. J., 331
Karl, K. A., 165
Karren, R. J., 108, 253
Kasabian, C., 474
Kasl, S. V., 433
Katz, D., 17, 309, 359, 380
Katzell, R. A., 15, 16, 259, 260, 261
Kavanagh, M. J., 169, 212
Kay, E., 227
Kazerooni, H., 512
Keck, S. L., 349
Keenan, P. A., 403
Kellogg, D. M., 369, 372, 373
Kelly, J. E., 281
Kelly, K. R., 471
Kelly, R. W., 178
Kendall, L. M., 213, 277
Kennedy, J. K., 314
Kent, R. L., 331
Kernan, M. C., 199, 207
Khojasteh, M., 214
Kienast, P., 262
Kiesswetter, E., 485
Kilcullen, R. N., 112
King, N., 241
Kintz, B. L., 51, 62
Kipnis, D., 322
Kiris, E. O., 515f
Kirk, R. E., 42
Kirkpatrick, D. L., 179, 180
Kirmeyer, S. L., 381, 434, 439, 444

Kissin, B., 475, 476
Kissler, G., 19
Kjelberg, A., 431
Klandermans, B., 434
Klich, N. R., 321
Klimoski, R., 117
Klimoski, R. J., 118
Kluger, A. N., 101
Knauth, P., 485
Knight, P. A., 22
Kochan, T. A., 409
Koenker, R. H., 61
Koestler, F. A., 188
Kofman, F., 359
Koopman, C., 368
Koopman, P. L., 333
Korabik, K., 298
Korman, A. K., 18, 240, 295
Kotch, D. A., 461
Krackhardt, D. M., 296
Kraiger, K., 180, 224, 225
Krantz, D. S., 472
Krau, E., 433
Krauss, R. M., 402
Krech, D., 156
Kroeker, L. P., 18
Krois, P. A., 371
Krzystofrak, R., 225
Kuder, G. F., 129
Kuhnert, K. W., 451
Kulka, R. A., 286
Kuna, D. P., 11, 13
Kunin, T., 280
Kushnir, T., 438, 439

L

Lahey, M. A., 78
Lambrinos, J., 512
Lamm, H., 398
Lance, C. E., 208, 269
Lancee, W., 420
Landy, F. J., 8, 9, 217, 224, 273
Lane, F. B., 244
Lane, I. M., 393
Langan-Fox, J., 245
LaPointe, J. A., 208
Lasek, M., 105
Latham, G. P., 43, 110, 133, 158, 166, 175, 208, 211, 216, 227, 252, 253, 258, 329, 388
Lattanzi, M. E., 420
Laville, A., 491
Lawler, E. E., 239, 246, 248, 251, 252, 261, 271, 272, 281, 283, 294, 295, 389
Lawler, E. E., III, 201, 318
Lawler, E. J., 402
Lawrence, P. R., 360, 362, 366
Lazarus, R. S., 417, 428
Leatherwood, M. L., 227
Lederman, S. J., 501
Lee, C., 420

Lee, R., 289
Lee, R. T., 441
Leirer, V. O., 461
Leiter, M. P., 441, 443
Leonard, J., 364
Leonard, R. L., 180
Levander, S., 462
Leviatan, U., 326
Levin, I., 286
Levin, L., 485
Levine, D. I., 283
Levine, E. L., 78, 81, 210, 224
Levy, P. E., 202
Levy-Leboyer, C., 6
Lewin, K., 308, 309, 370
Lichtman, R. J., 393
Likert, R., 309, 354, 382
Lin, L., 461
Lin, T., 381
Lincoln, J. R., 350
Linden, R. C., 227
Lindzey, G., 9, 236, 237
Lippitt, R., 308, 309
Liska, L. Z., 471
Litman, G. K., 475, 476
Littlepage, G. E., 394
Locke, E. A., 244, 252, 253, 254, 261, 267, 268, 270, 275, 277, 280, 283, 285, 294, 365, 388
Lockheed, M. E., 330
Loher, B. T., 281, 282
London, J., 332
London, M., 224
Long, R. J., 261, 511
Longenecker, C. O., 225, 227
Longley, J., 398
Lord, R. G., 305, 326, 327
Lorsch, J., 360, 362
Lorsch, J. W., 366
Love, K. G., 112
Lowell, E. L., 242
Lowman, R. L., 22
Lowry, P. E., 117, 118
Lozada-Larsen, S. R., 84
Ludwig, T. D., 468
Lundwall, L., 475, 476
Lupton, D. E., 20
Luthans, F., 258
Luz, J., 296
Lyness, S. A., 438

M

Mabe, P. A., 201
Macan, T. H., 109
Maccoby, N., 309
Mackie, R. R., 504
MacKinnon, D. W., 113
Mackworth, N. H., 504
Maeda, K., 456
Mael, F. A., 100
Magenau, J. M., 408
Mager, R. F., 35, 36

Mahar, L., 328
Mahoney, G. M., 318
Maier, N. R. F., 17, 397, 398, 467
Maitlis, S., 254
Makhijani, M. G., 331
Malott, J. M., 472
Malzahn, D. E., 492
Mann, R. B., 174
Manning, D. J., Jr., 254
Manning, F. J., 273
Manning, M. R., 433
Manz, C. C., 364, 365
Marics, M. A., 501
Marlatt, G. A., 472
Marras, W. S., 507
Marrow, A. J., 332
Martin, B. A., 254
Martin, J. C., 113
Martin, J. E., 408, 409
Martin, R., 43, 433, 487
Martinez, J., 432
Martocchio, J. J., 165, 363, 388, 435
Maslach, C., 420, 441
Maslow, A. H., 238, 354f
Mason, M. A., 166
Masuda, M., 422, 423
Mathieu, J. E., 166, 180
Matsui, T., 165, 249
Matteson, M. T., 419, 470
Matthews, K. A., 438
Mattson, J., 100
Maugham, W. S., 196
Maurer, S. D., 88, 111
Maurer, T. J., 130, 224, 327
Mausner, B., 241
Mawhinney, T. C., 234, 242
Mayes, B. T., 433, 436
Mayfield, E. C., 111
McAuliffe, T. G., 405
McBride, A., 420
McCanse, A. A., 310, 311
McClelland, D. C., 242, 244, 270
McCormick, E. J., 76, 77, 78, 84, 499, 506
McCormick, I. A., 419
McCrae, R. R., 147
McCullough, M., 286
McDaniel, M. A., 98, 107
McDonald, N., 485
McEvoy, G. M., 201, 297, 298
McFarlin, D. B., 270, 271, 283, 284, 436, 437
McFillen, J. M., 312
McGehee, W., 158
McGill, M. E., 359
McGrath, M. R., 371
McGregor, D., 383
McGregor, D. M., 352, 354
McGuire, W. J., 170, 269, 274
McIntosh, N. J., 420, 443

Riggio, R. E., 202
Rigny, A., 285
Riskind, J. H., 433
Roback, A. A., 7, 8, 10
Robbins, T. L., 225
Roberson, L., 286
Roberson, M. T., 57
Roberts, K. H., 484
Robertson, I. T., 167
Robeson, F. E., 485
Robinson, D. D., 20, 81
Robinson, V., 370
Roe, C. W., 395
Roehling, M. V., 87
Roethlisberger, F. J., 39, 267, 387, 389
Rogers, L. E., 190, 390
Rohmert, W., 493, 494
Roman, P. M., 472, 474, 475
Ronen, S., 483
Rosa, R. R., 483
Rose, R. M., 420, 433
Rosen, H., 409
Rosen, S., 419
Rosen, T. H., 459, 461, 462
Rosenberg, H., 476
Rosenman, R. H., 437, 438, 471
Rosin, H., 298
Ross, J., 286
Ross, R. A., 365
Ross, S., 90
Ross, T. L., 365
Rosse, J. G., 148
Rotchford, N. L., 484
Roth, S., 245
Roy, D. F., 387, 389
Rozier, C. K., 492
Roznowski, M., 288
Rubin, J. Z., 403
Rudolph, A. S., 117
Rush, M. C., 326
Russell, C. J., 88, 100, 363, 367
Russell, D. W., 269, 441, 443
Russell, J. S., 227, 329
Russell, J. T., 132
Russell, M. A. H., 462
Russell, R. D., 363, 367
Ryan, A. M., 105, 148
Ryan, T. A., 14
Rynes, S. L., 88

S

Saal, F. E., 22, 217
Saari, L. M., 166, 179, 189, 329
Sackett, P. R., 117, 148, 149
Sackmann, S., 363
Saks, A. M., 88
Salancik, G. R., 273
Salas, E., 166, 180
Salmaso, P., 169
Sanchez, J. I., 81

Sanders, M. S., 499, 506
Sankowsky, D., 312
Saunders, V., 100
Sauser, W. I., 77
Saxena, U., 506
Scandura, T. A., 283
Scarpello, V., 368
Schachter, V., 200, 465
Schaubroeck, J., 201, 202
Schay, B. W., 260
Scheid-Cook, T. L., 363
Scheier, M. F., 436
Schein, E. H., 362, 370
Schein, V. E., 224, 330, 331
Schendel, J. D., 162
Schmidt, F. L., 84, 96, 98, 101, 102t, 133, 139, 140
Schmidt, S. M., 322
Schmidt, W. H., 316
Schmit, M. J., 148
Schmitt, N., 22, 110, 112, 117, 141, 339
Schneider, A. M., 422
Schneider, B., 240, 248, 253, 277
Schneier, C. E., 157, 225, 331
Schoenfeldt, L. F., 98, 100
Schoenmarklin, R. W., 507
Schonpflug, W., 6
Schoorman, F. D., 203
Schriesheim, C. A., 57, 315, 319, 394, 395, 408
Schuler, R. S., 434
Schuman, H., 56, 57
Schwab, D. P., 283, 284
Schwab, R. L., 434
Schweiger, D. M., 261, 365, 419
Scott, K. D., 260, 296
Scott, W. D., 13
Scott, W. E., Jr., 295
Selye, H., 417, 421, 422
Sena, J. A., 26
Senge, P. M., 359
Seymore, J. D., 256
Shaffer, G. S., 100
Shahnavaz, H., 456
Shain, M., 458
Shani, A. B., 26
Sharfman, M. P., 362
Shaw, J. B., 273, 433
Shebilske, W. L., 164
Shenkar, O., 512
Sherif, M., 395, 403, 405, 406
Shouksmith, G., 420, 433
Shrader, C. B., 350
Shumaker, S. A., 432, 443
Shute, S. J., 491
Shuval, J. T., 432, 433
Siegel, A. I., 167
Silbey, V., 118
Silver, E. M., 143, 144
Skaggs, K. J., 258
Skinner, B. F., 255

Slack, A. K., 286
Slappendel, C., 452
Slocum, J. W., Jr., 359
Smith, D. E., 198, 212
Smith, F. J., 408
Smith, J. E., 84
Smith, L., 486t
Smith, M. J., 433, 468
Smith, P. B., 233, 353
Smith, P. C., 14, 213, 277
Smith, T. W., 438
Smither, J. W., 212
Snow, R. E., 166
Snyder, H. L., 511
Snyderman, B., 241
Solomon, J., 295
Solomon, R. L., 273
Sommer, R., 373
Sommer, S. M., 258
Sommese, T., 462, 472
Sonnenstuhl, W. J., 459, 471, 473, 474
Sorkin, R. D., 509
Sottolano, D., 321
Souza, J., 326
Spector, P. E., 297, 433, 434
Spelten, E., 486t
Spence, J. T., 438
Spencer, D. G., 298
Stagner, R., 409
Stahl, M., 248
Staines, G. L., 286
Stalker, G. M., 350, 366
Starr, A. F., 512
Starr, R. B., 204
Starr, S. J., 491
Staw, B. M., 286
Stecher, M. D., 148
Steele, P. D., 475
Steele, R. P., 253
Steels, M. J., 430
Steers, R. M., 244, 259, 295, 296, 298
Steiner, D. D., 321
Steinmetz, C. S., 176
Stephenson, B. B., 224
Sterkel-Powell, K., 187
Stewart, A. M., 208
Stewart, T., 510
Stieber, J., 199
Stockbauer, J. W., 405
Stogdill, R. M., 305, 306, 307
Stokes, J. P., 286
Stokols, D., 432
Stone, D. L., 461
Stone, G. L., 471
Stoyva, J., 469, 470
Strasser, S., 260
Strauss, R., 458
Streufert, S., 458
Strickland, W. J., 118
Stringfield, P., 201, 202

Struening, E. L., 424
Suarez, Y., 228
Suinn, R. M., 470, 471
Sulkunen, P., 458
Sulsky, L. M., 207, 212
Summers, R. J., 75
Summers, T. P., 252
Sundstrom, E., 59
Suttle, J. L., 239, 248
Sutton, H., 384
Sveback, S., 456
Swartz, J., 511

T

Tagalakis, V., 127
Tannenbaum, R., 316
Tannenbaum, S. I., 166, 169
Tansley, B., 501
Tarnopolosky, A., 430
Tarshis, B., 422
Taylor, F. W., 14, 266, 392
Taylor, G. S., 296
Taylor, H. C., 132
Taylor, H. L., 431
Taylor, M. A., 224
Taylor, S. H., 22, 70
Tenenbaum, D. R., 112
Tenopyr, M. L., 117, 139
Tepas, D. I., 485
Tepper, B. J., 315
Terborg, J. R., 296
Terkel, S., 266
Terpstra, D. E., 371
Tetrault, L. A., 315
Tetrick, L. E., 283
Thacker, R. A., 322
Tharenou, P., 295
Thayer, P. W., 158
Theriault, R., 283
Thomas, J. C., 326
Thompson, D. E., 225
Thorndike, E. L., 255
Thornton, G. C., III, 112
Tichauer, E. R., 507
Tiegs, R. B., 283
Tiffin, J., 204, 268
Tiggemann, M., 451
Timmreck, C., 111
Tippins, N., 209
Tjosvold, D., 401, 403, 405, 406
Tokunaga, R., 456
Tolliver, L., 25
Tolman, E. C., 255
Tomkiewicz, J., 331
Törner, M., 456
Tosi, H., 434
Totterdell, P., 485, 486t
Tougas, F., 75
Tourish, D., 190
Tracey, J. B., 169

Subject Index

International Association of
    Applied Psychology, 25
International business, 25, 27,
    332–33
Interpersonal conflict, 392
Interpersonal skills training,
    172–74
Interrater reliability, 95, 117,
    207, 214–15
Interview
        as communication mode,
           380–81
        in performance evaluation,
           227–28
        in survey research, 56
Interviewers, 109, 112–13
Interviews, selection, 94,
    106–13
        problems in, 107–12
        reliability of, 111
        unstructured and
           structured, 107–12
Intoxication, legal, 458
Intrinsic motivation, 165, 242,
    246, 260
Inverted pyramid, of authority,
    343–44
Inverted-U relationship, 431
I/O psychology
        around the world, 25
        careers in, 19–21, 24–25
        consulting in, 19–22
        future of, 23–27
        graduate study in, 22,
           517–19
        history of, 6–18
        licensing in, 20, 22
Irritant substances, 454
Item Response Theory, 150–51

J

Japanese management, 353,
    388, 419
JDI, 277, 278
Jenkins Activity Survey, 438
Job analysis, 18, 68, 76–85, 159
        in job evaluation, 77
        in selection, 109–10,
           112, 114
        in test validation, 137
        in training design,
           157–58, 169
Job attitudes, 267, 268–69, 273,
    281, 286
        measurement of, 274–77
Job characteristics model,
    281–83
Job component validity, 136
Job Descriptive Index, 277, 278
Job Diagnostic Survey, 281
Job Element Inventory, 84
Job element method of job
    analysis, 78, 82–84
Job enrichment, 241, 261, 281,
    352, 354, 355, 359

Job evaluation, 77
Job family, 76, 84
Job in General scale, 277
Job involvement, 268
Job marketing, 88
Job redesign, 241, 260–61, 443
Job rotation, 328
Jobs, simplified, 338, 340–42,
    348–49
Job satisfaction
        and age of employee,
           288–89
        and employee withdrawal,
           281–82, 295–98
        individual differences in,
           286–93
        and life satisfaction, 300
        measurement of, 274–80
        and motivation, 241, 266,
           270, 271, 281–82
        national levels of,
           286–88, 292
        and organizational
           commitment, 298
        with pay, 266, 283–84
        and productivity, 266, 268,
           271, 281–82, 294–95
        with supervision, 284–85
        theories of, 269–74
        of union members, 408
        with work itself,
           281–83, 289
Job standards, 127
Job study. *See* Job analysis
Job transfer, 432
Journal of Applied Psychology, 9, 15
Judgmental measures of
    performance, 203–4

K

Keyboards, 510
KR20, 129
KSAs, 81
Kuder-Richardson formula, 129

L

Laboratory training of
    supervisors, 328–29
Labor contract, 408–9
Labor-management negotiation,
    407–9
Labor unions, 199, 200
Laissez-faire leadership, 308–9
Language, 379–80
Lateral communication,
    339, 382
LBDQ, 310, 326
Leader
        effect on productivity and
           satisfaction, 284–85, 308–9,
           319, 322–24
        masculine and feminine
           traits of, 331
        need for, 335
        prototype of, 326–27, 331

        roles, 312–13, 316–19,
           322–24
        style, 313–14
*Leader Behavior Description
    Questionnaire,* 310
Leader Match, 328
Leaderless work group, 116, 335
Leader-member exchange
    model, 320–22
Leadership
        behavior, 306, 308–10, 319,
           322–23, 325–26
        cross-cultural patterns in,
           332–33
        effectiveness of, 308, 313,
           316, 320
        ethnic differences in, 331–32
        gender differences in,
           330–31
        group, 391, 398–99
        research on, 304–5
        theories of, 306–27
        training, 189–90, 308,
           328–29
Leadership motive pattern,
    244–45
*Leadership Opinion
    Questionnaire,* 310
Learning
        measures, 180
        and motivation, 165–66,
           236, 255
        organization, 359
        tasks, 161, 170–71
        and training, 156–57,
           162–69
Least Preferred Coworker
    Scale. *See* LPC scale
Left-handedness, 506–7
Legitimate power, 394–95
Leniency error, 208, 210, 217,
    219, 220
Lesson plans, 170–72
Letter's of recommendation,
    103–5
Licensing, 20, 22
Lie detector, 148
Lifting, 505–6
Lighting, workplace, 487–88
Likert scale, 277
Linear controls, 509
Line-staff organization, 342
Logical error, 208, 209
Lottery, behavior
    modification, 262
LPC scale, 313, 314–15, 328
Lung disease, 454–55, 467

M

Machine
        contributions to work,
           493, 496
        control, 507–9
        displays, 498–501
        monitoring, 513

Macro-organizational
    communication, 378
Management
        philosophy, 352, 360–61
        training, 157, 189–90
        women in, 188–89
Managerial assessment centers,
    113–16
Managerial differentiation,
    360–61
Managerial Grid, 328
Managers
        as leaders, 304
        motivation of, 243–45
        organizational power of,
           343–44
        performance evaluation
           of, 202
        roles of, 189–90
        stress of, 417, 419, 436
Manual materials handling, 505
Maslach Burnout Inventory, 441
Maslow's need hierarchy
    theory, 238–40, 354*f*
Massed practice, 163–64
Mass production industries,
    356–57
Matrix organization,
    345–46, 362
Maximum work area, 490
Meaning in work, 24, 266,
    281–83
Mechanical skills tests, 144–45
Median, 46–48
Mediation, in impasse
    resolution, 409
Medical professions, stress in,
    419–20, 433
Meditation, 442, 444
Mental ability tests, 143–44
Mental health problems, 450,
    451–52, 469–70
Mental practice, 162, 164–65
Mentors, 189, 328
Mergers, 368
Messages, in communication,
    385–86, 390
Meta-analysis, 26, 139–40
Michigan studies
    of leadership, 309
Micro-organizational
    communication, 379
Middle management, 340–41,
    383, 419, 436
Migration, 432–33
Miniature training and
    evaluation, 167
Minnesota Clerical Test, 143–44
*Minnesota Paper Form Board Test,
    Revised,* 144
*Minnesota Satisfaction
    Questionnaire,* 277, 279
Minority workers, 26
Mission statement, 338

Mixed Standards Rating Scale, 216–18
MMPI, 146–47
Mood disorder, 451
Moonlighting, 483
Morale, 268
Motivating employees, 227, 318–19, 322–24
Motivation
    early study of, 17–18, 234, 235
    and job satisfaction, 241–42, 266, 270, 281–82
    and performance, 236
    problems of, 349, 354
    related to training, 157, 165–66, 236
Motivational change programs, 259–62
Motivation theory, 238–58
    tension-reduction hypothesis in, 239
Motivator factor, 241–42
Motor vehicle accidents, 453, 458
Mouse, 510
MSRS, 216–17
Multicultural issues, in training, 186–88
Multifactor Leadership Questionnaire, 326
Multiple hurdles, 94
Multiple linkages model of leadership, 322–24
Münsterberg, Hugo, 4, 5, 6, 8–10, 32

N

Narcotics, 460
Narrative evaluation, 204
National Safety Council, 453, 454–55
Need for achievement, 243
Need for power, 244
Needs, 238, 239, 241–42, 252, 255, 270, 277, 280
Needs assessment, 35–37. *See also* Training, needs assessment
Need Satisfaction Questionnaire, 277, 279
Need theories of motivation, 238–45, 270
Negative affectivity, 286, 436
Negative correlation, 61–62
Negative-sum outcome, 404, 405
Negative transfer of training, 168–69
Negligent hiring, 105
Negotiation, 408–9
Neo Personality Inventory, 147
Nicotine use, 462, 472–73
Night work, 485

Noise, 429–31, 487
Noise dose, 487
Nominal hours, 482
Nonverbal communication, 379
Nonwork satisfaction, 300
Normal curve, 126, 222–23
Normal distribution, 47
Normal work area, 490
Normative models of leadership, 315–16
Nuisance variables, 41, 180–82
Null hypothesis, 40
Nurses, 419–20, 443

O

Objective tests, 126, 142
Observational research, 32–33, 52–62, 78–80
Observer reliability, 55
Obsolescence, 178, 188
Occupational disease, 453–56
Occupational Health and Safety Act, 464. *See also* OSHA
OD programs, 381. *See also* Organizational development
Ohio State studies of leadership, 309–10
Older workers, 126–27, 288–89
One-way communication, 382
On-the-job training, 176–78
Open communication, 383, 402
Open-ended question format, 58–59, 104, 276
Open systems, in organizational theory, 359
Operating core, 339, 341
Operational definitions, 40–41, 44
Operations goals, 339
Opponent process theory of job satisfaction, 273–74
Organization
    authority and power in, 343–45
    bureaucratic, 347–50, 352, 355, 357–58
    communication in, 378–86
    environment of, 349–51, 356–59, 360–62
    mechanistic, 350–51
    organic, 350–51, 357–58
    technical systems in, 357–58
    theories of, 347–63
Organizational analysis, in training needs assessment, 158
Organizational climate, 25, 169, 363, 380
Organizational commitment, 268–69, 298
Organizational culture, 325, 362–63, 367

Organizational development, 18, 369, 372–73
    action research in, 369–71
    interventions, 371–72
Organizational dynamics, theories of, 360–63
Organizational effectiveness, 339, 347, 349, 355, 357–58, 361–62, 367, 368
Organizational goals, 338–39
Organizational innovation, 366–67
Organizational stress, 424, 426
Organizational structure, 26
    centralized or decentralized, 344, 348, 350–51
    chart, 339–40
    design of, 338, 345–46, 347, 354–55, 357–58, 361–63
    differentiation in, 342–43, 346, 348, 360–62
    division of labor in, 339–42, 343
    formalized, 345, 349, 350
    hierarchy, 342–43
    matrix, 345–46
    theories emphasizing, 347–51
Organizational uncertainty, 366–67
Organizational values, 362–63, 367
OSHA, 464, 487
Otis Self-Administering Test of Mental Ability, 143
Out-group exchange, 321
Output
    goals, 338–39
    in human-machine systems, 494–95
    and motivation, 249
    organizational, 359
Overlapping group structure, 354
Overlearning, 162–63
Overpayment, 250–52
Overseas work, 187–88

P

Paired comparisons, 222
PAQ. See Position Analysis Questionnaire
Parallel processing of information, 502–3
Parasympathetic nervous system, 422
Partial reinforcement, 103–4,166, 256–57
Participant observer, 387
Participation in decision making, 261, 352, 354, 355, 364–66, 388–89

Participative management, 332–33, 352, 359, 388–89, 468
Part learning, 163–64
Part time work, 482, 483–84
Path-goal theory of leadership, 285, 318–19
Pay
    effect on motivation, 251, 257
    fairness, 69–70, 77, 250, 283–84
    incentive plans, 260–61
    satisfaction, 266–67, 283–84
    schedules, openness of, 252
Pay Satisfaction Questionnaire, 283
Pearson product-moment correlation, 62
Peer appraisals, 201–2
Pencil-and-paper tests, 143
Percentiles, 126
Perceptual abilities tests, 144–46
Perceptual processes, in human-machine systems, 499
Performance
    and arousal, 430–31
    effects of heat on, 431–32
    effects of noise on, 430–31
    feedback, 165–66
    improvement in, 256, 258, 261–62
    and job satisfaction, 281–82, 294–95
    and motivation, 236, 246–47, 250–52, 253, 255–56
    problems, 35–37, 157–58
    related to turnover, 298
    tests, 143
Performance evaluation, 42
    errors in, 207–12
    feedback interview, 226–28
    legal issues in, 198–200
    methods of, 202–5, 213–23
    personal factors in, 223–25
    purposes of, 159, 197–200
    supervisors and other sources of, 201–4
    validation of, 198–99, 202, 205–7
Permanent employment, 200
Personal growth, 239, 281–83
Personality
    Big five model of, 147–48
    and job satisfaction, 286
    and leadership, 307–8
    and stress, 436–39
    tests used in selection, 146–48
Personal protection, 467
Personal space, 432
Person analysis, in training needs assessment, 158–59
Person-Environment Fit Theory, 424–25